Teach Yourself VISUALLY™

Windows® 8

Visual™

Paul McFedries

WILEY
John Wiley & Sons, Inc.

Teach Yourself VISUALLY™ Windows® 8

Published by
John Wiley & Sons, Inc.
10475 Crosspoint Boulevard
Indianapolis, IN 46256

www.wiley.com

Published simultaneously in Canada

Library of Congress Control Number:

ISBN: 978-1-118-13528-0

Manufactured in the United States of America

10 9 8 7 6 5 4 3 2

Trademark Acknowledgments

Contact Us

For general information on our other products and services please contact our Customer Care Department within the U.S. at 877-762-2974, outside the U.S. at 317-572-3993 or fax 317-572-4002.

For technical support please visit www.wiley.com/techsupport.

WILEY **Sales** | Contact Wiley at (877) 762-2974 or fax (317) 572-4002.

Credits

Executive Editor
Jody Lefevere

Sr. Project Editor
Sarah Hellert

Technical Editor
Vince Averello

Copy Editor
Scott Tullis

Editorial Director
Robyn Siesky

Business Manager
Amy Knies

Sr. Marketing Manager
Sandy Smith

Vice President and Executive Group Publisher
Richard Swadley

Vice President and Executive Publisher
Barry Pruett

Project Coordinator
Sheree Montgomery

Graphics and Production Specialists
Carrie Cesavice
Tim Detrick
Noah Hart
Andrea Hornberger
Jennifer Mayberry
Jill A. Proll
Melissa K. Smith
Sarah Wright

Quality Control Technician
Dwight Ramsey

Proofreader
Tricia Liebig

Indexer
Potomac Indexing, LLC

About the Author

Paul McFedries is a full-time technical writer. Paul has been authoring computer books since 1991 and he has more than 75 books to his credit. Paul's books have sold more than three million copies worldwide. These books include the Wiley titles *Windows 8 Visual Quick Tips, Teach Yourself VISUALLY Excel 2010, The Facebook Guide for People Over 50, iPhone 4S Portable Genius,* and *The new iPad Portable Genius.* Paul is also the proprietor of Word Spy (www.wordspy.com), a website that tracks new words and phrases as they enter the language. Paul invites you to drop by his personal website at www.mcfedries.com.

Author's Acknowledgments

It goes without saying that writers focus on text, and I certainly enjoyed focusing on the text that you'll read in this book. However, this book is more than just the usual collection of words and phrases. A quick thumb through the pages will show you that this book is also chock full of images, from sharp screen shots to fun and informative illustrations. Those colorful images sure make for a beautiful book, and that beauty comes from a lot of hard work by Wiley's immensely talented group of designers and layout artists. They are all listed in the Credits section, and I thank them for creating another gem. Of course, what you read in this book must also be accurate, logically presented, and free of errors. Ensuring all of this was an excellent group of editors that included project editor Sarah Hellert, copy editor Scott Tullis, and technical editor Vince Averello. Thanks to all of you for your exceptional competence and hard work. Thanks, as well, to executive editor Jody Lefevere for asking me to write this book.

How to Use This Book

Who This Book Is For

This book is for the reader who has never used this particular technology or software application. It is also for readers who want to expand their knowledge.

The Conventions in This Book

1 Steps

This book uses a step-by-step format to guide you easily through each task. **Numbered steps** are actions you must do; **bulleted steps** clarify a point, step, or optional feature; and **indented steps** give you the result.

2 Notes

Notes give additional information — special conditions that may occur during an operation, a situation that you want to avoid, or a cross-reference to a related area of the book.

3 Icons and Buttons

Icons and buttons show you exactly what you need to click to perform a step.

4 Tips

Tips offer additional information, including warnings and shortcuts.

5 Bold

Bold type shows command names or options that you must click or text or numbers you must type.

6 Italics

Italic type introduces and defines a new term.

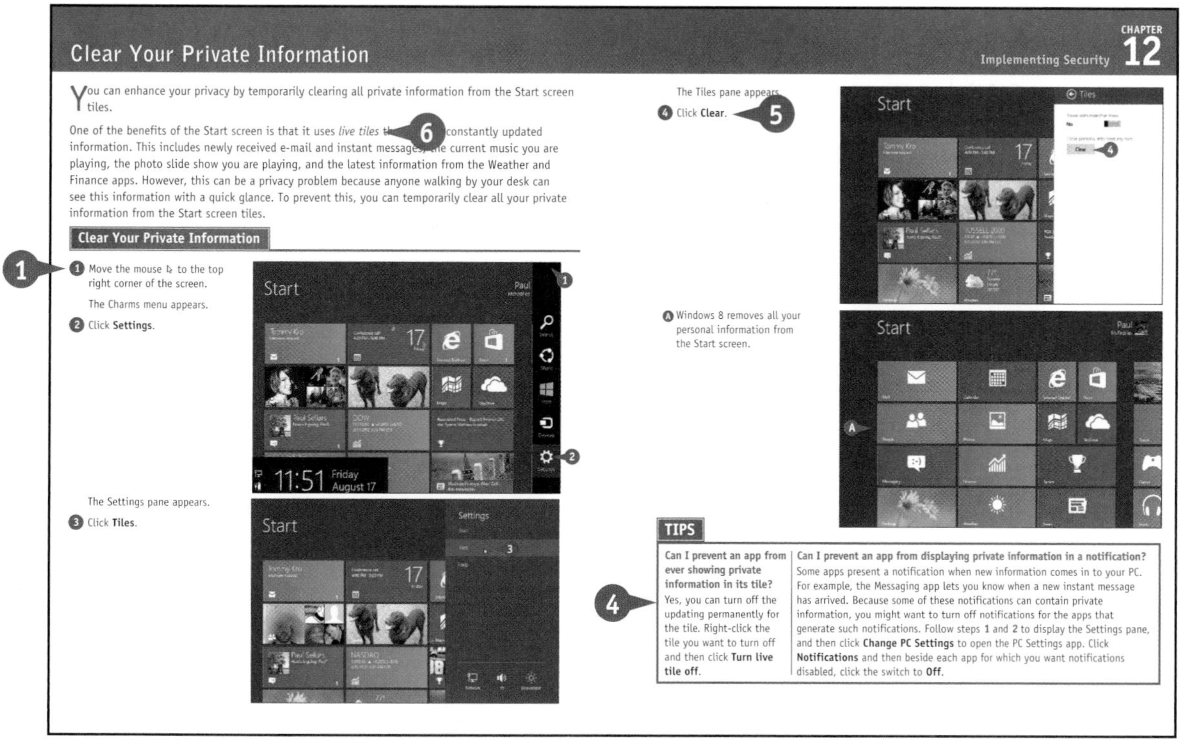

Clear Your Private Information

CHAPTER 12 Implementing Security

You can enhance your privacy by temporarily clearing all private information from the Start screen tiles.

One of the benefits of the Start screen is that it uses *live tiles* th 6 constantly updated information. This includes newly received e-mail and instant messages, the current music you are playing, the photo slide show you are playing, and the latest information from the Weather and Finance apps. However, this can be a privacy problem because anyone walking by your desk can see this information with a quick glance. To prevent this, you can temporarily clear all your private information from the Start screen tiles.

Clear Your Private Information

1 Move the mouse to the top right corner of the screen.

The Charms menu appears.

2 Click **Settings**.

The Settings pane appears.

3 Click **Tiles**.

The Tiles pane appears.

4 Click **Clear**. 5

A Windows 8 removes all your personal information from the Start screen.

TIPS 4

Can I prevent an app from ever showing private information in its tile?
Yes, you can turn off the updating permanently for the tile. Right-click the tile you want to turn off and then click **Turn live tile off**.

Can I prevent an app from displaying private information in a notification?
Some apps present a notification when new information comes in to your PC. For example, the Messaging app lets you know when a new instant message has arrived. Because some of these notifications can contain private information, you might want to turn off notifications for the apps that generate such notifications. Follow steps **1** and **2** to display the Settings pane, and then click **Change PC Settings** to open the PC Settings app. Click **Notifications** and then beside each app for which you want notifications disabled, click the switch to **Off**.

Table of Contents

Chapter 1 Getting Started with Windows 8

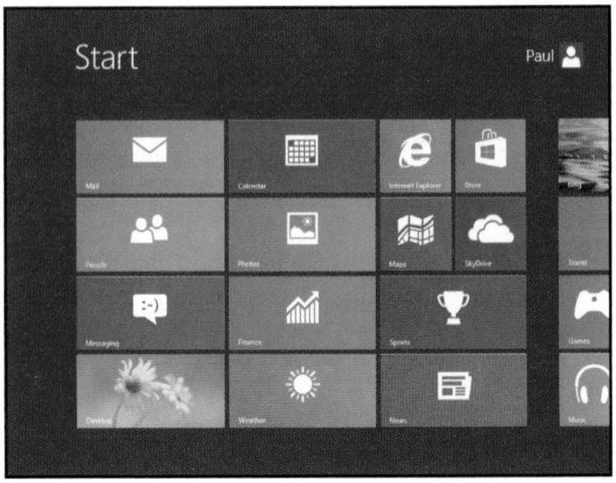

Chapter 2 Launching and Working with Apps

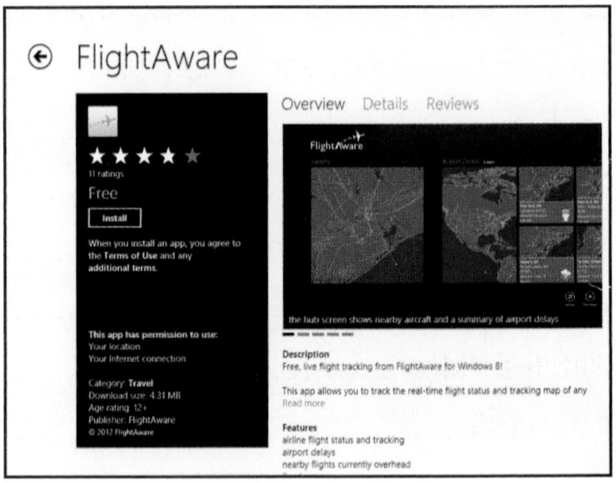

Chapter 3 Getting Connected to the Internet

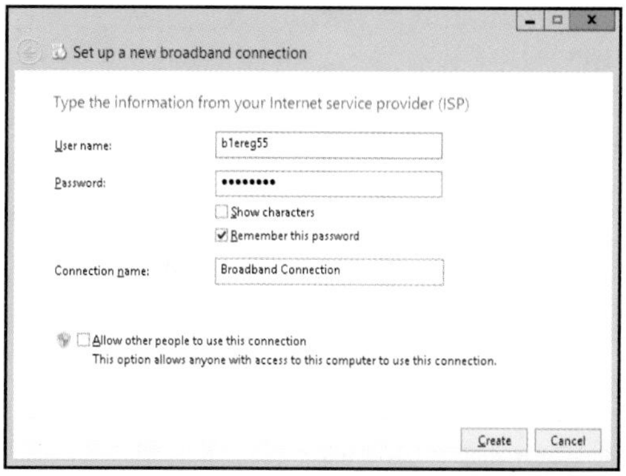

Chapter 4 Using the Windows 8 Apps

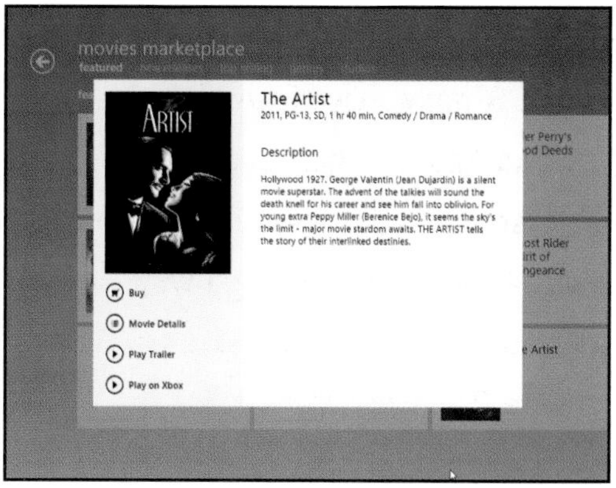

Table of Contents

Chapter 5 Surfing the World Wide Web

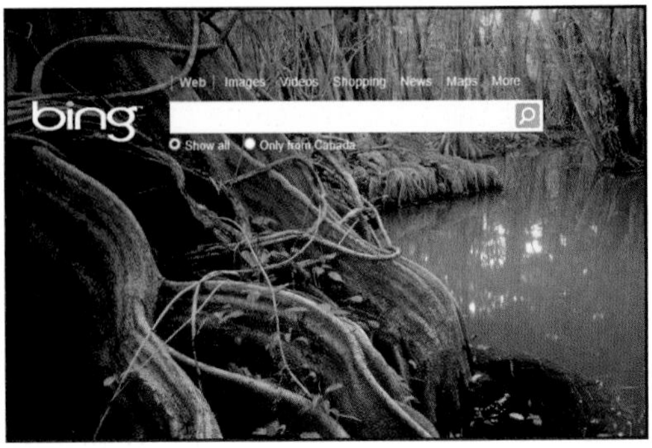

Chapter 6 Working with E-Mail and Calendars

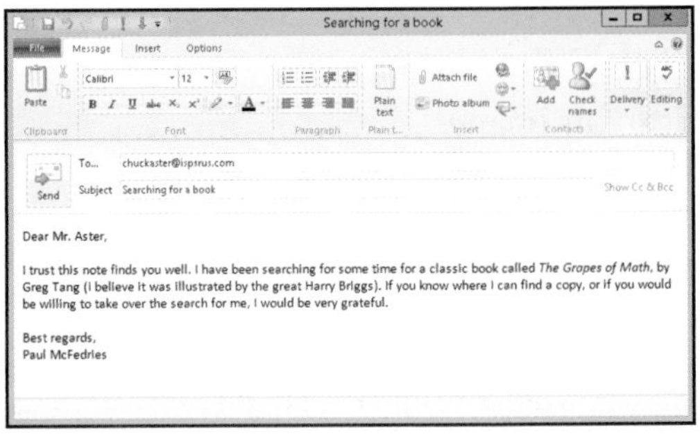

Chapter 7 Working with Images

Table of Contents

Chapter 8 Playing Music and Other Media

Chapter 9 Creating and Editing Documents

Chapter 10 Working with Files

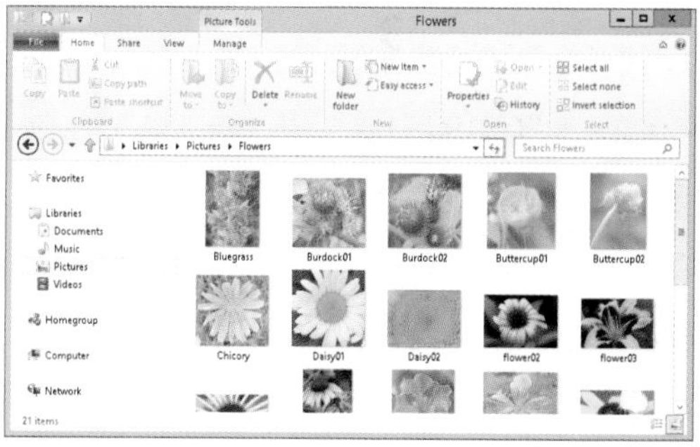

Table of Contents

Chapter 11 Sharing Your Computer

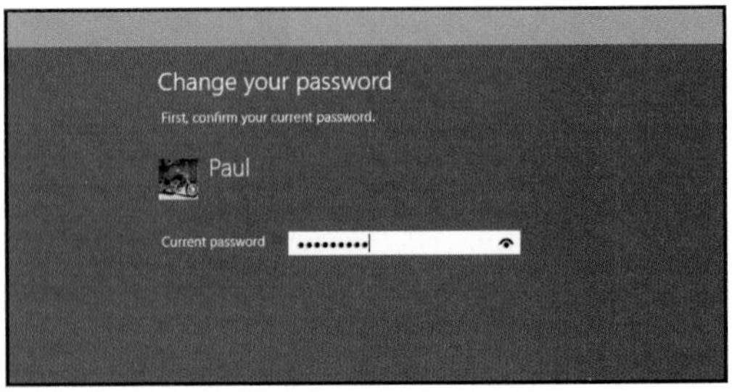

Chapter 12 Implementing Security

Chapter 13 Customizing Windows 8

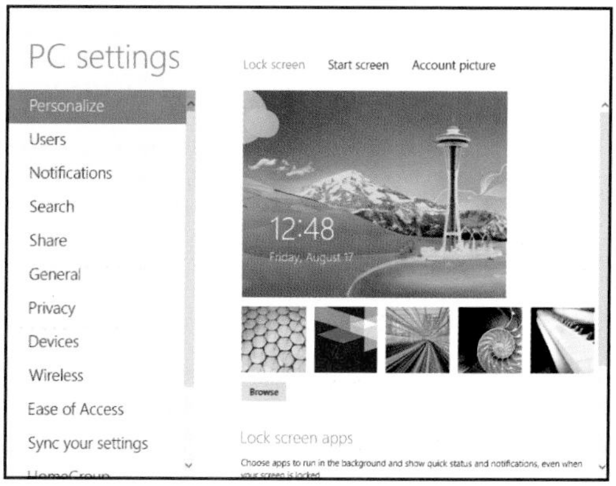

Chapter 14 Maintaining Windows 8

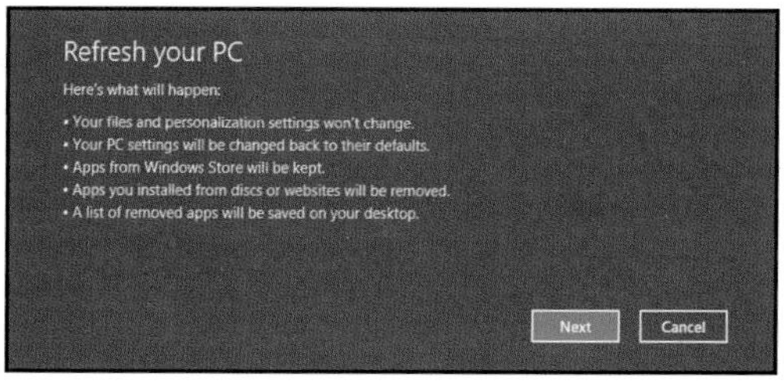

CHAPTER 1

Getting Started with Windows 8

Are you ready to discover Windows 8? In this chapter, you learn what you can do with Windows, tour the Start screen and desktop, learn about the mouse, and more.

Start Windows 8

When you turn on your computer, Windows 8 starts automatically, but you may have to navigate the sign on screen along the way.

To prevent other people from using your computer without your authorization, Windows 8 requires you to set up a username and password. You supply this information the very first time you start your computer, when Windows 8 takes you through a series of configuration steps. Each time you start your computer, Windows 8 presents the sign on screen and you must enter your username and password to continue.

Start Windows 8

1. Turn on your computer.

   A. After a minute or so, the Windows 8 Lock screen appears.

2. Press Enter.

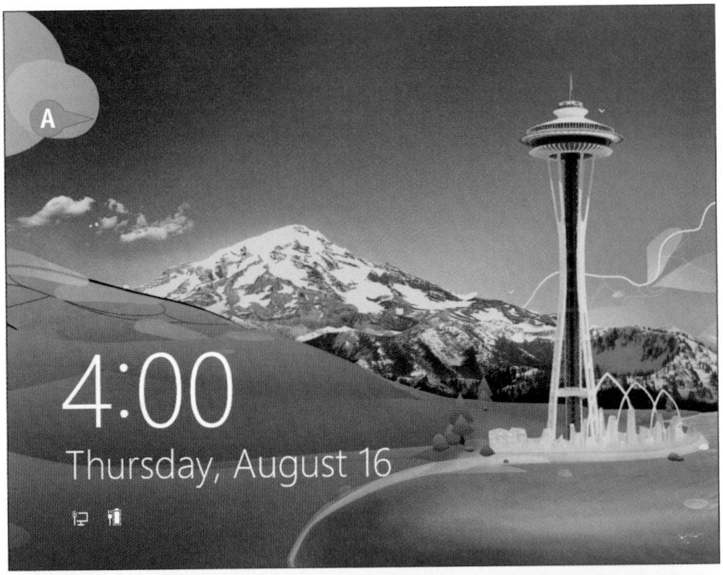

The Windows 8 sign on screen appears.

Note: If you have more than one user account on your computer, you must first click the icon that corresponds to your Windows 8 username.

3. Type your password.

Note: The password characters appear as dots as you type them so that no one else can read your password.

4. Click the **Submit** arrow (→) or press Enter.

   The Windows 8 Start screen appears.

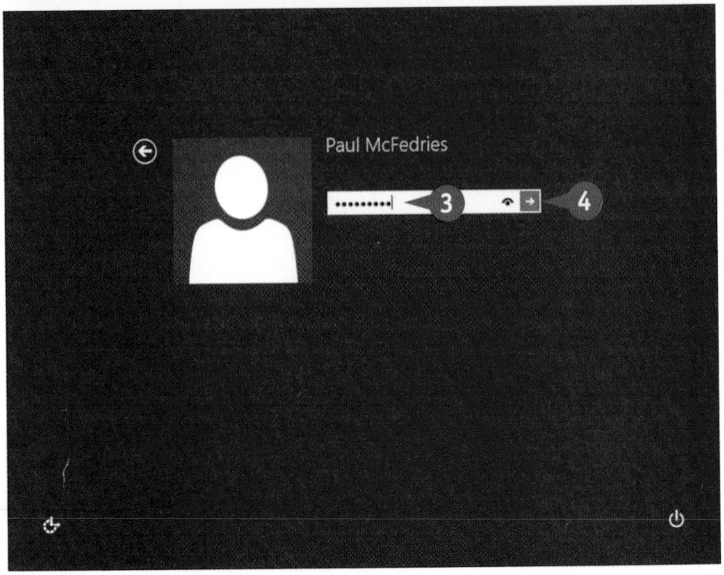

CHAPTER 1

What You Can Do with Windows 8

Windows 8 is an operating system that contains a collection of tools, applications, and resources. In this section you find out about the wide variety of tasks you can perform with Windows 8, including getting work done; organizing and editing photos; playing music, videos, and other media; surfing the web; and communicating with others.

Get Work Done

With Windows 8, you can run programs (also called applications or apps) that enable you to get your work done more efficiently, such as a word processor for writing memos and letters, a spreadsheet for making calculations, and a database for storing information. Windows 8 comes with some of these programs (such as the WordPad program you learn about in Chapter 9), and you can purchase and install others separately.

Morning Session

8:00 - 8:30	Opening Remarks
8:30 - 9:00	President's Welcome
9:00 - 9:45	Keynote Address
9:45 - 10:15	Coffee Break
10:15 - 11:00	Industry Trends
11:00 - 12:00	Advisory Panel
12:00 - 1:30	Lunch

Create and Edit Pictures

Windows 8 comes with a lot of features that let you work with images. You can create your own pictures from scratch, import images from a scanner or digital camera, or download images from the Internet. After you create or acquire an image, you can edit it, print it, or send it via e-mail. You can even create a photo slide show on a DVD. You learn about these and other picture tasks in Chapter 7.

Play Music and Other Media

Windows 8 has treats for your ears as well as your eyes. You can listen to audio CDs, play digital sound and video clips, copy tracks from a music CD, create your own music playlists, and copy audio files to a recordable CD. You can also play DVDs right on your computer. With the right cable, you can connect your computer to your TV and play music and movies and view photos on your TV. You learn about these multimedia tasks in Chapter 8.

Get on the Internet

Windows 8 makes connecting to the Internet easy (see Chapter 3). And after you are on the Net, Windows 8 has all the tools you need to get the most out of your experience. For example, you can get an account from Microsoft and use it to display messages, your calendar, and other online items on your Start screen. You can also use Internet Explorer to surf the World Wide Web (see Chapter 5) and Mail to send and receive e-mail, edit contacts, and create appointments (see Chapter 6).

The Windows 8 Start Screen

Before getting to the specifics of working with Windows 8, take a few seconds to familiarize yourself with the basic elements of the Start screen.

These elements include the Start screen's tiles and live tiles, the mouse pointer, and the Desktop tile.

Understanding where these elements appear on the Start screen and what they are used for will help you work through the rest of the sections in this book and will help you navigate Windows 8 and its applications on your own.

Ⓐ Tile

Each of these rectangles represents an application or a Windows 8 feature. An application you install often adds its own tile to the Start screen.

Ⓑ Mouse Pointer

When you move your mouse, this pointer moves along with it.

Ⓒ Desktop Tile

You use this tile to access the Windows 8 desktop, which you learn about in the next section.

Ⓓ Live Tile

Some tiles are *live* in the sense that they display frequently updated information, such as the weather data shown by the Weather tile.

Ⓔ User Account Tile

You use this tile to access commands related to your Windows 8 user account.

The Windows 8 Desktop

CHAPTER 1

Before getting to the specifics of working with Windows 8, take a few seconds to familiarize yourself with the basic screen elements.

These elements include desktop icons, the taskbar, and the notification area. Understanding these elements and what you use them for will help you throughout this book and will enable you to use Windows 8 and its applications on your own.

To get to the desktop from the Start screen, use your mouse to click the **Desktop** tile, or press Windows+D.

A Desktop Icon

An icon on the desktop represents a program or Windows 8 feature. A program you install often adds its own icon on the desktop.

B Desktop

This is the Windows 8 "work area," meaning that it is where you work with some of your programs and documents.

C Taskbar

The programs you have open appear in the taskbar. You use this area to switch between programs if you have more than one running at a time.

D Taskbar Icons

You use these icons as an alternative method for launching some Windows 8 programs.

E Notification Area

This area displays small icons that notify you about things happening on your computer. For example, you see notifications if your printer runs out of paper or if an update to Windows 8 is available over the Internet.

F Time and Date

This is the current time and date on your computer. To see the full date, position the mouse over the time. To change the date or time, click the time.

Using a Mouse with Windows 8

If you are using Windows 8 on a desktop or notebook computer, it pays to learn the basic mouse techniques early on because you will use them for as long as you use Windows.

If you have never used a mouse before, remember to keep all your movements slow and deliberate, and practice the techniques in this section as much as you can.

Using a Mouse with Windows 8

Click the Mouse

1. Position the mouse over the object you want to work with.
2. Click the left mouse button.

Windows 8 usually performs some operation in response to the click (such as displaying the desktop).

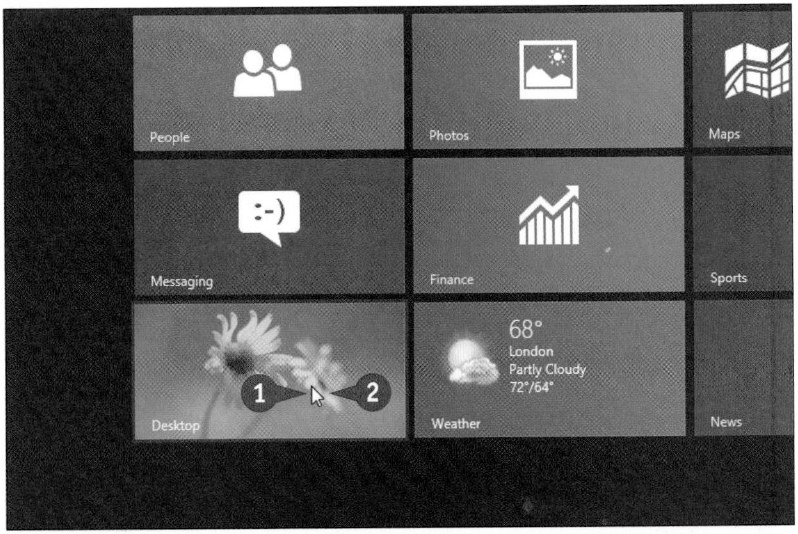

Double-Click the Mouse

1. Position the mouse over the object you want to work with.
2. Click the left mouse button twice in quick succession.

A. Windows 8 usually performs some operation in response to the double-click action (such as displaying the Recycle Bin window).

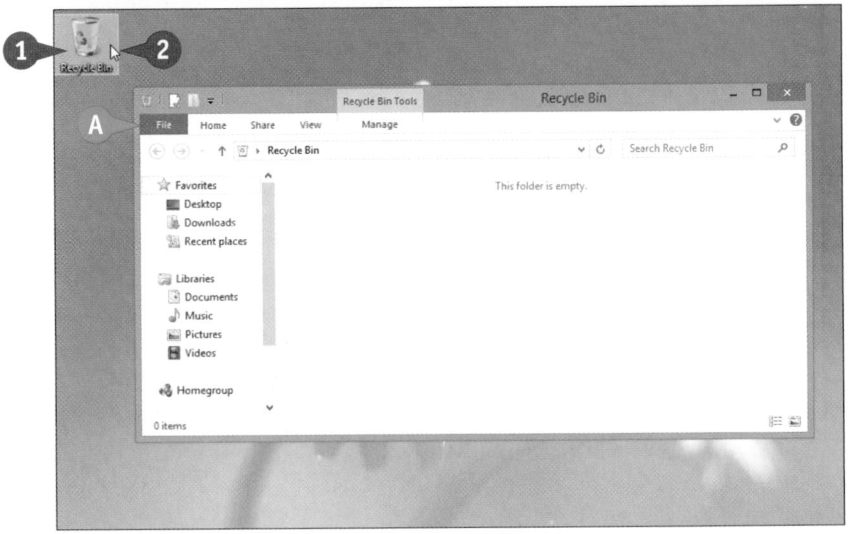

Right-Click the Mouse

1. Position the mouse over the object you want to work with.
2. Click the right mouse button.
- B Windows 8 displays a shortcut menu when you right-click something.

Note: The contents of the shortcut menu depend on the object you right-clicked.

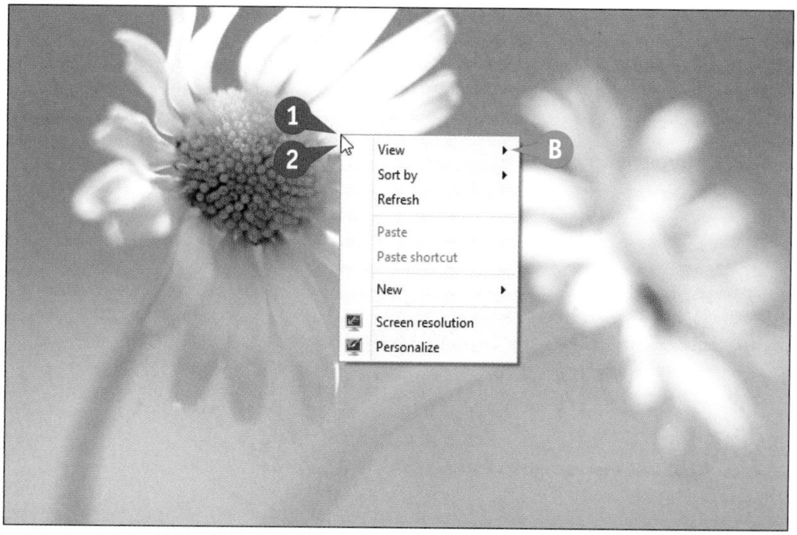

Click and Drag the Mouse

1. Position the mouse over the object you want to work with.
2. Click and hold the left mouse button.
3. Move the mouse to drag the selected object.
- C In most cases, the object moves along with the mouse.
4. Release the mouse button when the selected object is repositioned.

TIPS

Why does Windows 8 sometimes not recognize my double-clicks?

Try to double-click as quickly as you can, and be sure not to move the mouse between clicks. If you continue to have trouble, use the Start screen to type **mouse**, click **Settings**, and then click **Change mouse settings** to open the Mouse Properties dialog box. Click the **Buttons** tab. In the Double-Click Speed group, click and drag the slider to the left (toward Slow).

How can I set up my mouse for a left-hander?

You can switch the left and right mouse buttons. On the Start screen, type **mouse**, click **Settings**, and then click **Change mouse settings** to open the Mouse Properties dialog box. Click the **Buttons** tab. Click **Switch primary and secondary buttons** (☐ changes to ☑) and then use the right mouse button to click **OK**.

Using Windows 8 on a Tablet PC

If you are using Windows 8 on a tablet PC, you need to know the basic touch gestures available. Using a tablet PC is a different experience than using a regular computer, but Windows 8 was built with the tablet PC in mind, so it is intuitive and easy to learn.

If you have never used a tablet PC before, the main difference is that you use your fingers (or sometimes a stylus, if your tablet comes with one) to run applications, select items, and manipulate screen objects. This might seem awkward at first, but it will come to seem quite natural if you practice the techniques in this section as much as you can.

Using Windows 8 on a Tablet PC

Initiate an Action

1. Position your finger or the stylus over the object you want to work with.
2. Tap the screen.

   Depending on the object, Windows 8 either selects the object or performs some operation in response to the tap (such as displaying the desktop).

Swipe the Screen

1. Quickly move your finger or the stylus across the screen, as follows:

   Swipe left from the right edge of the tablet.

A. Windows 8 displays the Charms menu.

   Swipe right from the left edge of the tablet to switch between running applications.

   If an application takes up multiple screens, swipe right or left to navigate the screens.

   Swipe down from the top edge of the tablet to display a Windows 8 app's application bar.

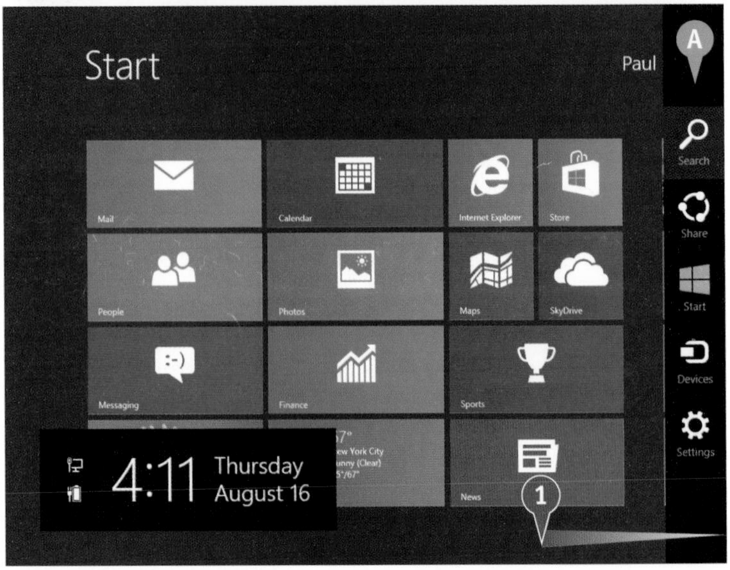

Display a Tile's Application Bar

1. Swipe down on the object you want to work with.

B Windows 8 displays the application bar.

Move an Item

1. Position your finger or the stylus over the item you want to work with.
2. Tap and hold the item and immediately begin moving your finger or the stylus.

C The object moves along with your finger or the stylus.

3. When the object is repositioned where you want it, lift your finger or the stylus off the screen to complete the move.

TIPS

How do I close an application using gestures?
This is slightly tricky, but with practice you can get the hang of it. Position your finger or the stylus at the top edge of the tablet and then slide it down the screen. At first you see the application's settings, as described in this section, so keep sliding. When you get about halfway, the application becomes a small window. Keep dragging that small window to the very bottom of the screen, and then lift your finger or stylus. Windows 8 shuts down the application.

After I tap the Desktop tile, how do I return to the Start screen?
You can do this a couple of ways. First, understand that the desktop is an application, so you can close it using the technique described in the previous tip. Alternatively, swipe left from the right edge of the tablet to display the Charms menu, and then tap the **Start** icon.

Restart Windows 8

You can restart Windows 8, which means it shuts down and starts up again immediately. This is useful if your computer is running slow or acting funny. Sometimes a restart solves the problem.

Knowing how to restart Windows 8 also comes in handy when you install a program or device that requires a restart to function properly. If you are busy right now, you can always opt to restart your computer yourself later, when it is more convenient.

Restart Windows 8

1. Shut down all your running programs.

Note: Be sure to save your work as you close your programs.

2. Press ⊞+I.

   A. The Start settings menu appears.

Note: To display the Start settings menu on a tablet PC, swipe from the right edge to open the Charms menu, and then tap **Settings**.

3. Click **Power**.
4. Click **Restart**.

   Windows 8 shuts down and your computer restarts.

Shut Down Windows 8

When you complete your work for the day, you should shut down Windows 8. However, do not just shut off your computer's power. Follow the proper steps to avoid damaging files on your system.

Shutting off the computer's power without properly exiting Windows 8 can cause two problems. First, if you have unsaved changes in some open documents, you may lose those changes. Second, you could damage one or more Windows 8 system files, which could make your system unstable.

Shut Down Windows 8

1. Shut down all your running programs.

Note: Be sure to save your work as you close your programs.

2. Press [Windows]+[I].

A. The Start settings menu appears.

Note: To display the Start settings menu on a tablet PC, swipe from the right edge to open the Charms menu, and then tap **Settings**.

3. Click **Power**.
4. Click **Shut down**.

Windows 8 shuts down and turns off your computer.

B. If you want Windows 8 to automatically reopen all the programs and documents currently on your screen, click **Power** and then click **Sleep**, instead.

CHAPTER 2

Launching and Working with Apps

To do something useful with your computer, you need to work with an app, one that comes with Windows 8 or one that you install yourself.

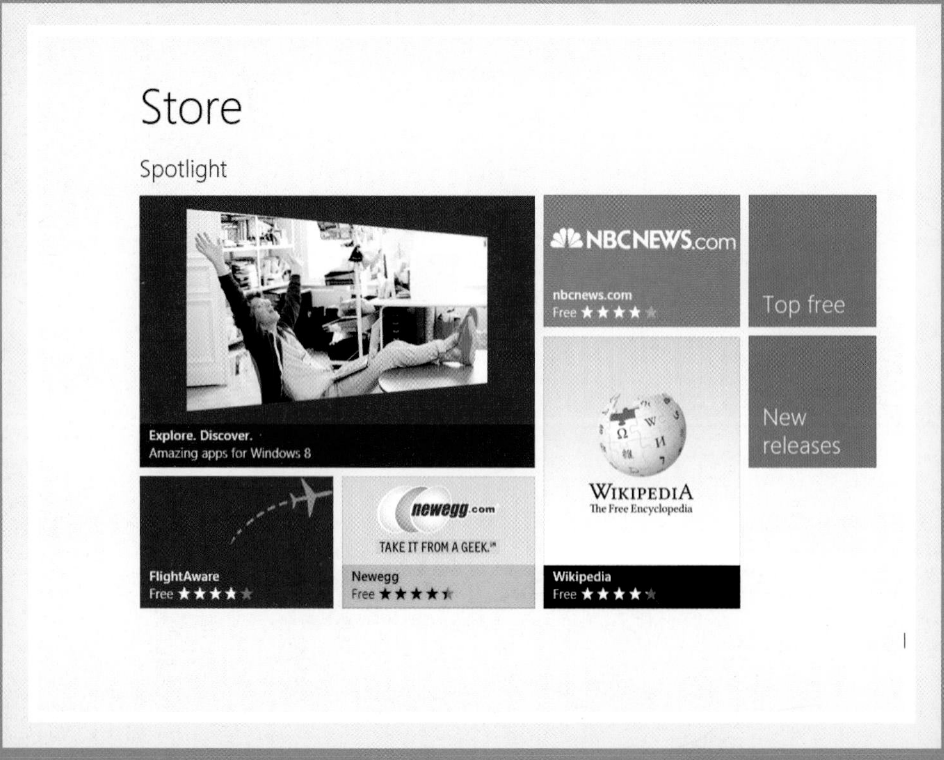

Install an App

If Windows 8 does not come with an app (short for application) that you need, you can obtain the app yourself and then install it on your computer. How you start the installation process depends on whether you obtained the app from the new Windows Store that comes with Windows 8 or you downloaded the app from the Internet. If you purchased the app from a retail store and received a physical copy of the software, you install the app using the CD or DVD disc that comes in the package.

Install an App

Install from the Windows Store

1. On the Start screen, click **Store**.

Note: You need a Microsoft account to install from the Windows Store. See Chapter 3.

The Windows Store appears.

2. Tap the app you want to install.

A. If you do not see the app you want to install, tap a category and then tap the app.

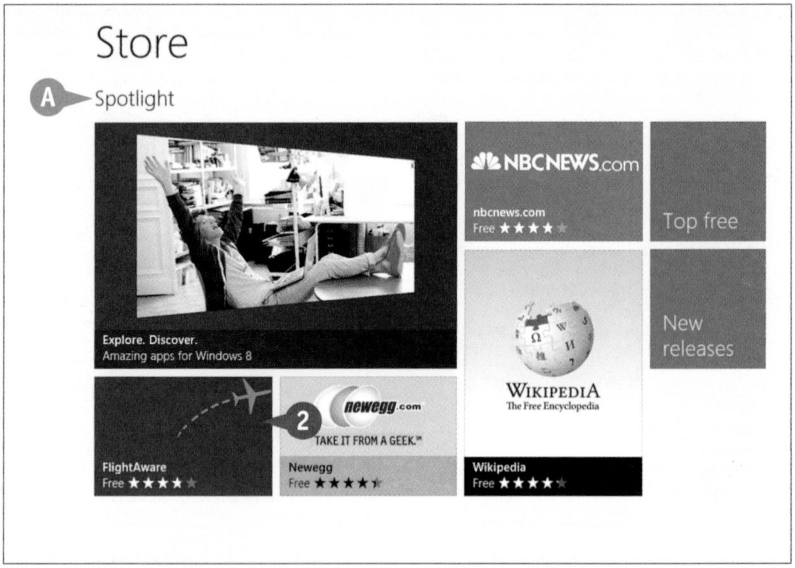

3. Tap **Install**.

Windows 8 installs the app.

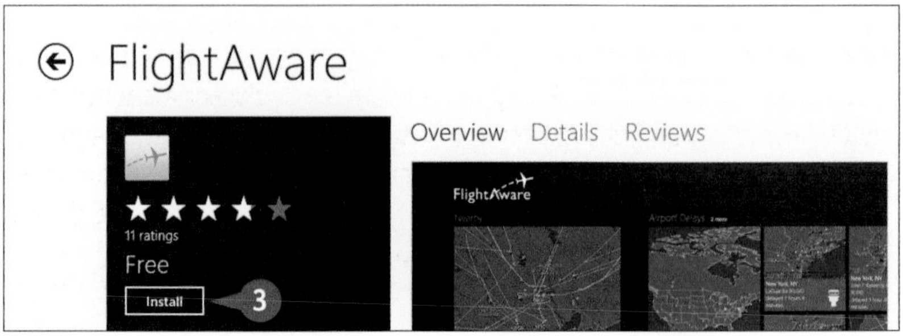

Install from a File Downloaded from the Internet

1. On the Start screen, type **downloads**.
2. Click **Downloads**.

Note: If you saved the downloaded file in a folder other than Downloads, use File Explorer to find the downloaded file. To view a file with File Explorer, see Chapter 10.

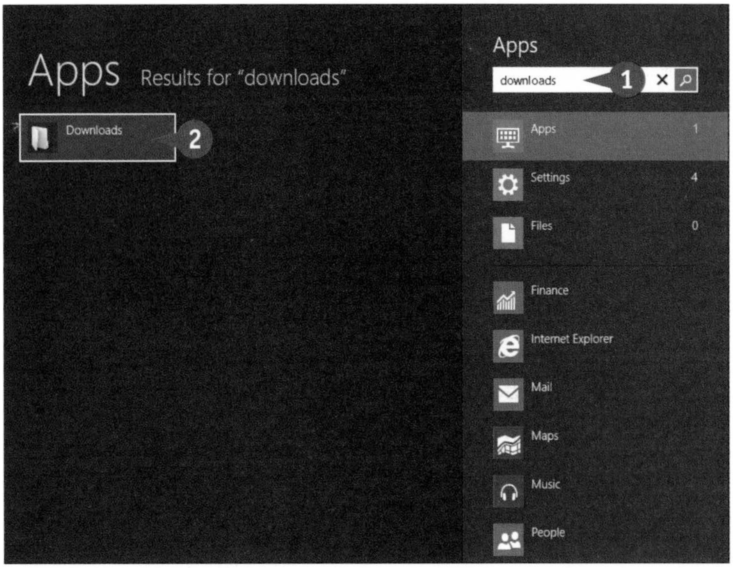

The Downloads folder appears.

3. Double-click the file.

The software's installation app begins.

Note: For compressed files, extract the files, and then double-click the setup file. See Chapter 10 for more information.

4. Follow the installation instructions the app provides.

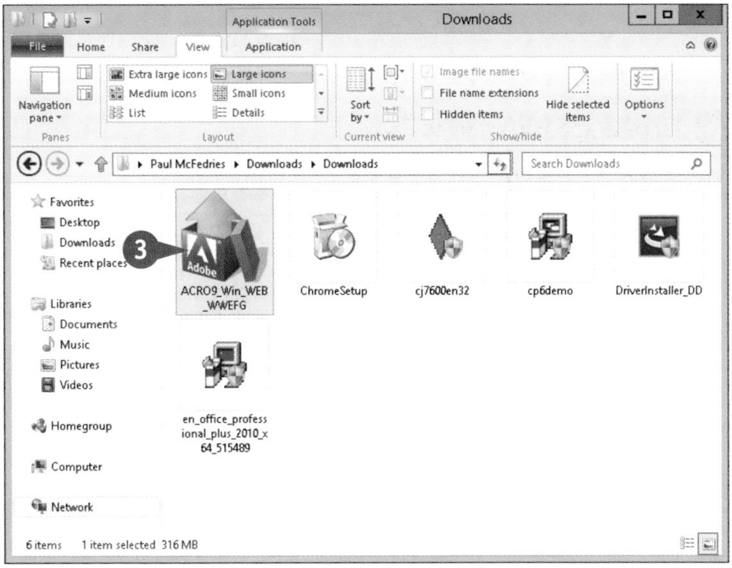

TIPS

How do I install software from a CD or DVD?
Insert the disc into your computer's CD or DVD drive. After a moment or two, the AutoPlay dialog box appears. Click **Run *file***, where *file* is the name of the installation app (usually SETUP.EXE). Then follow the installation instructions the app provides (these installation steps vary from app to app).

How do I find my software's product key or serial number?
The product key or serial number is crucial because many apps do not install until you enter the number. Look for a sticker attached to the back or inside of the CD case. Also look on the registration card, the CD itself, or the back of the box. If you downloaded the app, the number should appear on the download screen and on the e-mail receipt you receive.

Install Windows Live Essentials Programs

You can make your Windows 8 computer more powerful and more useful by installing one or more of the Windows Live Essentials programs available over the web from Microsoft.

The default Windows 8 apps that come with Windows 8 are decent programs, but most of them offer only a limited number of features. To do more with your Windows 8 PC, you can install the Windows Live Essentials programs. These programs include Mail (covered in Chapter 6) and Photo Gallery (covered in Chapter 7). You can also install Movie Maker (to create your own digital movies) and Messenger (to carry on instant messaging conversations).

Install Windows Live Essentials Programs

1. On the Start screen, type **Windows Live Essentials.**
2. Click **Internet Explorer.**
3. Click the **Windows Live Essentials - Download Windows Live Essentials** link.

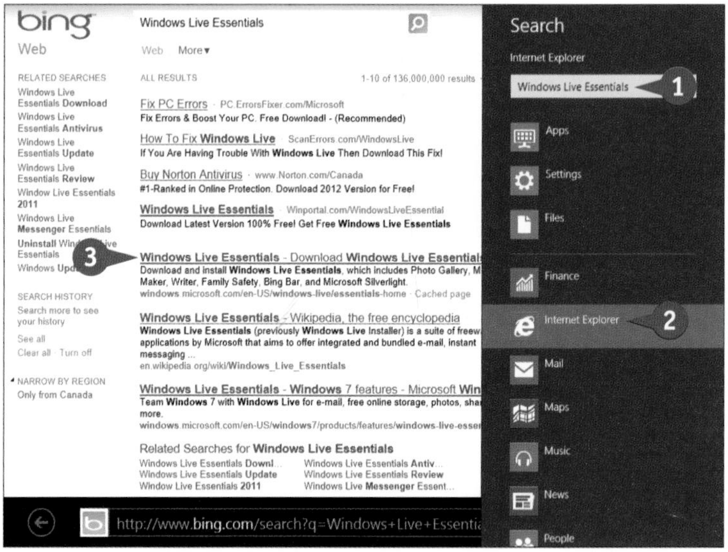

The Windows Live Essentials web page appears.

4. Click **Download now.**
5. Click **Run.**

The User Account Control dialog box appears.

6. Click **Yes.**

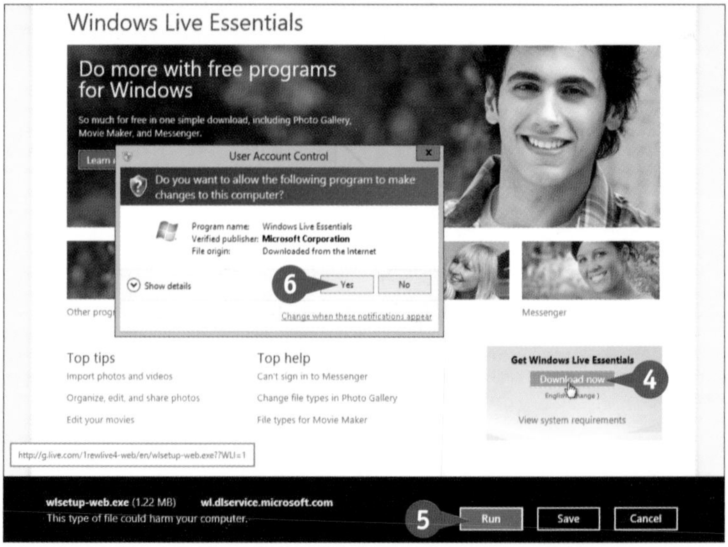

The What Do You Want to Install? dialog box appears.

7 Click **Choose the programs you want to install.**

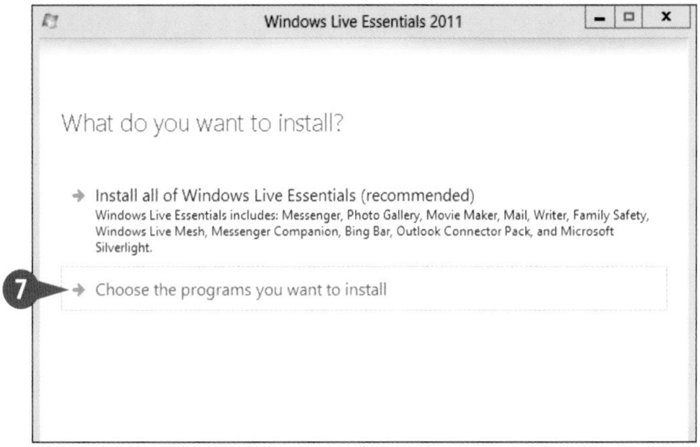

The Select Programs to Install dialog box appears.

8 Click the check box beside each program you want to install (☐ changes to ☑).

9 Click **Install.**

Windows 8 installs your selected Windows Live Essentials programs.

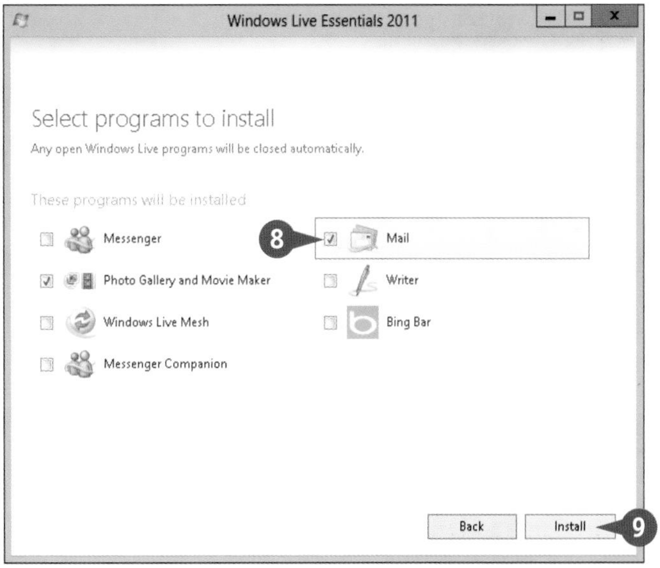

TIPS

Do I have to pay for any Windows Live Essentials programs?
No. All the programs available on the Windows Live Essentials website, including powerful programs such as Mail, Photo Gallery, and Movie Maker, are free. Microsoft created the Essentials programs as supplements to Windows 8, but did not include them in Windows 8 because many people prefer to use other programs, such as Microsoft Outlook for e-mail and contacts.

Can I remove a Windows Live Essentials program after it has been installed?
Yes, the Windows Live Essentials programs are just regular programs, so you launch and work with them using the same techniques that you learn throughout this chapter. This includes uninstalling any Windows Live Essentials programs you no longer require. You learn the steps for uninstalling an application later in this chapter.

Start an App

To perform tasks of any kind in Windows 8, you use one of the apps installed on your computer. The application you use depends on the task you want to perform. For example, if you want to surf the World Wide Web, you use a web browser application, such as the Internet Explorer app that comes with Windows 8.

Before you can use an application, however, you must first tell Windows 8 which application you want to run. In Windows 8, you can run selected apps using either the Start screen or the Apps screen.

Start an App

Using the Start Screen

1. Click the tile for the app you want to launch.

Note: If you have more apps installed than can fit on the main Start screen, scroll to the right and then click the app tile.

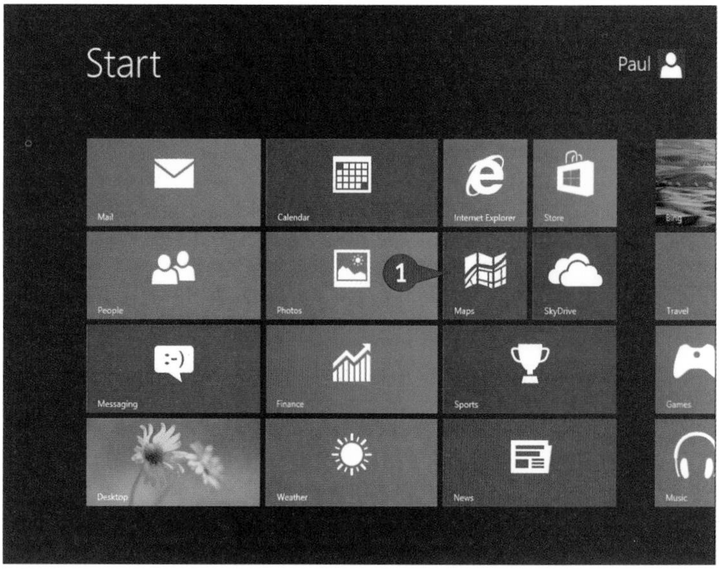

The app runs.

Ⓐ If you launched a Windows 8 app, it takes over the entire screen.

Note: To close a Windows 8 app, press Alt+F4.

Using the Apps Screen

1. Right-click an empty spot on the Start screen.
2. Click **All apps**.

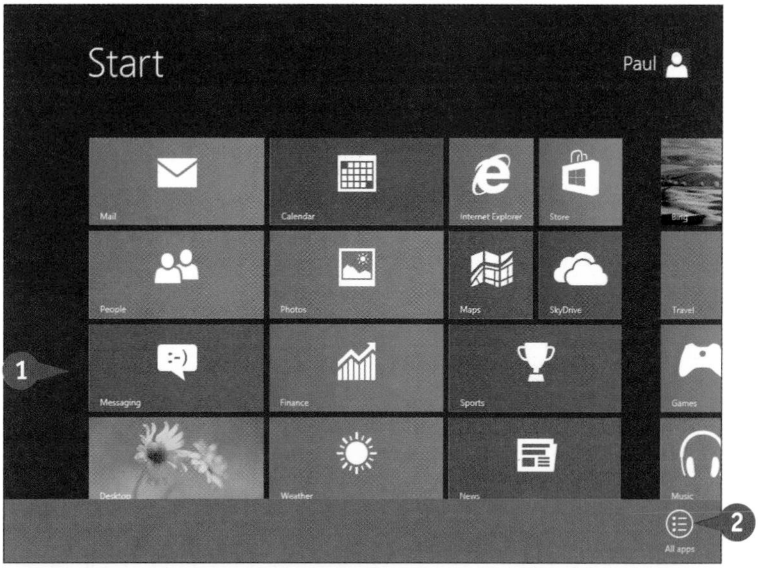

The Apps screen appears.

3. Click the app you want to run.

Windows 8 launches the app.

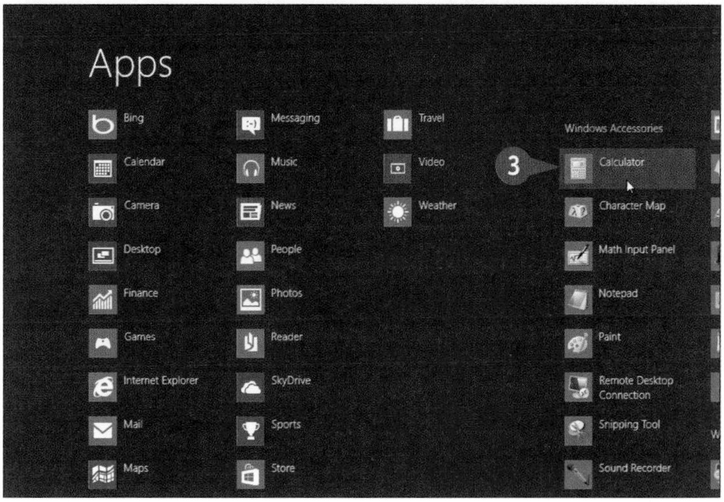

TIPS

Is there an easier way to locate an app, particularly when the Apps screen has dozens of icons?

Yes, you can perform an Apps search to locate it. Press ⊞+Q to open the Apps screen and display the Apps search pane. Begin typing the name of the app. As you type, Windows 8 displays a list of apps that match the characters. As soon as you see the app you want, click it to run the program.

How can I start an app that does not appear on the Start screen, the Apps screen, or in the Apps search results?

Windows 8 comes with some programs that do not appear in the Start screen, the Apps screen, or in the Apps search results. These are mostly Windows 8 tools and utilities, and Windows 8 recognizes these programs based only on their filenames, not their program names. Therefore, use the Apps search pane (as described in the previous tip) to run a search on the filename, if you know it.

Understanding Windows 8 App Windows

Windows 8 supports two quite different types of apps: Windows 8 and Desktop. A Windows 8 app is a new type of program and one designed to work specifically with Windows 8. Windows 8 apps take up the entire screen when they are running, and they hide their program features until you need them.

By contrast, a Desktop app runs on the Windows 8 desktop and runs inside a window.

This section focuses on Windows 8 apps; the next section covers Desktop apps.

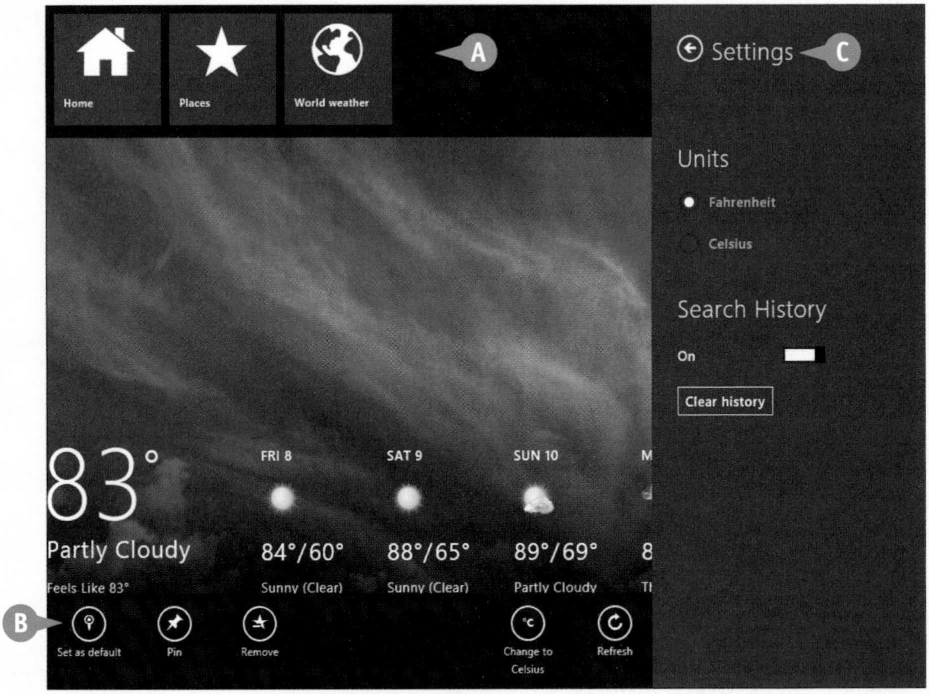

Ⓐ Toolbar

The toolbar offer buttons, lists, and other items that offer easy access to common app commands and features. Some buttons are commands and some have lists from which you can make a choice. Note that not all Windows 8 apps come with a toolbar. Right-click the screen or press ⊞+Z to display the toolbar. If you are using a tablet, swipe down from the top edge of the screen to display the toolbar.

Ⓑ Application Bar

The application bar contains icons that give you access to various app features and commands. Note that in some apps, the application bar appears at the top of the screen rather than at the bottom. You use the same techniques to display the application bar as for the toolbar.

Ⓒ Settings

The app settings are commands that you can select to configure and customize the app. To display the settings, press ⊞+I and then tap a command, such as **Settings**. On a tablet, swipe in from the right edge of the screen to display the Charms menu, tap **Settings**, and then tap a command.

Understanding Desktop App Windows

When you start a Desktop application, it appears on the Windows 8 desktop in its own window. Each application has a unique window layout, but almost all application windows have a few features in common.

Note that in Windows 8, some Desktop apps come with a ribbon and some come with a menu bar and toolbar. Both types are shown in this section.

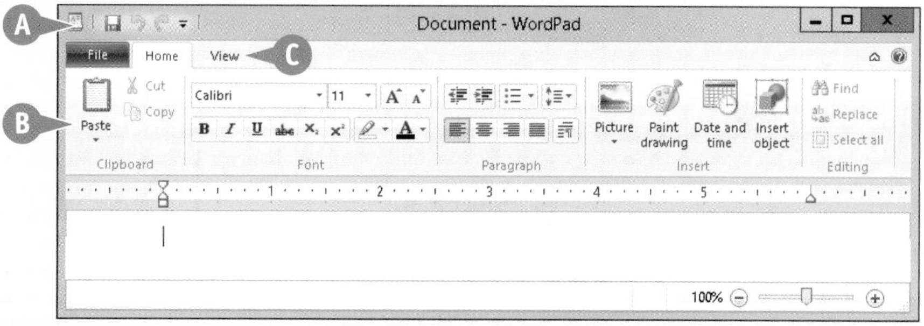

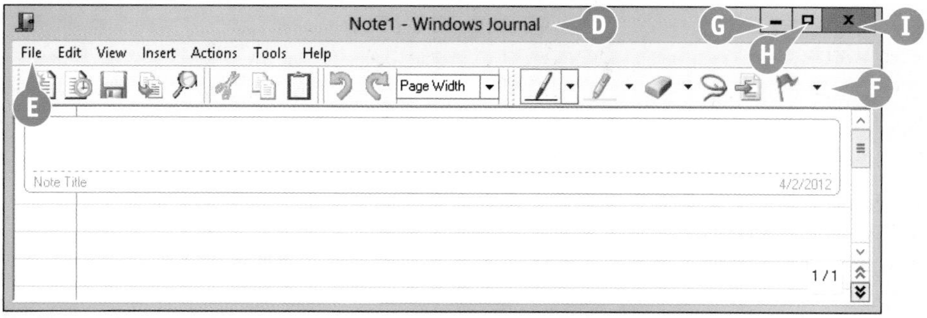

A Quick Access Toolbar

In a ribbon-style app, this part of the window gives you one-click access to a few common commands.

B Ribbon

This appears only in ribbon-style apps, and it offers buttons that give you access to all the app's features. Some buttons are commands and some are lists from which you can make a choice.

C Ribbon Tabs

Clicking a tab displays a different selection of related ribbon buttons.

D Title Bar

The title bar displays the name of the app. In some apps, the title bar also displays the name of the open document. You can also use the title bar to move the window.

E Menu Bar

The menu bar contains the pull-down menus for the Desktop app. In some apps you must press Alt to see the menu bar.

F Toolbar

Buttons that offer easy access to common app commands and features appear in the toolbar. Some buttons are commands, and some have lists from which you can make a choice.

G Minimize Button

You click the **Minimize** button (▭) to remove the window from the desktop and display only the window's taskbar button. The window is still open, but not active.

H Maximize Button

To enlarge the window either from the taskbar or so that it takes up the entire desktop, you click the **Maximize** button (▫).

I Close Button

When you click the **Close** button (×), the app shuts down.

Using a Ribbon

Many of the Windows 8 Desktop apps come with a ribbon, so you need to know how to use the ribbon to properly operate and control the app.

As described in the previous section, the ribbon is the strip that lies just below the title bar. The ribbon gives you access to all or most of the app's features and options. These items are organized into various tabs, such as File and Home.

Windows 8 apps that come with a ribbon include File Explorer, the desktop version of WordPad, and Paint. Also, many of the Windows Live Essentials programs — including Mail, Photo Gallery, and Movie Maker — come with a ribbon.

Using a Ribbon

Execute Commands

1. Click the ribbon button that represents the command or list.

Note: If the ribbon button remains "pressed" after you click it, the button toggles a feature on and off, and the feature is now on. To turn the feature off, click the button to "unpress" it.

- A The app executes the command or, as shown here, drops down the list.

2. If a list appears, click the list item that represents the command.

   The app runs the command.

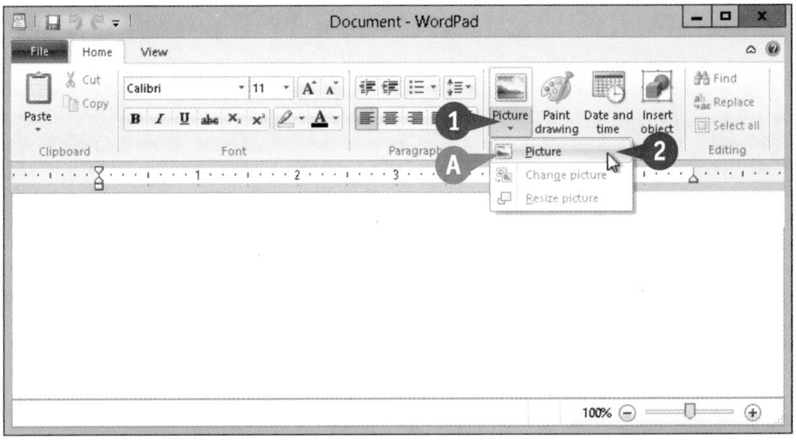

Select a Tab

1. Click the tab name.

- B The app displays the new set of buttons represented by the tab.

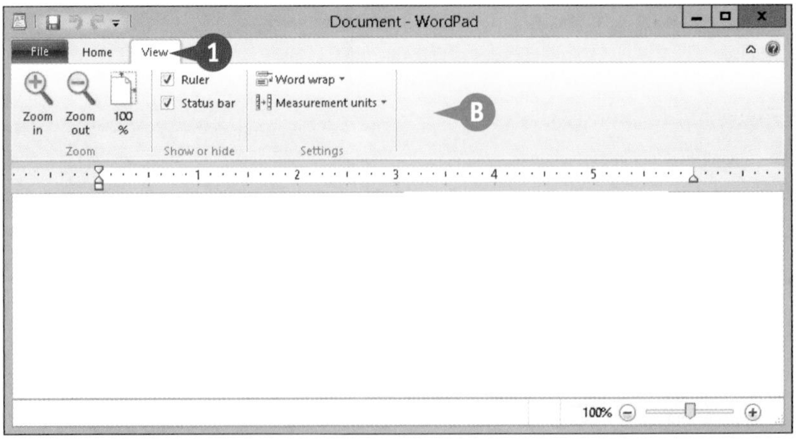

Access File-Related Commands

1 Click the **File** tab.

C The app displays a menu of file-related commands.

2 Click the command you want to run.

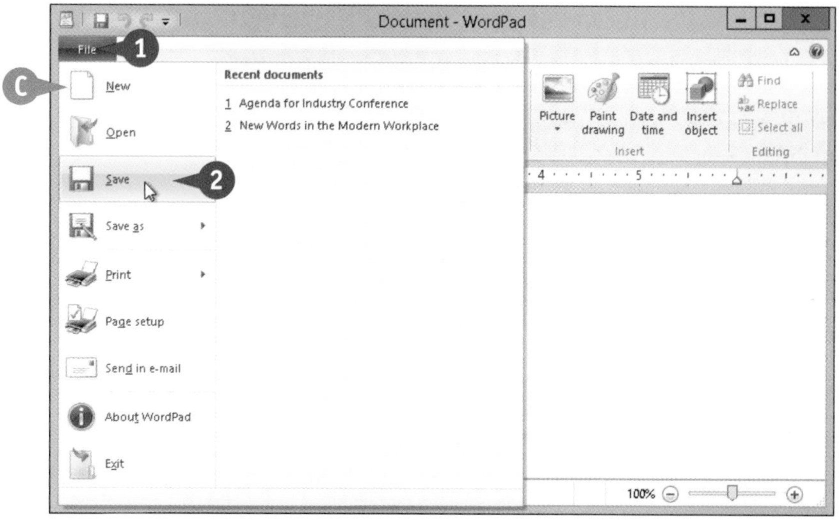

Hide and Display the Ribbon

1 Click **Minimize the Ribbon** (⌃).

The app hides the ribbon and changes ⌃ to ⌄.

To display the ribbon, click ⌄.

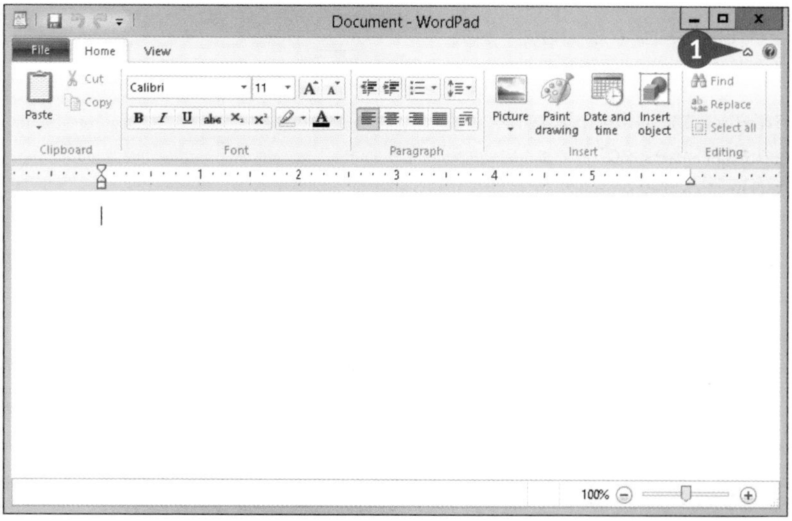

TIPS

Can I add other commands to the Quick Access toolbar?

Yes, you can add as many commands as can fit on the Quick Access toolbar. Taking advantage of this feature is a good idea because commands on the Quick Access toolbar are always just one click away, even when you hide the ribbon. To add a command to the Quick Access toolbar, locate the command on the ribbon, right-click it, and then click **Add to Quick Access Toolbar**.

My Quick Access toolbar is full. How can I get more of my preferred commands on the Quick Access toolbar?

You have a couple of options. The first option is to remove any commands that you do not use. Click the **Customize Quick Access Toolbar** icon (▾) and then click the check mark (☑) beside an existing command. The second option is to move the Quick Access toolbar under the ribbon to get more room. Right-click the ribbon and then click **Show Quick Access Toolbar below the Ribbon**.

Using a Pull-Down Menu

When you are ready to work with an app, use the pull-down menus to access the app's commands and features.

Each item in the menu bar represents a *pull-down menu*, a collection of commands usually related to each other in some way. For example, the File menu commands usually deal with file-related tasks such as opening and closing documents.

The items in a pull-down menu are either commands that execute some action in the app, or features that you turn on and off. If you do not see any menus, you can often display them by pressing Alt.

Using a Pull-Down Menu

Run Commands

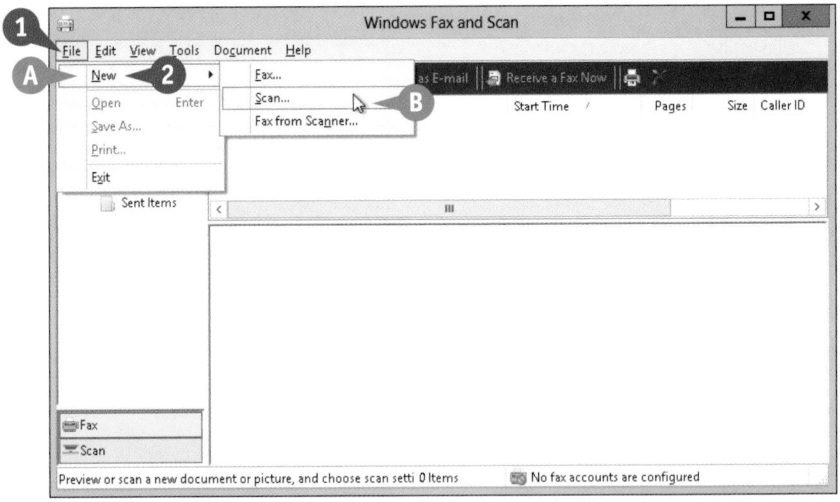

1 Click the name of the menu you want to display.

A The app displays the menu.

You can also display a menu by pressing and holding Alt and pressing the underlined letter in the menu name.

2 Click the command you want to run.

The app runs the command.

B If your command is in a submenu, click the submenu and then click the desired command.

Turn Features On and Off

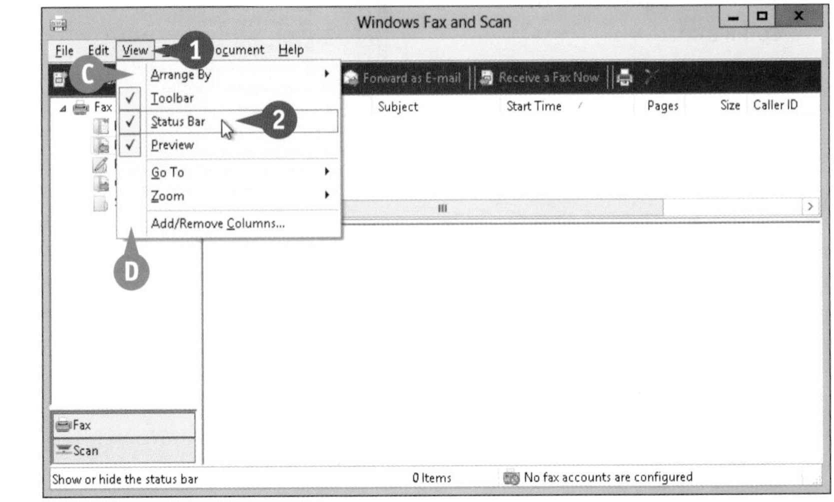

1 Click the name of the menu you want to display.

C The app displays the menu.

2 Click the menu item.

Click a submenu if your command is not on the main menu.

D Toggle features are either turned on (indicated by ☑) or off (no check mark appears).

Using a Toolbar

CHAPTER 2

You can access many app commands faster by using the toolbar. Many apps come with a toolbar, which is a collection of buttons, lists, and other controls displayed in a strip, usually across the top of the app window, just below the menu bar.

Because the toolbar is always visible, you can always use it to select commands, which means that the toolbar often gives you one-click access to the app's most common features. This is faster than using the menu bar method, which often takes several clicks, depending on the command.

Using a Toolbar

Execute Commands

1. Click the toolbar button that represents the command or list.

Note: If the toolbar button remains "pressed" after you click it, the button toggles a feature on and off, and the feature is now on. To turn the feature off, click the button to "unpress" it.

A The app executes the command or, as shown here, drops down the list.

2. If a list appears, click the list item that represents the command.

   The app runs the command.

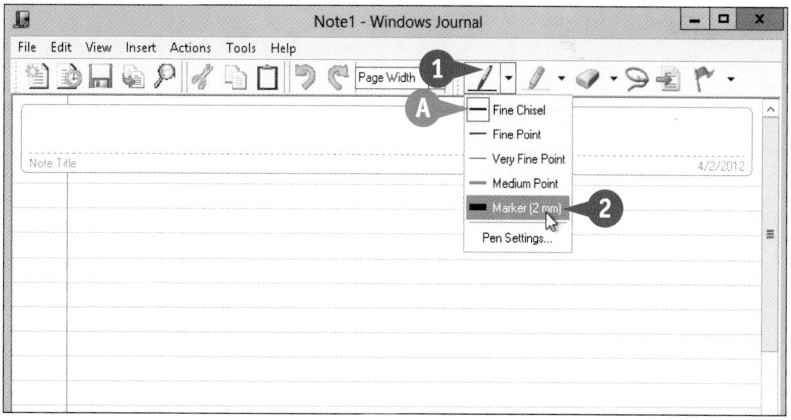

Display and Hide the Toolbar

1. Click **View**.
2. Click **Toolbars**.
3. Click a toolbar.

B If the toolbar is currently displayed (indicated by ☑ in the View menu), the app hides the toolbar.

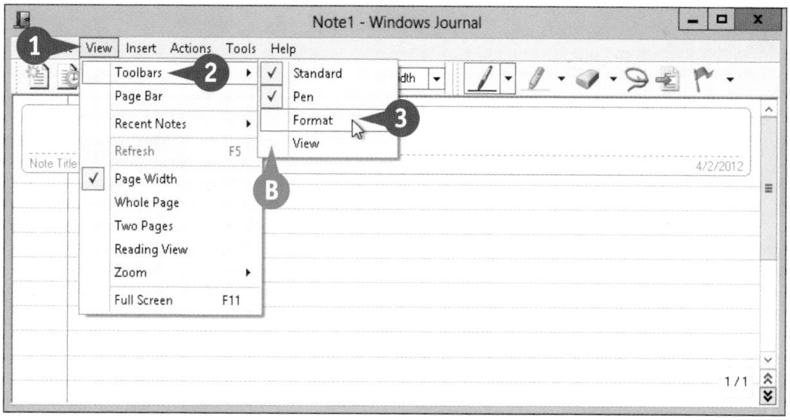

If the toolbar is currently hidden, the app displays the toolbar (indicated by ☑ in the View menu).

Note: Some apps have only a single toolbar. In this case, you click **View** and then click **Toolbar** to toggle the toolbar on and off.

Understanding Dialog Box Controls

You often interact with an app by selecting options or typing text using a dialog box.

A *dialog box* is a small window that appears when an app has information for you, or needs you to provide information. For example, when you select the Print command to print a document, you use the Print dialog box to specify the number of copies that you want to print.

You provide that and other information by accessing various types of dialog controls. To provide information to an app quickly and accurately, you need to know what these dialog controls look like and how they work.

A Option Button

Clicking an option button turns on an app feature. Only one option button in a group can be turned on at a time. When you click an option button, it changes from ○ to ◉.

B Check Box

Clicking a check box toggles an app feature on and off. If you are turning a feature on, the check box changes from ☐ to ☑; if you are turning the feature off, the check box changes from ☑ to ☐.

C Command Button

Clicking a command button executes the command written on the button face. For example, you can click **OK** to put settings you choose in a dialog box into effect and close the dialog box; you can click **Apply** to put the settings into effect and leave the dialog box open; or you can click **Cancel** to close the dialog box without changing the settings.

D Tab

The various tabs in a dialog box display different sets of controls. You can choose from these settings in a dialog box to achieve a variety of results.

E Spin Button

The spin button (⬍) enables you to choose a numeric value.

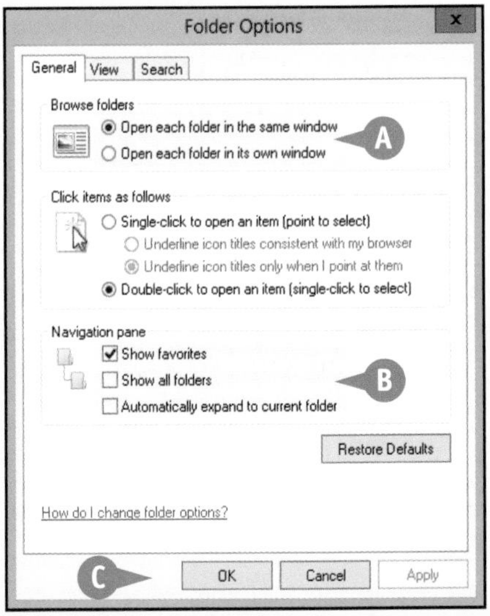

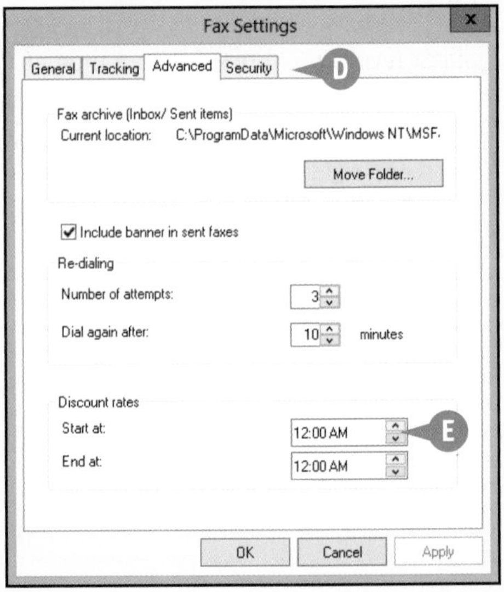

F List Box

A list box displays a relatively large number of choices, and you click the item you want. If you do not see the item you want, you can use the scrollbar to bring the item into view; see "Using Scrollbars," later in this chapter.

G Text Box

A text box enables you to enter typed text.

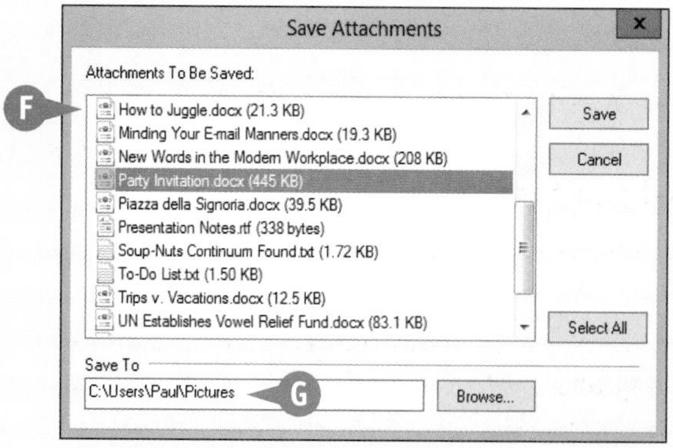

H Combo Box

The combo box combines both a text box and a list box. This means that you can either type the value you want into the text box, or you can use the list to click the value you want.

I Drop-Down List Box

A drop-down list box displays only the selected item from a list. You can open the list to select a different item.

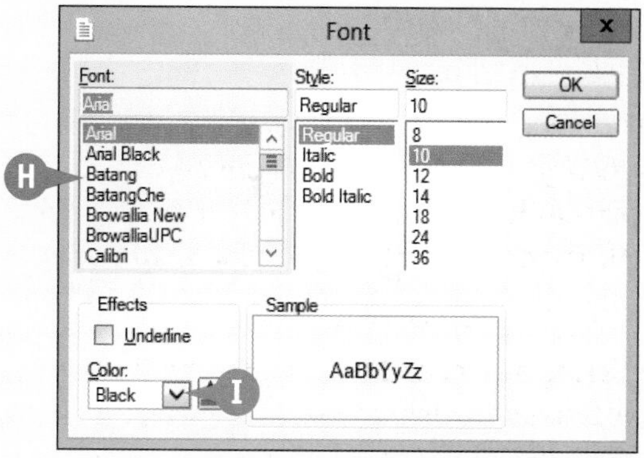

J Slider

A slider lets you choose from a range of values. Use your mouse to drag the slider bar (▯) to the left (which usually means choosing lower values) or the right (which usually means choosing higher values).

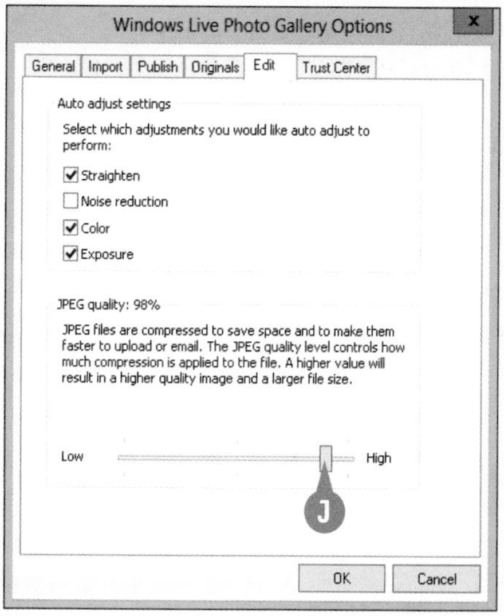

Using Dialog Boxes

After learning about the various types of dialog box controls available (see the previous section), you need to know how to use each of these controls to get the most out of any app.

Many dialog box controls are straightforward. For example, you click an option button to select it; you click a check box to toggle it on and off; you click a tab to view its controls; and you click a command button to execute the command written on its face.

Other dialog box controls are not so simple, and in this section, you learn how to use text boxes, spin buttons, list boxes, and combo boxes.

Using Dialog Boxes

Using a Text Box

1. Click inside the text box.

   A. A blinking, vertical bar (called a *cursor* or an *insertion point*) appears inside the text box.

2. Use **Backspace** or **Delete** to delete any existing characters.
3. Type your text.

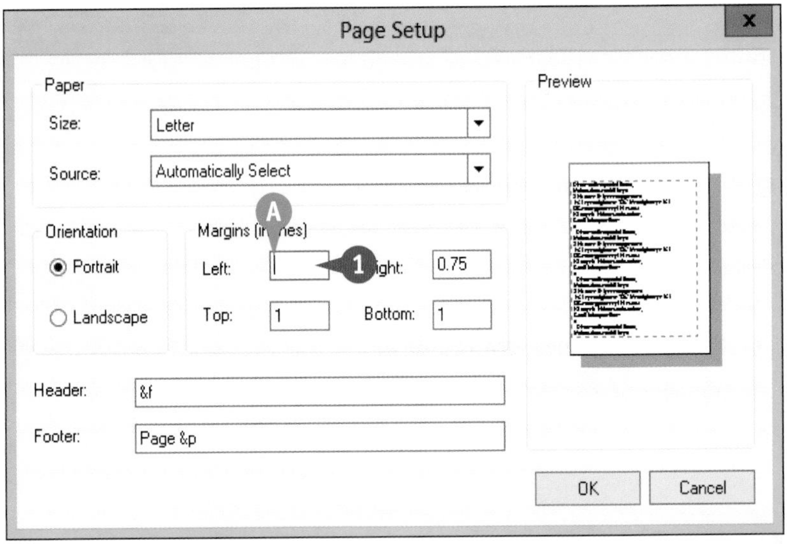

Enter a Value with a Spin Button

1. Click the top arrow on the spin button ( ) to increase the value.
2. Click the bottom arrow on the spin button ( ) to decrease the value.

   B. You can also type the value in the text box.

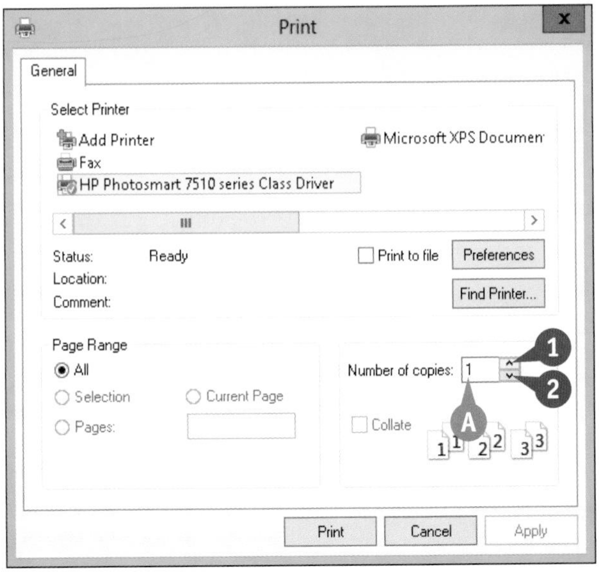

Select a List Box Item

1. If necessary, click the down arrow (▾) to scroll down the list and bring the item you want to select into view.

Note: See the "Using Scrollbars" section to learn how to use scrollbars.

2. Click the item.

C. Click the up arrow (▴) to scroll back up through the list.

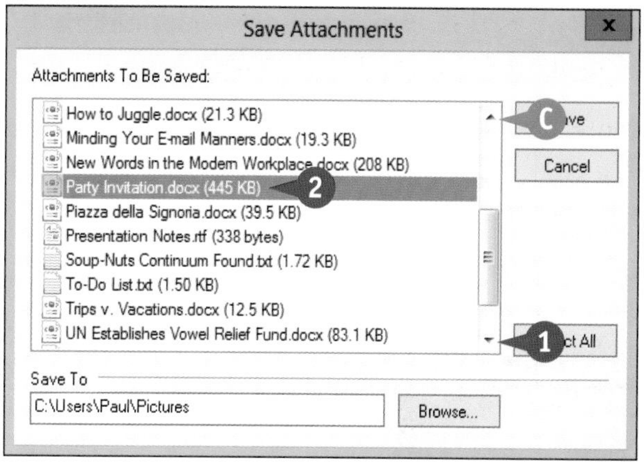

Select an Item Using a Combo Box

1. Click the item in the list box to select it.

D. You can also type the item name in the text box.

Select an Item from a Drop-Down List Box

2. Click the drop-down arrow (⌄).

E. The list appears.

3. Click the item in the list that you want to select.

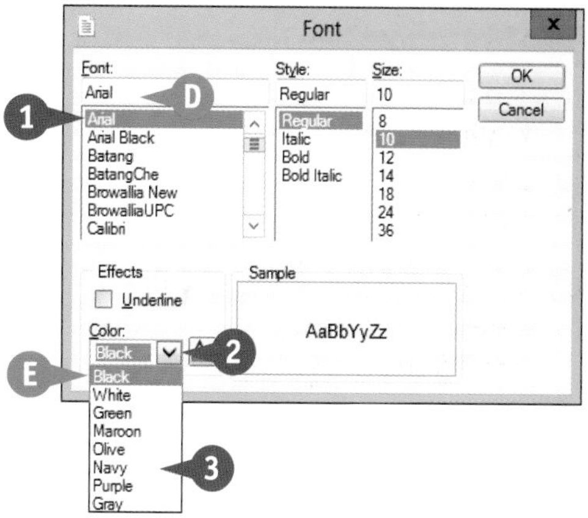

TIP

Are there keyboard shortcuts I can use to make dialog boxes easier to work with?

Yes. Here are the most useful shortcuts:

Enter	Selects the default command button (which is indicated with a highlight around it).
Esc	Cancels the dialog box (which is the same as clicking **Cancel**).
Alt+*letter*	Selects the control that has the *letter* underlined.
Tab	Moves forward through the dialog box controls.
Shift+Tab	Moves backward through the dialog box controls.
↑ and ↓	Moves up and down within the current option button group.
Alt+↓	Drops down the selected combo box or drop-down list box.

Using Scrollbars

If the entire content of a document does not fit inside a window, you can see the rest of the document by using the window's scrollbars to move the contents into view.

If the content is too long to fit inside the window, use the window's vertical scrollbar to move the content down or up as required. If the content is too wide to fit inside the window, use the horizontal scrollbar to move the content right or left as needed. Scrollbars also appear in many list boxes, so knowing how to work with scrollbars also helps you use dialog boxes.

Using Scrollbars

Scroll Up or Down in a Window

1. Click and drag the vertical scroll box down or up to scroll through a window.

   You can also click the up arrow (⌃) or down arrow (⌄).

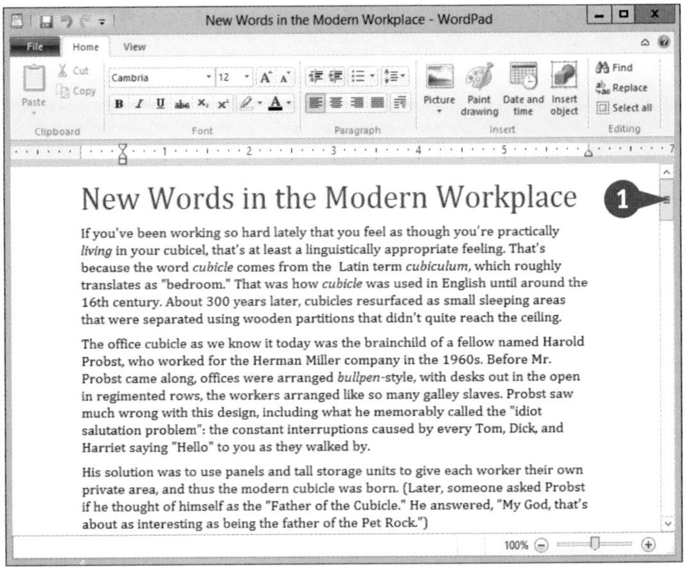

New Words in the Modern Workplace - WordPad
1
New Words in the Modern Workplace
If you've been working so hard lately that you feel as though you're practically living in your cubicel, that's at least a linguistically appropriate feeling. That's because the word cubicle comes from the Latin term cubiculum, which roughly translates as "bedroom." That was how cubicle was used in English until around the 16th century. About 300 years later, cubicles resurfaced as small sleeping areas that were separated using wooden partitions that didn't quite reach the ceiling.
The office cubicle as we know it today was the brainchild of a fellow named Harold Probst, who worked for the Herman Miller company in the 1960s. Before Mr. Probst came along, offices were arranged bullpen-style, with desks out in the open in regimented rows, the workers arranged like so many galley slaves. Probst saw much wrong with this design, including what he memorably called the "idiot salutation problem": the constant interruptions caused by every Tom, Dick, and Harriet saying "Hello" to you as they walked by.
His solution was to use panels and tall storage units to give each worker their own private area, and thus the modern cubicle was born. (Later, someone asked Probst if he thought of himself as the "Father of the Cubicle." He answered, "My God, that's about as interesting as being the father of the Pet Rock.")

Ⓐ The content scrolls down or up.

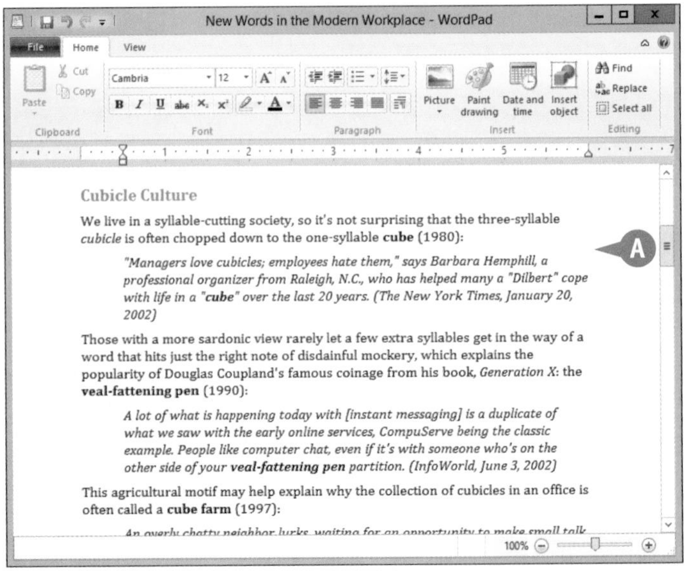

New Words in the Modern Workplace - WordPad
A
Cubicle Culture
We live in a syllable-cutting society, so it's not surprising that the three-syllable cubicle is often chopped down to the one-syllable cube (1980):
"Managers love cubicles; employees hate them," says Barbara Hemphill, a professional organizer from Raleigh, N.C., who has helped many a "Dilbert" cope with life in a "cube" over the last 20 years. (The New York Times, January 20, 2002)
Those with a more sardonic view rarely let a few extra syllables get in the way of a word that hits just the right note of disdainful mockery, which explains the popularity of Douglas Coupland's famous coinage from his book, Generation X: the veal-fattening pen (1990):
A lot of what is happening today with [instant messaging] is a duplicate of what we saw with the early online services, CompuServe being the classic example. People like computer chat, even if it's with someone who's on the other side of your veal-fattening pen partition. (InfoWorld, June 3, 2002)
This agricultural motif may help explain why the collection of cubicles in an office is often called a cube farm (1997):

Scroll Right or Left in a Window

1 Click and drag the horizontal scroll box.

You can also click the right arrow (<) or the left arrow (>).

B The content scrolls left or right.

TIP

What is the wheel on my mouse used for?

Not everyone's mouse has a wheel, but if yours does, you can use the wheel for scrolling up or down in a document. It works the same way as clicking the up arrow (^) or the down arrow (v) does. Move the wheel backward, toward your arm, and the document scrolls down; move the wheel forward, toward your computer, and the document scrolls up.

Switch between Running Apps

If you plan on running multiple applications at the same time, you need to know how to easily switch from one application to another.

In Windows 8, after you start one application, you do not need to close that application before you open another one. Windows 8 supports a feature called *multitasking*, which means running two or more applications at once. This is handy if you need to use several applications throughout the day. For example, you might keep your word processing application, your web browser, and your e-mail application open all day.

Switch between Running Apps

Switch Windows 8 Apps Using the Mouse

1. Move the mouse ⇖ to the top left of the screen.

   Ⓐ Windows 8 displays the most recent app you used.

2. Move the mouse ⇖ down the left edge of the screen.

   Ⓑ Windows 8 displays a list of your running Windows 8 apps.

3. Click the app you want to use.

Switch All Apps Using the Keyboard

1. Press and hold Alt and press Tab.

   Ⓒ Windows 8 displays thumbnail versions of the open apps.

2. Press Tab until the window in which you want to work is selected.

3. Release Alt.

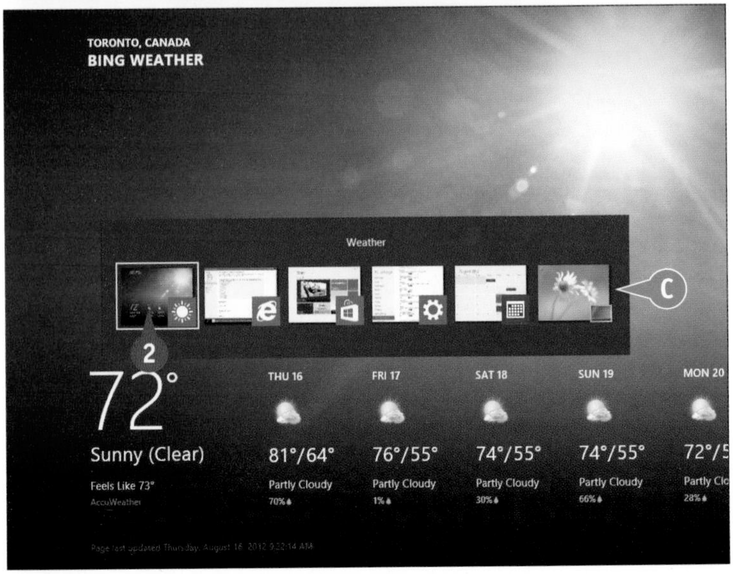

Switch Desktop Apps Using the Taskbar

1. Click the taskbar button of the app to which you want to switch.

Note: You can also switch to another window by clicking the window, even if it is the background.

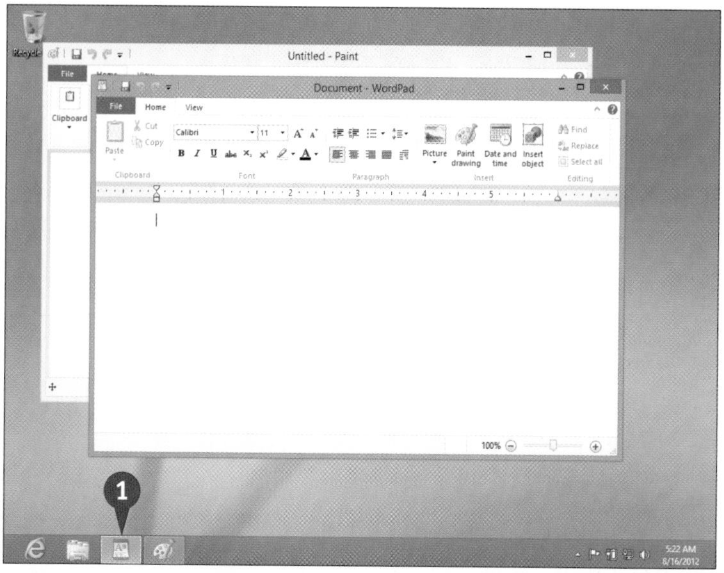

Switch Desktop Apps Using the Keyboard

1. Press and hold Alt and press Esc.

D Windows 8 brings the next Desktop app to the front.

2. Press Esc until you see the app you want to use.
3. Release Alt.

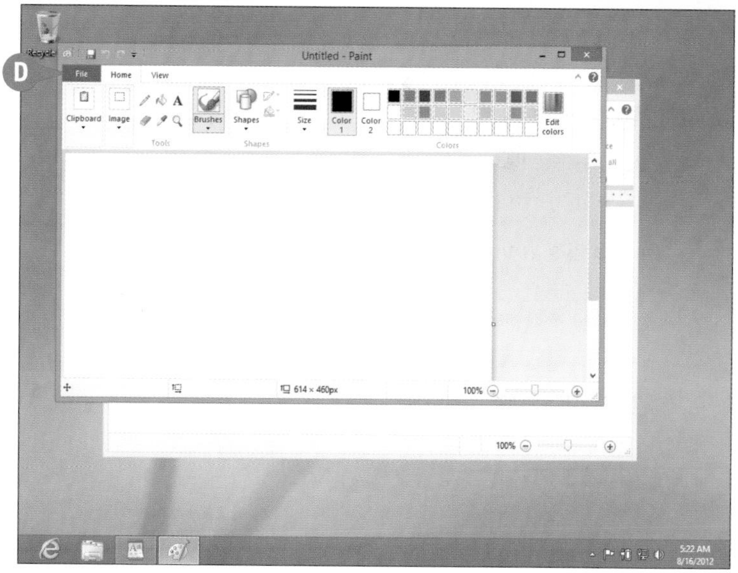

TIP

Can I switch between Windows 8 apps using a tablet?

Yes. In fact, Windows 8 gives you two different ways to do this:

- To cycle through your running Windows 8 apps, use a finger or stylus to swipe in from the left edge of the screen. As you swipe, your finger or stylus drags in the next app window. When you see the window you want, release your finger or stylus to switch to that app.
- To switch to a particular Windows 8 app, use a finger or stylus to swipe in from the left edge of the screen. When you see the next app window, drag it back to the left edge of the screen. Windows 8 displays a list of running apps, so you can now tap the one you want to use.

Uninstall an App

If you have an app that you no longer use, you can free up some disk space and reduce clutter on the Start screen by uninstalling that app.

When you install an app, the program stores its files on your computer's hard drive, and although most programs are quite small, many require hundreds of megabytes of disk space. Uninstalling an app you do not need frees up the disk space it uses and removes its tile (or tiles) from the Start screen (if it has any there) and the Apps screen.

Uninstall an App

Uninstall a Windows 8 App

1. Use the Start screen or the Apps screen to locate the Windows 8 app you want to uninstall.

Note: To display the Apps screen, right-click an empty section of the Start screen and then click **All apps**.

2. Right-click the app.

A. Windows 8 displays the application bar.

3. Click **Uninstall**.

Windows 8 asks you to confirm.

4. Click **Uninstall**.

Windows 8 removes the app.

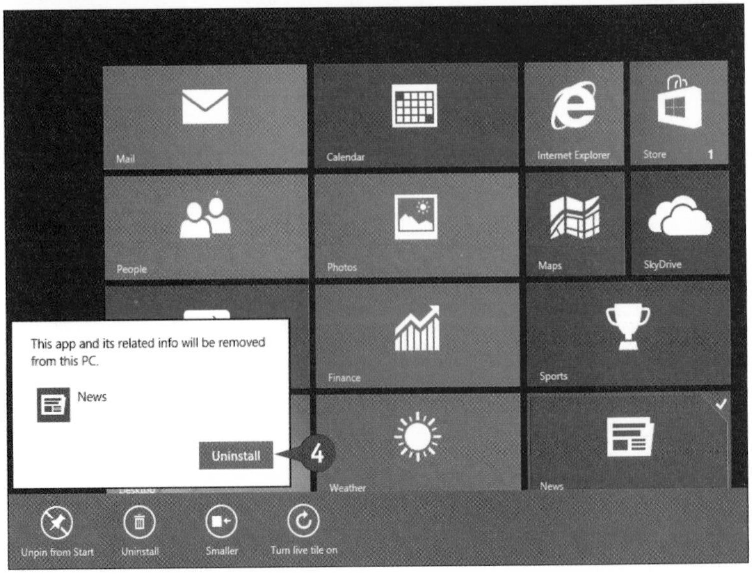

Uninstall a Desktop App

1. On the Start screen, type **uninstall**.
2. Click **Settings**.
3. Click **Uninstall a program**.

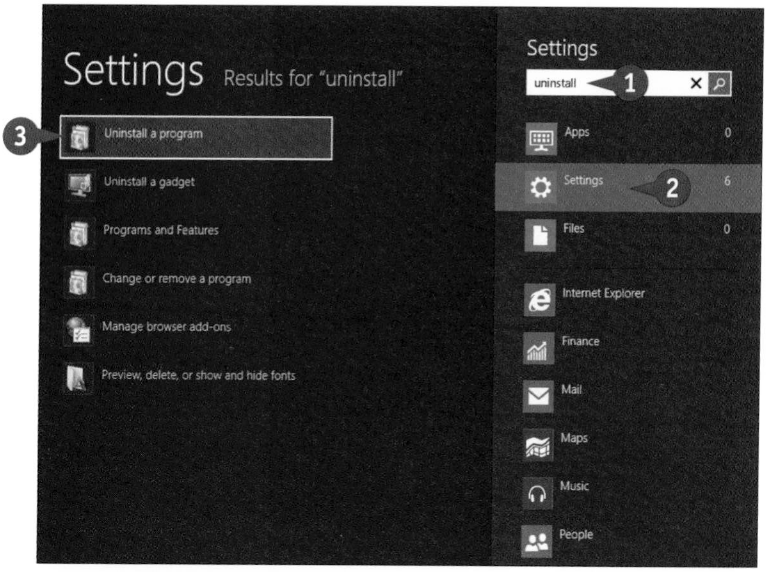

The Programs and Features window appears.

4. Click the app you want to uninstall.
5. Click **Uninstall** (or **Uninstall/ Change**).

   In most cases, the app asks you to confirm that you want to uninstall it.

6. Click **Yes**.

   The app's uninstall procedure begins.

7. Follow the instructions on the screen, which vary from app to app.

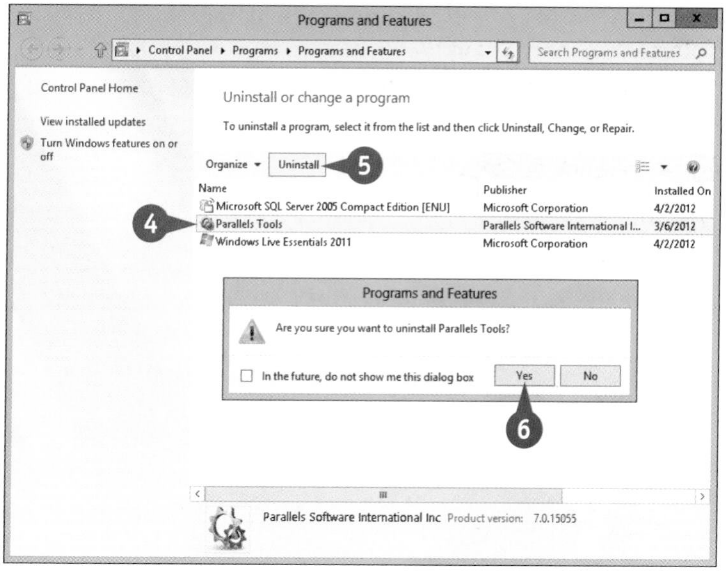

TIPS

How do I uninstall Windows Live Essentials programs?
Follow steps **1** to **3** in the second set of steps to open the Programs and Features window, click **Windows Live Essentials**, and then click **Uninstall/Change**. In the window that appears, click **Remove one or more Windows Live programs**. Select the check box beside each Windows Live program you want to remove (☐ changes to ☑), and then click **Uninstall**.

What is the difference between an Automatic and a Custom uninstall?
Some apps give you a choice of uninstall procedures. The Automatic uninstall requires no input from you. It is the easiest, safest choice and therefore the one you should choose. The Custom uninstall gives you more control, but is more complex and suitable only for experienced users.

CHAPTER 3

Getting Connected to the Internet

This chapter shows you how to connect your computer to the Internet, a global network that gives you a vast world of information.

Understanding Internet Connections

Before you connect to the Internet, you need to know some basic concepts and understand the different types of connections that exist.

For example, you need to know what an Internet service provider does, and you need to understand important concepts such as connection charges and connection speeds.

It is also important to know the difference between the three main types of connections: broadband, wireless broadband, and dialup. This section takes you through these concepts.

Internet Service Provider

An *Internet service provider* (ISP) supplies you with an account that enables you to access the Internet. As discussed later in this chapter, you use Windows 8 to set up a connection between your computer and the ISP, and then the ISP connects your computer to the Internet. The ISP charges you a monthly fee, which can range from a few dollars a month to $40 or $50 dollars a month, depending on the connection speed and how much data usage you are allowed each month.

Connection Speed

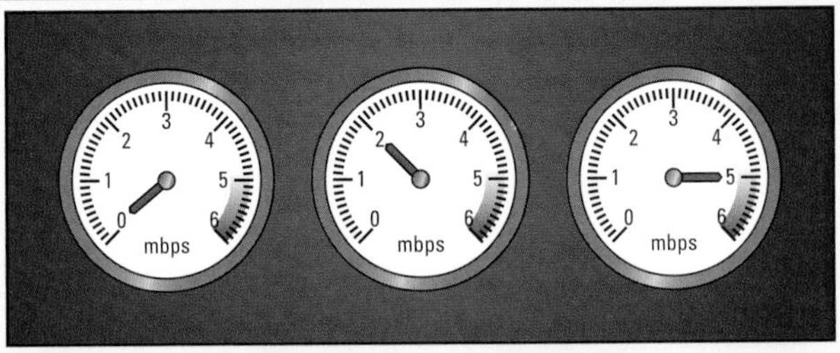

Internet connections have different speeds, and this speed determines how fast the Internet data is sent to your computer. High-speed connections offer speeds typically ranging from 1 megabit per second (Mbps) to 100 Mbps. ISPs typically advertise one speed for *downloads* (that is, data sent to your computer) and another for *uploads* (data sent from your computer). If you connect to your ISP using a dial-up modem, the connection speed may be up to 56 kilobits per second (Kbps).

Connection Usage

The connection usage — often called the connection *bandwidth* — is the amount of data that comes through the connection, both to and from your computer. Connection usage is measured in gigabytes per month, with typical offerings ranging from 15 gigabytes to 250 gigabytes. Note that your ISP charges you an extra fee per gigabyte if you exceed your allotted usage.

Broadband Internet Connection

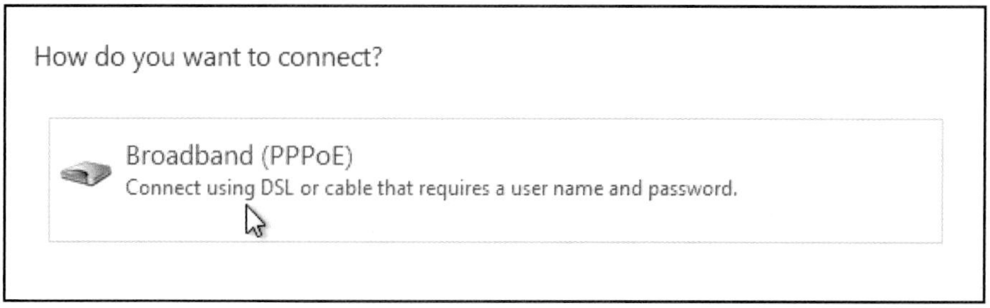

A *broadband* Internet connection is a high-speed connection, and the ISP is usually your local cable company, a phone provider (which usually calls the connection a digital subscriber line, or DSL), or via satellite. The broadband ISP gives you a device called a *broadband modem* that handles the connection. If you are the only person who will be using the Internet, you connect the modem directly to your computer.

Wireless Broadband Connection

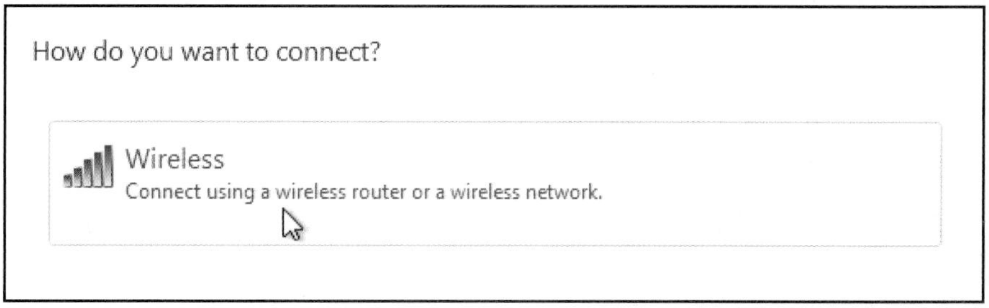

If you have a broadband ISP and you want to share that connection with other people in your home, or if you want to be able to access that connection from anywhere in your home, then you need to set up a wireless connection to the broadband modem. Some broadband ISPs offer modems that include built-in wireless capabilities. Otherwise, you need to purchase a separate device called a *wireless router*.

Dial-Up Internet Connection

If you do not have broadband access in your area, or if you find that broadband accounts are too expensive, you can still connect to the Internet using a dial-up account. A dial-up modem is needed to make the connection, although some computers come with a modem already installed. The main disadvantage to dialup is its exceptionally slow speed — about 100 to 1,000 times slower than broadband — so patience is required.

Set Up a Wireless Broadband Connection

The most common type of Internet connection is a broadband connection accessed over a wireless network, so you should know how to set up such a connection.

The first step in setting up a wireless broadband connection is to make the physical connections between the devices. You need a broadband modem from your ISP and a wireless router. Note, however, that some ISPs offer devices that combine the broadband modem and wireless router.

The second step is to configure your wireless router to connect to your ISP. For this step, your ISP will have provided you with data such as the connection type and the username and password.

Set Up a Wireless Broadband Connection

Connect the Broadband Modem and Wireless Router

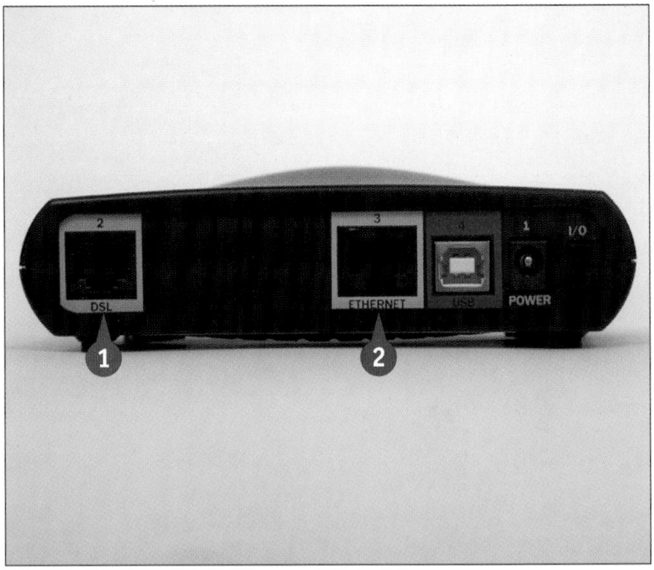

1. Attach the cable that provides the ISP's Internet connection:

   DSL: Run a phone line from the nearest wall jack to the appropriate port — usually labeled ADSL or DSL — on the back of the modem.

   Cable: Run a TV cable from the wall jack to the cable connector — usually labeled Cable — on the back of the modem.

2. Connect a network cable to the modem's network port.

Note: You can skip steps **2** and **3** if you have a device that combines both the modem and the router.

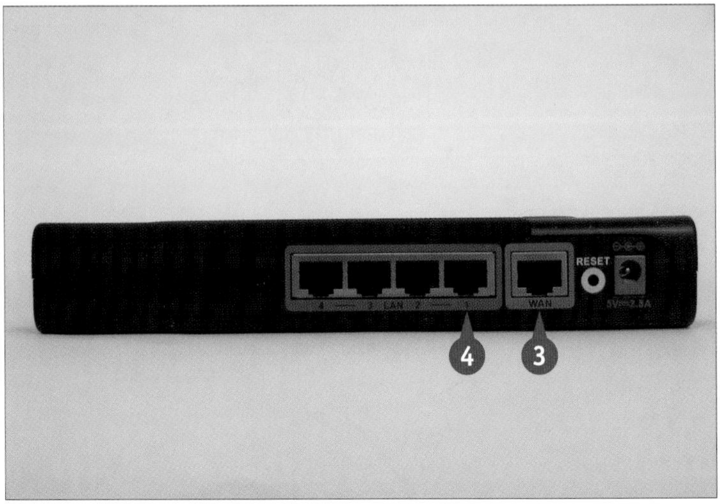

3. Run the network cable from the modem to the WAN (or Internet) port on the back of the router.
4. Connect a network cable to one of the router's network ports.
5. Run the router network cable to a network port on your computer (not shown).
6. Turn on the router and modem.

Configure the Wireless Router

1. On the computer connected to the router, click **Internet Explorer** ( ).
2. In Internet Explorer, type the router address.

Note: See the router manual to learn its address.

3. Type the username and password.

Note: See the router manual to learn username and password.

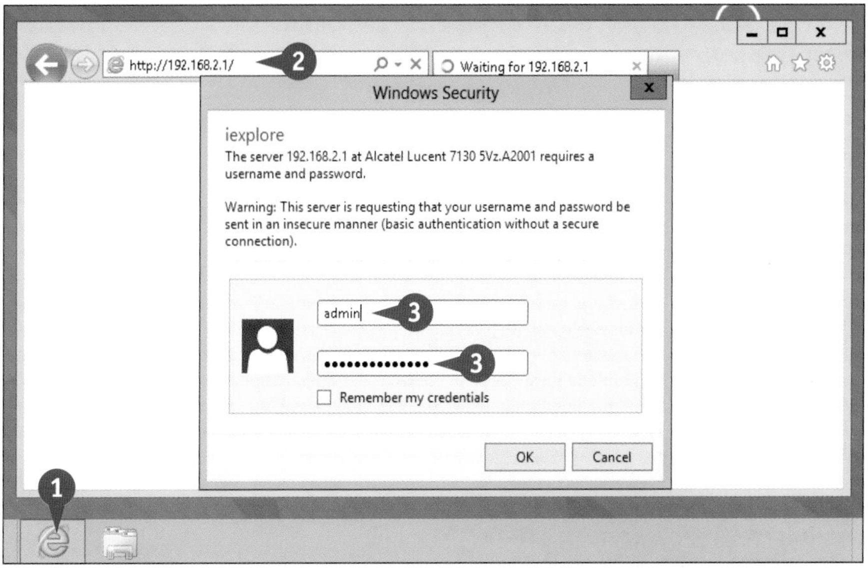

The router's setup page appears.

Note: The layout of the setup page varies depending on the router.

4. Select the type of broadband connection your ISP uses.
5. Type the connection's username and password.
6. Save your changes.

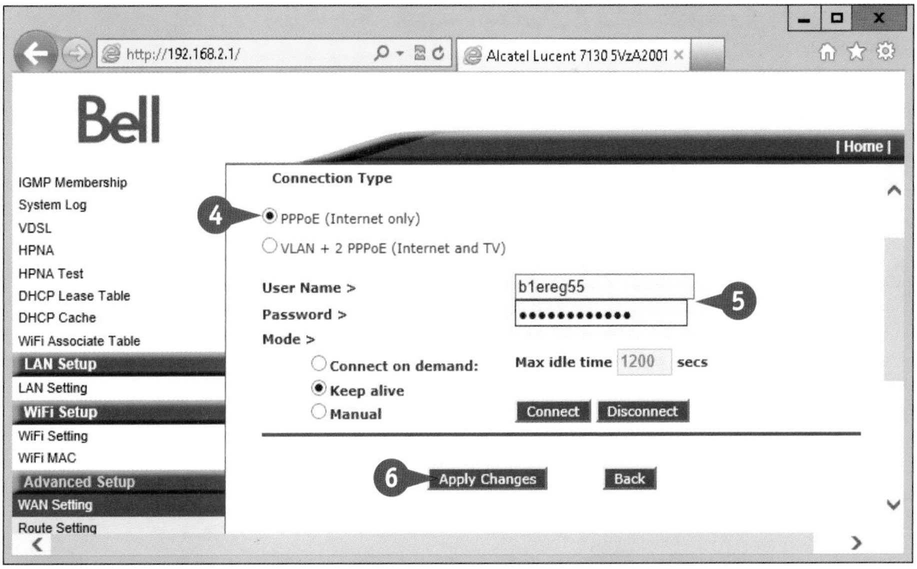

TIPS

Is there a way to access the router's setup page if I do not know the address?
Yes. On the Start screen, type **network** and then click the **Network** icon in the search results. In the Network window, look in the Network Infrastructure section for an icon that represents your router. Double-click the router icon. Internet Explorer appears and loads the router's setup page.

What information do I need to set up the router?
The most common connection types are DHCP and PPPoE. With DHCP, your ISP might require that you configure the router with a specific name, and also that you specify a service name and a domain name. With PPPoE, your ISP might require that you configure the router with a specific name as well as a username and password.

Connect a Broadband Modem

If you plan on using your broadband connection directly from your computer, then you need to know how to connect the broadband modem to your PC.

Although most people prefer to set up wireless access to their broadband connection, as described in the previous section, such a setup is not required for many situations. For example, if you have only one computer, then there is no need to set up wireless access to the Internet, so you should connect the broadband modem directly to your PC. Similarly, even if you have multiple computers, for safety reasons you might prefer that only one of them access the Internet.

Connect a Broadband Modem

1. Turn off the broadband modem.

2. Attach the cable that provides the ISP's Internet connection to the wall jack:

   DSL: Connect a phone line to the phone wall jack.

   Cable: Connect a TV cable to the cable wall jack.

3. Attach the other end of the cable to the modem:

   DSL: Connect the phone line to an appropriate port — usually labeled ADSL or DSL — on the back of the modem.

   Cable: Connect the TV cable to the cable connector — which is usually labeled Cable — on the back of the modem.

4 Attach a network cable to a network port on the back of the modem.

A On many modems, the network port is labeled Ethernet.

5 Attach the other end of the network cable to a network port on your computer.

6 Turn on the modem.

TIPS

How can I connect my broadband modem if my computer does not have a network port?

Most newer broadband modems also come with a USB port on the back. If you are working with a computer that does not have a network port, or if the network port already has a cable attached, you can use a USB port instead. Run a USB cable from the USB port on the modem to a free USB port on your computer. You also need to install the broadband modem's USB device driver, which should be on a disc that your ISP provided.

My ISP tells me I need to register my modem. How do I do that?

Nowadays, many ISPs insist that you register the broadband modem by accessing a page on the ISP's website and sometimes entering a code or the serial number of the modem. Read the instructions that come with your ISP's Internet kit to determine whether you must first register your broadband modem online. If so, follow the steps in this section and then use Internet Explorer to access the ISP's site and register your modem.

Create a Broadband Internet Connection

If you have a broadband account with your Internet service provider, and you have connected your broadband modem directly to your PC as described in the previous section, you can configure Windows 8 to use a broadband Internet connection.

This type of connection works with the PPPoE (this stands for Point-to-Point Protocol over Ethernet) connection type, so first make sure your ISP supports that type. To create the connection, you will also need to know the username and password that Windows 8 must enter to authorize the connection.

Create a Broadband Internet Connection

Create the Connection

1. On the Start screen, press ⊞+W to open the Settings search pane.
2. Type **broadband**.
3. Click the **Set up a broadband connection** item that appears in the search results.

   Windows 8 opens the Set Up a New Broadband Connection dialog box.
4. Type your username.
5. Type your password.
6. To avoid having to type the password when you connect in the future, click **Remember this password** (☐ changes to ☑).
7. Edit the connection name, if desired.

Note: The connection name is for your own use, so create a name that helps you remember what the connection is.

8. Click **Create**.

   Windows 8 sets up the connection and then connects to your ISP through the broadband modem.

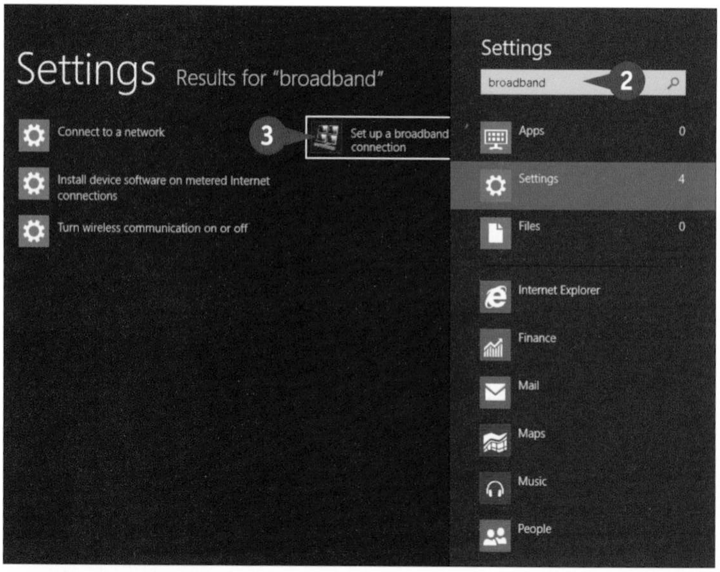

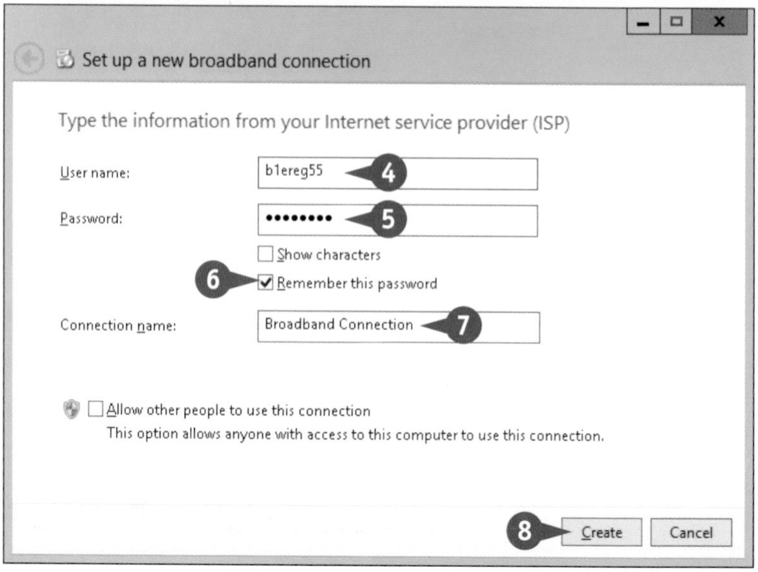

Connect to the Internet

1. On the Start screen, press ⊞+I.

   The Start settings pane appears.

2. Click **Network**.

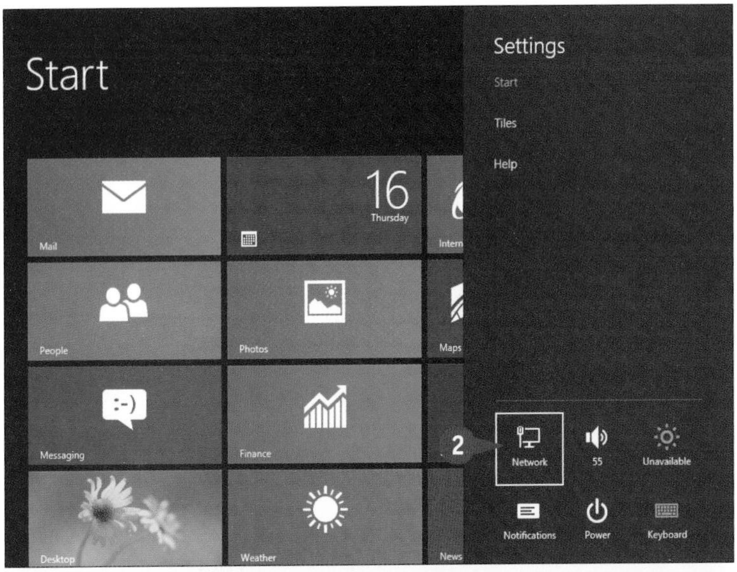

   The Networks pane appears.

3. Click the broadband connection.

4. Click **Connect**.

   Windows 8 connects to your ISP through the broadband modem.

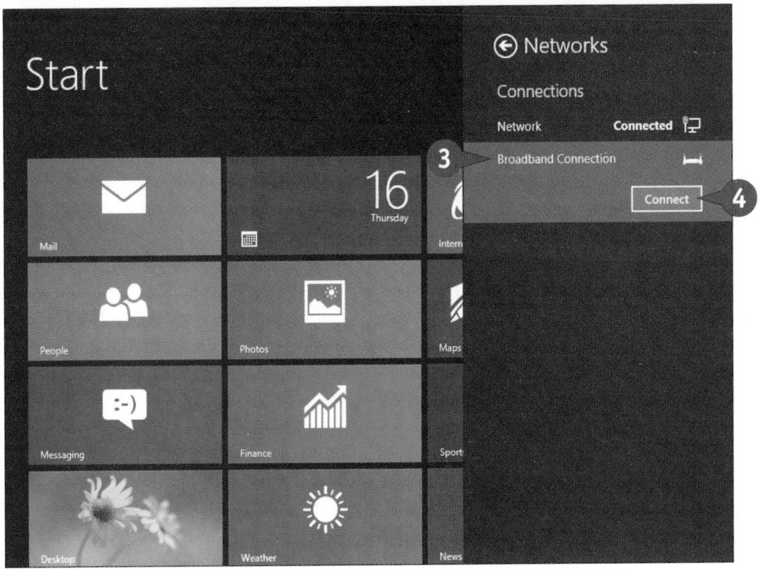

TIPS

How do I disconnect from the Internet?
If you do not want other people to use your computer to access the Internet while your computer is unattended, it is best to disconnect. To do this, press ⊞+I to open the Start settings pane, click **Network**, click the broadband connection, and then click **Disconnect**.

I have other user accounts on my computer. Can they use the same connection?
If you have other user accounts on your computer, you can save them time by making the Internet connection available when they log on. In the Set Up a New Broadband Connection dialog box, click **Allow other people to use this connection** (☐ changes to ☑).

Connect a Dial-Up Modem

If you signed up for a dial-up account with an ISP, then you need to know how to connect the dial-up modem to your PC.

Dial-up modems come in two varieties — internal and external — and which type you have determines how you set up the modem.

An internal modem resides inside your computer's case. With this modem type, you only need to connect the phone cables to get your modem ready to connect.

An external model is a separate device that sits outside the computer case. With this modem type, you must also connect a data cable between the modem and the PC.

Connect a Dial-Up Modem

Connect an Internal Modem

1. Attach a phone cable to a wall jack.

2. Attach the other end of the cable to your computer's modem jack.

Connect an External Modem

1. Attach a phone cable to a wall jack.
2. Attach the other end of the cable to the modem.

3. Attach the modem to a USB port on your computer.

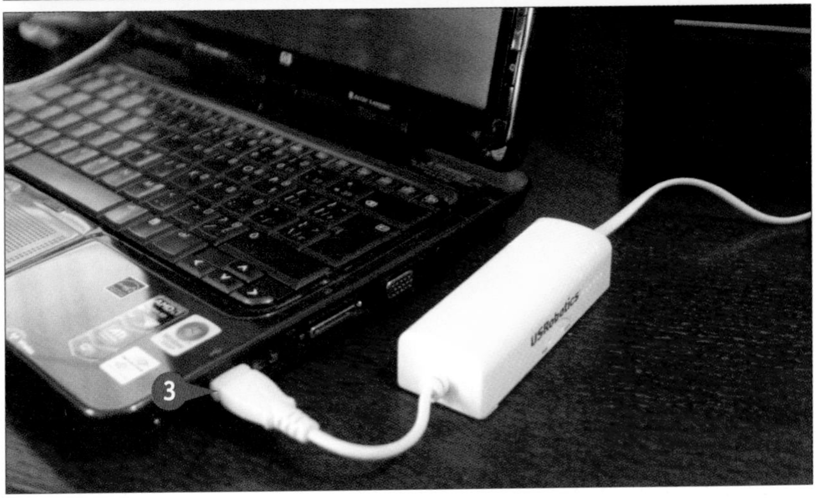

TIPS

Why does my modem have two phone jacks?

Having two phone jacks enables you to have your modem and your telephone connected at the same time. To set this up, be sure to connect the cable from the wall jack to the modem jack labeled Line (it may also be labeled Telco or it may just show a picture of a wall jack). Then attach a second phone cable to the jack labeled Phone (it may also just show a picture of a telephone) in the back of the external modem. Finally, attach the other end of this second cable to your telephone.

Can I talk on the telephone while my computer is using a dial-up connection to the Internet?

No, you cannot. When your computer is accessing the Internet using a dial-up connection, your phone line is engaged, so you cannot use it to make calls. This also means that people who attempt to call you either hear a busy signal or go straight to voice mail, if you have this feature on your phone line.

Create a Dial-Up Internet Connection

If you have a dial-up account with your Internet service provider and you have connected your dial-up modem as described in the previous section, you can configure Windows 8 to use a dial-up Internet connection.

To create the connection, you need to know the phone number that your modem must dial to connect with your ISP. You also need to know the username and password that Windows 8 must enter to authorize the connection.

If you have an external modem, be sure to turn the modem on before starting this section.

Create a Dial-Up Internet Connection

1. On the Start screen, press ⊞+W to open the Settings search pane.
2. Type **dial-up**.
3. Click the **Set up a dial-up connection** item that appears in the search results.

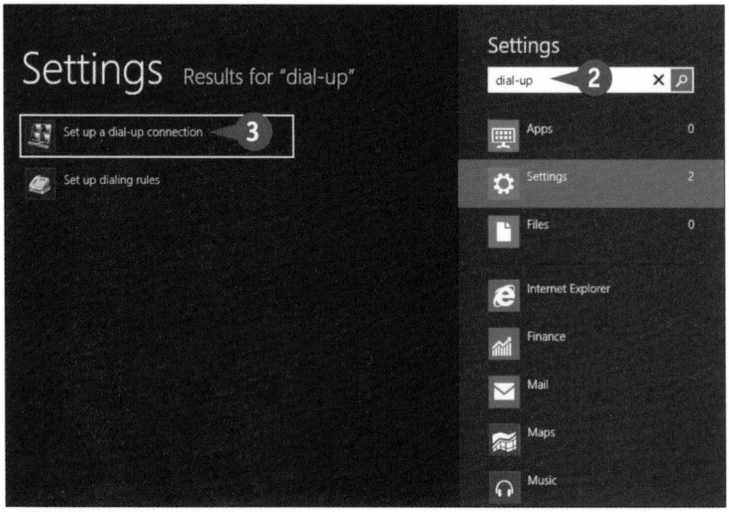

Windows 8 opens the Create a Dial-up Connection dialog box.

4. Type the dial-up phone number.
5. Type your username.
6. Type your password.
7. To avoid having to type the password when you connect in the future, click **Remember this password** (☐ changes to ☑).

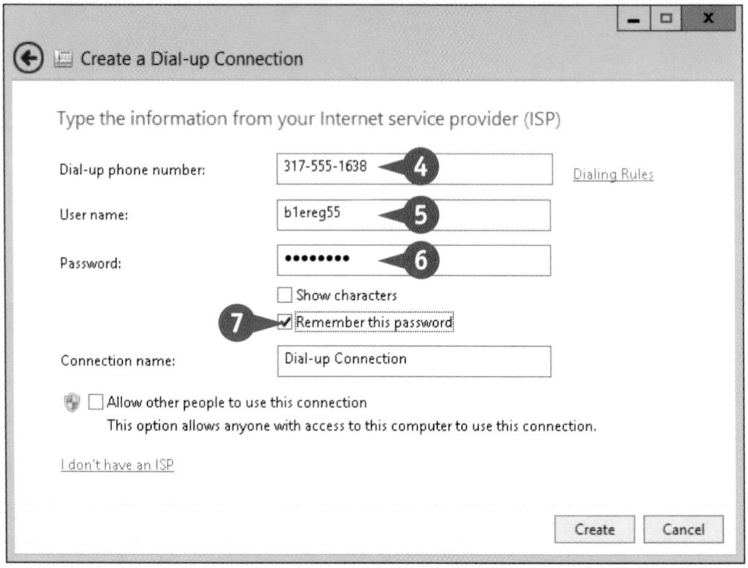

8 Edit the connection name, if desired.

Note: The connection name is for your own use, so create a name that helps you remember what the connection is.

9 Click **Create**.

Windows 8 sets up the connection and then connects to your ISP through the dial-up modem.

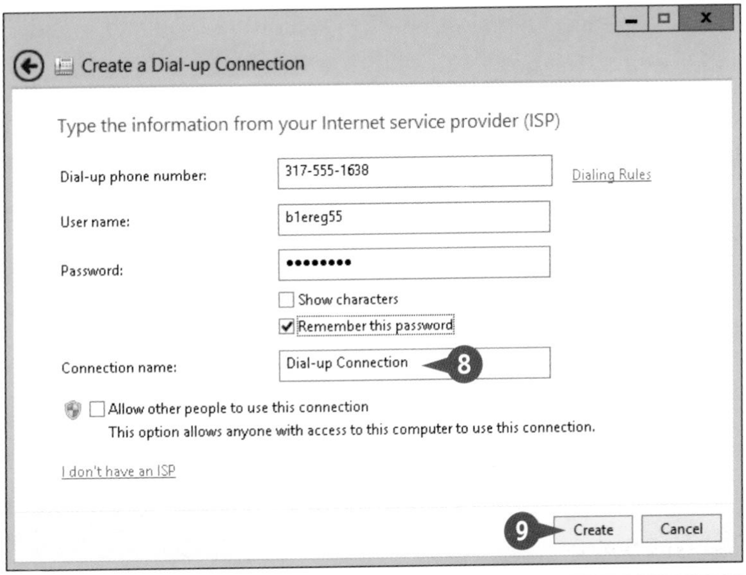

When the connection is complete, Windows 8 displays the Connection to the Internet Is Ready to Use dialog box.

10 Click **Close**.

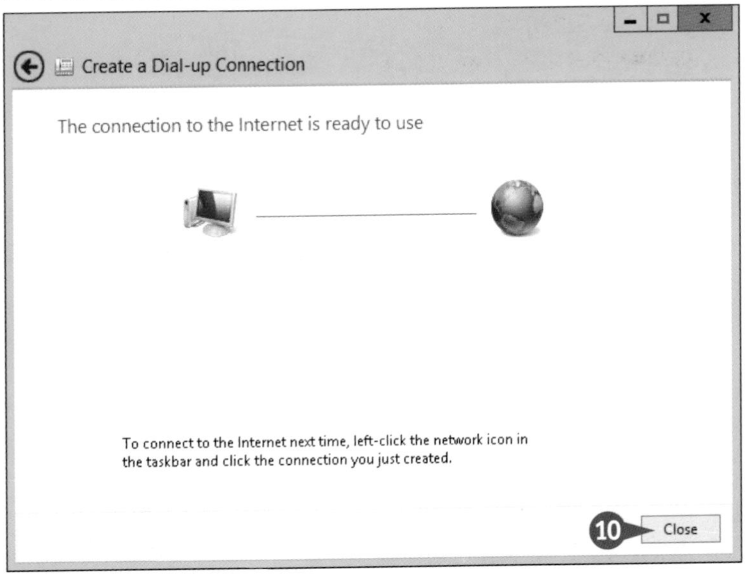

TIPS

How do I disconnect from and reconnect to the Internet?
After you have completed your dial-up Internet session, you should disconnect to avoid running up your connection time unnecessarily. To do this, press ⊞+I to open the Start settings pane, click **Network**, click the dial-up connection, and then click **Disconnect**. To reconnect, press ⊞+I to open the Start settings pane, click **Network**, click the dial-up connection, and then click **Connect**.

My area requires 10-digit dialing. How do I handle this?
When you fill in the ISP's phone number, add the area code in front of the phone number. For example, if the area code is 317 and the phone number is 555-1212, type **317-555-1212**.

Create a Microsoft Account

You can get much more out of Windows 8 by using a Microsoft account with your Windows 8 user account, so you need to know how to set up your own Microsoft account.

When you connect a Microsoft account to your Windows 8 user account, many previously inaccessible Windows 8 features become immediately available. For example, you can use the Mail app to access your e-mail and the Messages app to exchange text messages with other Microsoft account users. You can also download apps from the Store, access your photos and documents anywhere online, and even sync your settings with other PCs where you use the same account.

Create a Microsoft Account

Start the Creation of a Microsoft Account

1. Press ⊞+W to open the Settings search pane.
2. Type **microsoft**.
3. Click **Connect to a Microsoft account**.

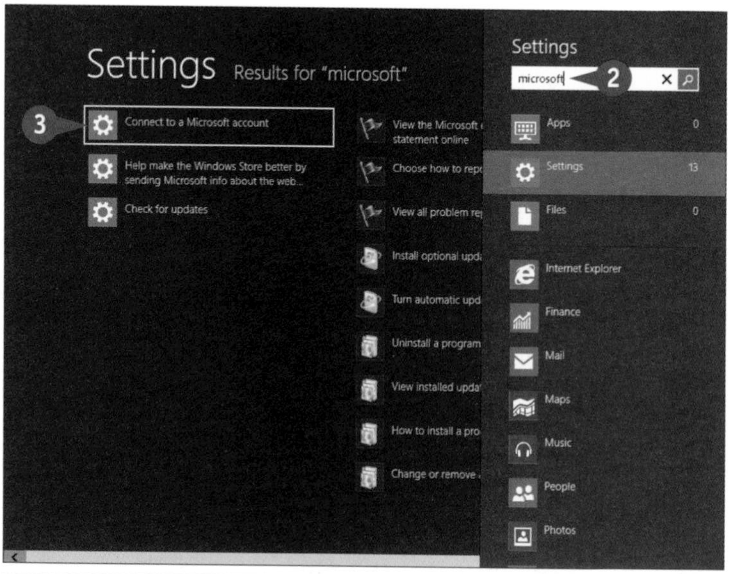

Windows 8 displays the PC Settings window with the Users tab selected.

4. Click **Switch to a Microsoft account**.

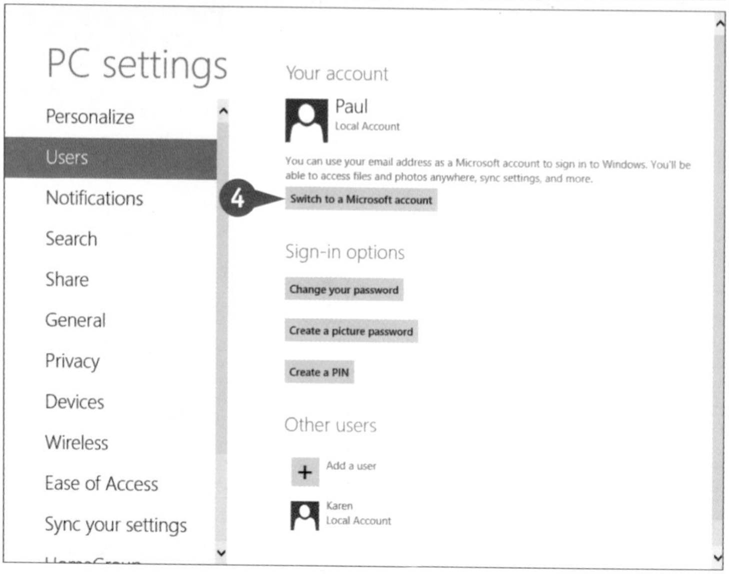

Windows 8 asks you to verify your current account password.

5 Type your password.

6 Click **Next**.

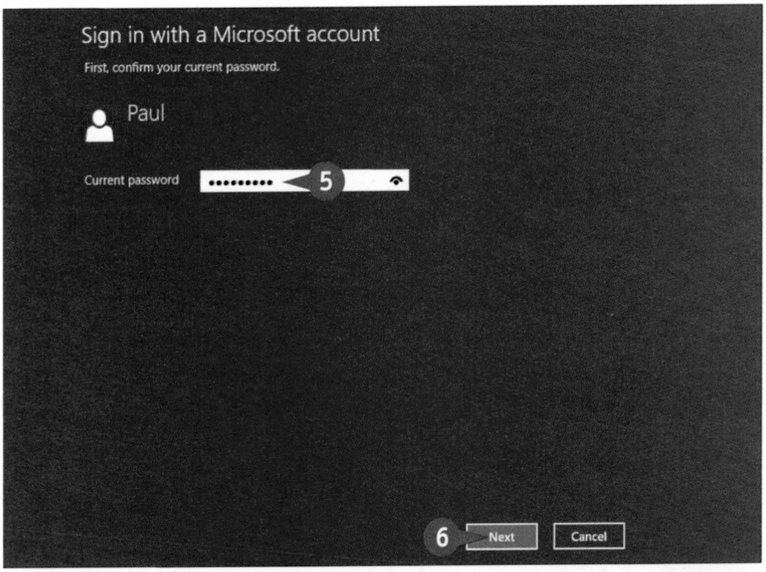
Sign in with a Microsoft account
First, confirm your current password.
Paul
Current password
5
6
Next
Cancel

Windows 8 asks you to enter your e-mail address.

7 Type your e-mail address.

8 Click **Next**.

Sign in with a Microsoft account
Use your favorite email address to sign in to Windows. If you already use an email address to sign in to PCs running Windows, enter it here.
myaddress@myisp.com
7
When you sign in to Windows with a Microsoft account, you can:
• Download apps from Windows Store.
• Get your online content in Microsoft apps automatically.
• Sync settings online to make PCs look and feel the same–this includes settings like browser favorites and history.
Privacy statement
Sign up for a new email address
8
Next
Cancel

TIPS

How do I create a new account using either Live.com or Hotmail.com?

When you type the e-mail address, type the username you prefer to use, followed by either **live.com** or **hotmail.com**. Assuming the username has not been taken, Windows 8 will recognize that this is a new address and create the new account automatically.

Can I use a non-Microsoft e-mail address?

Yes, you can. Windows 8 does not require that you use a Live.com or Hotmail.com e-mail address from Microsoft. If you have an e-mail address that you use regularly, you are free to use that same address with your Windows 8 account.

continued ▶

Create a Microsoft Account (continued)

How you proceed from here depends on whether you are creating a new Microsoft account or using an existing account. Using a Microsoft account with Windows 8 can also help you if you forget your account password and cannot log in. You can provide Microsoft with your mobile phone number, so that if you ever forget your password, Microsoft sends you a text message to help you reset your password. You can also give Microsoft an alternative e-mail address, or you can provide the answer to a secret question. Note that Windows 8 requires that you choose at least two of these three methods before it lets you complete your account.

Create a Microsoft Account (continued)

Configure a New Microsoft Account

1. Type your password in both text boxes.
2. Type your first name.
3. Type your last name.
4. Choose your country.
5. Type your ZIP code.
6. Click **Next**.

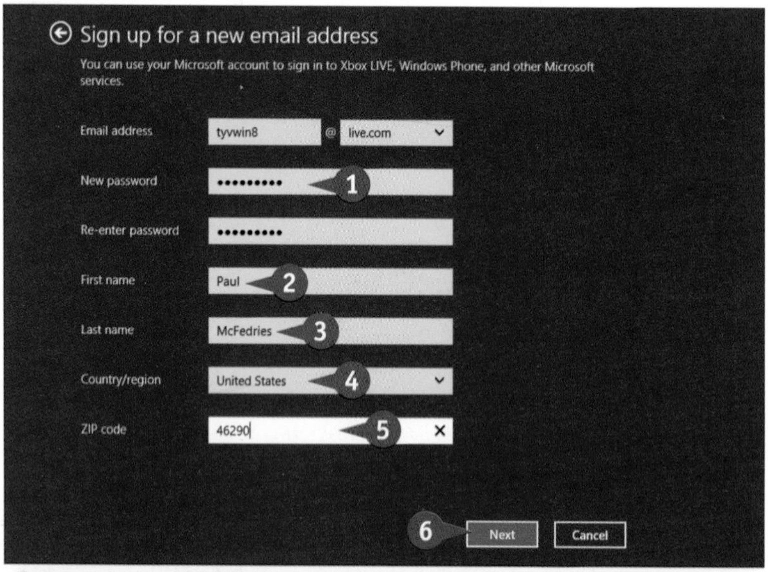

Configure an Existing Microsoft Account

1. Type your Microsoft account password.
2. Click **Next**.

Complete the Account

1. Type your mobile phone number.
2. Type an alternate e-mail address.
3. Choose a secret question.
4. Type the answer to the question.
5. Click **Next**.

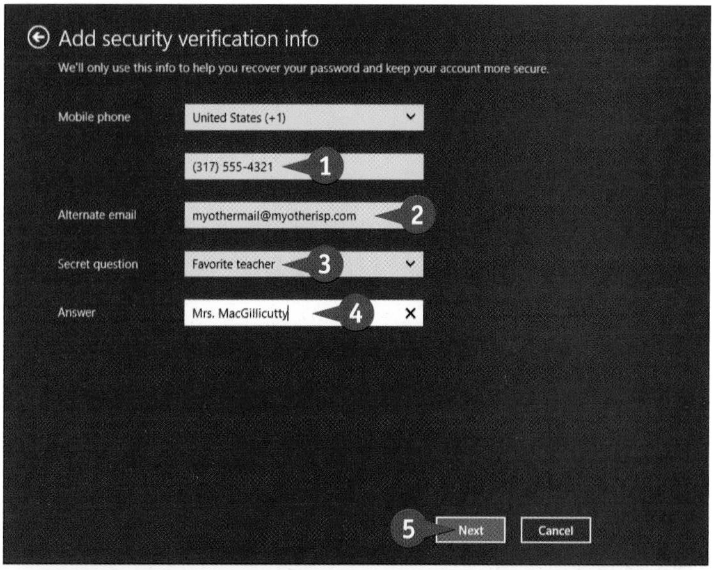

If you are creating a new account, Windows 8 asks for some extra information.

6. Choose the month, day, and year of your birth.
7. Click either **Male** or **Female** (○ changes to ◉).
8. Type the characters you see in the box.
9. Click the check box (☑ changes to ☐).
10. Click **Next**.
11. In the last window, click **Finish** (not shown).

Windows 8 connects the Microsoft account to your user account.

The next time you start Windows 8, use your Microsoft account e-mail address and password to log in.

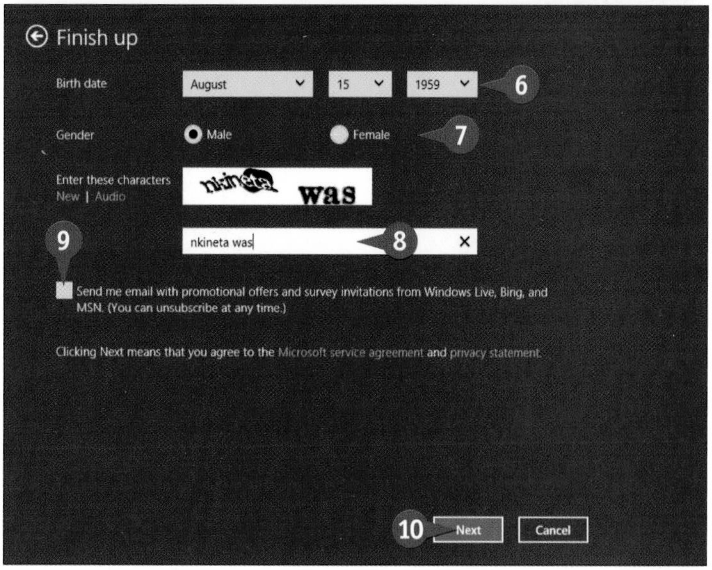

TIP

If I no longer want to use a Microsoft account with Windows 8, can I remove it?

Yes, you can revert to using your original user account at any time. Note, however, that you will no longer see any personal data on the Start screen, you will not be able to access your files online, and your settings will no longer sync between PCs.

To remove the Microsoft account, press ⊞+W to open the Settings search pane, type **microsoft**, and then click **Disconnect a Microsoft account**. In the PC Settings window, click **Switch to a local account**. Type your Microsoft account password, click **Next**, type your local account password (twice) and a password hint, and click **Next**. Click **Sign out and finish** to complete the removal.

CHAPTER 4

Using the Windows 8 Apps

The Start screen is home to a number of tiles, each of which represents a Windows 8 app. This chapter introduces you to most of the Windows 8 apps.

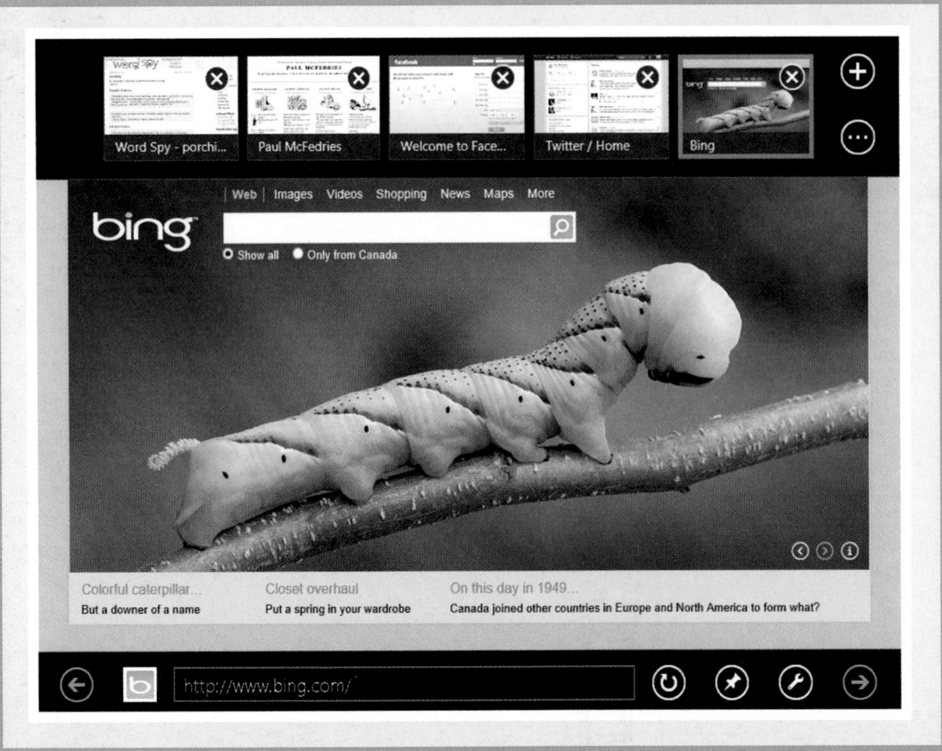

Surf the Web

After you have your Internet connection up and running, as described in Chapter 3, you can use a web browser application to navigate — or *surf* — the sites of the World Wide Web.

Windows 8 comes with two programs that you can use to surf the web: the desktop version of Internet Explorer, which you learn about in Chapter 5, and the Internet Explorer app, which is the subject of this section.

Surf the Web

Tour Internet Explorer

1 On the Start screen, click the **Internet Explorer** tile.

A The address bar shows the current page address.

B Links take you to different pages. They usually appear in a different color.

C When you point at a link, the mouse ⇖ changes to ☝.

D When you point at a link, this banner tells you the address of the linked page.

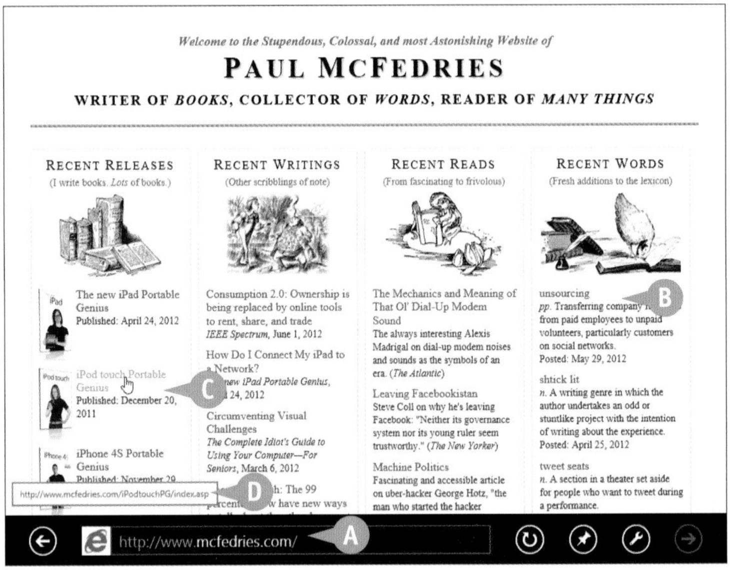

Enter a Web Page Address

1 If you know the address, click inside the address bar.

Note: If you do not see the address bar, right-click the screen.

E Internet Explorer displays a list of pages you have visited frequently.

If you see the page in this list, click it.

2 Type the address.

3 Click **Go** (➔) or press Enter.

Internet Explorer displays the page.

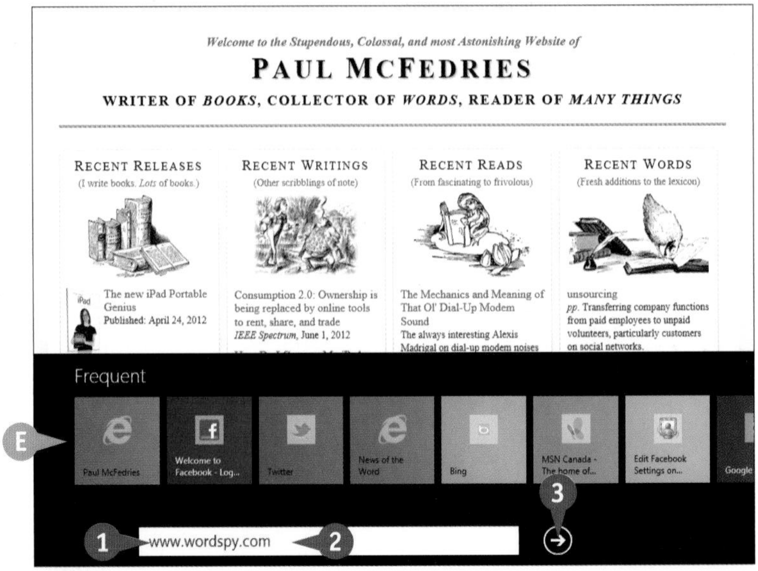

Select a Link

1. Position the mouse over a link (changes to).

   F The banner shows you the address of the linked page.

2. Click the link.

   Internet Explorer displays the page.

Navigate Web Pages

G Click **Back** () to return to the previous page. Repeat clicking until you return to the page you want to view.

H Click **Forward** () to return to the next page. Repeat clicking until you return to the page you want to view.

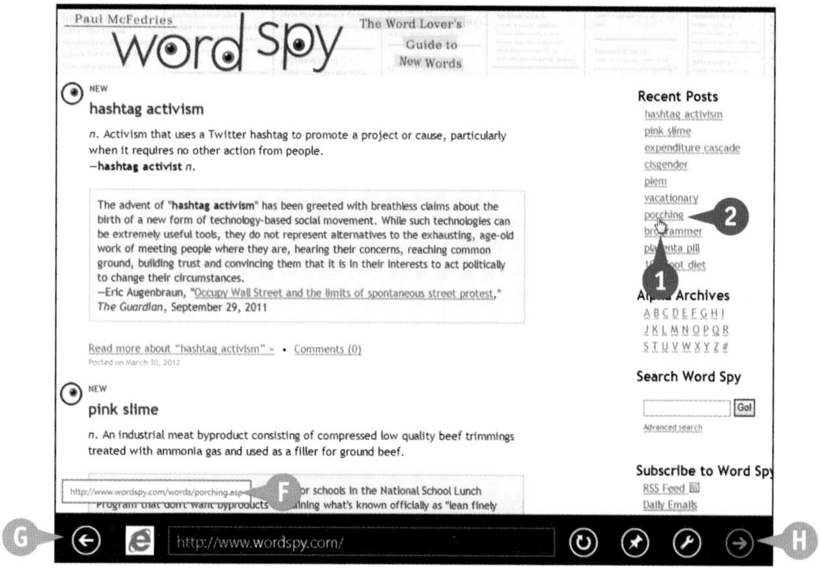

TIPS

Can I save my favorite websites rather than typing the address each time?

Yes. First, navigate to the page you want to save. To add a tile for the page to your Start screen, click **Pin site** () in the application bar, click **Pin to Start**, edit the page name, and then click **Pin to Start**. If you prefer to save the page within Internet Explorer, click and then click **Add to favorites**. Internet Explorer adds a tile for the page to the Favorites list, which appears to the right of the Frequent list.

Can I open multiple pages at the same time?

Yes. Internet Explorer offers a feature called *tabs* that enables you to open several pages at once, each in its own tab. Right-click the screen and Internet Explorer displays the tabs at the top of the screen. Click **New Tab** (), type the address, and then click (or press Enter). To open a link in a new tab, right-click the link and then click **Open in new tab**.

Send an E-Mail Message

If you know the e-mail address of a person or organization, you can use it to send an e-mail message to that address. An e-mail address is a set of characters that uniquely identifies the location of an Internet mailbox. Example e-mail addresses are paul@mcfedries.com and president@whitehouse.gov.

Windows 8 offers two methods for sending e-mail messages. If you have signed up for a Microsoft account as explained in Chapter 3, you can use the Mail app, as described here. You can also install the Mail program, which is discussed in detail in Chapter 6.

Send an E-Mail Message

1. On the Start screen, click the **Mail** tile.
2. Click **New** (⊕).

Note: You can also press Ctrl+N.

Live Inbox
2
Microsoft account
You've connected Twitter t... Wed
Microsoft account
You've connected Faceb... Wed
TechSmith
Snagit editor makes your im... Fri
Microsoft account
August 15, 2012 2:42 PM
To: Paul McFedries
You've connected Twitter to the People app
Never miss another Tweet!
The people you follow on Twitter have been added to the People app, so you'll see all their latest Tweets in What's new.
You can find more people to follow by searching for your contacts on Twitter.
Find friends on Twitter
Find more ways to connect, and review or change your Twitter connection settings at any time.
Notifications preferences | SMS notifications | Microsoft privacy statement

A message window appears.

3. Use the To text box to type the e-mail address of the recipient.

Note: You can add multiple e-mail addresses to the To line. Press Enter after each address.

A. To send a copy of the message to another person, use the Cc text box to type that person's e-mail address.

B. You can also click ⊕ beside **To** or **Cc** to select a person from the People app.

4. Click **Add a subject**.

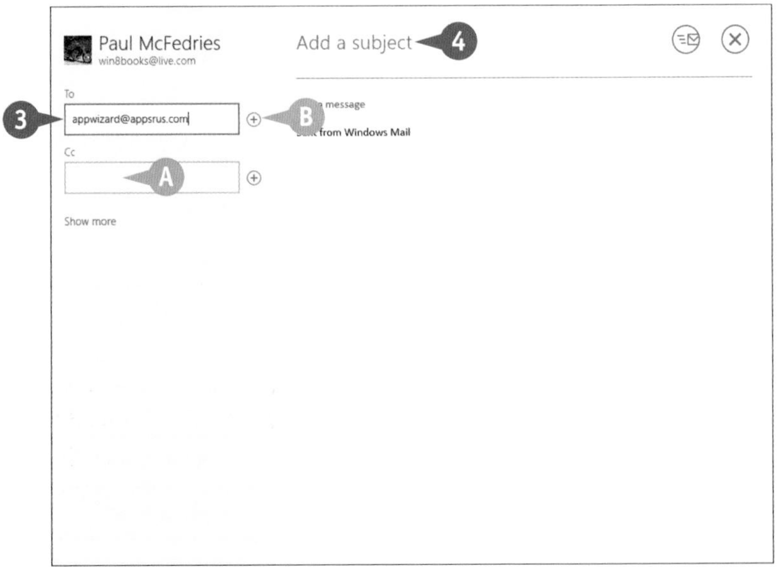

Paul McFedries
win8books@live.com
Add a subject
4
To
appwizard@appsrus.com
3
B
A
Cc
Show more
from Windows Mail

5. Type a title or short description for the message.
6. Type the message.
7. Right-click the screen.
8. Use the buttons in the application bar to format the message text.

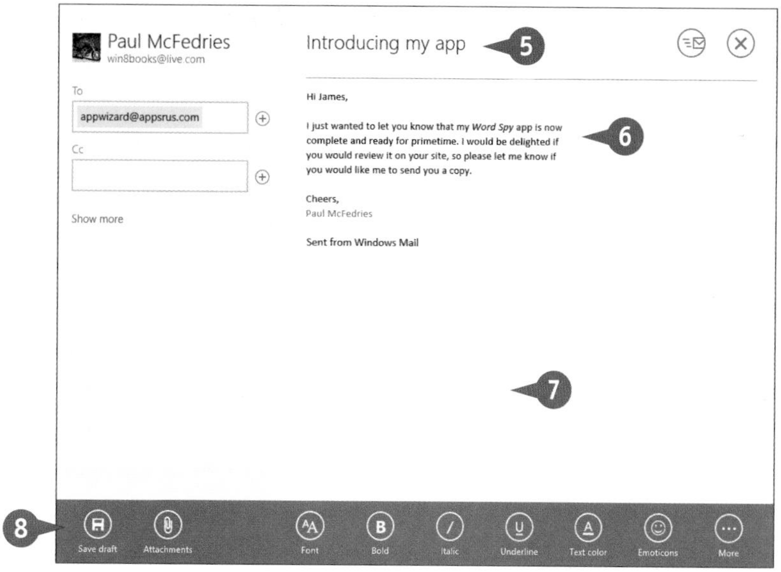
Paul McFedries
win8books@live.com
Introducing my app
5
To
appwizard@appsrus.com
Cc
Show more
Hi James,
I just wanted to let you know that my Word Spy app is now complete and ready for primetime. I would be delighted if you would review it on your site, so please let me know if you would like me to send you a copy.
6
Cheers,
Paul McFedries
Sent from Windows Mail
7
8
Save draft
Attachments
Font
Bold
Italic
Underline
Text color
Emoticons
More

9. Click **Send** (✉).

Mail sends your message.

Paul McFedries
win8books@live.com
Introducing my app
9
To
appwizard@appsrus.com
Cc
Show more
Hi James,
I just wanted to let you know that my Word Spy app is now complete and ready for primetime. I would be delighted if you would review it on your site, so please let me know if you would like me to send you a copy.
Cheers,
Paul McFedries
Sent from Windows Mail
Save draft
Attachments
Font
Bold
Italic
Underline
Text color
Emoticons
More

TIPS

Can I attach a file to my message?

Yes. This is useful if you have a document that you want another person to view or edit. In the message window, right-click the screen and then click **Attachments** to open the Files screen. Click **Files**, select the folder that contains the file you want to send, click the file, and then click **Attach**.

How do I a send a blind courtesy copy?

A *blind courtesy copy* (Bcc) is like a courtesy copy (Cc) in that the recipient receives a copy of your message. However, while other recipients can see the address of each Cc recipient, they cannot see the address of each Bcc recipient. To send a Bcc, click **Show more** and then, in the Bcc text box that appears, type the recipient's address.

Reply to an E-Mail Message

When a message you receive requires some kind of response — whether it is answering a question, supplying information, or providing comments — you can reply to that message.

Most replies go only to the person who sent the original message. However, it is also possible to send the reply to all the people who were included in the original message's To and Cc lines.

Mail includes the text of the original message in the reply, but you should edit the original message text to include only enough of the original message to put your reply into context.

Reply to an E-Mail Message

1. Click the message to which you want to reply.
2. Click **Respond** ( ).
3. Click the reply type you want to use:

   Click **Reply** to respond only to the first address displayed on the To line.

   Click **Reply all** to respond to all the addresses in the To and Cc lines.

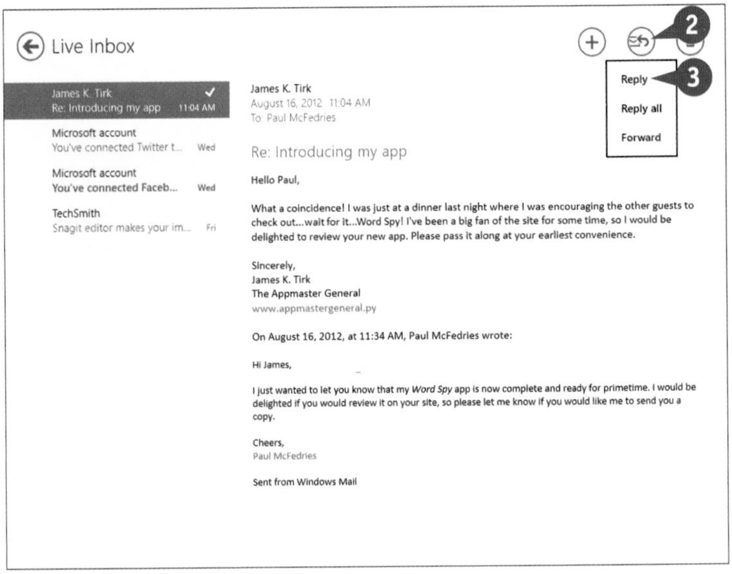

Live Inbox
2
Reply
3
Reply all
Forward
James K. Tirk
Re: Introducing my app 11:04 AM
Microsoft account
You've connected Twitter t... Wed
Microsoft account
You've connected Faceb... Wed
TechSmith
Snagit editor makes your im... Fri
James K. Tirk
August 16, 2012 11:04 AM
To: Paul McFedries
Re: Introducing my app
Hello Paul,
What a coincidence! I was just at a dinner last night where I was encouraging the other guests to check out...wait for it...Word Spy! I've been a big fan of the site for some time, so I would be delighted to review your new app. Please pass it along at your earliest convenience.
Sincerely,
James K. Tirk
The Appmaster General
www.appmastergeneral.py
On August 16, 2012, at 11:34 AM, Paul McFedries wrote:
Hi James,
I just wanted to let you know that my Word Spy app is now complete and ready for primetime. I would be delighted if you would review it on your site, so please let me know if you would like me to send you a copy.
Cheers,
Paul McFedries
Sent from Windows Mail

A message window appears.

- **A** Mail automatically addresses the reply to the sender.
- **B** Mail also inserts the subject line, preceded by RE.
- **C** Mail includes the original message's addresses (To and From), date, subject, and text at the bottom of the reply.

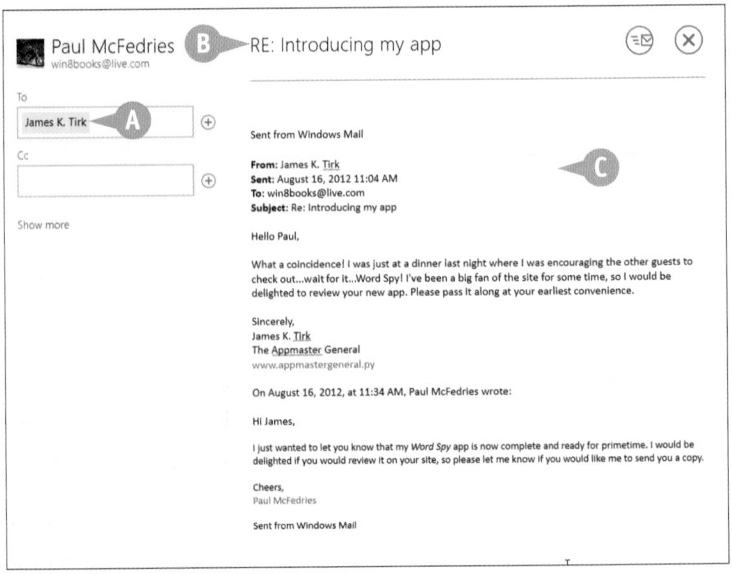

Paul McFedries
win8books@live.com
B
RE: Introducing my app
To
James K. Tirk
A
Cc
Show more
Sent from Windows Mail
From: James K. Tirk
Sent: August 16, 2012 11:04 AM
To: win8books@live.com
Subject: Re: Introducing my app
C
Hello Paul,
What a coincidence! I was just at a dinner last night where I was encouraging the other guests to check out...wait for it...Word Spy! I've been a big fan of the site for some time, so I would be delighted to review your new app. Please pass it along at your earliest convenience.
Sincerely,
James K. Tirk
The Appmaster General
www.appmastergeneral.py
On August 16, 2012, at 11:34 AM, Paul McFedries wrote:
Hi James,
I just wanted to let you know that my Word Spy app is now complete and ready for primetime. I would be delighted if you would review it on your site, so please let me know if you would like me to send you a copy.
Cheers,
Paul McFedries
Sent from Windows Mail

4. Edit the original message to include only the text relevant to your reply.

Note: If the original message is fairly short, you usually do not need to edit the text. However, if the original message is long, and your response deals only with part of that message, you will save the recipient time by deleting everything except the relevant portion of the text.

5. Click the area above the original message text.

Paul McFedries
win8books@live.com
RE: Introducing my app
To
James K. Tirk
Cc
Show more
5
Sent from Windows Mail
From: James K. Tirk
Sent: August 16, 2012 11:04 AM
To: win8books@live.com
Subject: Re: Introducing my app
Hello Paul,
What a coincidence! I was just at a dinner last night where I was encouraging the other guests to check out...wait for it...Word Spy! I've been a big fan of the site for some time, so I would be delighted to review your new app. Please pass it along at your earliest convenience.
Sincerely,
James K. Tirk
The Appmaster General
www.appmastergeneral.py
4

6. Type your reply.
7. Click **Send** ( ).

   Mail sends your reply.

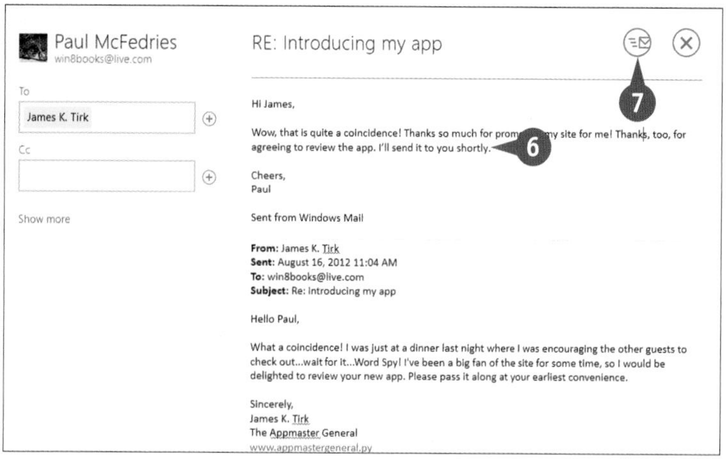
Paul McFedries
win8books@live.com
RE: Introducing my app
To
James K. Tirk
Cc
Show more
7
Hi James,
Wow, that is quite a coincidence! Thanks so much for prom my site for me! Thanks, too, for agreeing to review the app. I'll send it to you shortly.
6
Cheers,
Paul
Sent from Windows Mail
From: James K. Tirk
Sent: August 16, 2012 11:04 AM
To: win8books@live.com
Subject: Re: Introducing my app
Hello Paul,
What a coincidence! I was just at a dinner last night where I was encouraging the other guests to check out...wait for it...Word Spy! I've been a big fan of the site for some time, so I would be delighted to review your new app. Please pass it along at your earliest convenience.
Sincerely,
James K. Tirk
The Appmaster General

TIPS

What does the Forward command do?

The Forward command sends a copy of the message to another person. If a message has information that is relevant to or concerns another person, you can forward a copy of the message to that person. When you select the Forward command, Mail creates a new message, inserts the subject line preceded by FW, and adds the original message text. You can also include your own comments in the forward.

How often does the Mail app check for new messages?

The Mail app automatically checks for incoming e-mail messages when you first start the app. If you are using a Microsoft account (see Chapter 3), any messages addressed to that account are automatically sent to the Mail app as soon as they arrive. For other types of accounts, the Mail app automatically checks for new messages periodically. To check for new messages manually, either press F5 or right-click the app and then click **Sync**.

Create a Contact

You can make it easier to store information about your friends, family, and colleagues, as well as send messages to those people, by using the People app to create a contact for each person.

Each contact can store a wide variety of information. For example, you can store a person's first and last names, company name, e-mail address, phone number, street address, and more.

If you already have contacts in a social network such as Facebook or LinkedIn, you can also connect your social network account to your Microsoft account to access those contacts within the People app.

Create a Contact

1. On the Start screen, click the **People** tile.

   The People app loads.

2. Right-click an empty section of the screen.
3. Click **New**.

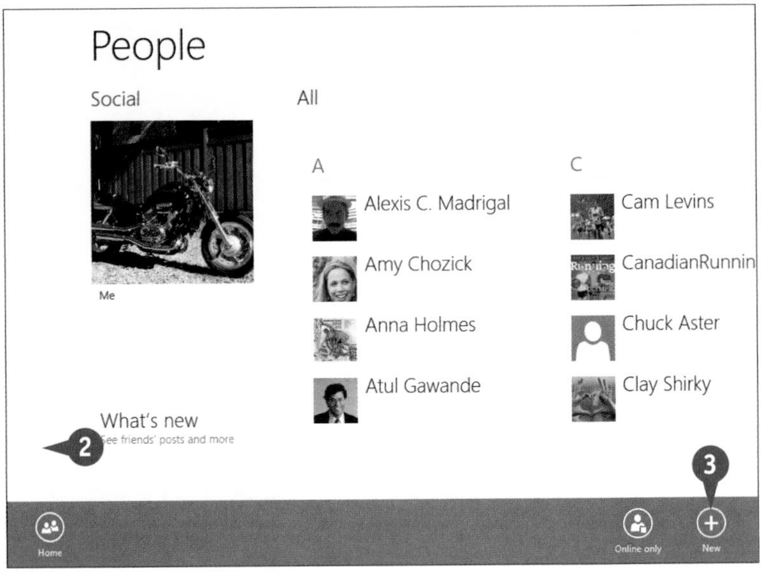

   The New Contact screen appears.

4. Type the contact's first name.
5. Type the contact's last name.
6. Type the contact's company name.
7. Click the **Email** label and then click the type of e-mail address you want to enter.

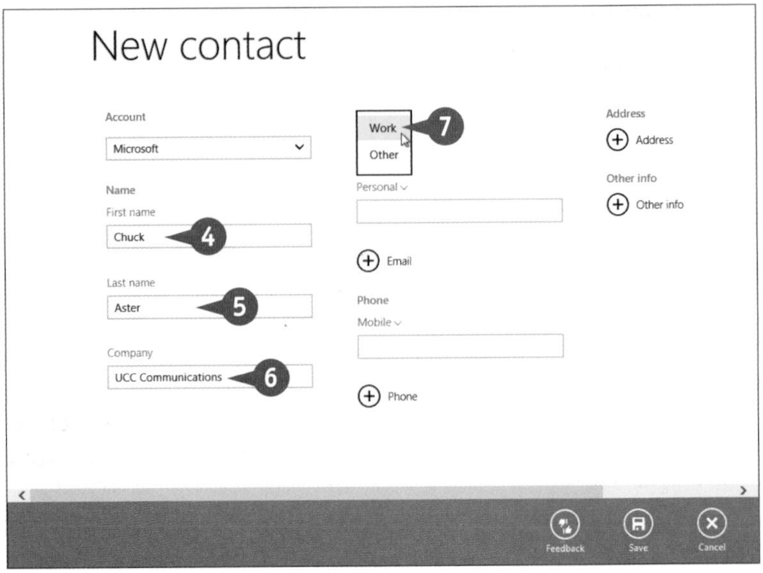

8 Type the contact's e-mail address.

A To add another e-mail address for the contact, click the **Email** ⊕, click a label, and then type the address in the field that appears.

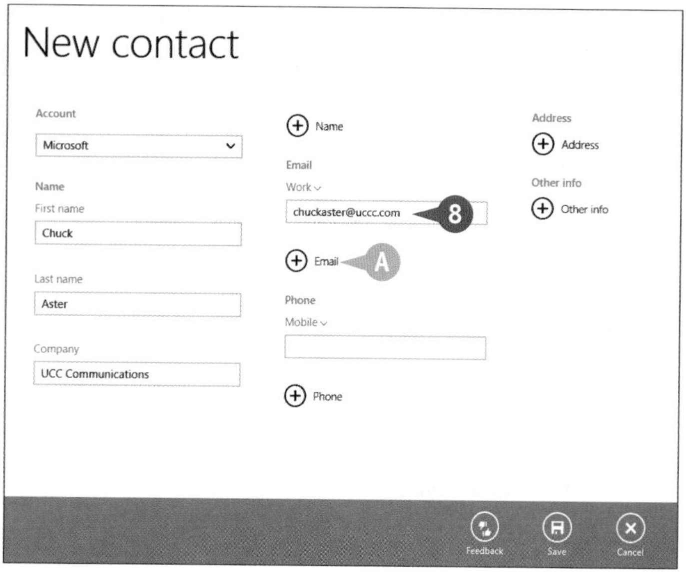

9 Click the **Phone** label and then click the type of phone number address you want to enter.

10 Type the contact's phone number.

B To add another e-mail address for the contact, click the **Phone** ⊕, click a label, and then type the number in the field that appears.

11 To add an address for the contact, click the **Address** ⊕.

12 Click **Save**.

The People app creates the new contact.

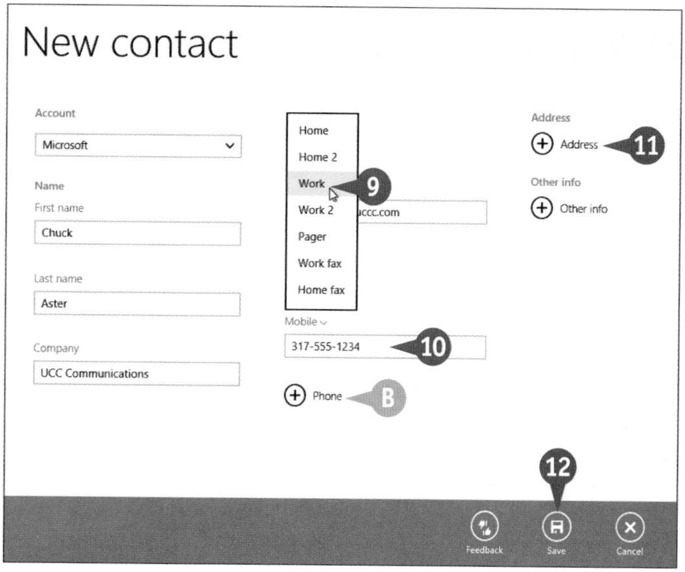

TIPS

Is there an easy way to send an e-mail to a contact?
Yes. Normally you would open the Mail app, begin a new message as described earlier in this chapter, and then click the **To** button to open the People app and choose a recipient. If you are already working in the People app, however, it is easier and faster to click the person's tile to open the contact and then click **Send email**.

Are there other types of information I can record for a contact?
Yes, you can also add notes about the contact, the contact's job title, the contact's website address, and the name of the contact's significant other. To add one of these categories, click the **Other info** ⊕, click the category you want to add, and then type the information in the new field that appears.

Add Social Network Contacts

If you are using a Microsoft account with Windows 8, you can connect several types of social network contacts to that account, including Facebook, Twitter, LinkedIn, and Google.

One of Microsoft's goals when designing the Start screen was to give you a single place that shows you what is happening in your life, whether it is the current weather, your most recently received e-mail or instant messages, or the currently running slide show. The People app can show you the latest messages from Facebook, Twitter, and other social networks. All you have to do is connect your social networks to your Microsoft account.

Add Social Network Contacts

1. On the Start screen, click the **People** tile.

   The People app loads.

2. Click **Connected to**.
3. Click **Add an account.**
4. Click the social network you want to add to the People app.

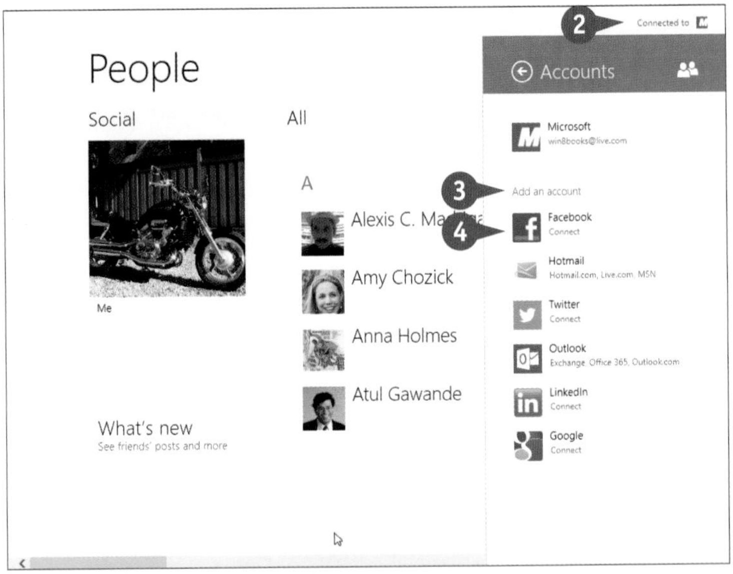

   The People app displays a description of the connection you are creating.

5. Click **Connect**.

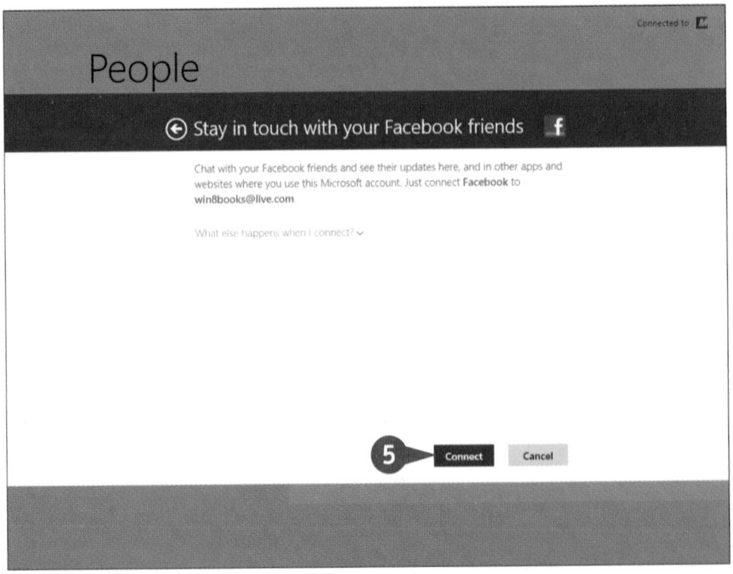

The social network prompts you to log in to your account.

6 Type your username or e-mail address.

7 Type your password.

8 Select the check box (☐ changes to ☑).

9 Click **Log In**.

Note: The name of the button you click depends on the social network. For example, with Twitter you click **Authorize app**, instead.

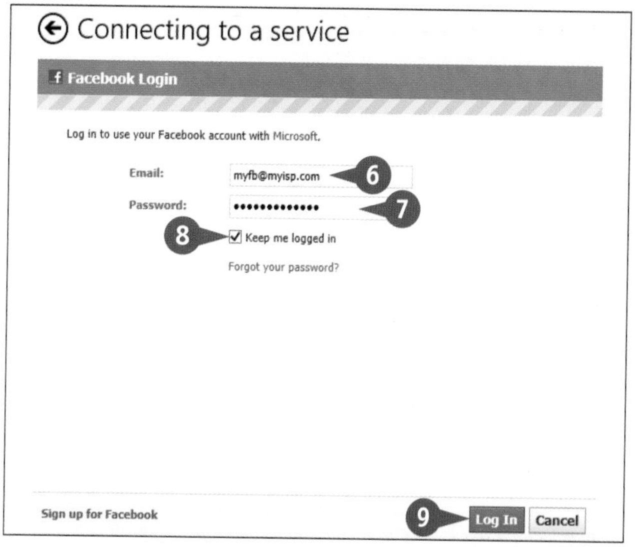
Connecting to a service
Facebook Login
Log in to use your Facebook account with Microsoft.
Email:
myfb@myisp.com
6
Password:
7
8
Keep me logged in
Forgot your password?
Sign up for Facebook
9
Log In
Cancel

Windows 8 connects the social network to your Microsoft account.

10 Click **Done**.

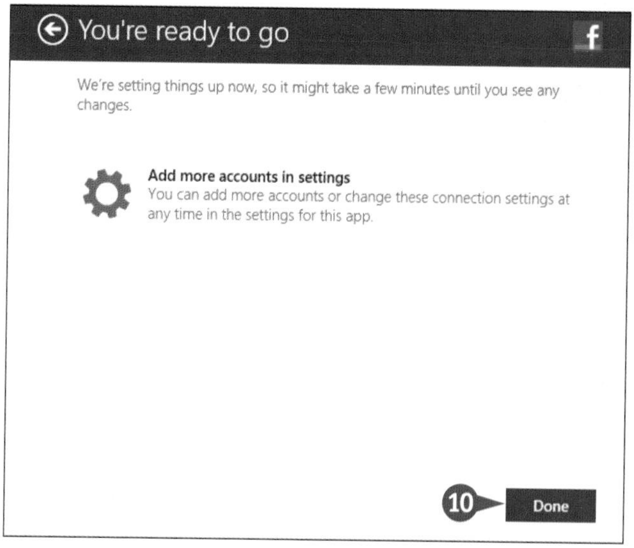
You're ready to go
We're setting things up now, so it might take a few minutes until you see any changes.
Add more accounts in settings
You can add more accounts or change these connection settings at any time in the settings for this app.
10
Done

TIPS

How do I see updates from my social networking friends?

After a few minutes, you should start seeing Facebook updates and notifications on the People app tile on the Start screen. To see updates from all your connected social networks, click the **People** app and then click the **What's new** tab. To see messages you have posted as well as notifications sent to you from the social network service, click the **Me** tab.

Can I interact with the social network messages that I receive in the People app?

Yes. For example, to "like" a Facebook post, click it and then click the **Like** icon. You can also click **Comment** to comment on the post. For a tweet, click it and then click **Retweet** to retweet it, click **Favorite** to save it as a favorite, or click **Reply** to send a reply to the person.

View Your Photos

If you want to look at several photos on your computer, you can use Windows 8 to navigate backward and forward through the photos in your Pictures library. You can navigate the photos manually, or you can start a slide show that displays each photo for a few seconds and then automatically switches to the next photo.

Windows 8 comes with two programs that you can use to view your photos: Windows Photo Viewer, a desktop program discussed in Chapter 7, and Photos, a Windows 8 app covered in this section.

View Your Photos

1. On the Start screen, click the **Photos** tile.

Windows 8 launches the Photos app.

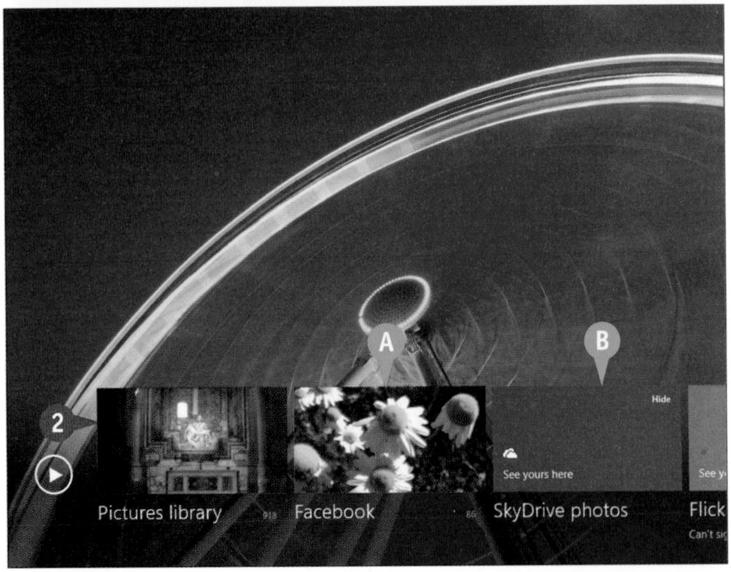

2. Click **Pictures library**.

A. If you connected your Facebook account to your Microsoft account, as described in the previous section, you can click **Facebook** to see your photos.

B. If you have uploaded photos to your SkyDrive, as described later in this chapter, click **SkyDrive photos** to see them.

The Photos app displays the albums and images in your Pictures library.

3. To view the photos in an album, click the album.

The Photos app opens the album.

4. Click the first photo you want to view.

C. If you want to run a slide show, instead, right-click the screen and then click **Slide show**.

5. Navigate the photos by pressing → to view the next photo and ← to view the previous photo.

TIPS

When I return to the Start screen, the Photos tile shows random images from my Pictures library. Can I turn this off?
Yes. If you find that the constantly changing images that Windows 8 displays on the Photos tile to be a distraction, you can disable this feature. Right-click the Photos tile to open the application bar, and then click **Turn live tile off**.

Can I use Photos to remove an image from my Pictures library?
Yes. If you have photos you no longer want to view, removing them is a good idea because this makes it easier and faster to view the rest of your photos. To remove a photo, use the Photos app to display the image, right-click the screen, and then click **Delete**. When Photos asks you to confirm, click **Delete**.

Watch a Video

If you have digital video files or recorded videos on your computer, you can use the Video app to watch one of those videos and control the playback. The Video app plays the video full-screen on your computer, so you get the best viewing experience. You can then pause and restart the playback, and you can use a tool called the scrubber to quickly fast forward or rewind.

Windows 8 comes with three programs that you can use to watch your videos: Windows Media Player and Windows Media Center are desktop programs discussed in Chapter 8; Video, a Windows 8 app, is the subject of this section.

Watch a Video

Start a Video

1. On the Start screen, click the **Video** tile.
2. Scroll left and then click **my videos.**

   A. If you see the video you want to play, click it and skip the rest of these steps.

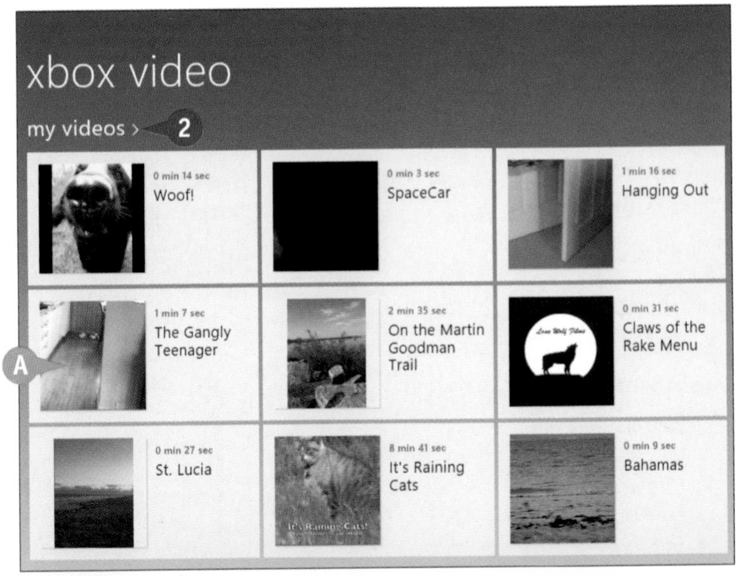

3. Click the tab that contains the video you want to play.

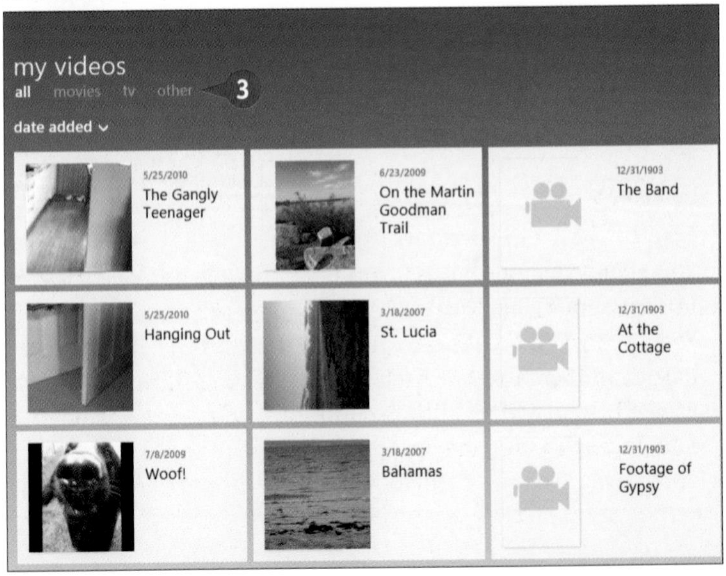

4 Click the video.

The Video app begins playing the video.

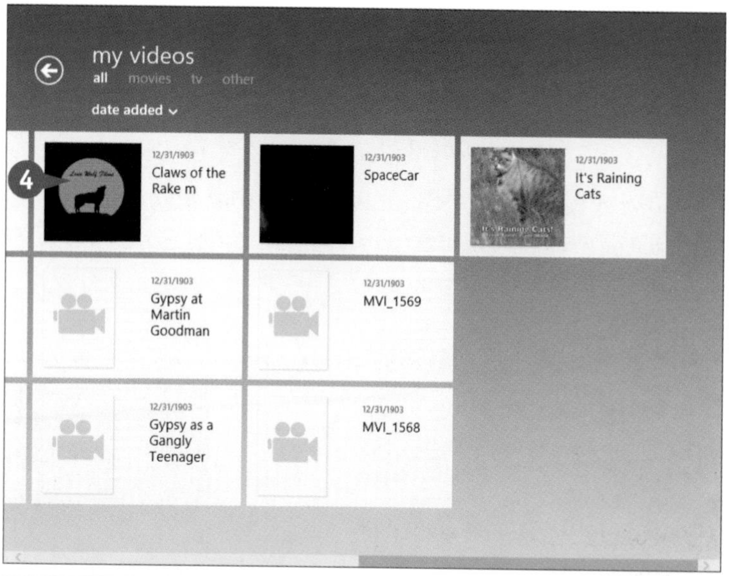

Control Video Playback

1 Click the screen.

The Video app displays the playback controls.

B Click **Pause** to stop and restart the playback.

C Click and drag the scrubber to rewind or fast-forward the video.

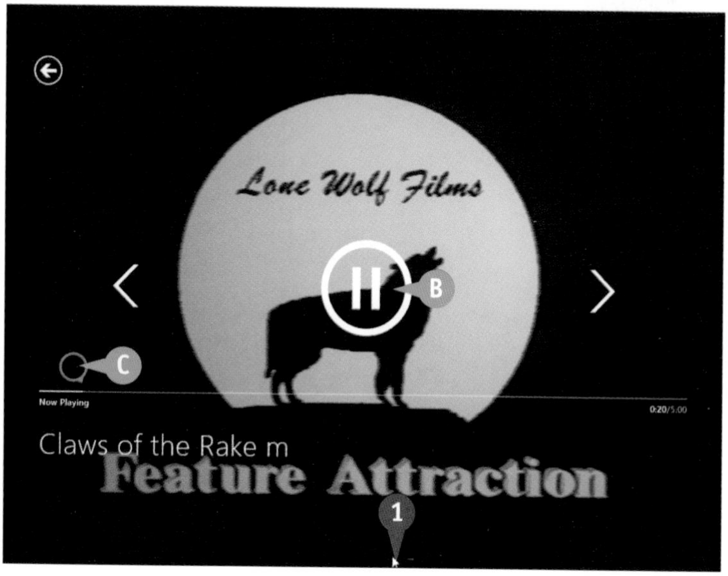

TIP

How do I get content into the Movies and TV tabs?

The main Video app screen contains three other tabs besides My Videos. The Spotlight tab lists popular movies and TV shows. You can use Movies Store to buy or rent movies and TV Store to buy or rent TV episodes. In these last two tabs, click the tab name to enter and then use tabs such as Featured and Genres to look for a video you want to view. Click the video, click **Buy** (or **Rent**, if available), and then enter your identification and payment information.

Play Music

If you want to listen to music while at your computer, you can use Windows 8 to play tunes from your Music library. You can listen to all the songs on an album, all the songs from a particular artist, or individual songs. You can also play albums, artists, and songs in random order and play albums and artists repeatedly.

Windows 8 comes with three programs that you can use to play music: Windows Media Player and Windows Media Center are desktop programs covered in Chapter 8; Music, a Windows 8 app, is the subject of this section.

Play Music

Start Music

1. On the Start screen, click the **Music** tile.
2. Scroll left and then click **my music**.

   A. If you see the album you want to play, click it and skip the rest of these steps.

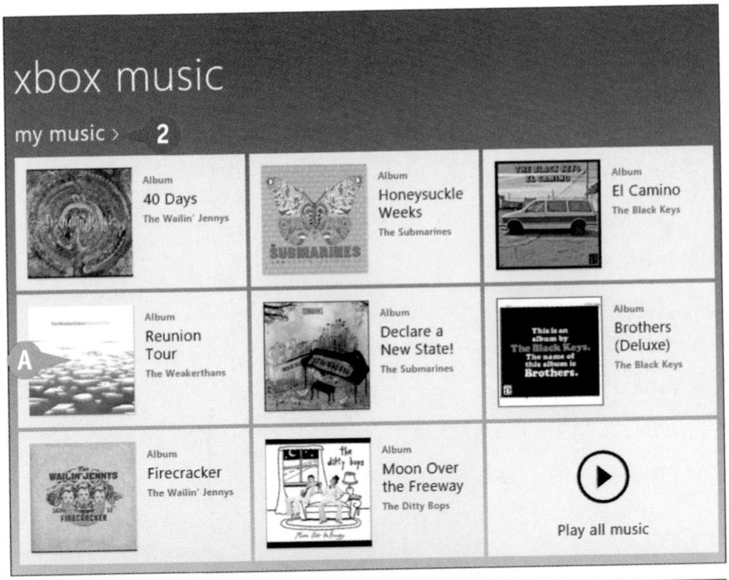

3. Click the tab that contains the music you want to play.
4. Click the album, artist, or song.

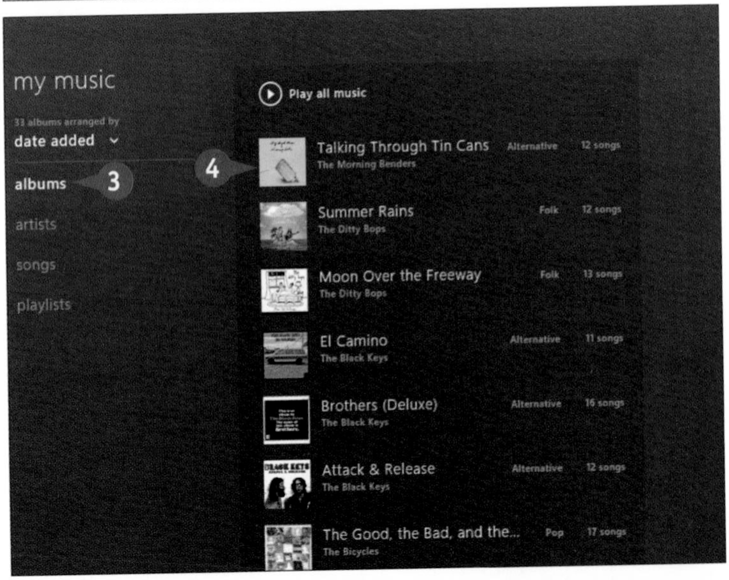

The Music app opens the album and displays a list of songs.

5 Click **Play**.

B You can also click a song and then click **Play**.

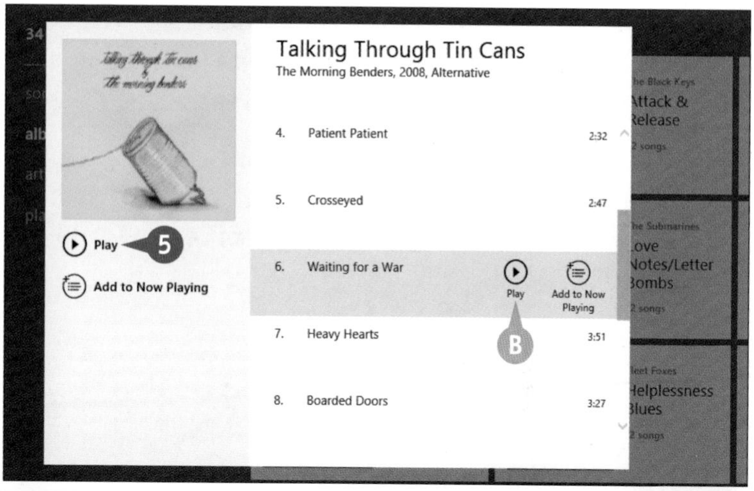

Control Music Playback

1 Right-click the screen.

The Music app displays the playback controls.

C Click **Pause** to stop and restart the playback.

D Click **Next** to jump to the next song.

E Click **Previous** to jump to the previous song.

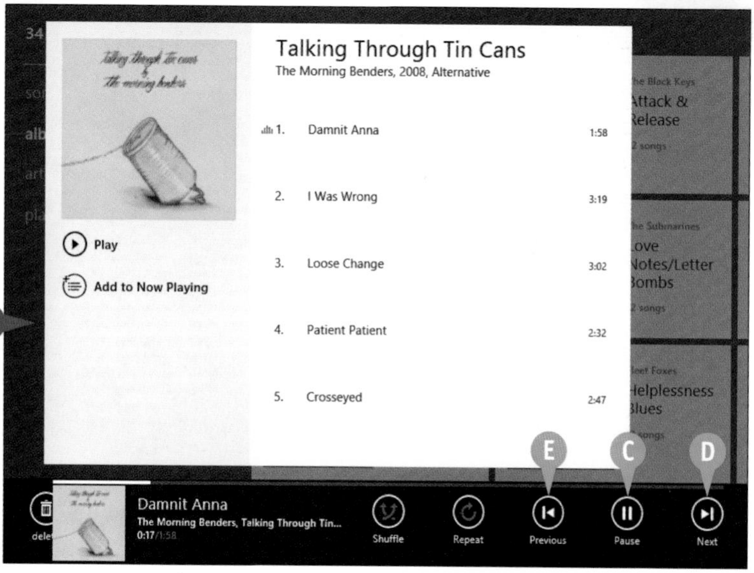

TIP

Can I buy music?

Yes you can, by using the two other tabs besides My Music that appear on the main Music app screen. Click the **xbox music store** tab to shop the entire music store. Click the **most popular** tab to see a list of popular singers and bands, organized by genre.

When you open an album, you can click **Preview** to hear each song, and click **Buy album** to purchase it. For individual songs, click a song and then click either **Preview** or **Buy song**. You then enter your identification and payment information.

View Your Calendar

Windows 8 comes with a Calendar app to enable you to manage your schedule. Before you create an event such as an appointment or meeting, or an all-day event such as a conference or trip, you must first select the date when the event occurs.

Calendar also lets you change the calendar view to suit your needs. For example, you can show just a single day's worth of events if you want to concentrate on that day's activities. Similarly, you can view a week's or a month's worth of events if you want to get a larger sense of what your overall schedule looks like.

View Your Calendar

View Events by Month

1. On the Start screen, click the **Calendar** tile.
2. Right-click the screen.
3. Click **Month.**
4. Move the mouse ⇘.
5. Click the arrows to navigate the months.

View Events by Week

1. Right-click the screen.
2. Click **Week.**
3. Move the mouse ⇘.
4. Click the arrows to navigate the weeks.

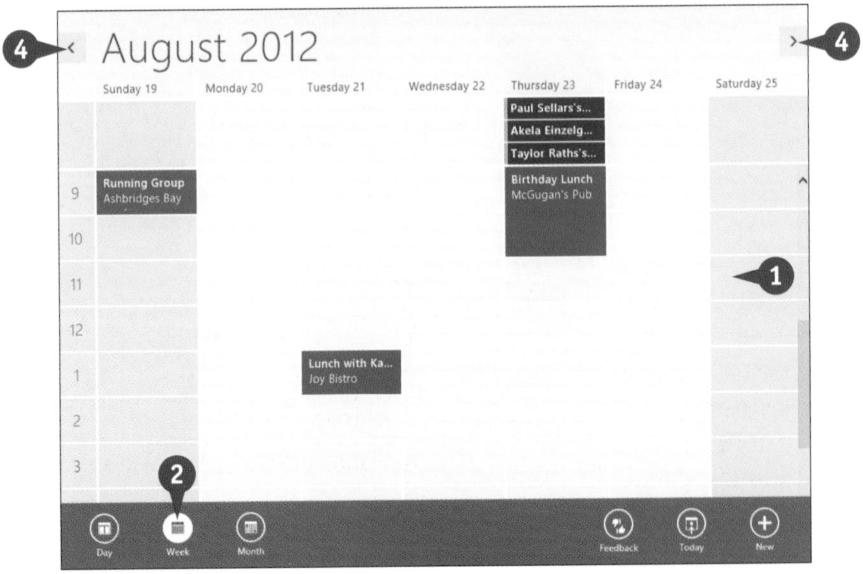

View Events by Day

1. Right-click the screen.
2. Click **Day**.
3. Move the mouse ↖.
4. Click the arrows to navigate the days.

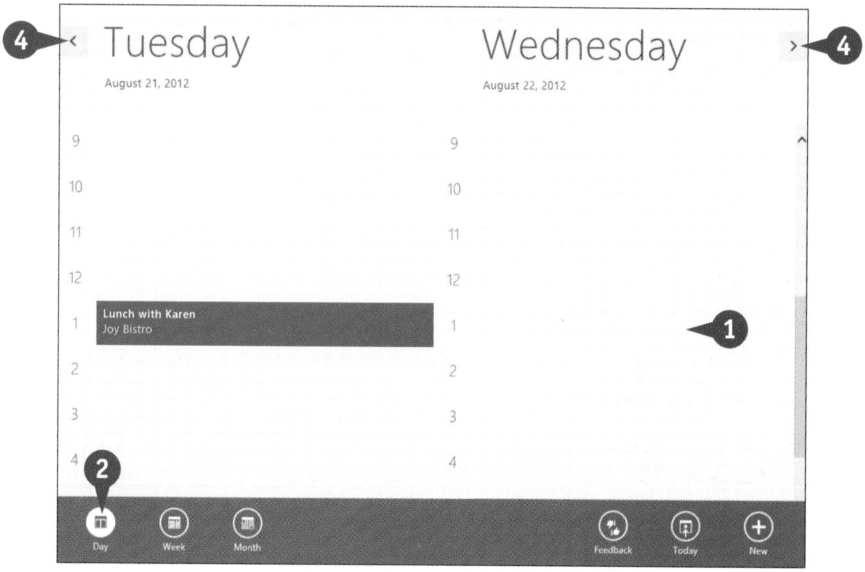

View Today's Events

1. Right-click the screen.
2. Click **Today**.

   Calendar navigates the current view to include today's date.

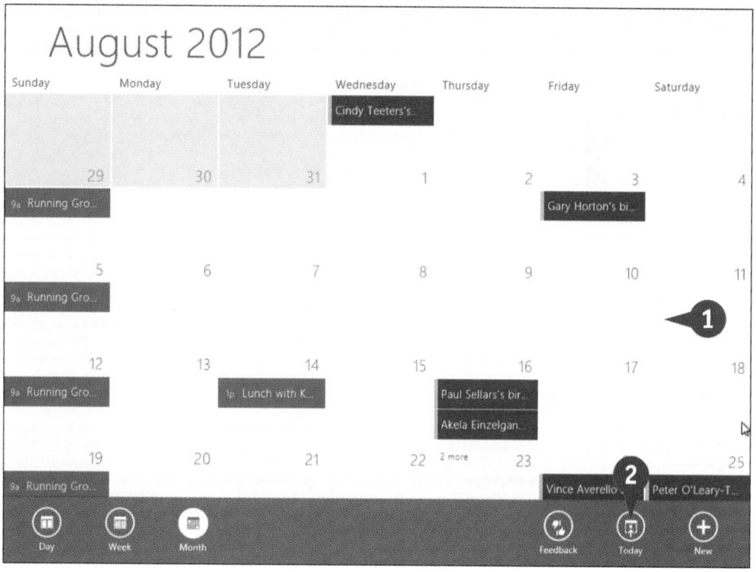

TIP

Are there any shortcut methods I can use to navigate the calendar?
Yes, the Calendar app offers several keyboard shortcuts that you can use to change the view:

Press	To
Ctrl + 1	Switch to Day view.
Ctrl + 2	Switch to Week view.
Ctrl + 3	Switch to Month view.
Ctrl + T	View today's events.
→	Navigate to the next screen in the current view.
←	Navigate to the previous screen in the current view.

Add an Event to Your Calendar

You can help organize your life by using the Calendar app to record your events — such as appointments, meetings, phone calls, and dates — on the date and time they occur.

If the event has a set time and duration — for example, a meeting or a lunch date — you add the event directly to the calendar as a regular appointment. If the event has no set time — for example, a birthday, anniversary, or multiple-day event such as a sales meeting or vacation — you can create an all-day event.

Add an Event to Your Calendar

1. Navigate to the date when the event occurs.
2. Click the time when the event starts.

Note: If you are currently in Month view, click the day the event occurs.

Note: You can also start a new event by right-clicking the screen and then clicking **New**, or by pressing Ctrl+N.

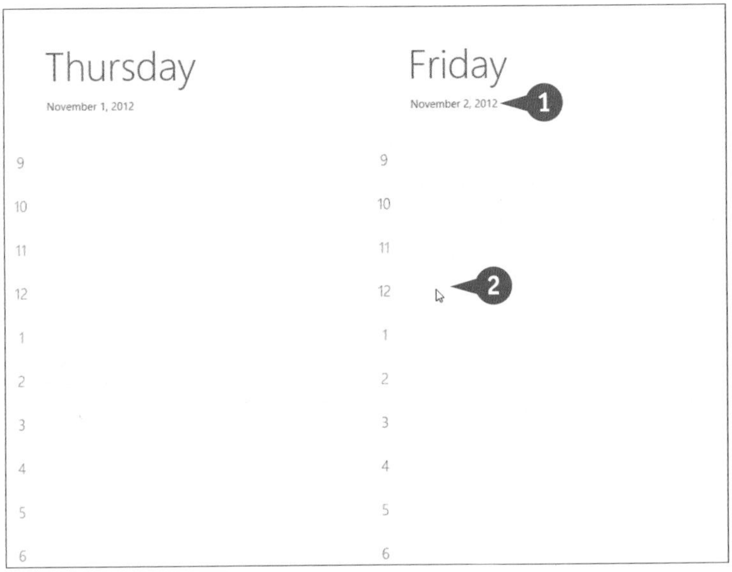

Calendar displays the New Event screen.

3. Type a name for the event.
4. If the start time is incorrect, use the Start controls to select the correct time.
5. Use the Where text box to type the event location.
6. Click the **How long** ☑.

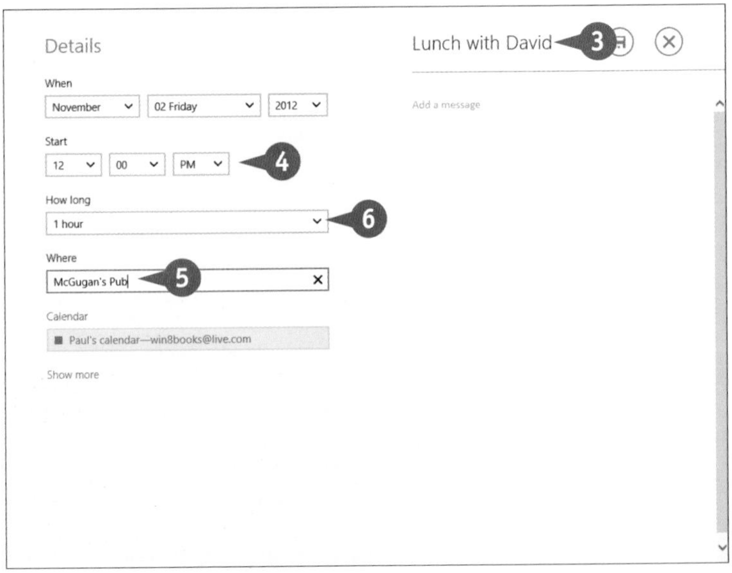

7. Click the duration of the event.

   A. If the event is an anniversary or other event that lasts all day, click **All day**.

   B. To choose a specific end time, click **Custom**.

8. Use the large text area to type notes related to the event.

9. Click **Save this event** (⊟).

   C. Calendar adds the event to your schedule.

Note: To make changes to the event, double-click it.

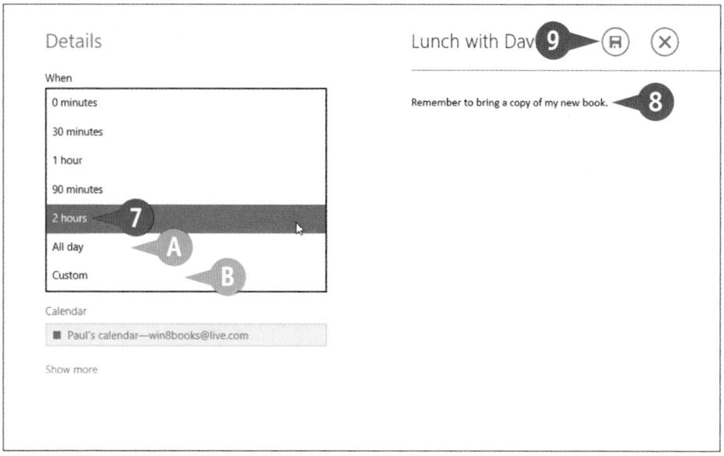

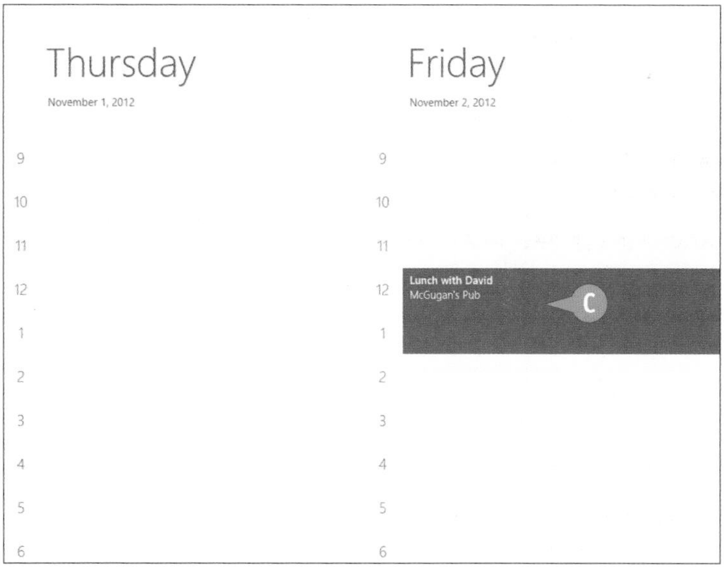

TIP

Is there an easy way to schedule an event that occurs at a regular interval?

Yes, you can set up a recurring event. Calendar can repeat an event at regular intervals such as daily, weekly, monthly, or yearly. Here are the steps to follow:

1. Repeat steps **1** to **8** to set up a new regular event, or double-click an existing event.
2. Click **Show more**.
3. Click the **How often** ☑.
4. Click the interval you want to use.

Calendar repeats the event at the interval you specified.

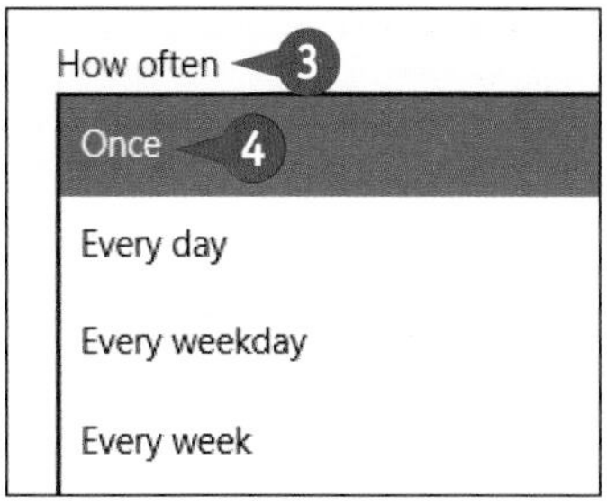

Search Your Computer

You can save time and make your Windows PC easier to use by learning how to search for the apps, settings, or files that you need.

After you have used your computer for a while and have created many documents, you might have trouble locating a specific file. You can save a great deal of time by having Windows 8 search for your document. You can also use the Start screen to search for apps and system settings.

If you are working with the Desktop app, you can also perform file searches using the search box in a folder window.

Search Your Computer

Search for Apps

1. On the Start screen, type your search text.

   The Apps search screen appears.

   A. As you type, Windows 8 adds your text to the search box.

   B. Windows 8 also displays each app with a name that includes your search text.

2. If you see the app you want, click it to open it.

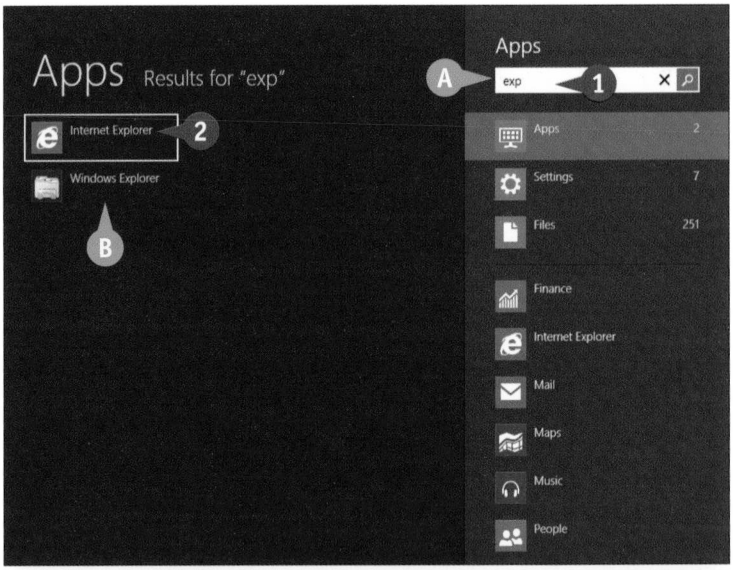

Search for Settings

1. On the Start screen, press ⊞+W.

   The Settings search screen appears.

2. Type your search text.

   C. Windows 8 displays each setting that matches your search text.

3. If you see the setting you want, click it to open it.

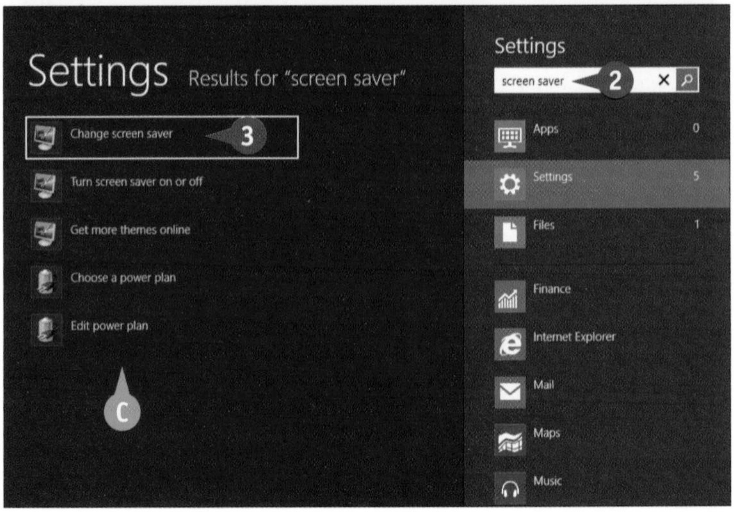

Search for Files

1. On the Start screen, press ⊞+F.

   The Files search screen appears.

2. Type your search text and then press Enter.

   D. Windows 8 displays each file that matches your search text.

3. If you see the file you want, click it to open it.

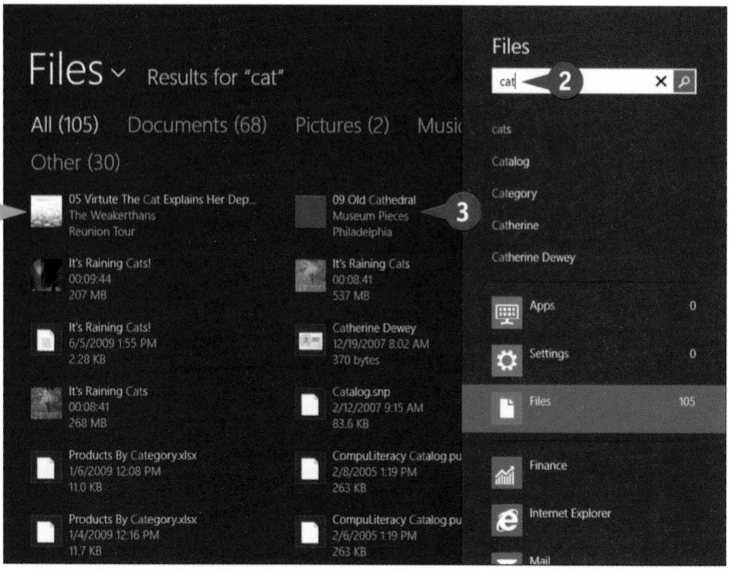

Search from a Folder Window

1. Open the folder in which you want to search.

2. Use the search box to type your search text.

   E. As you type, Windows 8 displays the folders and documents in the current folder with names, contents, or keywords that match your search text.

3. If you see the folder or document you want, double-click it to open it.

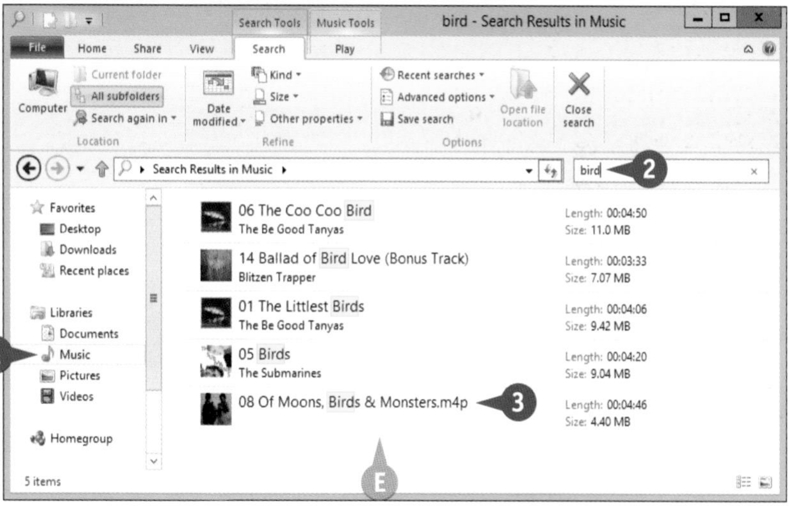

TIPS

In Start screen searches, why does the search pane list various apps, such as Mail and Internet Explorer?
You can use those apps to tell Windows 8 that you want to run your search within the app itself. For example, if you want to search only your e-mail messages, type your search text and then click **Mail**. Similarly, you can run a web search by typing your search text and then clicking **Internet Explorer**.

Can I remove apps from the search pane?
Yes. This is a good idea because removing apps you never use for searching makes it easier to navigate and find the remaining apps in the search pane. To remove an app, press ⊞+I, click **Change PC Settings**, click **Search**, and then click the app's switch to **Off**.

Get Directions to a Location

You can use the Maps app to get specific directions for traveling from one location to another.

Maps is a Windows 8 app that displays digital maps that you can use to view just about any location. Maps also understands the roads and highways found in most cities, states, and countries. This means that you can also use Maps to specify a starting point and destination for a trip, and Maps then provides you with directions for getting from one point to the other. Maps highlights the trip route on a digital map and also gives you specific directions for negotiating each leg of the trip.

Get Directions to a Location

1. On the Start screen, tap the **Maps** tile.

   The first time you start Maps it asks if it can use your location.

2. Click **Allow**.
3. Right-click the screen and then click **Directions**.

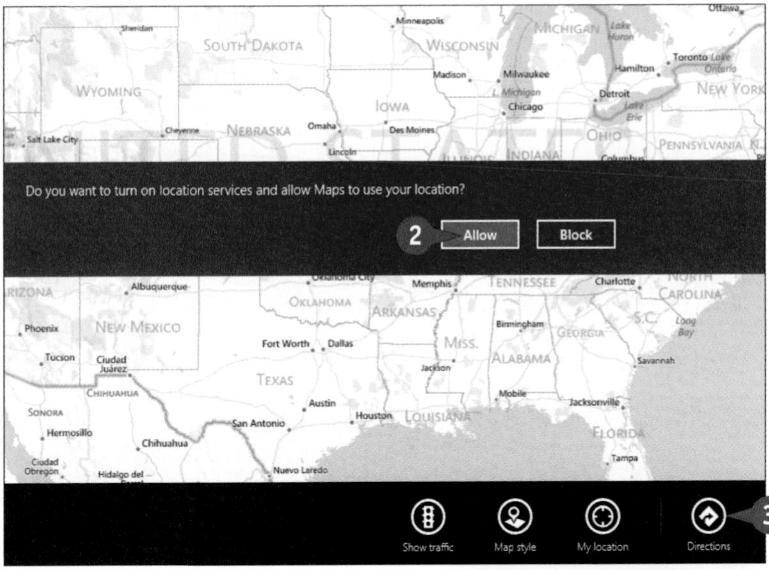

4. Type the name or address of the location where your journey will begin.

Note: Maps assumes you want to start at your current location. If that is true, skip step **4**.

5. Type the name or address of your destination.
6. Click the **Get directions** arrow (➔).

Ⓐ Maps displays an overview of your journey.

Ⓑ This area tells the distance and approximate traveling time by car.

Ⓒ This area displays the various legs of the journey.

7 Click the first leg of the trip.

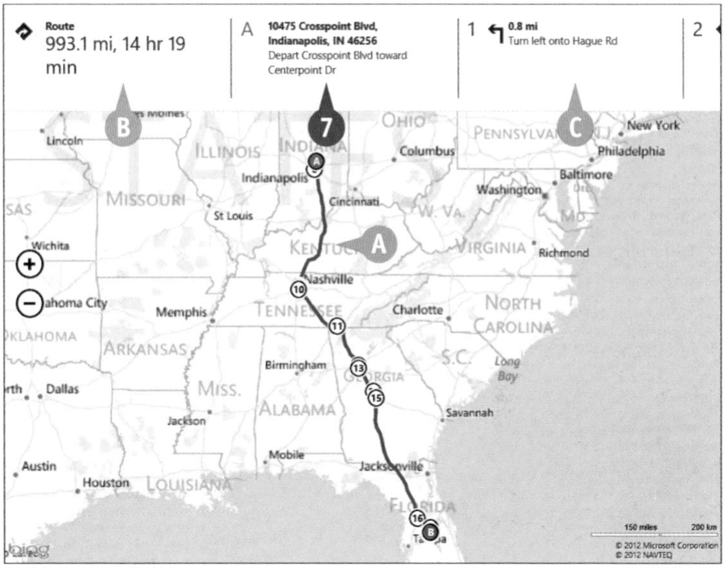

Ⓓ Maps zooms in to show you just that leg of the trip.

8 As you complete each leg of the trip, click the next leg for further instructions.

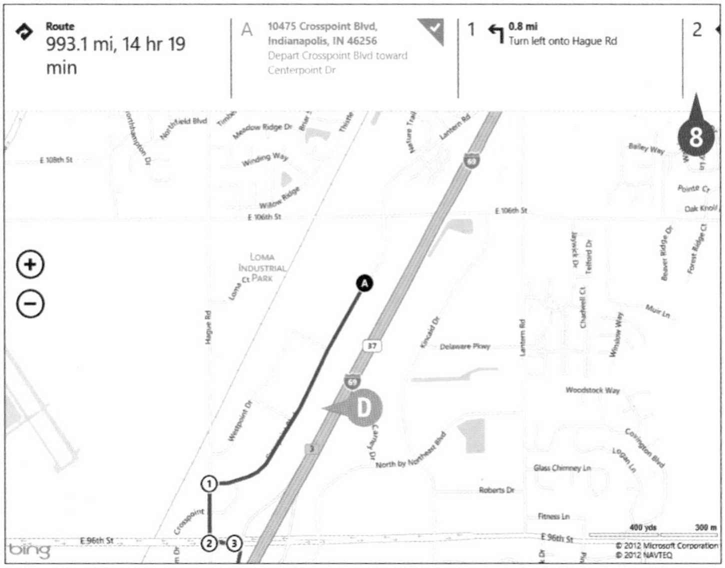

TIPS

How does the Maps app know my location?

The Maps app uses as many as three different bits of data to determine your location. First, it looks for known Wi-Fi hotspots, which are commercial establishments such as coffee shops that offer wireless Internet access. Second, if you are connected to the Internet, Maps uses the location information embedded in your unique Internet Protocol (IP) address. Third, if your computer or tablet has a Global Positioning System (GPS) receiver, Maps uses this GPS data to pinpoint your location to within a few feet.

Can I get more information about the trip?

Yes. Right-click the map to display the application bar. You can then click **Show Traffic** to see the current traffic conditions, where green means traffic is moving normally, orange means traffic is slow, and red means traffic is heavy.

Add a File to SkyDrive

You can use the SkyDrive app to send a file to the online storage area that comes with your Microsoft account.

If you are using Windows 8 under a Microsoft account, then as part of that account you get a free online storage area called SkyDrive. You can use the SkyDrive app to add any of your files to SkyDrive. This is useful if you are going to be away from your computer but still require access to a file. Because the SkyDrive is accessible anywhere you have web access, you can view and work with your file without having to be at your computer.

Add a File to SkyDrive

1. On the Start screen, click the **SkyDrive** tile.
2. Click the SkyDrive folder you want to use to store the file.

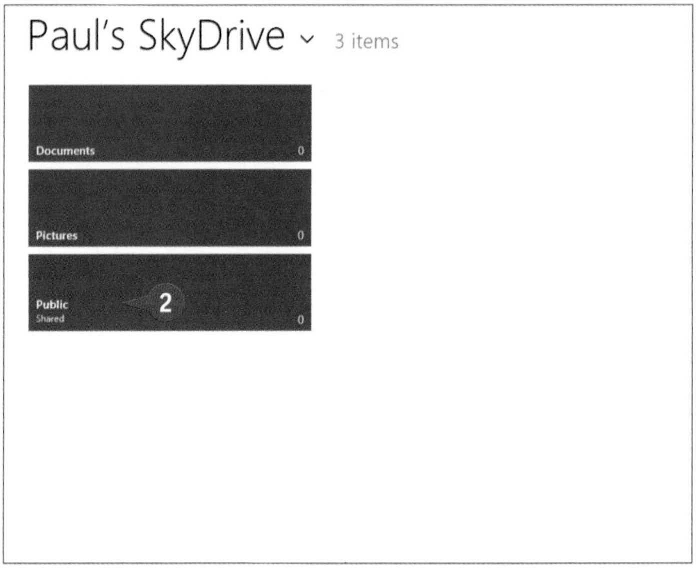

3. Right-click the screen.
4. Click **Add**.

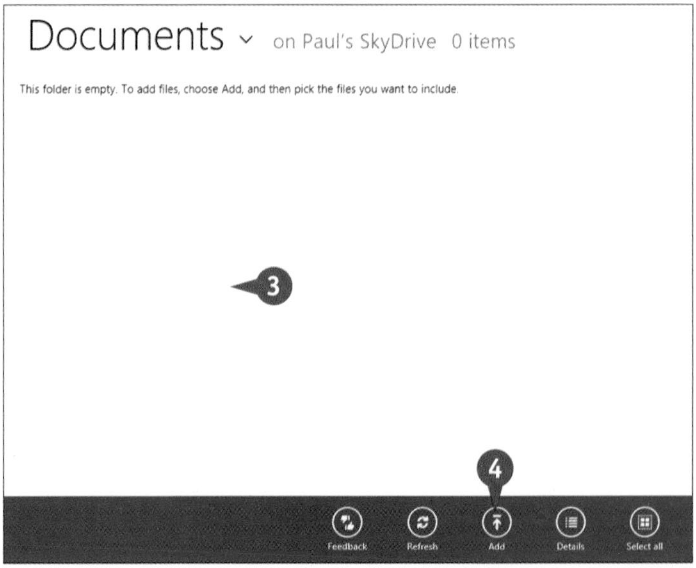

The SkyDrive app displays the Files screen.

5. Click **Files**.
6. Click the folder that contains the file you want to upload.

   The SkyDrive app displays a list of the files in the selected folder.

7. Click the file you want to send to SkyDrive.
8. Click **Add to SkyDrive**.

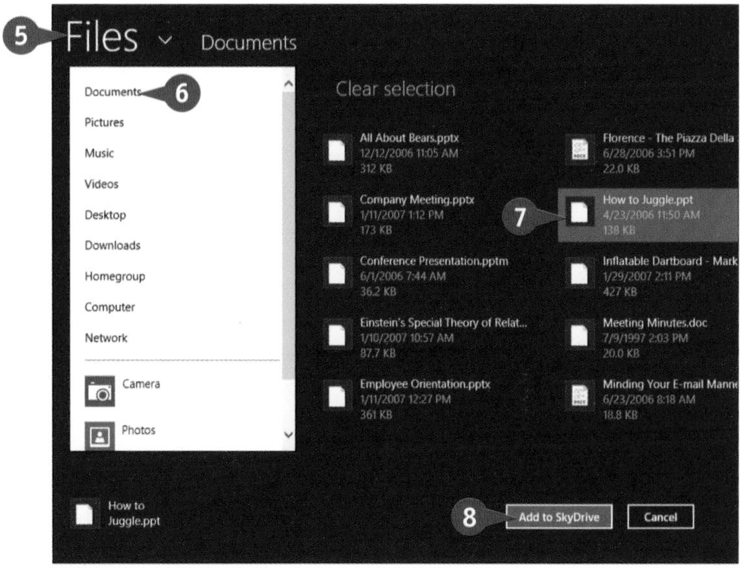

The SkyDrive app uploads the file.

A When the transfer is complete, the file appears in the SkyDrive folder.

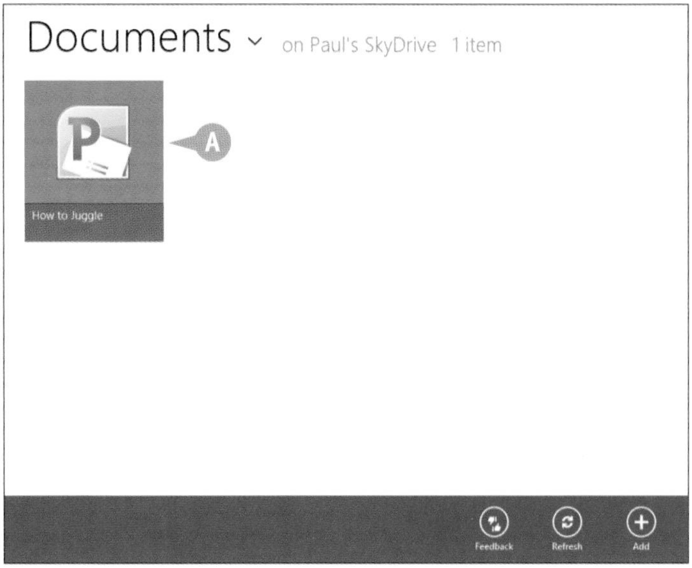

TIPS

How do I access my SkyDrive online?

The SkyDrive app only allows you to upload existing files. To do more with your SkyDrive, access the SkyDrive site (https://skydrive.live.com). There, you can create new folders, rename files, delete files, and more.

Can I create new documents using SkyDrive?

Yes. As part of your SkyDrive, Microsoft gives you access to the Office Web Apps, which are scaled-down, online versions of Word, Excel, PowerPoint, and OneNote. To create a document using one of these programs, navigate to your online SkyDrive and then click **Create Word document** ( ), **Create Excel workbook** ( ), **Create PowerPoint presentation** ( ), or **Create OneNote notebook** ( ).

Share App Data

You can enhance your social contacts and share more of your life with other people by using Windows 8's Share feature to send data, such as a photo or web page address.

In these days of ubiquitous social networking, we are immersed in a world of sharing: happenings, links, information, and much more. Windows 8 gets into the spirit by offering the Share feature, which lets you share app data with other people. For example, you can send a photo, alert a person about a web page, or let someone know about some cool music.

Share App Data

1. Using an app, open or select the data you want to share.

2. Move the mouse to the upper right corner of the screen.

   The Charms menu appears.

Note: You can also display the Charms menu by pressing ⊞+C.

3. Click **Share**.

The Share pane appears.

4 Click the app you want to use to send the selected item.

5 Fill in any data required to send the item, and then initiate the send.

A In Mail, for example, you type the recipient's address, add a subject line, and then click **Send** (✉).

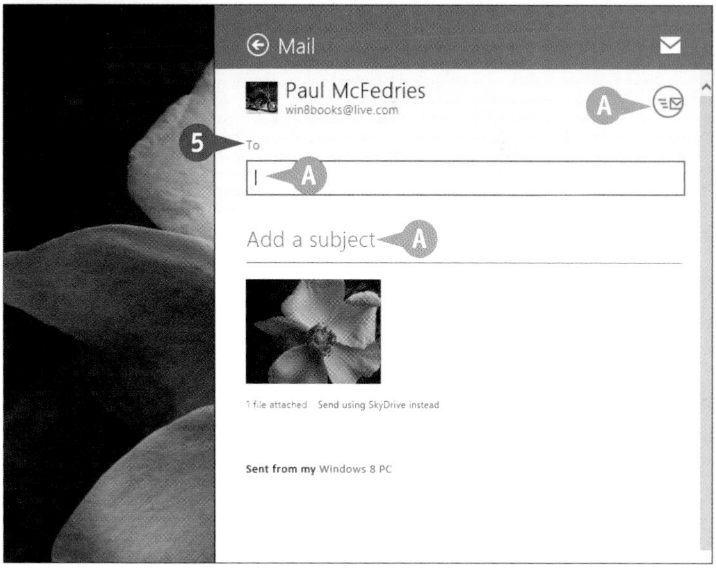

TIP

When I open an app and select an item, why does Windows 8 tell me that "App can't share," where App is the name of the app I am using?
Windows 8's Share feature is supported only by certain apps. In a default Windows 8 installation, for example, Share works only with Mail app (for example, to e-mail a photo) and the People app (for example, to share a link with your Facebook friends). However, you may be able to share a wider variety of items by installing third-party apps that extend the Share feature.

CHAPTER 5

Surfing the World Wide Web

This chapter explains the web and shows you how to use the desktop version of Internet Explorer to navigate from site to site.

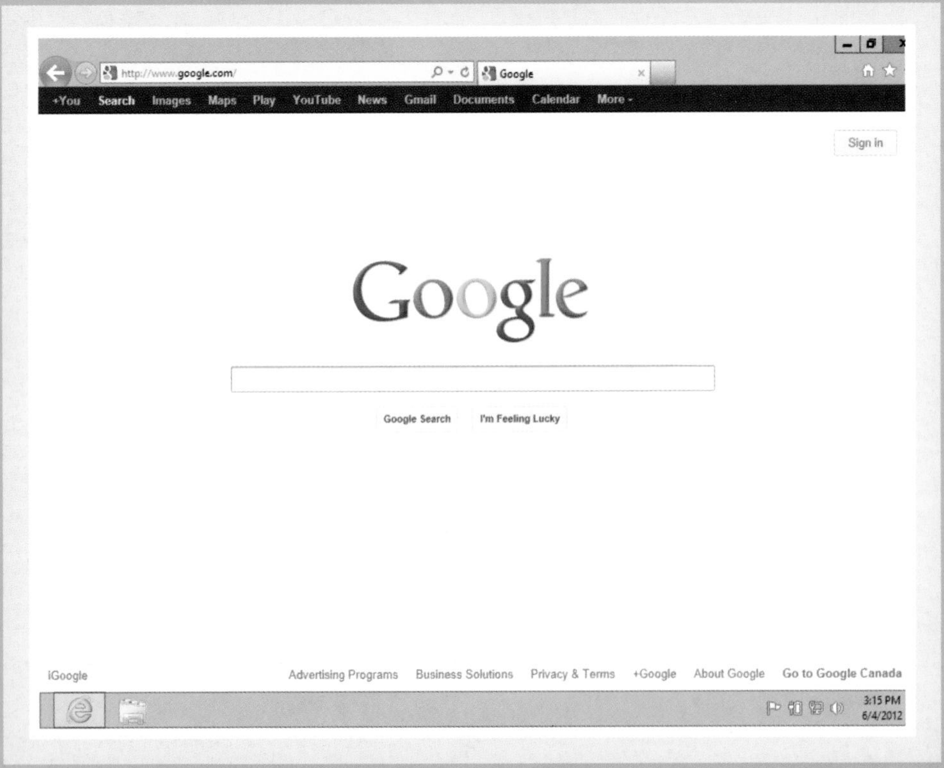

Understanding the World Wide Web

The World Wide Web — the web, for short — is a massive storehouse of information that resides on computers, called *web servers,* located all over the world.

You will probably find that you spend the majority of your online time browsing the web. That is not surprising because the web is useful, entertaining, fun, interesting, and provocative.

This section introduces you to the web. In particular, you learn about four crucial web concepts: the web page, the website, the web address, and the link. Understanding these ideas can help you get the most out of your web excursions.

Web Page

World Wide Web information is presented on web pages, which you download to your computer using a web browser program, such as Windows 8's Internet Explorer. Each web page can combine text with images, sounds, music, and even video to present you with information on a particular subject. The web consists of billions of pages covering almost every imaginable topic.

Website

A website is a collection of web pages associated with a particular person, business, service, government, school, or organization. Websites are stored on a web server, a special computer that makes web pages available for people to browse. A web server is usually a powerful computer capable of handling thousands of site visitors at a time. The largest websites are run by *server farms,* which are networks that may contain dozens, hundreds, or even thousands of servers.

Web Address

Every web page has its own web address that uniquely identifies the page. This address is sometimes called a *URL* (pronounced *yoo-ar-ell* or *erl*), which is short for Uniform Resource Locator. If you know the address of a page, you can plug that address into your web browser to view the page.

Links

A *link* (also called a hyperlink) is a kind of "cross-reference" to another web page. Each link is a bit of text (usually shown underlined and in a different color) or an image that, when you click it, loads the other page into your web browser automatically. The other page is often from the same site, but links that take you to pages anywhere on the web are also common.

Start Internet Explorer

To access websites and view web pages, you must use a web browser program. In Windows 8, the default web browser is Internet Explorer, which you can use to surf websites when your computer is connected to the Internet.

The desktop version of Internet Explorer offers a number of features that make it easier to browse the web. For example, you can open multiple pages in a single Internet Explorer window, save your favorite sites for easier access, and perform Internet searches from the Internet Explorer window.

To use these features, you must know how to start the Internet Explorer application. When you have finished surfing the web, you also need to know how to shut down Internet Explorer to save system resources on your computer.

Start Internet Explorer

1. Press ⊞+D.

   Windows 8 displays the desktop.

2. Click **Internet Explorer** (e).

2

The first time you start desktop Internet Explorer, the Set Up Internet Explorer 10 dialog box appears.

3. Click **Use recommended security and compatibility settings** (○ changes to ◉).

4. Click **OK**.

   The Internet Explorer window appears.

A. When you are finished with the web, click the **Close** button (x) to shut down Internet Explorer.

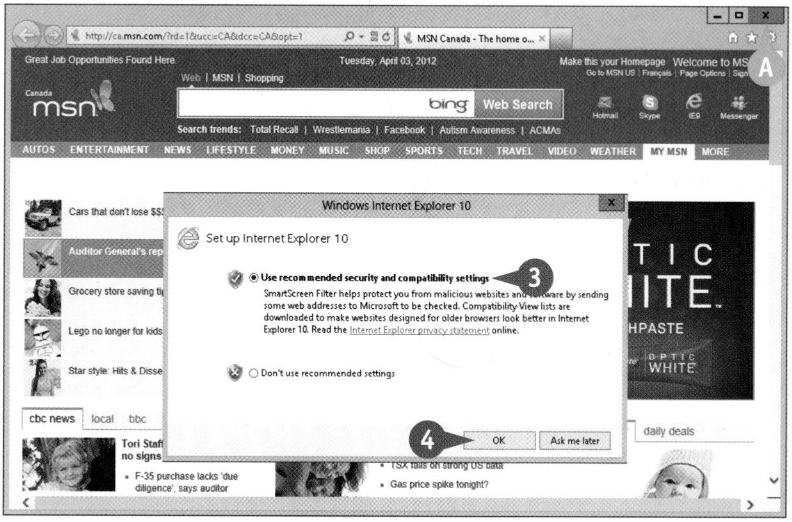
MSN Canada - The home o...
msn
Web Search
Windows Internet Explorer 10
Set up Internet Explorer 10
Use recommended security and compatibility settings
SmartScreen Filter helps protect you from malicious websites and software by sending some web addresses to Microsoft to be checked. Compatibility View lists are downloaded to make websites designed for older browsers look better in Internet Explorer 10. Read the Internet Explorer privacy statement online.
Don't use recommended settings
OK
Ask me later
3
4
A

Navigate Internet Explorer

You can easily surf the web if you know your way around the Internet Explorer web browser. In particular, you need to familiarize yourself with important Internet Explorer features such as the address bar and where the program displays the web page title. You also need to understand links, how to recognize the current link, and how to determine where a link will take you before clicking it.

A Address Bar

This text box displays the address of the displayed web page. You can also use the address bar to type the address of a web page that you want to visit to search for information on the web.

B Web Page Title

This part of the Internet Explorer title bar shows the title of the displayed web page.

C Links

Links appear either as text or as images. On most pages (although not the page shown here), text links appear underlined and in a different color (usually blue) than the regular page text.

D Current Link

This is the link that you are currently pointing at with your mouse. The mouse pointer changes from ↖ to 👆. On some pages (such as the one shown here), the link text also becomes underlined and changes color.

E Link Address

When you point at a link, Internet Explorer displays a banner that shows you the address of the page associated with the link.

Select a Link

Almost all web pages include links to other pages that contain related information. When you select a link, your web browser loads the other page.

Web page links come in two forms: text and images. Text links consist of a word or phrase that usually appears underlined and in a different color from the rest of the page text. However, web page designers can control the look of their links, so text links may not always stand out in this way.

Therefore, knowing which words, phrases, or images are links is not always obvious. The only way to tell for sure is to position the mouse ⇖ over the text or image; if ⇖ changes to ☝, you know the item is a link.

Select a Link

1. Position the mouse ⇖ over the link (⇖ changes to ☝).
2. Click the text or image.

A. This banner shows the address of the linked page.

Note: The link address shown when you point at a link may be different than the one shown when the page is downloading. This happens when the website "redirects" the link, which happens frequently.

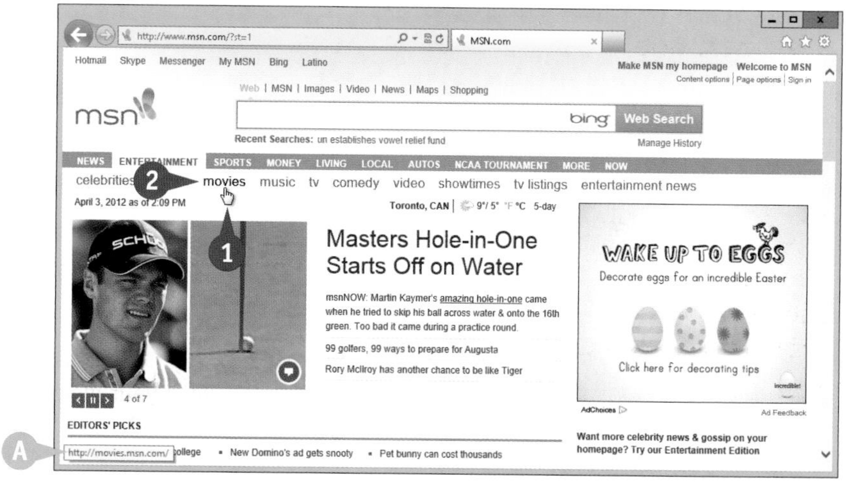

The linked web page appears.

B. The web page title and address change after the linked page is loaded.

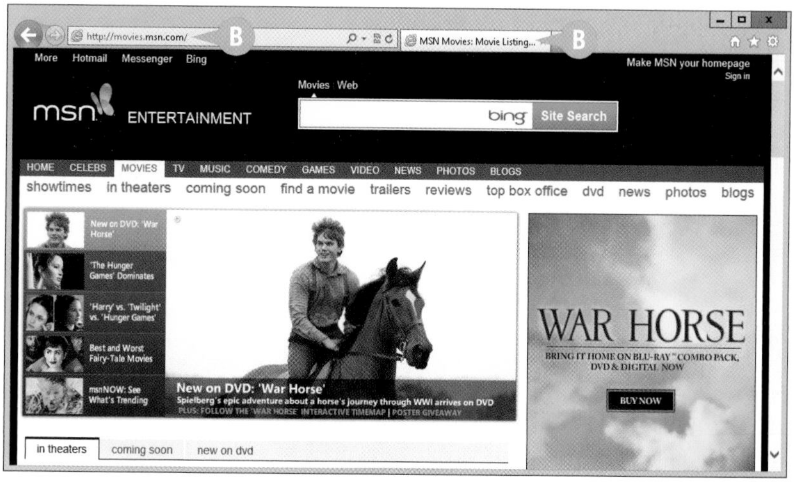

Enter a Web Page Address

If you know the address of a specific web page, you can type it into the web browser to display the page. Every web page is uniquely identified by an address called the Uniform Resource Locator, or URL.

The URL is composed of four basic parts: the *transfer method* (usually HTTP, which stands for Hypertext Transfer Protocol), the website *domain name*, the *directory* where the web page is located on the server, and the *web page filename*.

The website domain name suffix most often used is .com (commercial), but other common suffixes include .gov (government), .org (nonprofit organization), .edu (education), and country domains such as .ca (Canada).

Enter a Web Page Address

Type a Web Page Address

1. Click in the address bar.
2. Type the address of the web page.

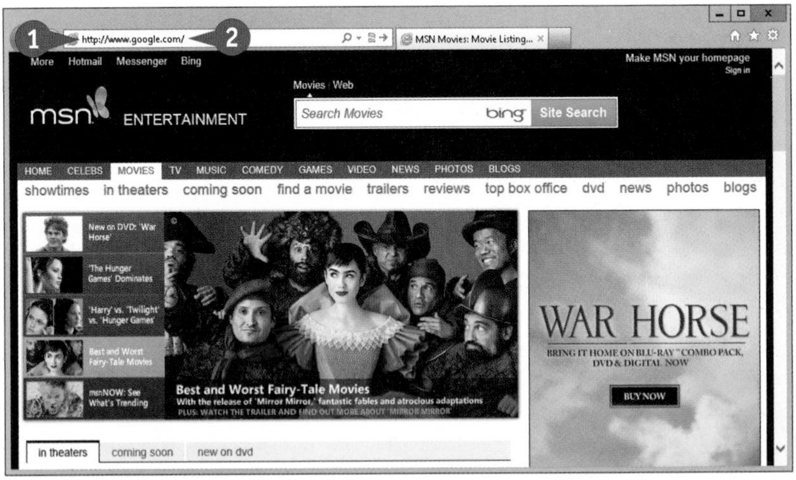

3. Click the **Go** button (→).

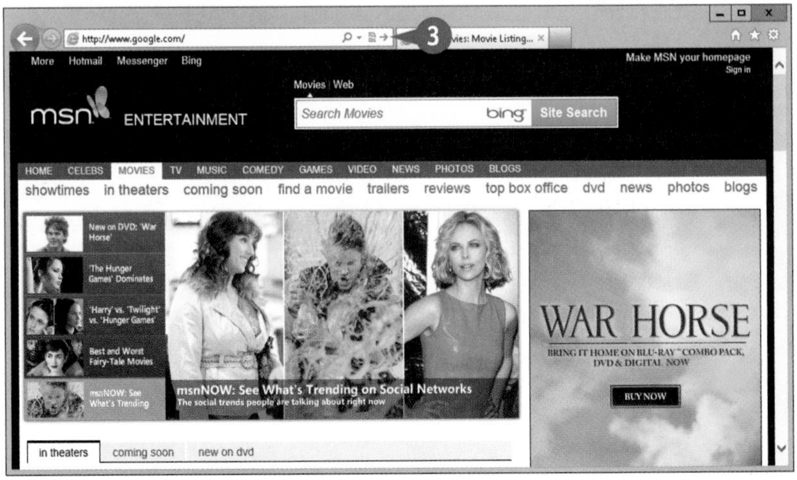

The web page appears.

Ⓐ The web page title changes after the page is loaded.

Redisplay a Web Page

1. Click the address bar (▾).

   A list of the addresses you have typed appears.

2. Click the address you want to display.

   The web page appears.

Note: If you type the first few letters of the address (such as **goog**), the address bar displays a list of addresses that match what you have typed. If you see the address you want, click it to load the page.

TIPS

Are there any shortcuts I can use to enter web page addresses?

Here are some useful keyboard techniques:

- After you finish typing the address, press Enter instead of clicking the **Go** button (→).
- Most web addresses begin with *http://*. You can leave off these characters when you type your address; Internet Explorer adds them automatically.
- If the address uses the form http://www.something.com, type just the "something" part and press Ctrl+Enter. Internet Explorer automatically adds *http://www.* at the beginning and *.com* at the end.

When I try to load a page, why does Internet Explorer tell me "The page cannot be displayed"?

This message means that Internet Explorer is unable to contact a web server at the address you typed. This is often a temporary glitch, so click **Refresh** (↻) or press F5 to try loading the page again. If the trouble persists, double-check your address to ensure that you typed it correctly. If you did, the site may be unavailable for some reason. Try again in a few hours.

Open a Web Page in a Tab

You can make it easier to work with multiple web pages and sites simultaneously by opening each page in its own tab. As you surf the web, you may come upon a page that you want to keep available while you visit other sites. That page may contain important information that you need to reference, or it might be a page that you want to read later on.

Instead of leaving the page and trying to find it again when you need it, Internet Explorer lets you keep the page open in a special section of the browser window called a *tab*. You can then use a second tab to visit your other sites, and to resume viewing the first site you need only click its tab.

Open a Web Page in a Tab

Open a Web Page in a Tab

1. Right-click the link you want to open.
2. Click **Open in new tab**.

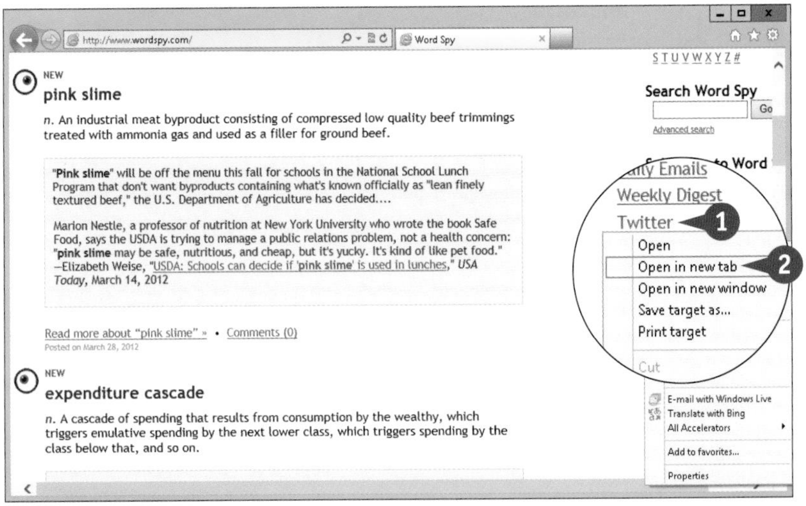

http://www.wordspy.com/
Word Spy
STUVWXYZ#
NEW
pink slime
n. An industrial meat byproduct consisting of compressed low quality beef trimmings treated with ammonia gas and used as a filler for ground beef.
"Pink slime" will be off the menu this fall for schools in the National School Lunch Program that don't want byproducts containing what's known officially as "lean finely textured beef," the U.S. Department of Agriculture has decided....
Marion Nestle, a professor of nutrition at New York University who wrote the book Safe Food, says the USDA is trying to manage a public relations problem, not a health concern: "pink slime may be safe, nutritious, and cheap, but it's yucky. It's kind of like pet food." —Elizabeth Weise, "USDA: Schools can decide if 'pink slime' is used in lunches," USA Today, March 14, 2012
Read more about "pink slime" » • Comments (0)
Posted on March 28, 2012
NEW
expenditure cascade
n. A cascade of spending that results from consumption by the wealthy, which triggers emulative spending by the next lower class, which triggers spending by the class below that, and so on.
Search Word Spy
Go
Advanced search
Weekly Digest
Twitter
1
Open
Open in new tab
2
Open in new window
Save target as...
Print target
Cut
E-mail with Windows Live
Translate with Bing
All Accelerators
Add to favorites...
Properties

A. A new tab appears with the page title.

3. Click the tab to display the page.

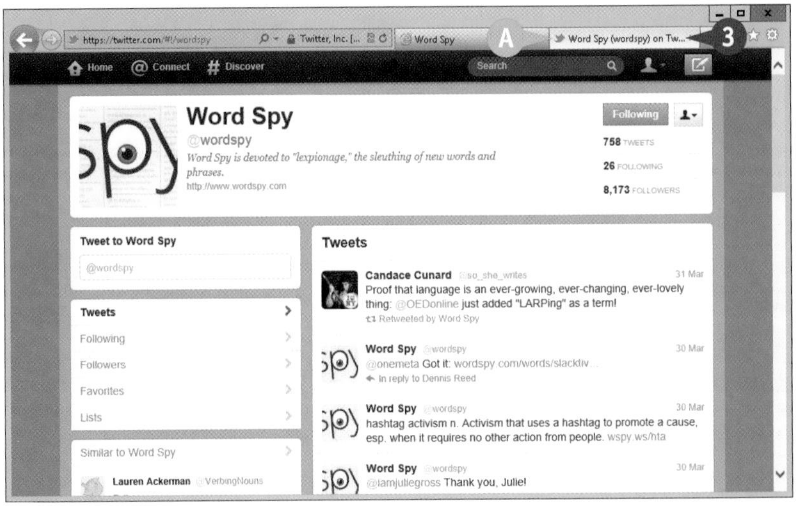

https://twitter.com/#!/wordspy
Twitter, Inc.
Word Spy
A
Word Spy (wordspy) on Tw...
3
Home
Connect
Discover
Search
Word Spy
@wordspy
Word Spy is devoted to "lexpionage," the sleuthing of new words and phrases.
http://www.wordspy.com
Following
758 TWEETS
26 FOLLOWING
8,173 FOLLOWERS
Tweet to Word Spy
@wordspy
Tweets
Following
Followers
Favorites
Lists
Similar to Word Spy
Lauren Ackerman @VerbingNouns
Tweets
Candace Cunard @so_she_writes 31 Mar
Proof that language is an ever-growing, ever-changing, ever-lovely thing: @OEDonline just added "LARPing" as a term!
Retweeted by Word Spy
Word Spy @wordspy 30 Mar
@onemeta Got it: wordspy.com/words/slacktiv...
In reply to Dennis Reed
Word Spy @wordspy 30 Mar
hashtag activism n. Activism that uses a hashtag to promote a cause, esp. when it requires no other action from people. wspy.ws/hta
Word Spy @wordspy 30 Mar
@iamjuliegross Thank you, Julie!

Navigate Tabs

1. Click the **Tab Left** button (◻) or the **Tab Right** button (◻) to display the tab you want.

Note: You see the Tab Left and Tab Right buttons only if Internet Explorer does not have enough room to display all the tabs.

2. Click the tab.

B The web page loaded in the tab appears.

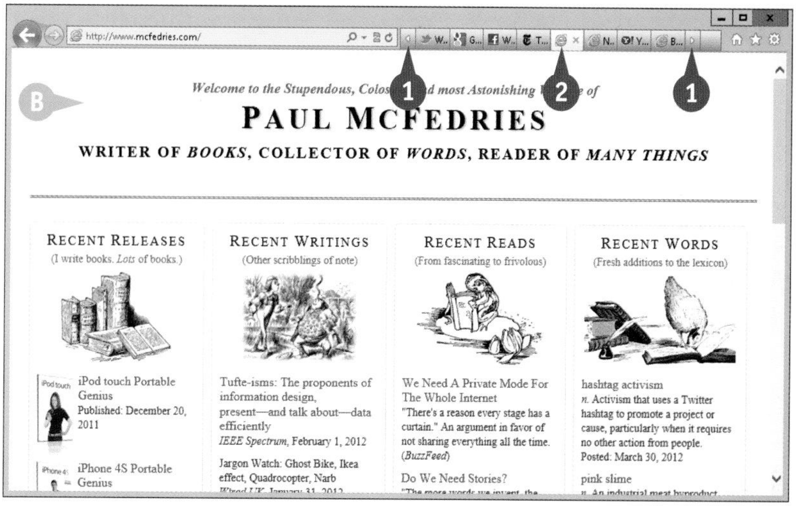

Close a Tab

1. Position the mouse ↖ over the tab you want to close.
2. Click **Close Tab** (☒).

TIP

Are there any shortcuts I can use to open web pages in tabs?

Here are some useful keyboard techniques:

- Press and hold Ctrl and click a link to open the page in a tab.
- Press and hold Ctrl + Shift and click a link to open the page in a tab and display the tab.
- Type an address and then press Alt + Enter to open the page in a new tab.
- Press Ctrl + Tab or Ctrl + Shift + Tab to cycle through the tabs.
- Press Ctrl + W to close the current tab.
- Press Ctrl + Alt + F4 to close every tab but the current one.

Navigate Web Pages

After you have visited several pages, you can return to a page you visited earlier. Instead of retyping the address or looking for the link, Internet Explorer gives you some easier methods.

When you navigate from page to page, you create a kind of "path" through the web. Internet Explorer keeps track of this path by maintaining a list of the pages you have visited. You can use that list to go back to a page you have visited.

After you have gone back to a page you have visited, you can also use the same list of pages to go forward through the pages again.

Navigate Web Pages

Go Back One Page

1. Click the **Back** button ( ).

   The previous page you visited appears.

1
https://twitter.com/#!/wordspy
Twitter, Inc. [...
Word Spy (wordspy) on Twi...
Home
Connect
Discover
Search
Word Spy
@wordspy
Word Spy is devoted to "lexpionage," the sleuthing of new words and phrases.
http://www.wordspy.com
758
26
8,174
Tweet to Word Spy
@wordspy
Tweets
Following
Followers
Favorites
Lists
Similar to Word Spy
Candace Cunard
Proof that language is an ever-growing, ever-changing,
thing: @OEDonline just added "LARPing" as a term!
Retweeted by Word Spy
Word Spy
@onemeta Got it: wordspy.com/words/slacktiv...
In reply to Dennis Reed
Word Spy
hashtag activism n. Activism that uses a hashtag to prom
esp. when it requires no other action from people.

Go Back Several Pages

1. Click and hold the mouse on the **Back** button ( ).

   A list of the sites you have visited appears.

   A The current site appears with a check mark ( ) beside it.

   B Items listed below the current site are ones you visited prior to the current site. When you position the mouse over a previous site, Internet Explorer displays the Go Back arrow ( ).

2. Click the page you want to display.

   The page appears.

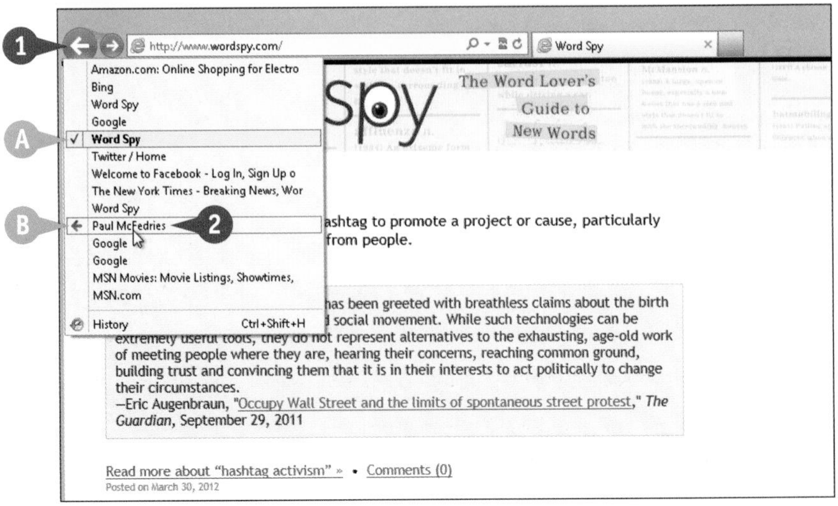

1
http://www.wordspy.com/
Word Spy
Amazon.com: Online Shopping for Electro
Bing
Word Spy
Google
A
Word Spy
Twitter / Home
Welcome to Facebook - Log In, Sign Up o
The New York Times - Breaking News, Wor
Word Spy
B
Paul McFedries
2
Google
Google
MSN Movies: Movie Listings, Showtimes,
MSN.com
History Ctrl+Shift+H
The Word Lover's Guide to New Words
ashtag to promote a project or cause, particularly
from people.
has been greeted with breathless claims about the birth
social movement. While such technologies can be
t represent alternatives to the exhausting, age-old work
of meeting people where they are, hearing their concerns, reaching common ground,
building trust and convincing them that it is in their interests to act politically to change
their circumstances.
—Eric Augenbraun, "Occupy Wall Street and the limits of spontaneous street protest," The Guardian, September 29, 2011
Read more about "hashtag activism" » • Comments (0)
Posted on March 30, 2012

Go Forward One Page

1. Click the **Forward** button (➡).

   The next page you visited appears.

Note: If you are at the last page viewed up to that point, the Forward button (➡) is not active.

Go Forward Several Pages

1. Click and hold the mouse on the **Forward** button (➡).

   A list of the sites you have visited appears.

   Ⓒ Items listed above the current site are ones you visited after the current site. When you position the mouse over a previous site, Internet Explorer displays the Go Forward arrow (➡).

2. Click the page you want to display.

   The page appears.

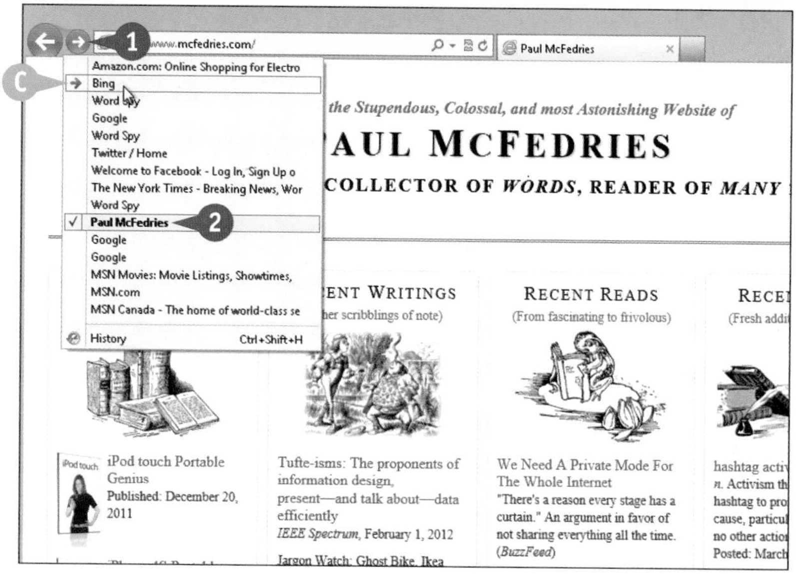

TIP

How do I go back or forward to a page, but also keep the current page on-screen?

You can do this by opening a second Internet Explorer window. Keep the current page in the original window and then use the second window to go back or forward. Here are the steps to follow:

1. Press Ctrl + N.

   Ⓐ A new Internet Explorer window appears.

2. Use the techniques described in this section to navigate to the page you want.

Change Your Home Page

Your home page is the web page that appears when you first start Internet Explorer. The default home page is usually the MSN.com page, but you can change that to any other page you want, or even to an empty page. This is useful if you do not use the MSN.com page, or if you always visit another page at the start of your browsing session. For example, if you have your own website, it might make sense to always begin there.

Internet Explorer also comes with a command that enables you to view the home page at any time during your browsing session.

Change Your Home Page

Change a Single Home Page

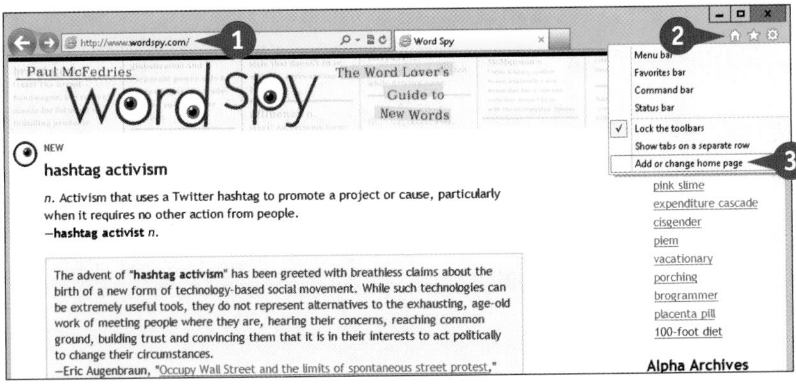

1. Display the web page that you want to use as your home page.
2. Right-click the **Home** button (🏠).
3. Click **Add or change home page**.

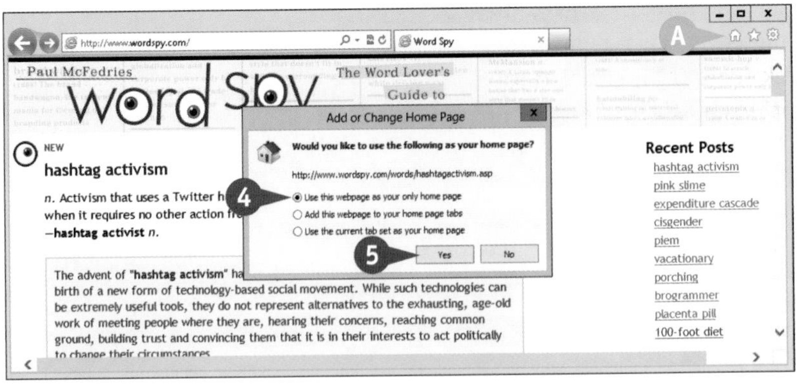

The Add or Change Home Page dialog box appears.

4. Click **Use this webpage as your only home page** (○ changes to ◉).
5. Click **Yes**.

Internet Explorer changes your home page.

A. You can click the **Home** button (🏠) to display the home page at any time.

Add a Page to Your Home Page Tabs

1. Display the web page that you want to add to your home page tabs.
2. Right-click the **Home** button ( ).
3. Click **Add or change home page**.

   The Add or Change Home Page dialog box appears.

4. Click **Add this webpage to your home page tabs** (○ changes to ◉).
5. Click **Yes**.

   Internet Explorer adds the page to your home page tabs.

B. You can click ( ) to display your home page tabs at any time.

Note: To return to using Internet Explorer's original home page, click **Tools** ( ), click **Internet Options**, click the **General** tab, click **Use default**, and then click **OK**.

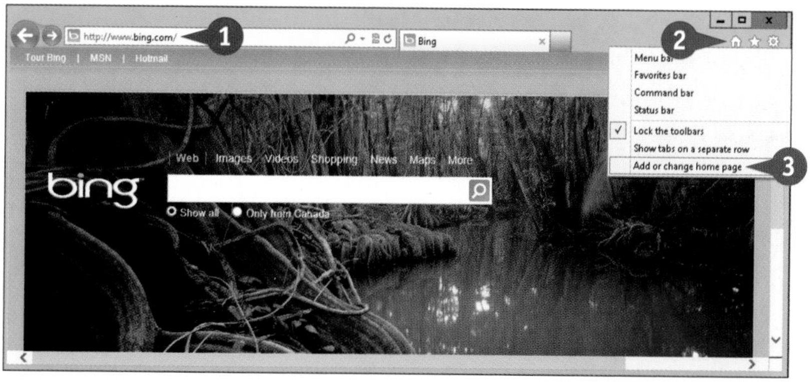

TIP

Can I get Internet Explorer to load without displaying a home page?

Yes, by following these steps:

1. Click **Tools** ( ).
2. Click **Internet Options**.
3. Click **Use new tab**.
4. Click **OK**.

Save Favorite Web Pages

If you have web pages that you visit frequently, you can save yourself time by saving those pages as favorites within Internet Explorer. This enables you to display the pages with just a couple of mouse clicks.

The Favorites feature is a list of web pages that you have saved. Instead of typing an address or searching for one of these pages, you can display the web page by selecting its address from the Favorites list.

Save Favorite Web Pages

Save a Favorite Web Page

1. Display the web page you want to save as a favorite.
2. Click the **View favorites** button (☆).
3. Click **Add to favorites**.

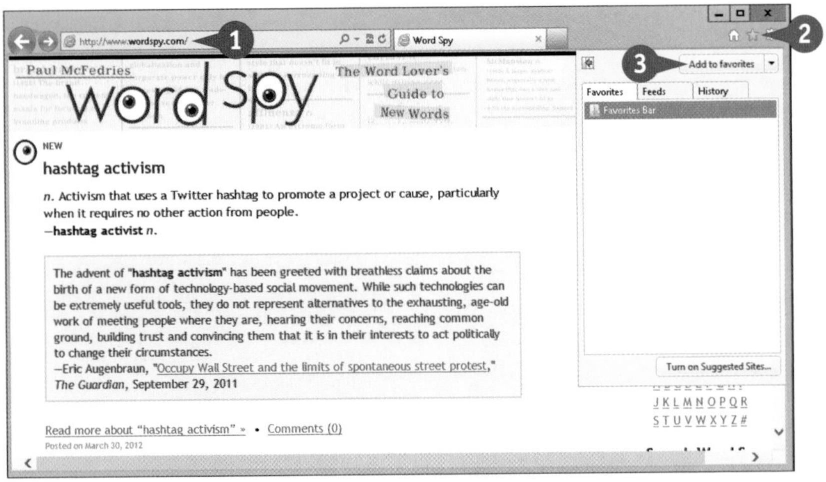

http://www.wordspy.com/
Word Spy
Paul McFedries
word spy
The Word Lover's Guide to New Words
Add to favorites
Favorites
Feeds
History
Favorites Bar
NEW
hashtag activism
n. Activism that uses a Twitter hashtag to promote a project or cause, particularly when it requires no other action from people.
—hashtag activist n.
The advent of "hashtag activism" has been greeted with breathless claims about the birth of a new form of technology-based social movement. While such technologies can be extremely useful tools, they do not represent alternatives to the exhausting, age-old work of meeting people where they are, hearing their concerns, reaching common ground, building trust and convincing them that it is in their interests to act politically to change their circumstances.
—Eric Augenbraun, "Occupy Wall Street and the limits of spontaneous street protest," The Guardian, September 29, 2011
Turn on Suggested Sites...
J K L M N O P Q R
S T U V W X Y Z #
Read more about "hashtag activism" » • Comments (0)
Posted on March 30, 2012
1
2
3

The Add a Favorite dialog box appears.

Note: You can also display the Add a Favorite dialog box by pressing Ctrl+D.

4. Edit the page name, as necessary.
5. Click **Add**.

Add a Favorite
Add a Favorite
Add this webpage as a favorite. To access your favorites, visit the Favorites Center.
Name:
Word Spy
Create in:
Favorites
New folder
Add
Cancel
4
5

Display a Favorite Web Page

1. Click the **View favorites** button (☆).
2. Click **Favorites.**

   The Favorites list appears.

3. Click the web page you want to display.

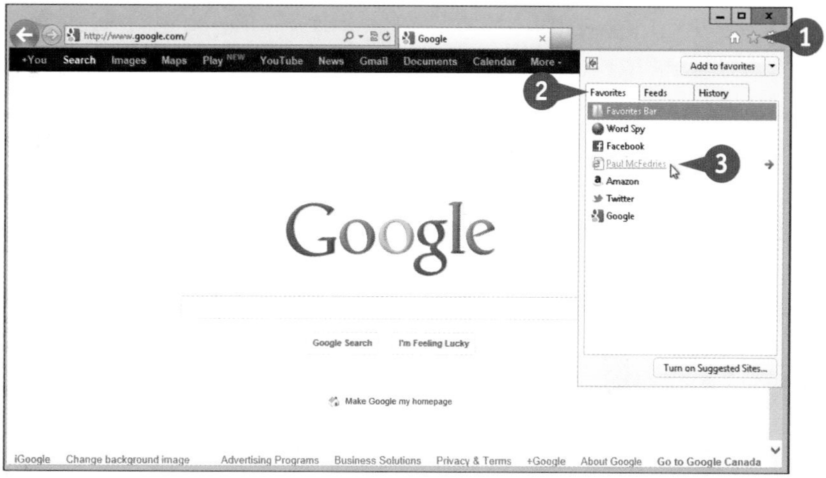

The web page appears.

Ⓐ If you use your Favorites list a lot, you can make it easier to display the pages by keeping the Favorites Center visible. Click the **View favorites** button (☆) and then click the **Pin the Favorites Center** button (⊞). Internet Explorer pins the Favorites Center to the left side of the window.

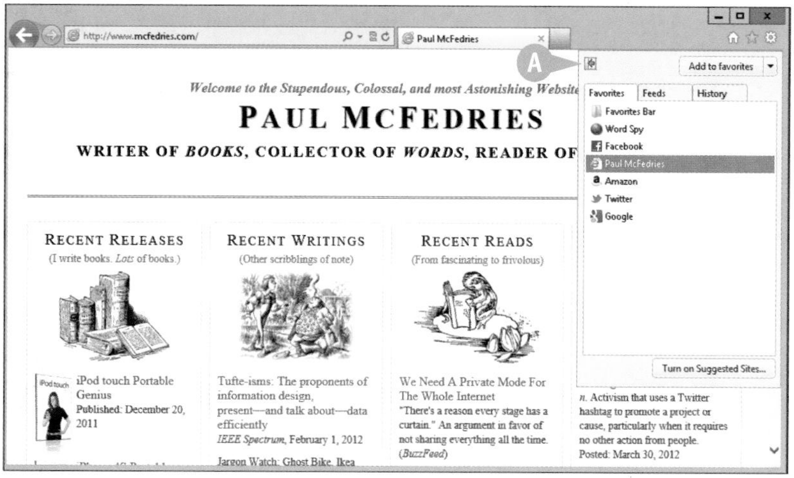

TIPS

Is there an easier way to display a favorite?

Yes, you can use Internet Explorer's Favorites bar, which appears just below the address bar and offers one-click access to your favorite pages. Note that the Favorites bar does not appear until you add at least one page. To do that, display the page you want to save, click the **View Favorites** button (☆), click the **Add to favorites** ▾, and then click **Add to Favorites bar**.

How do I delete a favorite?

If the site is on the Favorites bar, right-click the favorite and then click **Delete.** For all other favorites, click the **View Favorites** button (☆), click **Favorites**, right-click the favorite you want to delete, and then click **Delete.**

Search for Sites

If you need information on a specific topic, Internet Explorer has a built-in feature that enables you to quickly search the web for sites that have the information you require.

The web has a number of sites called *search engines* that enable you to find what you are looking for. By default, Internet Explorer uses the Bing search site.

Simple, one-word searches often return tens of thousands of *hits*, or matching sites. To improve your searching, type multiple search terms that define what you are looking for. To search for a phrase, enclose the words in quotation marks.

Search for Sites

1. In the address bar, click **Search** (🔍).

Note: You can also press Ctrl + E.

Internet Explorer turns the address bar into the search bar.

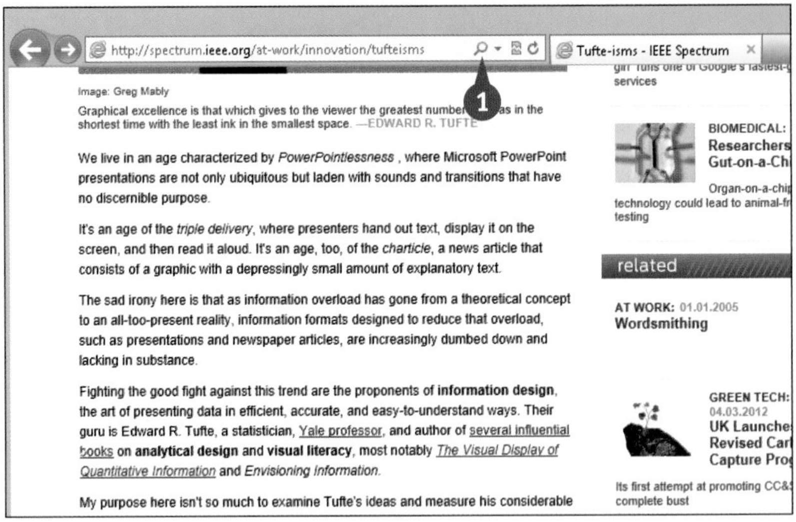

http://spectrum.ieee.org/at-work/innovation/tufteisms
Tufte-isms - IEEE Spectrum
1
Image: Greg Mably
Graphical excellence is that which gives to the viewer the greatest number of ideas in the shortest time with the least ink in the smallest space. —EDWARD R. TUFTE
We live in an age characterized by PowerPointlessness , where Microsoft PowerPoint presentations are not only ubiquitous but laden with sounds and transitions that have no discernible purpose.
It's an age of the triple delivery, where presenters hand out text, display it on the screen, and then read it aloud. It's an age, too, of the charticle, a news article that consists of a graphic with a depressingly small amount of explanatory text.
The sad irony here is that as information overload has gone from a theoretical concept to an all-too-present reality, information formats designed to reduce that overload, such as presentations and newspaper articles, are increasingly dumbed down and lacking in substance.
Fighting the good fight against this trend are the proponents of information design, the art of presenting data in efficient, accurate, and easy-to-understand ways. Their guru is Edward R. Tufte, a statistician, Yale professor, and author of several influential books on analytical design and visual literacy, most notably The Visual Display of Quantitative Information and Envisioning Information.
My purpose here isn't so much to examine Tufte's ideas and measure his considerable
services
BIOMEDICAL:
related
AT WORK: 01.01.2005
Wordsmithing
GREEN TECH:
04.03.2012

2. Type a word, phrase, or question that represents the information you want to find.

3. Press Enter.

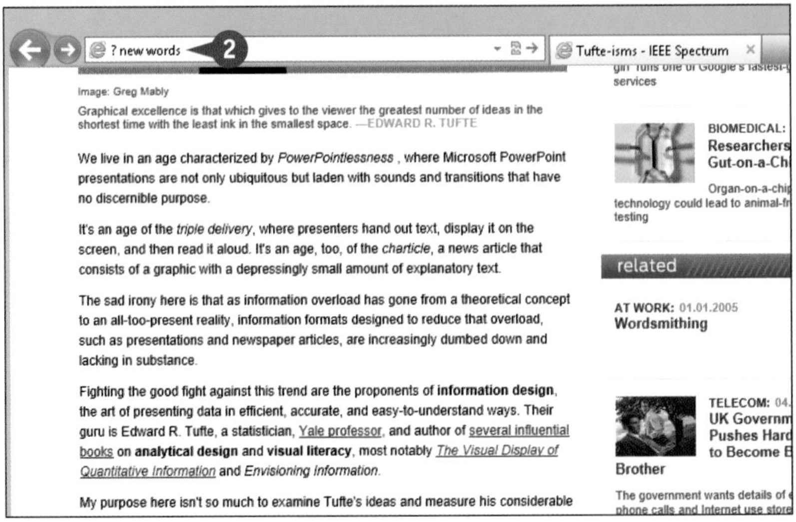

? new words
2
Tufte-isms - IEEE Spectrum
Image: Greg Mably
Graphical excellence is that which gives to the viewer the greatest number of ideas in the shortest time with the least ink in the smallest space. —EDWARD R. TUFTE
We live in an age characterized by PowerPointlessness , where Microsoft PowerPoint presentations are not only ubiquitous but laden with sounds and transitions that have no discernible purpose.
It's an age of the triple delivery, where presenters hand out text, display it on the screen, and then read it aloud. It's an age, too, of the charticle, a news article that consists of a graphic with a depressingly small amount of explanatory text.
The sad irony here is that as information overload has gone from a theoretical concept to an all-too-present reality, information formats designed to reduce that overload, such as presentations and newspaper articles, are increasingly dumbed down and lacking in substance.
Fighting the good fight against this trend are the proponents of information design, the art of presenting data in efficient, accurate, and easy-to-understand ways. Their guru is Edward R. Tufte, a statistician, Yale professor, and author of several influential books on analytical design and visual literacy, most notably The Visual Display of Quantitative Information and Envisioning Information.
My purpose here isn't so much to examine Tufte's ideas and measure his considerable
services
BIOMEDICAL:
related
AT WORK: 01.01.2005
Wordsmithing
Brother

Ⓐ A list of pages that match your search text appears.

❹ Click a web page.

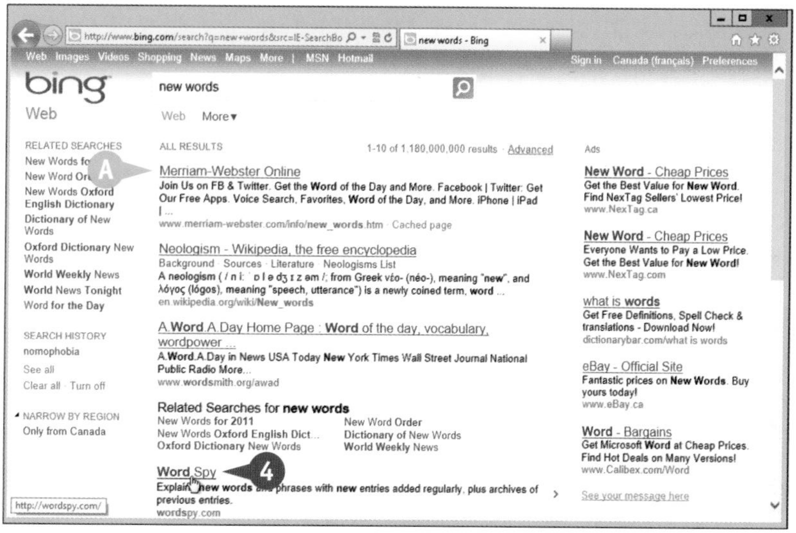

The page appears.

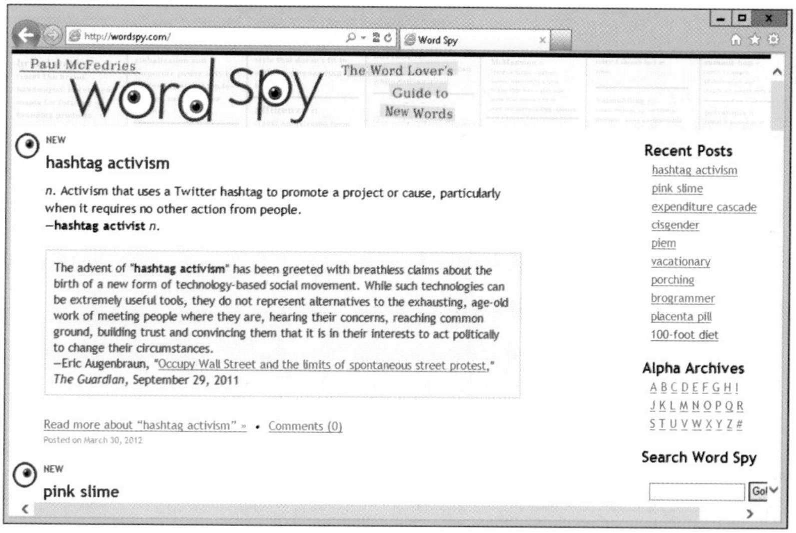

TIP

Can I use another search engine?

Yes. To add another search engine, click the address bar ▾ and then click **Add**. Internet Explorer takes you to the Internet Explorer Gallery site. Click the **search** category and then click the search engine you want to use with Internet Explorer. Click **Add to Internet Explorer**, and then click **Add** when you are asked to confirm.

To use the search engine, click the address bar ▾ and then click the search engine icon at the bottom of the list.

Navigate with the History List

The Back and Forward buttons (◼ and ◼) enable you to navigate pages only in the current browser session. To redisplay sites that you have visited in the past few days or weeks, you need to use the History list, which is a collection of the websites and pages you have visited over the past month.

If you visit sensitive places such as an Internet banking site or your corporate site, you can increase security by clearing the History list so that other people cannot see where you have been.

Navigate with the History List

1. Click the **View favorites** button (◼).
2. Click **History**.

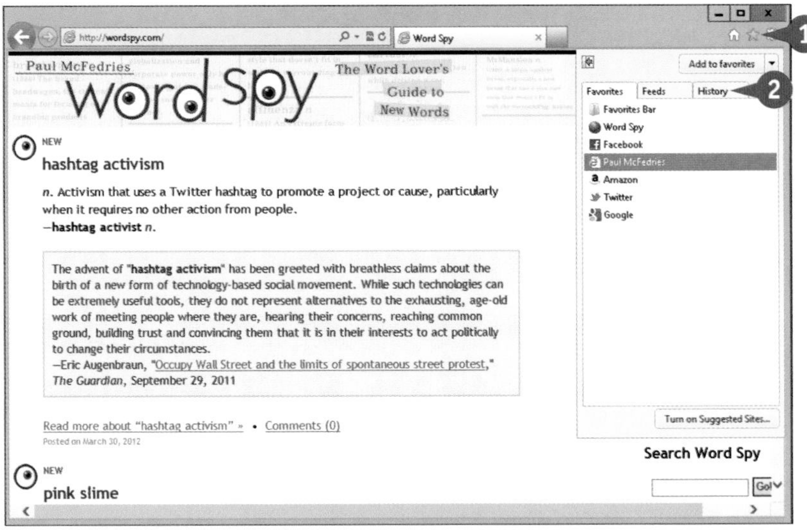

http://wordspy.com/
Word Spy
Paul McFedries
word spy
The Word Lover's Guide to New Words
NEW
hashtag activism
n. Activism that uses a Twitter hashtag to promote a project or cause, particularly when it requires no other action from people.
—hashtag activist n.
The advent of "hashtag activism" has been greeted with breathless claims about the birth of a new form of technology-based social movement. While such technologies can be extremely useful tools, they do not represent alternatives to the exhausting, age-old work of meeting people where they are, hearing their concerns, reaching common ground, building trust and convincing them that it is in their interests to act politically to change their circumstances.
—Eric Augenbraun, "Occupy Wall Street and the limits of spontaneous street protest," The Guardian, September 29, 2011
Read more about "hashtag activism" » • Comments (0)
Posted on March 30, 2012
NEW
pink slime
Add to favorites
Favorites
Feeds
History
Favorites Bar
Word Spy
Facebook
Paul McFedries
Amazon
Twitter
Google
Turn on Suggested Sites...
Search Word Spy
Go!
1
2

Ⓐ The History list appears.

3. Click the day or week that you visited the site.

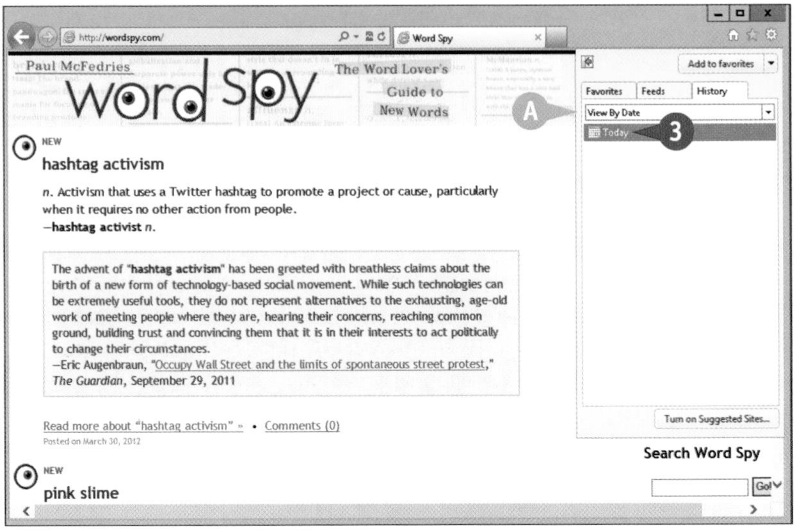

http://wordspy.com/
Word Spy
Paul McFedries
word spy
The Word Lover's Guide to New Words
NEW
hashtag activism
n. Activism that uses a Twitter hashtag to promote a project or cause, particularly when it requires no other action from people.
—hashtag activist n.
The advent of "hashtag activism" has been greeted with breathless claims about the birth of a new form of technology-based social movement. While such technologies can be extremely useful tools, they do not represent alternatives to the exhausting, age-old work of meeting people where they are, hearing their concerns, reaching common ground, building trust and convincing them that it is in their interests to act politically to change their circumstances.
—Eric Augenbraun, "Occupy Wall Street and the limits of spontaneous street protest," The Guardian, September 29, 2011
Read more about "hashtag activism" » • Comments (0)
Posted on March 30, 2012
NEW
pink slime
Add to favorites
Favorites
Feeds
History
View By Date
Today
Turn on Suggested Sites...
Search Word Spy
Go!
A
3

A list of sites that you visited during that day or week appears.

4. Click the site that contains the page you want to display.

A list of pages you visited in the site appears.

5. Click the page you want to display.

B. The page appears.

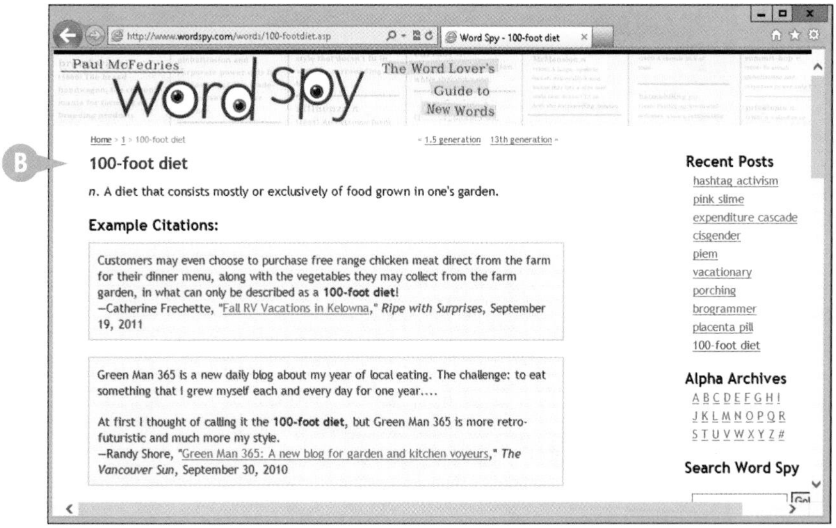

TIPS

How do I clear my History list?

Click **Tools** (⚙), click **Safety**, and then click **Delete browsing history** to open the Delete Browsing History dialog box. (Note that you can display this dialog box directly by pressing Ctrl+Shift+Delete.) Click to activate the **History** check box (☐ changes to ☑). Click to deactivate the other check boxes (☑ changes to ☐). Click **Delete**.

Can I control the length of time that Internet Explorer keeps track of the pages I visit?

Yes. Click **Tools** (⚙) and then click **Internet options** to open the Internet Options dialog box. Click the **General** tab and then click **Settings** to open the Website Data Settings dialog box. Click the **History** tab and then use the **Days to keep pages in history** spin box to set the amount of time you want Internet Explorer to track your history. Click **OK**.

CHAPTER 6

Working with E-Mail and Calendars

If you have installed Mail, you can use it to send and read e-mail messages. You can also use Mail for contacts and to track your events.

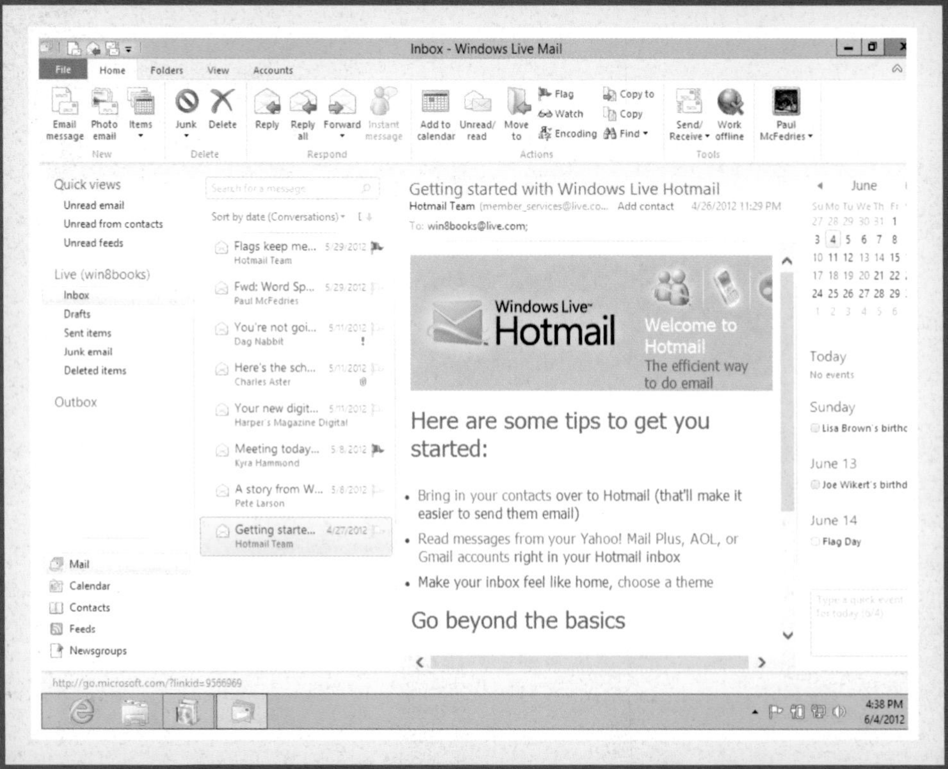

Open and Close Mail

The Mail application enables you to use an e-mail account to exchange and manage e-mail messages. E-mail is one of the most popular Internet services because it offers three main advantages: It is universal, fast, and convenient.

E-mail is universal because nearly anyone who can access the Internet has an e-mail address. E-mail is fast because messages are generally delivered within a few minutes. E-mail is convenient because you can send messages at any time of day, and your recipient does not need to be at the computer or connected to the Internet.

Before you can send messages, you must know how to start the Mail application.

Open and Close Mail

Open Mail

1 On the Start screen, click **Mail**.

Start
Paul
McFedries
1
Windows Live Mail
Windows Live Photo Gallery
Windows Live Movie Maker
Store
SkyDrive
Travel
Games
Camera

Windows 8 may display a dialog box telling you that your PC needs a feature to continue.

2 Click **Download and install this feature**.

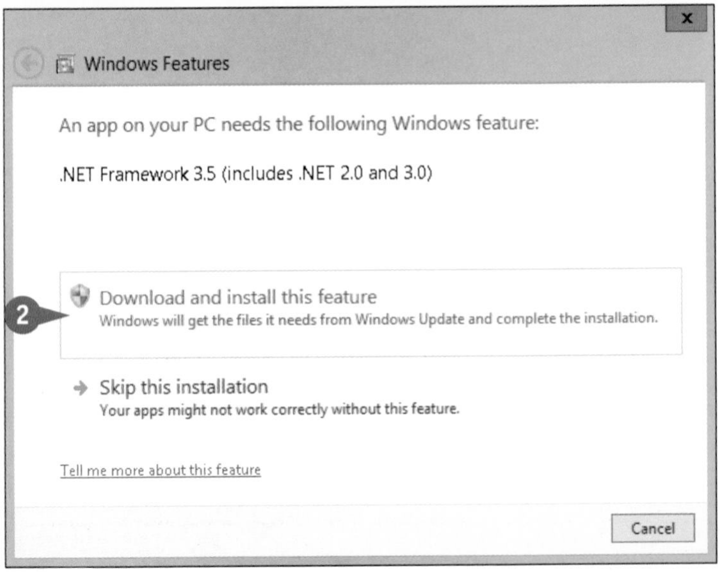

Windows Features
An app on your PC needs the following Windows feature:
.NET Framework 3.5 (includes .NET 2.0 and 3.0)
Download and install this feature
Windows will get the files it needs from Windows Update and complete the installation.
2
Skip this installation
Your apps might not work correctly without this feature.
Tell me more about this feature
Cancel

If you are using a Microsoft account as your Windows 8 user account (see Chapter 3), Mail asks if you want to sign in.

3. Click **Yes**.
4. Click **Finish** (not shown).

The Mail window appears.

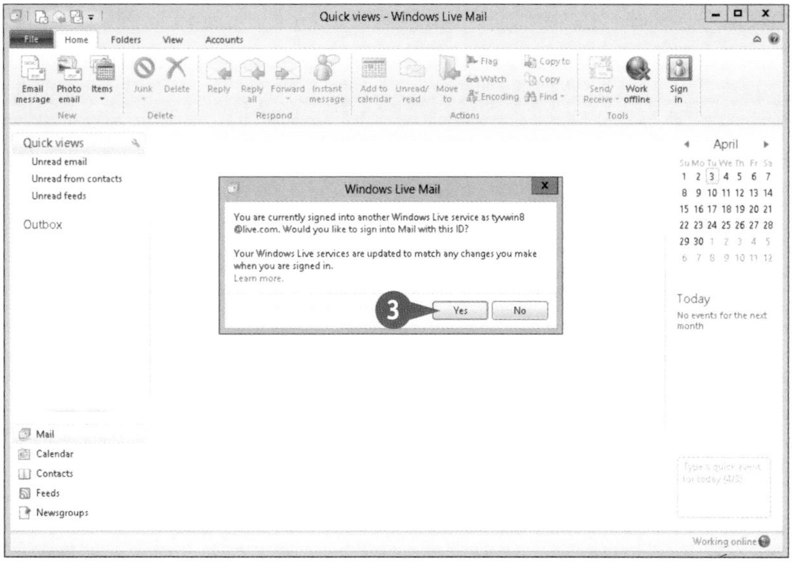
Quick views - Windows Live Mail
Windows Live Mail
You are currently signed into another Windows Live service as tyvwin8@live.com. Would you like to sign into Mail with this ID?
Your Windows Live services are updated to match any changes you make when you are signed in.
Learn more.
3
Yes
No

Close Mail

1. Click the **File** tab.
2. Click **Exit**.

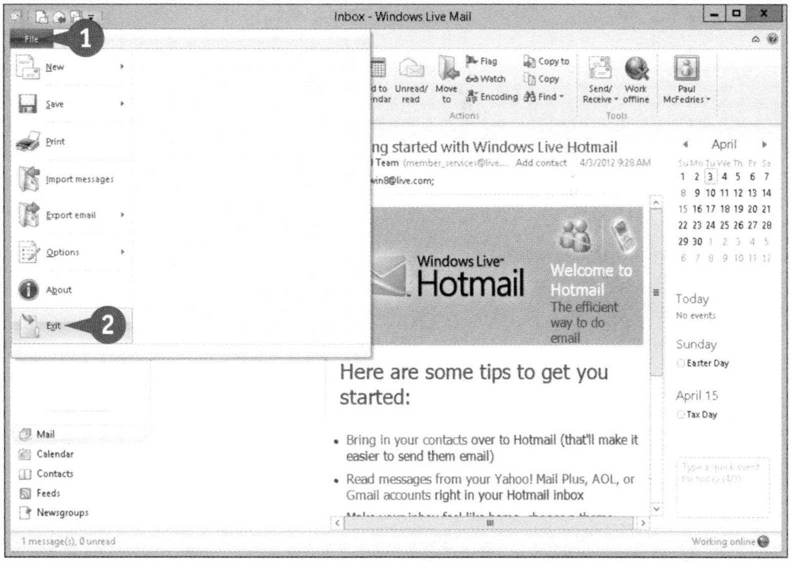
Inbox - Windows Live Mail
1
New
Save
Print
Import messages
Export email
Options
About
Exit
2
Windows Live Hotmail
Here are some tips to get you started:

TIPS

Are there other methods I can use to open Mail?
If you have unpinned the Mail icon from the Start screen, you can still start the program. First, press the Windows key to return to the Start screen. Now type **Mail** and then click **Mail** in the search results. You can also pin Windows Live Mail to the taskbar by starting the program, right-clicking its taskbar icon, and then clicking **Pin this program to taskbar**.

Are there faster methods I can use to close Mail?
Probably the fastest method you can use to quit Mail is to click its **Close** button (x). You can also right-click its taskbar icon and then click **Close window**. If your hands are closer to the keyboard than to the mouse, you can quit Mail by switching to the application and then pressing Alt + F4.

Configure an E-Mail Account

Before you can send an e-mail message, you must add your e-mail account to the Mail application. This also enables you to use Mail to retrieve the messages that others have sent to your account.

You can set up web-based e-mail accounts with services such as Hotmail and Gmail. A web-based account is convenient because it enables you to send and receive messages from any computer. You can also configure a POP (Post Office Protocol) account supplied by your Internet service provider (ISP), which should have supplied you with the POP account details.

Configure an E-Mail Account

1. Click the **Accounts** tab.
2. Click **Email**.

Note: If you signed in with your Live.com or Hotmail account, then you do not need to configure an e-mail account.

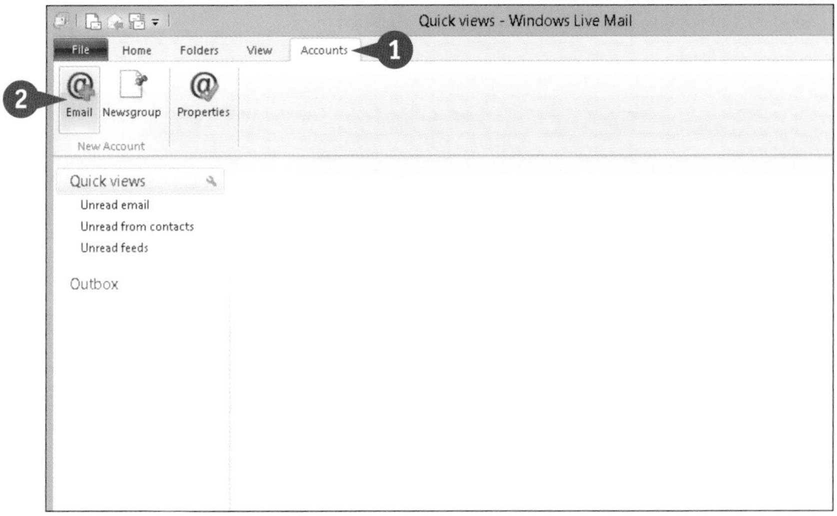

3. Type your e-mail address.
4. Type your e-mail password.
5. Click **Remember this password** (☐ changes to ☑).
6. Type your name.
7. Click **Next**.

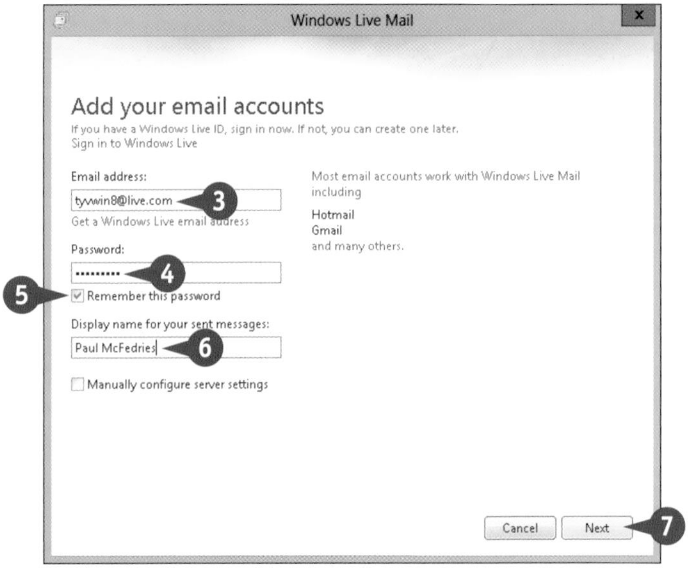

If you are configuring a Microsoft account, the program asks if you want to sign in to your account.

Note: If you see the Configure Server Settings dialog box, see the first tip to learn how to proceed.

8 Click **Yes**.

Mail tells you that your account was added.

9 Click **Finish**.

Mail begins using your e-mail account.

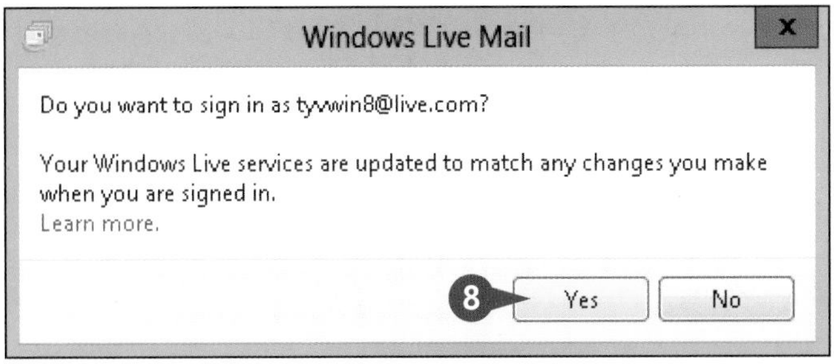
Windows Live Mail
Do you want to sign in as tywin8@live.com?
Your Windows Live services are updated to match any changes you make when you are signed in.
Learn more.
8
Yes
No

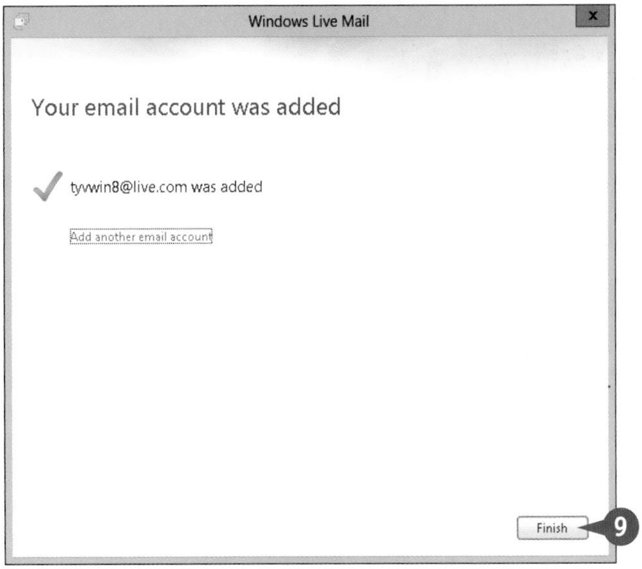
Windows Live Mail
Your email account was added
tywin8@live.com was added
Add another email account
Finish
9

TIPS

What do I do if Mail cannot configure my account automatically?
In this case, you use the Configure Server Settings dialog box to provide your e-mail account's server information. For your ISP's incoming mail server, you need to provide the name of the server and your e-mail account login username. For your ISP's outgoing mail server, you need to provide the name of the server. Check with your ISP to see if its outgoing mail server uses a different port number and requires authentication.

How do I make changes to an e-mail account?
After you configure your e-mail account, Mail adds the account to the Folder pane on the left side of the program window. To make changes to the account, right-click the account name and then click **Properties**. In the Properties dialog box that appears, use the tabs to make changes to your settings.

Send an E-Mail Message

If you know the e-mail address of a person or organization, you can send an e-mail message to that address. An e-mail address is a set of characters that uniquely identifies the location of an Internet mailbox. Each e-mail address takes the form *username@domain*, where *username* is the name of the person's account with the ISP or within his or her organization, and *domain* is the Internet name of the company that provides the person's e-mail account.

When you send an e-mail message, it travels through your ISP's outgoing mail server. This server routes the messages to the recipient's incoming mail server, which then stores the message in the recipient's mailbox.

Send an E-Mail Message

1. Click the **Home** tab.
2. Click **Email message**.

Note: You can also press Ctrl + M.

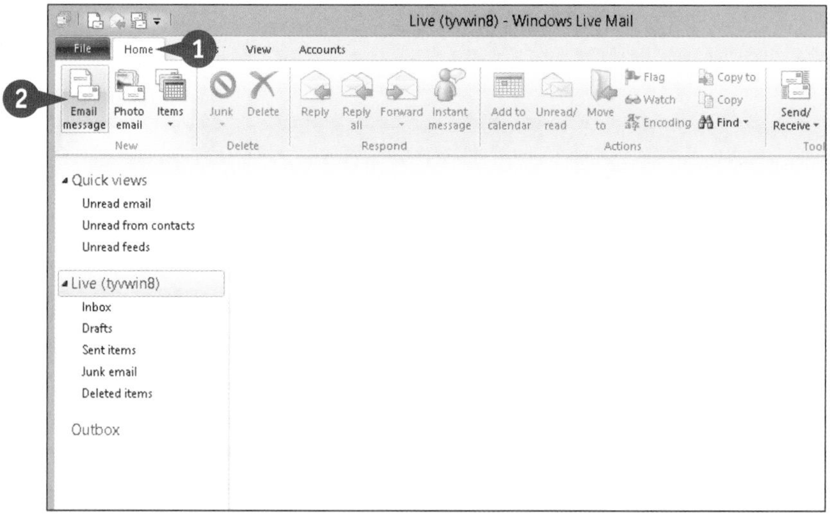

A message window appears.

3. Type the e-mail address of the recipient.

Note: You can add multiple e-mail addresses to the To line. Separate each address with a semicolon (;).

A. To send a copy of the message to another person, click **Show Cc & Bcc** and then type that person's e-mail address in the Cc field that appears.

4. Type a title or short description for the message.

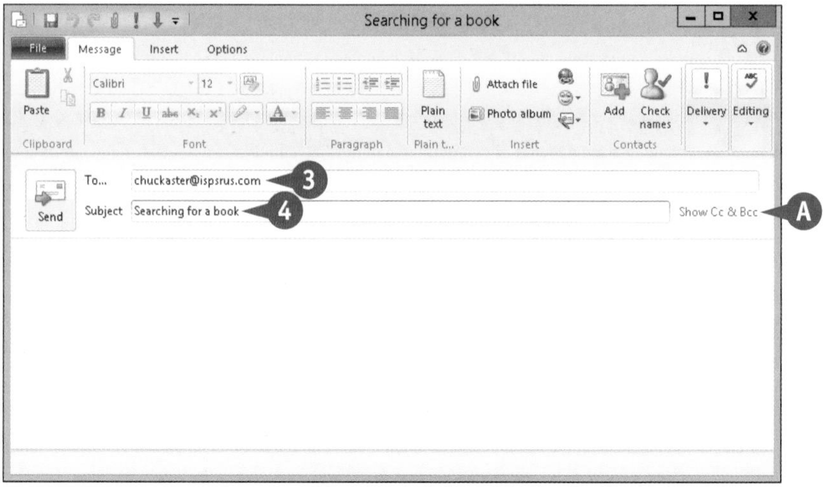

5. Type the message.
6. Use the buttons in the Message tab to format the message text.

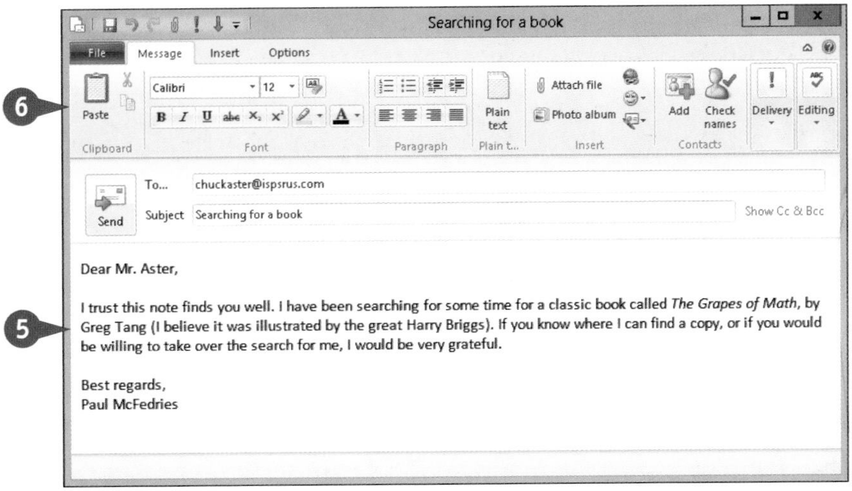
Searching for a book
File
Message
Insert
Options
Paste
Clipboard
Calibri
12
Font
Paragraph
Plain text
Plain t...
Attach file
Photo album
Insert
Add
Check names
Contacts
Delivery
Editing
To...
chuckaster@ispsrus.com
Subject
Searching for a book
Show Cc & Bcc
Send
Dear Mr. Aster,
I trust this note finds you well. I have been searching for some time for a classic book called The Grapes of Math, by Greg Tang (I believe it was illustrated by the great Harry Briggs). If you know where I can find a copy, or if you would be willing to take over the search for me, I would be very grateful.
Best regards,
Paul McFedries
6
5

7. Click **Send**.

   Mail sends your message.

Note: Mail stores a copy of your message in the Sent Items folder.

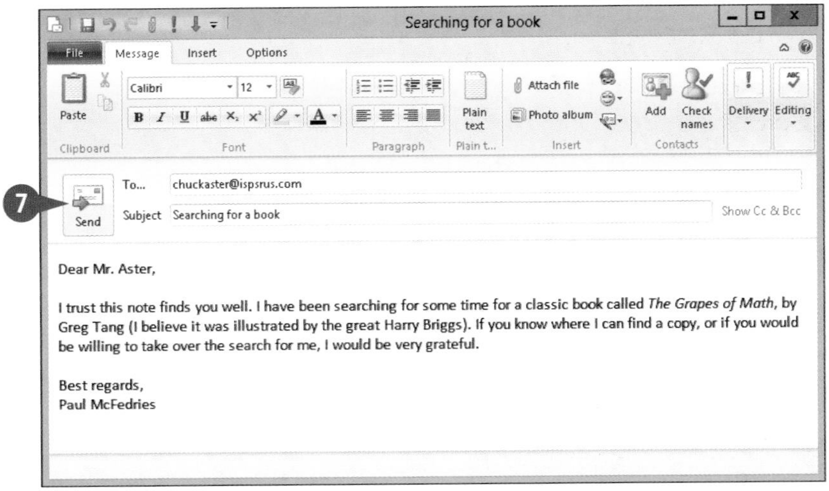
Searching for a book
File
Message
Insert
Options
Paste
Clipboard
Calibri
12
Font
Paragraph
Plain text
Plain t...
Attach file
Photo album
Insert
Add
Check names
Contacts
Delivery
Editing
To...
chuckaster@ispsrus.com
Subject
Searching for a book
Show Cc & Bcc
Send
Dear Mr. Aster,
I trust this note finds you well. I have been searching for some time for a classic book called The Grapes of Math, by Greg Tang (I believe it was illustrated by the great Harry Briggs). If you know where I can find a copy, or if you would be willing to take over the search for me, I would be very grateful.
Best regards,
Paul McFedries
7

TIP

I have a large number of messages to compose. Do I have to be online to do this?

No, you can compose all the messages while you are offline. Follow these steps:

1. While disconnected from the Internet, start Mail, and click **Cancel** if the program asks you to connect to the Internet.

   Mail displays Working Offline in the status bar.

2. Compose and send the message. Each time you click **Send**, your messages are stored temporarily in the Outbox folder.
3. After you are done, connect to the Internet.
4. In the Home tab, click **Go online**.

   Mail changes the status bar text to Working Online.

5. Click **Send/Receive**.

Add Someone to Your Contacts

You can use Contacts to store information about people with whom you frequently correspond. You do that by creating a new contact, which is an item that stores data about a person or company.

Each card can store a wide variety of information. For example, you can store a person's name, company name, phone numbers, e-mail address and instant messaging data, street address, notes, and much more.

When you choose a name from Contacts while composing a message, Mail automatically adds the contact's e-mail address. This is faster and more accurate than typing the address by hand.

Add Someone to Your Contacts

1. Click **Contacts** ( ).

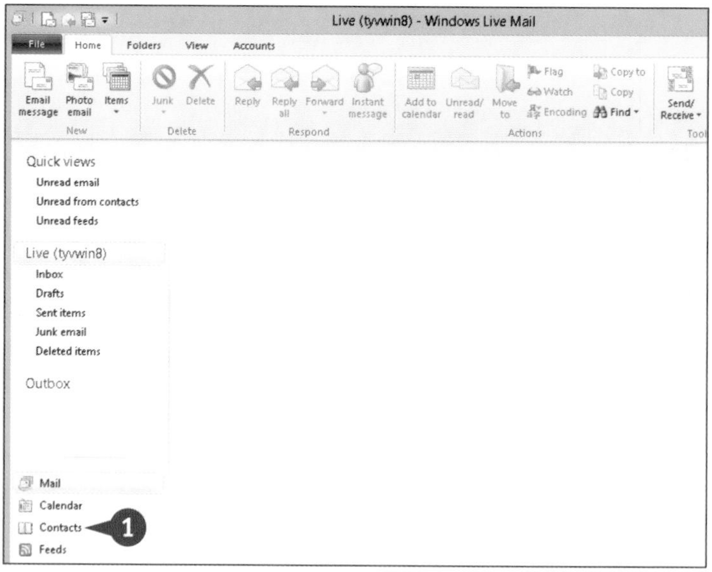

The Contacts window appears.

2. Click the **Home** tab.
3. Click **Contact**.

Note: You can also start a new contact by pressing Ctrl+N.

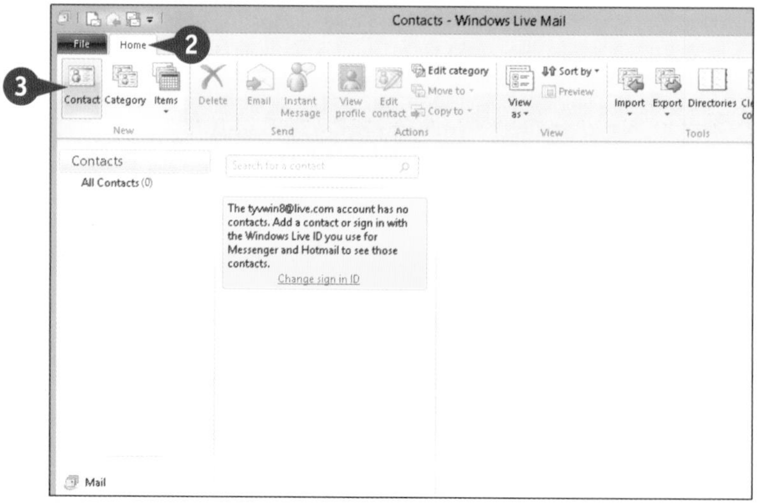

The Add a Contact dialog box appears.

4 Type the person's first name.

5 Type the person's last name.

6 Type the person's e-mail address.

Note: You can use the other tabs in the Add a Contact dialog box to store more information about the contact, including home and business addresses and phone numbers, spouse name, birthday, and more.

7 Click **Add contact**.

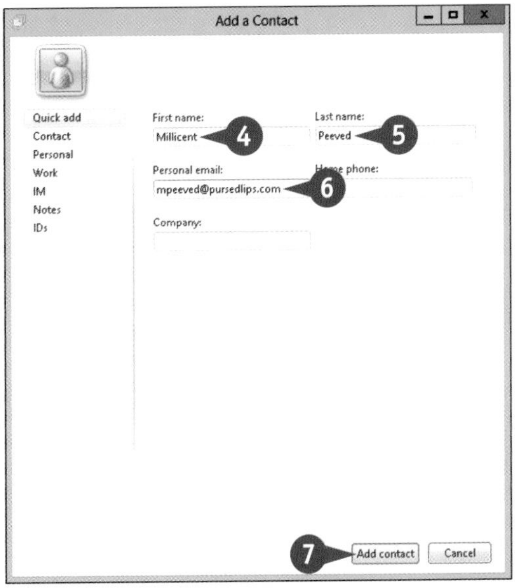

A Contacts adds the person to the Contacts list.

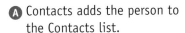

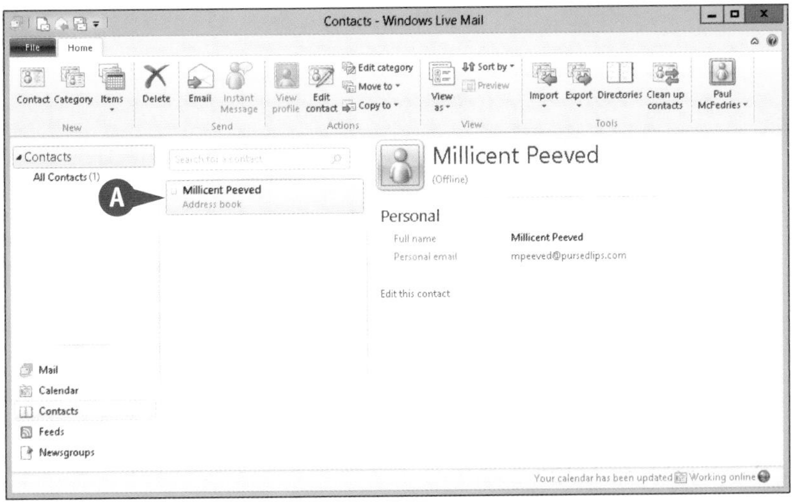

TIPS

How do I edit a person's contact data?

In the Contacts window, click the person you want to work with, click the **Home** tab, and then click **Edit contact**. (You can also double-click the person's name or click the **Edit this contact** link that appears in the contact's data section.) Use the Edit Contact dialog box to make your changes, and then click **Save**.

How do I delete someone from my Contacts?

In the Contacts window, click the person you want to work with, click the **Home** tab, and then click **Delete**. When Mail asks you to confirm the deletion, click **OK**.

Create a Contact Category

You can organize your contacts into one or more categories, which is useful if you want to view just a subset of your contacts. For example, you could create one category for your work colleagues, another for your family members, a third for people working on a current project, and so on.

Categories are particularly handy if you have a large number of contacts. By creating and maintaining categories, you can navigate your contacts more easily. You can also perform categorywide tasks, such as sending a single e-mail message to everyone in the group.

Create a Contact Category

1. Click the **Home** tab.
2. Click **Category**.

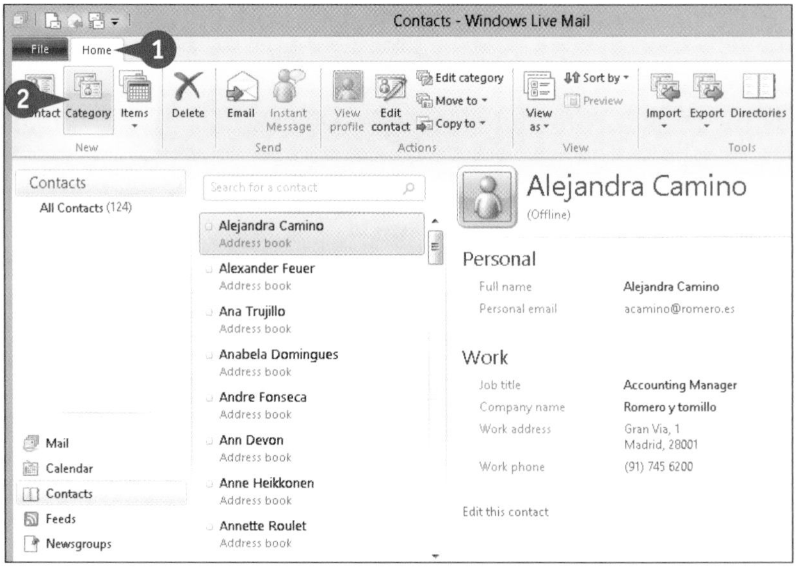

The Create a New Category dialog box appears.

3. Type a name for the category.
4. Click a contact that you want to include in the category.

Ⓐ Mail adds the contact to the category.

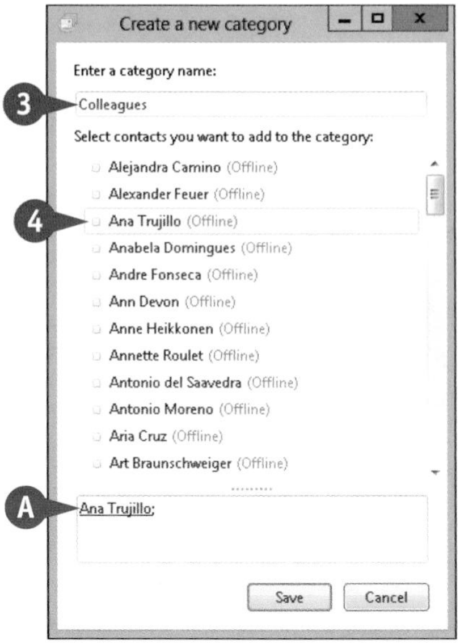

5 Repeat step **4** for the other contacts you want to add to the category.

Note: If you add the wrong contact by accident, you can remove it by clicking the contact name again.

6 Click **Save**.

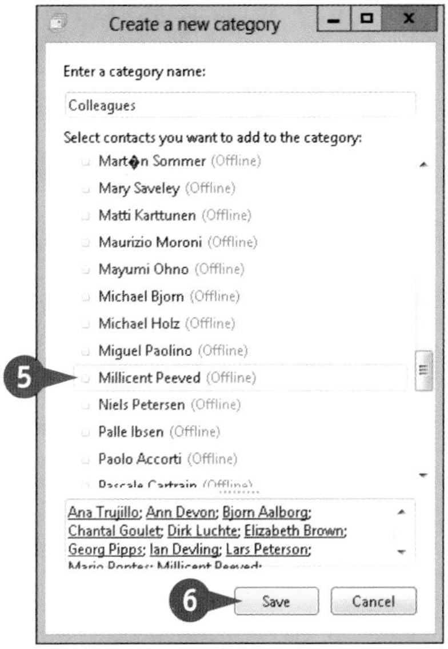

B Mail adds the category.

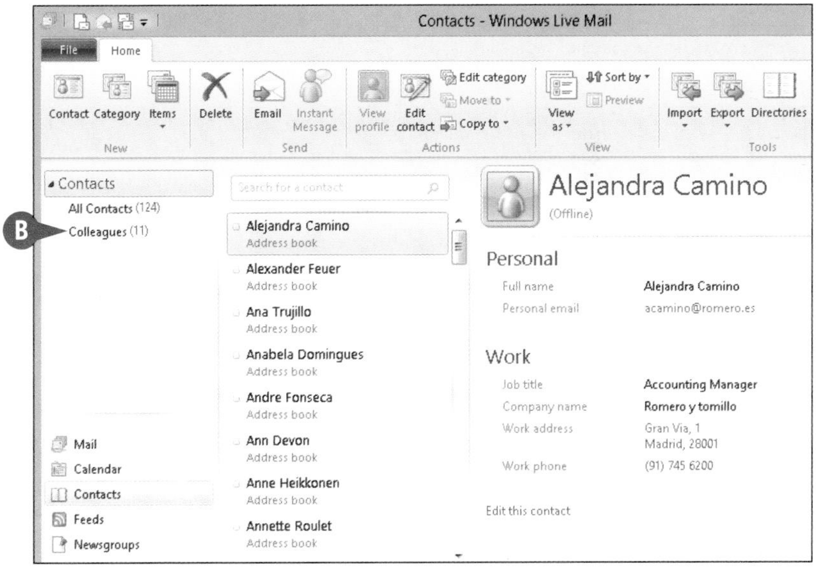

TIPS

Can I send an e-mail message to all the contacts in a category?

Yes, this is one of the best reasons to create a category. Normally, sending an e-mail message to multiple contacts involves typing or selecting multiple addresses. With a category, however, you send a single message to the category, and Mail automatically sends a copy to each member. Right-click the category and then click **Send e-mail**.

How do I edit or delete a category?

If you want to add new contacts to the category or delete existing contacts, right-click the category and then click **Edit Category**. If you want to delete a category, right-click the category and then click **Delete Category**. When Mail asks you to confirm the deletion, click **OK**.

Select a Contact Address

After you have some e-mail addresses and names in your Contacts list, when composing a message, you can select the address you want directly from the Contacts list.

As discussed earlier, when you compose a new e-mail message, one of your first tasks is to type the e-mail address of the message recipient. This can be problematic not only because it means you must memorize or otherwise keep track of the person's address, but you can easily make a mistake when typing the address. By storing this information in the Contacts list, you need only select the contact instead of typing the address.

Select a Contact Address

1. If you are still in Contacts, click **Mail** ( ).
2. Click the **Home** tab.
3. Click **Email message** to start a new message.
4. Click **To**.

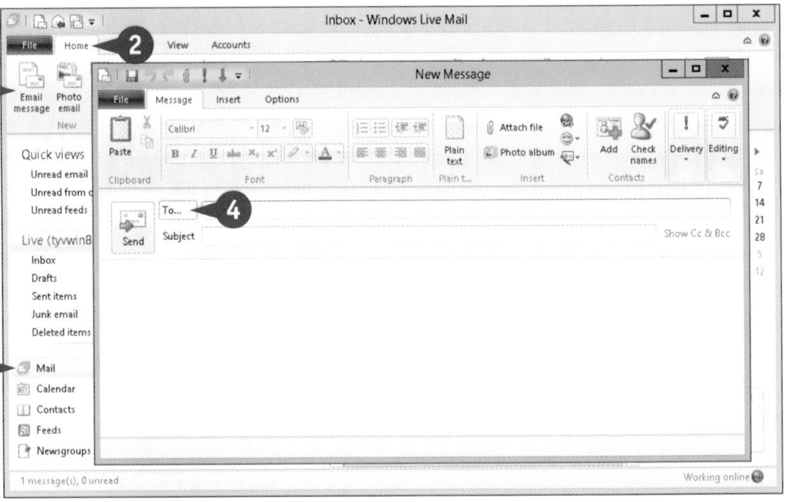

The Send an Email dialog box appears.

5. Click the person to whom you want to send the message.
6. Click **To**.

   Ⓐ The person's name appears in the To box.

7. Repeat steps **5** and **6** to add other recipients to the To box.

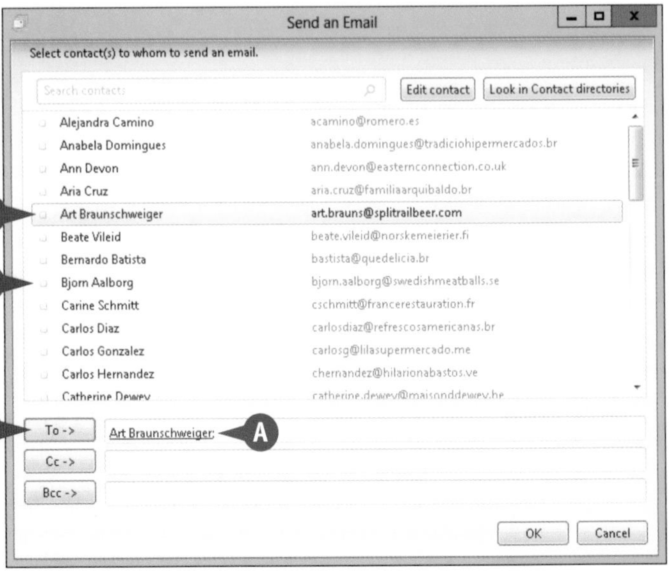

8 To send a copy of the message to a recipient, click the person's name.

9 Click **Cc**.

B The person's name appears in the message recipients box.

10 Repeat steps **8** and **9** to add other recipients to the Cc line.

11 Click **OK**.

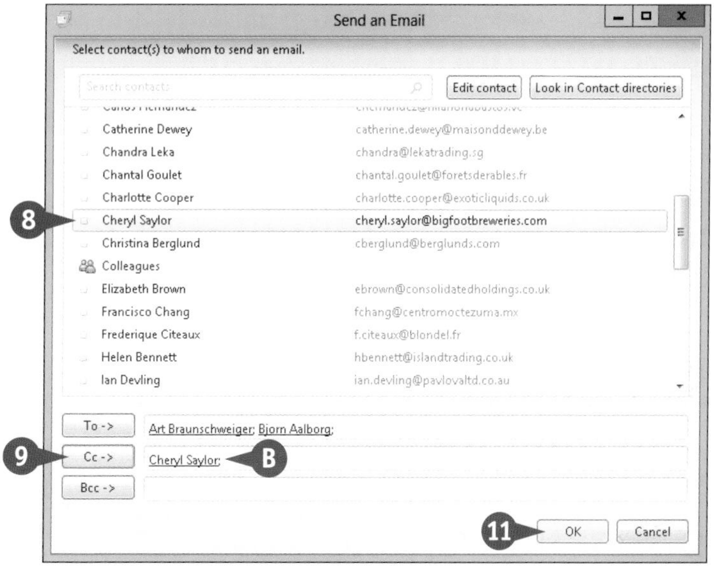

C Mail adds the recipients to the To and Cc lines of the new message.

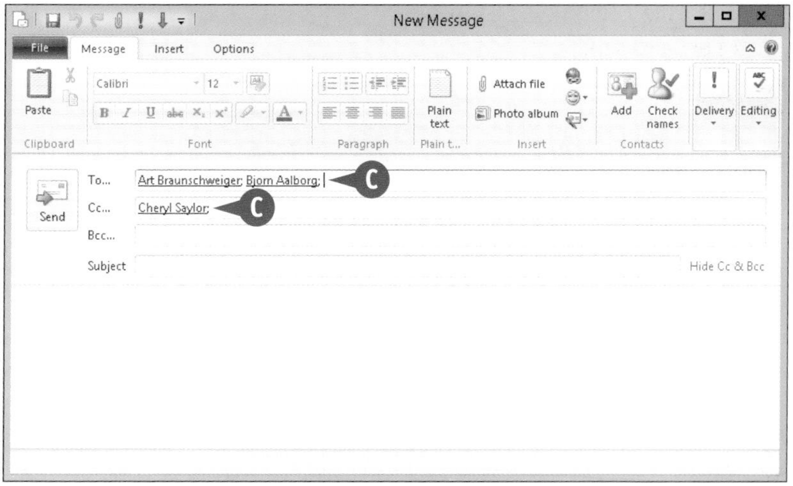

TIPS

Can I send a message from Contacts?

Yes. In Mail, click **Contacts** to open Contacts. Click the name of the person you want to send a message to, click the **Home** tab, and then click **Email**. You can also position the mouse over the contact and then click **Send email**. Mail creates a new message and adds the contact's name to the To field automatically.

In the Send an Email dialog box, what does the Bcc button do?

You click **Bcc** to add the current contact to the message's Bcc field. Bcc stands for *blind courtesy copy* and it means that any addresses in the Bcc field are not displayed to the other message recipients. If you do not want Mail to display the Bcc field in the message window, click **Hide Cc & Bcc**.

Add a File Attachment

If you have a document that you want to send to another person, you can attach the document to an e-mail message. A typical e-mail message is fine for short notes, but you may have something more complex to communicate, such as budget numbers or a slide show, or some form of media that you want to share, such as an image or a song.

Because these more complex types of data usually come in a separate file — such as a spreadsheet, presentation file, or picture file — it makes sense to send that file to your recipient. You do this by attaching the file to an e-mail message.

Add a File Attachment

Add an Attachment from a Dialog Box

1. Click the **Home** tab.
2. Click **Email message** to start a new message.
3. Click the **Message** tab.
4. Click **Attach file**.

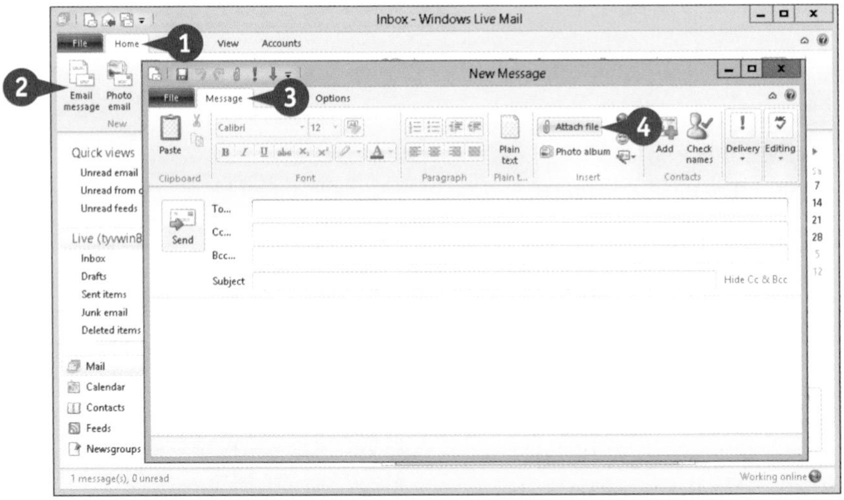

The Open dialog box appears.

5. Click the file you want to attach.
6. Click **Open**.

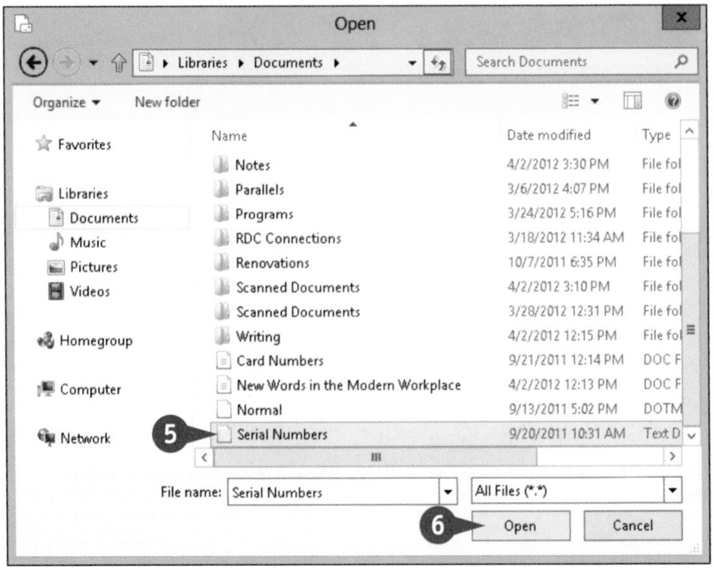

Ⓐ Mail attaches the file to the message.

7 Repeat steps **4** to **6** to attach additional files to the message.

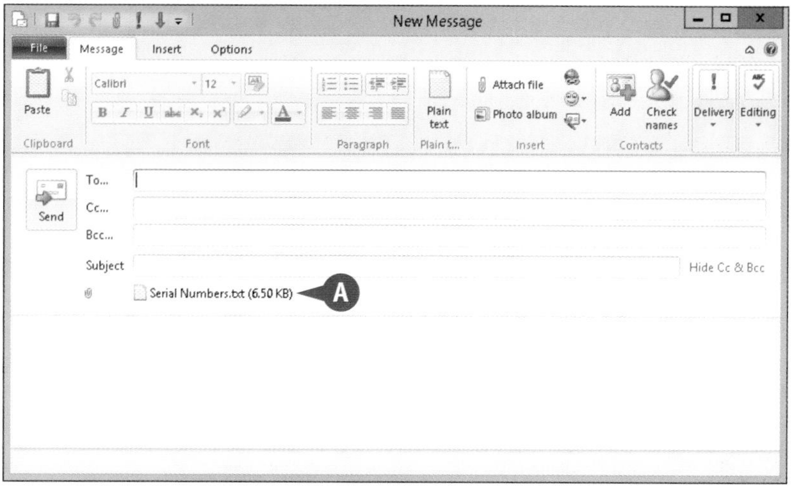

Add an Attachment Directly

1 Open the folder that contains the file you want to send as an attachment.

2 Click the file.

3 Click the **Share** tab.

4 Click **Email**.

Note: If you are sending a photo, Windows 8 also asks you to choose an image size. Use the **Picture size** list to select a size, and then click **Attach**.

Mail creates a new message and attaches the file.

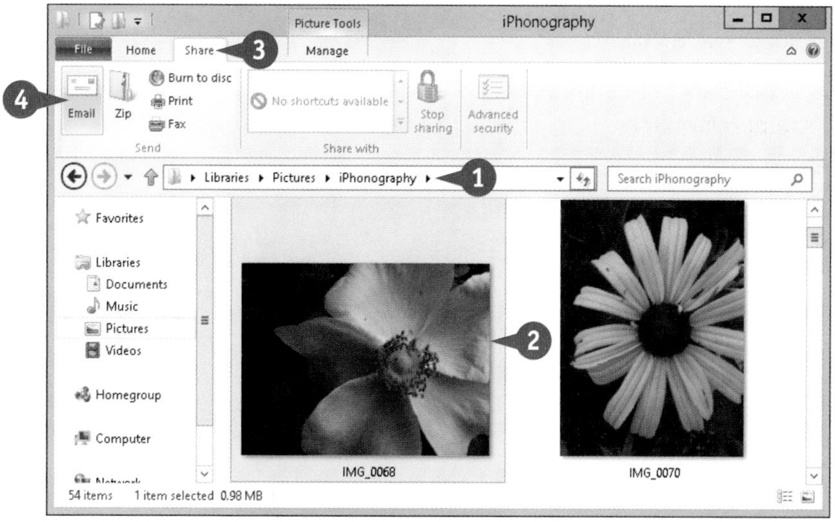

TIP

Is there a limit to the number of files I can attach to a message?

There is no practical limit to the number of files you can attach to the message. However, you should be careful with the total *size* of the files you send. If you or the recipient has a slow Internet connection, sending or receiving the message can take an extremely long time. Also, many Internet service providers (ISPs) place a limit on the size of a message's attachments, which is usually between 2MB and 10MB. In general, use e-mail to send only a few small files at a time.

Add a Signature

In an e-mail message, a *signature* is a small amount of text that appears at the bottom of the message. Instead of typing this information manually in each message, you can save the signature in your Mail options. When you compose a new e-mail message, reply to an existing message, or forward a message, you can click a button to have Mail add the signature to your outgoing message.

Signatures usually contain personal contact information, such as your phone numbers, business address, and e-mail and website addresses. Mail supports multiple signatures, which is useful if you use Mail with multiple accounts or for different purposes such as business and personal.

Add a Signature

Add a Signature

1. Click the **File** tab.
2. Click **Options.**
3. Click **Mail.**

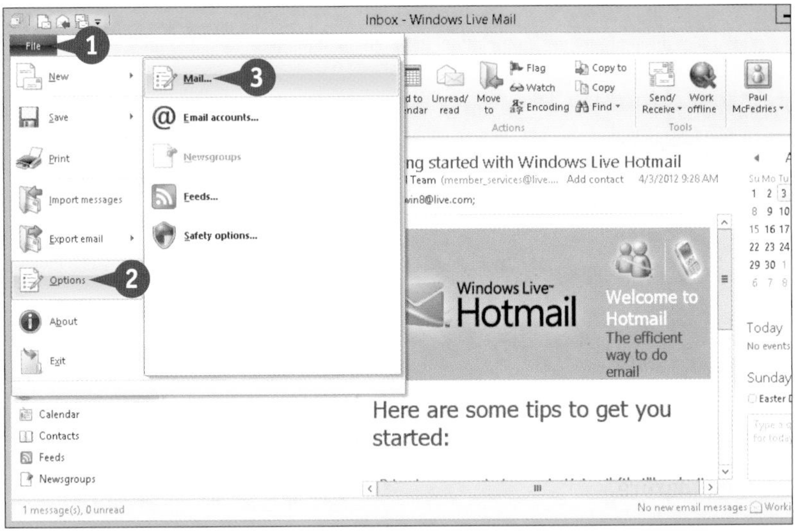

The Options dialog box appears.

4. Click the **Signatures** tab.
5. Click **New.**

A. Mail adds a new signature.

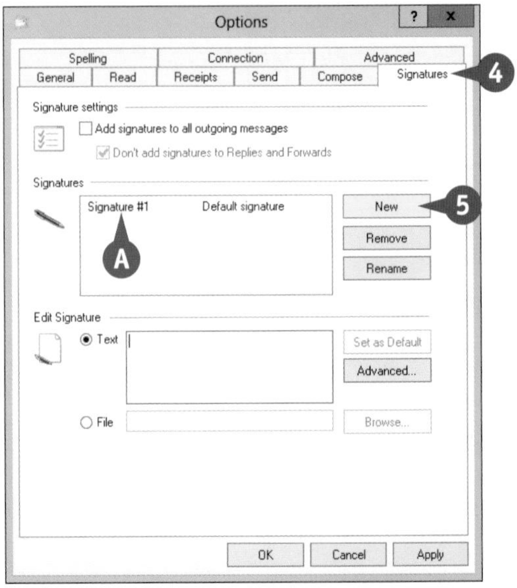

6. Type the signature text.
7. Click **Rename**.
8. Type a name for the signature.
9. Press Enter.
10. Click **OK**.

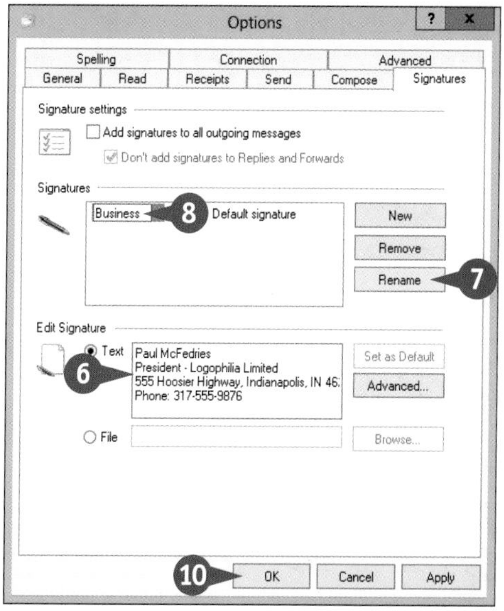

Insert the Signature Manually

1. Click the **Home** tab.
2. Click **Email message** to start a new message.
3. In the message text area, move the insertion point to the location where you want the signature to appear.
4. Click **Insert**.
5. Click **Signature**.
6. Click your signature.

B The signature appears in the message.

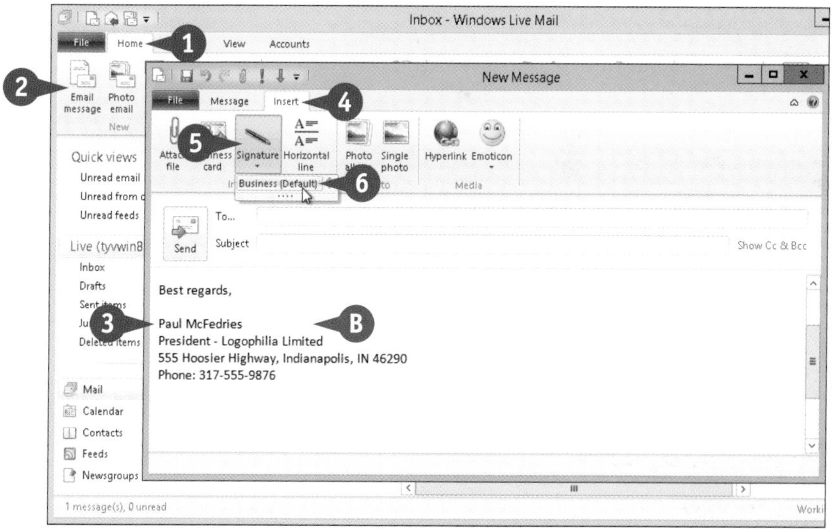

TIPS

Can I have more than one signature?

Yes, you can add as many signatures as you want. For example, you may want to have one signature for business use and another for personal use. To add multiple signatures, follow steps **1** to **4** to display the Signatures tab, and then follow steps **5** to **9** for each signature. Be sure to give each signature a descriptive name.

Can I get Mail to add my signature automatically?

Yes. First, follow steps **1** to **4** in the second set of steps to display the Signatures tab. Click **Add signatures to all outgoing messages** (☐ changes to ☑) to have Mail add your signature to the bottom of every new message. Click **Don't add signatures to Replies and Forwards** (☑ changes to ☐) if you want Mail to add your signature when you reply to and forward messages.

Receive and Read E-Mail Messages

You must connect to your mail provider's incoming mail server to retrieve and read messages sent to you.

When another person sends you an e-mail message, that message ends up in your e-mail account's mailbox on the incoming mail server maintained by your ISP or e-mail provider. However, that company does not automatically pass along that message to you. Instead, you must use Mail to connect to your mailbox on the incoming mail server and then retrieve any messages waiting for you.

By default, Mail automatically checks for new messages every ten minutes while you are online, but you can also check for new messages at any time.

Receive and Read E-Mail Messages

Receive E-Mail Messages

1. Click the **Home** tab.
2. Click **Send/Receive**.

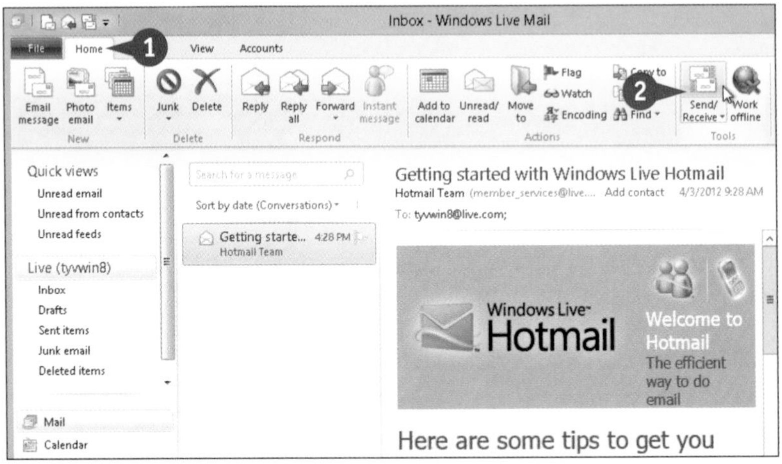

A If you have new messages, they appear in your Inbox folder in bold type.

B This symbol (!) means the message was sent as high priority.

C This symbol (↓) means the message was sent as low priority.

D This symbol (📎) means that the message came with a file attached.

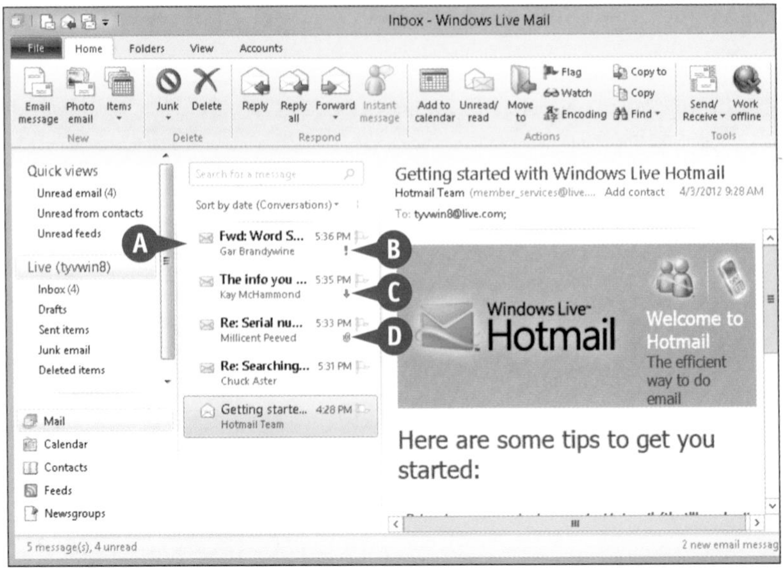

Read a Message

1. Click the message.
2. Read the message text in the preview pane.

E. If the message comes with an attached file, double-click the file icon to open it.

Note: If you want to open the message in its own window, double-click the message.

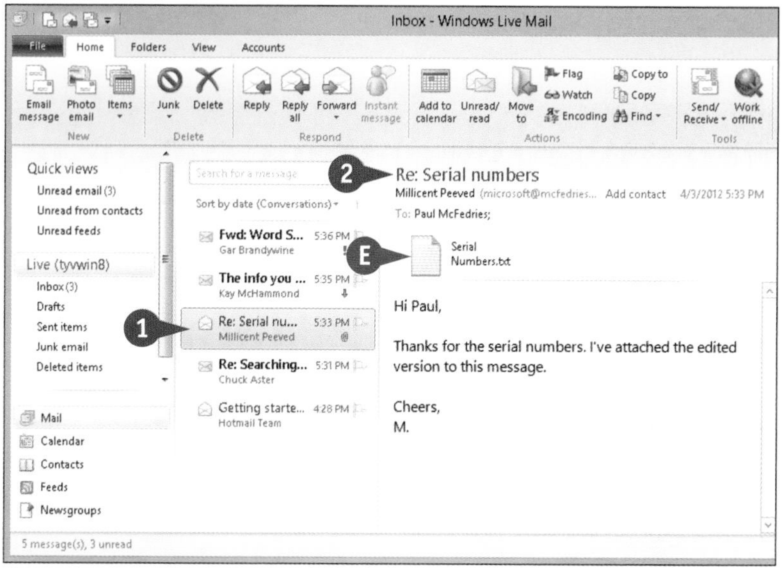

TIP

Can I change how often Mail automatically checks for messages?

Yes, by following these steps:

1. Click the **File** tab, click **Options**, and then click **Mail**.
2. In the Options dialog box, click the **General** tab.
3. If you do not want Mail to check for messages when the program starts, click **Send and receive messages at startup** (☑ changes to ☐).
4. Type a new time interval, in minutes, that you want Mail to use when automatically checking for new messages.
5. Click **OK**.

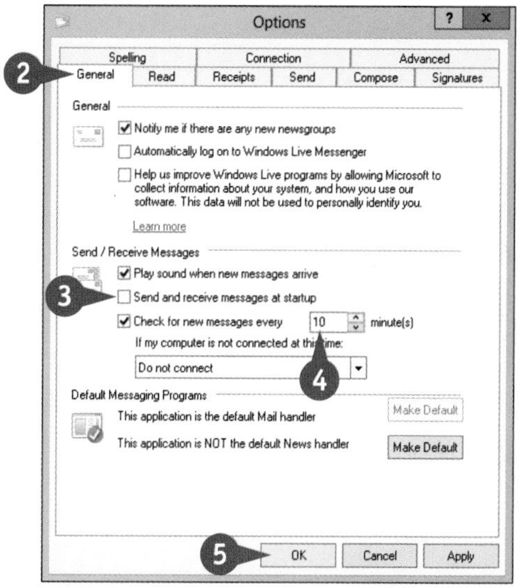

Reply to a Message

When a message you receive requires some kind of response — whether it is answering a question, supplying information, or providing comments — you can reply to that message.

Most replies go only to the person who sent the original message. However, you can also send the reply to all the people who were included in the original message's To and Cc lines.

Mail includes the text of the original message in the reply, but you should edit the original message text to include only enough of the original message to put your reply into context.

Reply to a Message

1. Click the message to which you want to reply.
2. Click the **Home** tab.
3. Click the reply type you want to use:

   Click **Reply** to respond only to the first address displayed on the To line.

   Click **Reply all** to respond to all the addresses in the To and Cc lines.

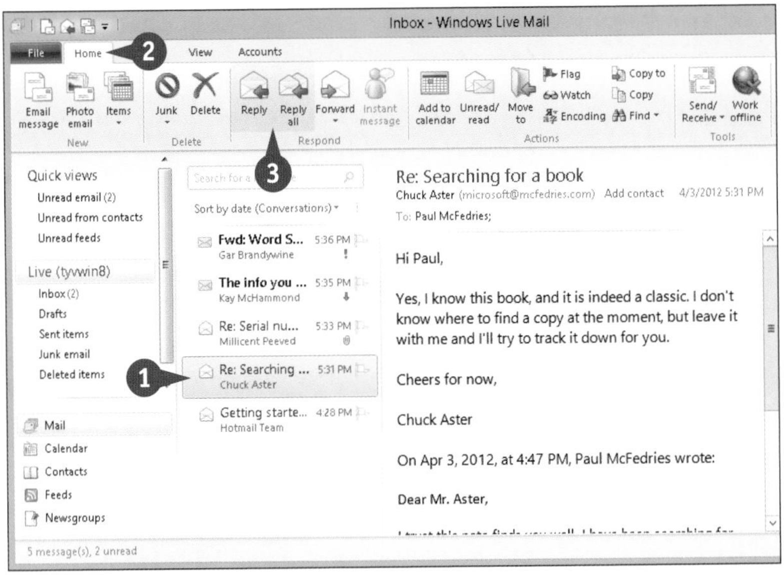

A message window appears.

- **A** Mail automatically inserts the recipient addresses.
- **B** Mail also inserts the subject line, preceded by Re.
- **C** Mail includes the original message's addresses (To and From), date, subject, and text at the bottom of the reply.

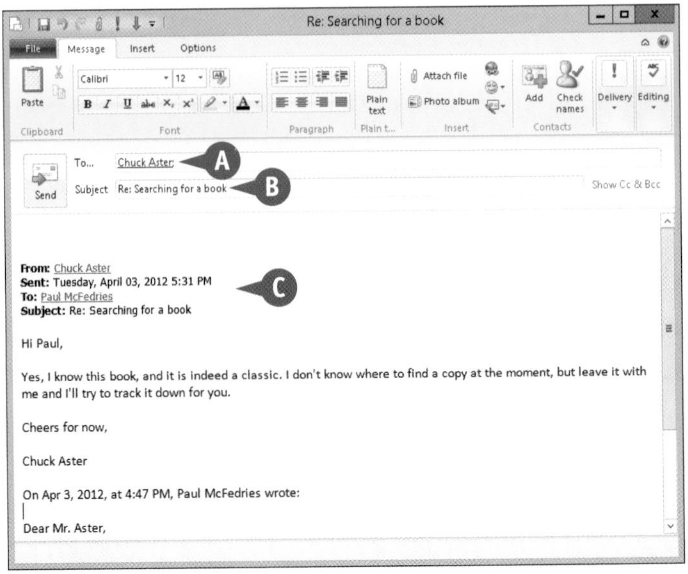

4 Edit the original message to include only the text relevant to your reply.

Note: If the original message is fairly short, you usually do not need to edit the text. However, if the original message is long, and your response deals only with part of that message, you will save the recipient time by deleting everything except the relevant portion of the text.

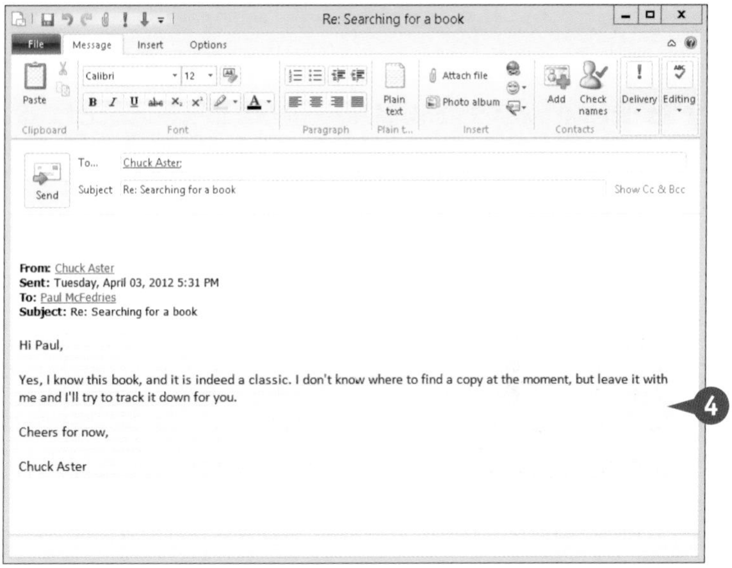

5 Click the area above the original message text and type your reply.

6 Click **Send**.

Mail sends your reply.

Note: Mail stores a copy of your reply in the Sent Items folder.

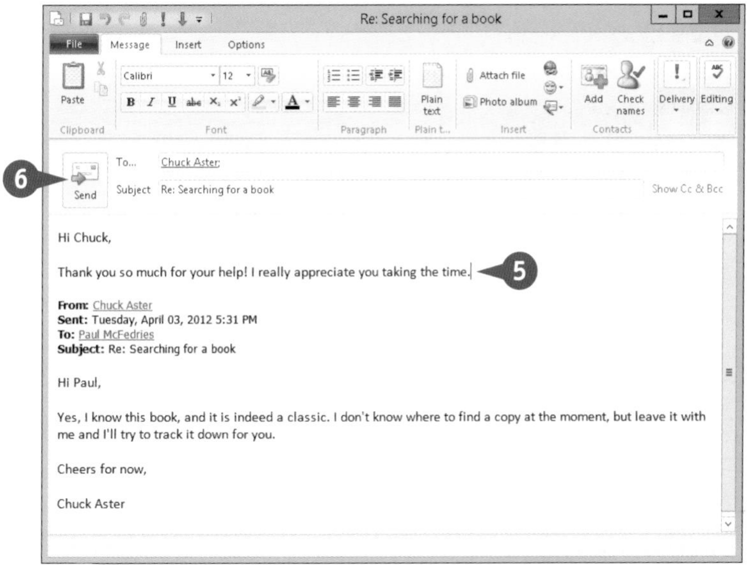

TIP

After I reply to a message, Mail sometimes adds the recipient to my Contacts list. How do I prevent this?

By default, Mail adds a person to your Contacts list after the third time you send that person a reply. To turn this off, follow these steps:

1 Click the **File** tab.

2 Click **Options**.

3 Click **Mail**.

The Options dialog box appears.

4 Click the **Send** tab.

5 Click **Automatically put people I reply to in my address book after the third reply** (☑ changes to ☐).

6 Click **OK**.

Forward a Message

If a message has information that is relevant to or concerns another person, you can forward a copy of the message to that person. You can also include your own comments in the forward.

In the body of the forward, Mail includes the original message's addresses, date, and subject line. Below this information Mail also includes the text of the original message. In most cases you will leave the entire message intact so your recipient can see it. However, if only part of the message is relevant to the recipient, you should edit the original message accordingly.

Forward a Message

1. Click the message that you want to forward.
2. Click the **Home** tab.
3. Click the top half of the **Forward** button.

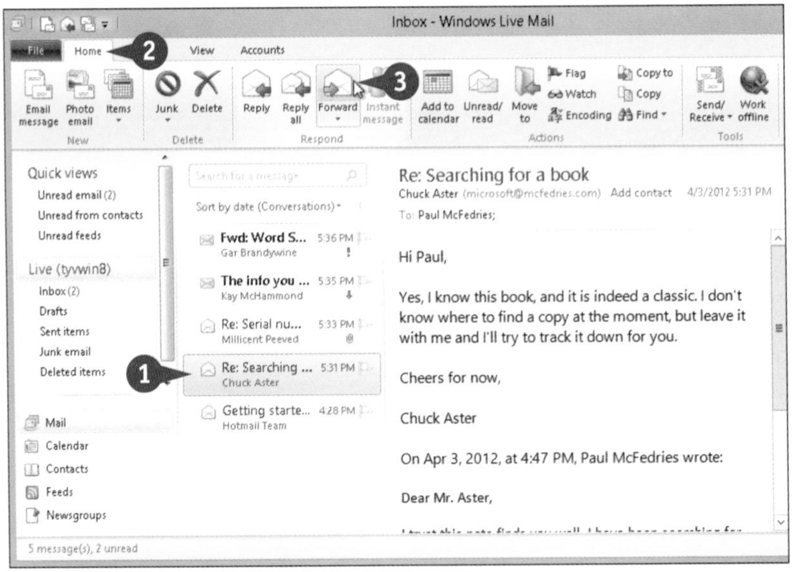

A message window appears.

- **A** Mail inserts the subject line, preceded by Fw.
- **B** The original message's addresses (To and From), date, subject, and text are included at the bottom of the forward.

4. Select or type the e-mail address of the person to whom you are forwarding the message.

- **C** To send a copy of the message to another person, click **Show Cc & Bcc** and then type that person's e-mail address in the Cc field that appears.

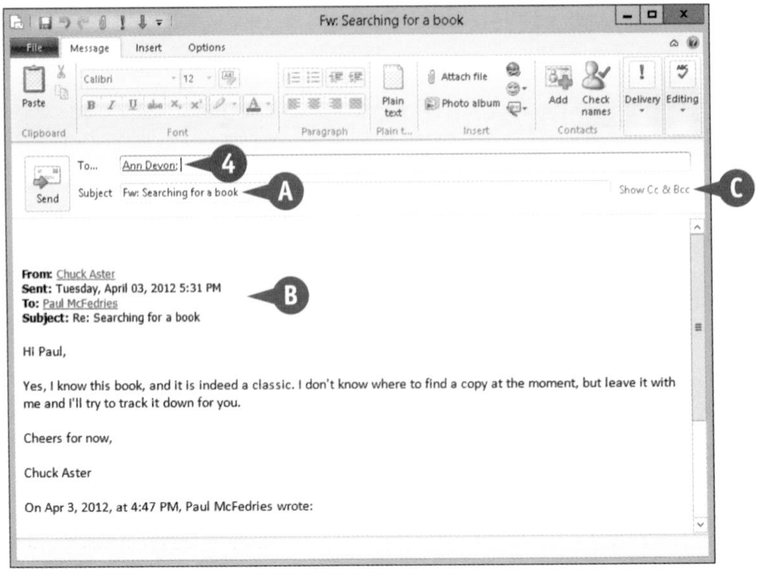

5. Edit the original message to include only the text relevant to your forward.
6. Click the area above the original message text.

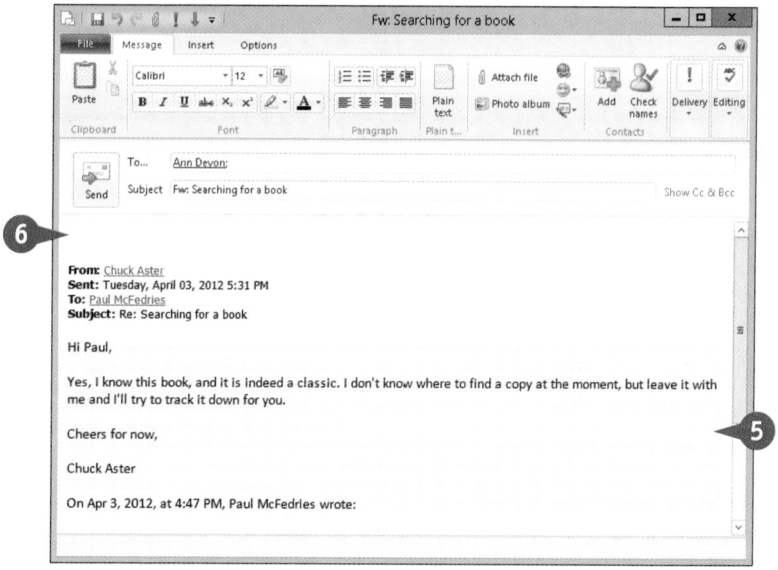

7. Type your comments.
8. Click **Send**.

   Mail sends your forward.

Note: Mail stores a copy of your forward in the Sent Items folder.

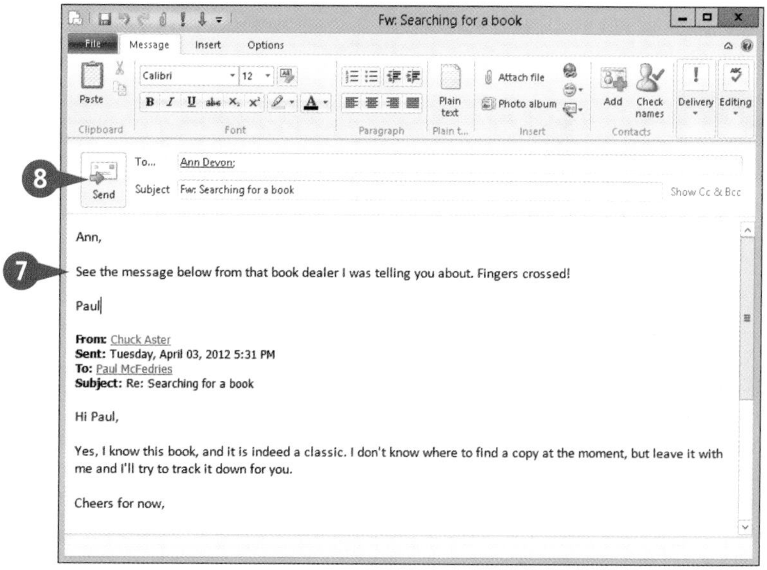

TIPS

How do I forward someone a copy of the actual message rather than just a copy of the message text?

Click the message, click the **Home** tab, click the bottom half of the **Forward** button, and then click **Forward as attachment**. Mail creates a new message and includes the original message as an attachment.

My replies and forwards do not always use the same format. How can I make Mail use a single format?

Click **File**, click **Options**, and then click **Mail** to open the Options dialog box. Click the **Send** tab and then click the **Reply to messages using the format in which they were sent** check box (☑ changes to ☐). In the Mail Sending Format area, click the format you want to use (○ changes to ◉) and then click **OK**.

Open and Save an Attachment

If you receive a message that has a file attached, you can open the attachment to view the contents of the file. You can also save the attachment as a file on your computer.

When a message comes in and displays the Attachment symbol (a paperclip), it means that the sender has included a file as an attachment to the message. If you just want to take a quick look at the file, you can open it directly from Mail. Alternatively, if you want to keep a copy of the file on your computer, you can save it to your hard drive.

Be careful when dealing with attached files. Computer viruses are often transmitted by e-mail attachments.

Open and Save an Attachment

Open an Attachment

1 Click the message that has the attachment, as indicated by the Attachment symbol (📎).

A A list of the message attachments appears.

2 Double-click the attachment you want to open.

Mail asks you to confirm that you want to open the file.

3 Click **Open**.

The file opens in the appropriate program.

Note: Instead of opening the file, Windows 8 may display a dialog box saying that the file "does not have a program associated with it." This means you need to install the appropriate program for the type of file. If you are not sure, ask the person who sent you the file what program you need.

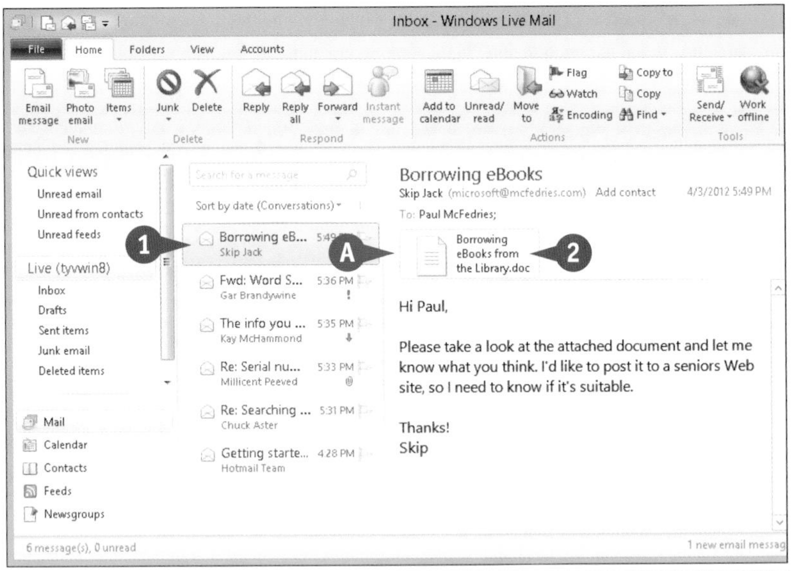

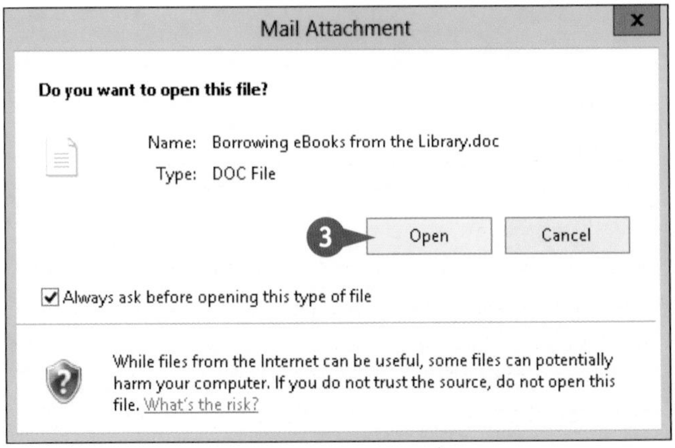

Save an Attachment

1. Click the message that has the attachment, as indicated by the Attachment symbol (@).

   B A list of the message attachments appears.

2. Right-click the attachment you want to save.
3. Click **Save as**.

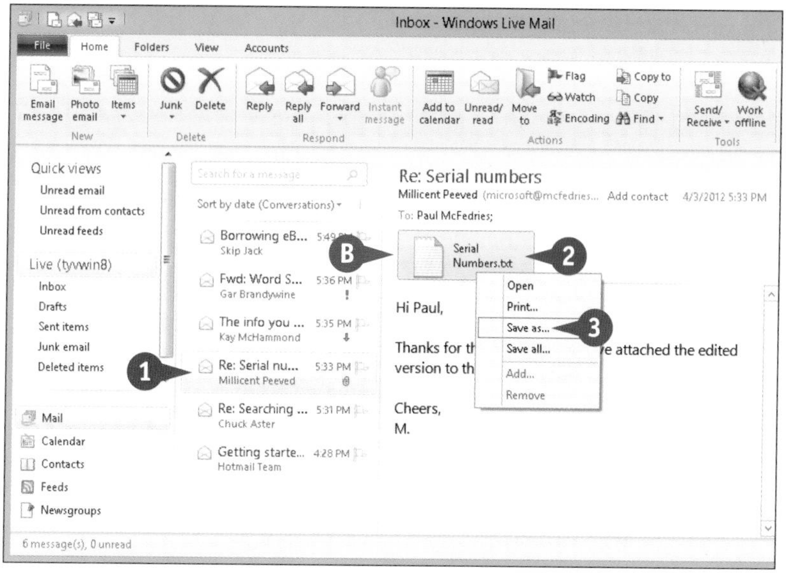

The Save Attachment As dialog box appears.

4. Use the File Name text box to edit the filename, if desired.
5. Select the folder into which you want the file saved.
6. Click **Save**.

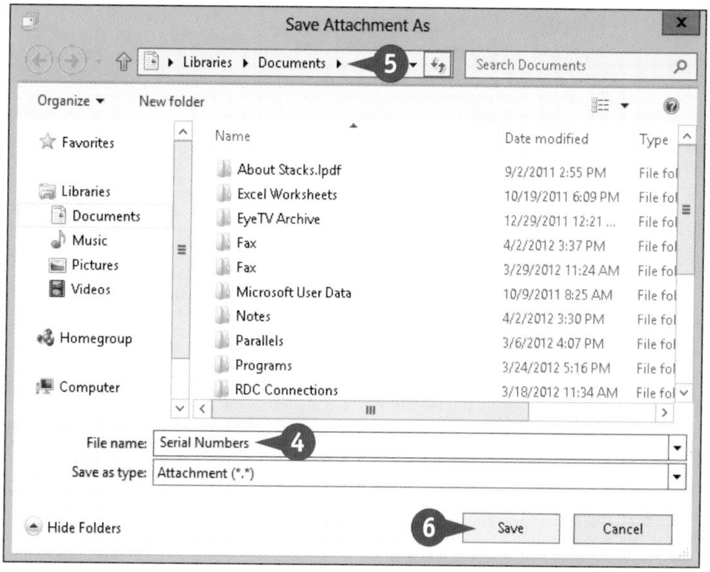

TIP

When I right-click an attached file, why am I unable to click the Save As command?

Mail has determined that the attached file may be unsafe, meaning that the file may harbor a virus or other malicious code. To confirm this, double-click the message to open it. Below the ribbon, you should see a message saying, "Prohibited file type: This message contains an attachment whose file type is considered dangerous." If you are absolutely certain the file is safe, turn off this feature by clicking the **File** tab, **Options**, **Safety Options**, the **Security** tab, and then **Do not allow attachments to be saved or opened that could potentially be a virus** (☑ changes to ☐). Be sure to reactivate this feature after you have opened or saved the attachment.

Create a Folder for Saving Messages

After you have used Mail for a while, you may find that you have many messages in your Inbox folder. To keep the Inbox uncluttered, you can create new folders and then move messages from the Inbox to the new folders.

To help keep your messages organized, you should use each folder you create to save related messages. For example, you could create separate folders for people you correspond with regularly, projects you are working on, different work departments, and so on. By saving each message to the appropriate folder, you make it easier to find your messages in the future.

Create a Folder for Saving Messages

Create a Folder

1. Click the **Folders** tab.
2. Click **New folder**.

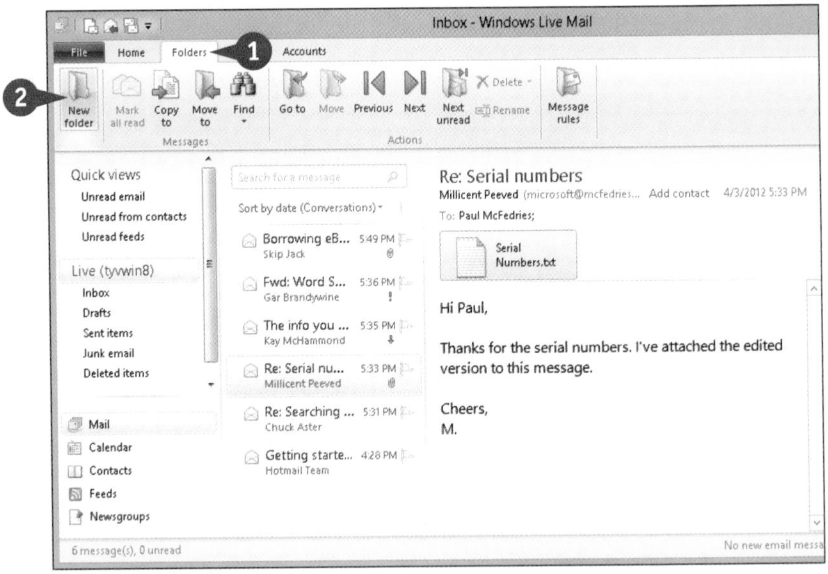

The Create Folder dialog box appears.

3. Type the name of the new subfolder.
4. Click the folder in which you want to create the new folder.
5. Click **OK**.

Ⓐ The new subfolder appears in the Folders list.

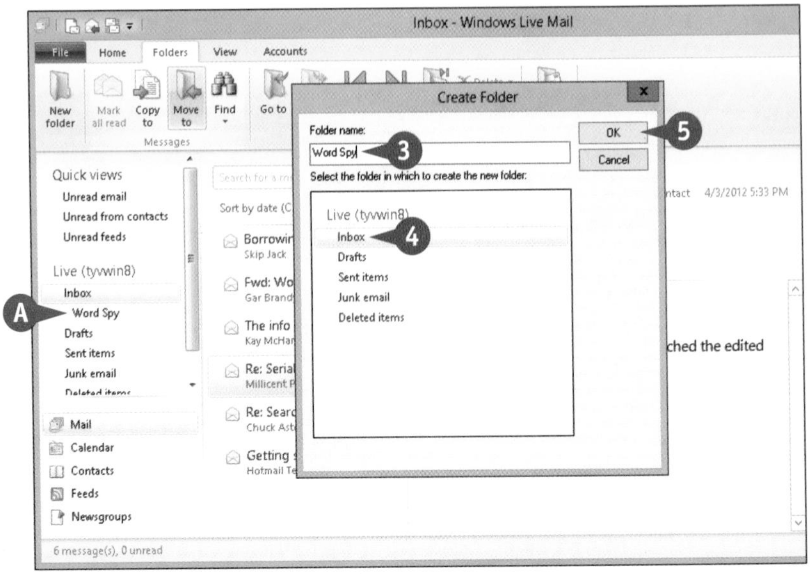

Move a Message to another Folder

1. Click the folder that contains the message you want to move.
2. Click the message you want to move.
3. Click the **Folders** tab.
4. Click **Move to**.

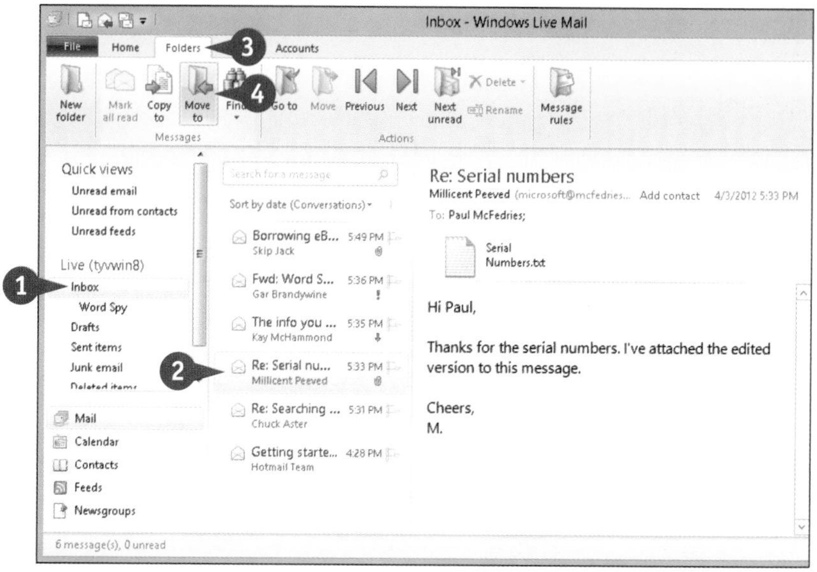

The Move dialog box appears.

5. Click the folder you want to use as the destination.
6. Click **OK**.

Mail moves the message.

B You can also move a message to another folder by clicking and dragging the message and then dropping it on the folder.

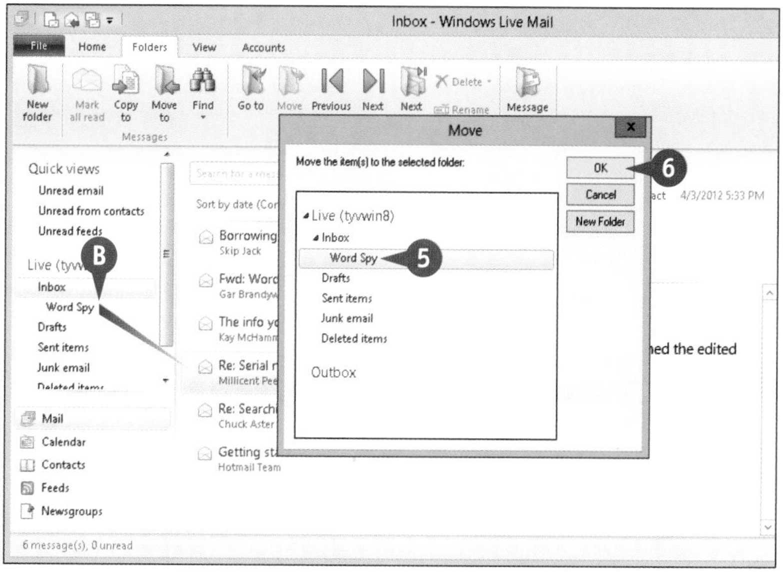

TIPS

How do I rename a folder?

Click the folder you want to rename, click the **Folders** tab, and then click **Rename**. Use the Rename Folder dialog box to type the new name and then click **OK**. Note that Mail only allows you to rename those folders that you have created yourself.

How do I delete a folder?

Click the folder you want to delete, click the **Folders** tab, and then click **Delete**. When Mail asks you to confirm the deletion, click **Yes**. Note that Mail only allows you to delete those folders that you have created yourself. Remember, too, that when you delete a folder, you also delete any messages stored in that folder.

Create Rules to Filter Incoming Messages

You can make your e-mail chores faster and more efficient if you create *rules* that handle incoming messages automatically.

A rule combines a condition and an action. The condition part of the rule consists of one or more message criteria. These criteria could be the address of the sender, a word or phrase in the subject line or body of the message, or whether the message has an attachment.

The action part of the rule specifies what happens to a message that satisfies the condition. For example, you could move the message to another folder, delete the message, or send a reply that includes a specific message.

Create Rules to Filter Incoming Messages

1. Click the **Folders** tab.
2. Click **Message rules.**

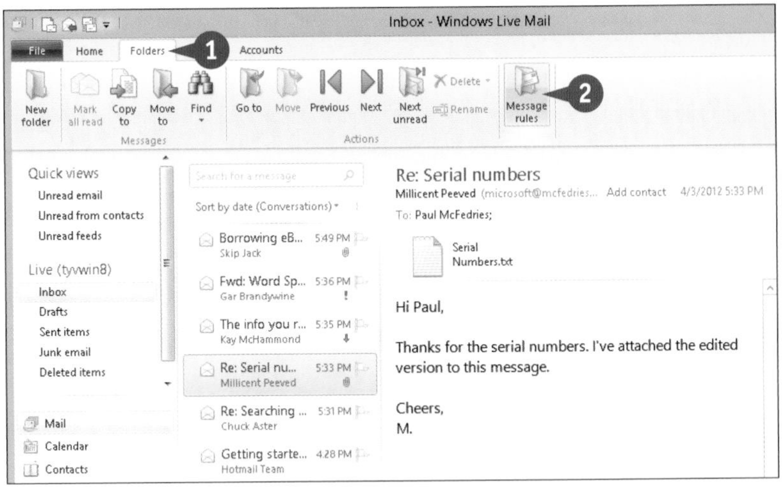

3. If you have already created at least one rule, the Rules dialog box appears. In that case, click **New**.

   The New Mail Rule dialog box appears.

4. In the Select One or More Conditions box, click the condition you want to use (☐ changes to ☑).
5. If the condition requires editing, click the underlined text.

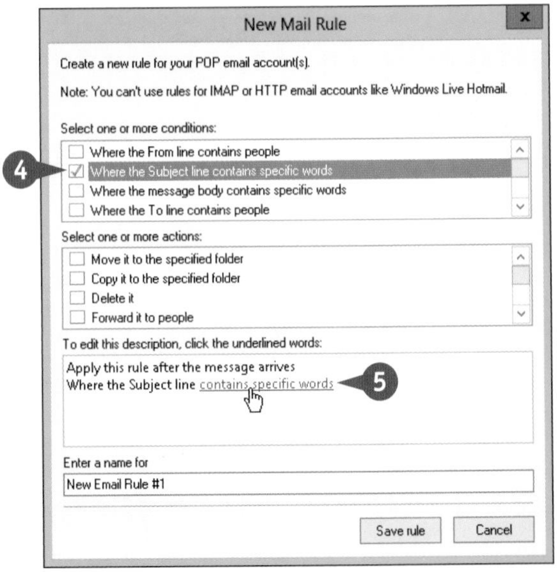

A dialog box appears, the layout of which depends on the condition.

6. Enter the text, address, or other required information.
7. Click **Add**.
8. Repeat steps **6** and **7** to add other data to the rule.
9. Click **OK**.

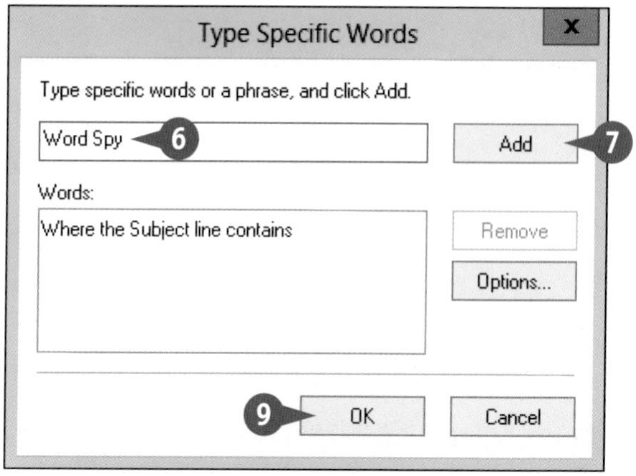

10. In the Select One or More Actions box, click the action you want to use (☐ changes to ☑).
11. If the action requires editing, follow steps **5** to **7**.
12. Type a name for the rule.
13. Click **Save rule.**

Mail adds the rule to the Rules dialog box.

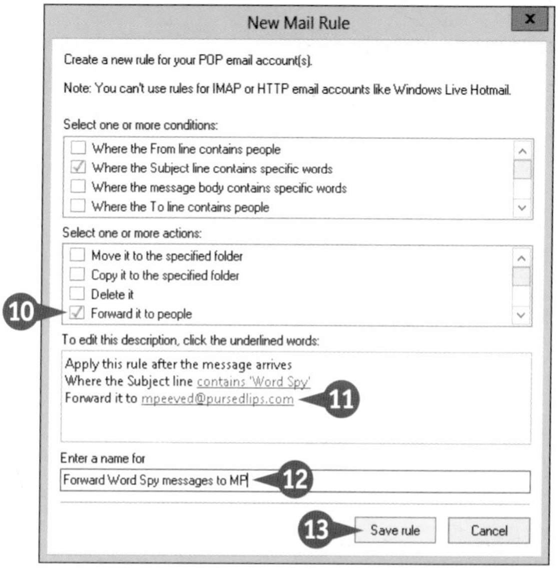

TIPS

I created my rule, but Mail did not perform the action on my existing messages. Why?

By default, Mail applies a new rule only on messages that you receive after you create the rule. If you want to apply the rule to existing messages, follow steps **1** and **2** from this section to open the Rules dialog box. Click **Apply now** to open the Apply Mail Rules Now dialog box. Click the rule you want to apply, and then click **Apply Now**.

How do I make changes to a rule?

Follow steps **1** and **2** from this section to open the Rules dialog box. Click the rule you want to change and then click **Modify**. In the Edit Mail Rule dialog box that appears, follow steps **4** to **13** to make your changes to the rule, and then click **OK**.

Switch to Calendar

Mail comes with a Calendar feature to enable you to manage your schedule. Calendar enables you to create and work with events, which are either scheduled appointments such as meetings, lunches, and visits to the dentist, or all-day activities, such as birthdays, anniversaries, or vacations. You can also use Calendar to set up events that happen at recurring intervals.

Before you can add or work with events (appointments, meetings, all-day activities, and so on), you must first switch to the Calendar feature.

Switch to Calendar

1. Click **Calendar** (📅).

Note: You can also open the Calendar by pressing Ctrl + Shift + X.

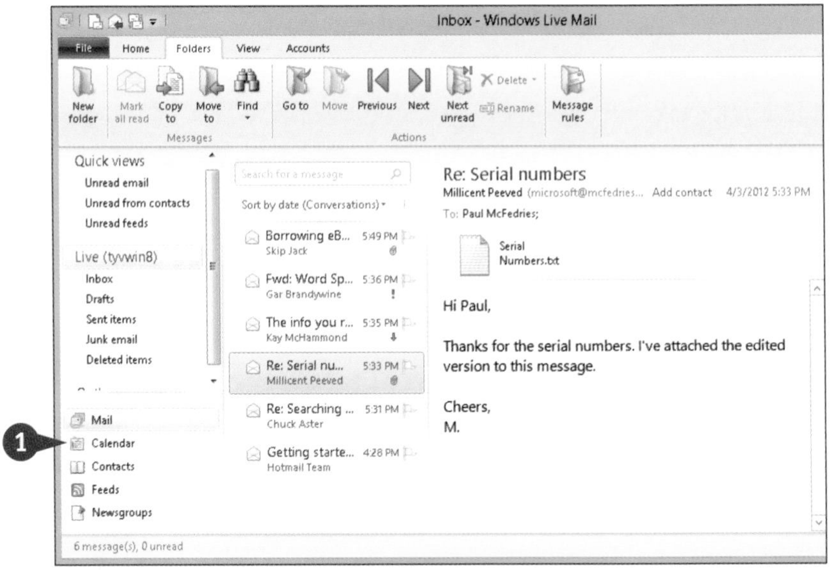

The Calendar window appears.

2. When you finish your scheduling chores, click **Mail** (📧), or press Ctrl + Shift + J, to return to the Mail feature.

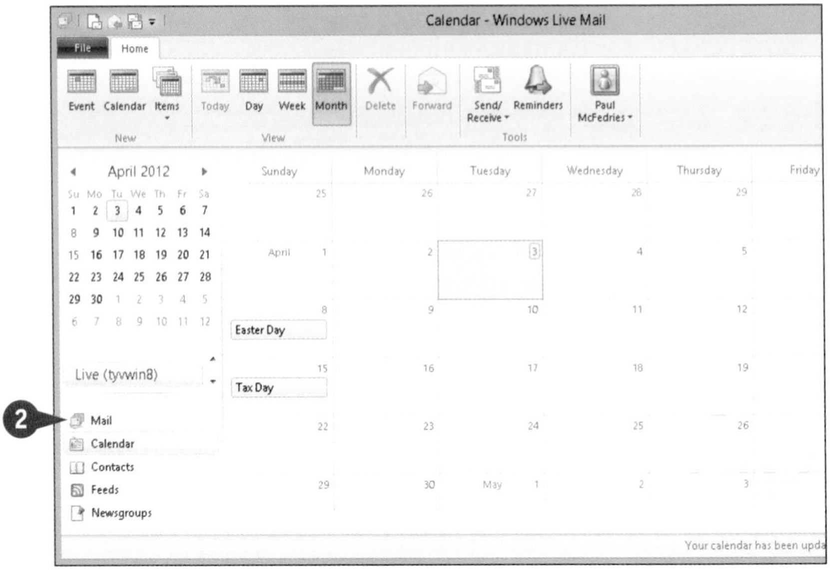

Navigate the Calendar

CHAPTER 6

Mail's Calendar makes scheduling easy. However, you can make it even easier by taking some time now to learn the layout of the Calendar window.

In particular, you need to familiarize yourself with the Date Navigator, the event list, the available views, and the list of calendars that you can use.

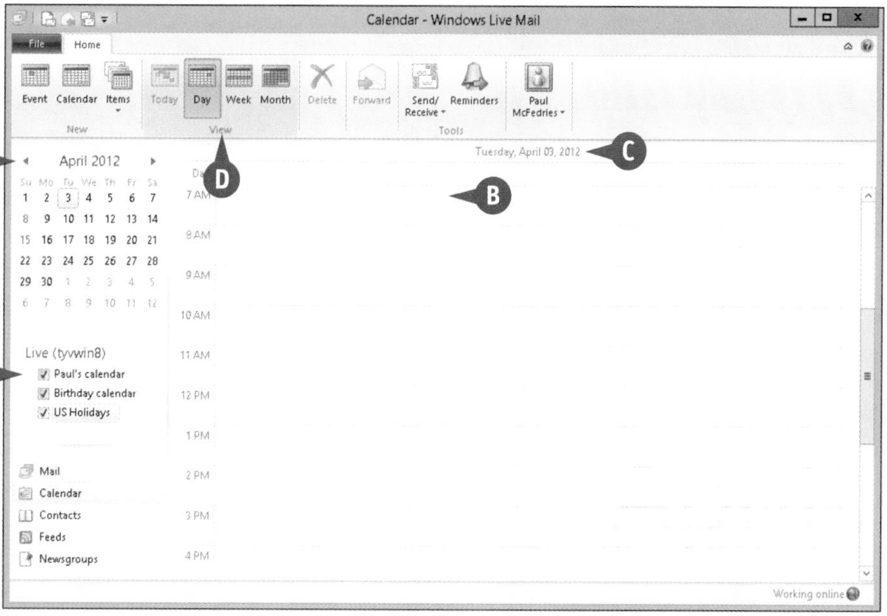

A Date Navigator

This area shows the current month, and you use the Date Navigator to select the date on which you want to schedule an event, all-day event, or task. See the "Display a Different Date" section, later in this chapter, to learn how to use the Date Navigator.

B Event List

This area shows the events that you have scheduled. In Day view, as shown here, the event list is divided into half-hour increments.

C Current Date

This area shows the date currently selected in the Date Navigator.

D Views

Click these buttons to determine how Calendar displays your events, as shown in the "Display a Different Date" section.

E Calendars

This area shows a list of your calendars. You get a single calendar to start with, but you can add more calendars as described in the "Add a Calendar" section, later in this chapter.

Display a Different Date

Before you create an event such as an appointment or meeting, or an all-day event such as a conference or trip, you must first select the date when the event occurs. You do that in Calendar by using the Date Navigator to display a different date.

Calendar also lets you change the calendar view to suit your needs. For example, you can show just a single day's worth of events if you want to concentrate on that day's activities. Similarly, you can view a week's worth of events if you want to get a larger sense of what your overall schedule looks like.

Display a Different Date

Navigate by Month

1. In the Date Navigator, click the **Next Month** button (▶) until the month of your event appears.

   A. If you go too far, click the **Previous Month** button (◀) to move back to the month you want.

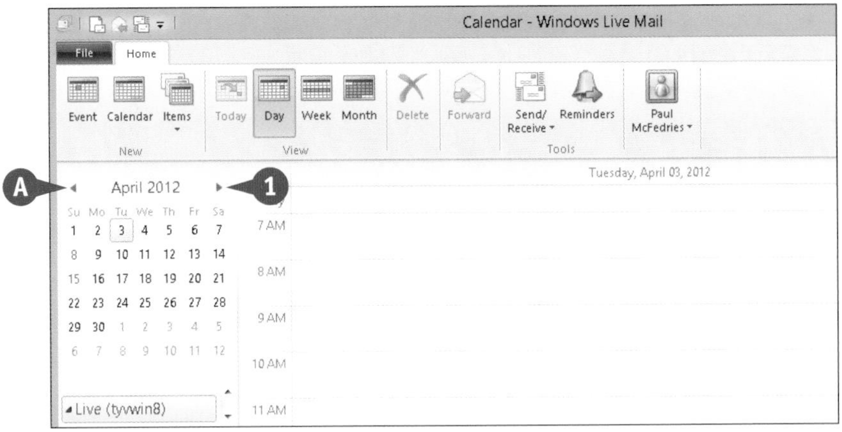

2. Click the date.

   B. The date appears in the events list.

   C. If you want to return to today's date, click **Go to today** or click **Today** in the ribbon.

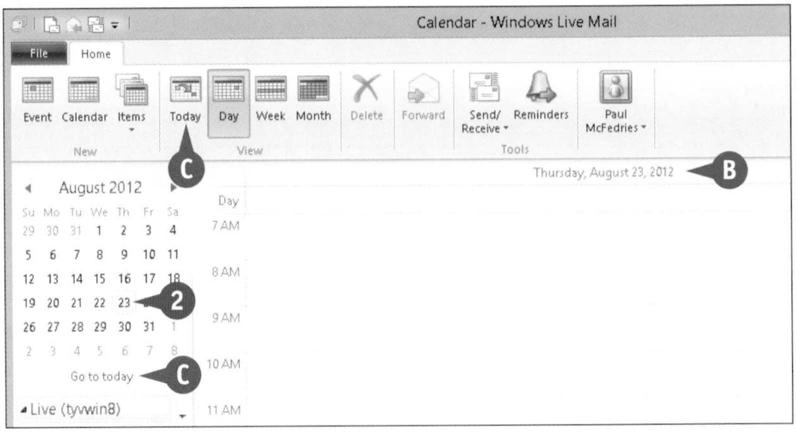

Navigate by Year

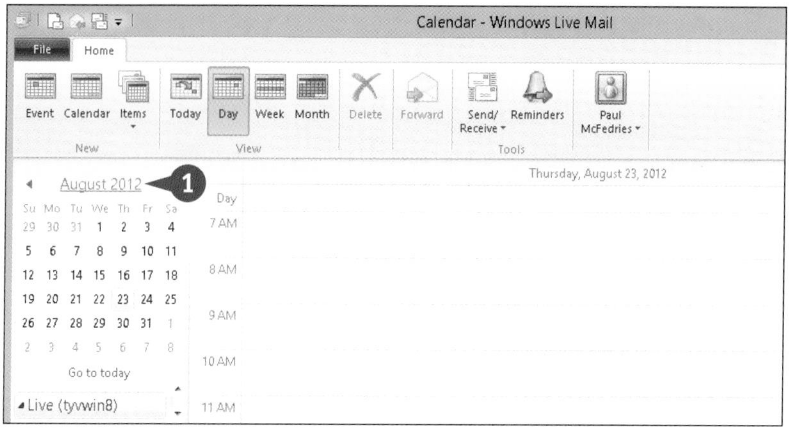

1 In the Date Navigator, click the month.

Calendar switches to Year view.

2 Click the **Next Year** button (▶) until the year of your event appears.

D If you go too far, click the **Previous Year** button (◀) to move back to the year you want.

3 Click the month when your event occurs.

Calendar switches back to Month view.

4 Use steps **1** and **2** in the first set of steps to display and select the date when your event occurs.

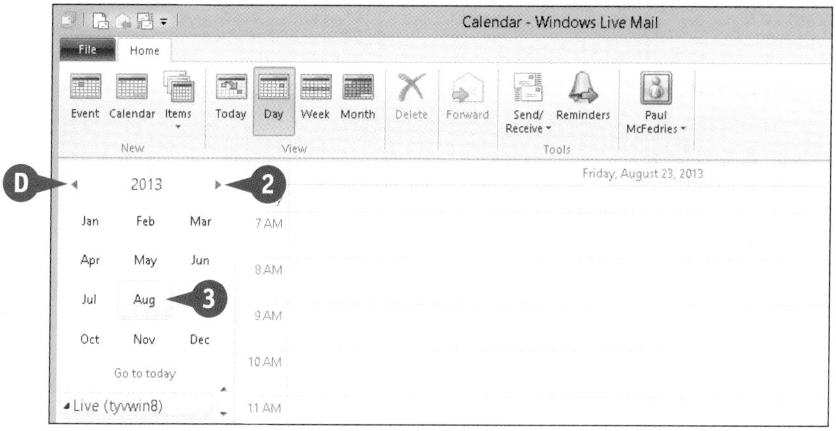

TIP

Can I see more than one day at a time in the events list?

Yes. Use the following ribbon buttons to select the view you want:

A **Day**. Shows the date currently selected in the Date Navigator. (You can also press Ctrl+Alt+1.)

B **Week**. Shows the full week that includes the date currently selected in the Date Navigator. (You can also press Ctrl+Alt+2.)

C **Month**. Shows the month that includes the date currently selected in the Date Navigator. (You can also press Ctrl+Alt+3.)

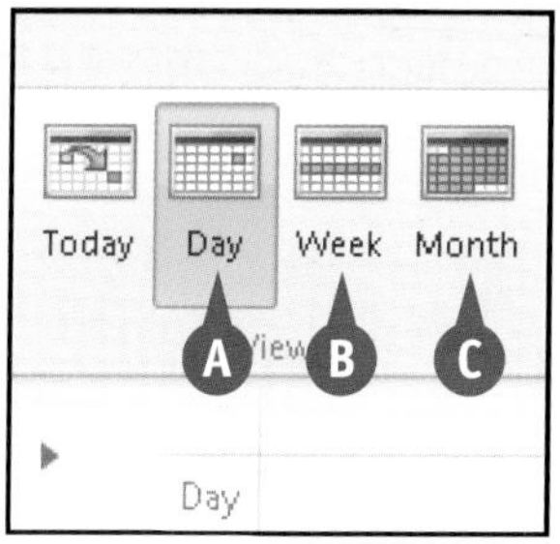

Create an Event

You can help organize your life by using Mail's Calendar to record your events — such as appointments, meetings, phone calls, and dates — on the date and time they occur.

If the event has a set time and duration — for example, a meeting or a lunch date — you add the event directly to the calendar as a regular appointment. If the event has no set time — for example, a birthday, anniversary, or multiple-day event such as a sales meeting or vacation — you can create an all-day event.

Create an Event

1. Navigate to the date when the event occurs.
2. Click the time when the event starts.

Note: If the event is more than half an hour, you can also click and drag the mouse over the full event period.

3. Click the **Home** tab.
4. Click **Event**.

Note: Another way to start a new event is to press Ctrl+Shift+E.

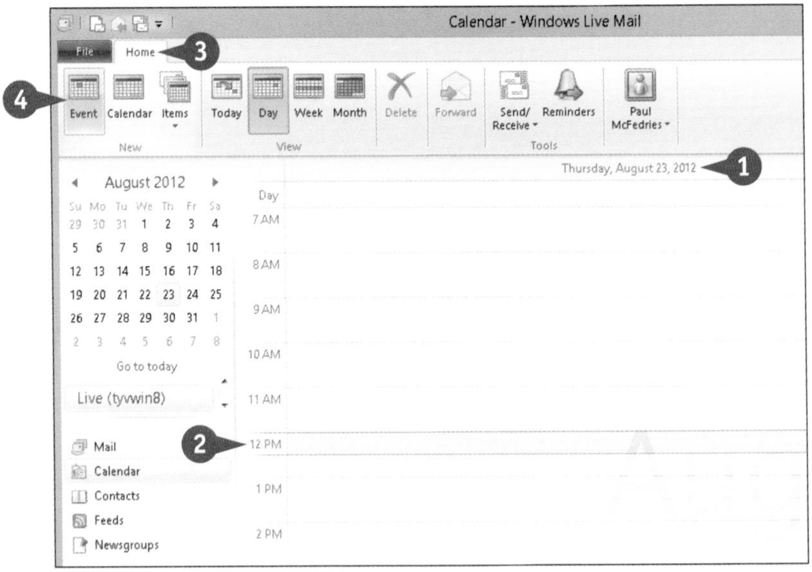

Calendar displays the New Event dialog box.

5. Type a name for the event.
6. Use the Location text box to type the event location.
7. If the event is an anniversary or other event that lasts all day, click **All day** (☐ changes to ☑).

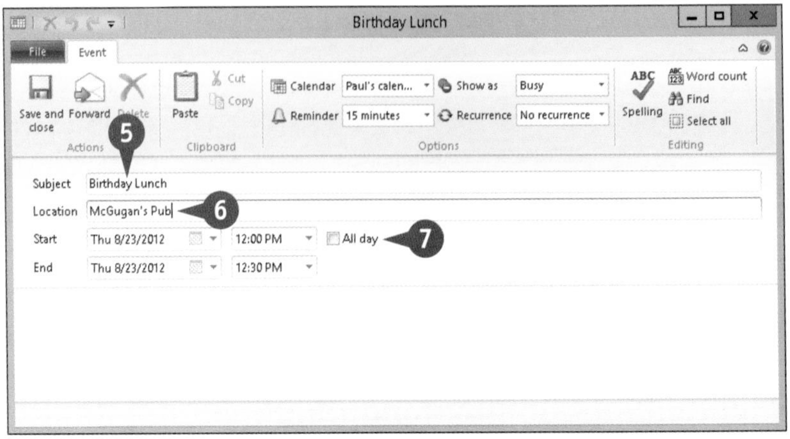

8. If the start time is incorrect, use the Start text box to type the correct time.
9. If the end time is incorrect, use the End text box to type the correct time.
10. Use the large text area to type notes related to the event.
11. Click **Save and close**.

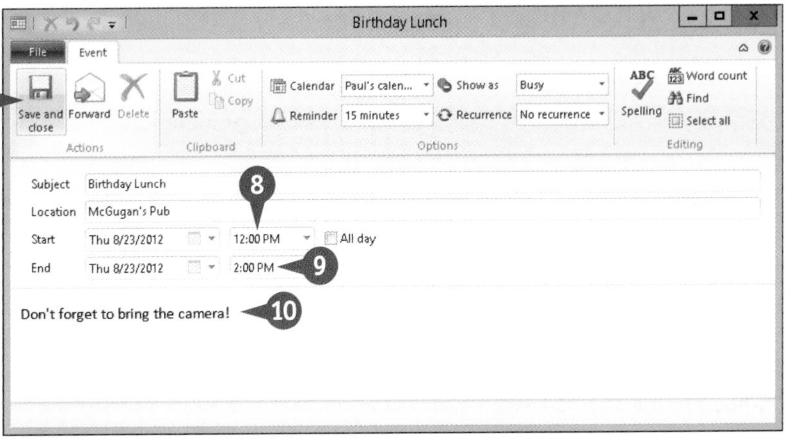

A. Calendar adds the event to the list.

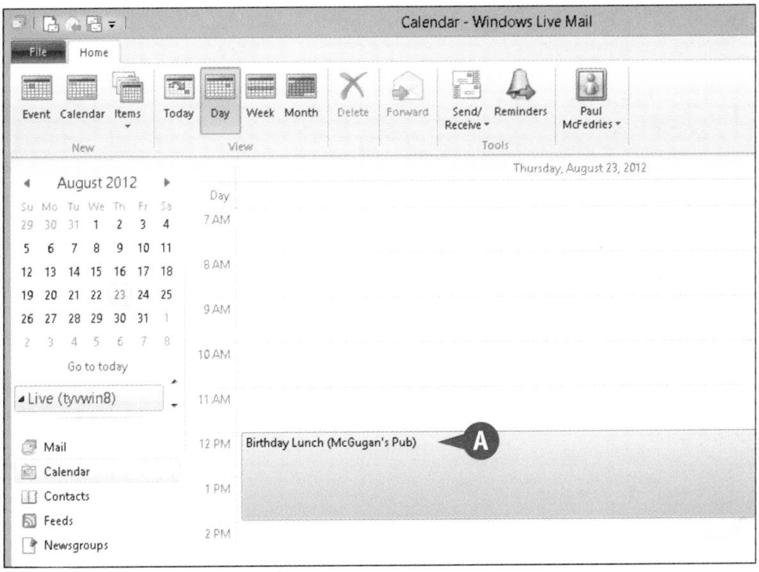

TIP

Is there an easy way to schedule an event that occurs at a regular interval?

Yes, you can set up a recurring event. Calendar can repeat an event at regular intervals such as daily, weekly, monthly, or yearly. You can also set up an advanced recurrence that uses a custom interval that you specify. Here are the steps to follow:

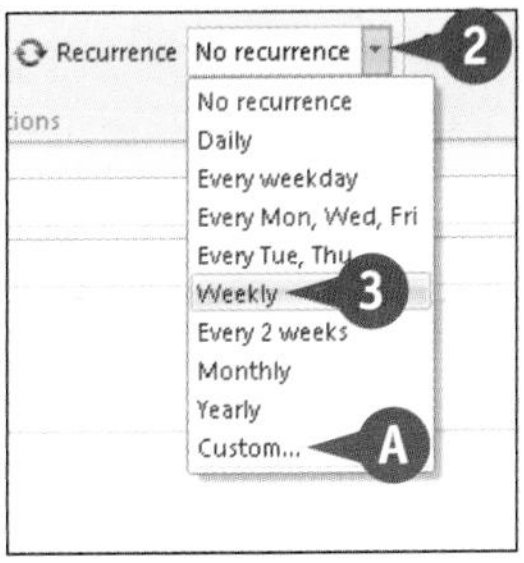

1. Follow steps **1** to **10** to set up a regular event.
2. Click the **Recurrence** ▾.
3. Click the interval you want to use.

A. If you want to set up your own recurrence, click **Custom** and use the Event Recurrence dialog box to specify your custom interval.

Windows Calendar repeats the event at the interval you specified.

Add a Calendar

If you have different schedules that you want to keep separate, you can add another calendar. For example, you might want to have one calendar for work events and a second calendar for personal events.

Separating your events into different calendars is a good idea because it makes it easier to maintain separate schedules and to keep track of which event belongs to which part of your life. To make this tracking even easier, you can assign different colors to each calendar, which helps you to see at a glance which event belongs to which calendar.

Add a Calendar

1. Click the **Home** tab.
2. Click **Calendar**.

Note: Another way to start a new calendar is to press Ctrl + Shift + D.

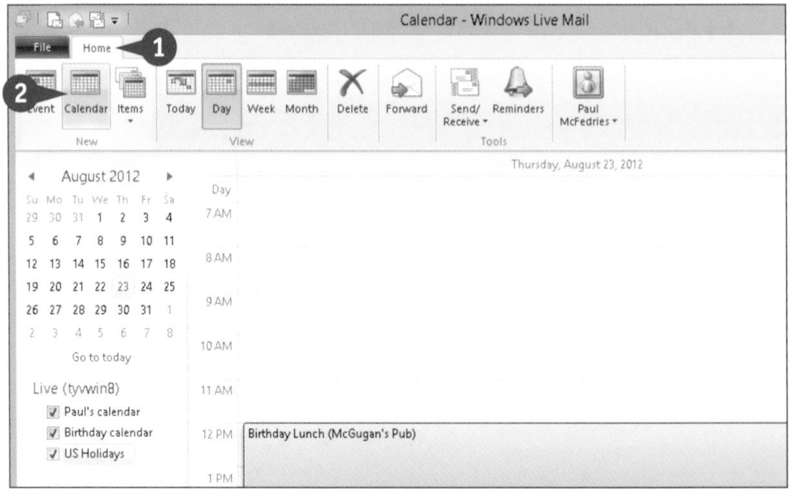

The Add a Calendar dialog box appears.

3. Type a name for the calendar.
4. Click the color you want to use for the calendar.

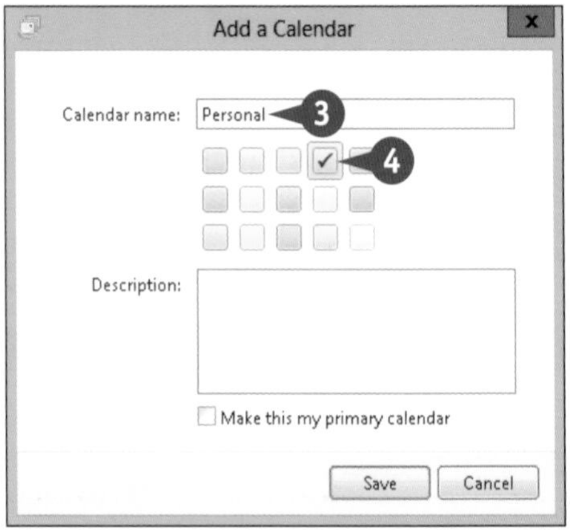

5 Type an optional description for the calendar.

6 If you want Mail to use this calendar as the default for new events, click **Make this my primary calendar** (☐ changes to ☑).

7 Click **Save**.

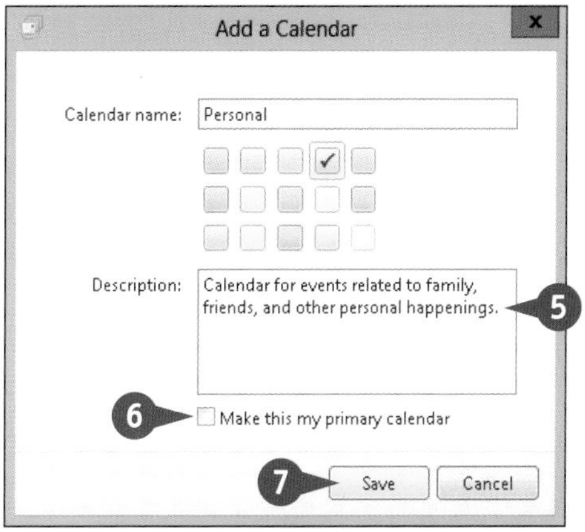

A The new calendar appears in the Calendars list.

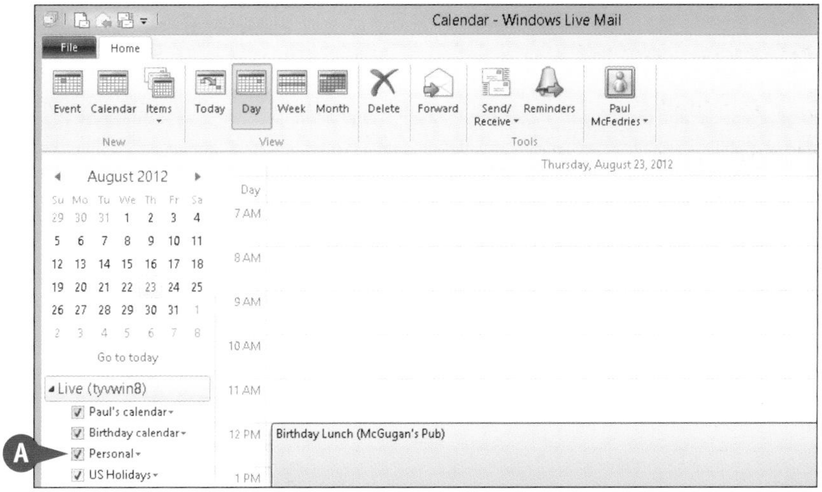

TIPS

How do I assign an event to a particular calendar?
Click the calendar you want to use, and then click **New event** in the menu that appears. You can also click the **Home** tab, click **Event** to open the New Event window, click the **Calendar** ▾, and then click the calendar you want to use. For existing events, double-click the event to open it, click the **Calendar** ▾, and then click the calendar.

Can I rename the original calendar?
Yes. The default name of "Calendar" is not very descriptive, so renaming it to something more useful is a good idea. In the Calendars list, click **Calendar** and then click **Properties** in the menu that appears. Use the Calendar Name text box to type a new name, and then click **Save**.

CHAPTER 7

Working with Images

Whether you load your images from a digital camera or a scanner, download them from the Internet, or draw them yourself, Windows 8 comes with a number of useful tools for working with those images. In this chapter you learn how to view your images, import images from a scanner or camera, fix photo problems, and print images.

Open the Pictures Library

Before you can work with your images, you need to view them on your computer. You do that by opening the Windows 8 Pictures library, which is a special folder designed specifically for storing images.

This section assumes you already have some images on your computer. If you do not yet have any images to view, see the sections later in this chapter that show you how to scan images and import images from a digital camera.

Open the Pictures Library

1. On the Start screen, click **Desktop**.

2. Click **File Explorer**.
3. Click **Pictures**.

Ⓐ The Pictures library appears.

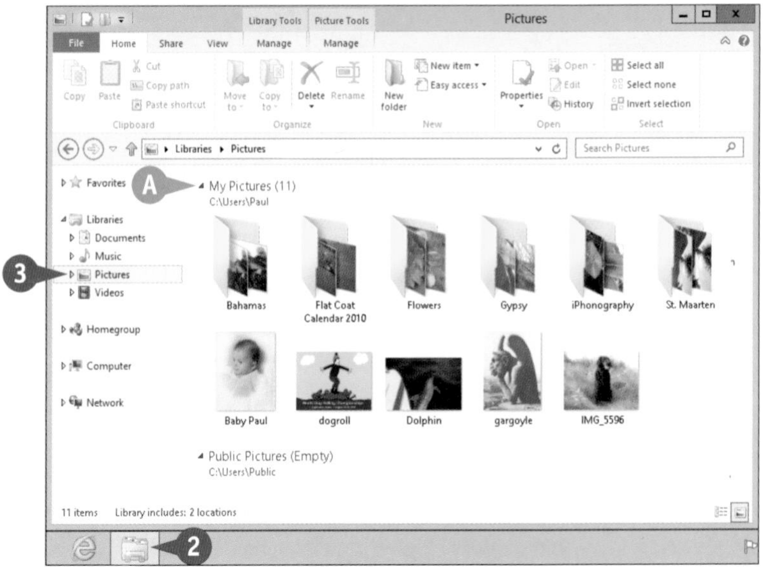

Preview an Image

Although Windows 8 displays a small version of each image in the Pictures library, you can take a closer look at a particular image by previewing it.

You can preview any image file using the Preview pane in the Pictures library. The Preview pane, which when active appears on the right side of the window, displays a larger version of the image so that you can see its details. You can also use the Preview pane to preview images stored in *subfolders* — folders stored within the main Pictures library.

Preview an Image

1. If the image you want to preview is located inside a subfolder, double-click that subfolder.

   A. Subfolders are shown in the Pictures library with a yellow folder icon, each of which also displays a couple of images stored in the folder.

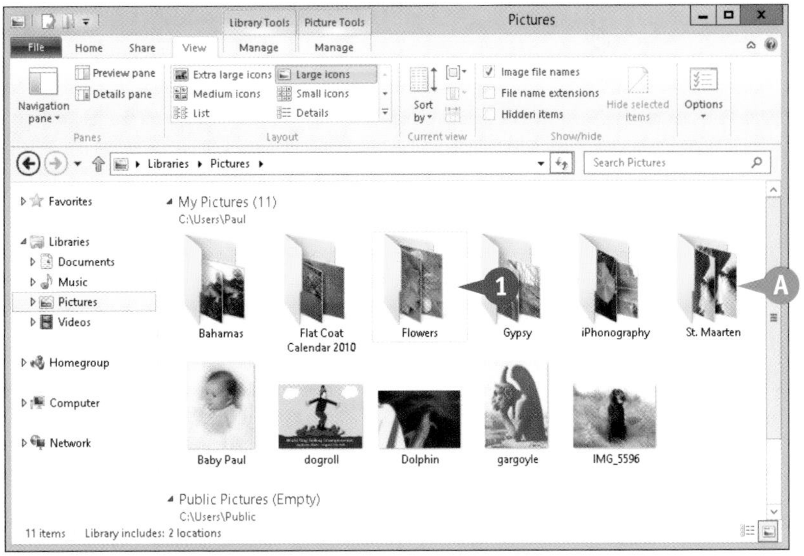

2. Click the image file you want to preview.
3. Click the **View** tab.
4. Click **Preview pane**.

   B. Windows 8 opens the Preview pane and displays a larger version of the image.

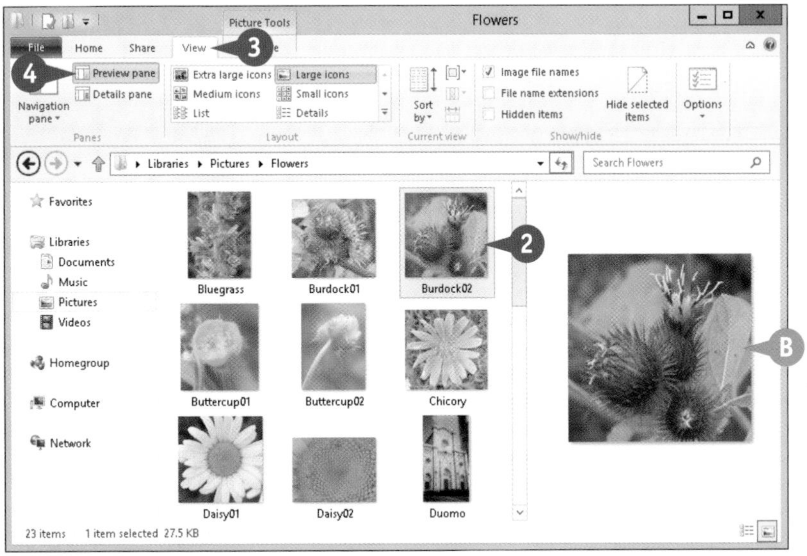

View Your Images

If you want to look at several images, Windows 8 offers a couple of tools that you can use to navigate backward and forward through the images in the Pictures library.

By default, Windows 8 comes with the Windows Photo Viewer. Alternatively, you can install Photo Gallery and use it to view your images. See Chapter 2 to learn how to install Photo Gallery.

You can also use either program to zoom in and out of an image and to run an image slide show.

View Your Images

View Images Using Windows Photo Viewer

1. Click the image.
2. Click the **Home** tab.
3. Click the **Open** ▾.
4. Click **Windows Photo Viewer**.

Note: If you see a notification telling you there are new programs that can open this type of file, you can ignore the message.

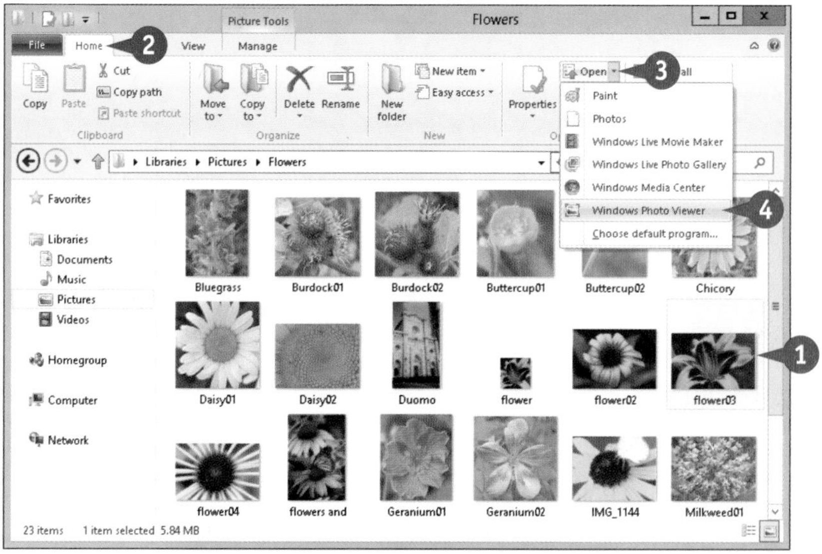

The image opens in Windows Photo Viewer.

5. To get a closer look at the image, click the magnifying glass and then click and drag the slider up.
6. To view the next image in the folder, click the **Next** button (▶|).
7. To view the previous image in the folder, click the **Previous** button (|◀).
8. To start a slide show of all the images in the folder, click the **Play Slide Show** button (▣).

Note: To stop the slide show, press Esc.

View Images Using Photo Gallery

1. Click the image.
2. Click the **Home** tab.
3. Click the **Open** ▾.
4. Click **Photo Gallery**.

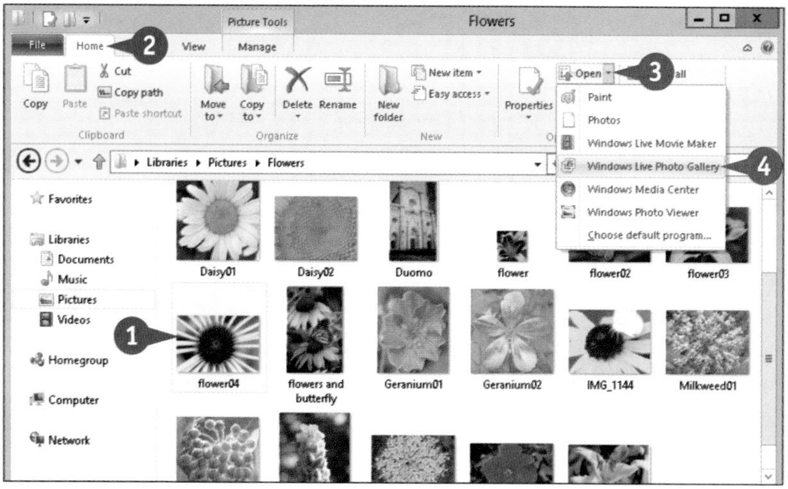

The image opens in Photo Gallery.

5. To see more of the image, click and drag the slider to the right.
6. To view the next image in the folder, click the **Next** button (⏭).
7. To view the previous image in the folder, click the **Previous** button (⏮).
8. To start a slide show of all the images in the folder, click the **Play Slide Show** button (▣).

Note: To stop the slide show, press Esc.

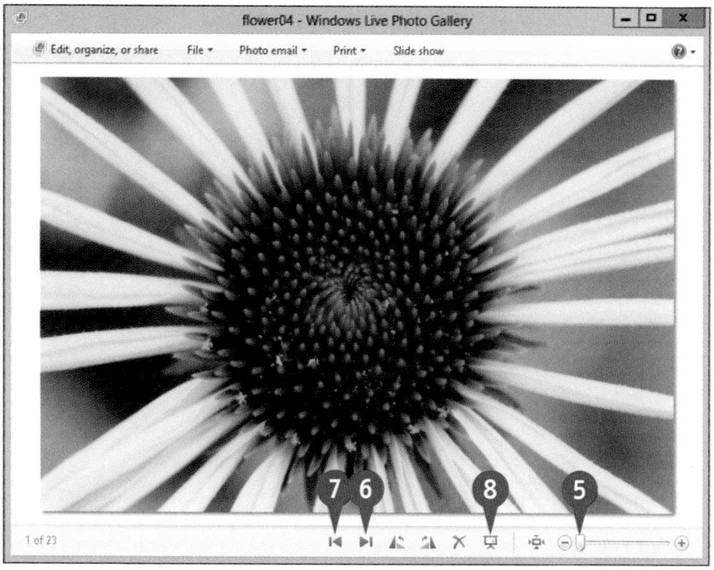

TIP

Is there a way I can view my pictures without using the Photo Gallery Viewer?

Yes, you can change the Picture folder's view to display large *thumbnails* — scaled-down versions of the actual images:

1. Click the **View** tab.
2. Click **Extra large icons.**

Ⓐ Windows 8 displays the images as thumbnails.

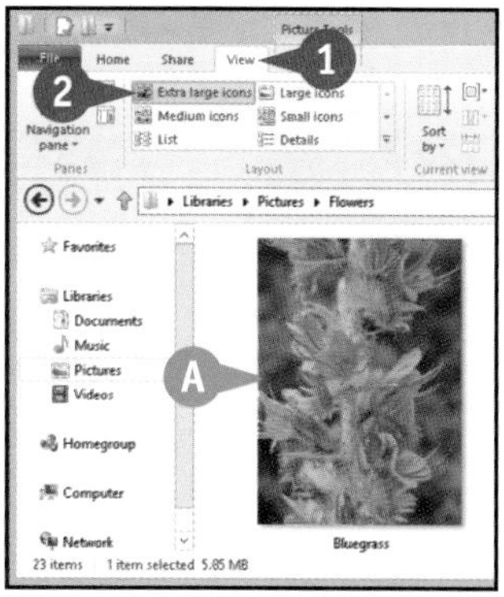

Scan an Image

You can create a digital copy of a photo or other image by using a document scanner, or the scanner component of an all-in-one printer. The scanner copies the image to your computer, where you can then store it as a file on your hard drive.

You can use a scanned image in many ways. For example, you can scan a photo to e-mail to friends or publish on a web page. You can also scan a logo or other image to use in a document.

Scan an Image

1. Turn on your scanner or all-in-one printer and position a photo or other image on the scanner bed.
2. On the Start screen, press ⊞+W.

   The Settings search pane appears.
3. Type **devices.**
4. Click **Devices and Printers.**

The Devices and Printers window appears.

5. Click the device you want to use to perform the scan.
6. Click **Start scan.**

The New Scan dialog box appears.

7 Click the **Profile** and then click **Photo**.

8 Click the **Resolution** to specify the scan resolution.

Note: The higher the resolution, the sharper the image, but the larger the resulting file.

9 Click **Preview**.

A A preview of the scan appears here.

10 Click and drag the edges of the dashed rectangle to set the scan area.

11 Click **Scan**.

Windows 8 scans the image.

The Import Pictures and Videos dialog box appears.

12 Click **Import all new items now** (○ changes to ◉).

13 Type a word or phrase that describes the scan.

14 Click **Import**.

Windows 8 imports the image to your computer.

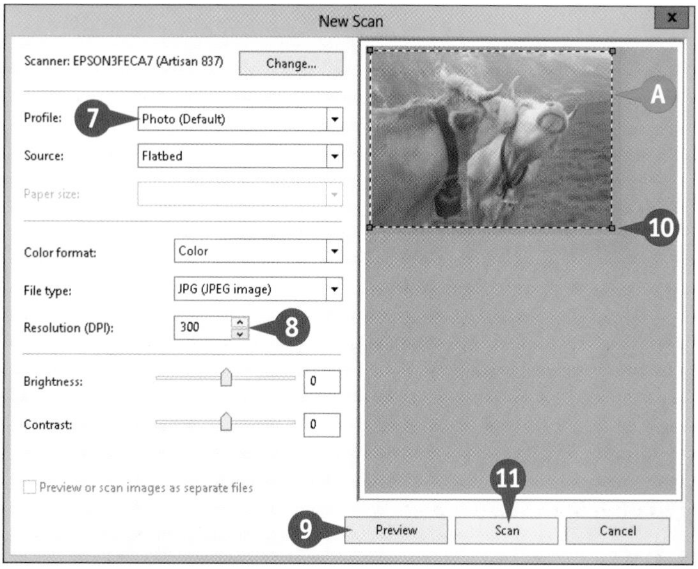

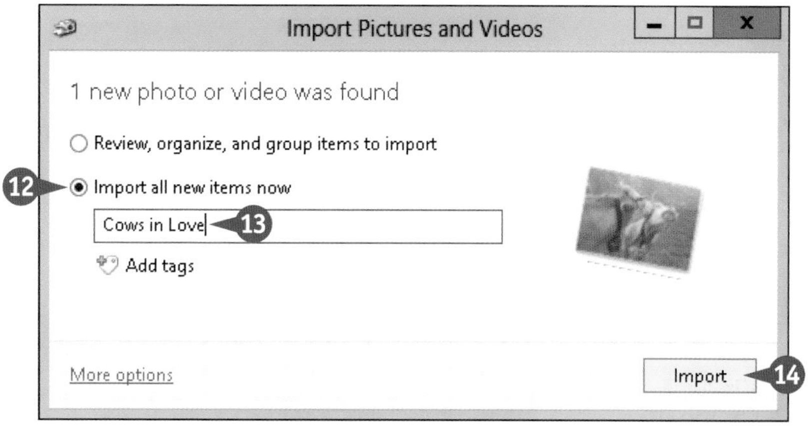

TIPS

How do I view a picture I have previously scanned?
Windows 8 stores the image in the Pictures library. It creates a new folder, the name of which is the current date followed by whatever word or phrase you type in the Import Pictures and Videos dialog box; for example, 2012-10-27, Flower. Open the subfolder to see your scanned picture.

Are there other methods I can use to scan an image?
Yes. Most scanners or all-in-one printers come with a Scan button that you can push to start a new scan. You can also use the Start screen to type **fax**, click **Windows Fax and Scan**, and then click **New Scan**. In Paint (type **paint** and then click **Paint**), click the **File** menu and then click **From scanner or camera**. In Photo Gallery (on the Start screen, click **Photo Gallery**), click **File** and then click **Import photos and videos**.

Import Images from a Digital Camera

You can import photos from a digital camera and save them on your computer. If your camera stores the photos on a memory card, you can also use a memory card reader attached to your computer to upload the digital photos from the removable drive that Windows 8 sets up after you insert the card.

To perform the import directly from your digital camera, you need a cable to connect your camera to your PC. Most digital cameras come with a USB cable.

Once you have the digital photos on your system, you can view, make repairs to, or print the images.

Import Images from a Digital Camera

1. Plug in your camera or memory storage card reader.

   A notification appears.

2. Click the notification.

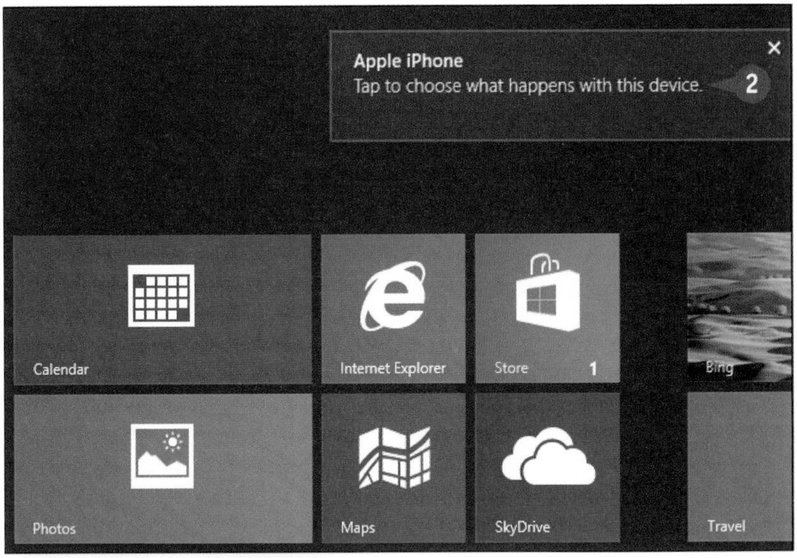

Windows 8 displays a list of actions you can perform.

3. Click **Import pictures and videos.**

Note: You see the Import option only if you have Photo Gallery installed. Otherwise, click **Open device to view files**, double-click your camera, and then keep double-clicking folders until you see your images. You can then copy the images to your Pictures library.

The Import Photos and Videos dialog box appears.

4 Click **Import all new items now** (○ changes to ◉).

5 Type a word or phrase that describes the photos.

6 Click **Import**.

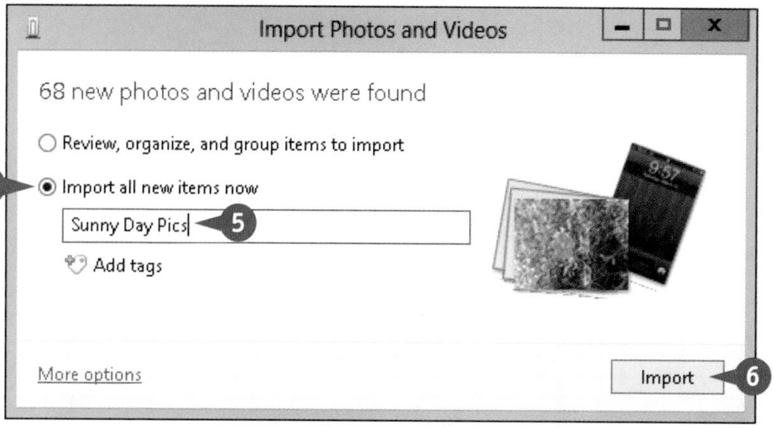

Windows 8 begins importing the digital photos.

7 To have Windows 8 erase the photos from the camera or card, click **Erase after importing** (☐ changes to ☑).

When the import is complete, Photo Gallery appears and displays the imported photos.

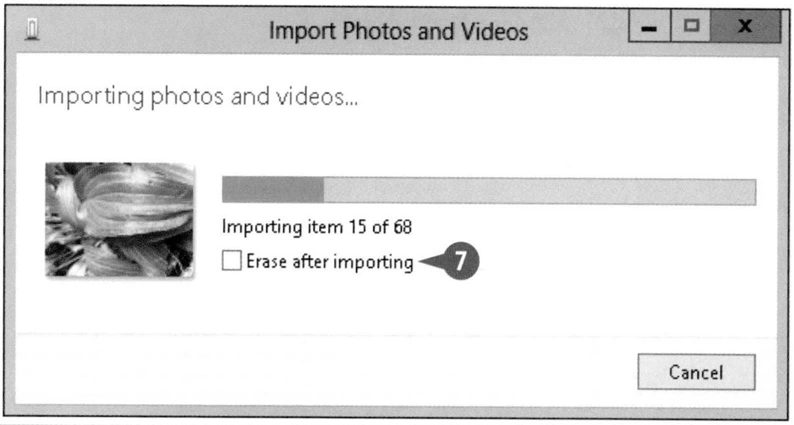

TIPS

What do I do if I want to import only some of the photos on my camera?

In the Import Photos and Videos dialog box, click **Review, organize, and group items to import** (○ changes to ◉) and then click **Next**. Click the check box beside a group of photos you want to import (☐ changes to ☑), type a name for the group, and then click **Import**.

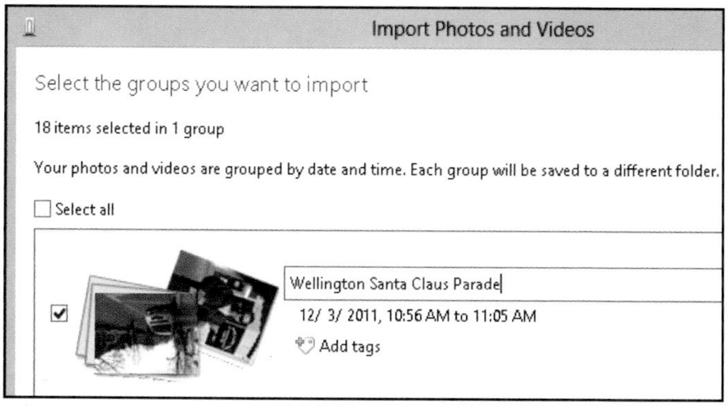

How do I view the imported photos?

If you have closed Picture Gallery, note that Windows 8 stores the imported digital photos in the Pictures library. It creates a new subfolder, the name of which is whatever word or phrase you type in the Import Photos and Videos dialog box. To view the photos, click the **Photos** app, click **Pictures library**, and then click the subfolder that holds your imported photos.

Repair a Digital Image

You can use Photo Gallery to improve the look of digital photos and other images. When you open an image in Photo Gallery, the ribbon offers a number of tools for repairing various image attributes.

The image window enables you to reduce the image noise problems, which are small flaws in the image. Photo Gallery also offers a set of tools that automatically adjust your image. Using the image window, you can automatically adjust an image's brightness, contrast, color temperature, tint, and saturation. See Chapter 2 to learn how to download and install Photo Gallery.

Repair a Digital Image

1 Click **Photo Gallery**.

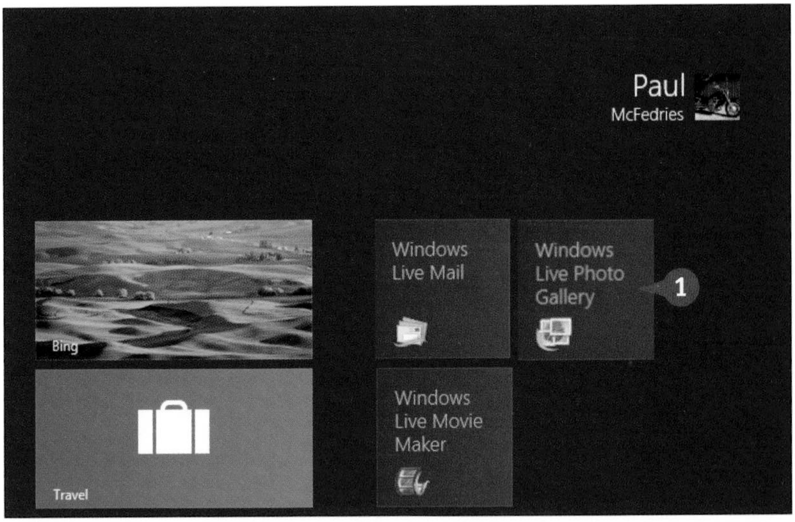

Photo Gallery appears.

Note: The first time you run the program, it asks if you want to use the program to open certain file types. Click **Yes**.

2 Double-click the image you want to repair.

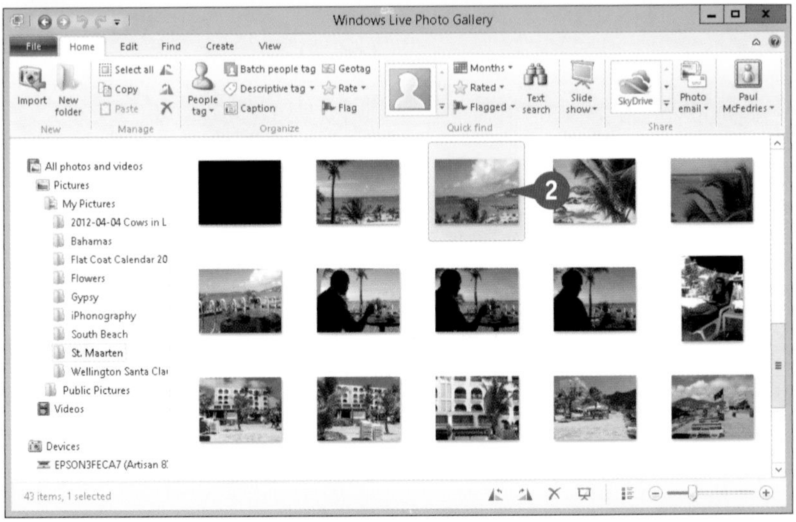

Photo Gallery opens the image and displays the Edit tab.

3 To fix small flaws, click **Noise reduction**.

4 To fix the colors, click **Color** and then click **Auto adjust color**.

5 To fix the exposure, click **Exposure** and then click **Auto adjust exposure**.

A To adjust all these properties at once, click **Auto adjust**.

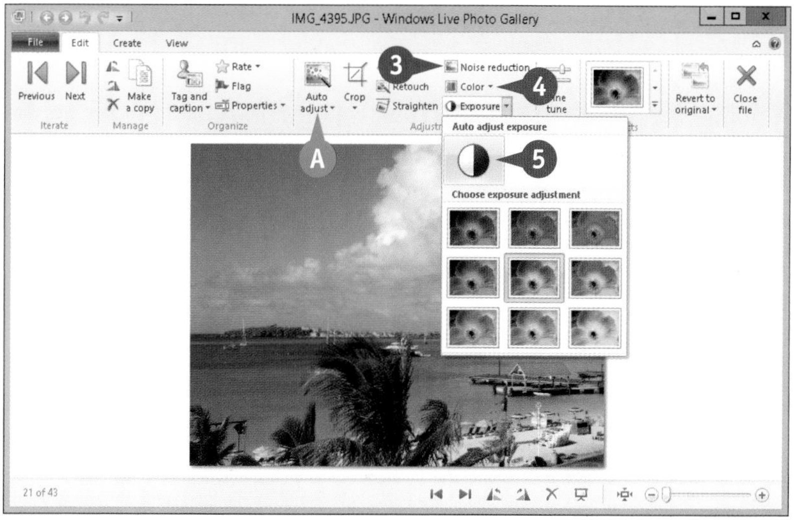

6 To remove red eye from a photo, click **Red eye** and then drag a rectangle around the red eye.

7 When you are done, click **Close file**.

Photo Gallery applies the repairs.

TIP

I do not like the repairs I made to my image. Can I get the original image back?

Yes, you can. Photo Gallery always keeps a backup copy of the original image, just in case. To undo all your changes and get the original image back, double-click the image to open it. In the image window's **Edit** tab, click **Revert to original** (or press Ctrl + R), and then click **Revert**.

Crop an Image

If you have an image containing elements that you do not want or need to see, you can often cut out those elements. This is called *cropping*, and you can do this with Photo Gallery.

When you crop a photo, you specify a rectangular area of the photo that you want to keep. Photo Gallery discards everything outside the rectangle.

Cropping is a useful skill to have because it can help give focus to the true subject of a photo. Cropping is also useful for removing extraneous elements that appear on or near the edges of a photo.

Crop an Image

1 Click **Photo Gallery**.

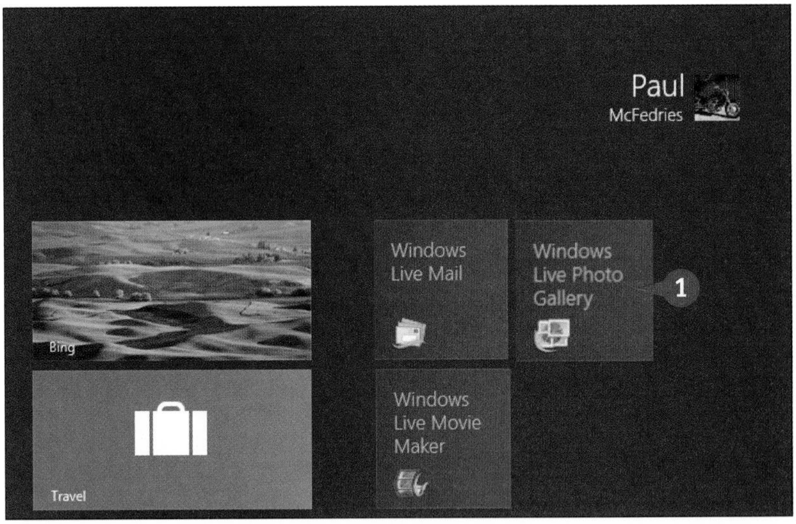

Photo Gallery appears.

2 Double-click the image you want to repair.

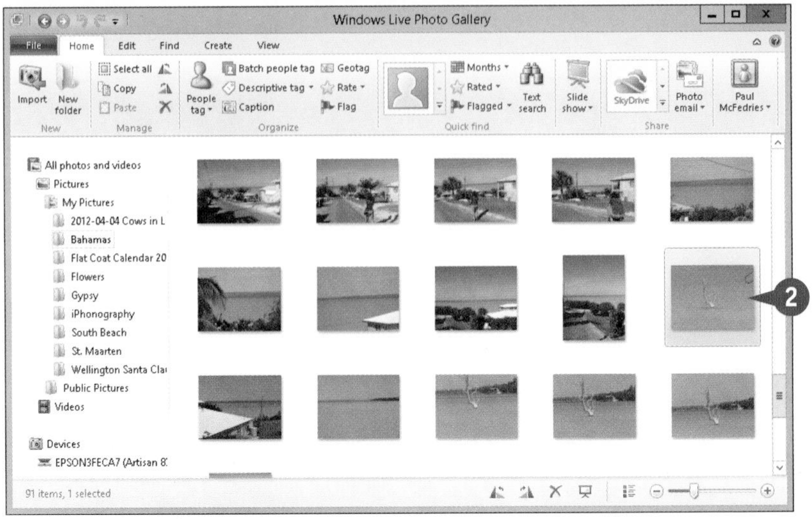

Photo Gallery opens the image and displays the Edit tab.

3. Click the top half of the **Crop** button.

   Photo Gallery displays a cropping rectangle on the photo.

4. Click and drag a corner or side to define the area you want to keep.

Note: Remember that Photo Gallery keeps the area inside the rectangle.

5. Click the bottom half of the **Crop** button.

6. Click **Apply crop**.

7. Click **Close file**.

   Photo Gallery closes the image.

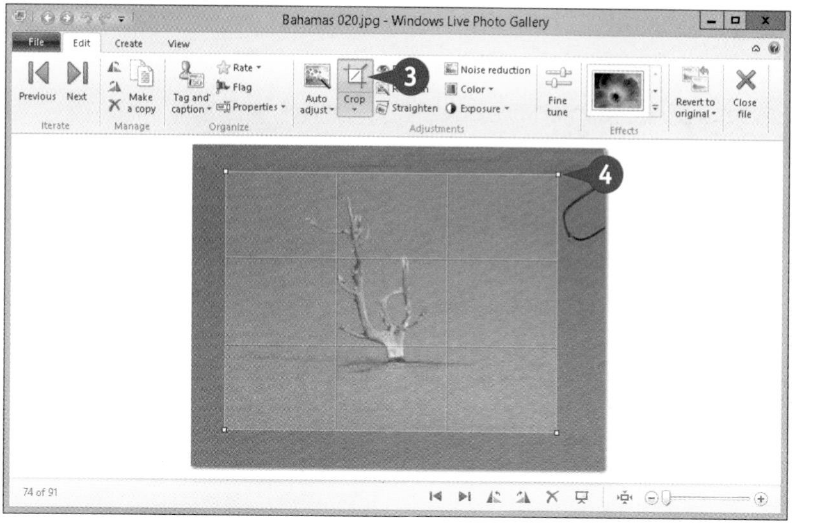

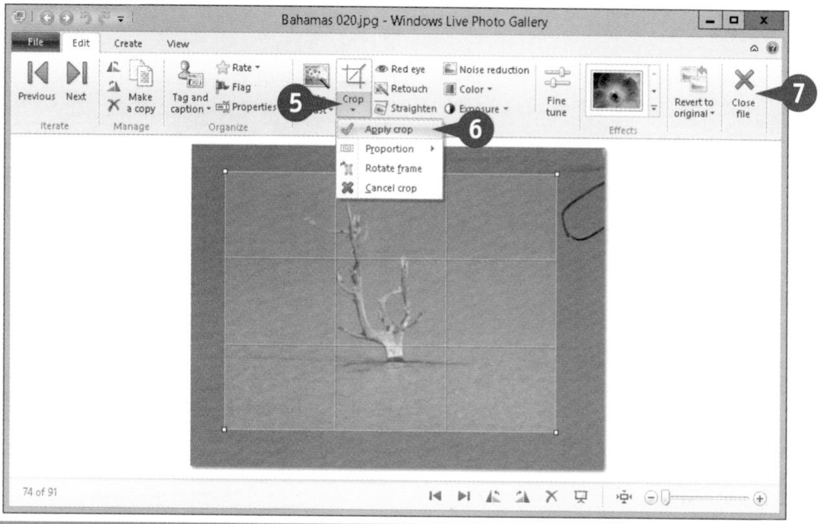

TIP

Is there a quick way to crop a photo to a certain size?

Yes, Photo Gallery enables you to specify a specific ratio, such as 4 × 6 or 5 × 7. Follow these steps:

1. Repeat steps **1** and **2** to open the image.
2. Click the bottom half of the **Crop** button.
3. Click **Proportion**.
4. Click the ratio you want to use.
5. To maintain the size, drag the inside of the crop rectangle rather than the corners or sides.
6. Click **Close file**.

   Photo Gallery exits edit mode.

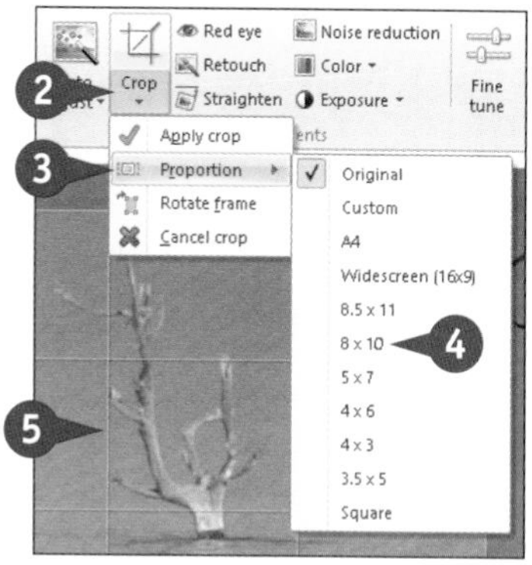

Rotate and Straighten an Image

You can rotate and straighten a photo using Photo Gallery.

Depending on how you held your camera when you took a shot, the resulting photo might show the subject sideways or upside down. To fix this problem, you can use Photo Gallery to rotate the photo so that the subject appears right-side up. You can rotate a photo either clockwise or counterclockwise.

Despite your best efforts, you might end up with a photo that is not quite level. To fix this problem, you can use Photo Gallery to nudge the photo clockwise or counterclockwise so that the subject appears straight.

Rotate and Straighten an Image

Open the Image for Editing

1 Click **Photo Gallery**.

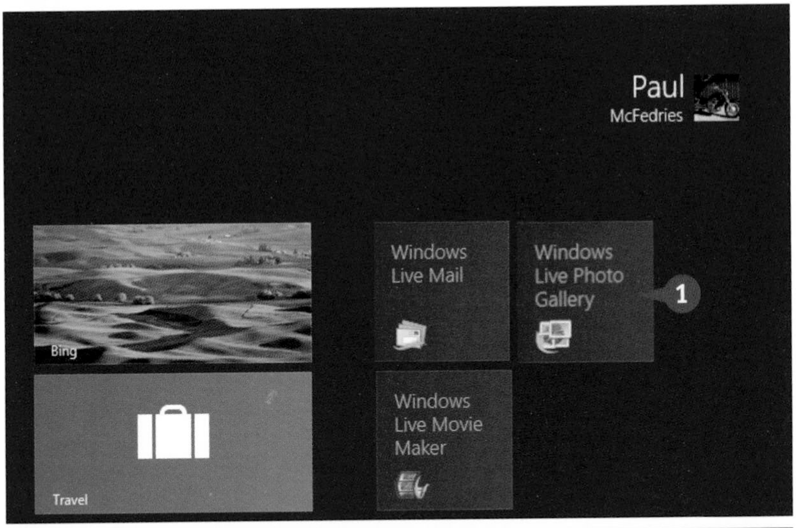

Photo Gallery appears.

2 Double-click the image you want to repair.

Photo Gallery opens the image and displays the Edit tab.

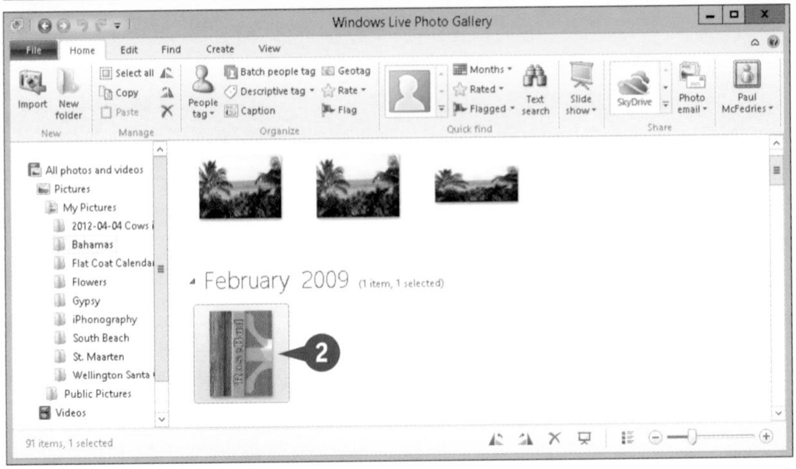

Rotate the Image

1. Rotate the image in the direction you want:

   A. Click **Rotate left** ( ) to rotate the image counterclockwise.

   B. Click **Rotate right** ( ) to rotate the image clockwise.

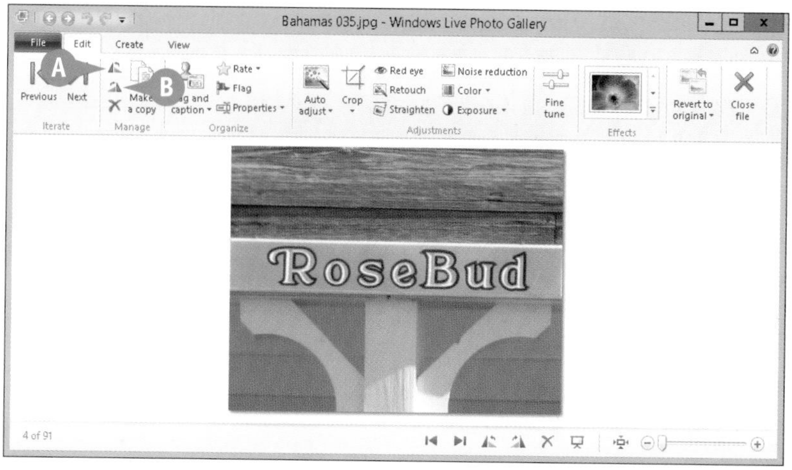

Straighten the Image

1. Click **Fine tune**.

   C. Photo Gallery displays extra repair tools.

2. Click **Straighten photo**.
3. Drag the slider bar ( ) left or right to adjust the angle of the image.

   D. You can also click **Straighten** to have Photo Gallery straighten the image automatically.

4. Click **Close file**.

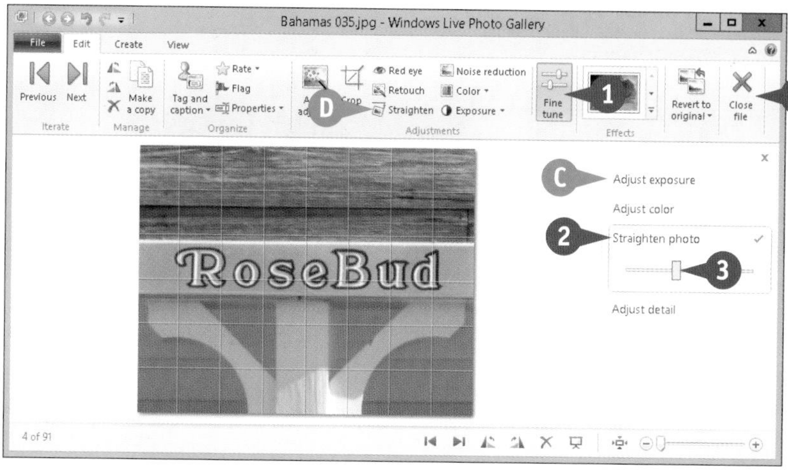

TIPS

How do I know when my photo is level?

Use the gridlines that Photo Gallery places over the photo. Locate a horizontal line in your photo, and then rotate the photo so that this line is parallel to the nearest horizontal line in the grid. You can also match a vertical line in the photo with a vertical line in the grid.

Is there an easier way to straighten an image?

Yes, in many cases you can get Photo Gallery to straighten the image automatically. The easiest way to do this is to click the **Straighten** button in the ribbon. This feature is also part of the image automatic adjustment, so you can also click the top half of the **Auto adjust** button (which also adjusts the image colors and exposure).

Print an Image

You can print an image from the Pictures library, or from any subfolder in the Pictures library. When you activate the Print command, the Print Pictures dialog box appears. You can use this dialog box to choose a printer and a layout, and to send the image to the printer.

You can print a single image or multiple images. If you work with multiple images, you can print them individually or print two or more images per sheet.

Print an Image

1. On the Start screen, type **pictures**.
2. Click **Pictures**.

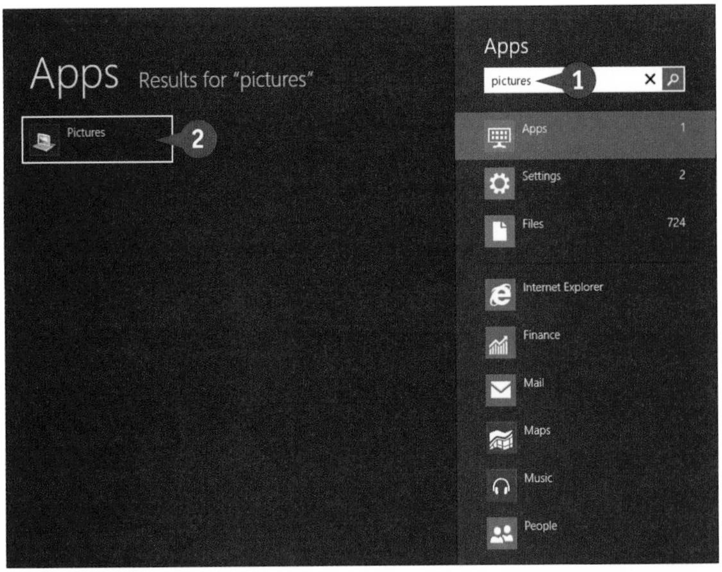

Windows 8 displays the Pictures library.

3. Click the image or images you want to print.

Note: To select multiple images, press and hold Ctrl and click each image.

4. Click the **Share** tab.
5. Click **Print**.

The Print Pictures dialog box appears.

6. If you use more than one printer with your computer, click ▾ and click the printer you want to use.
7. Click ▾ and click the size of paper you are using.
8. Click ▾ and click the printout quality you prefer.

Note: Print quality is measured in dots per inch (dpi). The higher the dpi value, the better the print quality.

9. Click the layout you want to use for the printed image.
10. Click ⬍ to select the number of copies you want.

A. Windows 8 displays a preview of the printout.

11. Click **Print**.

Windows 8 sends your image or images to the printer.

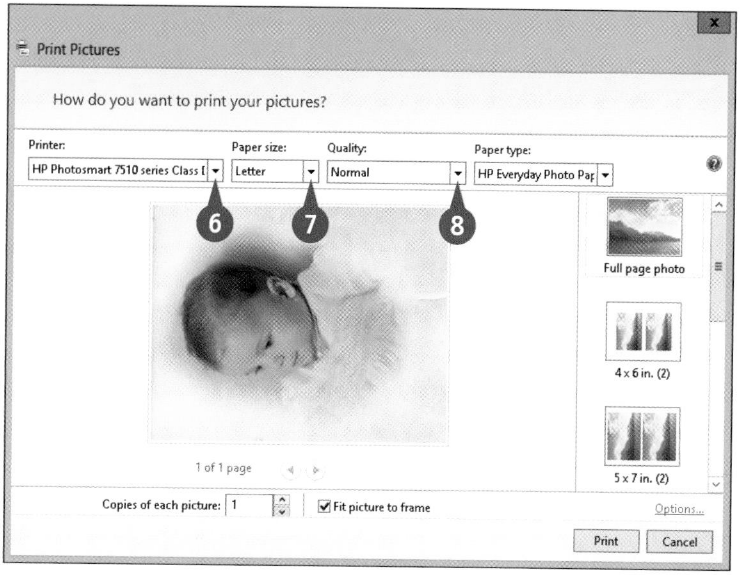

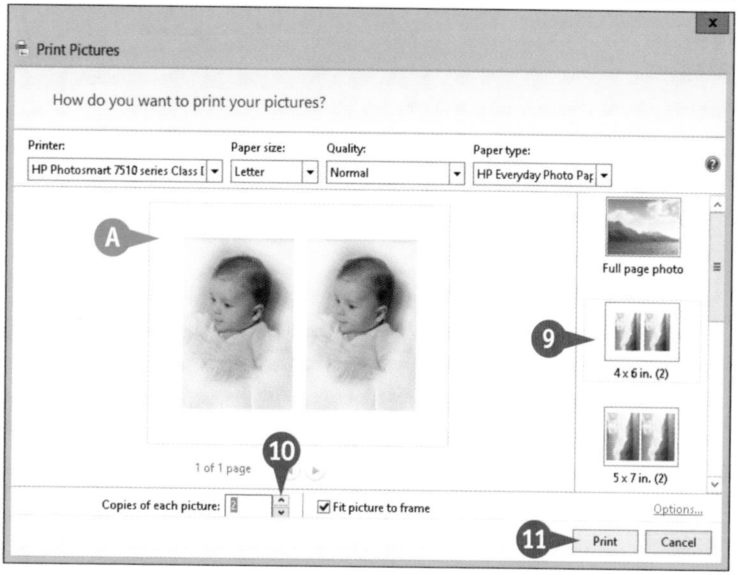

TIP

What type of paper should I use for my photo printouts?

Depending on the kind of printer you are using, you can find a variety of photo-quality paper types for printing out your digital photographs. Photo-quality paper, though more expensive than multipurpose paper, is designed to create a more permanent image and improve the resolution and color of the printed images. Photo-quality paper comes in glossy and matte finishes, as well as variations of each. Be sure to select a photo-quality paper that your printer manufacturer recommends.

CHAPTER 8

Playing Music and Other Media

Besides the Music and Video Windows 8 apps, Windows 8 comes with two other media applications: Windows Media Player and Windows Media Center. Using Windows Media Player, you can listen to audio files and music CDs, watch video files, and even create your own music CDs. Using Windows Media Center, you can view pictures and videos on your TV, play DVD discs, and listen to audio files through your stereo.

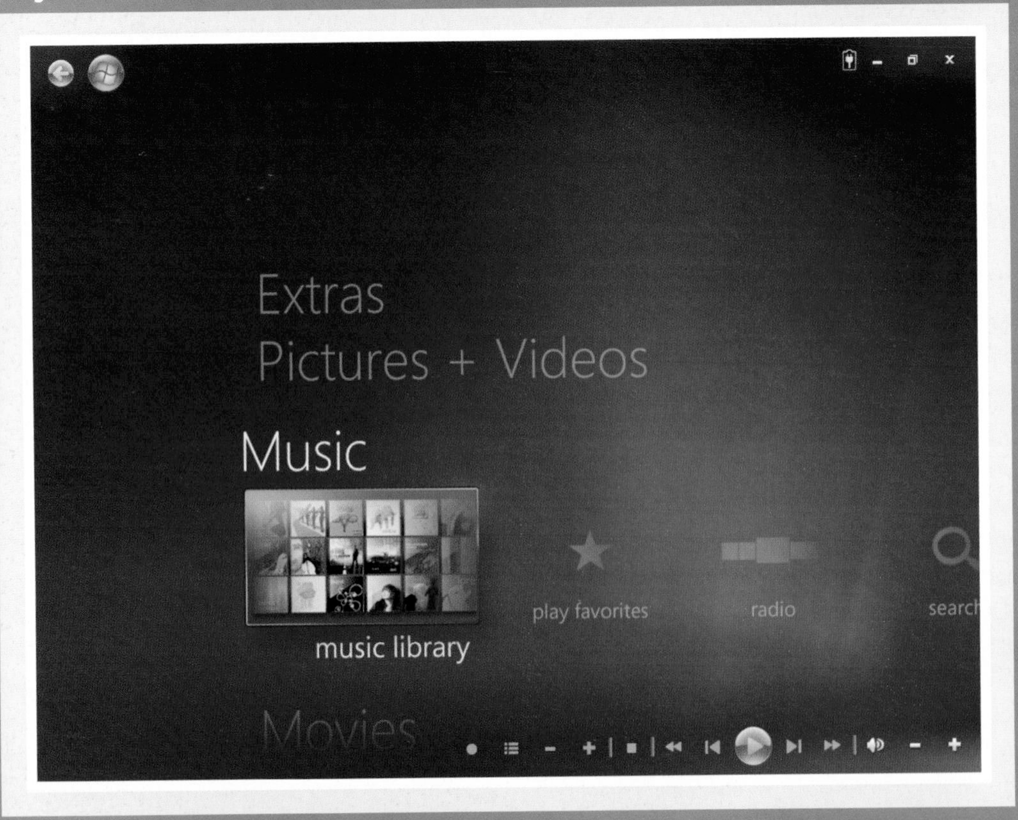

Open and Close Windows Media Player

Windows 8 includes Windows Media Player to enable you to play back and record audio as well as view video. Windows Media Player also includes features for playing videos, watching movies and TV shows, and viewing pictures, but this chapter focuses on Media Player's audio and video features.

To begin using the program, you must first learn how to open the Windows Media Player window. When you finish using the program, you can close the Windows Media Player window to free up computer processing power.

Open and Close Windows Media Player

1. On the Start screen, type **media**.
2. Click **Windows Media Player**.

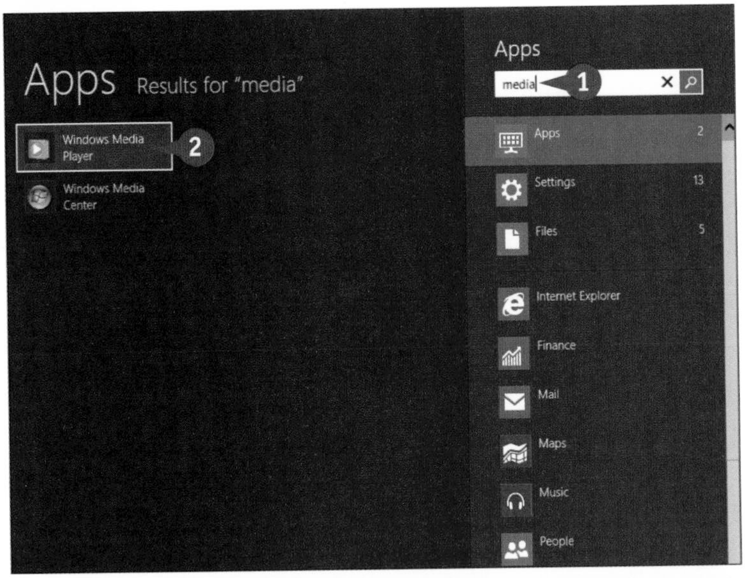

Apps Results for "media"
Windows Media Player
Windows Media Center
Apps
media
1
2
Apps 2
Settings 13
Files 5
Internet Explorer
Finance
Mail
Maps
Music
People

The first time you start the program, the Welcome to Windows Media Player dialog box appears.

3. Click **Recommended settings** (○ changes to ◉).
4. Click **Finish**.

The Windows Media Player window appears.

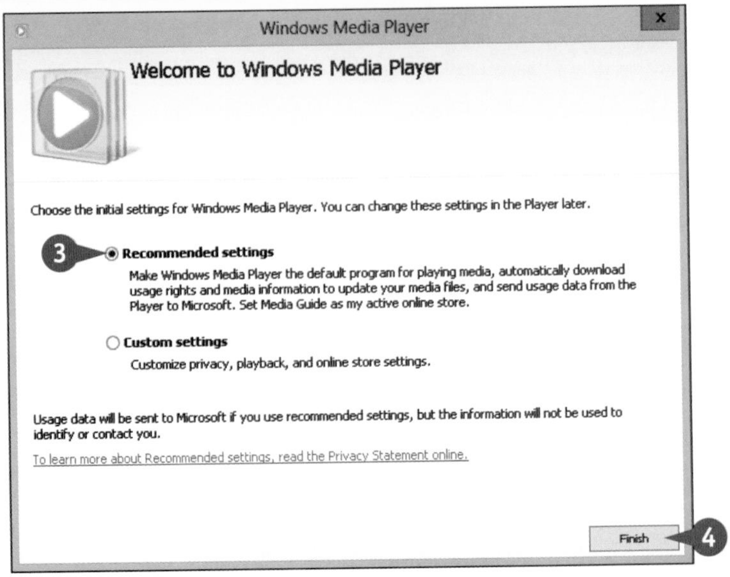

Windows Media Player
Welcome to Windows Media Player
Choose the initial settings for Windows Media Player. You can change these settings in the Player later.
3
Recommended settings
Make Windows Media Player the default program for playing media, automatically download usage rights and media information to update your media files, and send usage data from the Player to Microsoft. Set Media Guide as my active online store.
Custom settings
Customize privacy, playback, and online store settings.
Usage data will be sent to Microsoft if you use recommended settings, but the information will not be used to identify or contact you.
To learn more about Recommended settings, read the Privacy Statement online.
Finish
4

Navigate the Media Player Window

Familiarizing yourself with the various elements of the Windows Media Player window is a good idea so that you can easily navigate and activate elements when you are ready to play audio files or view videos and DVDs.

Ⓐ Address Bar

This area shows your current location in the Media Player library.

Ⓑ Tabs

The tabs are links to the key features of Windows Media Player.

Ⓒ Toolbar

You can use the Media Player toolbar to access commands, change the view, and search for media.

Ⓓ Navigation Pane

You use this pane to navigate the Media Player library's categories.

Ⓔ Playback Controls

These buttons control how a video or music file plays, and enable you to make adjustments to the sound.

Ⓕ Details Pane

This pane displays information about the contents of the current library location, such as the album art and title, and the title and length of the song or video.

Using the Library

You can use the library feature in Windows Media Player to manage all the media files on your computer, including audio files and videos. The library also enables you to organize other digital content, such as music CDs.

When you first start using Windows Media Player, the program automatically updates the library with the files already in your computer's media folders, such as Music and Videos.

To get the most out of using Windows Media Player, you need to know how to navigate the library and how to change the view.

Using the Library

Navigate the Library

1. In the navigation pane, click the category you want to use.
2. If the category includes subcategories, click a subcategory to see its contents.
3. Double-click the item you want to use.

Media Player displays the contents of the item in the details pane.

- **A** You can also click the items in the address bar to return to a category or subcategory.
- **B** Click an arrow to see the contents of any address bar item.

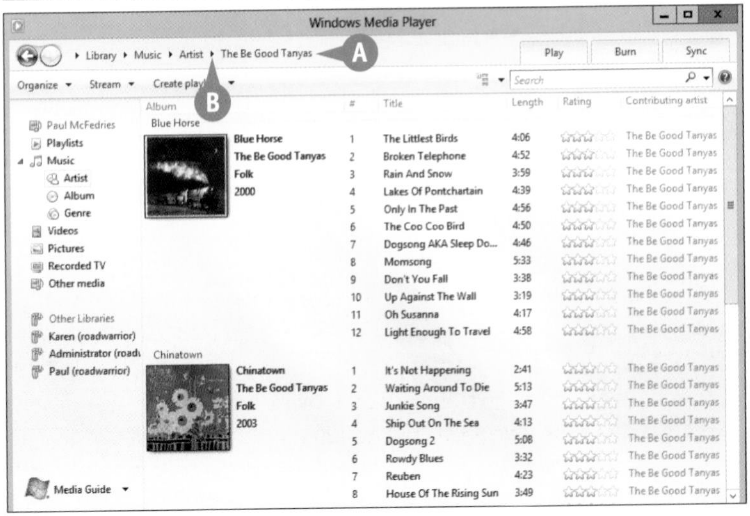

Change the Library View

1. Click the **View options** ▾.
2. Click the view you want to use.

   Click **Icon** to see just the images associated with each item, such as album covers.

   Click **Tile** to see icons and some item data.

   Click **Details** to see extra information about each item.

Note: Not all views are available with all categories or subcategories.

   Media Player changes the view.

TIPS

My library is quite large. How do I search for a specific file?

If you want to search the entire library, click **Library** in the address bar. Otherwise, click the category you want to search, such as **Music**. Click in the search box on the right side of the toolbar. Type a word or phrase that represents the media you want to find. The matching media appear in the library.

How does the library create its folders and subfolders?

The library automatically groups music into the categories based on their media content information. Media content information, also called *metadata* or *tags*, includes information such as the artist name, song title, rating, play count, and composer. Media content information also identifies the file type.

Play an Audio or a Video File

Windows Media Player uses the library to play audio files that you store on your computer. Although Windows Media Player offers several methods to locate the song you want to play, the easiest method is to display the albums you have in your Media Player library, and then open the album that contains the song you want to play.

When you select an audio file from a library folder and play it in Windows Media Player, you can also switch to the Now Playing view to see the album cover along with the song.

Play an Audio or a Video File

1. Use the library to navigate to the folder that contains the audio or video file that you want to play.

Note: See "Using the Library" to learn more about working with the library's folders.

2. Click the audio or video file.
3. Click the **Play** button (▶).
4. Click **Switch to Now Playing** to view the album art while an audio file plays.

Windows Media Player begins playing the audio or video file.

5. Move the mouse into the Now Playing window.

(A) The playback buttons appear, which enable you to control how the song or video plays.

Note: See "Play a Music CD" to learn more about the playback buttons.

(B) You can click **Switch to Library** to return to the Media Player library.

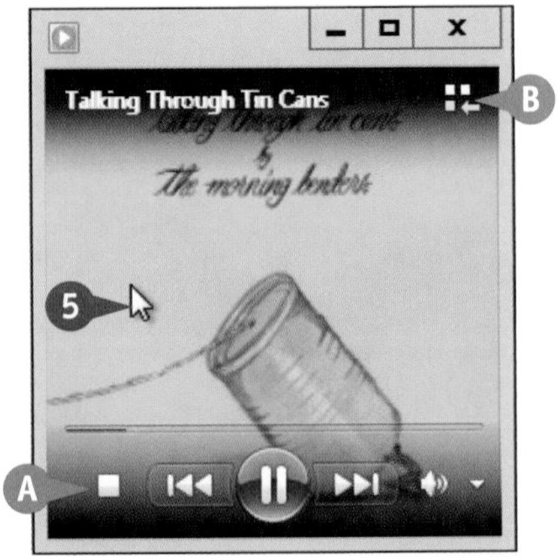

Adjust the Volume

While an audio or video file is playing, you can adjust the volume in Windows Media Player up or down to get the audio just right.

If you are listening to media by yourself, you can adjust the volume to suit the music and your mood. However, if other people are nearby, you should use Windows Media Player's volume control to keep the playback volume low to avoid disturbing others. If you need to silence the media temporarily — for example, if a telephone call comes in — you can mute the playback.

Adjust the Volume

Adjust the Volume Using the Library

1. Click and drag the **Volume** slider left (to reduce the volume) or right (to increase the volume).

A. If you want to silence the playback, click the **Mute** button ( ).

Note: To restore the volume, click the **Sound** button ( ).

Adjust the Volume in the Now Playing Window

1. Position the mouse within the Now Playing window.

   The playback controls appear.

2. Click here and then drag the **Volume** slider left (to reduce the volume) or right (to increase the volume).

B. To silence the playback, click the **Mute** button ( ).

Note: To restore the volume, click the **Sound** button ( ).

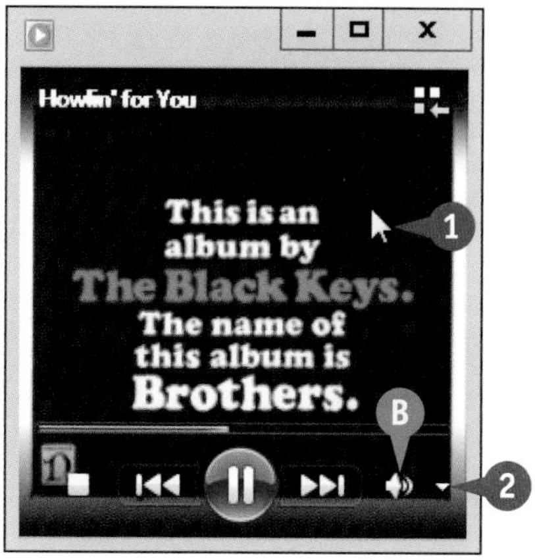

Play a Music CD

You can play your favorite music CDs in Windows Media Player. When you first insert an audio disc in your PC's optical drive (that is, a drive capable of reading CDs and DVDs), Windows 8 asks what action you want to perform with audio CDs, and you can tell it to play them using Windows Media Player.

The CD appears in the Now Playing window, and if you have an Internet connection you see the name of each track as well as other track data.

You can control some playback options using the Now Playing window, but you can also switch to the Media Player library for more options.

Play a Music CD

Play a CD

1. Insert a music CD into your computer's optical drive.

A. Windows 8 displays an audio CD notification.

2. Click the notification.

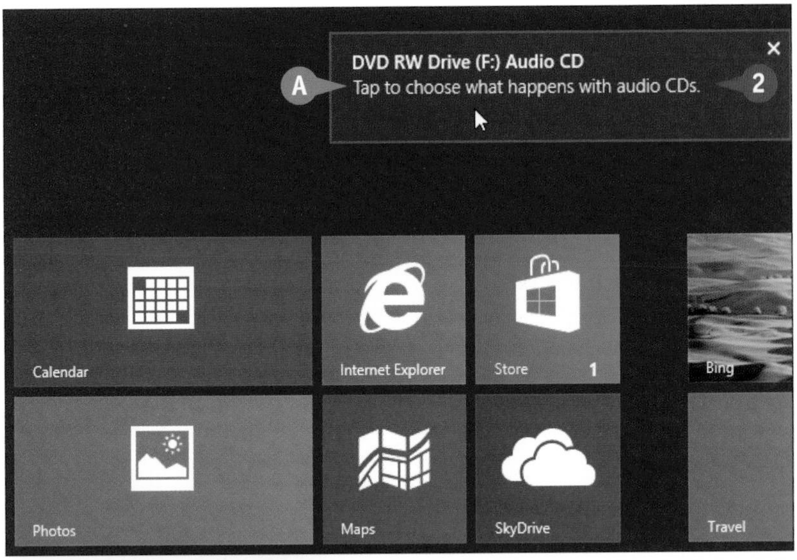

Windows 8 displays a list of actions you can take when you insert an audio CD.

3. Click **Play audio CD**.

Windows Media Player's Now Playing window appears and begins playing the audio CD.

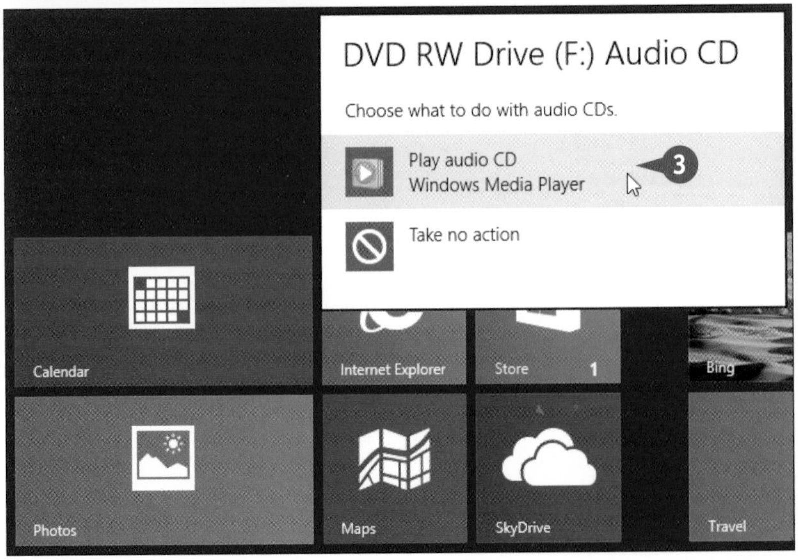

Skip a Track

4 Click the **Next** button (⏭) to skip to the next track.

5 Click the **Previous** button (⏮) to skip to the previous track.

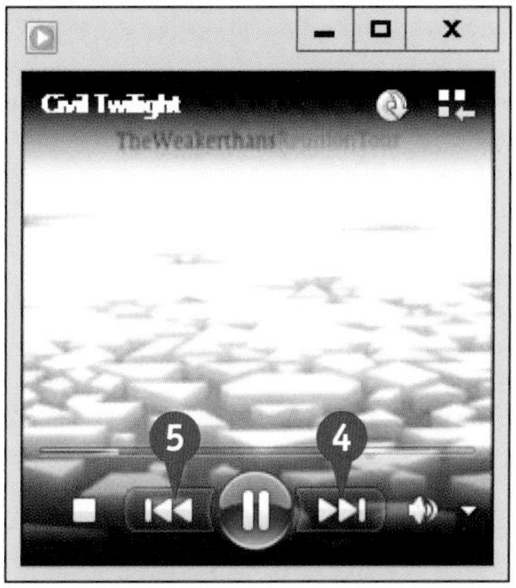

Pause and Resume Play

6 Click the **Pause** button (⏸).

Windows Media Player pauses playback.

7 Click the **Play** button (▶).

Windows Media Player resumes playback where you left off.

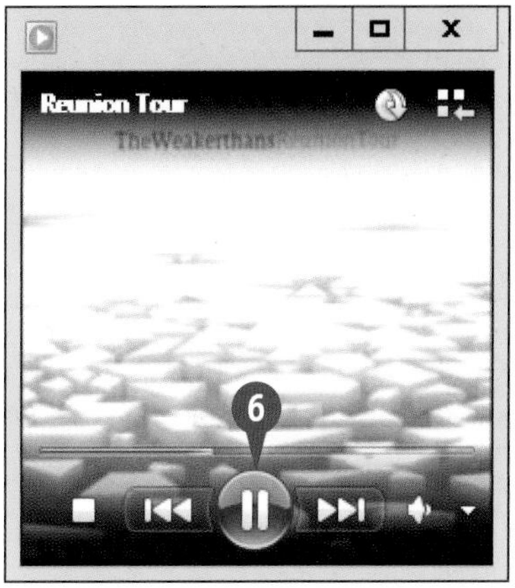

TIPS

Can I change the CD's audio levels?
Yes, Windows Media Player has a graphic equalizer component you can work with. To display it, right-click the **Now Playing** window, click **Enhancements**, and then click **Graphic equalizer**. To choose a predefined set of levels, click **Default**, and then click a preset value such as Rock or Classical. Alternatively, use the sliders to set your own audio levels.

Can I display something other than album art during playback?
Yes. Right-click the **Now Playing** window and then click **Visualizations** to see a list of visualization categories. Click a category and then click the visualization you want to view. The visualizations in the Battery category are fun to play with, as their names suggest: Dance of the Freaky Circles, Green Is Not Your Enemy, Spider's Last Moment, and My Tornado Is Resting.

continued ▶

You can use the playback buttons at the bottom of the Windows Media Player library to control how a CD plays. For example, you can easily switch from one song to another on the CD. You can also use the Repeat feature to tell Media Player to start the CD over from the beginning after it has finished playing the CD. Media Player also offers the Shuffle feature, which plays the CD's tracks in random order.

If you want to learn how to import music from the CD to Media Player, see the section "Copy Tracks from a Music CD."

Play a Music CD (continued)

Stop Play

8 Click the **Stop** button (■).

Windows Media Player stops playback.

If you click the **Play** button (▶) after clicking the **Stop** button (■), the current song starts over again.

9 Click **Switch to Library** (⊞) to open the Media Player library window.

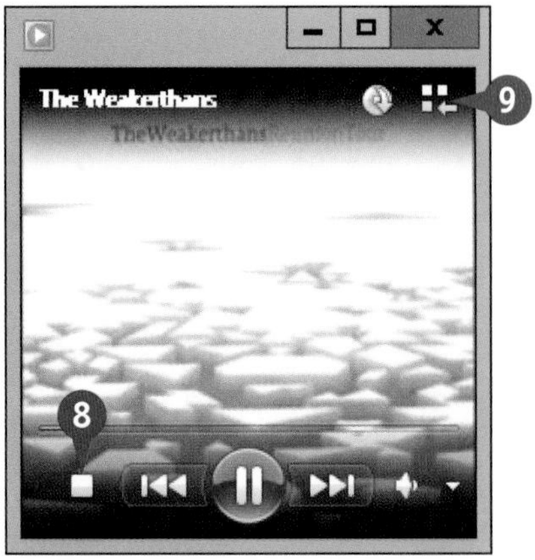

Play another Song

10 In the details pane, double-click the song you want to play.

Windows Media Player begins playing the song.

A This area displays the current song title, the album title, and the song composer (if one is listed).

Repeat the CD

11 Click the **Turn Repeat On** button (⟳).

Windows Media Player restarts the CD after the last track finishes playing.

Note: To turn on Repeat from the Now Playing window, press Ctrl+T.

Play Songs Randomly

12 Click the **Turn Shuffle On** button (⤮).

Windows Media Player shuffles the order of play.

Note: To turn on Shuffle from the Now Playing window, press Ctrl+H.

TIPS

My details pane does not list the song titles. Why not?

Windows Media Player tries to gather information about the album from the Internet. If it cannot ascertain song titles, then it displays track numbers instead. To add your own titles, right-click the song title you want to change and click **Edit.** Type your text and press Enter. You can also press F2 and then Tab to edit a song title.

Is there a way to keep the Now Playing window in view at all times?

Yes. You can configure the Now Playing window so that it stays on top of any other window that you have open on your desktop. This enables you to control the playback no matter what other programs are running on your PC. Right-click the Now Playing window and then click **Always show Now Playing on top**.

Copy Tracks from a Music CD

You can add tracks from a music CD to the library in Windows Media Player. This enables you to listen to an album without having to put the CD into your optical drive each time. The process of adding tracks from a CD is called *copying,* or *ripping,* in Windows 8.

You can either rip an entire CD directly from the Now Playing window, or you can rip selected tracks using the library. You can also use the tracks to create your own playlists and to create your own custom CDs.

Copy Tracks from a Music CD

Rip an Entire CD Using the Now Playing Window

1. Insert a CD into your computer's optical drive.

   The Now Playing window appears.

2. Click **Rip CD** (◙).

   Media Player begins ripping the entire CD.

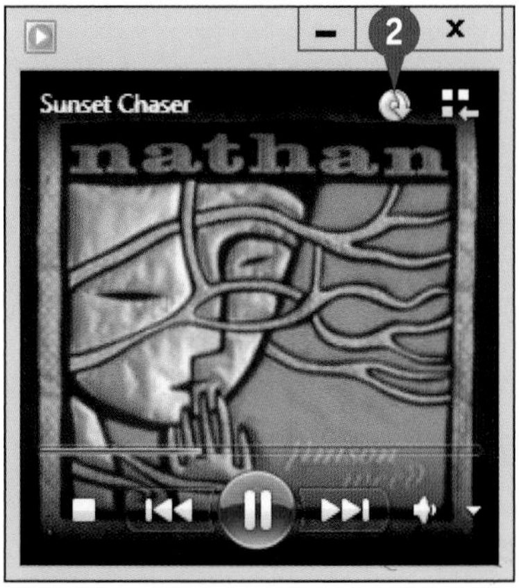

Rip Selected Tracks Using the Library

1. Insert a CD into your computer's optical drive.

   If the Now Playing window appears, click **Switch to Library** (▣).

   Ⓐ Media Player displays a list of the CD's tracks.

2. Click the CD tracks that you do not want to copy (☑ changes to ☐).

3. Click **Rip CD**.

Windows Media Player begins copying the track or tracks.

B The Rip Status column displays the copy progress.

C After each file is copied, the Rip Status column displays a Ripped to Library message.

D The copy is complete when all the tracks you selected display the Ripped to Library status.

TIPS

I ripped a track by accident. How do I remove it from the library?

In the library, click **Music**, click **Album**, and then double-click the album that you ripped to display a list of the tracks. Right-click the track that you want to remove, and then click **Delete** from the menu that appears.

Can I adjust the quality of the copies?

Yes. You do that by changing the *bit rate*, which is a measure of how much of the CD's original data gets copied to your computer. This is measured in kilobits per second (Kbps); the higher the value the higher the quality, but the more disk space each track takes up. Click **Rip Settings**, click **Audio Quality** from the menu that appears, and then click the value you want.

Create a Playlist

A *playlist* is a collection of songs, or music tracks you copy from a music CD, store on your computer hard drive, or download from the Internet. You can create customized playlists in Windows Media Player that play only the songs that you want to hear.

For example, you might want to create a playlist of upbeat or festive songs to play during a party or celebration. Similarly, you might want to create a playlist of your current favorite songs to burn to a CD.

Create a Playlist

1 Click **Create playlist**.

A Windows Media Player creates a new playlist folder.

2 Type a name for the new playlist.

3 Press Enter.

4. Click and drag items from the library and drop them on the playlist.

5. Click the playlist.

The details pane shows the songs you added.

6. Click and drag the songs to change the playlist order.

7. Click **Play** (▶) to listen to the playlist.

TIPS

Can I add items to an existing playlist?
Yes, there are a couple of methods you can use. The first method is to repeat step **4** for any other items you want to add to the playlist. The second method is to locate the song you want to add, right-click the song, click **Add to**, and then click the name of the playlist in the menu that appears.

Why does Media Player show only my most recently created playlists in the navigation pane?
By default, Media Player's navigation pane is configured to show only the five most recent playlists. If you prefer to see all your playlists, right-click any item in the navigation pane and then click **Customize navigation pane**. In the Customize Navigation Pane dialog box, click the **All** check box that appears under the **Playlists** branch (☐ changes to ☑).

Burn Music Files to a CD

You can copy, or *burn*, music files from your computer onto a CD. Burning CDs is a great way to create customized CDs that you can listen to on the computer or in a portable device that plays CDs.

You can burn music files from within the Windows Media Player window. The easiest way to do this is to create a playlist of the songs you want to burn to the CD. You then organize the playlist by sorting the tracks in the order you want to hear them.

To burn music files to a CD, your PC must have a recordable optical drive.

Burn Music Files to a CD

1. Insert a blank CD into your computer's recordable optical drive.
2. Click the **Burn** tab.

Ⓐ The Burn list appears.

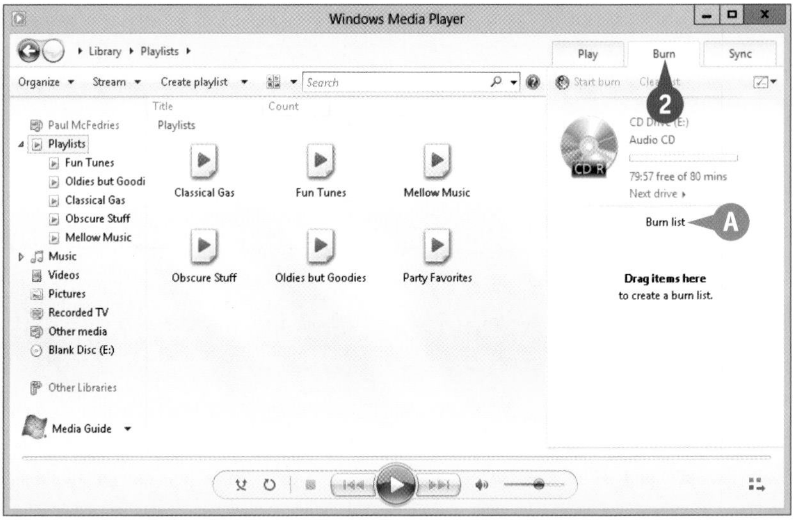

3. Click and drag items from the library and drop them inside the Burn list.

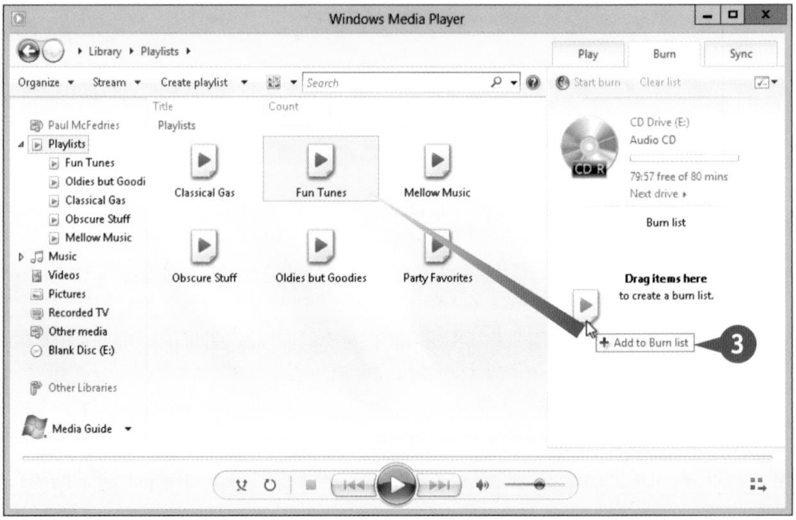

Ⓑ Windows Media Player adds the files to the Burn list.

Ⓒ Windows Media Player updates the approximate time remaining on the disc.

❹ Repeat step **3** to add more files to the Burn list.

❺ Click **Start burn**.

Windows Media Player converts the files to CD tracks and copies them to the CD.

Ⓓ The Burn tab shows the progress of the burn.

Note: When the recording is complete, Windows Media Player automatically ejects the disc. Do not attempt to eject the disc yourself before the burn is finished.

TIPS

Do I have to burn the songs in the order they appear in the list?

No, Media Player offers several options for rearranging the tracks before burning. Perhaps the easiest method is to click and drag a track and then drop it in the list location you prefer. You can also click **Burn options** (☑▾), click either **Shuffle list** or **Sort list by**, and then click a sort order.

What happens if I have more music than can fit on a single disc?

You can still add all the music you want to burn to the Burn list. Windows Media Player fills the first disc and then starts on a second disk (look for Disc 2 in the Burn list). After the program finishes burning the first disc, it prompts you to insert the next one.

Connect Your PC and Your Home Theater

With the appropriate hardware, you can connect your computer to your television and stereo system. You can then use the Media Center program to display DVDs and pictures on your TV and play music on your stereo.

In some cases, you can also attach a television cable to your computer and then watch and record TV shows on your PC. If you do not want to have a computer in the same room as your TV, there are other devices you can use to beam the signal from a remote PC and display it on the TV.

TV Connection

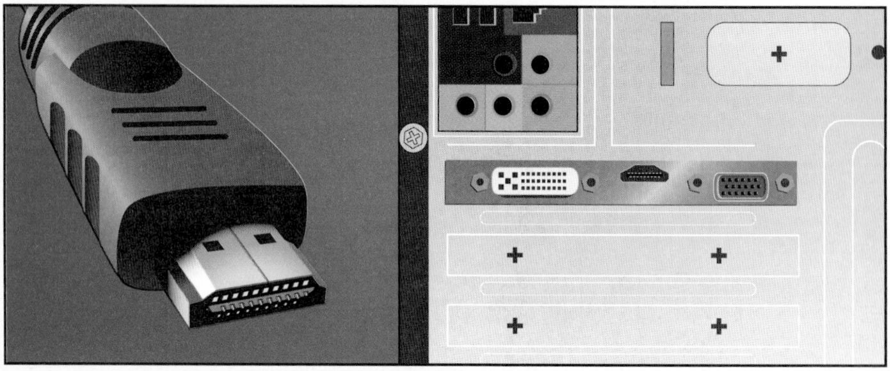

To view computer-based DVDs, images, and video files on your TV, run an HDMI cable from the HDMI output port on the back of your computer's video card to the HDMI input port on the back of your TV. (Older computers and TVs may require an S-Video connection, instead.)

Stereo Connection

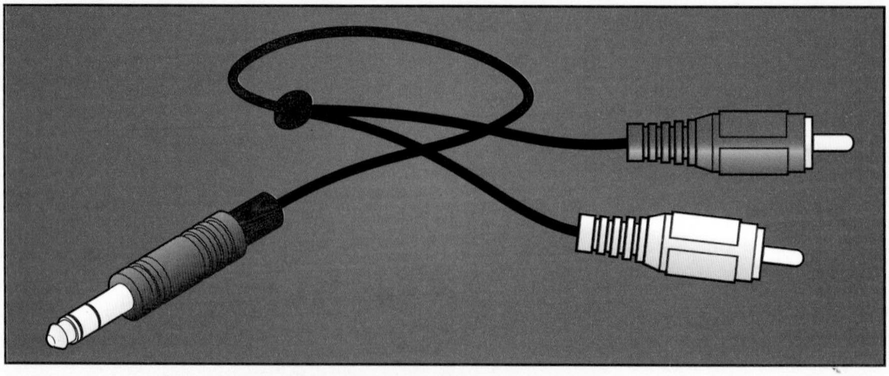

To listen to computer-based music and sound files through your stereo system, you need a Y-adapter cable, which has a single stereo plug on one end and two RCA-style plugs (one red and one white) on the other. Connect the single stereo plug to the green port in the back of your computer's sound card, and the two RCA plugs to the corresponding input jacks on the back of your stereo receiver.

TV-to-PC

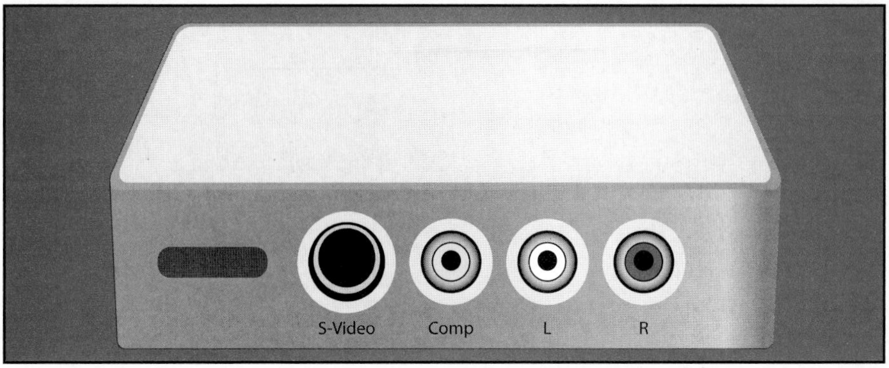

A *TV tuner* is an internal or external device that captures an incoming TV signal. You can use it to watch and record TV on your computer. Attach a TV cable to the TV tuner's cable jack. Alternatively, you can run RCA cables or an S-Video cable from your TV's output jacks (if it has them) to the corresponding ports on the TV tuner.

Remote Control

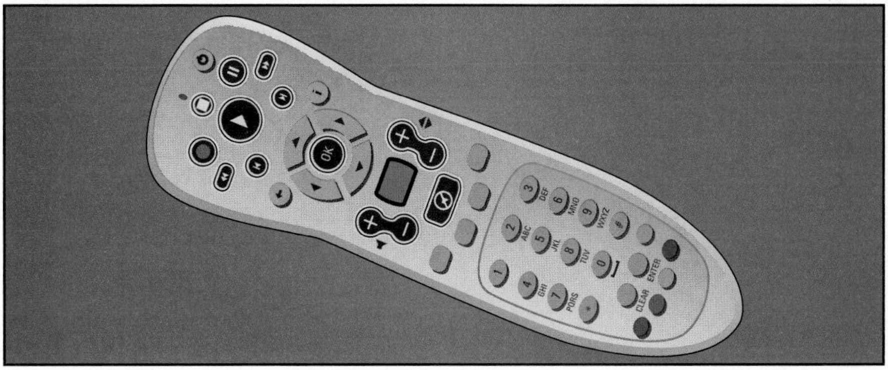

You can purchase a special remote control that enables you to use the Media Center program on your TV. This enables you to use Media Center from your couch because you do not need to use the computer directly. For those times when you must use the computer, you can also add a wireless keyboard and mouse to your system.

Media Extender

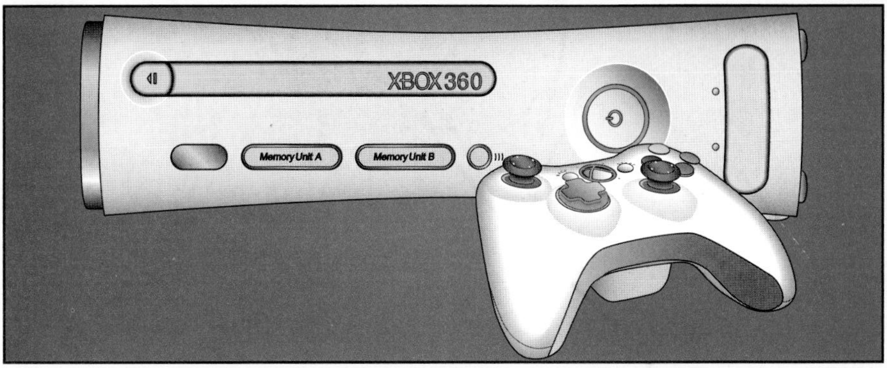

A *media extender* is a wireless device that takes the signal from a remote PC and relays it to your TV. This saves you from having a PC in the same room as your TV. An example of a media extender is the Xbox 360 gaming console.

What You Can Do with Media Center

The Media Center program is designed to be a hub around which you can view and work with all the media files on your computer as well as view and work with your TV and stereo system.

To get the most out of Media Center, you need to be familiar with the wide variety of things you can do with the program, including playing DVDs and music, showing images, accessing radio stations online, and recording TV shows.

Play DVDs

If your computer has a DVD drive, you can insert a DVD movie and then start the movie for playback on your computer monitor or on your TV.

Play Music

Media Center picks up the music files in your Music folder. You can view the music by title, artist, or genre, edit file data, and delete files. You also have many options for playing music, including shuffle and repeat.

View Pictures and Videos

Media Center picks up the images you have in your Pictures folder. You can manipulate the images and then display them in a slide show using animated transitions. You can also listen to music during the slide show. Media Center also locates the video files on your PC so that you can play them through the video library.

Listen to Internet Audio

Media Center offers links to a number of online sites that offer music, news, sports, and other audio content. You can also listen to some Internet-based radio stations.

Watch Live TV

Media Center can pick up a TV signal and display it on your PC. Media Center offers a program guide that enables you to choose the show you want to watch. You can also use Media Center to watch TV shows via the Internet.

Record TV

You can use Media Center as a *digital video recorder*, which enables you to record TV programs to your hard drive as you watch them, or at scheduled times. You can also pause, rewind, and fast-forward live TV, as well as watch instant replays.

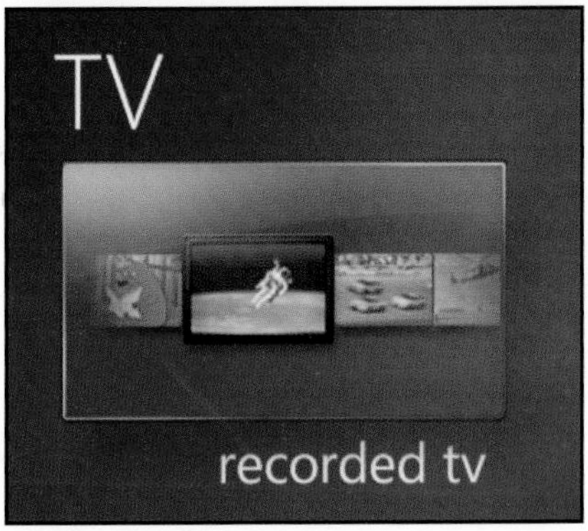

Open and Close Media Center

Media Center is a desktop app that comes with Windows 8. To begin using Media Center, you must first learn how to find and open the Media Center window. You learn how to navigate the Media Center window in the next section.

When you finish using the program, you can close the Media Center window to reduce memory usage and free up computer processing power.

Open and Close Media Center

1. On the Start screen, type **media center**.
2. Click **Windows Media Center**.

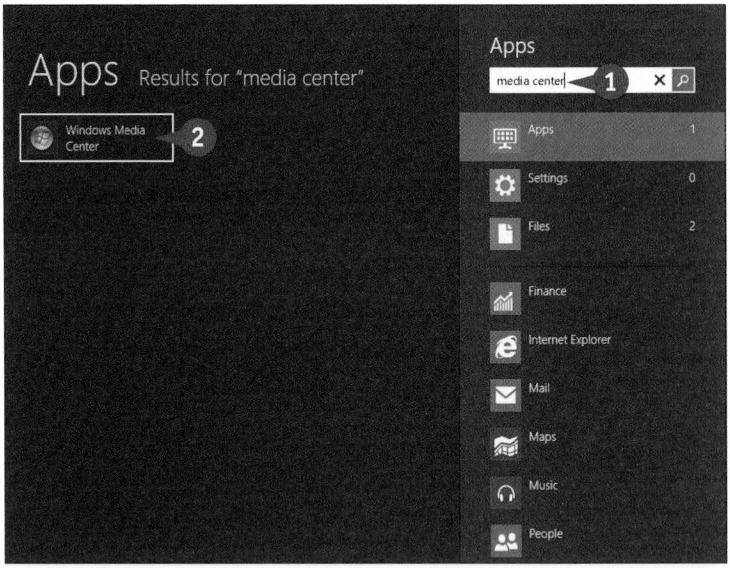

The Media Center window appears.

A. The first time you start Media Center, you must run through a set of screens designed to configure the program. Click **Continue** and then click **Express.**

3. When you have finished with Media Center, click the **Close** button (×) to close the window.

The Media Center window closes.

Navigate the Media Center Window

Familiarizing yourself with the various elements of the Media Center window is a good idea so that you can easily navigate and activate elements when you are ready to play audio files or view videos and DVDs.

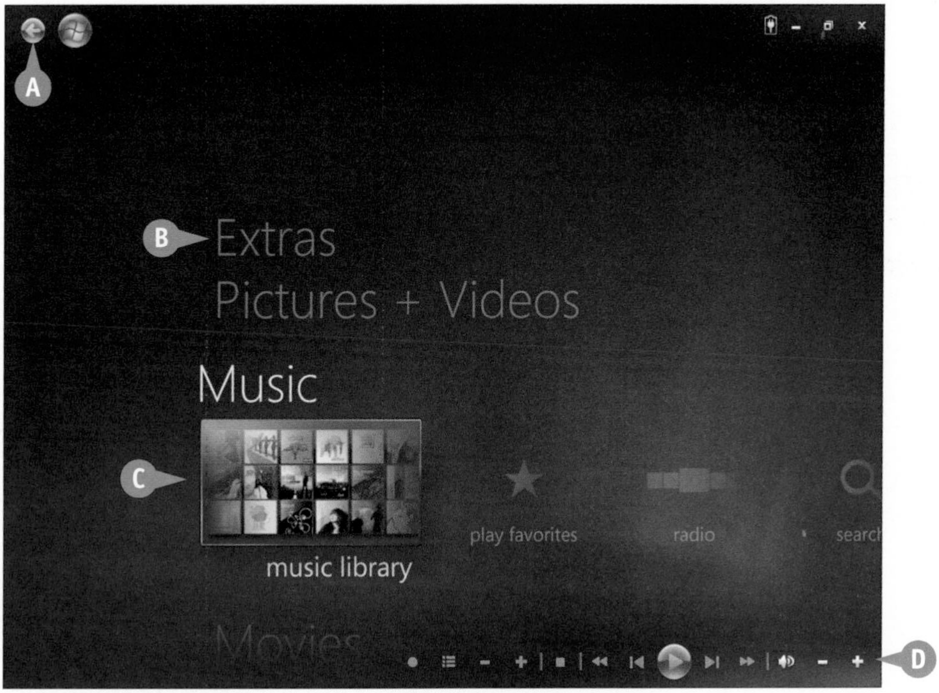

A Back

Click this button to return to the previous Media Center screen.

B Main Menu

These items represent the main Media Center features.

C Tasks

Each main menu item has one or more tasks that you can perform.

D Playback Controls

These buttons control how a DVD or music file plays, and they enable you to make adjustments to the sound.

Run a Media Center Slide Show

You can use Media Center to run a slide show of images in your Pictures folder. After you start the slide show, the feature automatically advances and displays each image in the folder as a slide.

Each image is displayed for 12 seconds, but you can customize the duration of each image. To add visual interest, Media Center displays each picture using *pan-and-zoom*, a technique that simultaneously moves the picture across the screen and zooms in on the picture. Media Center also uses an animated transition between images.

Run a Media Center Slide Show

1. In Media Center, navigate to the Pictures + Videos section.
2. Click **picture library**.

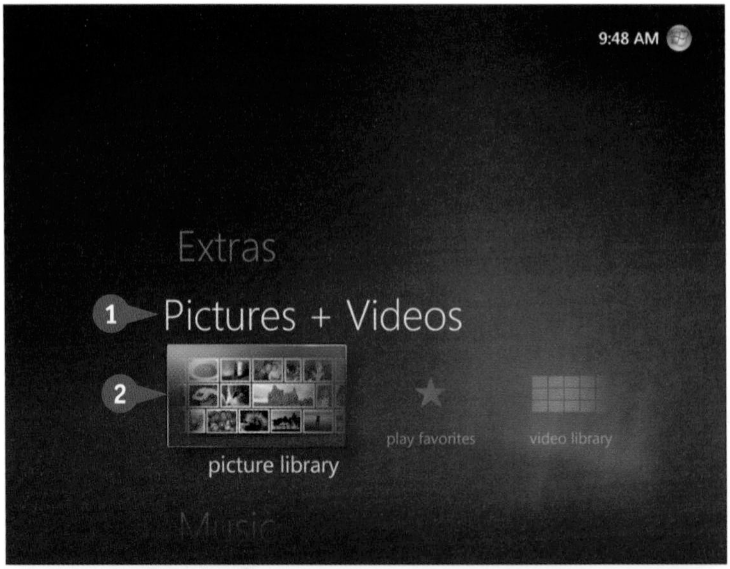

The Media Center picture library appears.

3. Click **play slide show**.

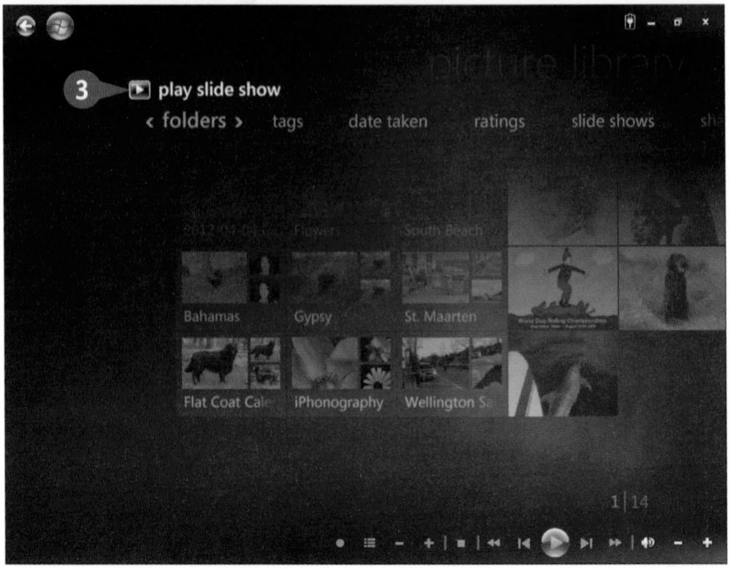

The slide show begins.

4. Click the **Next** button (▶) to advance to the next picture.
5. Click the **Previous** button (◀) to return to the previous picture.
6. Click the **Pause** button (⏸) to pause the slide show.

Note: If you do not see the playback controls, click the screen.

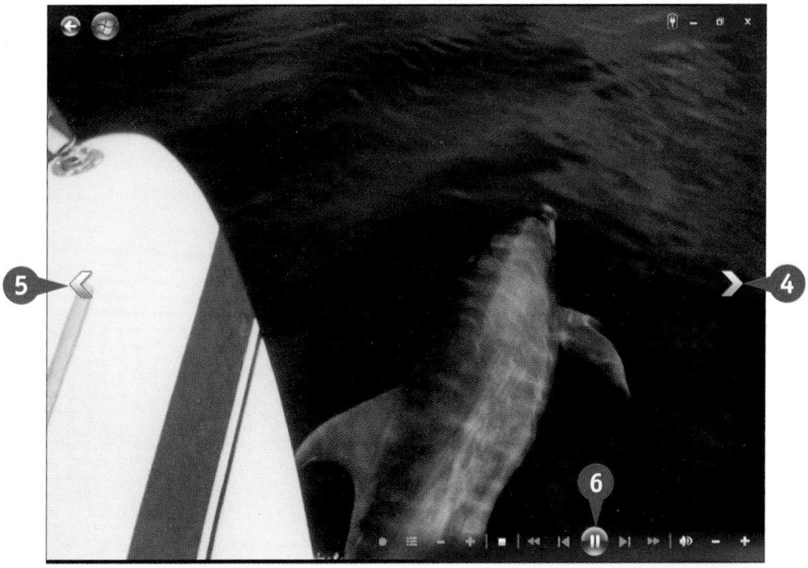

7. Click the **Play** button (▶) to resume the slide show.
8. Click the **Stop** button (■) to stop the slide show.

TIPS

Can I display the slide show images in random order?
Yes, in the main Media Center menu, navigate to **Tools** and then click **settings**. Click **Pictures** to display the picture settings. Click **Show pictures in random order** (☐ changes to ☑). If you also want to see the name of the each picture and the date it was created, click **Show picture information** (☐ changes to ☑). Click **Save**.

How do I change the amount of time that Media Center displays each image?
In the main Media Center menu, navigate to **Tasks** and then click **settings**. Click **Pictures** and then use the **Show pictures for** controls to set the time each image is displayed: click **plus** (+) to increase the time; click **minus** (–) to decrease the time. Click **Save** when you are done.

Play a DVD

You can use Windows Media Center to play DVDs. Windows Media Center also enables you to watch any multimedia items stored on a DVD, such as movies and video footage.

By default, Windows 8 is not set up to start playing DVDs automatically. When you insert your first DVD, you can configure Windows 8 to launch Media Center and automatically play the DVD, which then displays its main menu. See the section "Navigate a DVD" to learn how to control DVD playback.

To play DVDs, your PC must have an optical drive capable of reading DVD discs.

Play a DVD

Configure Windows 8 to Play DVDs Automatically

1. Insert a DVD into your computer's DVD drive.

   After a few moments, Windows 8 displays a notification for the DVD.

2. Click the notification.

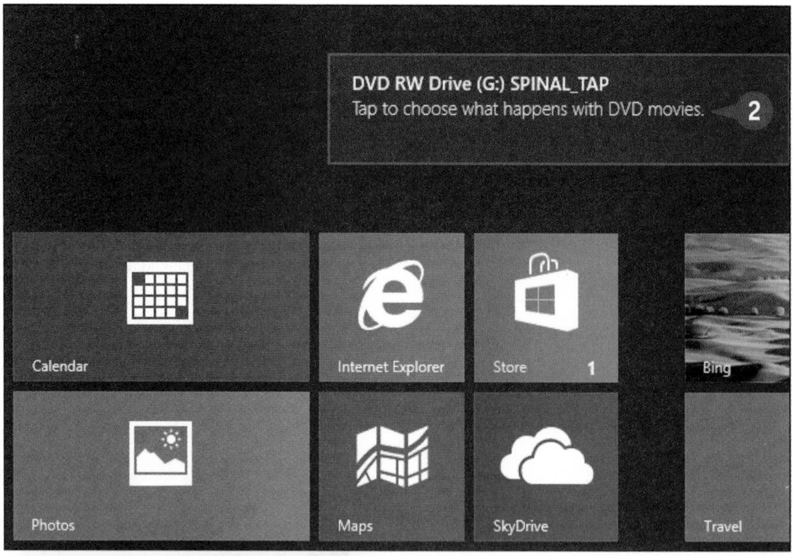

   Windows 8 displays a list of actions you can take whenever you insert a DVD.

3. Click **Play DVD movie.**

   From now on, whenever you insert a DVD, Media Center automatically begins playing the DVD.

Note: If the DVD does not start, open Media Center, click **Movies**, and then click **play dvd**.

Display the DVD Controls

1. Position the mouse within the DVD window.

A. Media Player displays the playback controls.

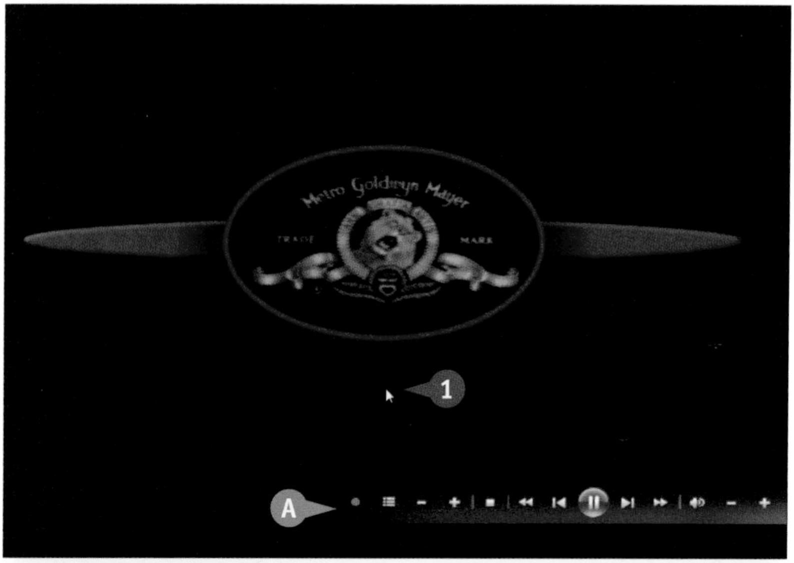

Select a DVD Feature

B. After a few moments, Media Center displays the DVD's main menu.

DVD menu items can vary in appearance and use different layouts.

1. Click the menu item or feature you want to access.

TIP

Can I restrict the DVDs my kids watch?

Yes. First, set up your kids with Standard user accounts (Chapter 11). Then, in Windows Media Player:

1. Click **Tasks** and then click **settings**.
2. Click **General**.
3. Click **Parental Controls**.
4. Type a 4-digit access code and then repeat the code.
5. Click **Movie/DVD Ratings**.
6. Click **Turn on movie blocking** (☐ changes to ☑).
7. In the Maximum Allowed Movie Rating list, click plus (+) or minus (–) to select the maximum rating you want.
8. Click **Save**.

Navigate a DVD

You can control how a DVD plays by using the various navigation controls in the Windows Media Player window. The window includes volume and playback controls. You can also navigate to different scenes using the list of tracks in the Playlist pane. All scenes, or tracks, stem from a root menu that directs you to the DVD's contents.

Throughout this section, note that you must position the mouse ↖ within the DVD window to display the playback controls.

Navigate a DVD

Stop and Start a DVD

1. Click the **Stop** button (■).

   Windows Media Player stops the DVD playback.

2. Click the **Play** button (▶).

   Windows Media Player restarts the playback from the beginning.

   You can also click the **Pause** button (⏸) to pause the playback if you want to resume playing in the same scene.

Navigate Scenes

1. Click the **Previous** button (⏮).

   Windows Media Player jumps to the previous scene.

2. Click the **Next** button (⏭).

   Windows Media Player jumps to the next scene.

Ⓐ You can also rewind or fast-forward the DVD by clicking and dragging the **Seek** slider.

Return to the Root Menu

1. Right-click the **screen**.
2. Click **controls**.
3. Click **Root Menu**.

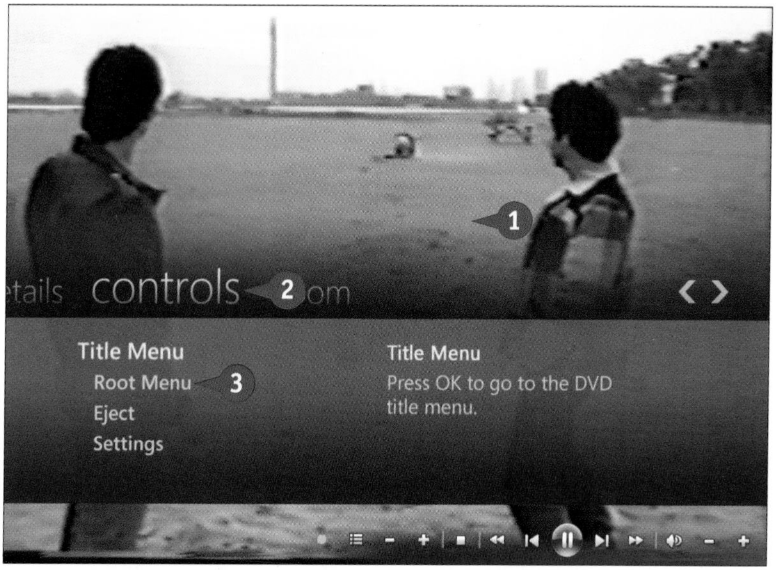

The DVD's opening menu appears in the Windows Media Player window.

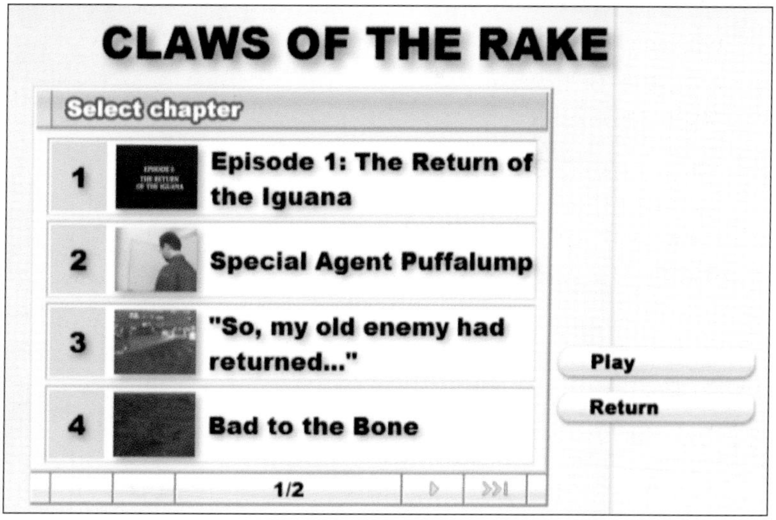

TIPS

What is a root menu?

The *root menu* is the opening menu of a DVD, and it typically displays links to the various segments, features, or clips on the DVD. You can return to the root menu at any time to access other DVD elements. In full-screen view, you can quickly access the root menu with a shortcut menu. Right-click over the DVD screen, click **DVD features**, and then click **Root menu**.

Can I change the language or display subtitles?

Yes, as long as your DVD offers multiple languages or subtitles you can activate these features. To choose a different language, right-click the playback screen, scroll to the right and click **language**, and then click the language you want to use. To activate subtitles, right-click the screen, scroll to the right and click **subtitles**, and then click the subtitle language you want to see.

CHAPTER 9

Creating and Editing Documents

To get productive with Windows 8, you need to know how to work with documents. In this chapter, you learn what documents are, and you learn how to create, save, open, edit, and print documents.

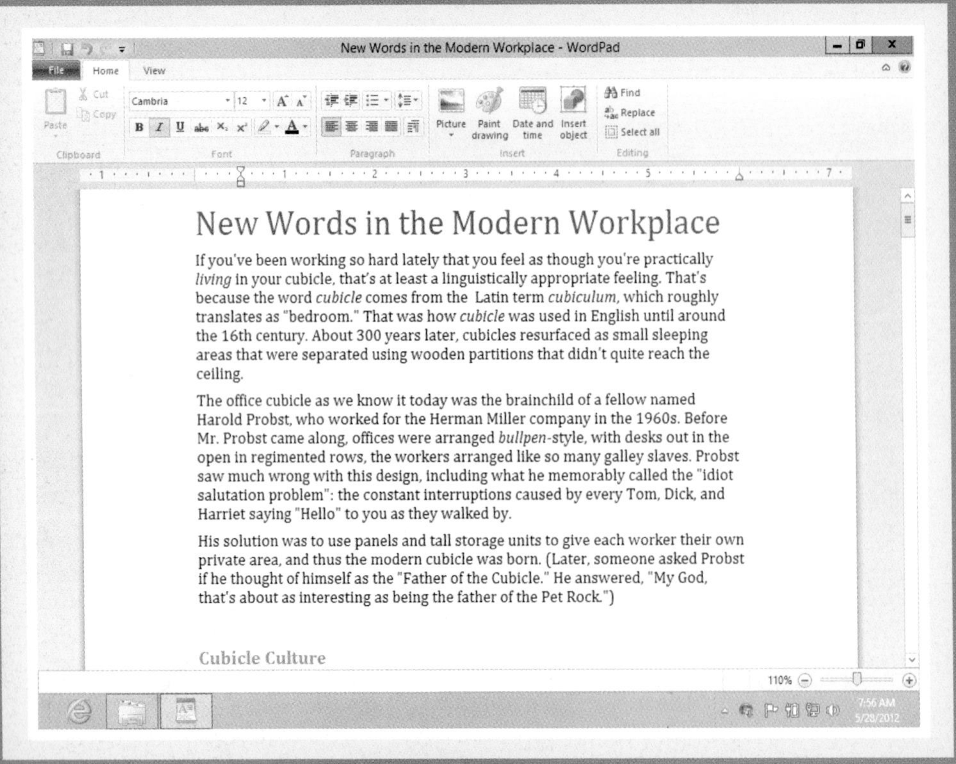

New Words in the Modern Workplace - WordPad
New Words in the Modern Workplace
If you've been working so hard lately that you feel as though you're practically living in your cubicle, that's at least a linguistically appropriate feeling. That's because the word cubicle comes from the Latin term cubiculum, which roughly translates as "bedroom." That was how cubicle was used in English until around the 16th century. About 300 years later, cubicles resurfaced as small sleeping areas that were separated using wooden partitions that didn't quite reach the ceiling.
The office cubicle as we know it today was the brainchild of a fellow named Harold Probst, who worked for the Herman Miller company in the 1960s. Before Mr. Probst came along, offices were arranged bullpen-style, with desks out in the open in regimented rows, the workers arranged like so many galley slaves. Probst saw much wrong with this design, including what he memorably called the "idiot salutation problem": the constant interruptions caused by every Tom, Dick, and Harriet saying "Hello" to you as they walked by.
His solution was to use panels and tall storage units to give each worker their own private area, and thus the modern cubicle was born. (Later, someone asked Probst if he thought of himself as the "Father of the Cubicle." He answered, "My God, that's about as interesting as being the father of the Pet Rock.")
Cubicle Culture

Understanding Documents

Documents are files that you create or edit yourself. The four examples shown here are the basic document types that you can create using the programs that come with Windows 8.

Text Document

A text document is one that includes only the characters that you see on your keyboard, plus a few others (see the "Insert Special Symbols" section in this chapter). A text document contains no special formatting, such as colored text or bold formatting, although you can change the font. In Windows 8 you normally use the Notepad program to create text documents (although you can also use WordPad).

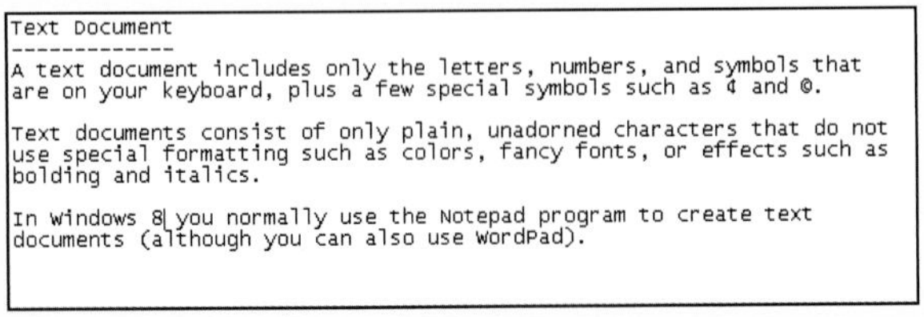
Text Document

A text document includes only the letters, numbers, and symbols that are on your keyboard, plus a few special symbols such as ¢ and ©.

Text documents consist of only plain, unadorned characters that do not use special formatting such as colors, fancy fonts, or effects such as bolding and italics.

In Windows 8 you normally use the Notepad program to create text documents (although you can also use WordPad).

Word Processing Document

A word processing document contains text and other symbols, but you can format those characters to improve the look of the document. For example, you can change the size, color, and typeface, and you can make words bold or italic. In Windows 8, you use the WordPad program to create word processing — or Rich Text Format — documents.

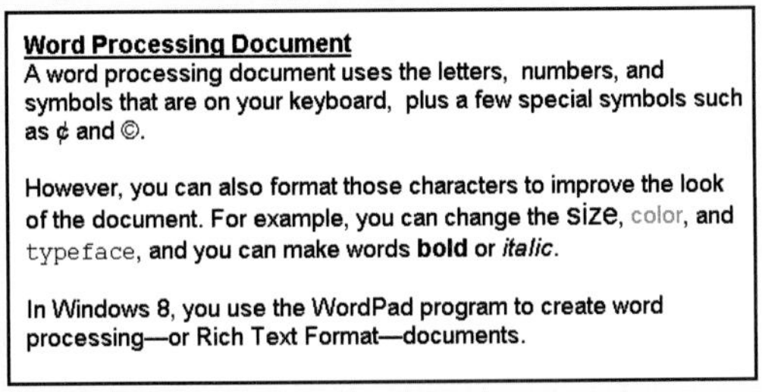
Word Processing Document
A word processing document uses the letters, numbers, and symbols that are on your keyboard, plus a few special symbols such as ¢ and ©.

However, you can also format those characters to improve the look of the document. For example, you can change the size, color, and typeface, and you can make words **bold** or *italic*.

In Windows 8, you use the WordPad program to create word processing—or Rich Text Format—documents.

Drawing

A drawing in this context is a digital image you create using special "tools" that create lines, boxes, polygons, special effects, and free-form shapes. In Windows 8, you use the Paint program to create drawings.

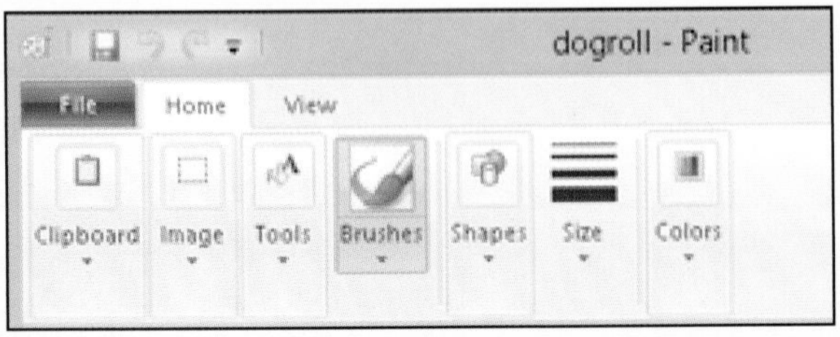

E-Mail Message

An e-mail message is a document that you send to another person via the Internet. Most e-mail messages use plain text, but some programs support formatted text, images, and other effects. In Windows 8, you can create and send e-mail messages using either the Mail Windows 8 app (see Chapter 4) or the Mail desktop program (see Chapter 6).

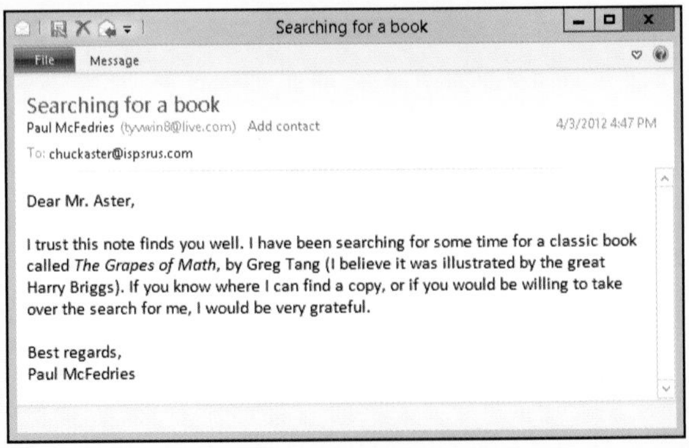
Searching for a book
File Message

Searching for a book
Paul McFedries (tyvwin8@live.com) Add contact 4/3/2012 4:47 PM
To: chuckaster@ispsrus.com

Dear Mr. Aster,

I trust this note finds you well. I have been searching for some time for a classic book called *The Grapes of Math*, by Greg Tang (I believe it was illustrated by the great Harry Briggs). If you know where I can find a copy, or if you would be willing to take over the search for me, I would be very grateful.

Best regards,
Paul McFedries

Create a Document

When you are ready to create something using Windows 8, in most cases you begin by launching a program and then using that program to create a new document to hold your work.

Many Windows 8 programs (such as WordPad and Paint) create a new document for you automatically when you begin the program. However, you can also use these programs to create another new document after you have started the program.

Create a Document

1. Start the program you want to work with.
2. Click **File**.
3. Click **New**.

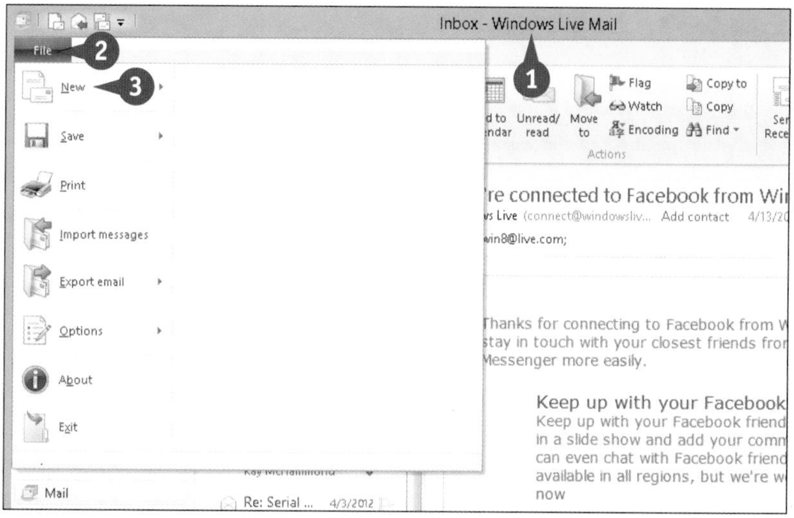

A. If the program supports more than one type of file, the program asks which type you want to create.

Note: Some programs display a dialog box with a list of document types.

4. Click the document type you want.

   The program creates the new document.

Note: In most programs, you can also press Ctrl+N to create a new document.

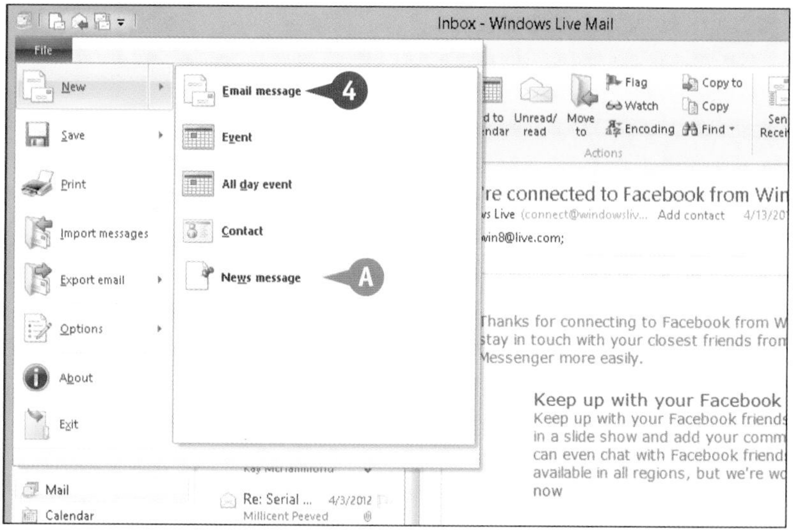

Save a Document

After you create a document and make any changes to it, you can save the document to preserve your work.

When you work on a document, Windows 8 stores the changes in your computer's memory. However, Windows erases the contents of your PC's memory each time you shut down or restart the computer. This means that the changes you have made to your document are lost when you turn off or restart your PC.

Saving the document preserves your changes on your computer's hard drive.

Save a Document

1. Click **File**.
2. Click **Save**.

Note: In most programs, you can also press Ctrl + S or click the **Save** button ( ).

Note: If you saved the document previously, your changes are now preserved. You do not need to follow the rest of the steps in this section.

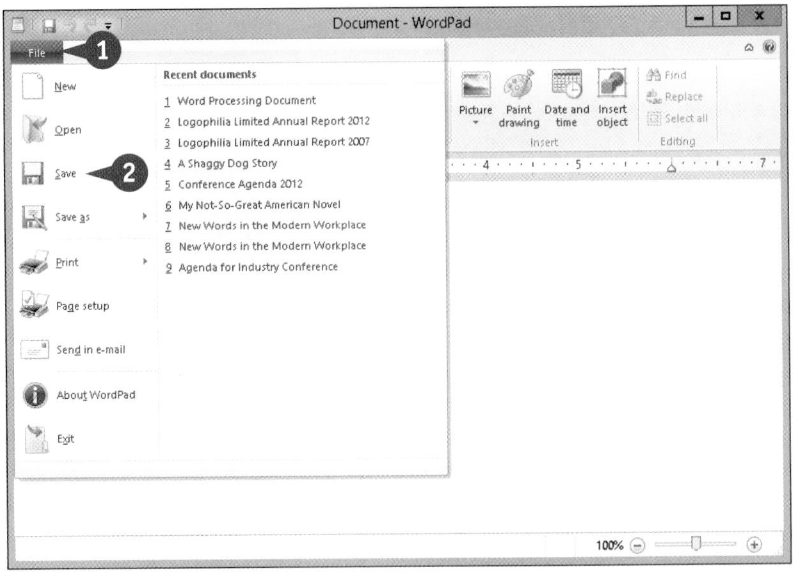

If this is a new document that you have never saved before, the Save As dialog box appears.

3. Click **Documents**.

Note: In most programs, the Documents library is selected automatically when you save a document.

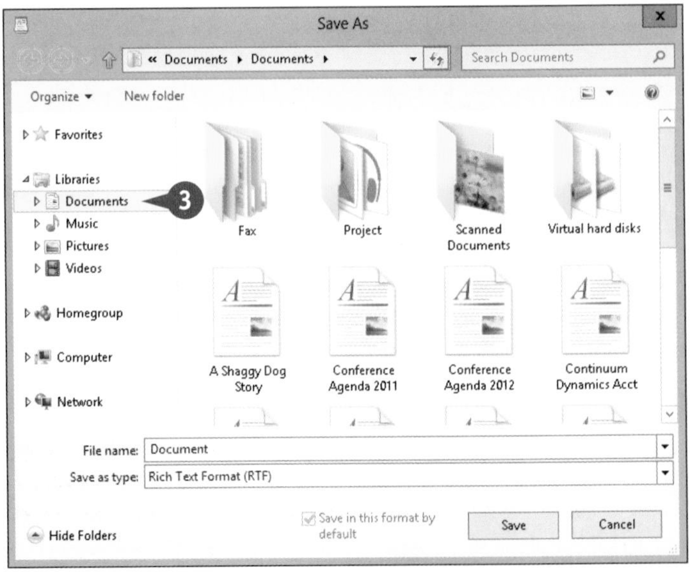

Ⓐ Windows 8 opens the Documents library.

4. Click in the File Name text box and type the name you want to use for the document.

Note: The name you type can be up to 255 characters long, but it cannot include the following characters: < > , ? : " \ *.

5. Click **Save**.

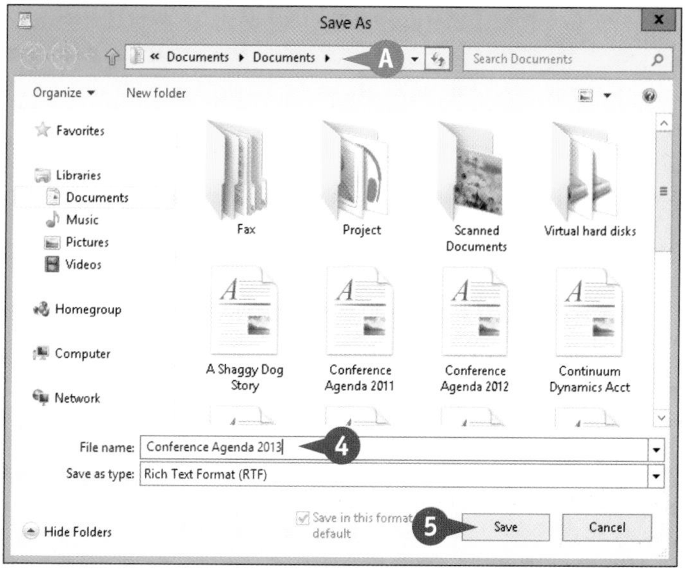

Ⓑ The filename you typed appears in the program's title bar.

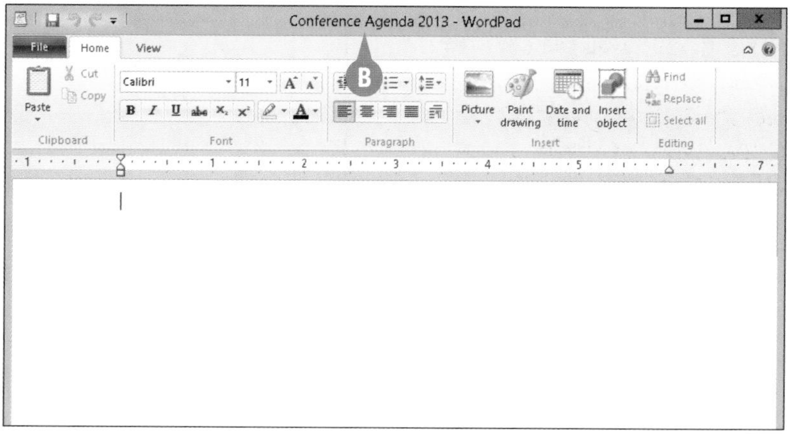

TIPS

Can I create different types of documents in a program?

Yes, in most programs. With WordPad, for example, you can create both word processing documents and text documents. However, a program such as Notepad supports only text documents. If the program supports multiple document types, the Save As dialog box includes a drop-down list named Save As Type (or something similar). Use that list to choose the document type you want.

Do I have to save all my files to the Documents library?

No, not necessarily. The Documents library is a convenient place because having everything in one location makes it easier to find your files. However, if you have several related files, you can create a subfolder within Documents and use it to store the related files. In the Save As dialog box, click **New folder**, type the name of the folder, press Enter, double-click the new folder, and then follow steps **4** and **5**.

Open a Document

To work with a document that you have saved in the past, you need to open the document in the program that you used to create it.

When you save a document, you save its contents to your PC's hard drive, and those contents are stored in a separate file. When you open the document using the same application that you used to save it, Windows loads the file's contents into memory and displays the document in the application. You can then view or edit the document as needed.

Open a Document

1. Start the program you want to work with.
2. Click **File**.

   A. If you see the document you want in a list of the most recently used documents on the File menu, click the name to open it. You can skip the rest of the steps in this section.

3. Click **Open**.

Note: In most programs, you can also press Ctrl+O or click the **Open** button ( ).

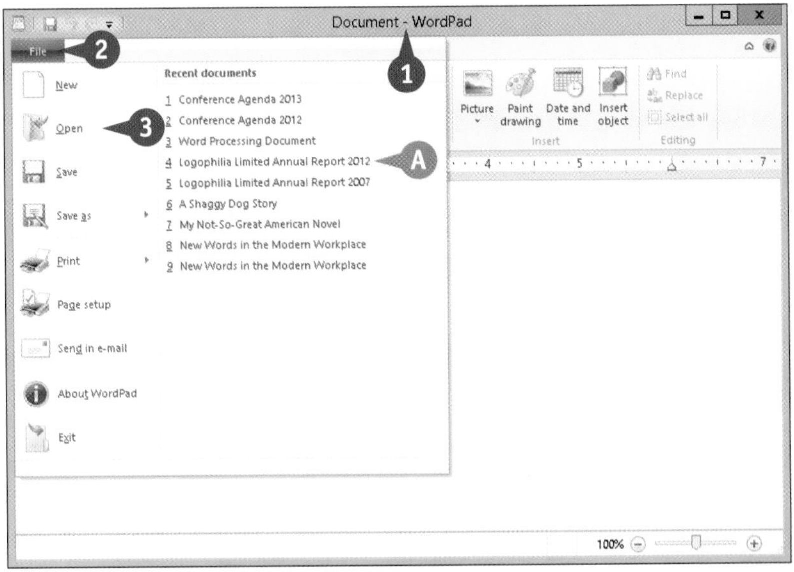

The Open dialog box appears.

4. Click **Documents**.

Note: In most programs, the Documents library is selected automatically when you open a document.

   B. If you want to open the document from some other folder, click here, click your username, and then double-click the folder.

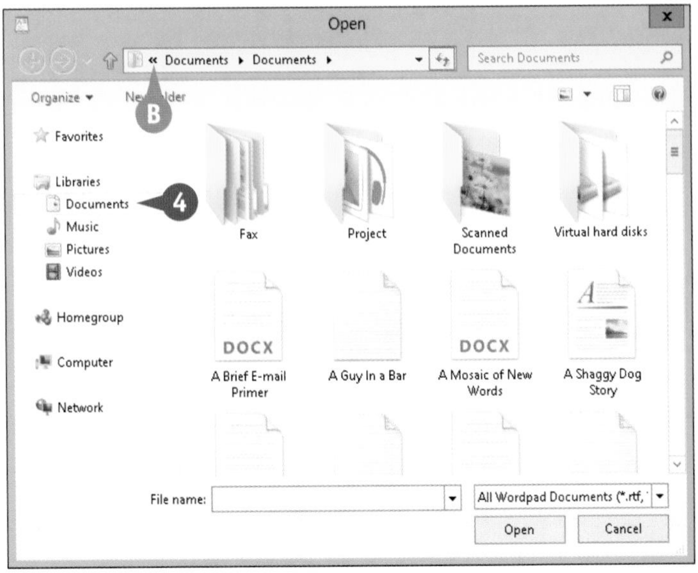

Ⓒ Windows 8 opens the Documents library.

5 Click the document name.

6 Click **Open**.

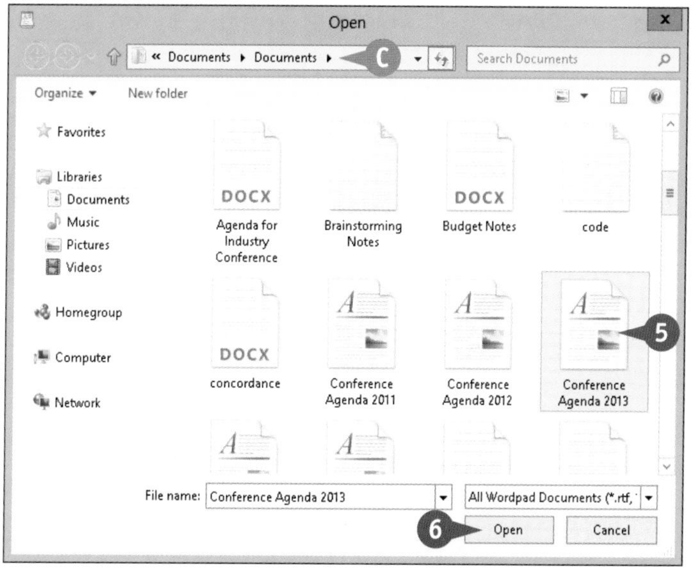

Ⓓ The document appears in the program window.

TIPS

Is there a more direct way to open a document?

Yes, there is. You do not always need to open the program first. Instead, open the folder that contains the document and then double-click the document. Windows 8 automatically launches the program and opens the document.

Is there a quick way to locate a document?

Yes, Windows 8 offers a file search feature, which is handy if your Documents library contains many files. On the Start screen, press ⊞+F to open the Files search pane. (On a tablet, swipe from the right edge, tap **Search**, and then tap **Files**.) Type some or all of the document's filename and then double-click the document in the search results.

Edit Document Text

When you work with a character-based file, such as a text or word processing document or an e-mail message, you need to know the basic techniques for editing, selecting, copying, and moving text.

Text you enter into a document is rarely perfect the first time through. The text likely contains errors that require correcting, or words, sentences, or paragraphs that appear in the wrong place.

To get your document text the way you want it, you need to know how to edit text, including deleting characters, selecting the text you want to work with, and copying and moving text.

Edit Document Text

Delete Characters

1. Click immediately to the left of the first character you want to delete.

   A. The cursor appears before the character.

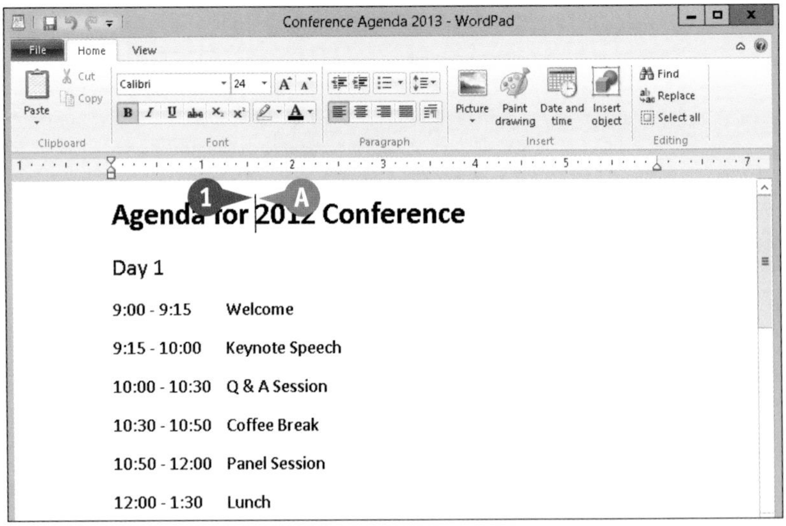

2. Press Delete until you have deleted all the characters you want.

Note: An alternative method is to click immediately to the right of the last character you want to delete and then press Backspace until you have deleted all the characters you want.

Note: If you make a mistake, immediately press Ctrl+Z or click the **Undo** button (↶). Alternatively, click **Edit**, and then click **Undo**.

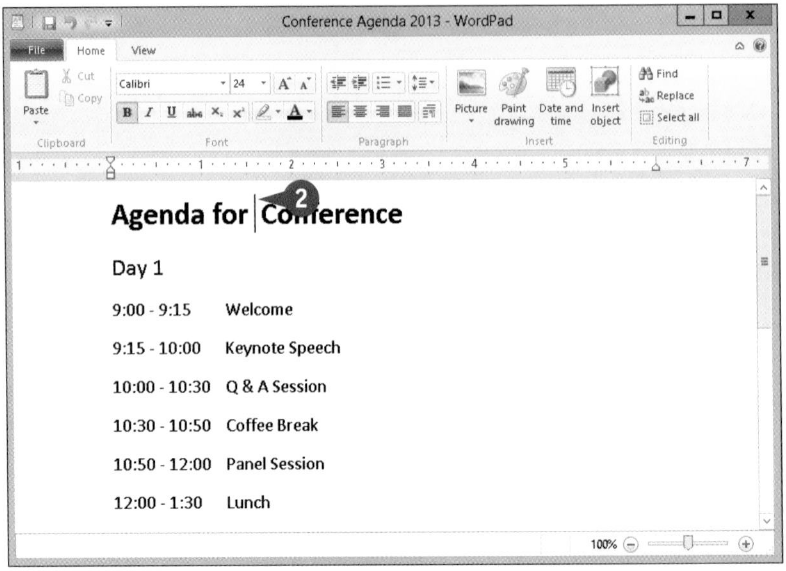

Select Text for Editing

1 Click and drag across the text you want to select.

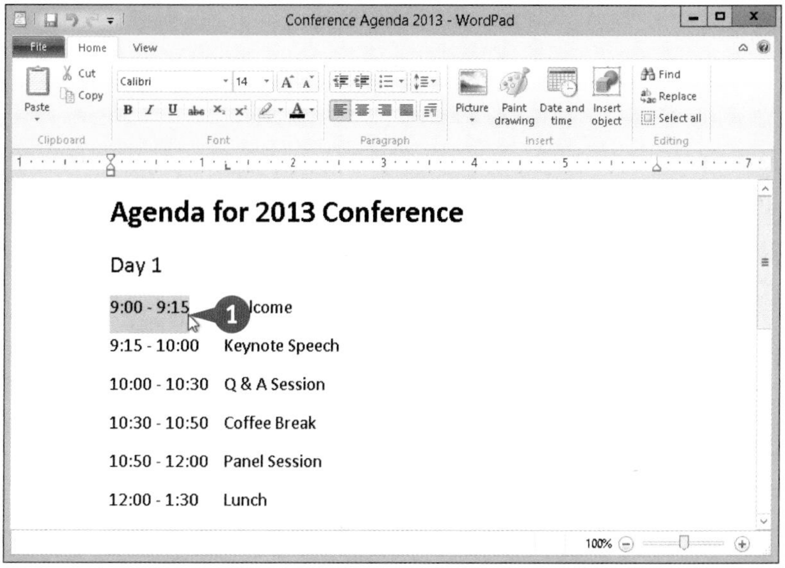

2 Release the mouse button.

B The program highlights the selected text.

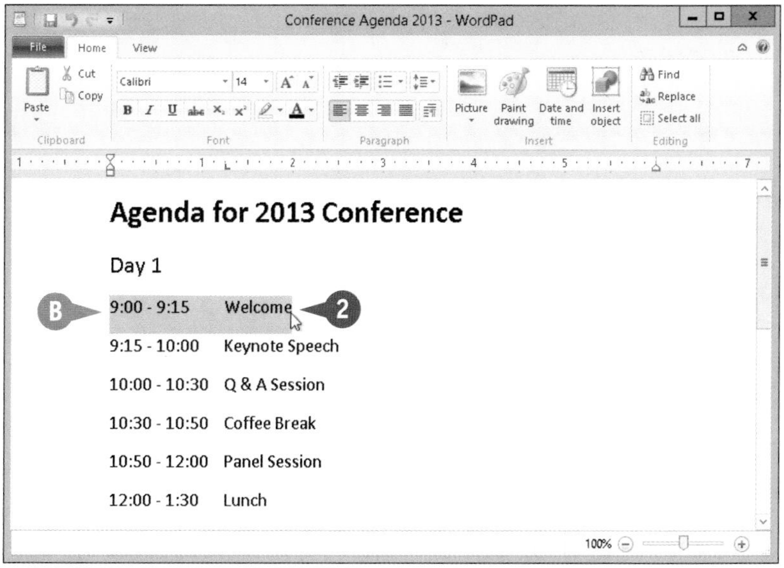

TIP

Are there any shortcut methods I can use to select text in WordPad?

Yes. Here are the most useful ones:

- Click in the whitespace to the left of a line to select the line.
- Double-click a word to select it.
- Triple-click inside a paragraph to select it.
- Press Ctrl + A to select the entire document.
- For a long selection, click to the left of the first character you want to select, scroll to the end of the selection using the scroll bar, press and hold Shift, and then click to the right of the last character you want to select.

continued ▶

Once you select some text, you can then copy or move the text to another location in your document.

Copying text is often a useful way to save work. For example, if you want to use the same passage of text elsewhere in the document, you can copy it instead of typing it from scratch. Similarly, if you need a similar passage in another part of the document, copy the original and then edit the copy as needed.

If you entered a passage of text in the wrong position within the document, you can fix that by moving the text to the correct location.

Edit Document Text (continued)

Copy Text

1. Select the text you want to copy.
2. Click **Copy** (📋).

Ⓐ In WordPad, you display the Clipboard options by clicking the **Home** tab.

Note: In most programs, you can also press Ctrl+C or click the **Edit** menu and then click **Copy**.

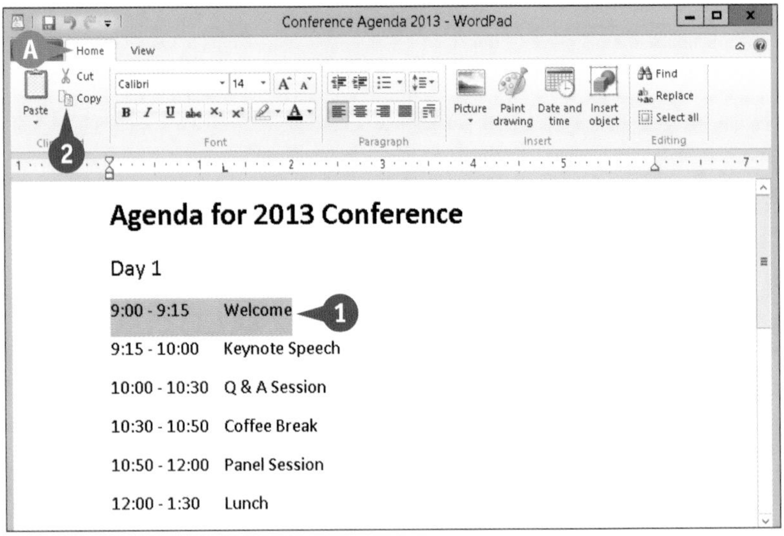

3. Click inside the document at the position where you want the copy of the text to appear.

   The cursor appears in the position you clicked.

4. Click **Paste** (📋).

Note: In most programs, you can also press Ctrl+V or click the **Edit** menu and then click **Paste**.

Ⓑ The program inserts a copy of the selected text at the cursor position.

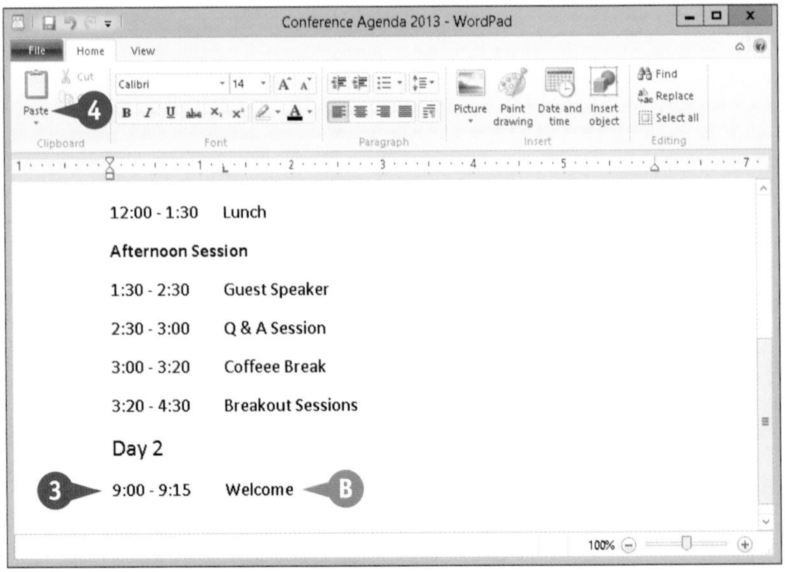

Move Text

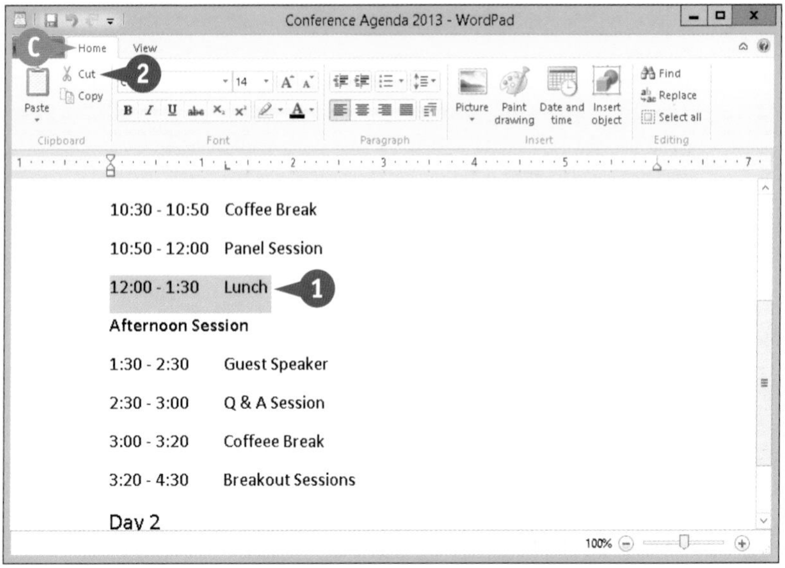

1. Select the text you want to move.
2. Click **Cut** (✂).

   C In WordPad, you display the Clipboard options by clicking the **Home** tab.

Note: In most programs, you can also press Ctrl+X or click the **Edit** menu and then click **Cut**.

The program removes the text from the document.

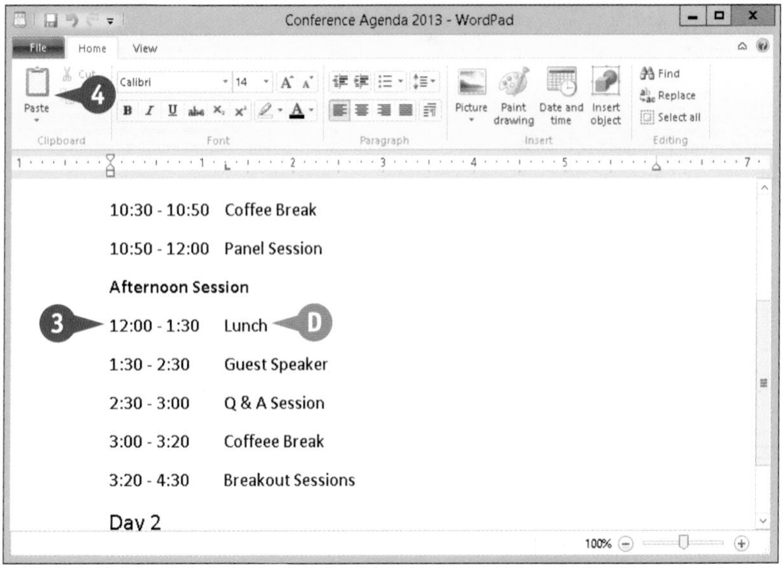

3. Click inside the document at the position where you want to move the text.

   The cursor appears at the position you clicked.

4. Click **Paste** (📋).

Note: In most programs, you can also press Ctrl+V or click the **Edit** menu and then click **Paste**.

D The program inserts the text at the cursor position.

TIP

How do I move and copy text with my mouse?

First, select the text you want to work with. To move the selected text, position the mouse over the selection, and then click and drag the text to the new position within the document.

To copy the selected text, position the mouse over the selection, press and hold Ctrl, and then click and drag the text to the desired position within the document.

Change the Text Font

When you work in a word processing document, you can add visual appeal by changing the font formatting.

The font formatting includes attributes such as the typeface, style, size, or special effects.

A *typeface* — also called a *font* — is a distinctive character design that you can apply to the selected text in a document. The *type style* refers to formatting applied to text, such as **bold** or *italics*. The *type size* refers to the height of each character, which is measured in *points*; 72 points equal one inch. *Special effects* are styles that change the appearance of the text. The most common examples are underline and ~~strikethrough~~.

Change the Text Font

1 Select the text you want to format.

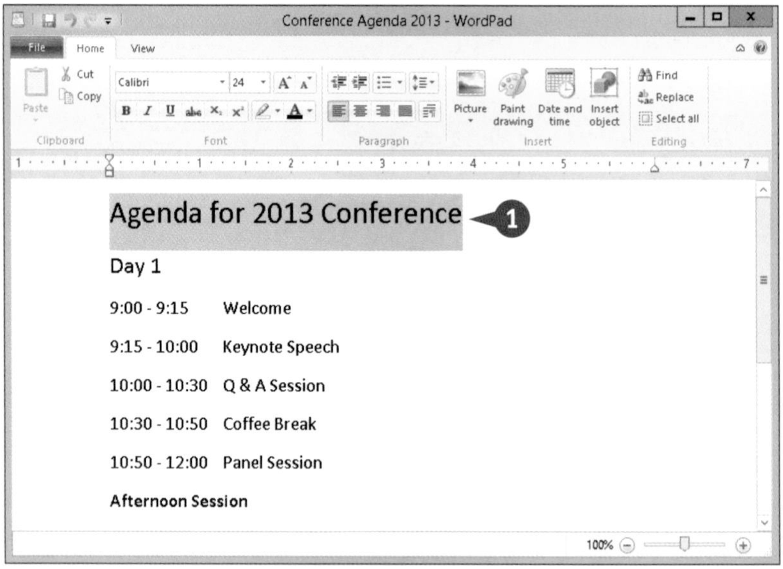

2 Display the font options.

A In WordPad, you display the font options by clicking the **Home** tab.

Note: In many other programs, you display the font options by clicking **Format** in the menu bar and then clicking the **Font** command.

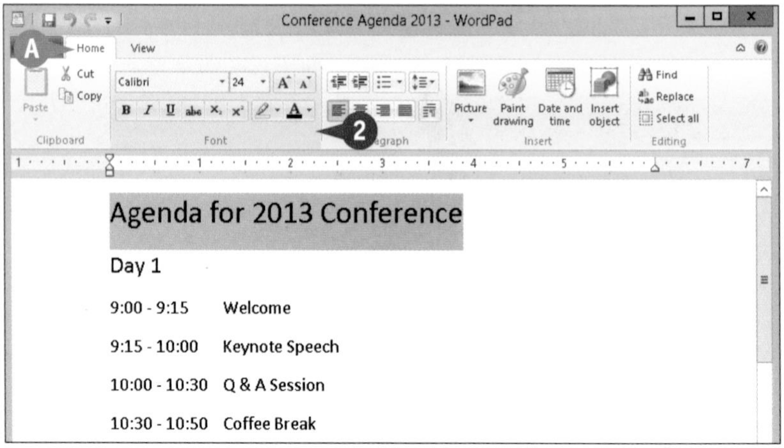

3. In the Font list, click ▾ and then click the typeface you want.
4. In the Size list, click the type size you want.

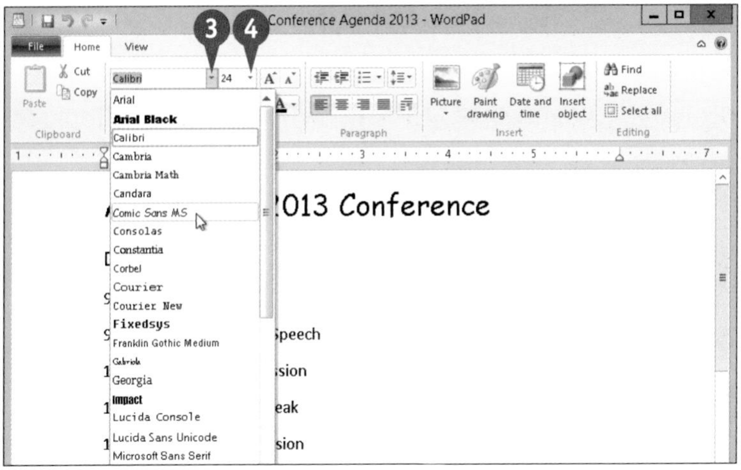

5. For bold text, click **Bold** (B).
6. For italics, click **Italic** (I).
7. For underlining, click **Underline** (U).
8. For color, click the **Font color** ▾ and then click a color.

B. The program applies the font formatting to the selected text.

Note: Here are some shortcuts that work in most programs: For bold, press Ctrl+B; for italics, press Ctrl+I; for underline, press Ctrl+U.

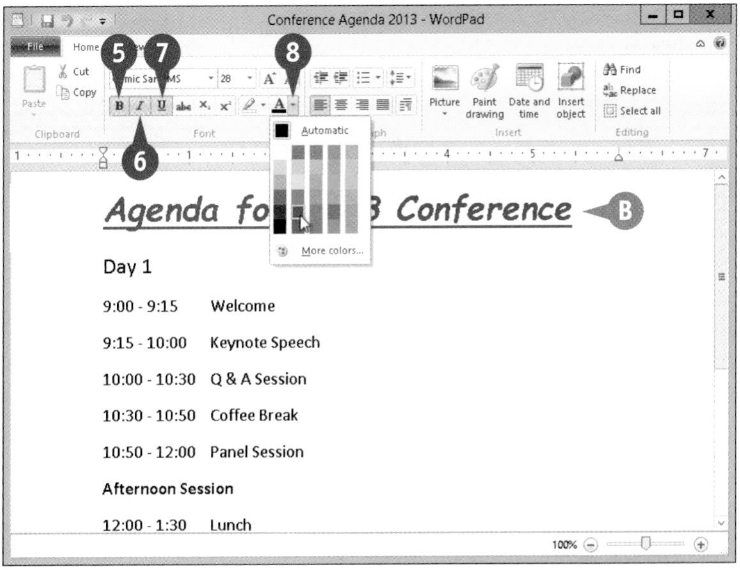

TIP

How can I make the best use of fonts in my documents?

- Do not use many different typefaces in a single document. Stick to one or at most two typefaces to avoid the "ransom note look."
- Avoid overly decorative typefaces because they are often difficult to read.
- Use bold only for document titles, subtitles, and headings.
- Use italics only to emphasize words and phrases, or for the titles of books and magazines.
- Use larger type sizes only for document titles, subtitles, and, possibly, headings.
- If you change the text color, be sure to leave enough contrast between the text and the background. In general, dark text on a light background is the easiest to read.

Find Text

In large documents, when you need to find specific text, you can save a lot of time by using the program's Find feature.

In short documents that contain only a few dozen or a couple hundred words, finding a specific word or phrase is usually not difficult. However, many documents contain hundreds or even thousands of words, so finding a word or phrase becomes much more difficult and time consuming. You can work around this problem by using the Find feature, which searches the entire document in the blink of an eye.

Most programs that work with text — including Windows 8's WordPad and Notepad programs — have the Find feature.

Find Text

1. Click **Find** (🔍).

   A. In WordPad, you display the Editing options by clicking the **Home** tab.

Note: In many programs, you run the Find command by clicking **Edit** in the menu bar and then clicking the **Find** command, or by pressing Ctrl+F.

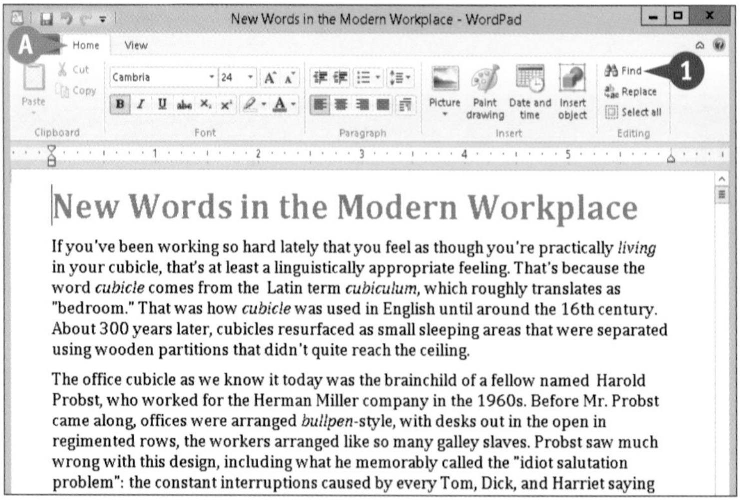

The Find dialog box appears.

2. Click in the Find What text box and type the text you want to find.
3. Click **Find Next**.

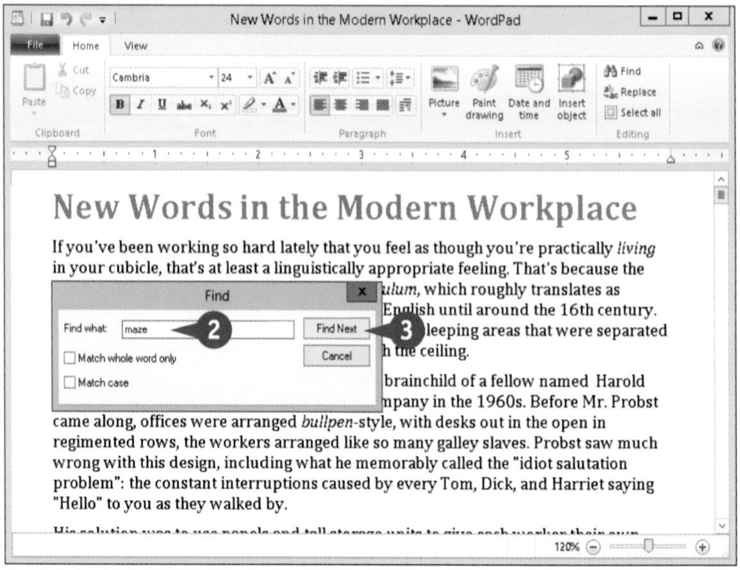

B The program selects the next instance of the search text.

Note: If the search text does not exist in the document, the program displays a dialog box to let you know.

4 If the selected instance is not the one you want, click **Find Next** until the program finds the correct instance.

5 Click the **Close** button (x) to close the Find dialog box.

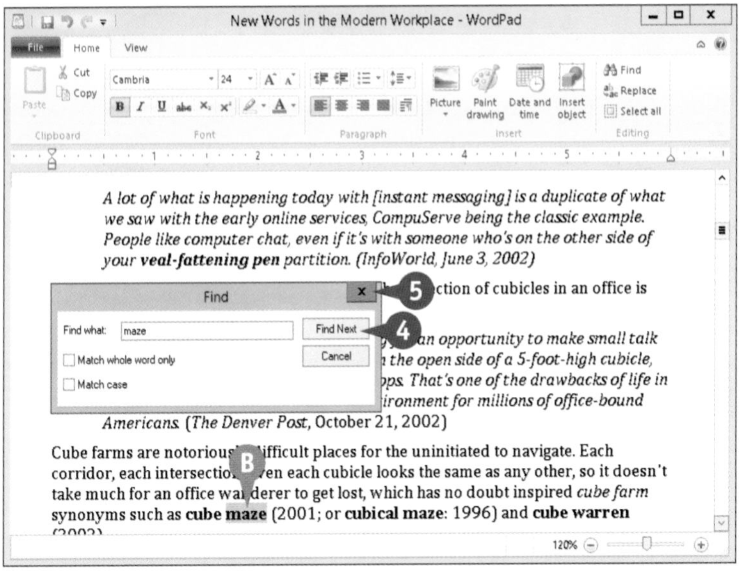

C The program leaves the found text selected.

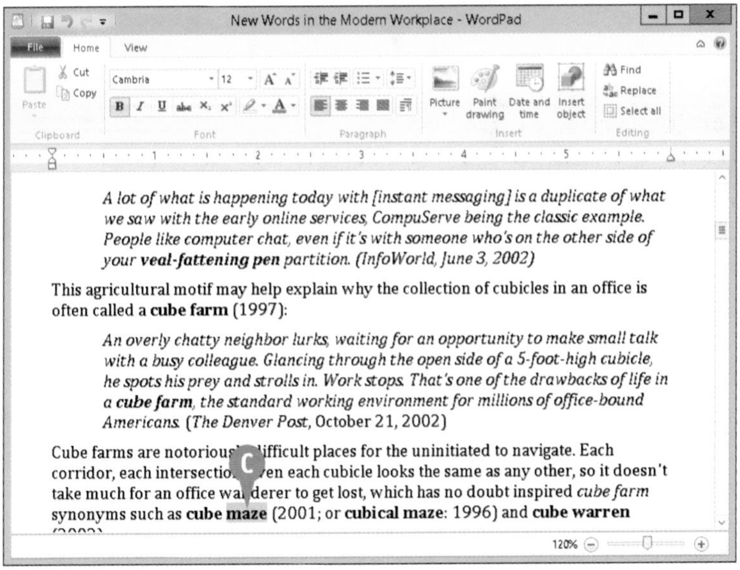

TIPS

When I search for a small word such as the, the program matches it in larger words such as theme and bother. How can I avoid this?

In the Find dialog box, click **Match whole word only** (☐ changes to ☑). This tells the program to match the search text only if it is a word on its own and not part of another word.

When I search for a name such as Bill, the program also matches the non-name bill. Is there a way to fix this?

In the Find dialog box, click **Match case** (☐ changes to ☑). This tells the program to match the search text only if it has the same mix of uppercase and lowercase letters that you specify in the Find What text box. If you type **Bill**, for example, the program matches only *Bill* and not *bill*.

Replace Text

You can make it easier to replace multiple instances of one word with another by taking advantage of the program's Replace feature.

Do you need to replace a word or part of a word with some other text? If you have several instances to replace, you can save time and do a more accurate job if you let the program's Replace feature replace the word for you.

Most programs that work with text — including Windows 8's WordPad and Notepad programs — have the Replace feature.

Replace Text

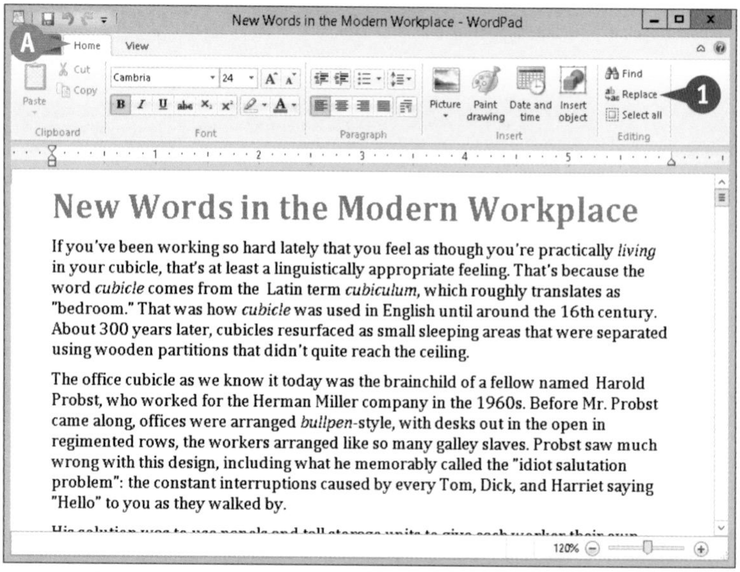

1. Click **Replace** (icon).

   A. In WordPad, you display the Editing options by clicking the **Home** tab.

Note: In many programs, you run the Find command by clicking **Edit** in the menu bar and then clicking the **Replace** command, or by pressing Ctrl+H.

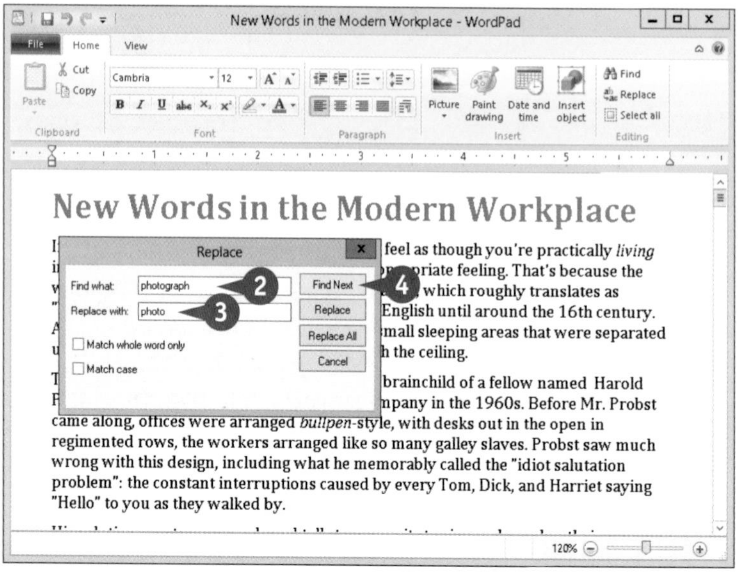

The Replace dialog box appears.

2. In the Find What text box, enter the text you want to find.
3. Click in the Replace With text box and type the text you want to use as the replacement.
4. Click **Find Next**.

B The program selects the next instance of the search text.

Note: If the search text does not exist in the document, the program displays a dialog box to let you know.

5 If the selected instance is not the one you want, click **Find Next** until the program finds the correct instance.

6 Click **Replace**.

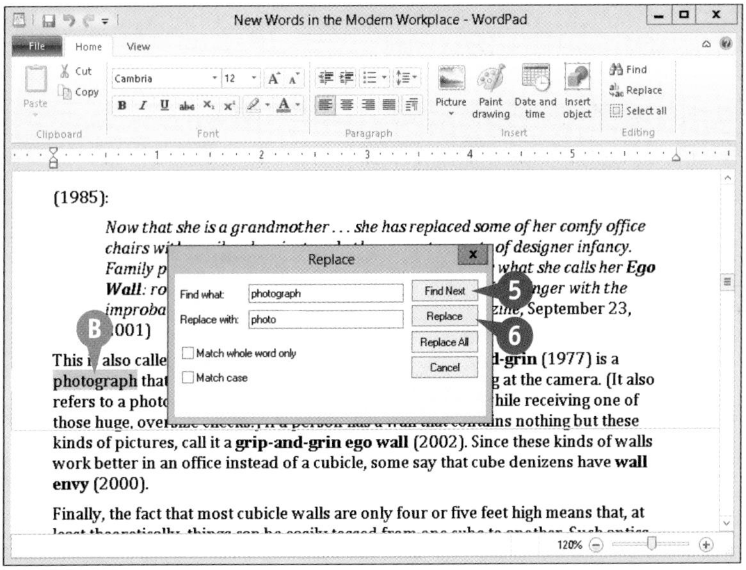

C The program replaces the selected text with the replacement text.

D The program selects the next instance of the search text.

7 Repeat steps **5** and **6** until you have replaced all the instances you want to replace.

8 Click the **Close** button (x) to close the Replace dialog box.

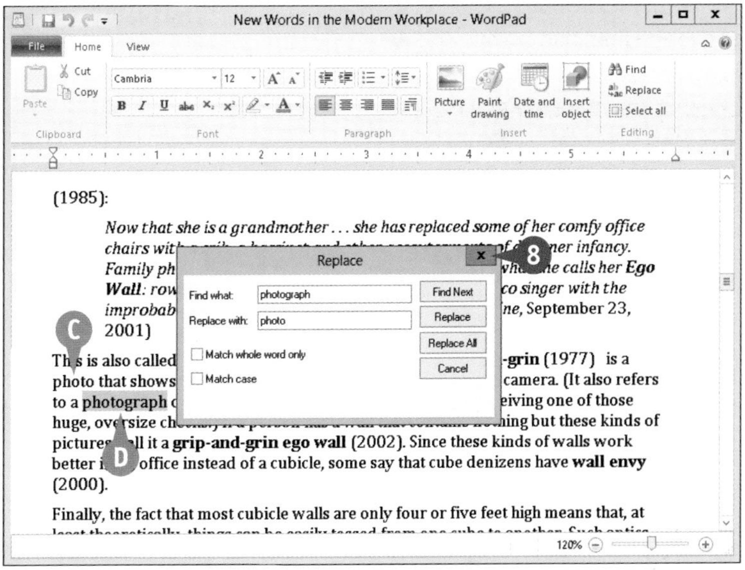

TIP

Is there a faster way to replace every instance of the search text with the replacement text?

Yes. In the Replace dialog box, click **Replace All**. This tells the program to replace every instance of the search text with the replacement text. However, you should exercise some caution with this feature because it may make some replacements that you did not intend. Click **Find Next** a few times to make sure the matches are correct. Also, consider clicking the **Match whole word only** and **Match case** check boxes (☐ changes to ☑), as described in the "Find Text" section in this chapter.

Insert Special Symbols

You can make your documents more readable and more useful by inserting special symbols that are not available via your keyboard.

The keyboard is home to a large number of letters, numbers, and symbols. However, the keyboard is missing some useful characters. For example, it is missing the foreign characters in words such as café and Köln. Similarly, your writing might require mathematical symbols such as ÷ and ½, financial symbols such as ¢ and ¥, or commercial symbols such as © and ®. These and many more symbols are available in Windows 8 via the Character Map program.

Insert Special Symbols

1. On the Start screen, type **char**.
2. Click **Character Map**.

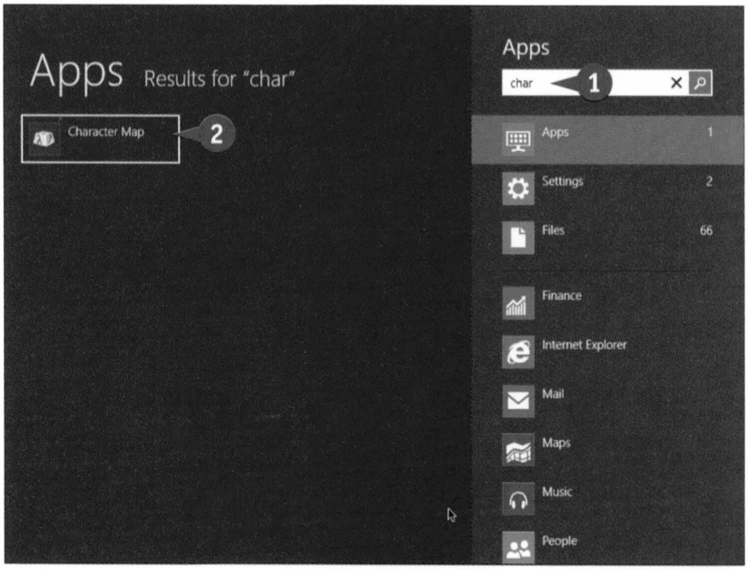

The Character Map window appears.

3. Click the symbol you want.
4. Click **Select**.

Ⓐ Character Map adds the symbol to the Characters to Copy text box.

5. Click **Copy**.
6. Click the **Close** button (×) to shut down Character Map after you choose all the characters you want.

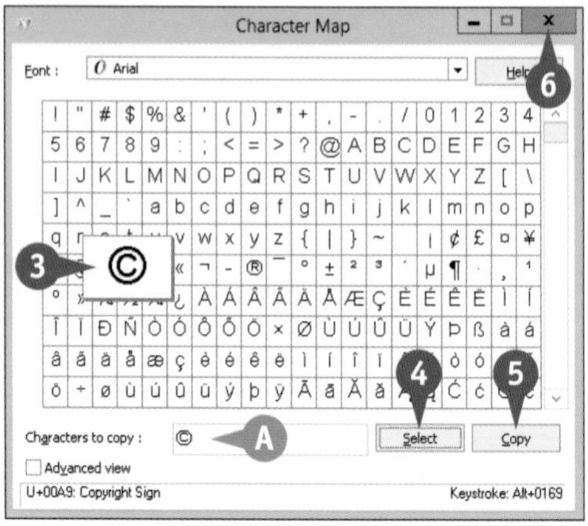

7. In your document, position the cursor where you want to insert the symbol.

B. In WordPad, you display the Clipboard options by clicking the **Home** tab.

8. Click **Paste** (📋).

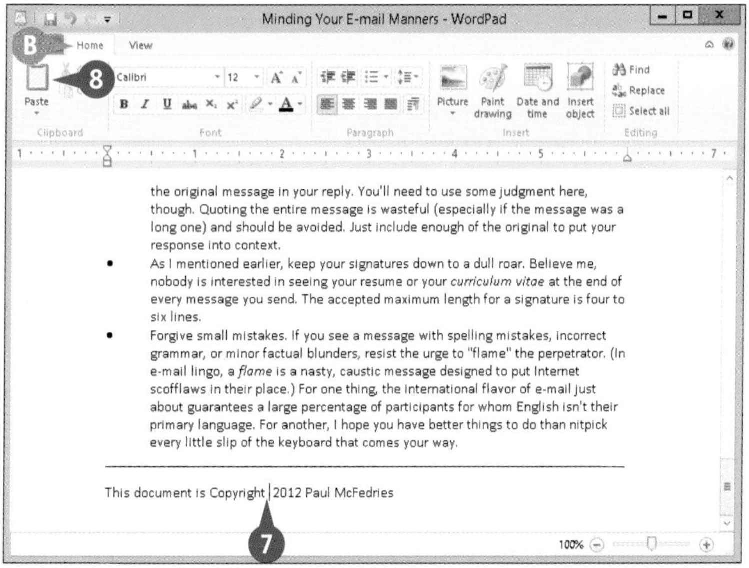
Minding Your E-mail Manners - WordPad
B
Home
View
8
Paste
Calibri
12
Picture
Paint drawing
Date and time
Insert object
Find
Replace
Select all
Clipboard
Font
Paragraph
Insert
Editing
the original message in your reply. You'll need to use some judgment here, though. Quoting the entire message is wasteful (especially if the message was a long one) and should be avoided. Just include enough of the original to put your response into context.
As I mentioned earlier, keep your signatures down to a dull roar. Believe me, nobody is interested in seeing your resume or your curriculum vitae at the end of every message you send. The accepted maximum length for a signature is four to six lines.
Forgive small mistakes. If you see a message with spelling mistakes, incorrect grammar, or minor factual blunders, resist the urge to "flame" the perpetrator. (In e-mail lingo, a flame is a nasty, caustic message designed to put Internet scofflaws in their place.) For one thing, the international flavor of e-mail just about guarantees a large percentage of participants for whom English isn't their primary language. For another, I hope you have better things to do than nitpick every little slip of the keyboard that comes your way.
This document is Copyright 2012 Paul McFedries
7
100%

C. The program inserts the symbol.

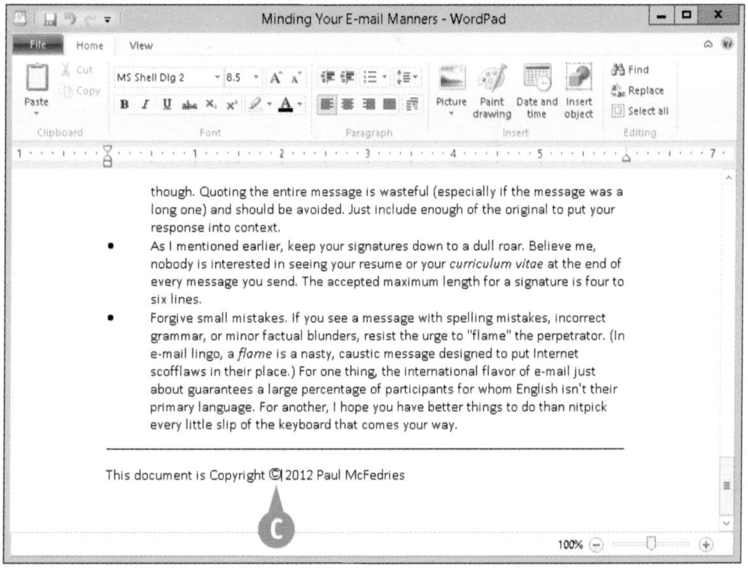
Minding Your E-mail Manners - WordPad
File
Home
View
Cut
Copy
Paste
MS Shell Dlg 2
8.5
Picture
Paint drawing
Date and time
Insert object
Find
Replace
Select all
Clipboard
Font
Paragraph
Insert
Editing
though. Quoting the entire message is wasteful (especially if the message was a long one) and should be avoided. Just include enough of the original to put your response into context.
As I mentioned earlier, keep your signatures down to a dull roar. Believe me, nobody is interested in seeing your resume or your curriculum vitae at the end of every message you send. The accepted maximum length for a signature is four to six lines.
Forgive small mistakes. If you see a message with spelling mistakes, incorrect grammar, or minor factual blunders, resist the urge to "flame" the perpetrator. (In e-mail lingo, a flame is a nasty, caustic message designed to put Internet scofflaws in their place.) For one thing, the international flavor of e-mail just about guarantees a large percentage of participants for whom English isn't their primary language. For another, I hope you have better things to do than nitpick every little slip of the keyboard that comes your way.
This document is Copyright © 2012 Paul McFedries
C
100%

TIPS

When I click a symbol, Character Map sometimes displays a "Keystroke" in the status bar. What does this mean?

This tells you that you can insert the symbol directly into your document by pressing the keystroke shown. For example, you can insert the copyright symbol (©) by pressing Alt+0 1 6 9. When you type the numbers, be sure to use your keyboard's numeric keypad.

Are there even more symbols available?

Yes, dozens of extra symbols are available in the Character Map program's Webdings and Wingdings typefaces. To see these symbols, click the **Font** ▾, and then click either **Webdings** or **Wingdings**.

Make a Copy of a Document

When you need to create a document that is nearly identical to an existing document instead of creating the new document from scratch, you can save time by making a copy of the existing document and then modifying the copy as needed.

For example, you might have a résumé cover letter that you want to modify for a different job application. Similarly, this year's conference agenda is likely to be similar to last year's. Instead of creating these new documents from scratch, it is much faster to copy the original document and then edit the copy as needed.

Make a Copy of a Document

1. Start the program you want to work with and open the original document.
2. Click **File**.
3. Click **Save as**.

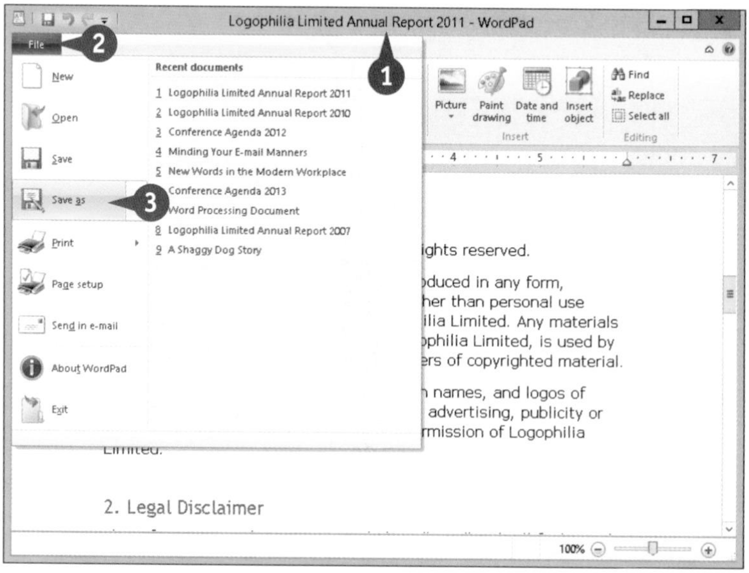

The Save As dialog box appears.

4. Click **Documents**.

Note: In most programs, the Documents library is selected automatically when you run the Save As command.

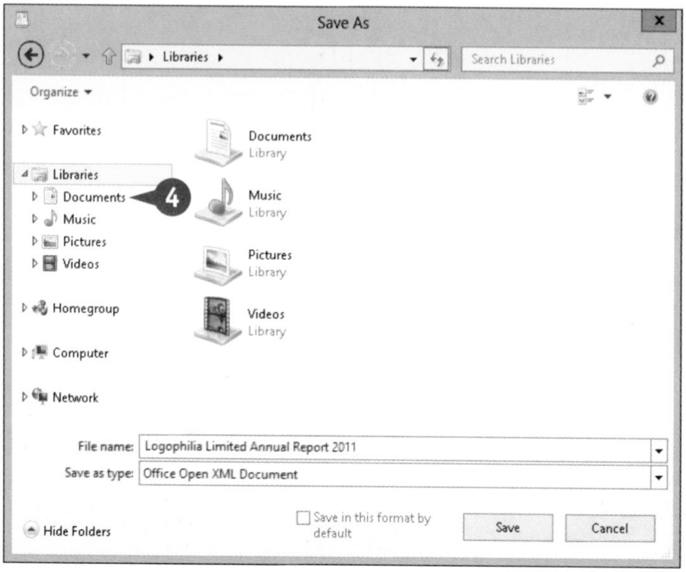

Ⓐ Windows 8 opens the Documents library.

5 Click in the File Name text box and type the name you want to use for the copy.

Note: The name you type can be up to 255 characters long, but it cannot include the following characters: < > , ? : " \ *.

6 Click **Save.**

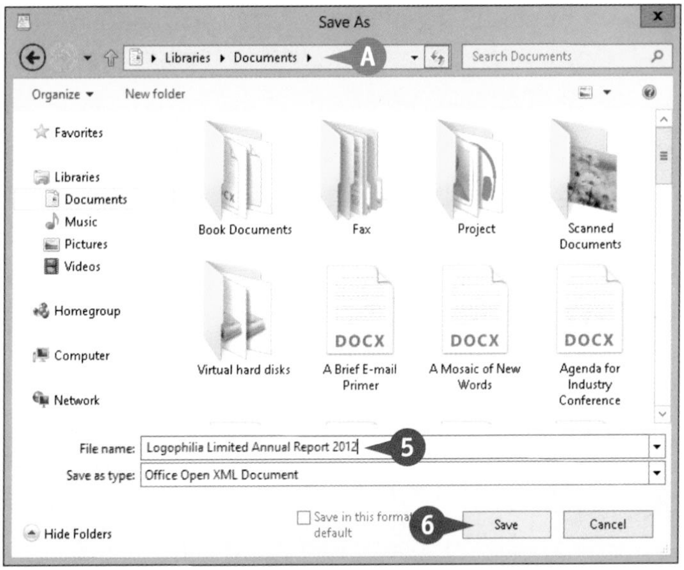

The program closes the original document and opens the copy you just created.

Ⓑ The filename you typed appears in the program's title bar.

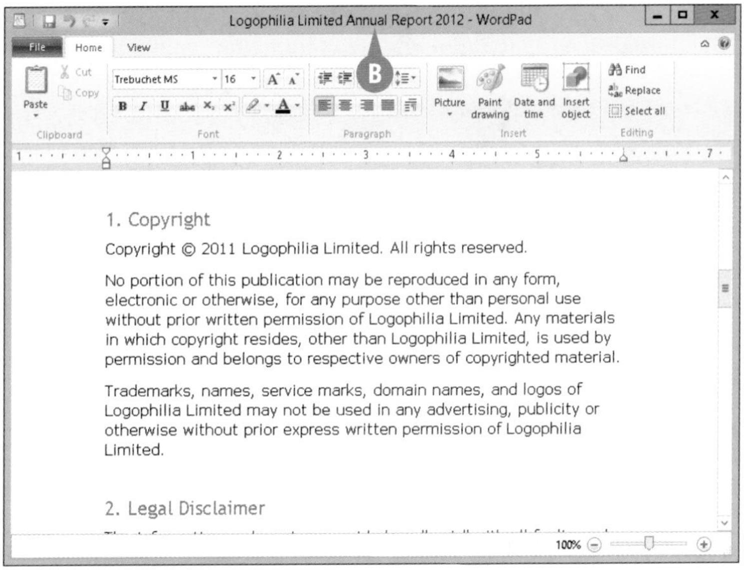

TIP

Can I use the Save As command to make a backup copy of a document?

Yes, Save As can operate as a rudimentary backup procedure. (For a better solution, see the "Keep a History of Your Files" section in Chapter 14.) Create a copy with the same name as the original, but store the copy in a different location. Good places to choose are a second hard drive, a USB flash drive, or a memory card. Remember, too, that after you complete the Save As steps, the *backup copy* will be open in the program. Be sure to close the copy and then reopen the original.

Print a Document

When you need a hard copy of your document, either for your files or to distribute to someone else, you can get a hard copy by sending the document to your printer.

Most applications that deal with documents also come with a Print command. When you run this command, the Print dialog box appears. You use the Print dialog box to choose the printer you want to use as well as to specify how many copies you want to print. Many Print dialog boxes also enable you to see a preview of your document before printing it.

Print a Document

1. Turn on your printer.
2. Open the document you want to print.

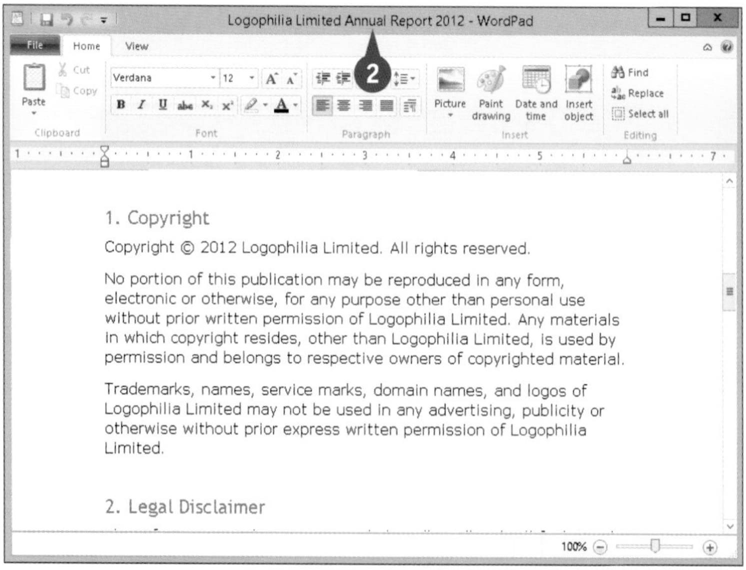

3. Click **File**.
4. Click **Print**.

Note: In many programs, you can select the Print command by pressing Ctrl+P or by clicking the **Print** button ( ).

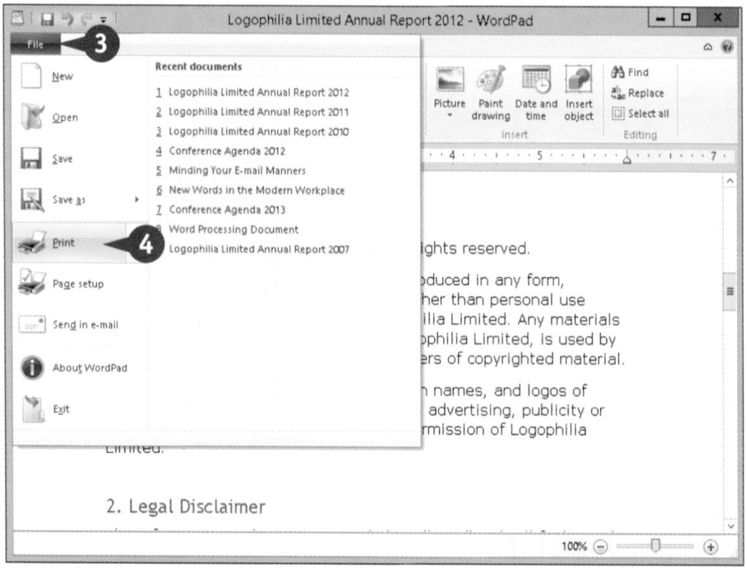

The Print dialog box appears.

Note: The layout of the Print dialog box varies from program to program. The WordPad version shown here is a typical example.

5 If you have more than one printer, click the printer you want to use.

6 Use the **Number of copies** (⬍) to specify the number of copies to print.

7 Click **Print**.

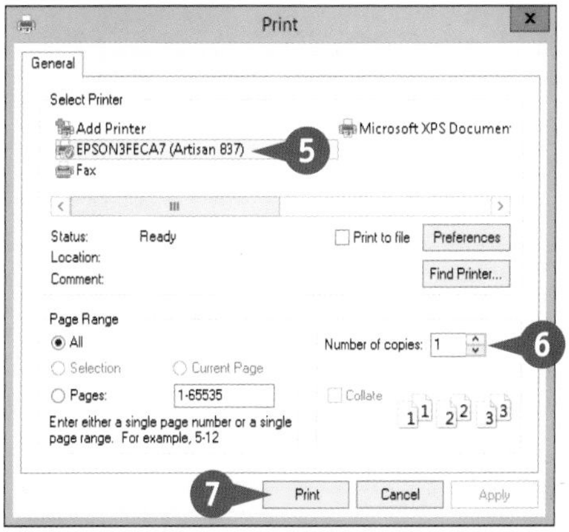

A Windows 8 prints the document. The print icon (🖶) appears in the taskbar's notification area while the document prints.

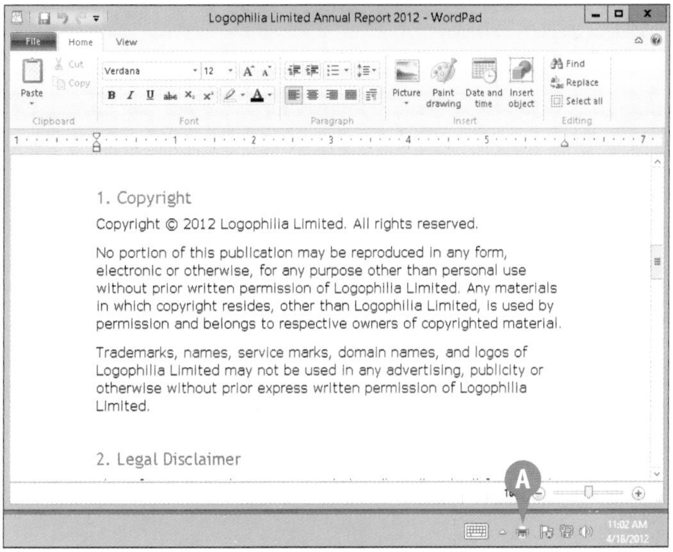

TIPS

How do I print only part of a document?

Most programs enable you to use the following methods to print only part of the document:

- Print selected text: Select the text you want to print. In the Print dialog box, click **Selection** (○ changes to ◉).
- Print a specific page: Place the cursor on the page you want to print. In the Print dialog box, click **Current Page** (○ changes to ◉).
- Print a range of pages: In the Print dialog box, click **Pages** (○ changes to ◉). In the text box, type the first page number, a dash (–), and the last page number (for example, 1–5).

Can I preview my document before I print it?

Yes. It is a good idea to preview the document before printing it to ensure that the document layout looks the way you want. To preview the document in WordPad, click **File**, click the **Print** (▸), and then click **Print preview**.

CHAPTER 10

Working with Files

This chapter shows you how to work with the files on your computer. These easy and efficient methods show you how to view, select, copy, move, rename, and delete files, as well as how to restore accidentally deleted files, how to copy files to a CD or DVD, and how to extract files from a compressed folder.

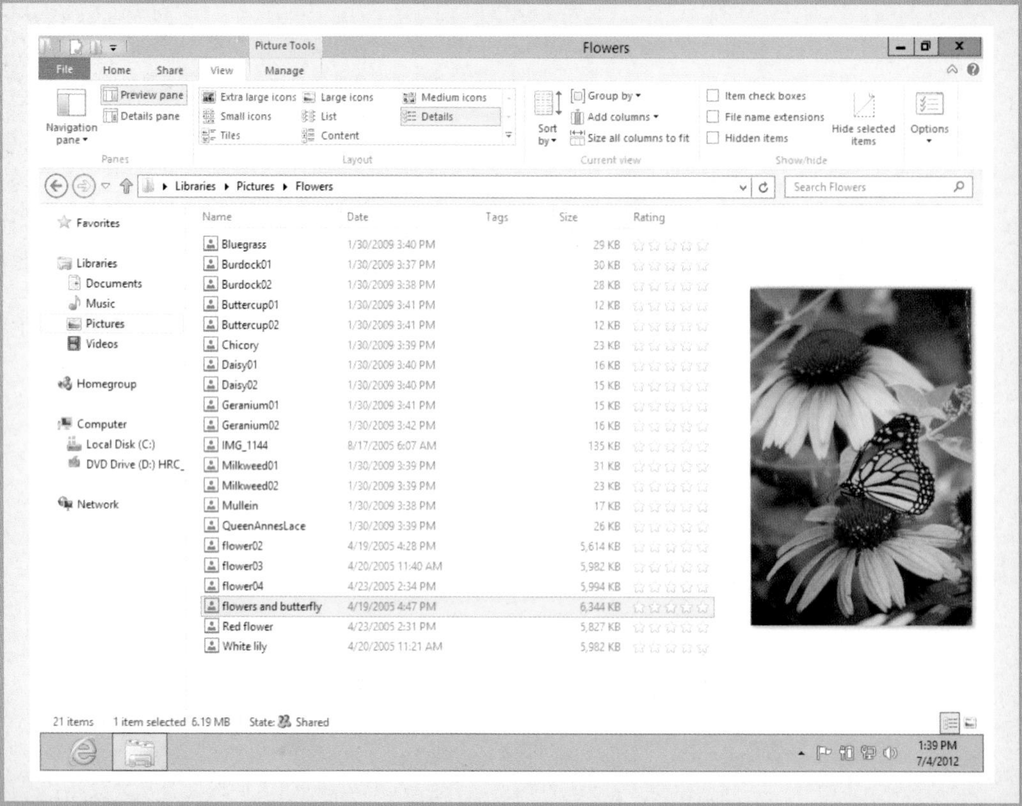

View Your Files

You can view the files you create, as well as those stored on your hard drive that you download and copy to your computer. If you want to open or work with those files, you first need to view them.

Windows 8 stores files on your hard drive using special storage areas called *folders*. A folder is a location on your hard drive that contains one or more related files. You can also store folders within folders, and these nested folders are known as *subfolders*. To view your files, you usually have to open one or more folders and subfolders.

View Your Files

1 Click **Desktop**.

2 Click **File Explorer**.

Windows 8 displays the Libraries window.

3 Double-click the folder you want to view.

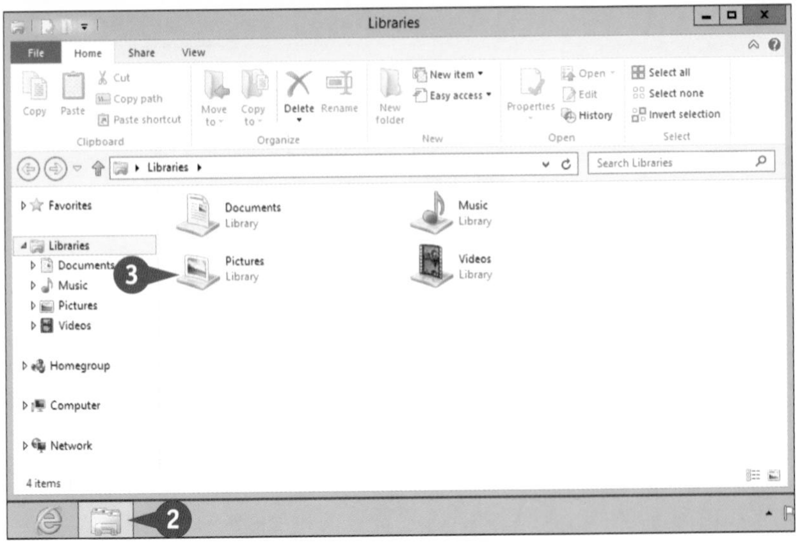

Windows 8 displays the contents of the folder including subfolders.

4 If the files you want to view are stored in a subfolder, double-click the subfolder.

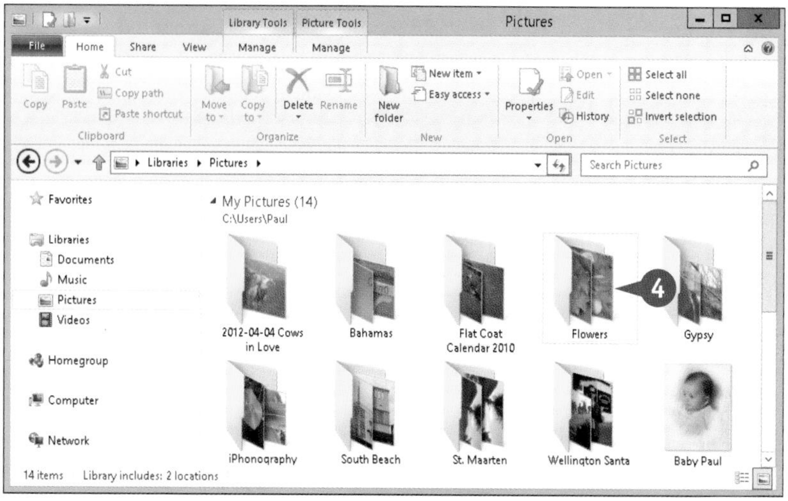

Windows 8 displays the contents of the subfolder.

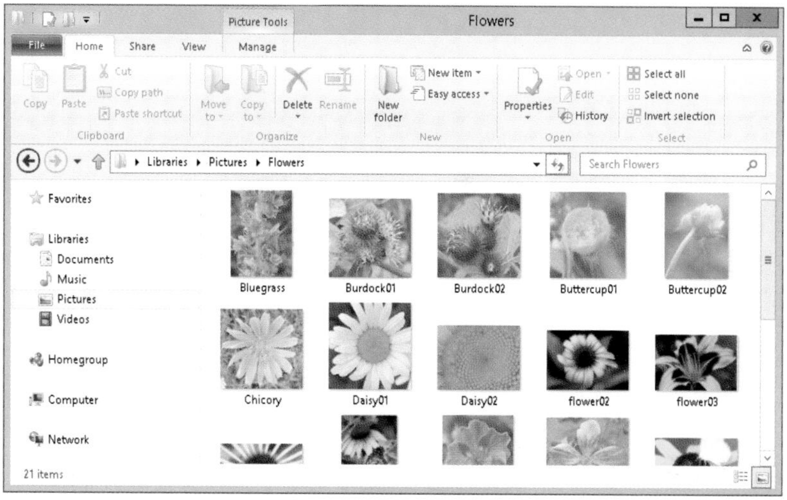

TIPS

How do I view the files I have on a CD, DVD, flash drive, memory card, or other media?

Insert the media into the appropriate drive or slot on your computer. If you see the AutoPlay notification, click it and then click **Open folder to view files**. Otherwise, click **File Explorer** and then click **Computer** to display the Computer folder, and then double-click the hard drive or device that contains the files you want to view. Windows 8 displays the contents of the media.

What is a file library?

In Windows 8, the four main document storage areas — Documents, Music, Pictures, and Videos — are set up as *libraries*, where each library consists of two or more folders. For example, the Documents library consists of your My Documents folder and the Public Documents folder. To add a folder to a library, open the folder, click the **Home** tab, click **Easy access**, click **Include in library**, and then click the library.

Select a File

Before you can do any work with one or more files, you first have to select the files so that Windows 8 knows exactly the ones you want to work with.

Later sections in this chapter cover how to copy several files to a different folder, how to move several files to a new location, how to rename a file, and how to delete one or more files. Before you can perform any of these operations, you must first select the files you want to work with.

Although you learn specifically about selecting files in this section, the technique for selecting folders is exactly the same.

Select a File

Select a Single File

1. Open the folder containing the file.
2. Click the file.

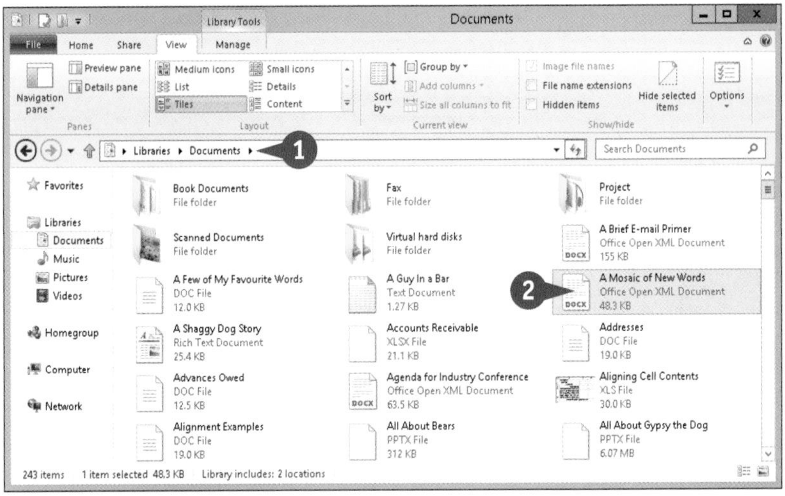

Select Multiple Files

1. Open the folder containing the files.
2. Click the first file you want to select.
3. Press and hold Ctrl and click each of the other files you want to select.

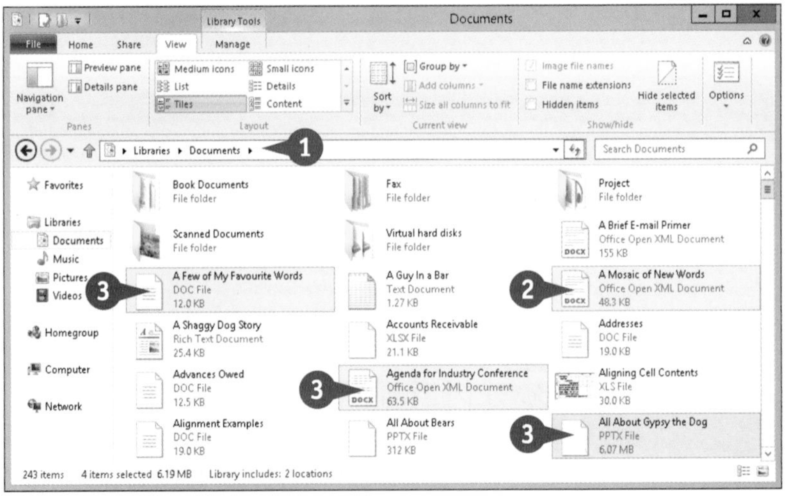

Select a Group of Files

1. Open the folder containing the files.
2. Position the mouse slightly above and slightly to the left of the first file in the group.
3. Click and drag the mouse down and to the right until all the files in the group are selected.

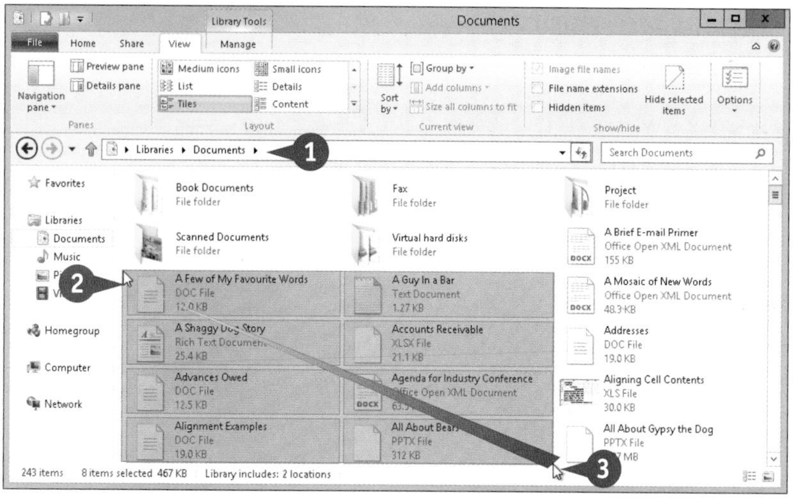

Select All Files

1. Open the folder containing the files.
2. Click the **Home** tab.
3. Click **Select all**.

Ⓐ File Explorer selects all the files in the folder.

Note: A quick way to select all the files in a folder is to press Ctrl+A.

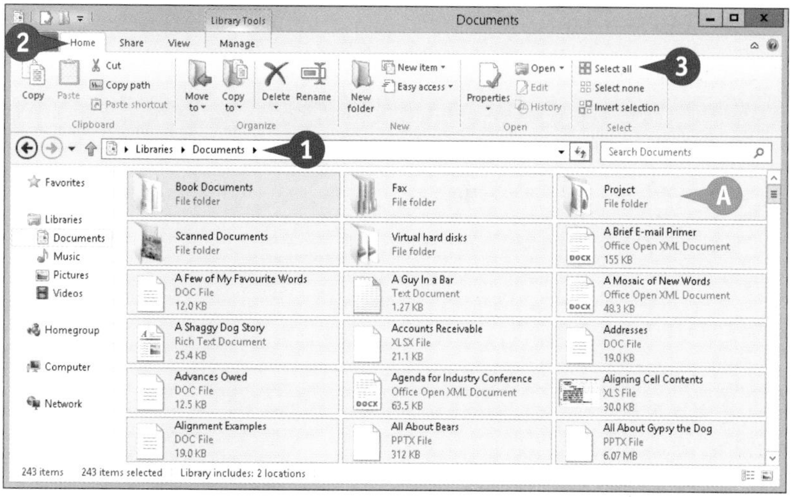

TIP

How do I deselect a file?

- To deselect a single file from a multiple-file selection, press and hold Ctrl and click the file you want to deselect.
- To deselect all files, either click the **Home** tab and then click **Select none**, or click an empty area within the folder.
- To reverse the selection — deselect the selected files and select the deselected files — click the **Home** tab, and then click **Invert selection**.

Change the File View

You can configure how Windows 8 displays the files in a folder by changing the file view. This enables you to see larger or smaller icons or the details of each file.

Choose a view such as Small Icons to see more files in the folder window. Choose a view such as Large Icons or Extra Large Icons when you are viewing images to see thumbnail versions of each picture. If you want to see more information about the files, choose either the Tiles view or Details view.

Change the File View

1. Open the folder containing the files you want to view.
2. Click the **View** tab.
3. In the Layout section, click **More** (▿).

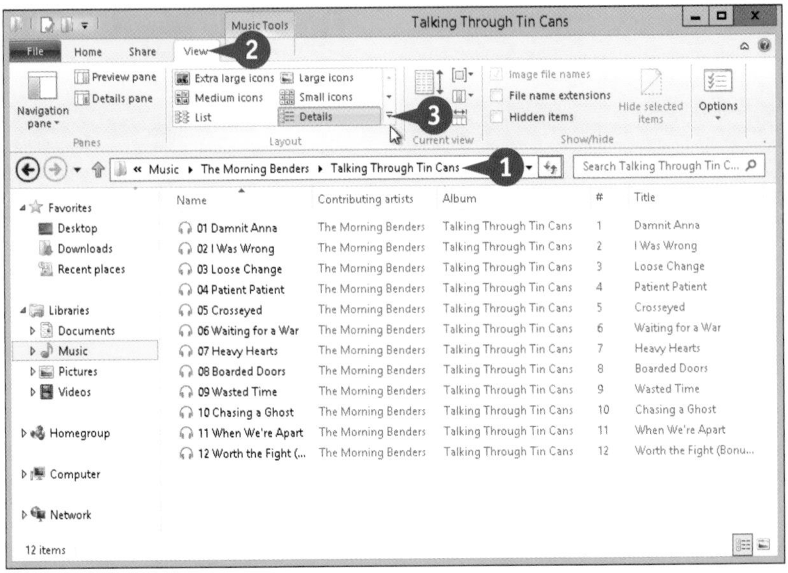

Windows 8 displays the Layout gallery.

4. Click the view you want.

Ⓐ File Explorer changes the file view (to Tiles, in this example).

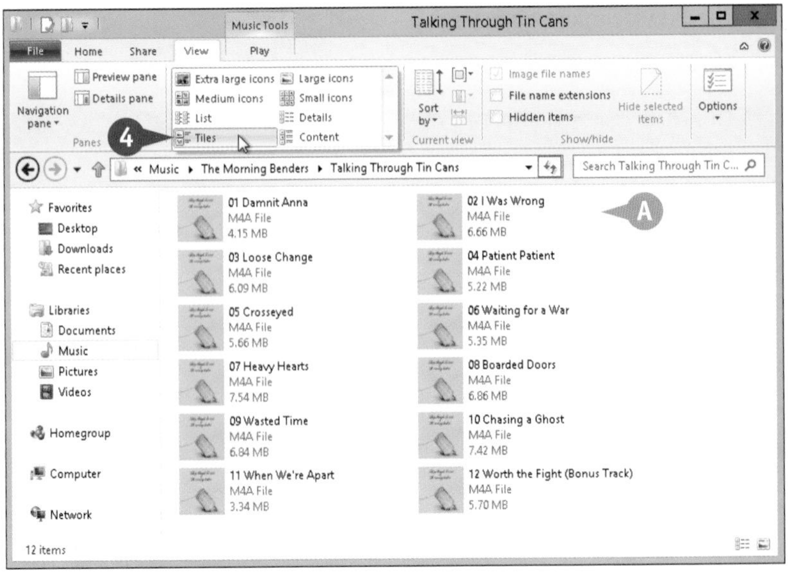

Preview a File

Windows 8 enables you to view the contents of some files without opening them. This makes it easier to select the file you want to work with because it means you do not have to run an application to see the file's contents. Previewing the file is faster and uses fewer system resources.

Windows 8 previews only certain types of files, such as text documents, rich text documents, web pages, images, and videos.

Preview a File

1. Open the folder containing the file you want to preview.
2. Click the **View** tab.
3. Click **Preview pane**.

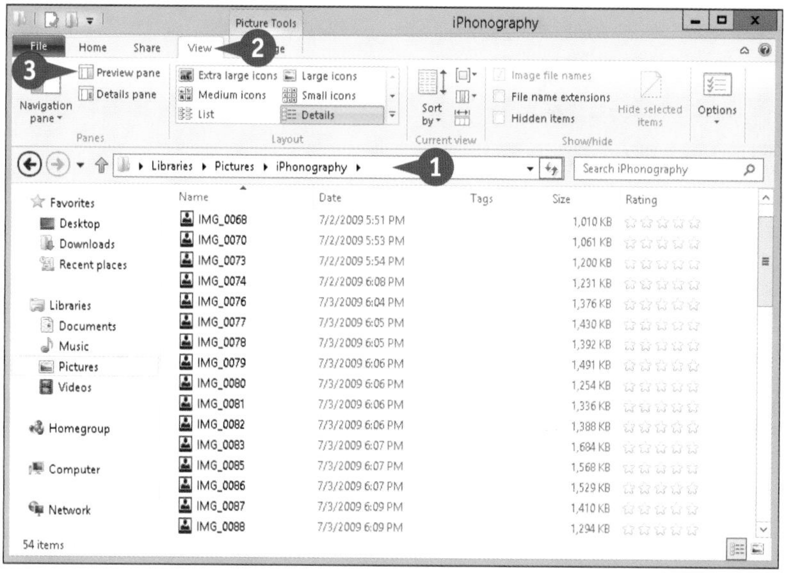

- Ⓐ The Preview pane appears.

4. Click a file.

- Ⓑ The file's contents appear in the Preview pane.
- Ⓒ You can click and drag the left border of the Preview pane to change its size.
- Ⓓ When you are finished with the Preview pane, click **Preview pane** to close it.

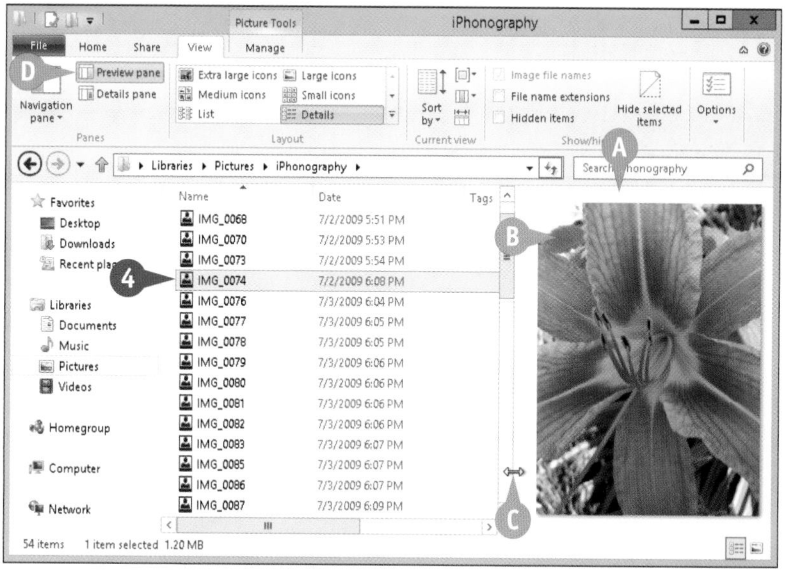

Copy a File

You can use Windows 8 to make an exact copy of a file. This is useful if you want to back up an important file by making an extra copy on a flash drive, memory card, or other removable disk. Similarly, you might require a copy of a file if you want to send the copy on a disk to another person.

This section shows you how to copy a single file, but the steps also work if you select multiple files. You can also use these steps to copy a folder.

Copy a File

1. Open the folder containing the file you want to copy.
2. Select the file.
3. Click the **Home** tab.
4. Click **Copy**.

Windows 8 places a copy of the file in a special memory location called the *Clipboard*.

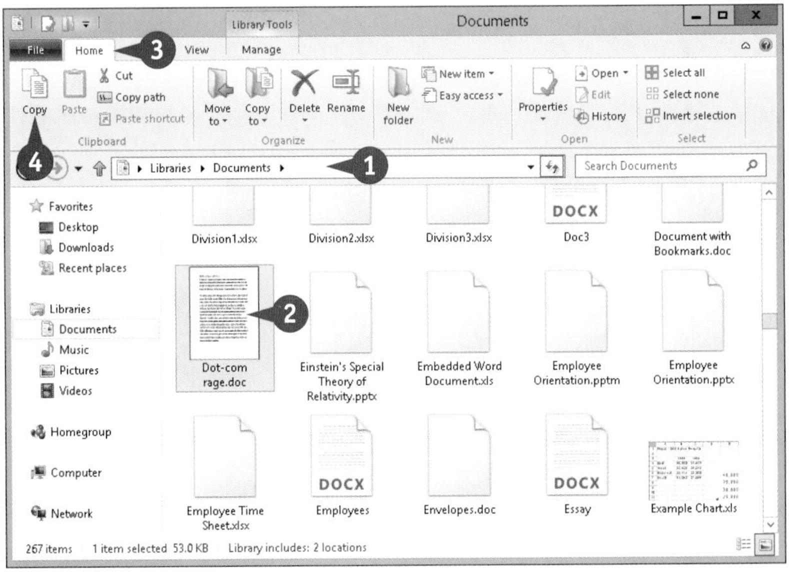

5. Open the location you want to use to store the copy.
6. Click the **Home** tab.
7. Click **Paste**.

Ⓐ Windows 8 inserts a copy of the file in the location.

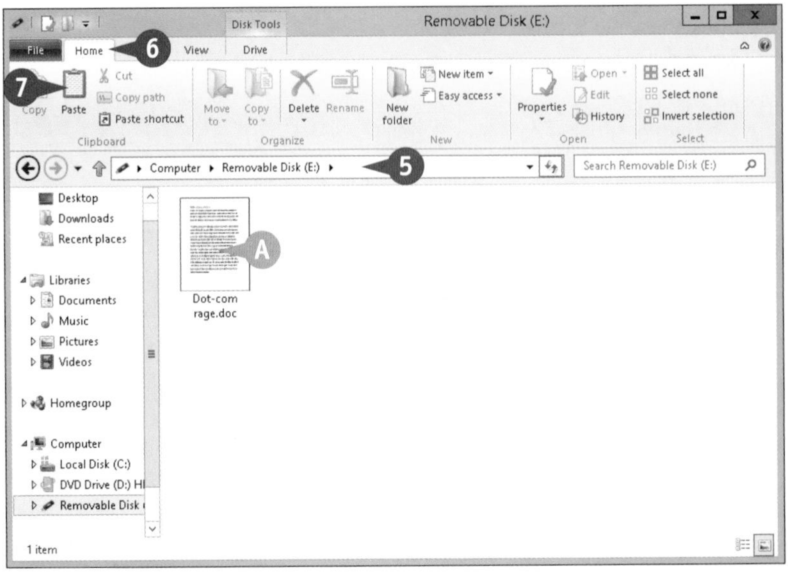

Move a File

When you need to store a file in a new location, the easiest way is to move the file from its current folder to another folder on your computer.

When you save a file for the first time, you specify a folder on your PC's hard drive. This original location is not permanent; you can move the file to another location on the hard drive.

This section shows you how to move a single file, but the steps also work if you select multiple files or move a folder.

Move a File

1. Open the folder containing the file you want to move.
2. Select the file.
3. Click the **Home** tab.
4. Click **Cut**.

   Windows 8 removes the file from the folder and places it in the Clipboard.

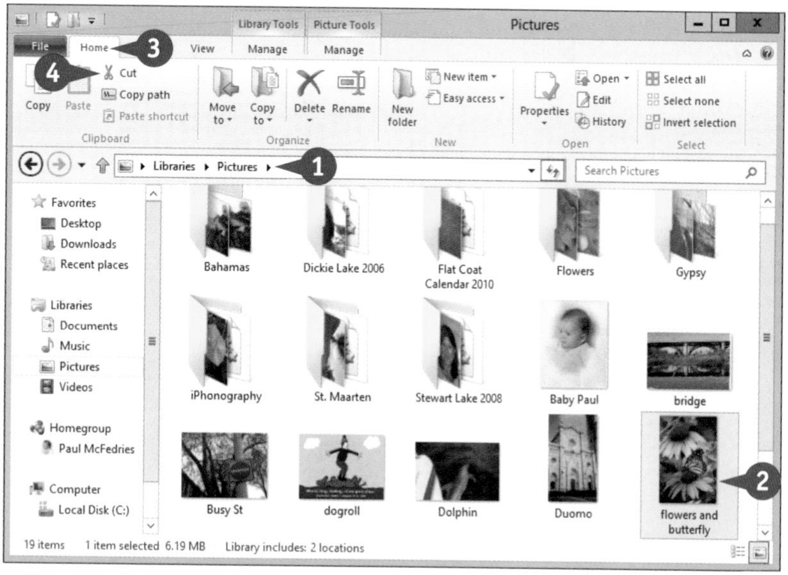

5. Click the new location you want to use for the file.
6. Click the **Home** tab.
7. Click **Paste**.

   Ⓐ Windows 8 inserts the file in the new location.

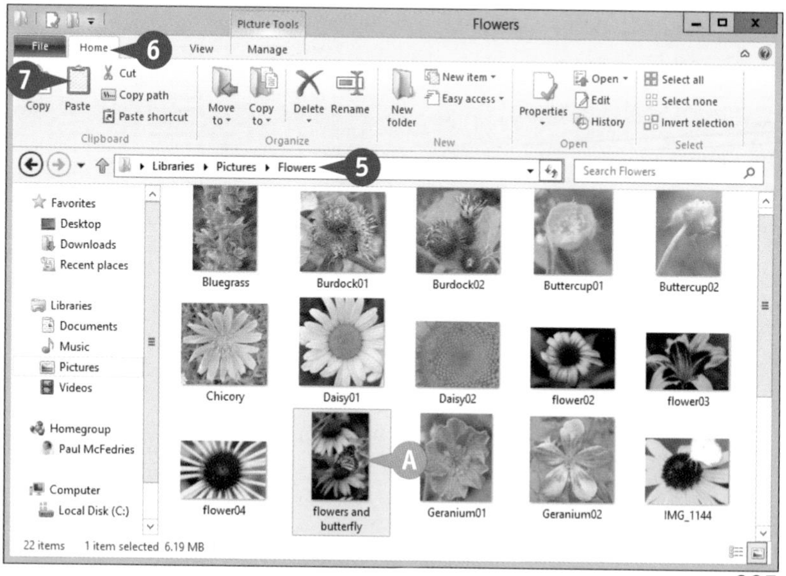

Rename a File

You can change the names of a file, which is useful if the current name of the file does not accurately describe the file's contents. By giving your document a descriptive name, you make it easier to find the file later.

Make sure that you rename only those documents that you have created yourself or that someone else has given to you. Do not rename any of the Windows 8 system files or any files associated with your programs, or your computer may behave erratically, or even crash.

Rename a File

1 Open the folder that contains the file you want to rename.

2 Click the file.

3 Click the **Home** tab.

Note: In addition to renaming files, you can also rename any folders that you created yourself.

4 Click **Rename**.

A text box appears around the filename.

Note: You can also select the Rename command by clicking the file and then pressing F2.

5 Type the new name you want to use for the file.

Note: If you decide that you do not want to rename the file after all, press Esc to cancel the operation.

Note: The name you type can be up to 255 characters long, but it cannot include the following characters: < > , ? : " \ *.

6 Press Enter or click an empty section of the folder.

The new name appears under the file's icon.

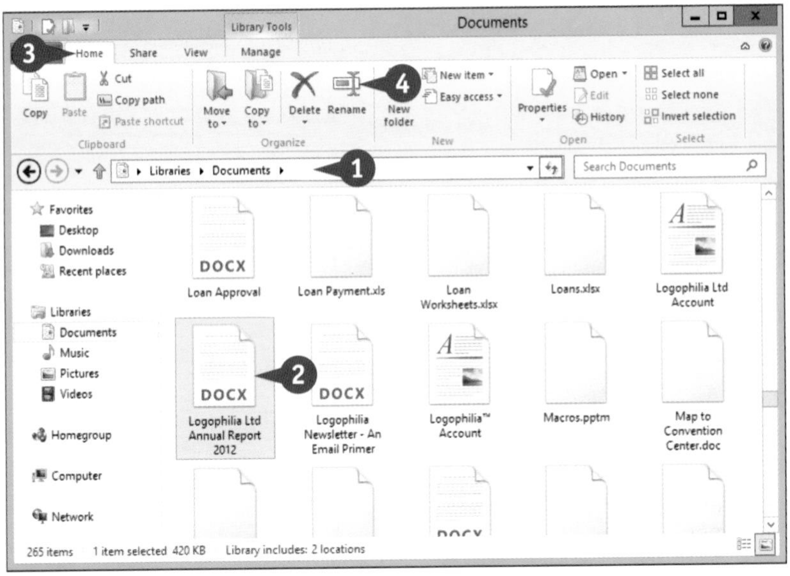

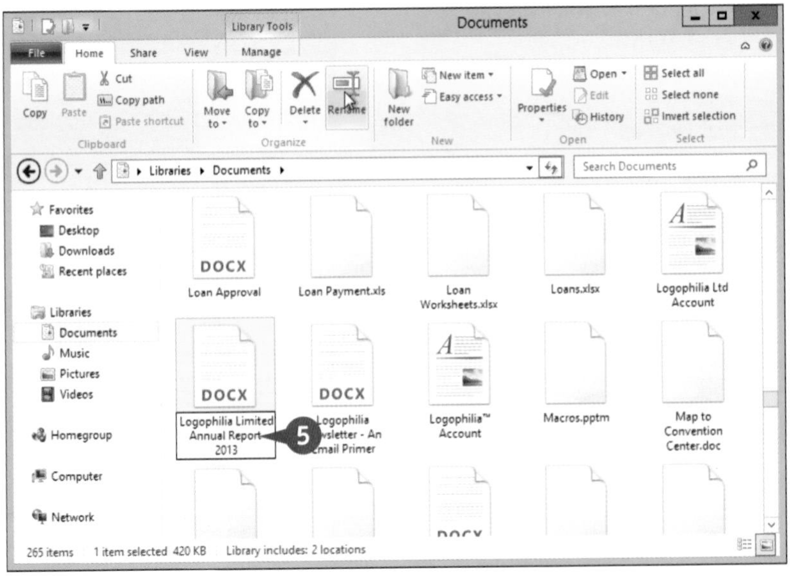

Create a New File

You can quickly create a new file directly within a file folder. This method is faster, and often more convenient, than running a program's New command, as explained in Chapter 9.

In Windows 8, you can create several different types of file, the most important of which are the Bitmap Image (a drawing), a Rich Text Document (a WordPad file), a Text Document (a Notepad file), and a Compressed (Zipped) Folder (which combines multiple files in a single file, as described later in this chapter). You can also create a new folder.

Create a New File

1. Open the folder in which you want to create the file.
2. Click the **Home** tab.
3. Click **New item**.
4. Click the type of file you want to create.

Note: If you click **Folder**, Windows 8 creates a new subfolder.

Note: The New Item menu on your system may contain more items than you see here because some programs install their own file types.

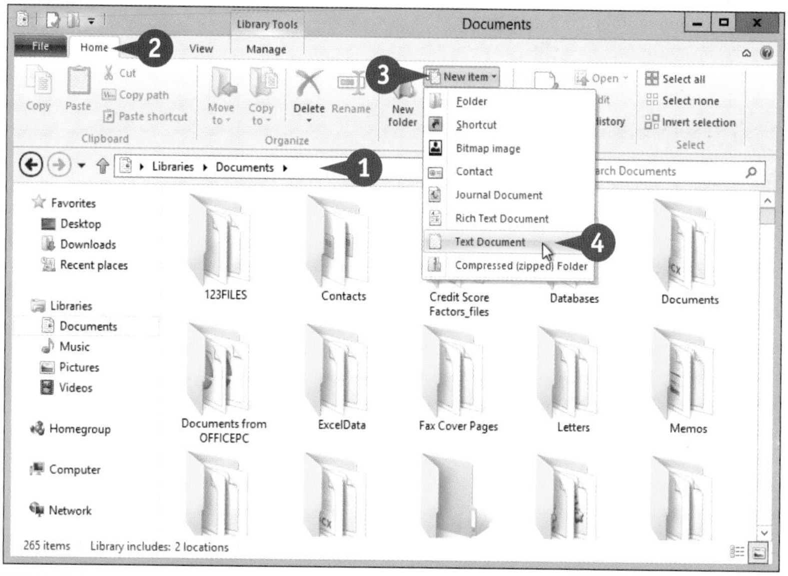

- (A) An icon for the new file appears in the folder.

5. Type the name you want to use for the new file.
6. Press Enter.

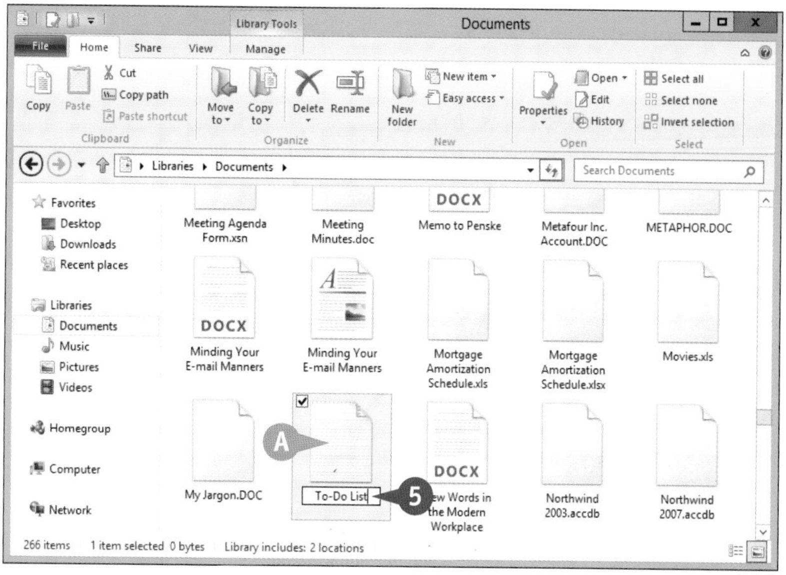

Delete a File

When you have a file that you no longer need, instead of leaving the file to clutter your hard drive, you can delete it.

Make sure that you delete only those documents that you have created yourself or that someone else has given to you. Do not delete any of the Windows 8 system files or any files associated with your programs, or your computer may behave erratically or crash.

Delete a File

1. Open the folder that contains the file you want to delete.
2. Click the file you want to delete.

Note: If you need to remove more than one file, select all the files you want to delete.

3. Click the **Home** tab.
4. Click the top half of the **Delete** button.

Note: Another way to select the Delete command is to press Delete.

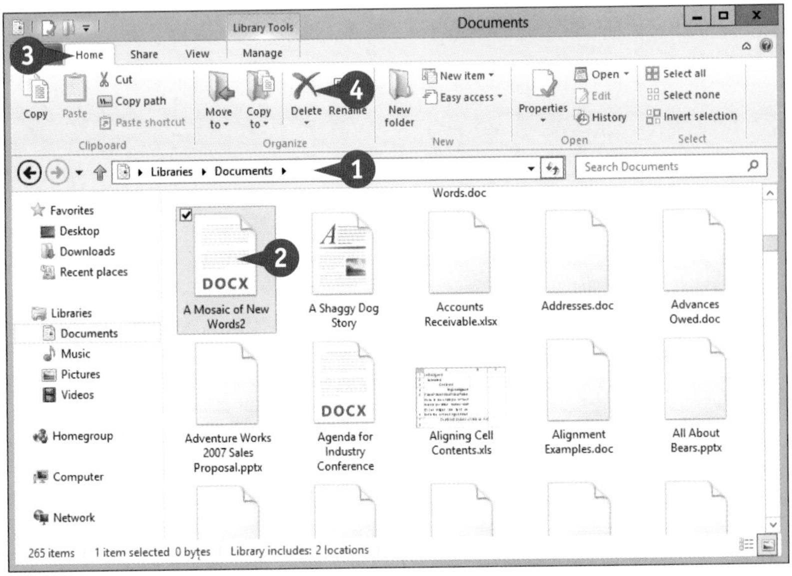

A. Windows 8 removes the file from the folder.

Note: Another way to delete a file is to click and drag it to the desktop's Recycle Bin icon.

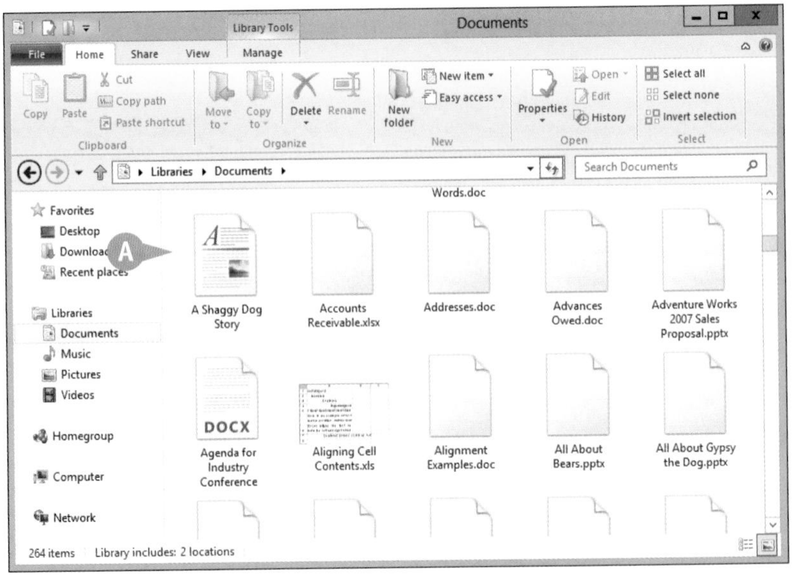

Restore a Deleted File

If you delete a file in error, Windows 8 enables you to restore the file by placing it back in the folder from which you deleted it.

You can restore a deleted file because Windows 8 stores each deleted file in a special folder called the Recycle Bin, where the file stays for a few days or a few weeks, depending on how often you empty the bin or how full the folder becomes.

Restore a Deleted File

1. Double-click the desktop **Recycle Bin** icon.

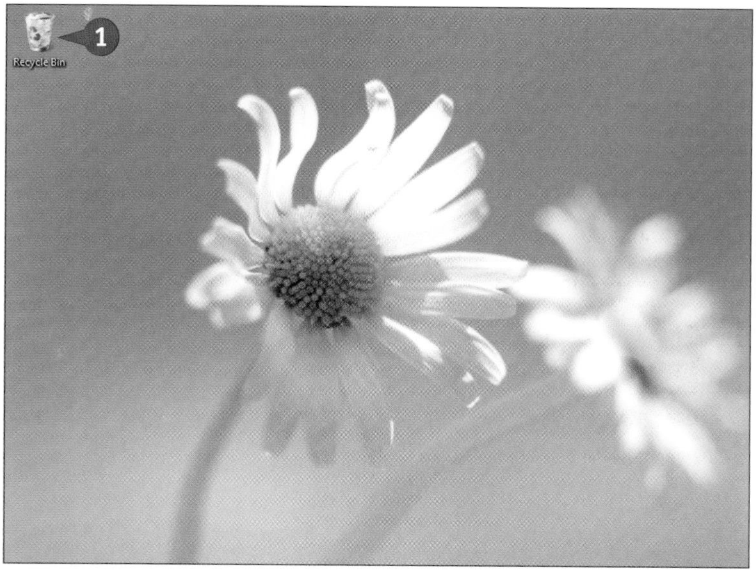

The Recycle Bin folder appears.

2. Click the file you want to restore.
3. Click the **Manage** tab.
4. Click **Restore the selected items**.

The file disappears from the Recycle Bin and reappears in its original folder.

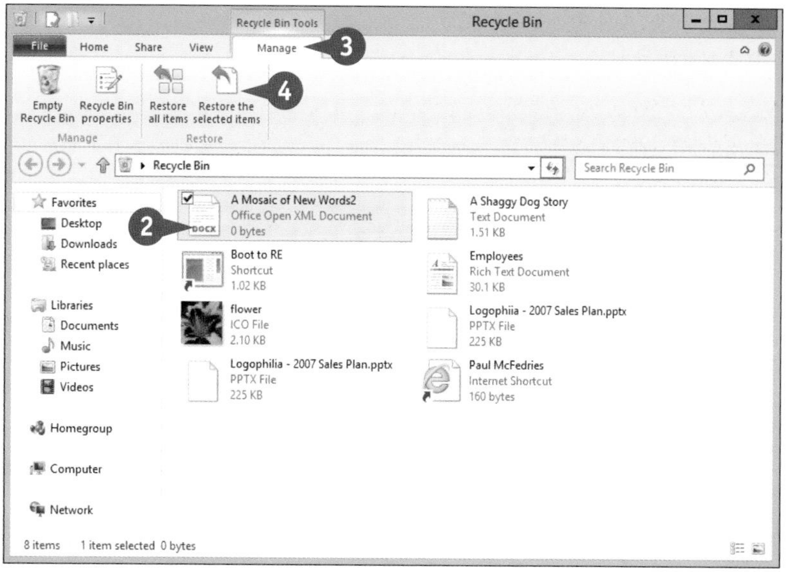

Burn Files to a CD or DVD

If your computer has a recordable CD or DVD drive, you can copy — or *burn* — files and folders to a recordable disc. This enables you to store a large amount of data in a single place for convenient transport, storage, or backup.

If you want to copy music files to a CD, see Chapter 8.

Burn Files to a CD or DVD

1. Insert a recordable disc into your recordable CD or DVD drive.

   The AutoPlay notification appears.

2. Click the notification.

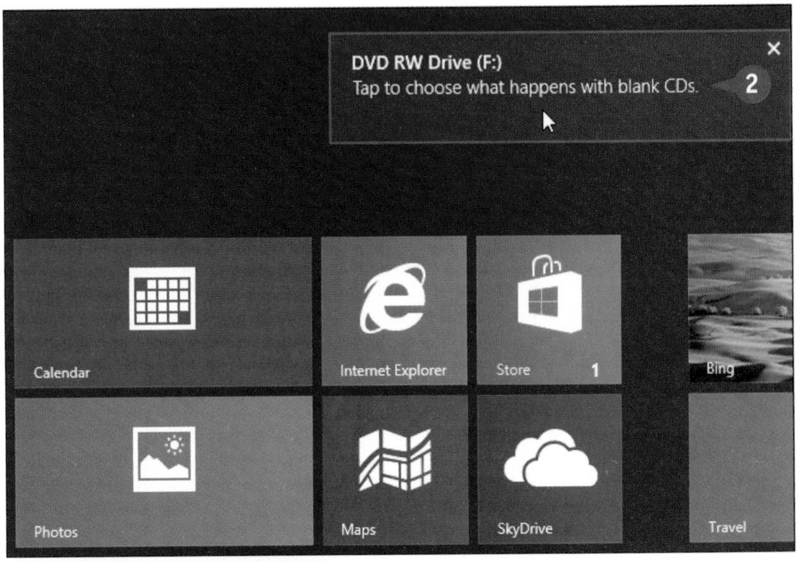

3. Click **Burn files to disc**.

If you have never used the disc for burning files, the Burn a Disc dialog box appears.

4 Type a title for the disc.

5 Click **Like a USB flash drive** (☐ changes to ☑).

6 Click **Next**.

Windows 8 formats the disc and displays a dialog box to show you the progress.

When the format is complete, the AutoPlay notification appears, but you can ignore it this time.

7 Open the folder containing the files you want to copy to the disc.

8 Select the files.

A If you selected more than 15 files and you want to see the total size of the selection, click **View**, click **Details pane**, and then click **Show more details**.

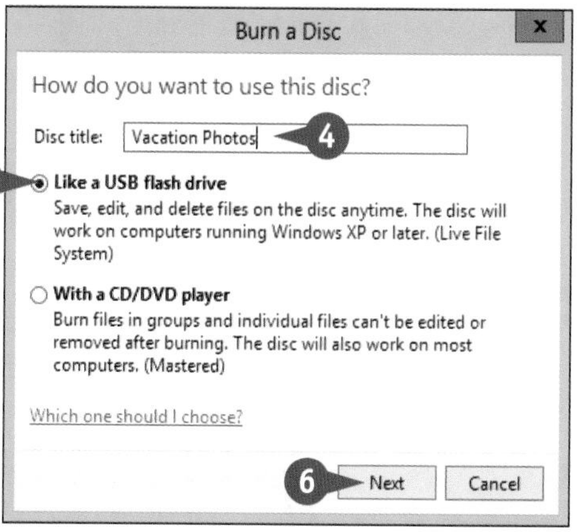

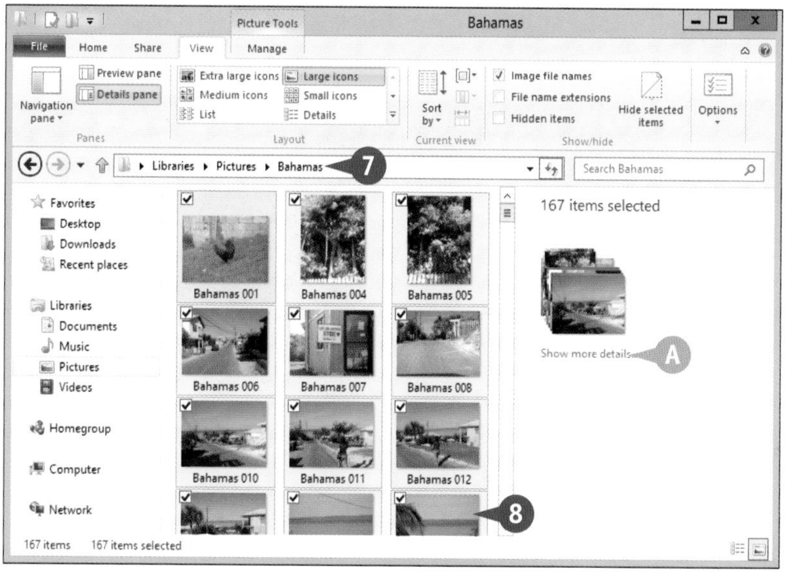

TIPS

Does it matter what type of recordable CD or DVD I use?

Not in Windows 8. Normally, CD-R and DVD-R discs allow you to copy files to the disc only once. After you finalize the disc, it is locked and you cannot copy more files to the disc, or delete files from the disc. However, Windows 8 uses a system that enables you to copy, recopy, and delete files with any type of recordable disc.

How much data can I store on a recordable CD?

Most recordable CDs can hold about 650MB (megabytes) of information. If a typical word processing document is about 50KB (kilobytes), this means you can store about 13,000 files on a recordable CD. For larger files, such as images, you can store about 650 1MB files on the disc.

continued ▶

Burn Files to a CD or DVD (continued)

Traditionally, CDs and DVDs only allow you to burn files to them once, and you can then no longer burn any more files to the disc. However, Windows 8 supports a different burning mode called Live File System that enables you to burn files to a disc multiple times, much like you can copy files multiple times to a USB flash drive.

With Windows 8's method for burning files to a CD or DVD, you only need to format the disc once. After that, you can burn more files to the disc, delete files from the disc, and more.

Burn Files to a CD or DVD (continued)

Ⓐ If you clicked Show More Details, the Size number shows the total size of the selected files.

9. Click the **Share** tab.
10. Click **Burn to disc**.

Note: If you want to copy everything in the folder to the disc, do not select any file or folder and click **Burn to disc**.

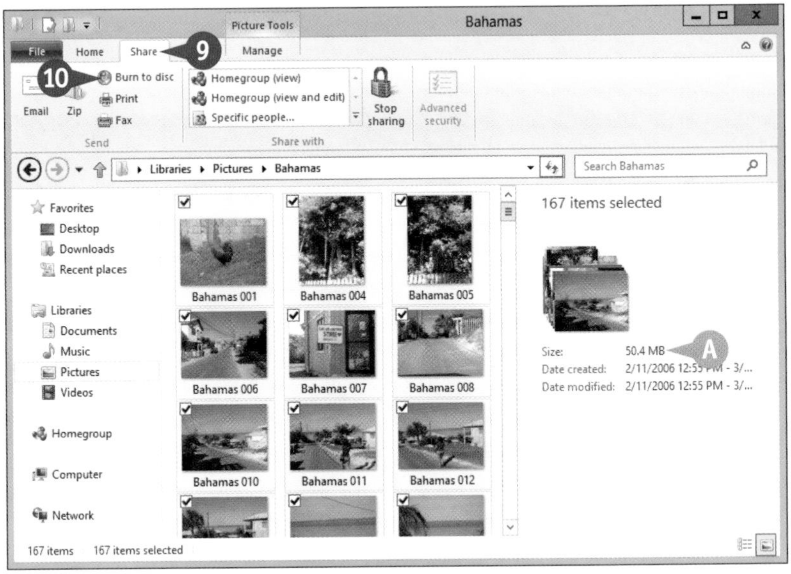

Ⓑ Windows 8 burns the files to the disc.

Ⓒ Windows 8 opens the disc and displays the copied files.

11. Repeat steps **8** to **10** to burn more files to the disc.

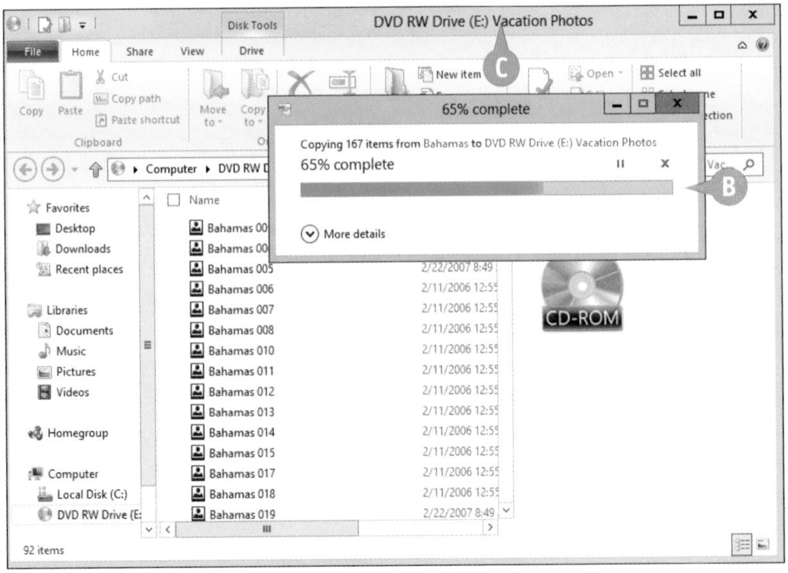

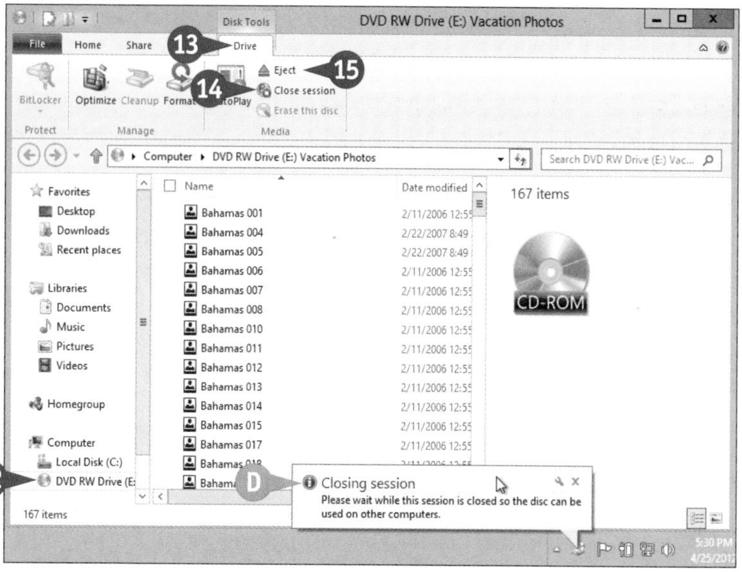

12. Open the disc folder.

13. Click the **Drive** tab.

14. Click **Close session**.

    Windows 8 closes the disc session to allow the disc to be used on other computers.

    D This message appears while the disc is being closed.

15. When the Closing Session message disappears, click **Eject**.

    Windows 8 ejects the disc.

TIP

I want to start over with a CD-RW or DVD-RW disc. Is there an easy way to erase the disc?

Yes. Follow these steps:

1. Open File Explorer.
2. Click **Computer**.
3. Click the disc icon.
4. Click the **Drive** tab.
5. Click **Format**.

   The Format dialog box appears.

6. Use the Volume Label text box to type a new name for the disc, if desired.
7. Click **Start**.

   Windows 8 warns you that all data on the disc will be erased.

Extract Files from a Compressed Folder

If someone sends you a file via e-mail, or if you download a file from the Internet, the file often arrives in a *compressed* form, which means the file actually contains one or more files that have been compressed to save space. To use the files on your computer, you need to extract them from the compressed file.

Because a compressed file can contain one or more files, it acts like a kind of folder. Therefore, Windows 8 calls such files *compressed folders*, *zipped folders*, or *Zip archives*.

Extract Files from a Compressed Folder

1. Open the folder containing the compressed folder.

   A. The compressed folder usually appears as a folder icon with a zipper.

2. Click the compressed folder.
3. Click the **Extract** tab.
4. Click **Extract all.**

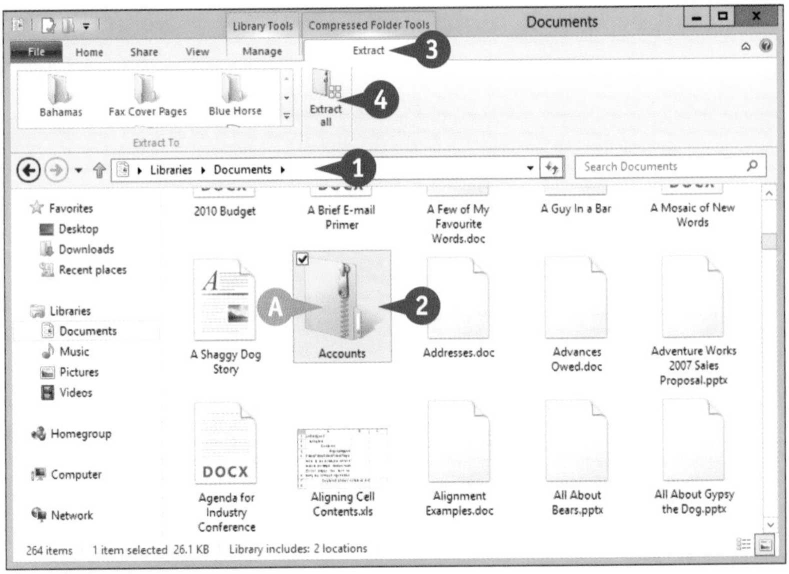

The Select a Destination and Extract Files dialog box of the Extract Wizard appears.

5. Type the location of the folder into which you want the files extracted.

   B. You can also click **Browse** and choose the folder using the Select a Destination dialog box.

6. If you want to open the folder into which you extracted the files, click **Show extracted files when complete** (☐ changes to ☑).
7. Click **Extract**.

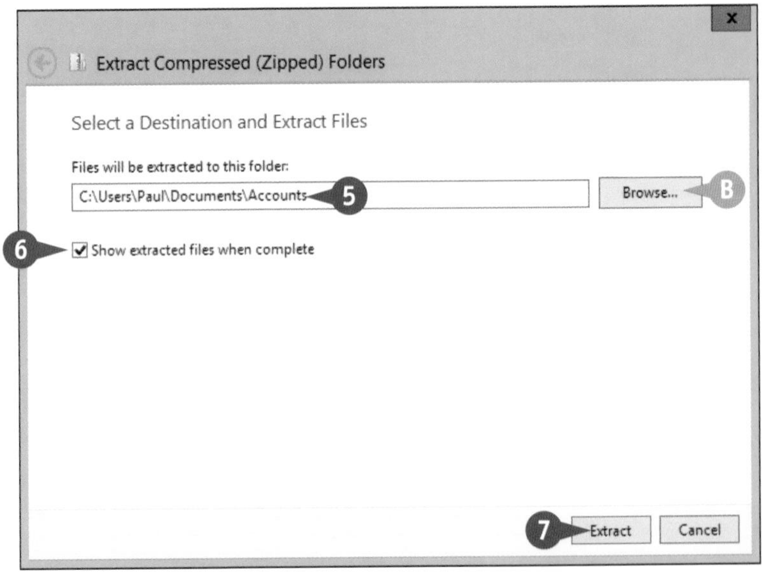

Windows 8 extracts the files.

Note: You can view the contents of a compressed folder before you extract the files. Double-click the compressed folder to open it. Windows 8 treats the compressed folder just like a regular subfolder, which means it displays the files in the window. In that window, you can click **Extract all** to launch the Extract Wizard.

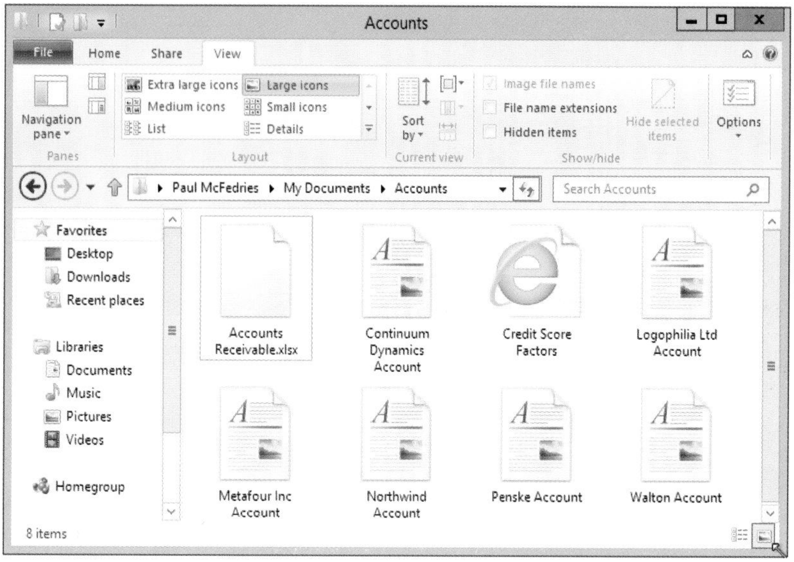

TIP

How can I create a compressed folder?

Follow these steps:

1. Select the files and folders you want to store in the compressed folder.
2. Right-click any selected item.
3. Click **Send to**.
4. Click **Compressed (zipped) folder**.

The compressed folder appears.

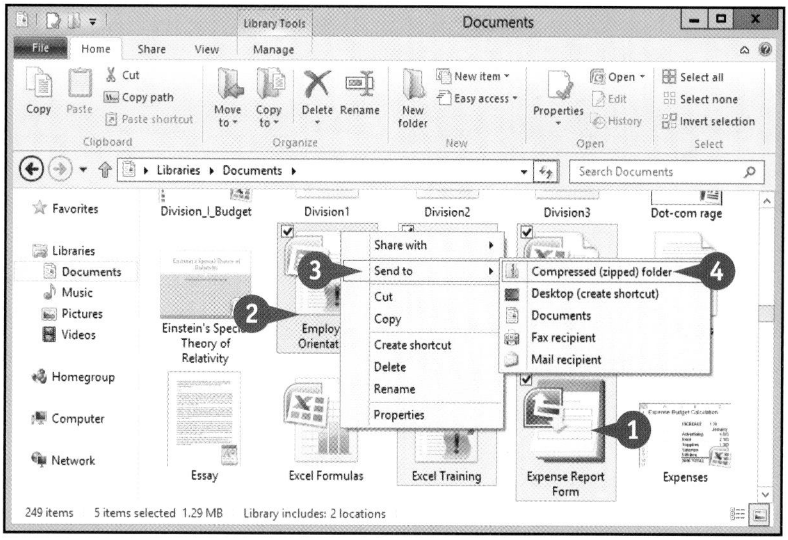

CHAPTER 11

Sharing Your Computer

If you share your computer with other people, you can create separate user accounts so that each person works only with his own documents, programs, and Windows 8 settings. This chapter shows you how to create and change user accounts, how to log on and off different accounts, how to share documents between accounts, and how to connect and work with a network and homegroup.

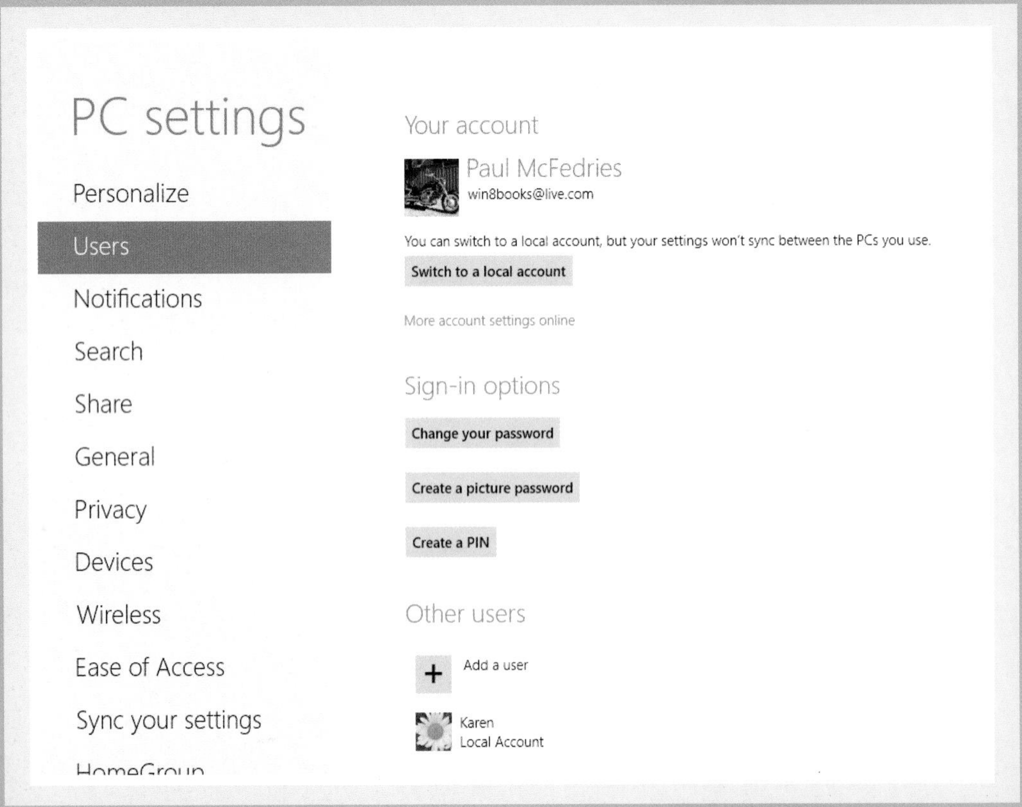

Display User Accounts

To work with user accounts, you need to display Windows 8's Users settings.

A *user account* is a collection of Windows 8 folders and settings associated with one person. In this chapter, you learn how to create new user accounts, change a user account's picture, change a user account's password, and delete a user account. To perform any of these tasks, you must first display the Users tab of the PC Settings app.

Display User Accounts

1. Move the mouse to the top right corner of the screen.

   The Charms menu appears.

Note: You can also display the Charms menu by press ⊞+C.

2. Click **Settings**.

   The Start settings pane appears.

3. Click **Change PC settings**.

The PC Settings app appears.

4. Click **Users**.

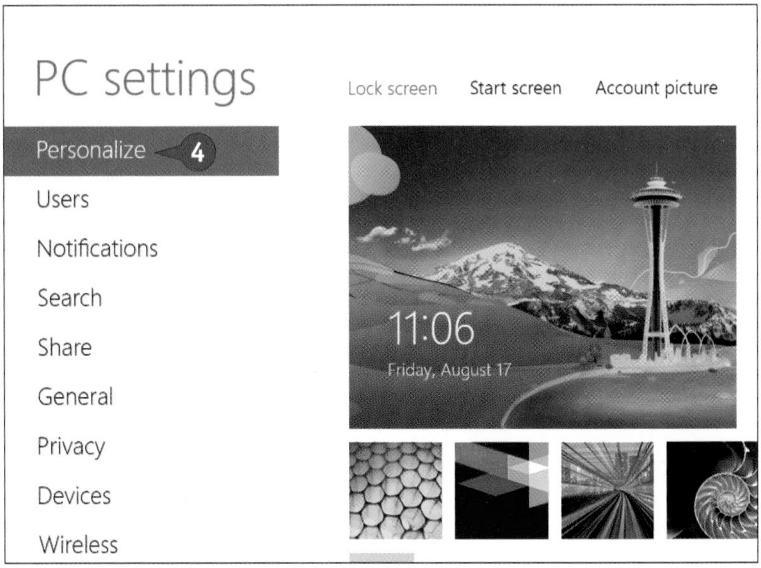

The Users tab appears.

A. Information about your account appears here. Later, after you have switched to another account, information for the current account appears in this spot.

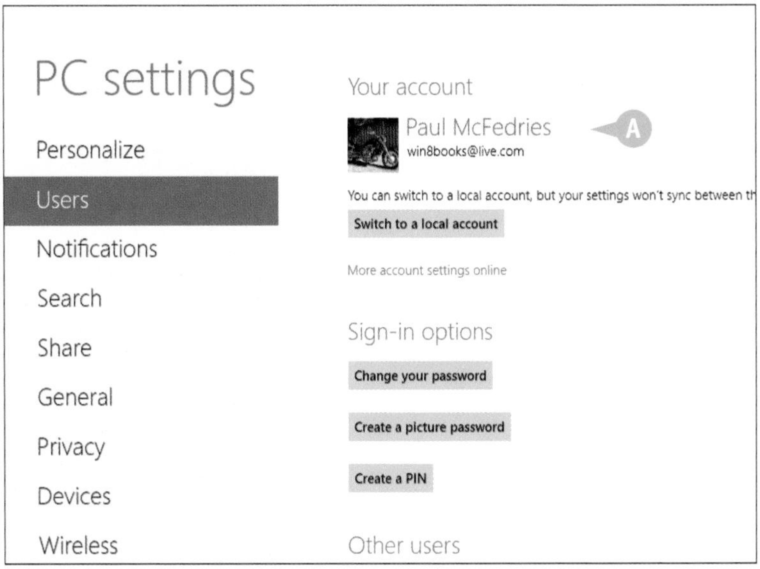

TIP

How do user accounts help me share my computer with other people?

Without user accounts, anyone who uses your computer can view and even change your documents, Windows 8 settings, e-mail accounts and messages, Internet Explorer favorites, and more.

With user accounts, users get their own libraries (Documents, Pictures, Music, and so on), personalized Windows 8 settings, e-mail accounts, and favorites. In short, users get their own versions of Windows 8 to personalize without interfering with anyone else's. Also, user accounts enable you to safely share documents and folders with people who use your computer and with people on your network.

Create a User Account

If you want to share your computer with another person, you need to create a user account for that individual. This enables the person to log on to Windows 8 and use the system. The new user account is completely separate from your own account. This means that the other person can change settings, create documents, and perform other Windows tasks without interfering with your own settings or data.

You can create a local user account or a Microsoft account. For maximum privacy, you should safeguard each account with a password.

Create a User Account

1 Display the Users tab of the PC Settings app.

Note: See "Display User Accounts," earlier in this chapter, to learn how to display the Users tab.

2 Click **Add a user**.

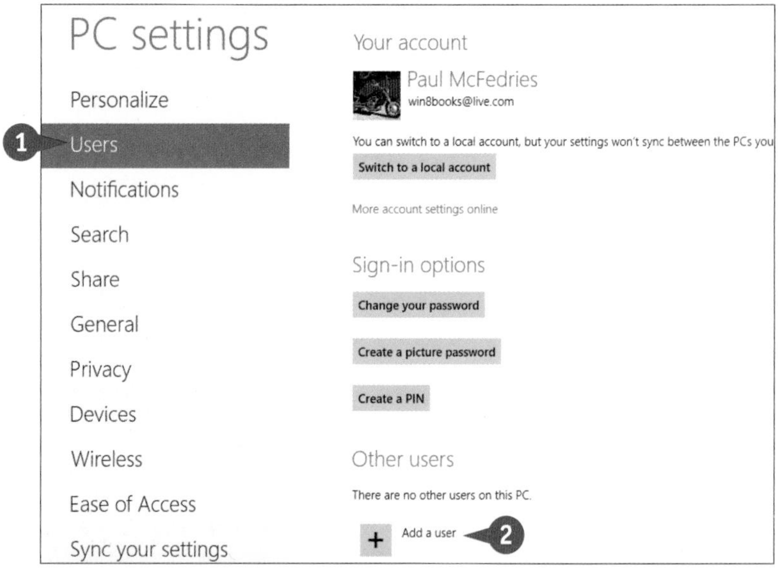

The Add a User screen appears.

3 For a local account, click **Sign in without a Microsoft account.**

Note: If you want to create a Microsoft account instead, follow the steps in the "Create a Microsoft Account" section in Chapter 3.

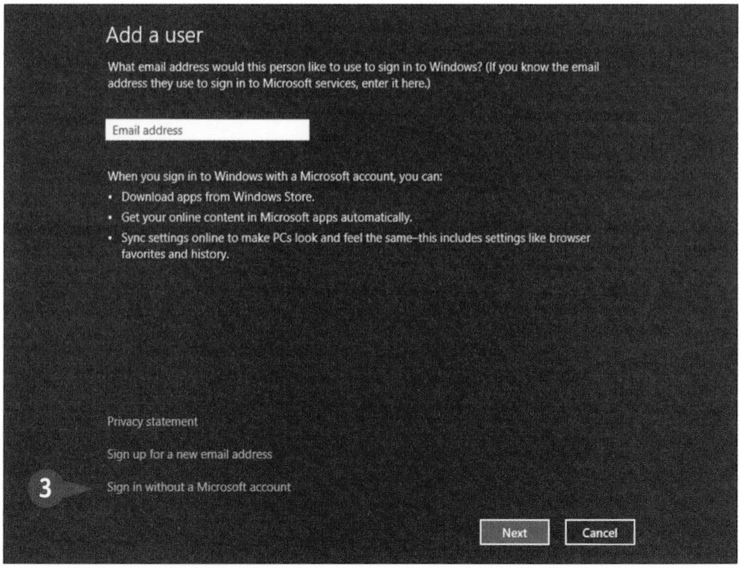

4 Click **Local account**.

The local account version of the Add a User screen appears.

5 Type the name you want to use for the new account.

6 Type the password.

Note: The password characters appear as dots for security reasons.

7 Type the password again.

8 Type a hint that will help you or the user remember the password.

9 Click **Next**.

Windows 8 creates the account.

A If you are setting up an account for a child, you can click this check box (☐ changes to ☑) to track and control the child's PC usage. See Chapter 12 for details.

10 Click **Finish** (not shown).

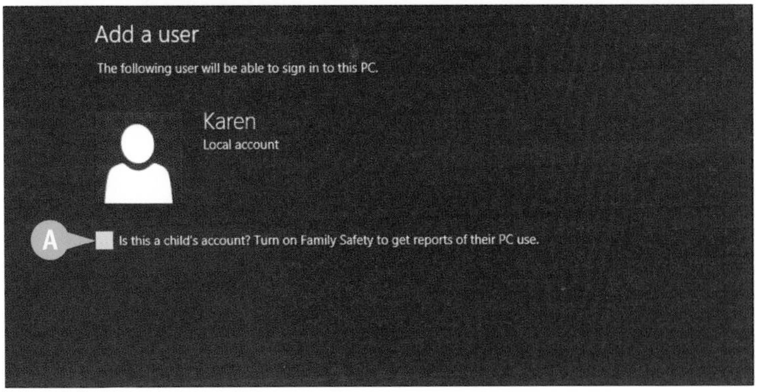

TIP

How do I create a secure password?

It is a good idea to use secure passwords that a nefarious user cannot guess. Here are some guidelines to follow:

- Do not use an obvious password such as the user's account name or the word "password."
- Make sure the password is at least eight characters long.
- Use at least one character from at least three of the following four sets: lowercase letters, uppercase letters, numbers, and symbols.

Switch between Accounts

After you have created more than one account on your computer, you can switch between accounts. This is useful when one person is already working in Windows 8 and another person needs to use the computer.

When you switch to a second account, Windows 8 leaves the original user's programs and windows running. This means that after the second person is finished, the original user can sign on again and continue working as before.

Switch between Accounts

1 On the Start screen, click your user account tile.

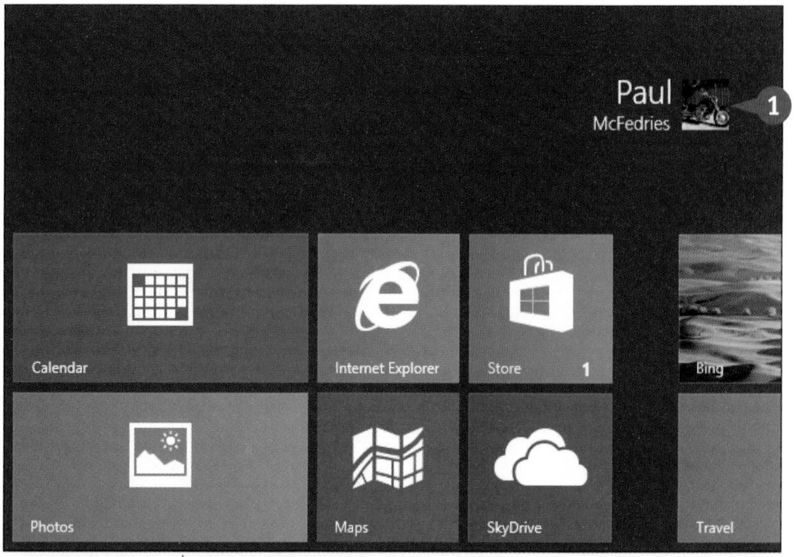

2 Click the user account you want to switch to.

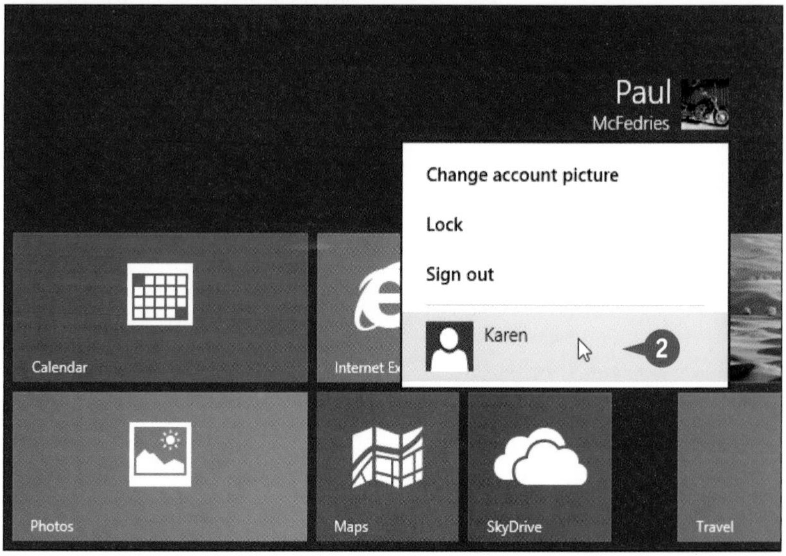

Windows 8 prompts you for the user account password.

3. Type the password.
4. Click the **Submit** arrow (→).

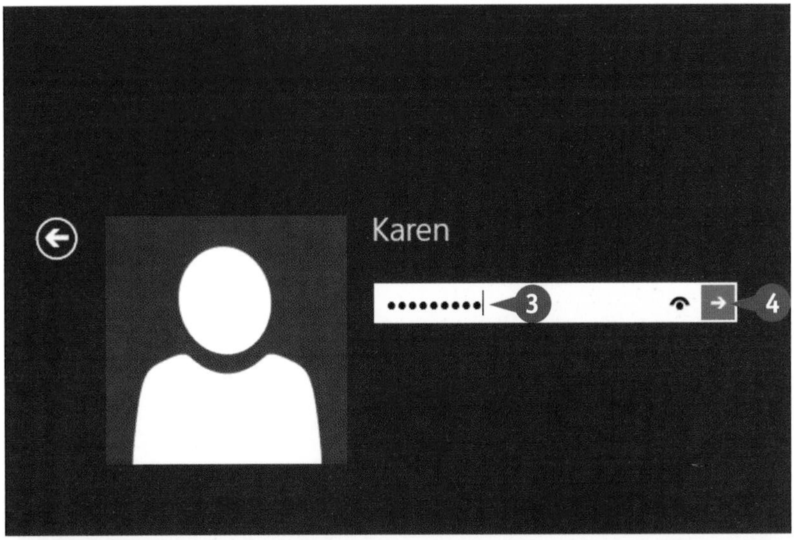

A. The user's name and picture now appear in the Start menu.

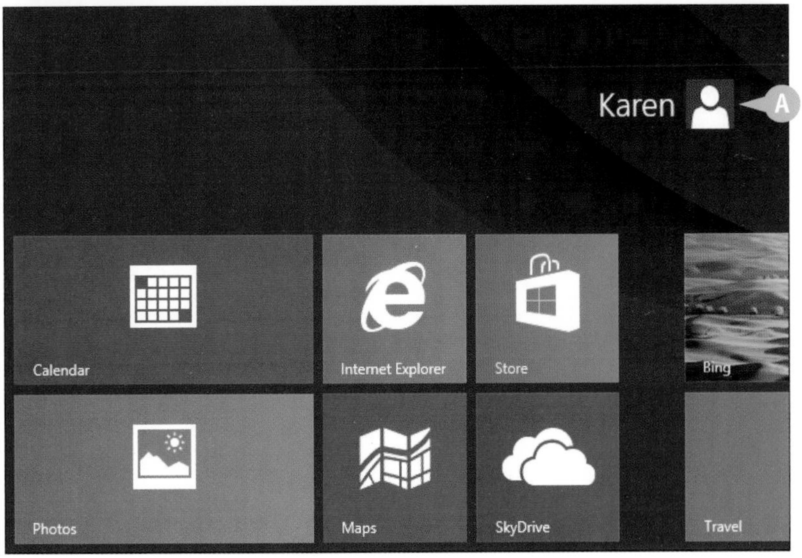

TIP

What happens if I forget my password?

When you set up your password as described in the previous section, Windows 8 asks you to supply a hint to help you remember the password. If you cannot remember your password, follow these steps:

1. In the sign-on screen, leave the password text box blank.
2. Click the **Submit** arrow (→).

   Windows 8 tells you the password is incorrect.

3. Click **OK** to return to the sign-on screen.

   Windows 8 displays the password hint.

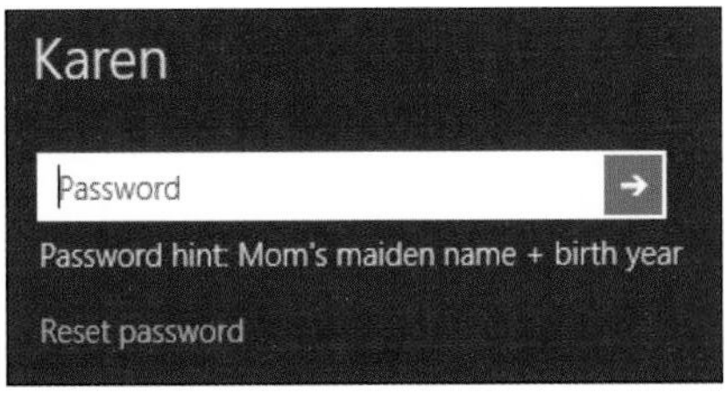

Change Your User Account Picture

You can add visual interest to your user account as well as make it a bit easier to tell one user account from another by adding a picture to the account.

When you create a user account, Windows 8 assigns a default picture to the account, and this picture appears in the user's Start screen tile, the Users tab of the PC Settings app, and the sign-on screen. Unfortunately, this default picture is a generic silhouette of a person's head and upper torso, so it is not very interesting or useful. If you have a more suitable picture that you would prefer to use, you can change your picture.

Change Your User Account Picture

1. On the Start screen, click your user account tile.
2. Click **change account picture**.

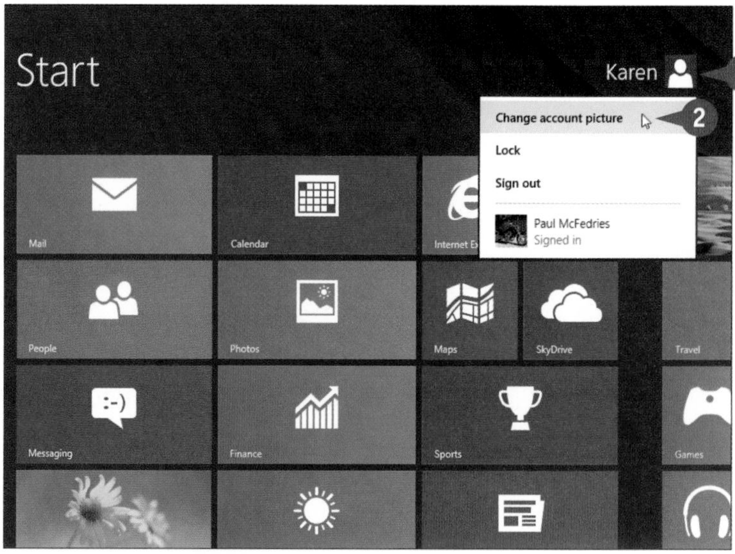

The PC Settings app appears with the Personalize tab displayed.

3. Click **Browse**.

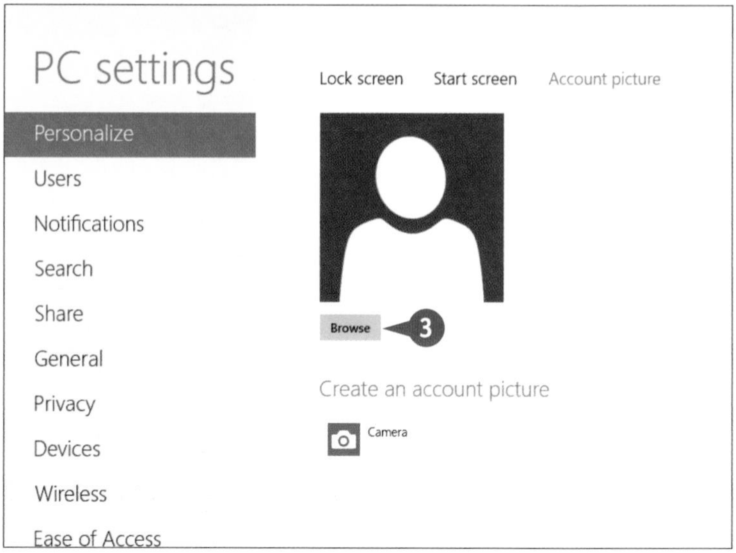

The Account Pictures screen appears.

4. Click **Files** and then click the folder that contains the picture you want to use.

5. Click the picture you want to use.

6. Click **Choose image**.

A. The Personalize tab appears and displays the new picture.

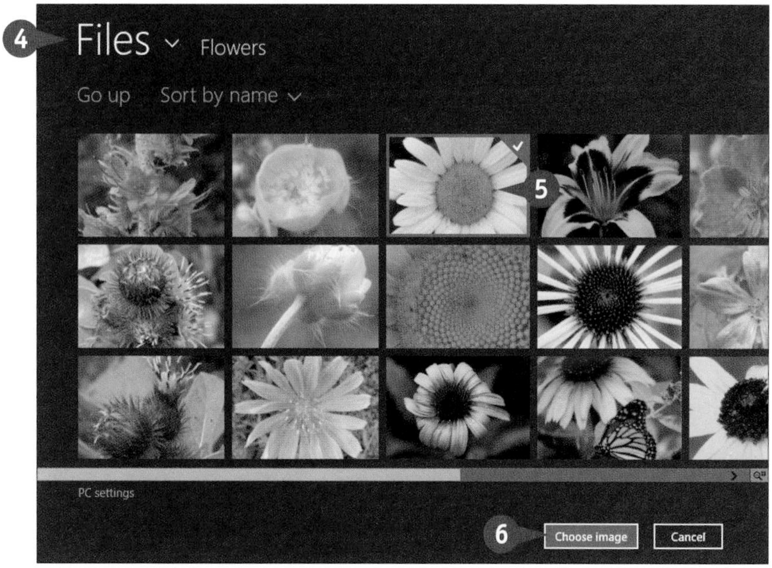

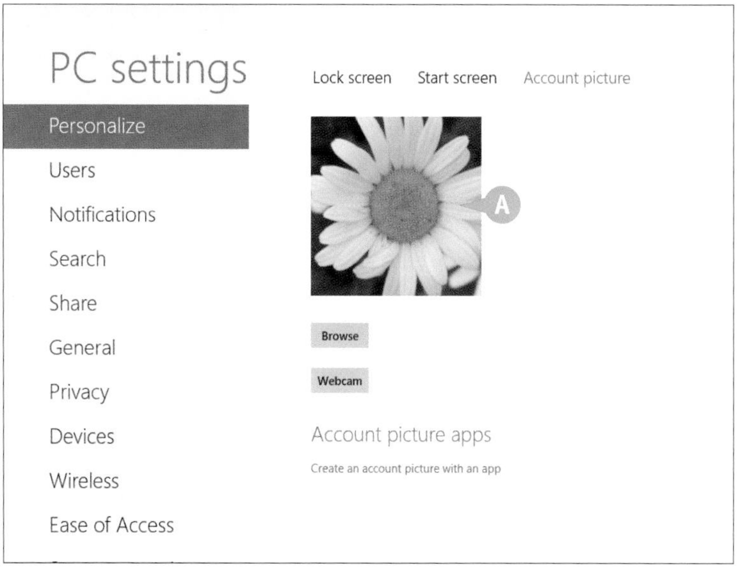

TIP

How do I use a webcam photo as my user account picture?

Follow these steps:

1. Repeat steps **1** and **2**.
2. Click **Camera**.

   The Camera app appears.
3. Position yourself within the screen.
4. Click the screen to take the picture.

   The Camera app displays the photo and adds a rectangle that defines the area of the photo it will use for your account picture.
5. Click and drag the rectangle to the position you want.
6. Click and drag the rectangle corners to set the size and shape of the rectangle.
7. Click **OK**.

Change a User's Password

If you set up a user account with no password, or if you find it difficult to remember your existing password, you can change the password.

Assigning a password to each user account is good practice because otherwise someone who sits down at the PC can sign in using an unprotected account. It is also good practice to assign a strong password to each account, so that a malicious user cannot guess the password and gain access to the system. Whether you want to assign a password or create a password that is stronger or easier to remember, you can use Windows 8 to change an existing password.

Change a User's Password

1. If you want to change another user's password, sign in as that user.
2. Display the Users tab of the PC Settings app.

Note: See "Display User Accounts," earlier in this chapter, to learn how to display the Users tab.

3. Click **Change your password.**

Note: If the account has no password, click **Create a password** instead.

The Change Your Password screen appears.

4. Type your old password.

Note: If the account has no password, you can skip step 4.

5. Click **Next.**

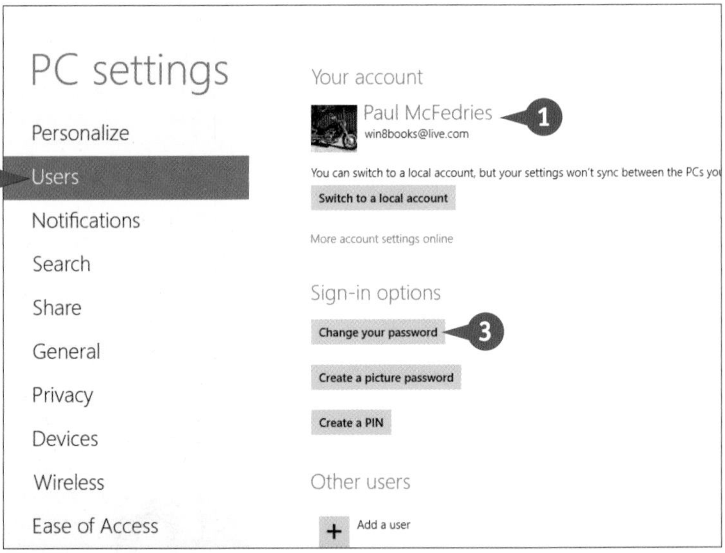

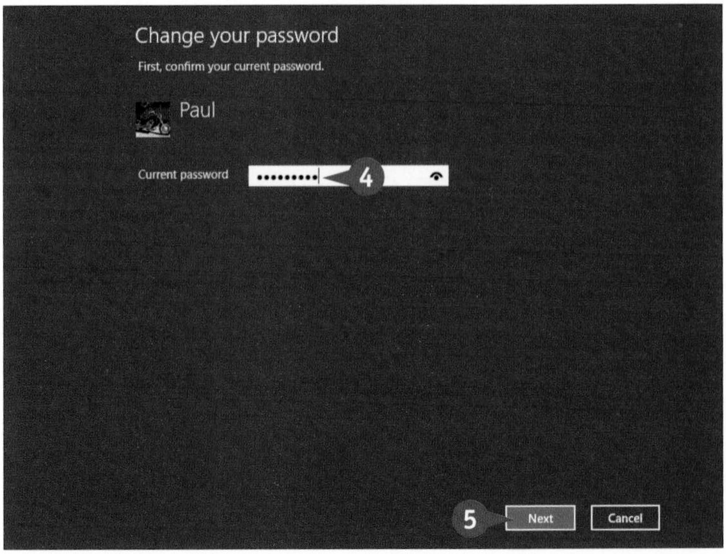

6 Type the new password.

7 Type the new password again.

A If you are not sure whether you typed a password correctly, click and hold the icon to temporarily display the password.

8 Type a password hint.

9 Click **Next**.

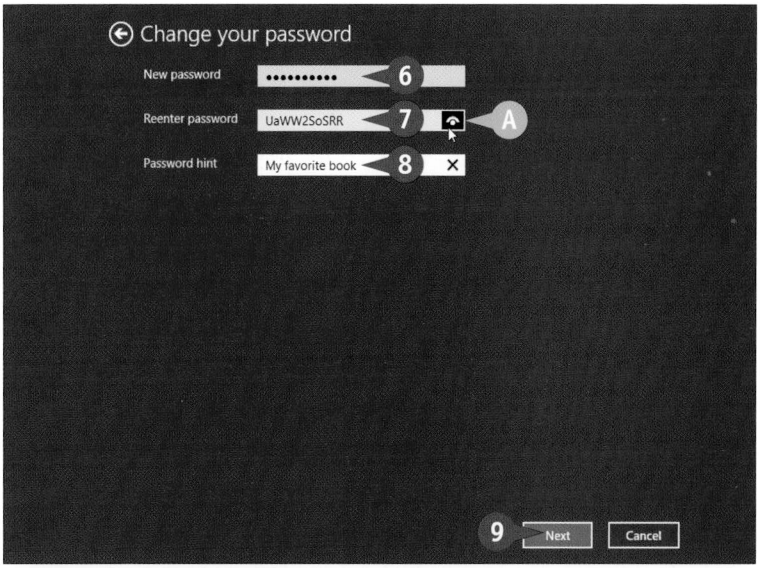

10 Click **Finish** (not shown).

Windows 8 updates the user account password.

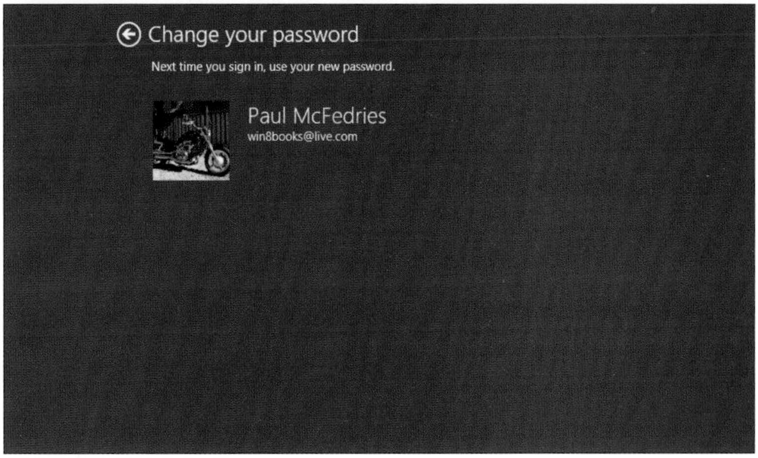

TIP

Are there any other precautions I can take to protect my password?

Yes, besides creating a strong password as described earlier in this chapter, you should also safeguard your password by following these guidelines:

- Do not tell anyone your password.
- Do not write down your password.
- Make your password easier to remember by using a mnemonic device. For example, you could use the first letters as well as any numbers that appear in the name of a favorite book or movie. For example, from the book *Unbroken: A World War II Story of Survival, Resilience, and Redemption*, you could get the password UaWW2SoSRR.

Delete an Account

If you created a user account temporarily, or if you have a user account that is no longer needed or no longer used, you can delete that account.

This reduces the number of users that appear in the Users tab of the PC Settings app, as well as the Windows 8 sign-on screen, which can make these screens a bit easier to navigate. Deleting a user account also means that Windows 8 reclaims the disk space that the account uses, which gives you more room to store files in your other accounts.

Delete an Account

1. Sign out of the user account you want to delete.

Note: To sign out of an account, click the user account tile on the Start screen, and then click **Sign out**.

2. On the Start screen, press ⊞ + W.

   The Settings search pane appears.

3. Type **remove user**.
4. Click **Remove user accounts**.

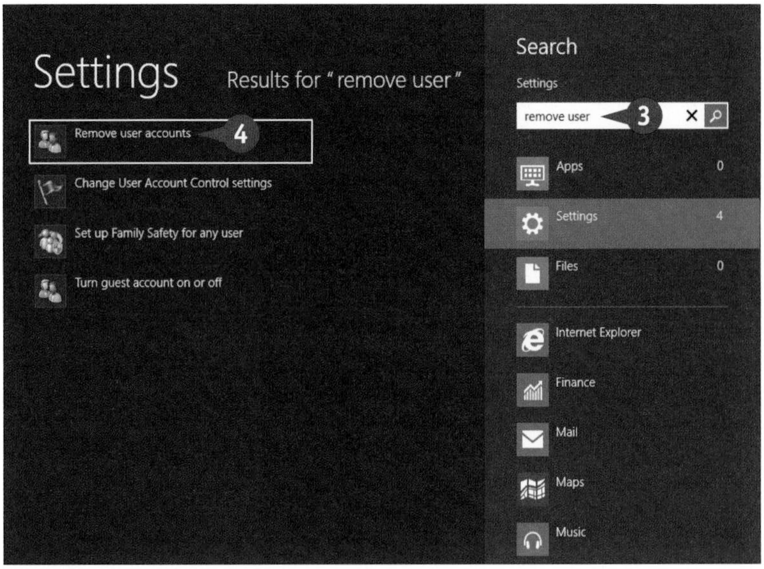

The Manage Accounts window appears.

5. Click the user account you want to delete.

The Change an Account window appears.

6 Click **Delete the account.**

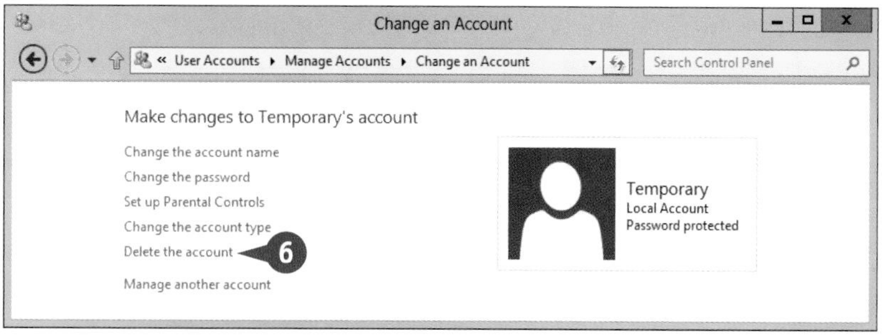

The Delete Account window appears.

7 Click to specify whether you want to keep or delete the user's personal files.

Note: See the tip to learn the difference between these two options.

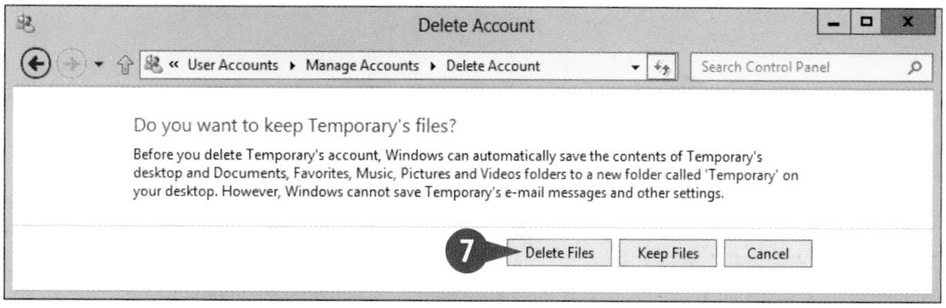

The Confirm Deletion window appears.

8 Click **Delete Account.**

Windows 8 deletes the account.

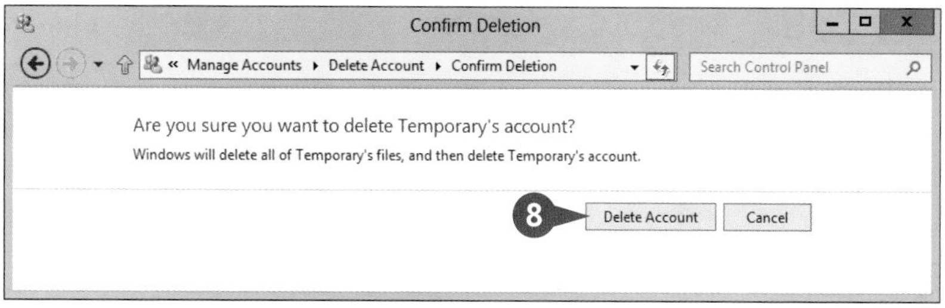

TIPS

My user account does not offer the Delete the account task. Why not?

If yours is the administrator account on the computer, Windows 8 does not allow you to delete it. Windows 8 requires that there always be at least one administrator account on the computer.

What is the difference between the Keep Files and Delete Files options?

The options enable you to handle user files two ways:

- Click **Keep Files** to retain the user's personal files — the contents of his or her Documents folder and desktop. These files are saved on your desktop in a folder named after the user. All other personal items — settings, e-mail accounts and messages, and Internet Explorer favorites — are deleted.
- Click **Delete Files** to delete all the user's personal files, settings, messages, and favorites.

Connect to a Wireless Network

If you have a wireless access point in your home or office and your computer has built-in wireless networking capabilities, you can connect to the wireless access point to access your network. If your wireless access point is connected to the Internet, then connecting to the wireless network gives your computer Internet access, as well.

Most wireless networks are protected with a security key, which is a kind of password. Be sure you know the key before attempting to connect. However, after you have connected to the network once, your PC remembers the password, and will connect again automatically the next time the network comes within range.

Connect to a Wireless Network

1. Press ⊞+I.

   The Settings pane appears.

2. Click the **Network** icon (📶).

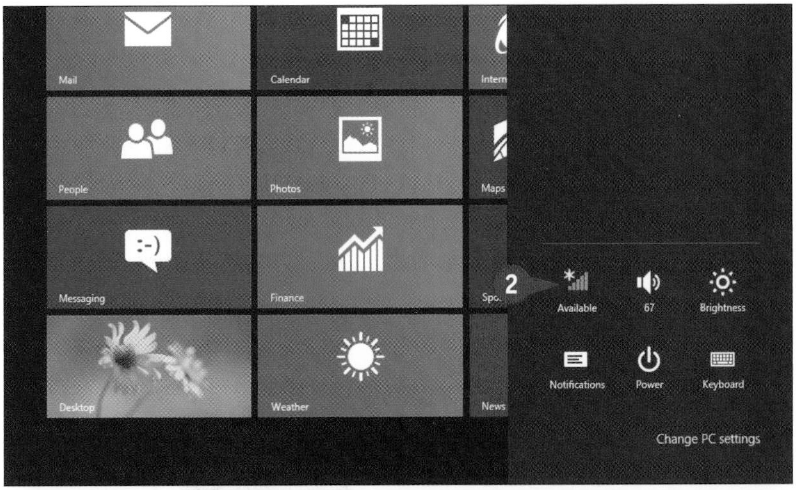

A. Windows 8 displays a list of wireless networks in your area.

3. Click your network.
4. To have Windows 8 connect to your network automatically in the future, click to activate the **Connect automatically** check box (☐ changes to ☑).
5. Click **Connect**.

If the network is protected by a security key, Windows 8 asks you to enter it.

6 Type the security key.

B If you want to be certain you typed the security key correctly, temporarily click and hold the **Display Password Characters** icon ( ).

7 Click **Next**.

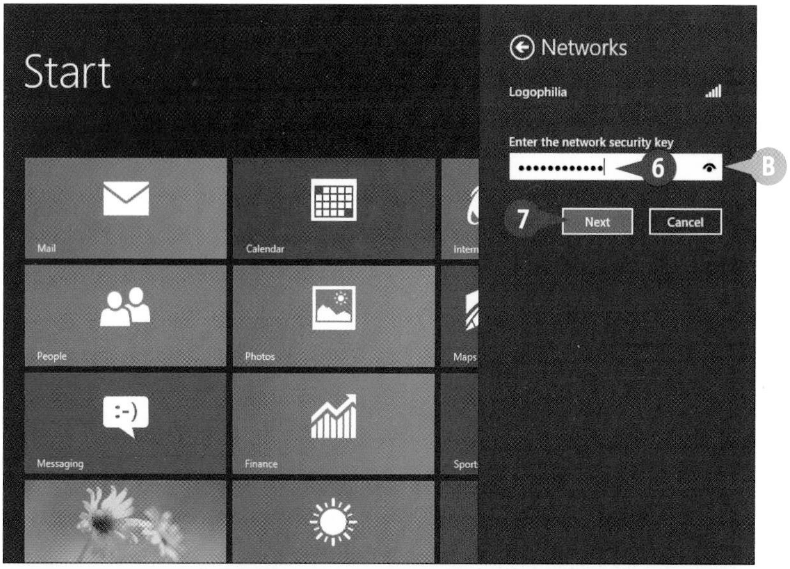

Windows 8 connects to the network.

8 Press + .

C The network icon changes from to to indicate that you now have a wireless network connection.

TIP

How do I disconnect from my wireless network?

To disconnect from the network, follow these steps:

1 Click the **Network** icon ( ).

2 Click your network.

3 Click **Disconnect**.

Windows 8 disconnects from the wireless network.

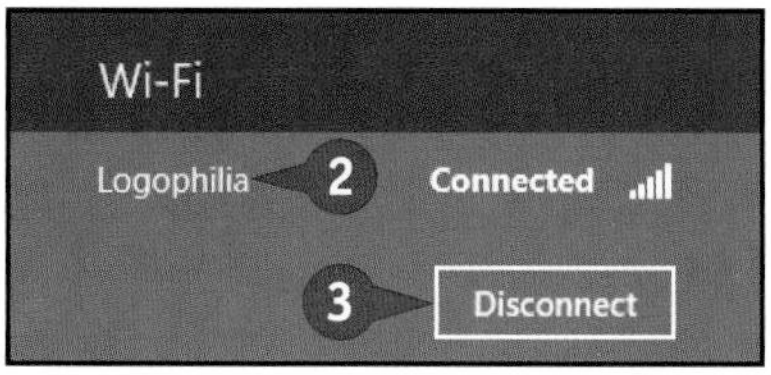

Create a Homegroup

You can share documents and media easily with other Windows 8 computers by creating a homegroup on your network. A homegroup simplifies network sharing by making it easy to create a homegroup and share documents.

You use one Windows 8 computer to create the homegroup, and then you use the homegroup password to join your other Windows 8 computers. See "Join a Homegroup," later in this chapter.

Create a Homegroup

1. On the Start screen, press ⊞+I.
2. Click **Change PC settings**.

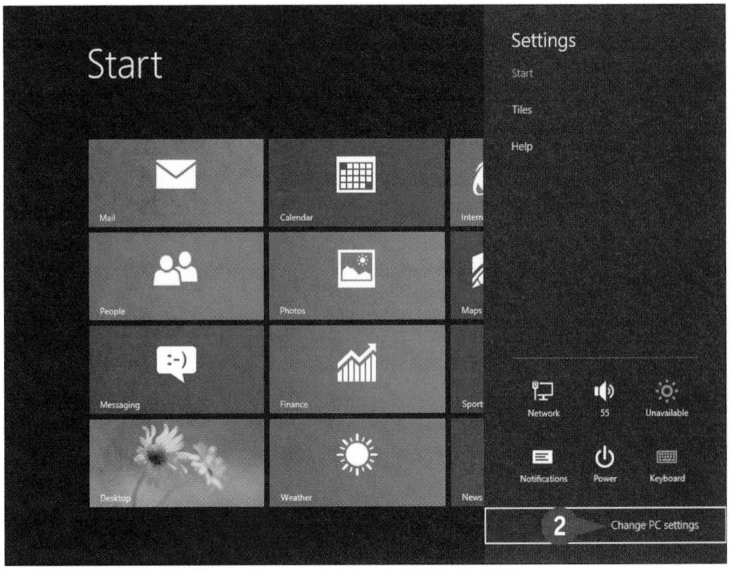

The PC Settings app appears.

3. Click **HomeGroup**.
4. Click **Create**.

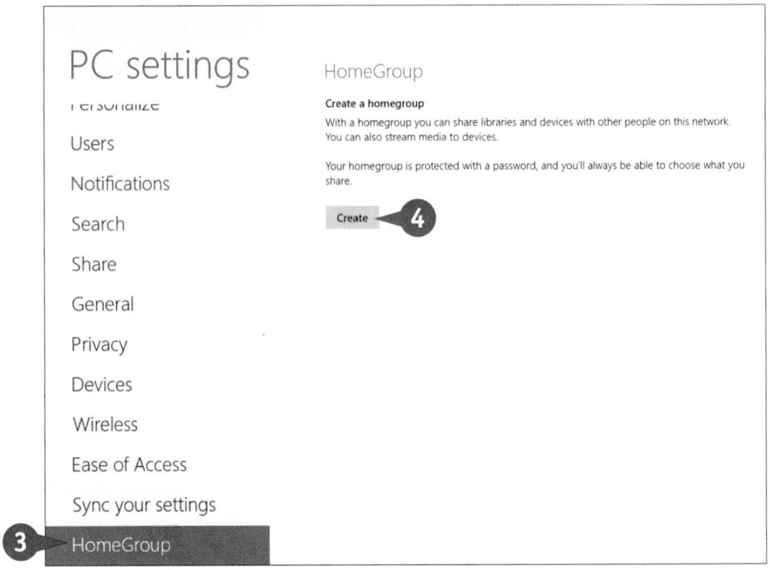

Windows 8 creates the homegroup and displays the Libraries and Devices screen.

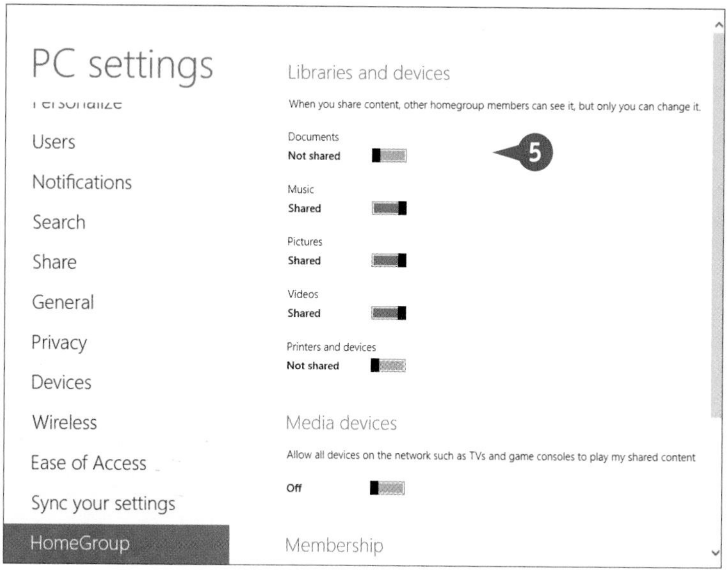

5 Click the switch to Shared for each type of file you want to share with the homegroup.

6 If you want devices on your network to be able to play your shared data, click this switch to **On**.

A Windows 8 displays the homegroup password.

7 Write down the homegroup password.

You can now join your other Windows 8 or Windows 7 computers to the homegroup, as described in the next section.

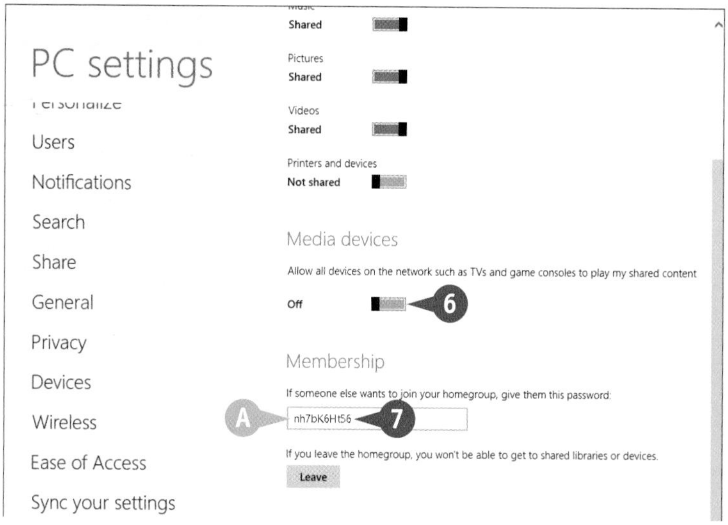

TIPS

I have lost my homegroup password. How do I view it again?
One method is to repeat steps **1** to **3**. Alternatively, press ⊞+W to open the Settings search pane, type **homegroup**, and then click **Change homegroup password**. Click the **View or print homegroup password** link to see your password. To print the password, click **Print this page**.

Is it possible to change the homegroup password?
Yes. On the Start screen, press ⊞+W to open the Settings search pane, type **homegroup**, and then click **Change homegroup password**. Click the **Change the password** link and then click **Change the password** to generate a new homegroup password. If one or more computers have already joined the homegroup, you need to provide them with the new password.

Join a Homegroup

If your network has a homegroup, you can join your Windows 8 computer to that homegroup. This enables you to access shared resources on other homegroup computers, and to share your own resources with the homegroup.

This section assumes you or someone else on your home network has already set up a homegroup as described in the "Create a Homegroup" section and that you have the homegroup password.

Join a Homegroup

1. On the Start screen, press ⊞+I.
2. Click **Change PC settings**.

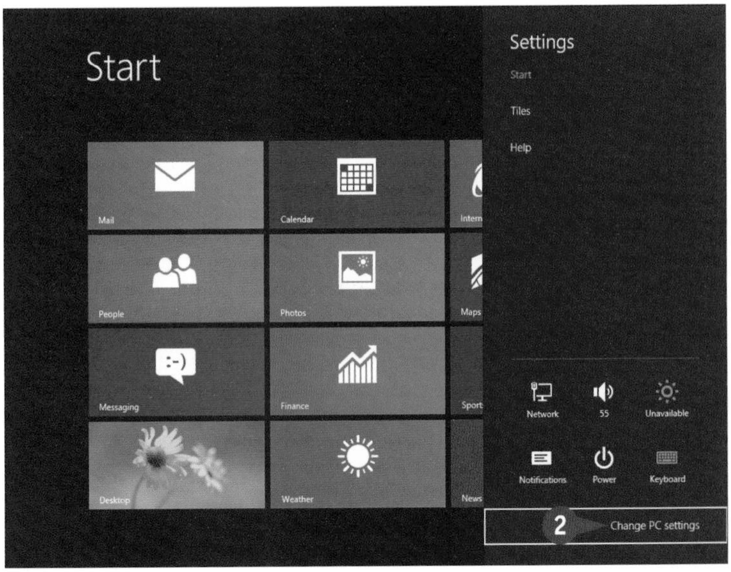

The PC Settings app appears.

3. Click **HomeGroup**.

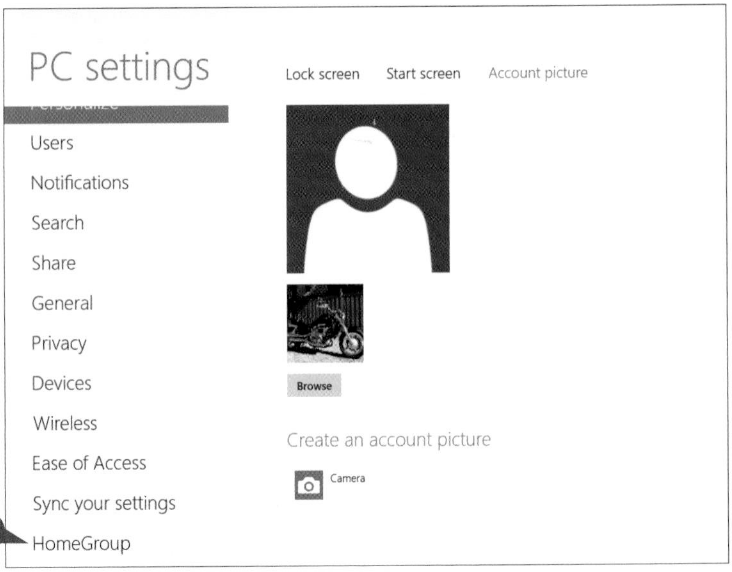

Windows 8 prompts you for the homegroup password.

4 Type the homegroup password.

5 Click **Join**.

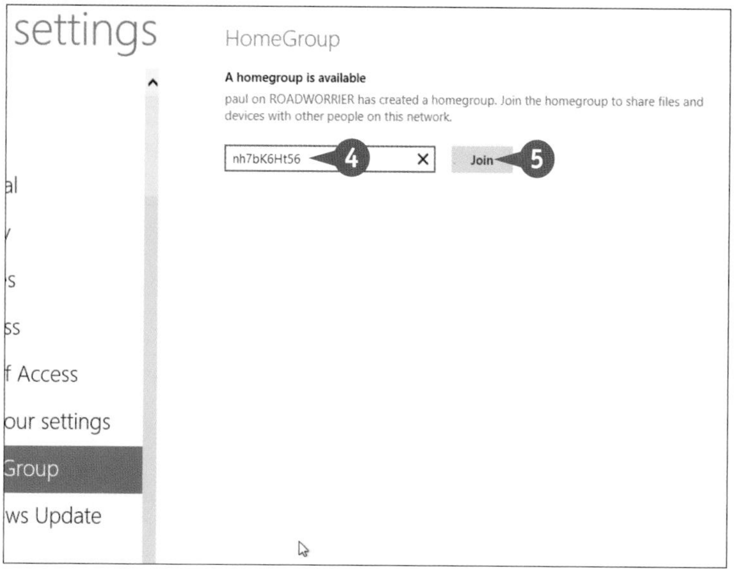

Windows 8 joins the homegroup and displays the Libraries and Devices screen.

6 Click the switch to Shared for each type of file you want to share with the homegroup.

7 If you want devices on your network to be able to play your shared data, click this switch to **On**.

You can now access other homegroup computers and share your files with the homegroup.

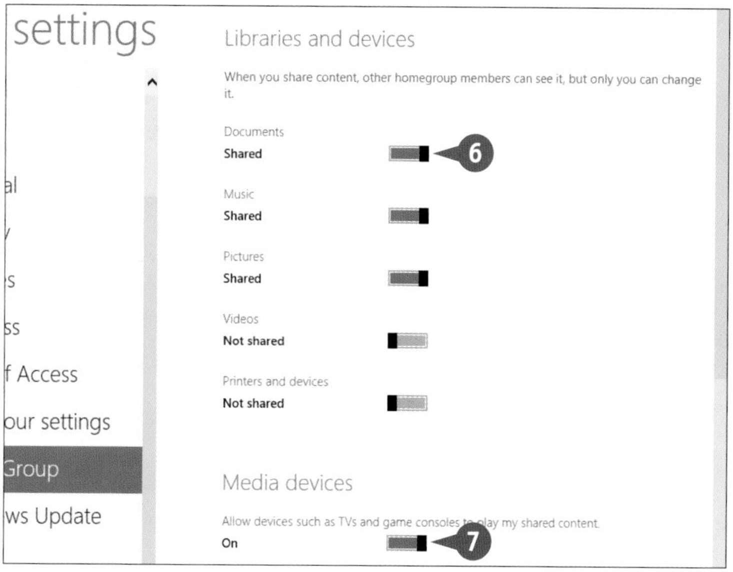

TIPS

When I try to join a homegroup, Windows 8 tells me my password is not correct. What am I doing wrong?

First, double-check that you have been given the correct homegroup password and that you are typing that password correctly. Second, understand that homegroup passwords are case-sensitive, so you must enter the uppercase and lowercase letters exactly as they appear in the original homegroup settings. Make sure your keyboard does not have Caps Lock turned on.

Can I leave a homegroup if I no longer need it?

Yes. On the Start screen, press ⊞ + I to open the Settings pane, and then click **Change PC Settings**. Click **HomeGroup**, and then click **Leave**. Windows 8 removes your computer from the homegroup.

Share a Document or Folder

You can share documents and folders of your choice with your homegroup, if your network has one. You can also share a document or folder with other users set up on your computer.

Sharing a document or folder enables you to work on a file with other people without having to send them a copy of the file. You can set up each document or folder with View or View and Edit permissions. View permission means that users cannot make changes to the document or folder; View and Edit permission means that users can also make changes to the document or folder.

Share a Document or Folder

Share with the Homegroup

1. On the Start screen, click **Desktop** (not shown).
2. Click **File Explorer**.
3. Open the folder containing the document or subfolder you want to share.
4. Click the document or subfolder.

Note: If you want to share more than one object, select all the objects you want to share.

5. Click the **Share** tab.
6. Click **Homegroup (view)**.

A. If you want homegroup users to make changes to the item, click **Homegroup (view and edit)** instead.

Share with a Specific User

1. Open the folder containing the document or subfolder you want to share.
2. Click the document or subfolder.
3. Click **Share**.
4. Click **Specific people**.

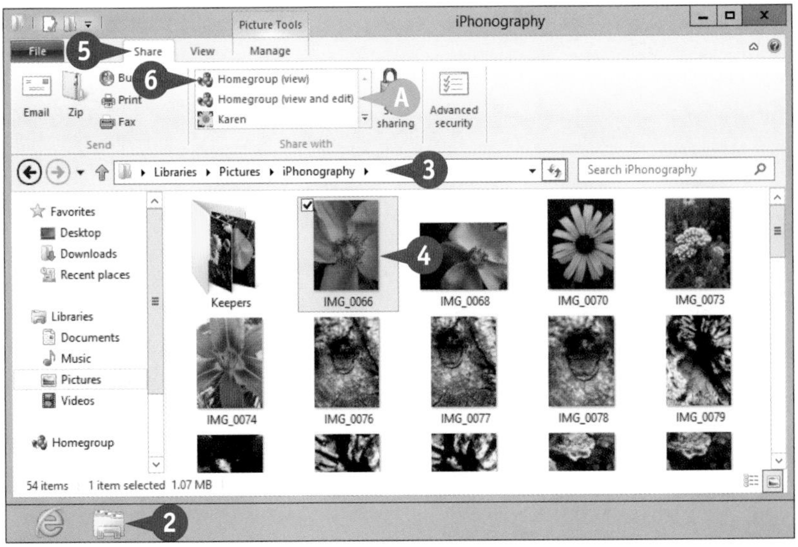

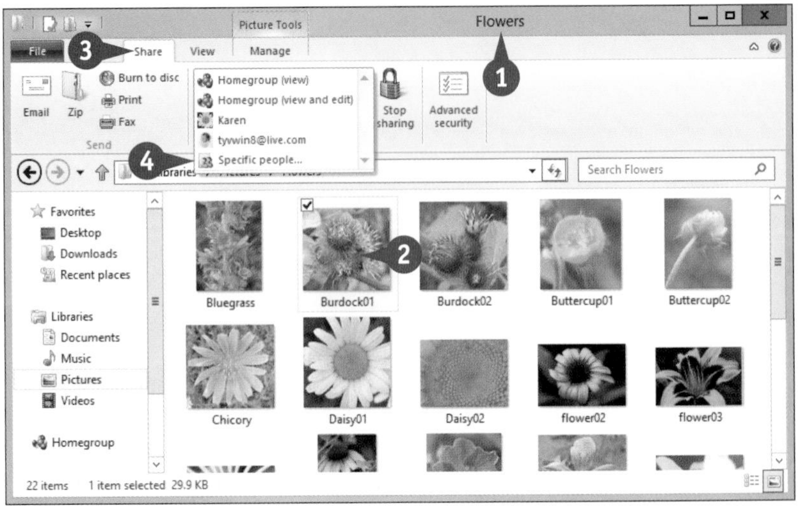

The File Sharing dialog box appears.

5. Click ▾ and then click the name of the user.
6. Click **Add**.
7. Click ▾ and then click the permission level.

Note: Read permission is the same as View, and Read/Write is the same as View and Edit.

8. Click **Share**.

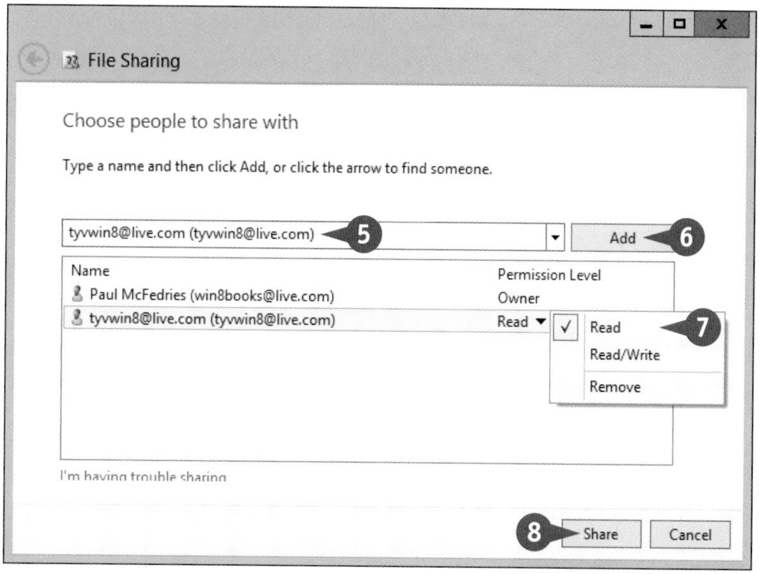

Windows 8 shares the document or folder.

- **B** Be sure to give the user the address that appears here.

9. Click **Done**.

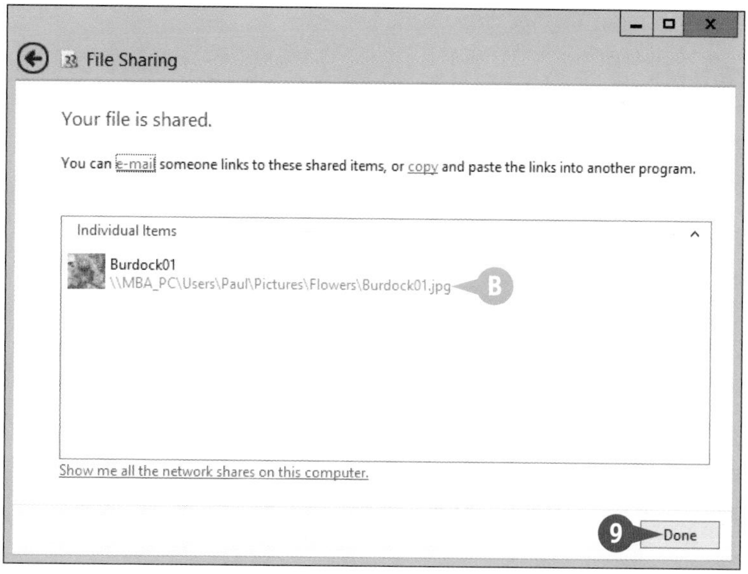

TIPS

How do the other users access the shared document or folder?

You need to send them the address that appears in the final File Sharing dialog box. You have two choices: Click **e-mail** to send the address via e-mail, or click **copy** to copy the address to memory. You can then open a program such as WordPad, click **Edit**, and then click **Paste** to paste the address.

Can I see all the documents and folders that I am sharing with other users?

Yes, you can do this in two ways. In the final File Sharing dialog box, click **Show me all the network shares on this computer**. Alternatively, in any folder window, click **Network** and then double-click your computer.

View Network Resources

To see what other network users have shared on your homegroup, you can use the Homegroup folder to view the other computers and see their shared resources. To get access to the shared homegroup resources, you must know the homegroup's password and have joined the homegroup, as described earlier in the "Join a Homegroup" section. If your network does not have a homegroup, you can use the Network folder instead.

A network resource can be a folder, hard drive, CD or DVD drive, removable disk drive, printer, scanner, or other shared device.

View Network Resources

View Homegroup Resources

1. On the Start screen, click **Desktop** (not shown).
2. Click **File Explorer**.
3. Click the **Homegroup** folder.

(A) Windows 8 displays icons for each user who is sharing data in the homegroup.

4. Double-click the user who is sharing the resource you want to access.

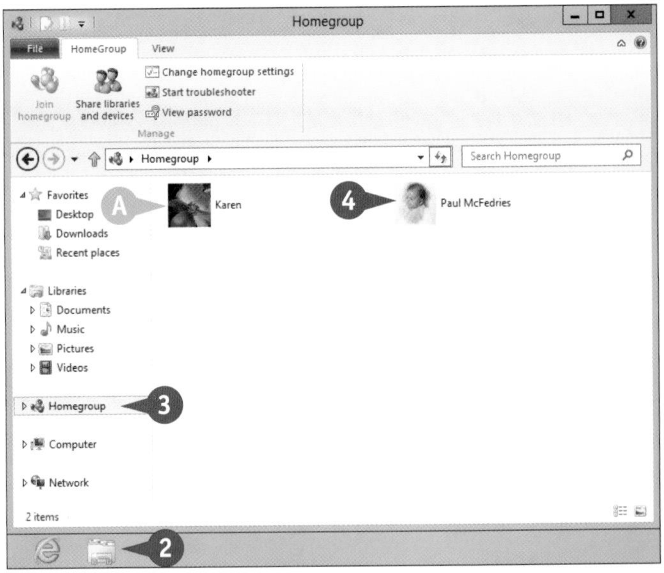

Windows 8 displays the resources the user is sharing.

(B) If the user has an account on multiple PCs, you see a section for each PC.

(C) The resources that the user is sharing on the computer appear here.

5. Double-click an icon to access the resource.

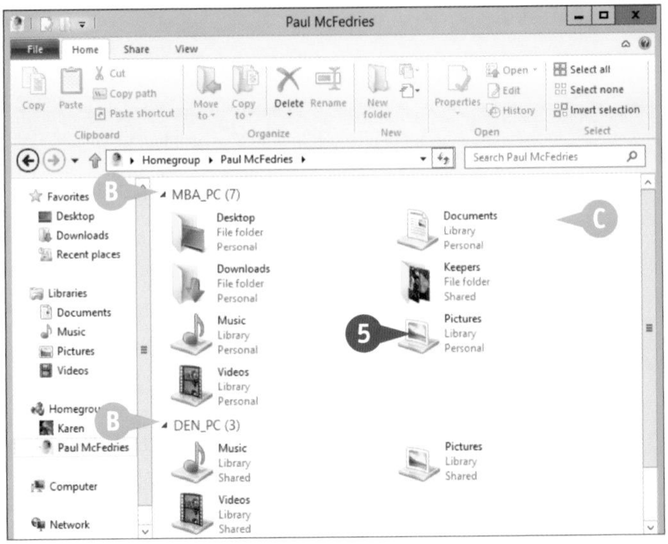

View Network Resources

1. On the Start screen, click **Desktop** (not shown).
2. Click **File Explorer**.
3. Click the **Network** folder.

D Windows 8 displays icons for each computer that is sharing resources.

4. Double-click the computer that is sharing the resource you want to access.

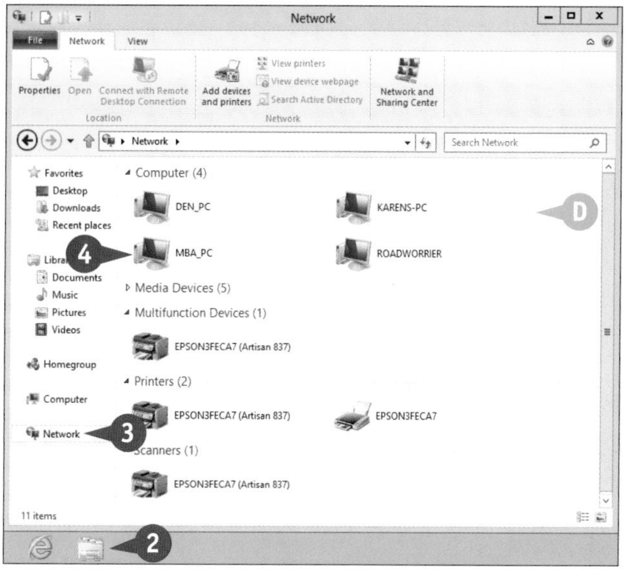

E The resources the computer is sharing appear here.

5. Double-click an icon to access the resource.

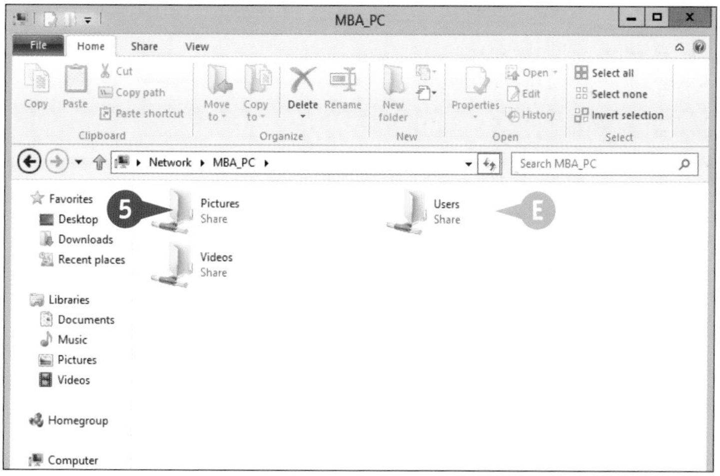

TIPS

My network is not working. Is there a way to fix the problem?

Yes. Windows 8 comes with troubleshooting tools for homegroups and networks. If you are having trouble with your homegroup, launch File Explorer, click the **Homegroup** folder, click the **Homegroup** tab, and then click **Start troubleshooter**. If you are having network trouble, right-click the network icon in the taskbar's notification area, and then click **Troubleshoot problems**. In both cases, follow whatever repair techniques Windows 8 suggests.

How do I change the network name of my computer?

On the Start screen, type **name** and then click **Rename this computer** in the search results to open the System Properties dialog box with the Computer Name tab displayed. Click **Change**, use the Computer Name text box to type the new name, and then click **OK**.

CHAPTER 12

Implementing Security

Threats to your computer-related security and privacy often come from the Internet in the form of system intruders, such as junk e-mail, viruses, and identity thieves. In addition, many security and privacy violations occur right at your computer by someone simply using your computer while you are not around. To protect yourself and your family, you need to understand these threats and know what you can do to thwart them.

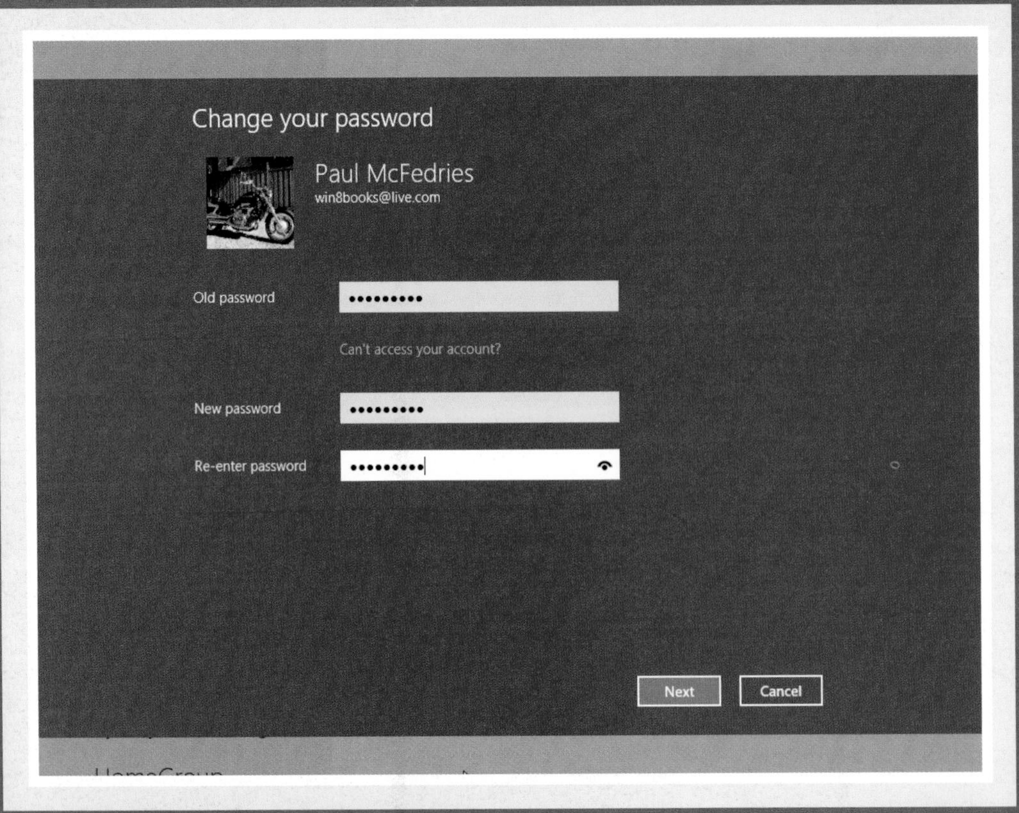

Understanding Windows 8 Security

Before getting to the details of securing your PC, it helps to take a step back and look at the security and privacy tools that Windows 8 makes available.

These tools include your Windows 8 user account password, User Account Control, parental controls, Windows Firewall, Windows Defender, Internet Explorer's anti-phishing features, and Mail's anti-spam features. Taken all together, these features represent a defense-in-depth security strategy that uses multiple layers to keep you and your data safe and private.

User Account Password

Windows 8 security begins with assigning a password to each user account on the computer. This prevents unauthorized users from accessing the system, and it enables you to lock your computer. See "Protect an Account with a Password" and "Lock Your Computer," later in this chapter.

User Account Control

User Account Control asks you to confirm certain actions that could conceivably harm your system. When you are using your main Windows 8 user account, which is your PC's administrative account, you click **Yes** to continue; for all other accounts, you must enter the administrative account's password to continue.

Family Safety

If one or more children use your computer, you can use the controls in the Windows 8 Family Safety feature to protect those children from inadvertently running certain programs, playing unsuitable games, and using the computer at inappropriate times. See "Set Up Family Safety," later in this chapter.

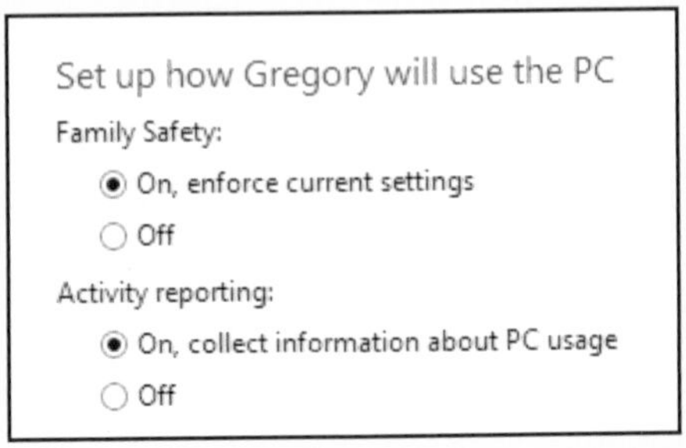

Windows Firewall

Windows 8 comes with its Windows Firewall feature turned on, because when your computer is connected to the Internet, another person on the Internet can possibly access your computer and infect it with a virus or cause other damage. Windows Firewall prevents intruders from accessing your computer while you are online.

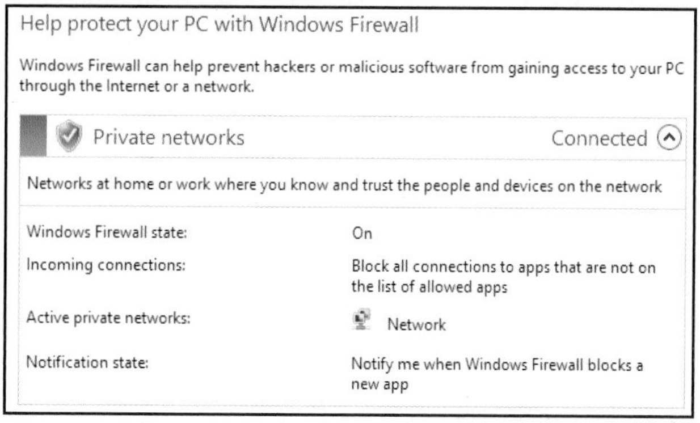
Help protect your PC with Windows Firewall
Windows Firewall can help prevent hackers or malicious software from gaining access to your PC through the Internet or a network.
Private networks
Connected
Networks at home or work where you know and trust the people and devices on the network
Windows Firewall state:
On
Incoming connections:
Block all connections to apps that are not on the list of allowed apps
Active private networks:
Network
Notification state:
Notify me when Windows Firewall blocks a new app

Windows Defender

Spyware is a software program that installs on your computer without your knowledge or consent. This program surreptitiously gathers data from your computer, steals your passwords, displays advertisements, and hijacks your web browser. To prevent spyware from installing on your computer, Windows 8 includes the Windows Defender program.

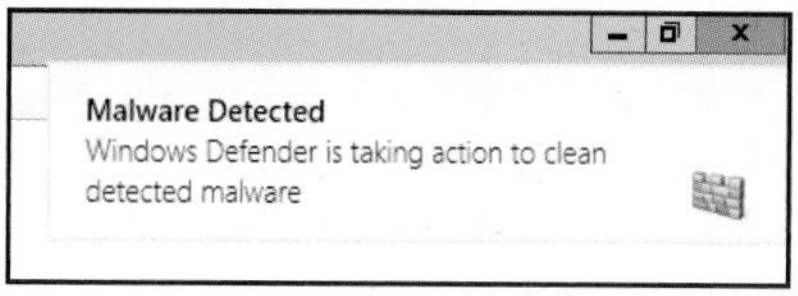
Malware Detected
Windows Defender is taking action to clean detected malware

Anti-Phishing

This website has been reported as unsafe
be.thegoodmama.com
We recommend that you do not continue to this website.

Phishing refers to e-mail messages or websites that appear to come from legitimate businesses and organizations, but actually come from a scam artist. The purpose of the message or site is to fool you into divulging personal or private data, such as passwords and credit card numbers. Internet Explorer and Mail come with anti-phishing features to help prevent this.

Junk E-Mail Filter

Junk e-mail — or *spam* — refers to unsolicited, commercial e-mail messages that advertise anything from baldness cures to cheap printer cartridges. Many spams advertise deals that are simply fraudulent, and others feature such unsavory practices as linking to adult-oriented sites, and sites that install spyware. Mail comes with a junk e-mail filter; see "Set the Junk E-Mail Protection Level," later in this chapter.

Windows Live Mail
Windows Live Mail has downloaded a message that appears to be junk email. This message was automatically moved to the Junk email folder.
You should check the Junk Email folder regularly to ensure that you don't miss email that you wish to receive.
Please do not show me this dialog again
Open Junk Email folder
Junk Email Options...
Close

Check Action Center for Security Problems

In Windows 8, the Action Center displays messages about the current state of your PC. In particular, Action Center warns you if your computer has any current security problems.

For example, Action Center tells you if your PC does not have virus protection installed, or if the Windows Defender spyware database is out of date. Action Center also warns you if your PC is not set up to download updates automatically and if important security features such as User Account Control are turned off.

Check Action Center for Security Problems

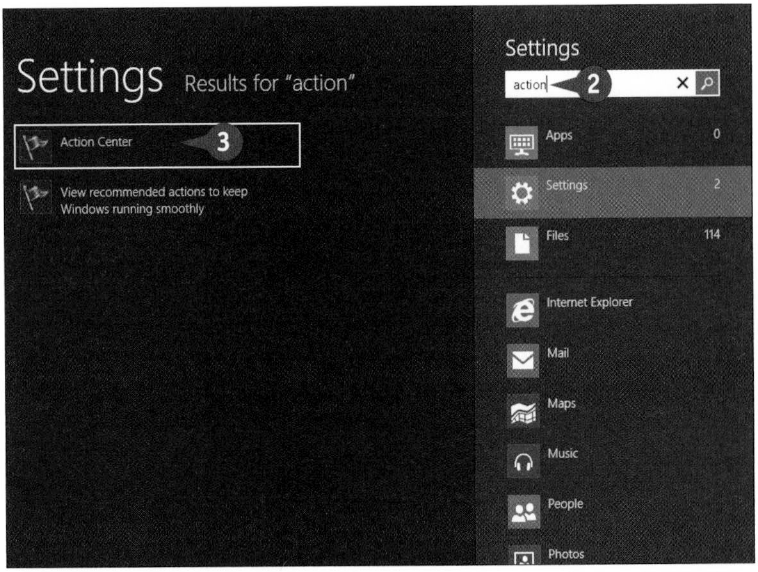

1 Press ⊞+W.

The Settings search pane appears.

2 Type **action**.

3 Click **Action Center**.

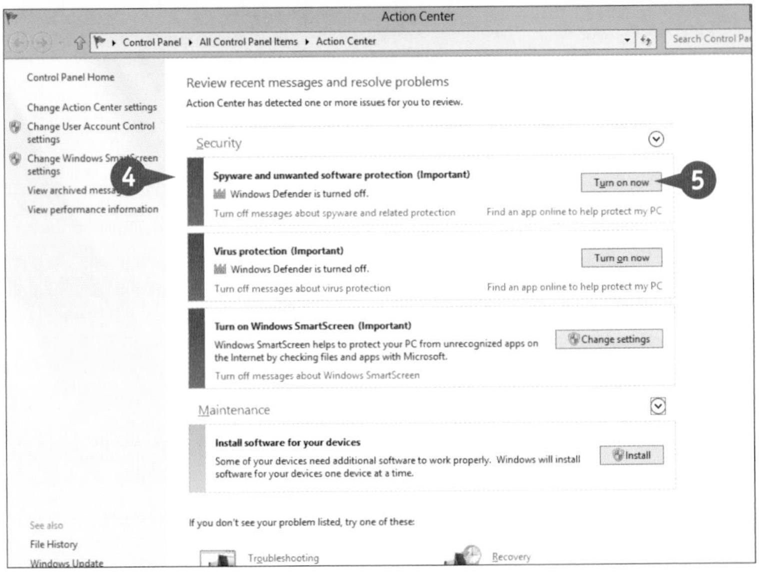

The Action Center window appears.

4 Review the messages in the Security section.

5 Click a message button to resolve the security issue, such as clicking **Turn on now** if Windows Defender is turned off.

6 Click **Security**.

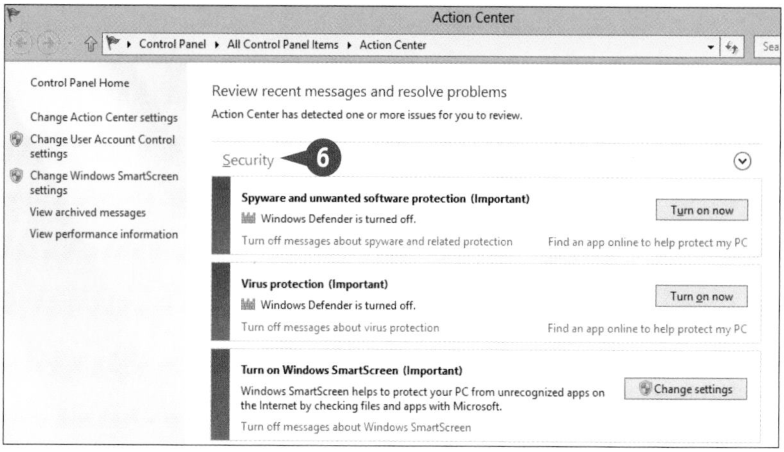

7 Scroll down the Action Center window.

A Action Center displays a summary of all your system's security settings.

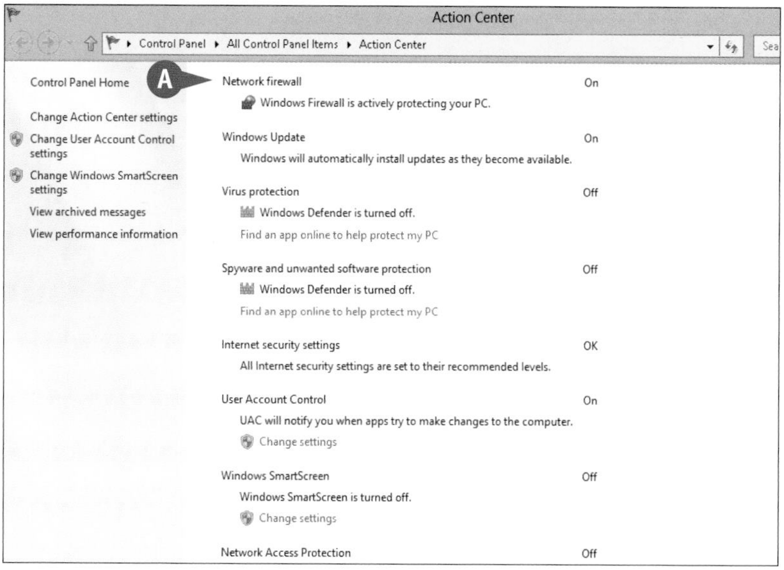

TIP

Is there a quicker way to see Action Center messages?

Yes, if you are working in the Desktop app, you can view Action Center messages and open the Action Center more quickly by following these steps:

1 Click the **Action Center** icon (⚑) in the taskbar's notification area.

A The current Action Center messages appear here.

2 To launch Action Center, click **Open Action Center**.

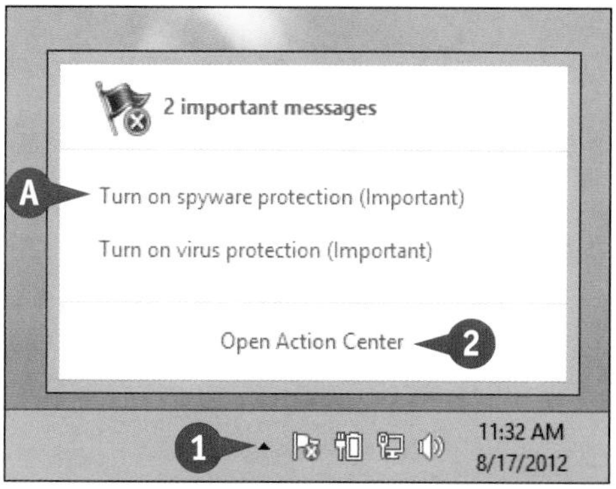

Protect an Account with a Password

You can enhance your PC's security by protecting your Windows 8 user accounts with a password.

Your main administrative account — that is, the one you set up when you first configured Windows 8 — must use a password; subsequent standard user accounts do not require a password. However, leaving an account unprotected is dangerous because another user can log on to the account just by clicking the username on the sign-on screen.

For maximum security, make sure that all your PC's user accounts are protected by a strong password that cannot be easily guessed or hacked. See the tip in this section.

Protect an Account with a Password

Display the Password Screen

1. Sign in with the account you want to protect.
2. Press ⊞+W.

   The Settings search pane appears.
3. Type **users**.
4. Click **Users**.

   The PC Settings app appears and displays the Users tab.
5. Click **Change your password**.

Note: If you are working with an account that has no password, click **Create a password**, instead.

The Change Your Password screen appears.

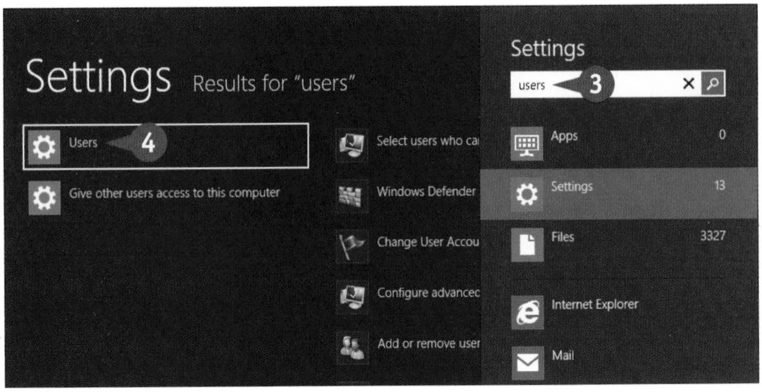

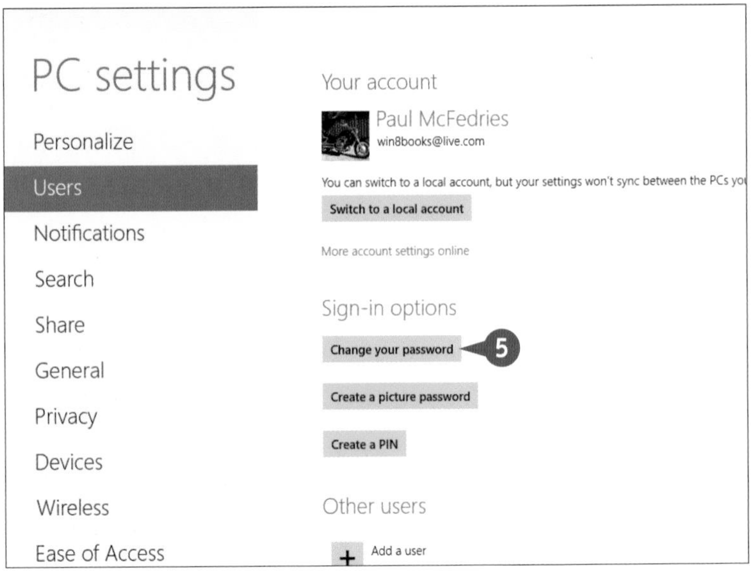

Change the Administrative User Password

1. Type your current password.
2. Type the new password.
3. Type the new password again.
4. Click **Next** (not shown).
5. Click **Finish** (not shown).

   Windows 8 updates the password.

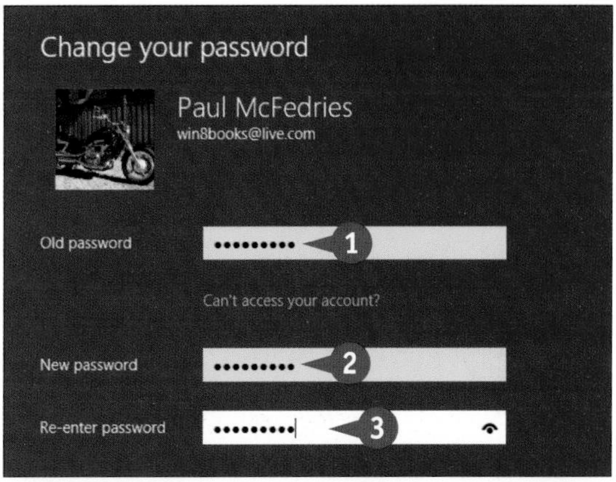

Change a Standard User Password

1. Type your current password.

Note: If you are working with an account that currently has no password, skip to step **3**.

2. Click **Next** (not shown).
3. Type the new password.
4. Type the new password again.
5. Type a word or phrase to use as a password hint in case you forget the password.
6. Click **Next** (not shown).
7. Click **Finish** (not shown).

   Windows 8 updates the password.

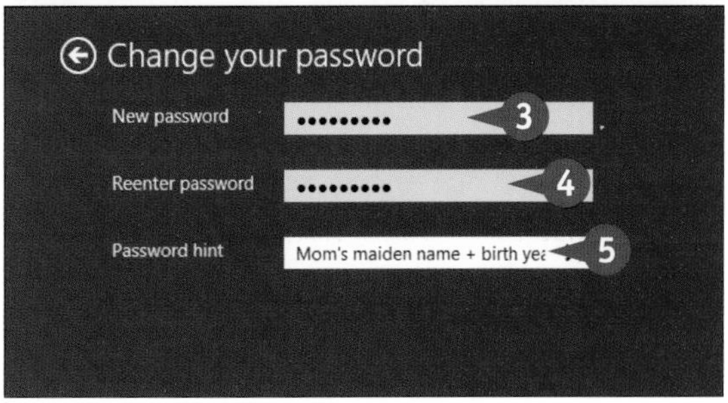

TIPS

What are the components of a strong password?
First, do not use obvious items such as your name or a word such as "password." Your password should be at least eight characters long, and it should include at least one character from each of the following three sets: lowercase letters, uppercase letters, and numbers. The strongest passwords also include at least one symbol such as % or &.

How can I guard against forgetting my password?
If you are using a Microsoft account, go to https://account.live.com/password/reset to reset your password. If you are using a local user account, create a password reset disk. Insert a USB flash drive, press ⊞+W, type **password reset**, click **Create a password reset disk**, and then follow the Forgotten Password Wizard's steps. To use the disk, insert it, attempt to sign on to Windows 8, click **OK** when it fails, and then click **Reset password**.

Lock Your Computer

You can enhance your computer's security by locking your system when you leave your desk.

Protecting your account with a password prevents someone from logging on to your account, but what happens when you leave your desk? If you remain logged on to the system, any person who sits down at your computer can use your account to view and change files. To prevent this, lock your computer.

Once your computer is locked, anyone who tries to use your computer will first have to enter your password.

Lock Your Computer

Lock Your Computer

1. On the Start screen, click your user account tile.
2. Click **Lock**.

Windows 8 locks your computer and displays the Lock screen.

Unlock Your Computer

1. On the Lock screen, press any key to display the sign-on screen.

A. The word "Locked" appears under your username.

2. Click inside the Password text box.

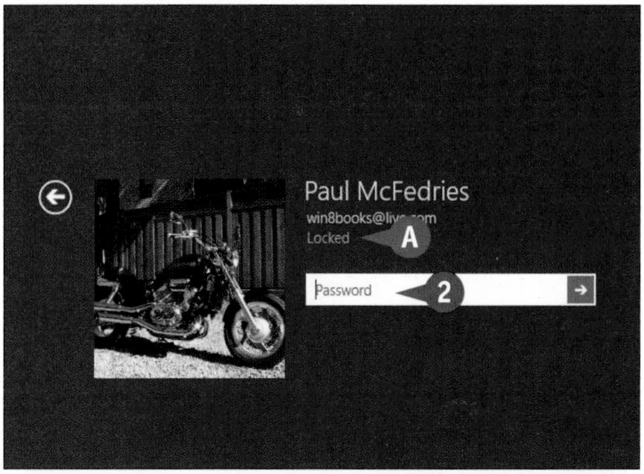

3. Type your password.
4. Click the **Submit** arrow (→).

   Windows 8 unlocks your computer and restores your desktop.

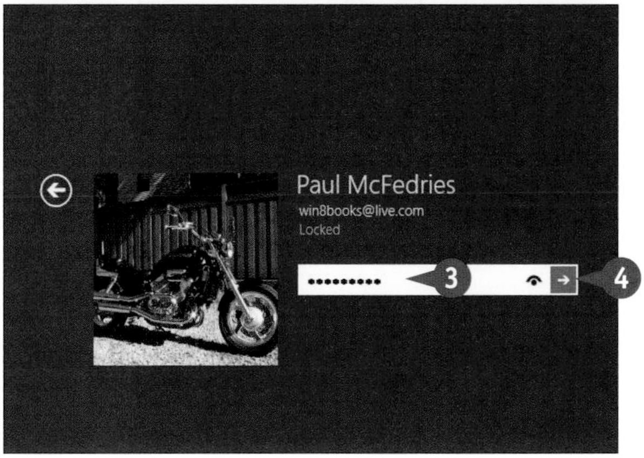

TIP

I use the Lock command frequently. Is there a way to make it easier to access?

Yes, you can use two faster methods. The first method is to press +L. The second method is to configure Windows 8 to automatically lock the computer after it has been idle for a specified amount of time:

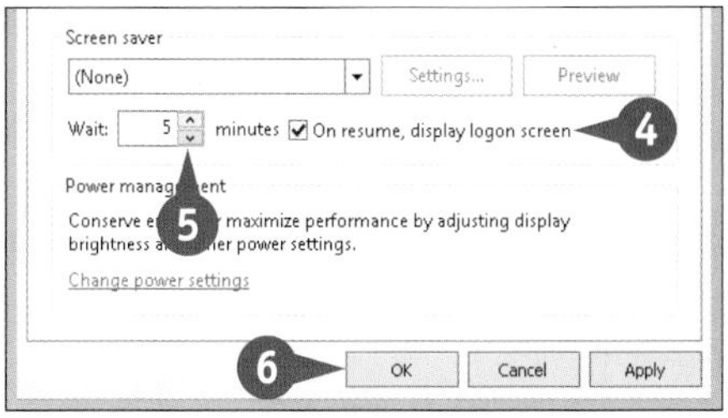

1. Press +W to open the Settings search pane.
2. Type **lock computer**.
3. Click **Lock the computer when I leave it alone for a period of time**.
4. Click **On resume, display logon screen** (☐ changes to ☑).
5. Click the **Wait** spin box to set the number of minutes of idle time after which Windows 8 locks your PC.
6. Click **OK**.

Set Up Family Safety

If your children have computer access, you can protect them from malicious content by setting up a set of parental controls called Family Safety for activities such as web surfing, playing games, and running programs.

Family Safety enables you to set specific limits on how your children perform various activities on the computer. For example, the Windows Web Filter lets you specify allowable websites, restrict sites based on content, and block file downloads.

Before you can apply the Family Safety controls, you must set up a Windows 8 user account for each child. See Chapter 11.

Set Up Family Safety

Activate Family Safety

1. Press ⊞+W.

   The Settings search pane appears.

2. Type **family**.
3. Click **Family Safety**.

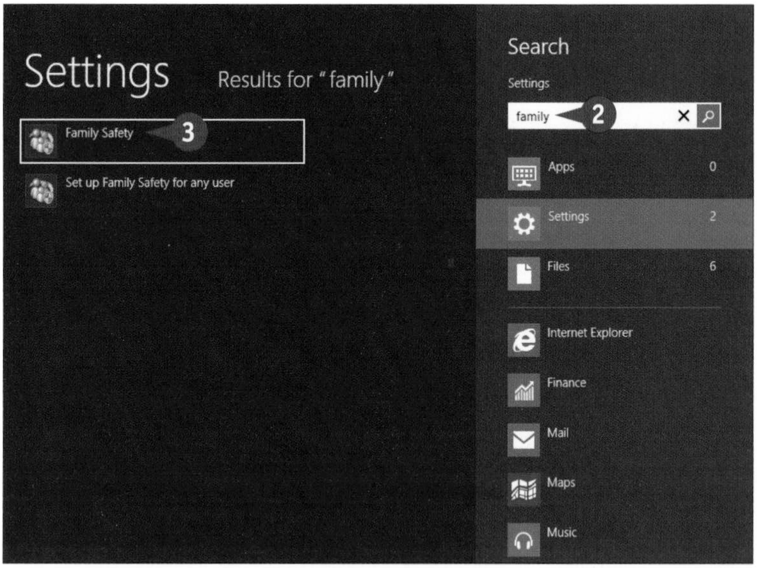

The Family Safety window appears.

4. Click the user you want to work with.

The User Settings window appears.

5. Click **On, enforce current settings** (○ changes to ◉).

   Windows 8 turns on parental controls for the user.

Set Web Restrictions

6. Click **Web filtering**.

   The Web Filtering window appears.

7. Click ***User* can only use the websites I allow** (○ changes to ◉) to block some web content.

8. Click **Web Restrictions** and then click a web restriction level (○ changes to ◉).

9. If you want to control specific sites, click **Allow or Block Websites**, type the site address, and then click **Allow** or **Block**.

10. Click **User Settings**.

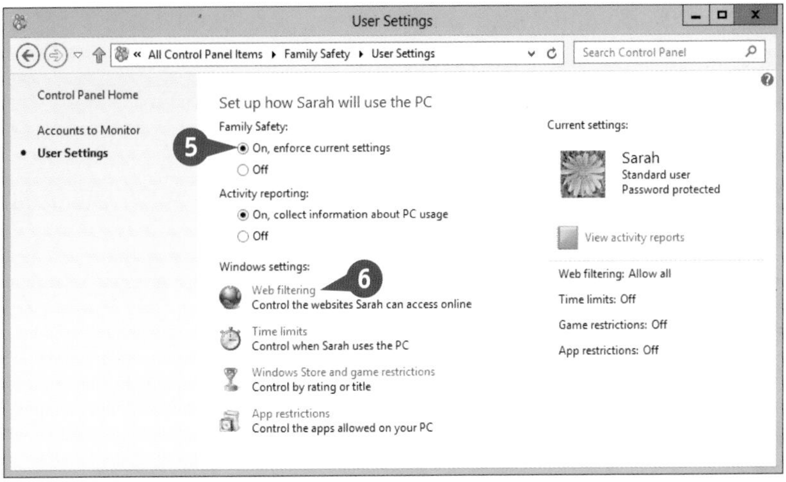

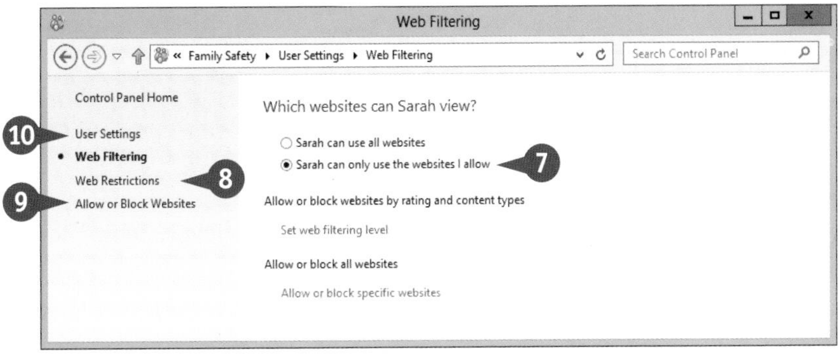

TIPS

How do I prevent my kids from downloading files?
Blocking downloads is a good idea because it reduces the risk of infecting the computer with viruses or other malicious software. In the User Settings window, click **Web Filtering**, and then click **Web Restrictions** to display the Web Restrictions window. Scroll down to the bottom of the window and click **Block file downloads** (☐ changes to ☑). Click **User Settings**.

Can I choose which game rating system Windows 8 uses?
Yes, Windows 8 supports several game rating systems, including classifications from the Entertainment Software Rating Board (this is the default system), Computer Entertainment Rating Organization, and Game Rating Board. Return to the Family Safety window, click **Rating Systems**, click the system you want to use (○ changes to ◉), and then click **Accounts to Monitor**.

continued ►

With the Family Safety controls activated, you can now set up specific restrictions. For example, as you saw earlier you can allow and block specific websites, and you can set the web restriction level to determine the types of sites your children can access.

Family Safety also enables you to set up times when children are not allowed to use the computer, set the maximum game rating that kids can play, and allow or block specific games and programs.

Set Up Family Safety (continued)

Set Computer Time Limits

11. Click **Time limits**.

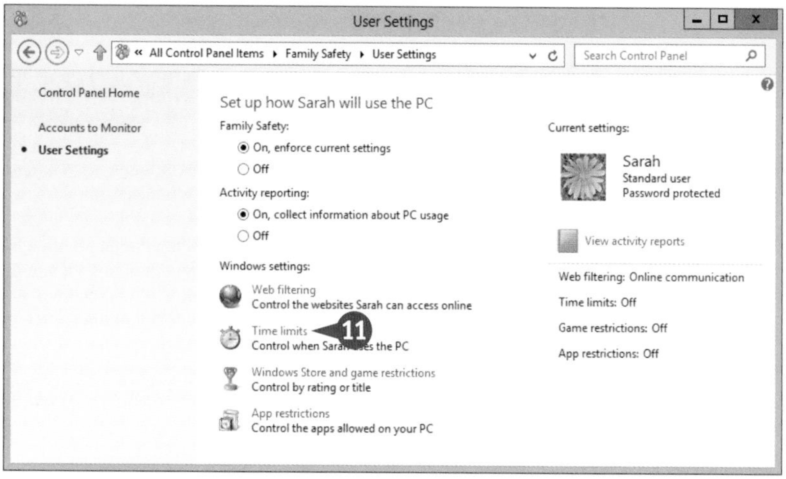

The Time Limits window appears.

12. Click **Curfew**.
13. Click ***User* can only use the PC during the time ranges I allow** (○ changes to ◉).
14. Click each hour that you want to block access to the computer.

A. Blocked hours appear in blue.

B. Allowed hours appear in white.

15. Click **User Settings**.

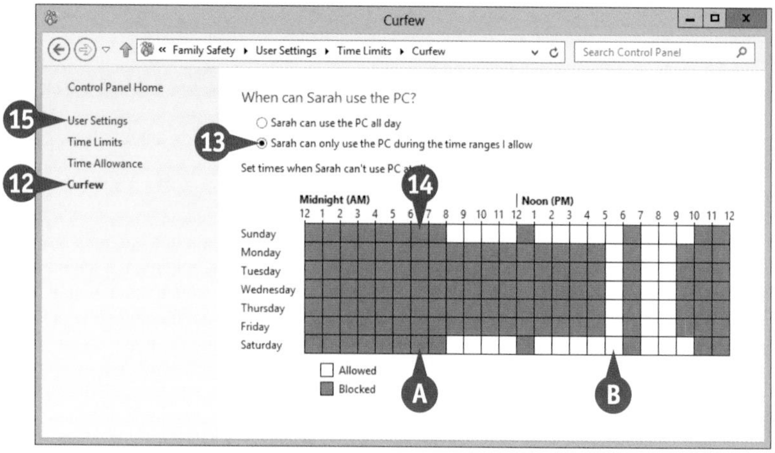

Restrict Game Usage

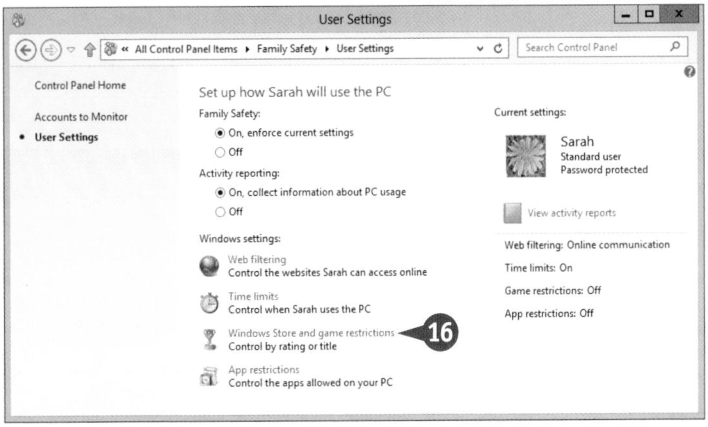
User Settings
All Control Panel Items ▸ Family Safety ▸ User Settings
Search Control Panel
Control Panel Home
Accounts to Monitor
User Settings
Set up how Sarah will use the PC
Family Safety:
On, enforce current settings
Off
Activity reporting:
On, collect information about PC usage
Off
Windows settings:
Web filtering
Control the websites Sarah can access online
Time limits
Control when Sarah uses the PC
Windows Store and game restrictions
Control by rating or title
App restrictions
Control the apps allowed on your PC
Current settings:
Sarah
Standard user
Password protected
View activity reports
Web filtering: Online communication
Time limits: On
Game restrictions: Off
App restrictions: Off
16

16. Click **Windows Store and game restrictions.**

    The Game and Windows Store Restrictions window appears.

Game and Windows Store Restrictions
User Settings ▸ Game and Windows Store Restrictions
Search Control Panel
Control Panel Home
User Settings
Game and Windows Store Restrictions
Rating Level
Allow or Block Games
Control which games and Windows Store apps Sarah can use
Sarah can play all games and view all Windows Store apps
Sarah can only use games and Windows Store apps I allow
Allow or block games and Windows Store apps by rating
Set game and Windows Store ratings
Maximum allowed rating: ADULTS ONLY, including unrated games
Allow or block any game on your PC by name
17
18

17. Click ***User* can only use games and Windows Store apps I allow** (○ changes to ◉).
18. Click **Rating Level.**

    The Rating Level window appears.

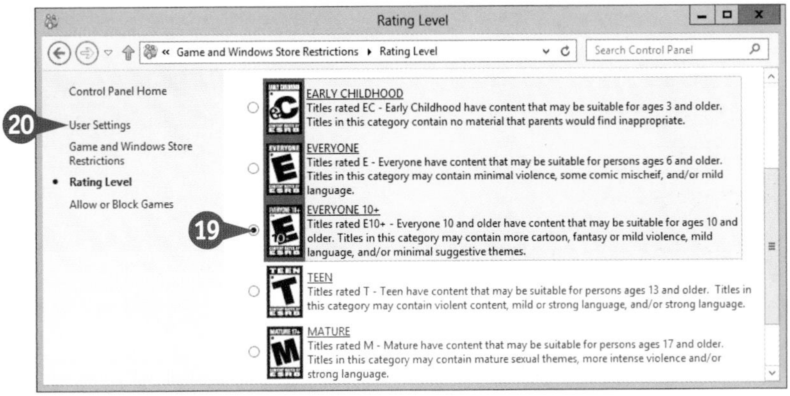
Rating Level
Game and Windows Store Restrictions ▸ Rating Level
Search Control Panel
Control Panel Home
User Settings
Game and Windows Store Restrictions
Rating Level
Allow or Block Games
EARLY CHILDHOOD
Titles rated EC - Early Childhood have content that may be suitable for ages 3 and older. Titles in this category contain no material that parents would find inappropriate.
EVERYONE
Titles rated E - Everyone have content that may be suitable for persons ages 6 and older. Titles in this category may contain minimal violence, some comic mischief, and/or mild language.
EVERYONE 10+
Titles rated E10+ - Everyone 10 and older have content that may be suitable for ages 10 and older. Titles in this category may contain more cartoon, fantasy or mild violence, mild language, and/or minimal suggestive themes.
TEEN
Titles rated T - Teen have content that may be suitable for persons ages 13 and older. Titles in this category may contain violent content, mild or strong language, and/or strong language.
MATURE
Titles rated M - Mature have content that may be suitable for persons ages 17 and older. Titles in this category may contain mature sexual themes, more intense violence and/or strong language.
19
20

19. Click the maximum rating that you want the user to play (○ changes to ◉).
20. Click **User Settings.**

TIPS

Can I block a specific game?

Yes. In the Game and Windows Store Restrictions window, click **Allow or Block Games** to display the Allow or Block Games window, which shows all the games installed on your computer. For the game you want to block, click the **Always Block** option (○ changes to ◉), and then click **User Settings.**

Can I prevent my kids from running certain programs?

Yes. In the User Settings window, click **App restrictions** to display the App Restrictions window. Click ***User* can only use the apps I allow** (where *User* is the name of the user). In the list, click the check box for each program you want the user to be able to run (☐ changes to ☑). Click **User Settings.**

Delete Your Browsing History

To ensure that other people who have access to your computer cannot view information from sites you have visited, you can delete your browsing history.

Your browsing history is a collection of data that Internet Explorer stores on your computer. Internet Explorer uses this data to make your web surfing faster and easier, but that data also exposes various aspects of your Internet activities, so it could compromise your privacy if other people have access to your computer. See the tip in this section to learn more about browsing history.

Delete Your Browsing History

1. Click **Tools** (⚙).
2. Click **Safety**.
3. Click **Delete browsing history**.

Note: You can also press Ctrl + Shift + Delete.

The Delete Browsing History dialog box appears.

4. To keep the browsing history associated with sites on your Favorites list, click **Preserve Favorites website data** (☐ changes to ☑).
5. To delete saved web page files, click **Temporary Internet files and website files** (☐ changes to ☑).

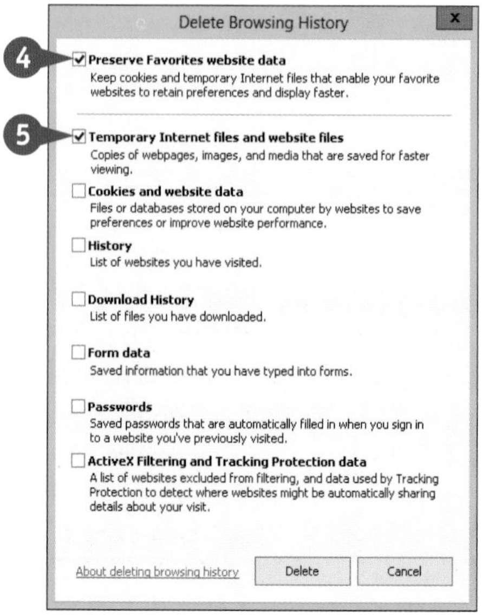

6. To delete cookie files and website data files, click **Cookies and website data** (☐ changes to ☑).

7. To delete the list of websites you have visited, click **History** (☐ changes to ☑).

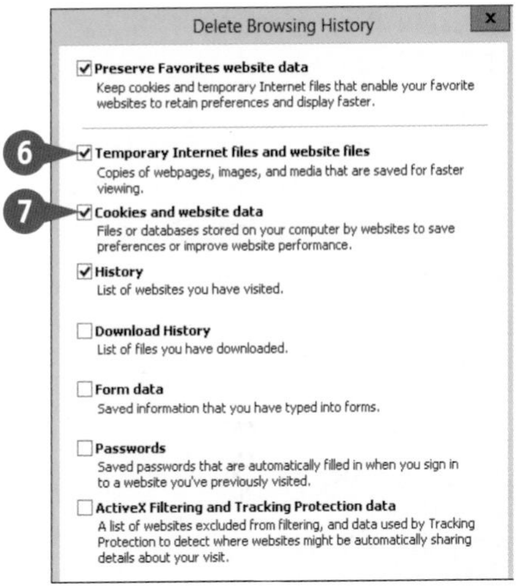
Delete Browsing History
Preserve Favorites website data
Keep cookies and temporary Internet files that enable your favorite websites to retain preferences and display faster.
6
Temporary Internet files and website files
Copies of webpages, images, and media that are saved for faster viewing.
7
Cookies and website data
Files or databases stored on your computer by websites to save preferences or improve website performance.
History
List of websites you have visited.
Download History
List of files you have downloaded.
Form data
Saved information that you have typed into forms.
Passwords
Saved passwords that are automatically filled in when you sign in to a website you've previously visited.
ActiveX Filtering and Tracking Protection data
A list of websites excluded from filtering, and data used by Tracking Protection to detect where websites might be automatically sharing details about your visit.

8. To delete the list of files that you have downloaded, click **Download History** (☐ changes to ☑).

9. To delete saved form data, click **Form data** (☐ changes to ☑).

10. To delete saved form passwords, click **Passwords** (☐ changes to ☑).

11. Click **Delete**.

    Internet Explorer deletes the selected browsing history.

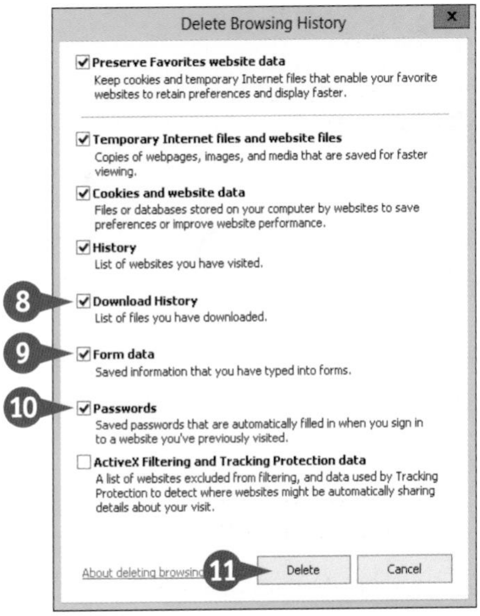
Delete Browsing History
Preserve Favorites website data
Keep cookies and temporary Internet files that enable your favorite websites to retain preferences and display faster.
Temporary Internet files and website files
Copies of webpages, images, and media that are saved for faster viewing.
Cookies and website data
Files or databases stored on your computer by websites to save preferences or improve website performance.
History
List of websites you have visited.
8
Download History
List of files you have downloaded.
9
Form data
Saved information that you have typed into forms.
10
Passwords
Saved passwords that are automatically filled in when you sign in to a website you've previously visited.
ActiveX Filtering and Tracking Protection data
A list of websites excluded from filtering, and data used by Tracking Protection to detect where websites might be automatically sharing details about your visit.
11
Delete
Cancel

TIP

What is browsing history?

Internet Explorer maintains a list of the sites you visit, as well as copies of page text, images, and other content so that sites load faster the next time you view them. Internet Explorer also saves text and passwords that you have typed into forms, the names of files you have downloaded, and *cookies*, which are small text files that store information such as site preferences and site logon data.

Saving this history makes surfing easier, but it is also dangerous because other people who use your computer can just as easily visit or view information about those sites. This can be a problem if you visit financial sites, private corporate sites, or some other page that you would not want another person to visit. You reduce this risk by deleting some or all of your browsing history.

Browse the Web Privately

If you visit sensitive or private websites, you can tell Internet Explorer not to save any browsing history for those sites.

If you regularly visit private websites or websites that contain sensitive or secret data, you can ensure that no one else sees any data for such sites by deleting your browsing history, as described in the previous section. However, if you visit such sites only occasionally, deleting your entire browsing history is overkill. A better solution is to turn on Internet Explorer's InPrivate Browsing feature before you visit private sites. This tells Internet Explorer to temporarily stop saving any browsing history.

Browse the Web Privately

1. Click **Tools** (⚙).
2. Click **Safety**.
3. Click **InPrivate Browsing**.

Note: You can also press Ctrl + Shift + P.

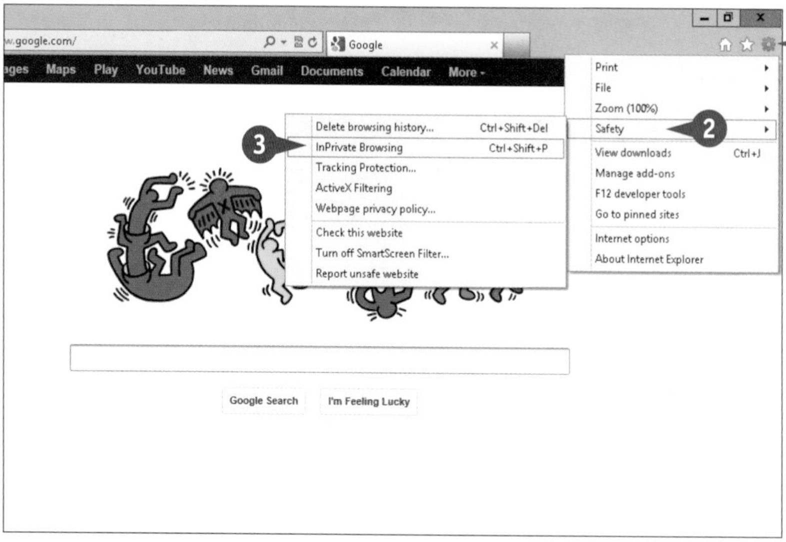

A new Internet Explorer window appears.

Ⓐ The InPrivate indicator appears in the address bar.

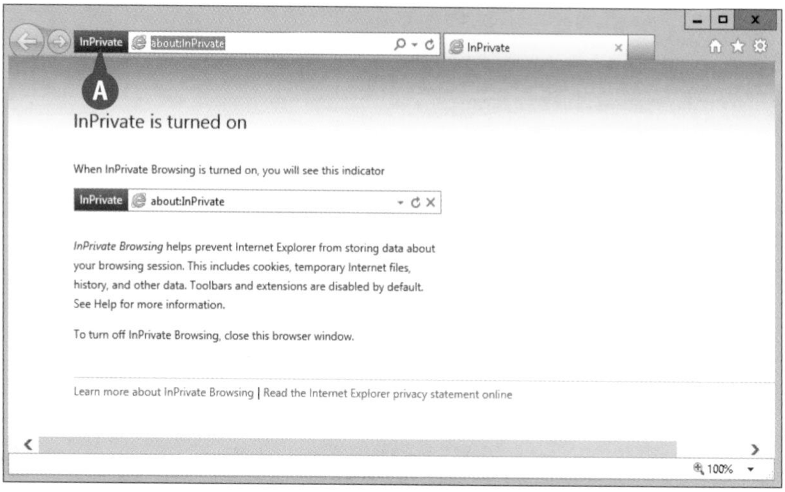

4. Surf to and interact with websites as you normally would, such as the banking site shown here.

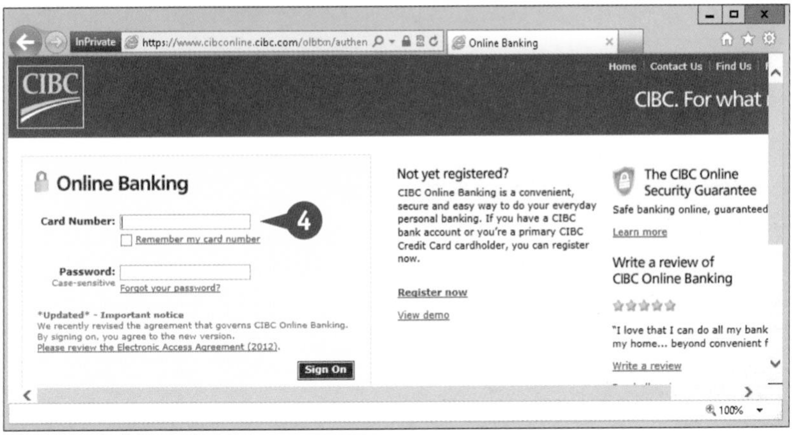

5. When you are done, click the **Close** button (x).

Internet Explorer closes the InPrivate Browsing window and turns off InPrivate Browsing.

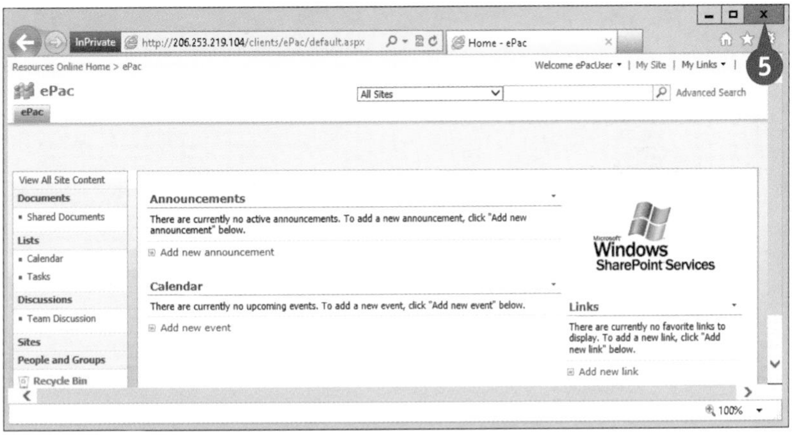

TIP

What does Tracking Protection do?

Some websites load content such as ads and maps from a third-party site. If a particular third-party company provides data for many different sites, that company could conceivably build up a profile of your online activity. Tracking Protection looks for third-party sites that provide data quite often to the places you visit, and begins blocking those sites' content so that they cannot build up a profile of your activity. To turn on this feature, click **Tools** ( ), click **Safety**, and then click **Tracking Protection**. Click **Get a Tracking Protection List online**, locate a list that suits the way you use the web, and then click **Add**.

Set the Junk E-Mail Protection Level

You can make junk messages easier to manage by setting the Mail junk e-mail protection level. You can set a higher level if you receive many junk messages each day, or you can set a lower level if you receive very few junk messages.

The higher the protection level, the more aggressively Mail checks for junk e-mail. All suspected junk messages get moved to the Junk Email folder. If a legitimate message is moved to Junk E-mail by accident, you can mark the message as not junk.

Set the Junk E-Mail Protection Level

Set the Junk E-Mail Protection Level

1. Click **File**.
2. Click **Options**.
3. Click **Safety options**.

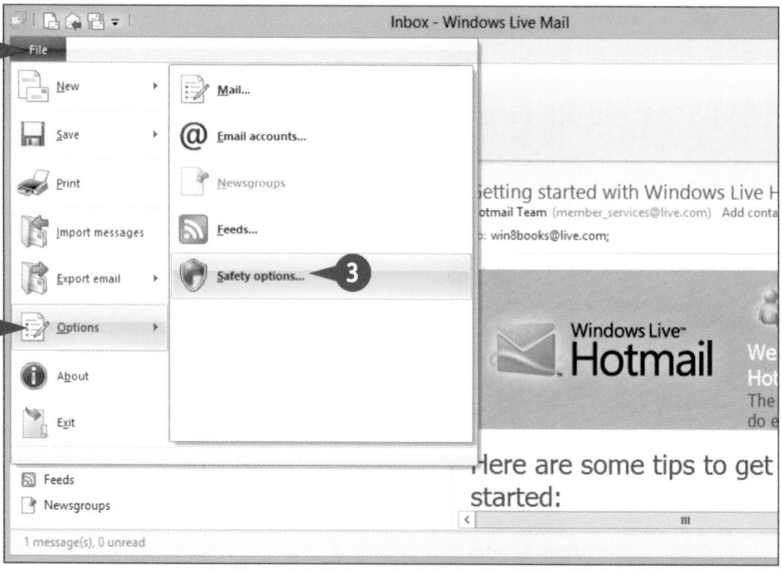
Inbox - Windows Live Mail
1
File
New
Save
Print
Import messages
Export email
2
Options
About
Exit
Mail...
Email accounts...
Newsgroups
Feeds...
Safety options...
3
Feeds
Newsgroups
1 message(s), 0 unread
Windows Live
Hotmail
started:

The Safety Options dialog box appears.

4. Click the **Options** tab.

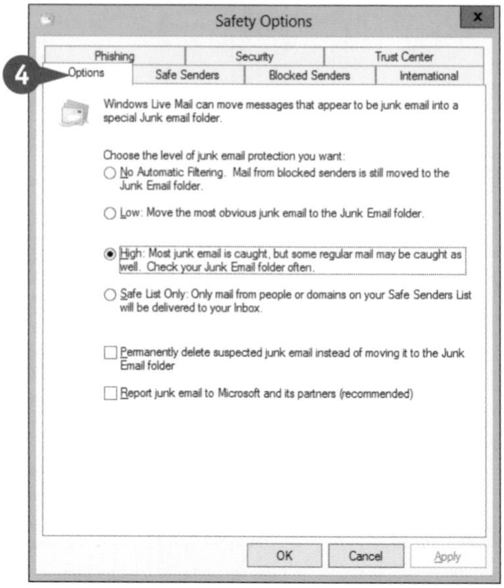
Safety Options
Phishing
Security
Trust Center
4
Options
Safe Senders
Blocked Senders
International
Windows Live Mail can move messages that appear to be junk email into a special Junk email folder.
Choose the level of junk email protection you want:
No Automatic Filtering. Mail from blocked senders is still moved to the Junk Email folder.
Low: Move the most obvious junk email to the Junk Email folder.
High: Most junk email is caught, but some regular mail may be caught as well. Check your Junk Email folder often.
Safe List Only: Only mail from people or domains on your Safe Senders List will be delivered to your Inbox.
Permanently delete suspected junk email instead of moving it to the Junk Email folder
Report junk email to Microsoft and its partners (recommended)
OK
Cancel
Apply

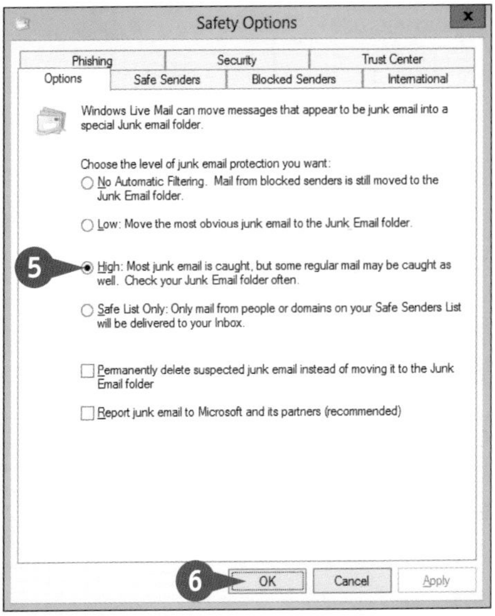

5 Click the protection level you want (○ changes to ◉):

Click **No Automatic Filtering** if you receive very few junk messages each day.

Click **Low** if you receive a moderate number of junk messages.

Click **High** if you receive many junk messages each day.

6 Click **OK**.

Mail puts the new protection level into effect.

Mark a Message as Not Junk

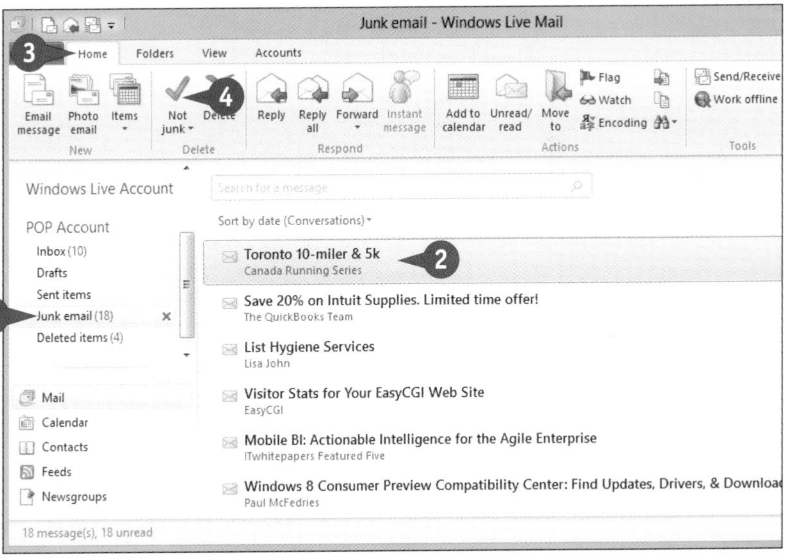

1 Click the **Junk email** folder.

2 Click the message.

3 Click the **Home** tab.

4 Click the top half of the **Not junk** button.

Mail returns the message to the Inbox folder.

TIPS

What is a false positive?

A false positive is a legitimate message that Mail has mistakenly marked as spam and moved to the Junk Email folder. When you use the High protection level, which is the Mail default level, you run a greater risk of false positives, so you should check your Junk Email folder often to look for legitimate messages.

How does the Safe List Only protection level work?

Safe List Only means that Mail treats every message as junk, unless the sender's e-mail address is on your Safe Senders list. To populate this list, follow steps **1** to **4** in the first set of steps, click the **Safe Senders** tab, click **Add**, type an address, click **OK**, and repeat as necessary. Alternatively, follow steps **1** to **3** in the second set of steps, click the bottom half of the **Not junk** button, and then click **Add sender to safe sender list.**

Block a Person Who Sends You Junk Mail

You can reduce the amount of junk mail you have to deal with by blocking those people who send you such messages. Mail automatically moves existing and future messages from that person to the Junk Email folder.

You can use two methods to add a person to your blocked senders list. If you have an example message from that person, you can tell Mail to block future messages from the address that sent the example message. If you do not currently have an example message, but you know the sender's e-mail address, you can add that address directly to the blocked senders list.

Block a Person Who Sends You Junk Mail

Block a Sender Using a Message

1. Click the junk e-mail message.
2. Click the **Home** tab.
3. Click the bottom half of the **Not junk** button.
4. Click **Add sender to blocked sender list**.

   Mail adds the sender's e-mail address to the list of blocked senders.

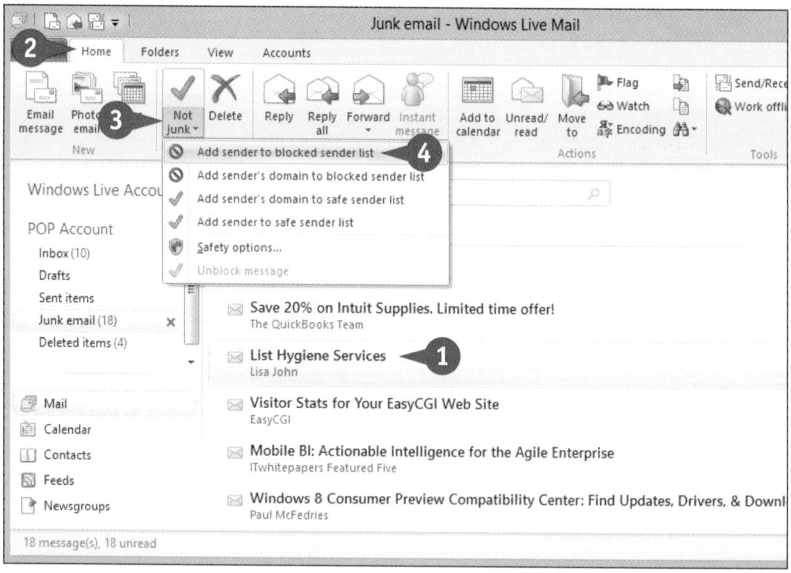

Block a Sender By Hand

1. Click **File**.
2. Click **Options**.
3. Click **Safety options**.

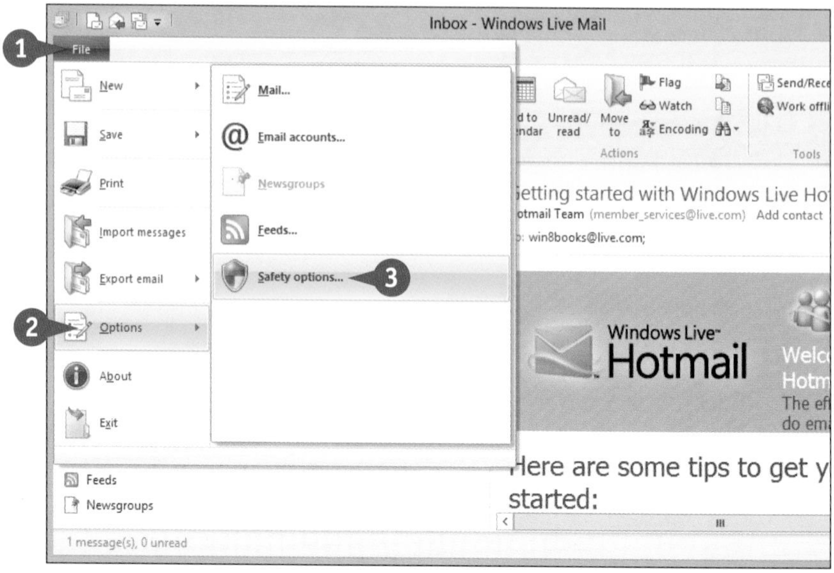

The Safety Options dialog box appears.

4 Click the **Blocked Senders** tab.

5 Click **Add**.

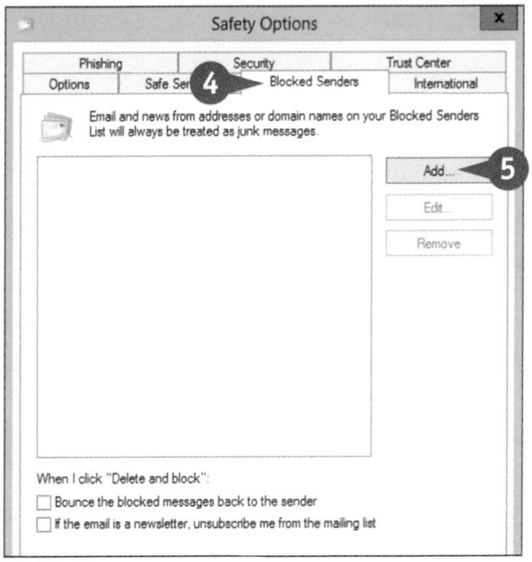
Safety Options
Phishing
Security
Trust Center
Options
Safe Ser
4
Blocked Senders
International
Email and news from addresses or domain names on your Blocked Senders List will always be treated as junk messages.
Add...
5
Edit...
Remove
When I click "Delete and block":
Bounce the blocked messages back to the sender
If the email is a newsletter, unsubscribe me from the mailing list

The Add Address or Domain dialog box appears.

6 Type the sender's address.

7 Click **OK**.

A Mail includes the address on the list of blocked senders.

8 Follow steps **5** to **7** to add more addresses.

9 Click **OK**.

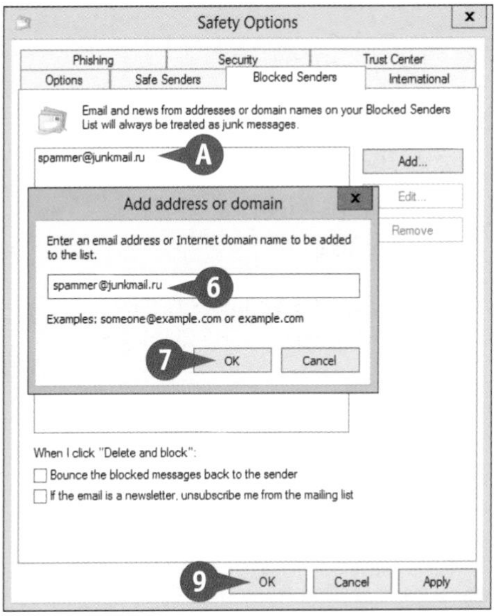
Safety Options
Phishing
Security
Trust Center
Options
Safe Senders
Blocked Senders
International
Email and news from addresses or domain names on your Blocked Senders List will always be treated as junk messages.
spammer@junkmail.ru
A
Add...
Edit...
Remove
Add address or domain
Enter an email address or Internet domain name to be added to the list.
spammer@junkmail.ru
6
Examples: someone@example.com or example.com
7
OK
Cancel
When I click "Delete and block":
Bounce the blocked messages back to the sender
If the email is a newsletter, unsubscribe me from the mailing list
9
OK
Cancel
Apply

TIPS

How do I take someone off the blocked senders list?

If you add someone by mistake, you should take that person off the blocked senders list as soon as possible. Follow steps **1** to **4** to display the Block Senders tab, click the person's e-mail address, click **Remove**, and then click **OK**.

I get lots of unwanted messages from a particular country. Can I block messages from that country?

Yes, in most cases. Messages sent using a foreign address usually include a country code as part of the address. These so-called top-level domains include ru for the Russian Federation, cn for China, and kr for South Korea. To block a country, follow steps **1** to **3** to display the Safety Options dialog box, click the **International** tab, click **Blocked Top-Level Domain List**, click the check box beside the country (☐ changes to ☑), and then click **OK**.

Clear Your Private Information

You can enhance your privacy by temporarily clearing all private information from the Start screen tiles.

One of the benefits of the Start screen is that it uses *live tiles* that display constantly updated information. This includes newly received e-mail and instant messages, the current music you are playing, the photo slide show you are playing, and the latest information from the Weather and Finance apps. However, this can be a privacy problem because anyone walking by your desk can see this information with a quick glance. To prevent this, you can temporarily clear all your private information from the Start screen tiles.

Clear Your Private Information

1. Move the mouse to the top right corner of the screen.

   The Charms menu appears.

2. Click **Settings**.

   The Settings pane appears.

3. Click **Tiles**.

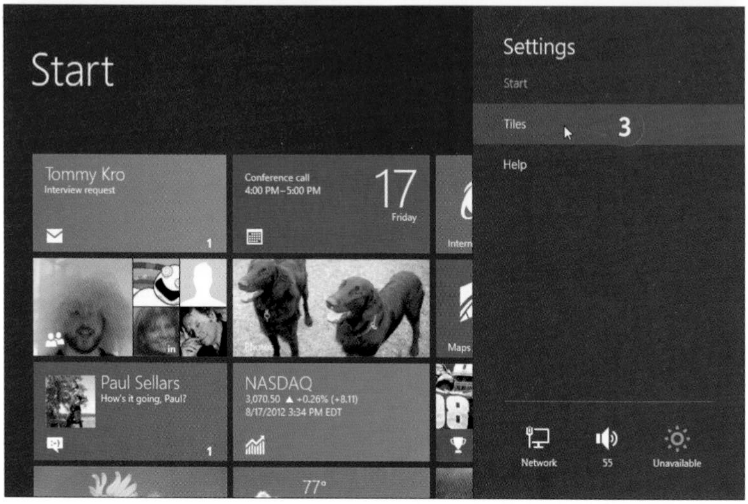

The Tiles pane appears.

4 Click **Clear**.

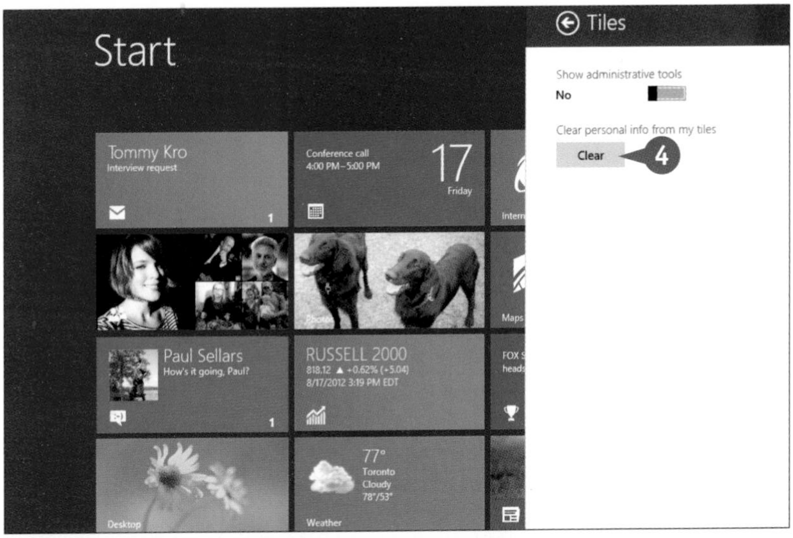

A Windows 8 removes all your personal information from the Start screen.

TIPS

Can I prevent an app from ever showing private information in its tile?

Yes, you can turn off the updating permanently for the tile. Right-click the tile you want to turn off and then click **Turn live tile off**.

Can I prevent an app from displaying private information in a notification?

Some apps present a notification when new information comes in to your PC. For example, the Messaging app lets you know when a new instant message has arrived. Because some of these notifications can contain private information, you might want to turn off notifications for the apps that generate such notifications. Follow steps **1** and **2** to display the Settings pane, and then click **Change PC Settings** to open the PC Settings app. Click **Notifications** and then beside each app for which you want notifications disabled, click the switch to **Off**.

Reset Your Computer to Preserve Privacy

If you are selling or giving away your PC, you can prevent the recipient from seeing your personal data by resetting the computer.

As you use your computer, you accumulate a large amount of personal data: documents, installed apps, Internet Explorer favorites, e-mail messages, photos, and much more. If you are selling your PC or giving it away, you probably do not want the recipient to have access to all that personal data. To prevent this, you can reset the PC, which deletes all your personal data and reinstalls a fresh copy of Windows 8.

Reset Your Computer to Preserve Privacy

Note: This section assumes you have copied your personal files to a backup destination, such as an external hard drive. See Chapter 14.

1. Insert your Windows 8 installation disc.
2. Press ⊞+I.

   The Settings pane appears.
3. Click **Change PC settings.**

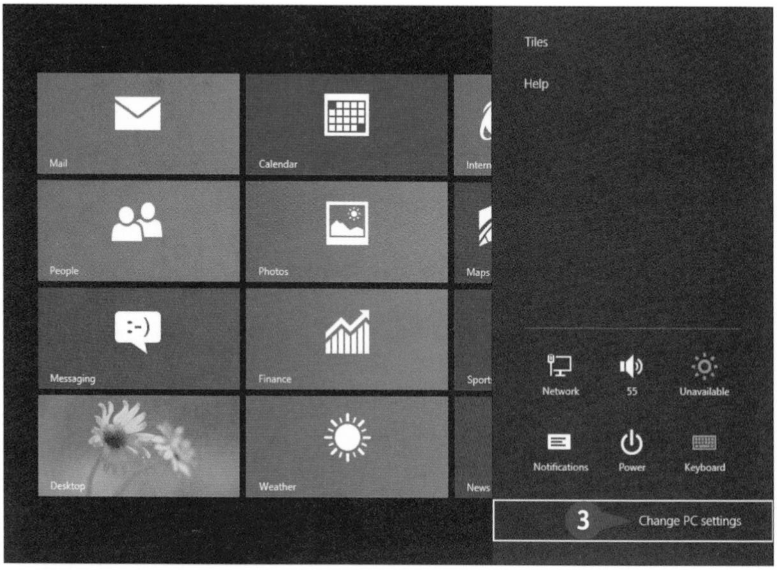

Tiles
Help
Mail
Calendar
People
Photos
Maps
Messaging
Finance
Desktop
Weather
News
Network
55
Unavailable
Notifications
Power
Keyboard
3
Change PC settings

   Windows 8 starts the PC Settings app.
4. Click **General.**
5. Under Remove Everything and Reinstall Windows, click **Get started.**

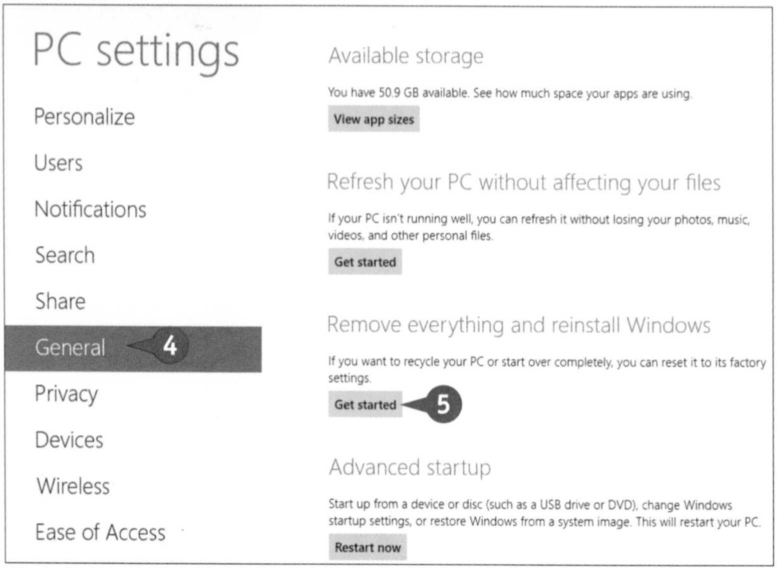

PC settings
Personalize
Users
Notifications
Search
Share
General
4
Privacy
Devices
Wireless
Ease of Access
Available storage
You have 50.9 GB available. See how much space your apps are using.
View app sizes
Refresh your PC without affecting your files
If your PC isn't running well, you can refresh it without losing your photos, music, videos, and other personal files.
Get started
Remove everything and reinstall Windows
If you want to recycle your PC or start over completely, you can reset it to its factory settings.
Get started
5
Advanced startup
Start up from a device or disc (such as a USB drive or DVD), change Windows startup settings, or restore Windows from a system image. This will restart your PC.
Restart now

Windows 8 displays an overview of the reset process.

6 Click **Next**.

Note: If you see a message about your PC having more than one drive, click **All drives**.

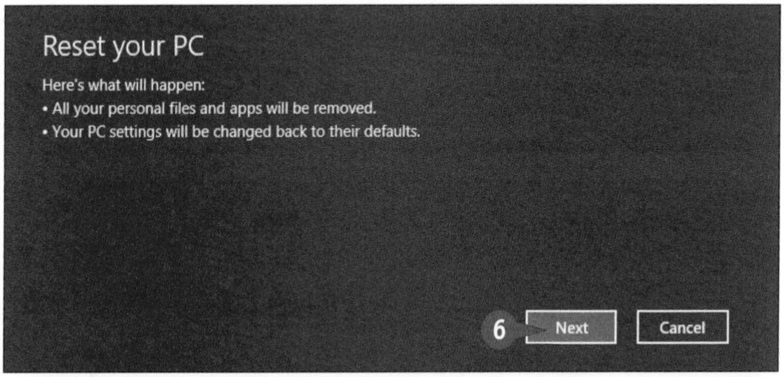
Reset your PC
Here's what will happen:
• All your personal files and apps will be removed.
• Your PC settings will be changed back to their defaults.
6
Next
Cancel

Windows 8 asks how you want to your personal files removed.

7 Click the removal option you want to use.

Note: For more information about the removal options, see the first tip in this section.

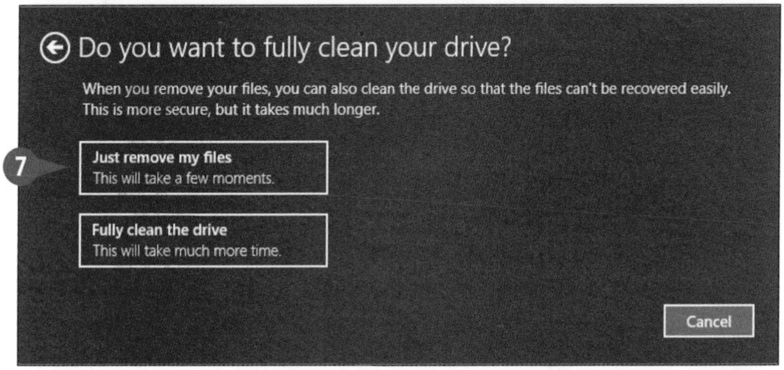
Do you want to fully clean your drive?
When you remove your files, you can also clean the drive so that the files can't be recovered easily. This is more secure, but it takes much longer.
7
Just remove my files
This will take a few moments.
Fully clean the drive
This will take much more time.
Cancel

8 Click **Reset**.

Windows 8 resets your PC.

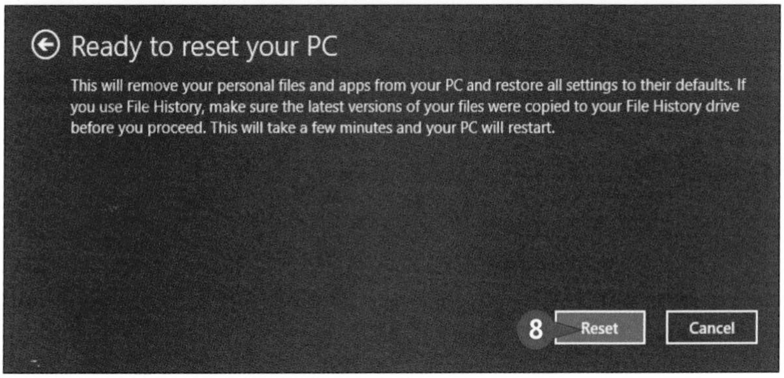
Ready to reset your PC
This will remove your personal files and apps from your PC and restore all settings to their defaults. If you use File History, make sure the latest versions of your files were copied to your File History drive before you proceed. This will take a few minutes and your PC will restart.
8
Reset
Cancel

TIPS

What is the difference between removing my files and fully cleaning the hard drive?

Removing your files deletes your data in the sense that after Windows is reset, it can no longer work with or see the data. However, the data remains on the PC's hard drive, so a person with special tools can access the data. The clean option prevents this by overwriting your information with random data, which can take quite a bit of time, but is much more secure.

Can I still reset my PC if I do not have my Windows 8 installation disc?

Yes, you can use a Windows 8 recovery drive, instead. This is a USB flash drive that contains the Windows 8 recovery tools. To learn how to create such a drive, see the section "Create a Recovery Drive" in Chapter 14.

CHAPTER 13

Customizing Windows 8

Windows 8 comes with a number of features that enable you to personalize your computer. Not only can you change the appearance of Windows 8 to suit your taste, but you can also change the way Windows 8 works to make it easier to use and more efficient.

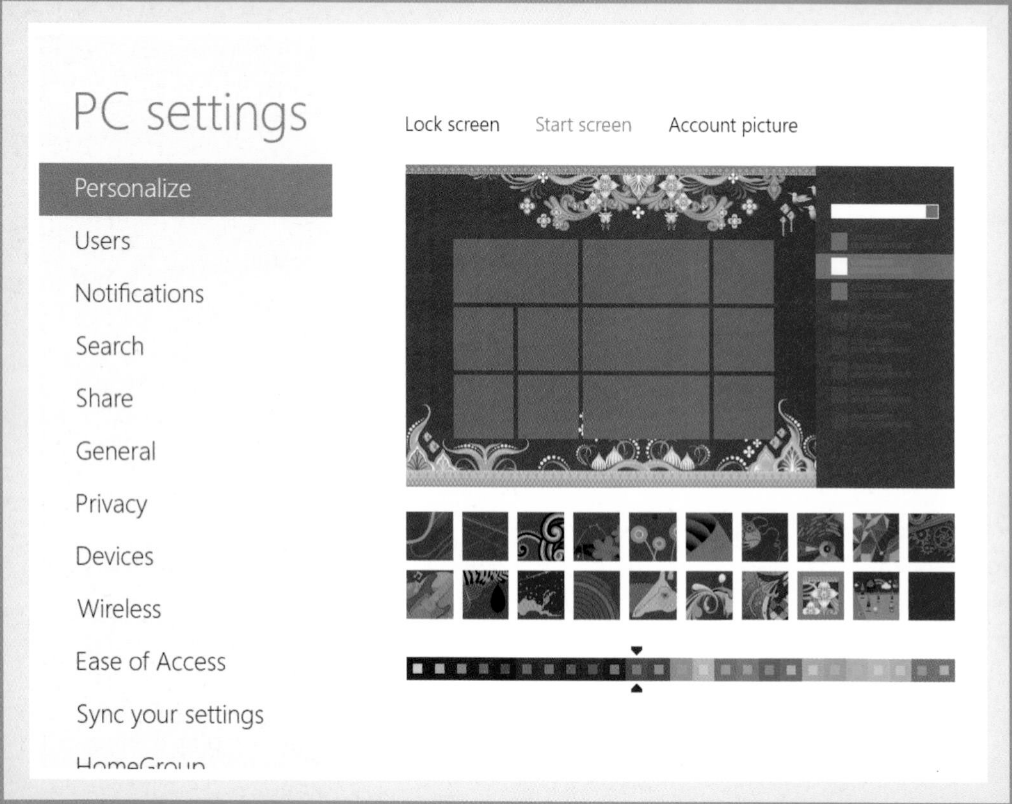

Configure the Start Screen

You can personalize how the Start screen looks and operates to suit your style and the way you work. For example, you can rearrange the Start screen tiles so that the apps you use most often appear together on the screen.

You can also make your Start screen more useful or more efficient by resizing some of the Windows 8 app screen tiles. The Start screen supports two sizes of Windows 8 app tiles: small and large. They are both the same height, but the larger size is twice as wide as the smaller.

Configure the Start Screen

Move a Tile

1 On the Start screen, click the tile of the app you want to move.

A Windows 8 reduces the tile sizes slightly and adds extra space between the tiles.

2 Drag the tile to the position you prefer.

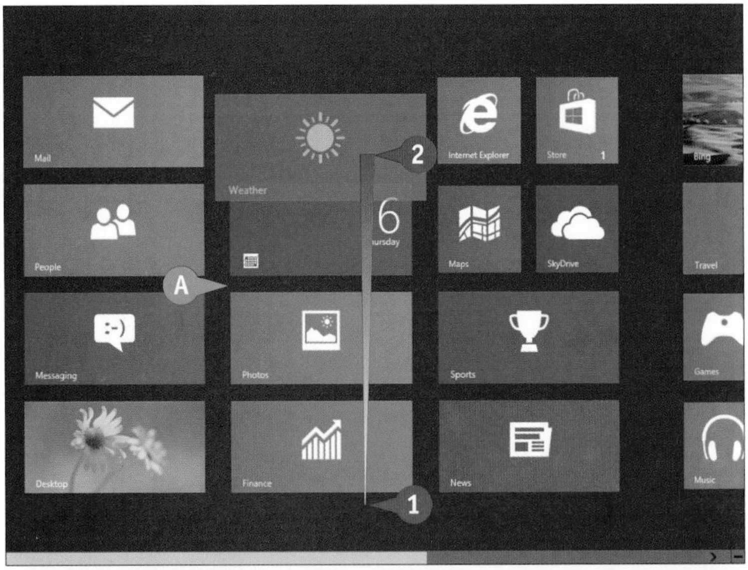

3 Release the tile.

B Windows 8 moves the tile to the new position.

Change a Tile Size

1. Right-click the Start screen tile you want to resize.

Ⓒ Windows 8 displays the application bar.

2. Click **Smaller**.

Note: If the tile is small and you prefer to enlarge it, click **Larger**, instead.

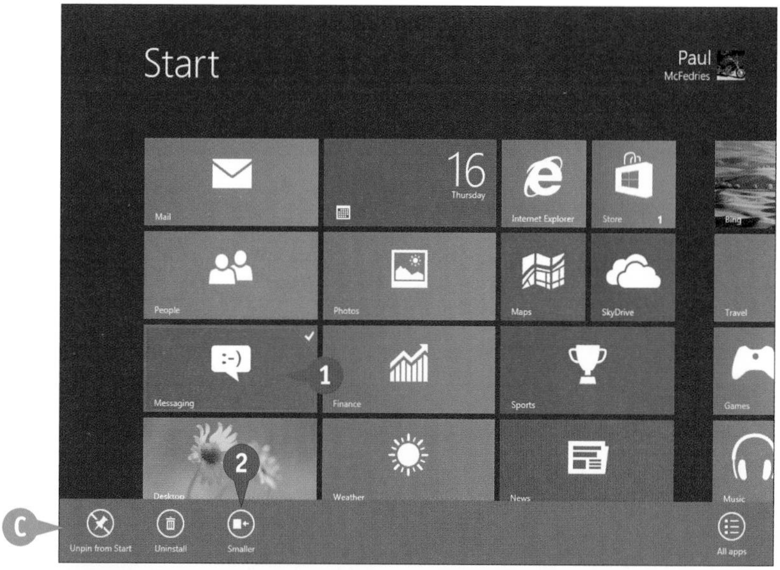

Ⓓ Windows 8 resizes the tile.

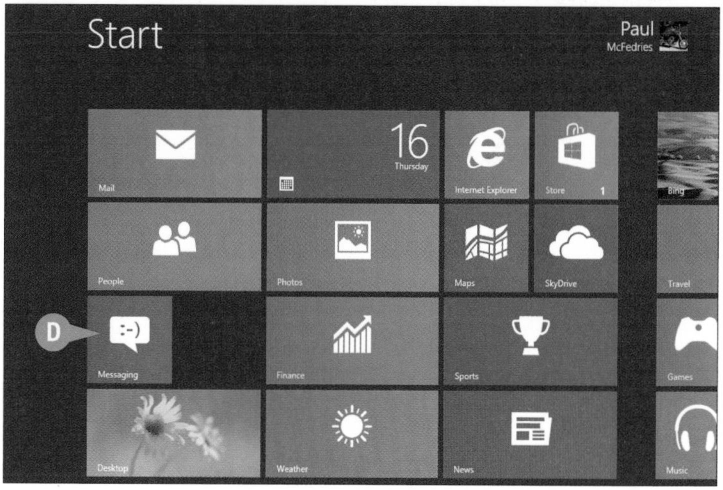

TIPS

Can I combine similar apps into a single group of tiles?

Yes. For example, you might want to break out all the game-related apps into their own group. To create a group, drag the first app tile all the way to left edge of the screen until you see a vertical bar, and then release the mouse button. Windows 8 creates a new group for the app tile. To add other tiles to the new group, drag and drop the tiles within the group.

Can I name an app group?

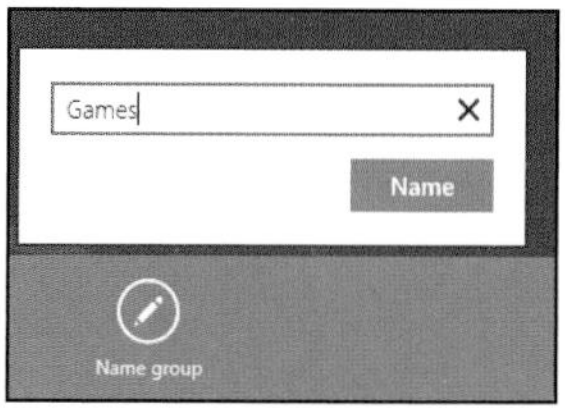

Yes. This is a good idea because it makes the Start screen even easier to use and navigate. To name a group, press Ctrl + - (dash) to zoom out of the Start screen. Right-click any tile in the group, click **Name group**, type the group name, and then click **Name**. Press Ctrl + + to zoom back in to the Start screen.

Pin an App to the Start Screen

You can customize the Start screen to give yourself quick access to the programs that you use most often.

If you have an app that does not appear on the Start menu, you usually open the app by right-clicking the Start screen and then clicking All Apps. For those apps you use most often, you can avoid this extra work by *pinning* their icons permanently to the main Start screen.

All pinned apps appear to the right of the main Start screen tiles. This means that once you have pinned an app to your Start screen, you can launch that app by scrolling right and then clicking the app.

Pin an App to the Start Screen

1. Right-click an empty section of the Start screen.

   A The application bar appears.

2. Click **All apps**.

The Apps screen appears.

3. Locate the app you want to pin.
4. Right-click the app.

Ⓑ The application bar appears.

5 Click **Pin to Start**.

6 Press ⊞.

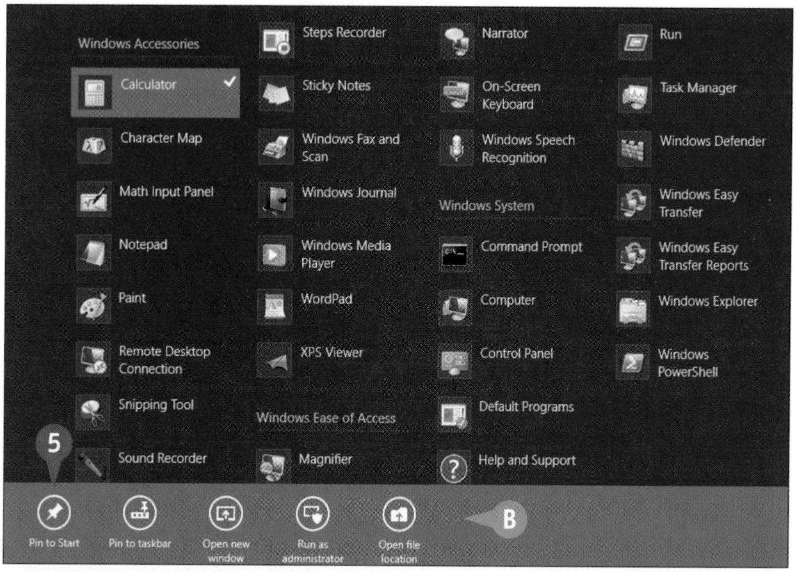

Windows 8 returns you to the Start screen.

7 Scroll to the right.

Ⓒ A tile for the pinned app appears on the Start screen.

TIPS

Can I remove an app from the Start screen?

Yes, you can remove any app tile from the Start screen, even the default apps that come with Windows 8. To remove an app from the Start screen, right-click the app's tile and then click **Unpin from Start**.

What happens if the app I want to pin does not appear in the Apps screen?

If you do not see the app in the Apps screen, you can still pin the app to the Start screen by searching for it. Switch to the Start screen and begin typing the name of the app you want to pin. Windows 8 switches to the Apps search screen and begins displaying a list of apps with names that match your text. Keep typing until you see the app, right-click the app, and click **Pin to Start**.

Open the PC Settings App

You can configure and customize many aspects of your Windows 8 system using the PC Settings app.

PC Settings is the Windows 8 app that you use for customizing and tweaking your PC. Many of the tasks that follow in this chapter, including changing the Start and Lock screen backgrounds and adding an app to the Lock screen, are performed using the PC Settings app. PC Settings also offers a wealth of other options that you can use to customize your PC.

Open the PC Settings App

1 Move the mouse to the top right corner of the screen.

The Charms menu appears.

2 Click **Settings**.

The Settings pane appears.

3 Click **Change PC settings**.

The PC Settings app appears.

A Use the tabs on the left side of the screen to navigate the PC Settings app.

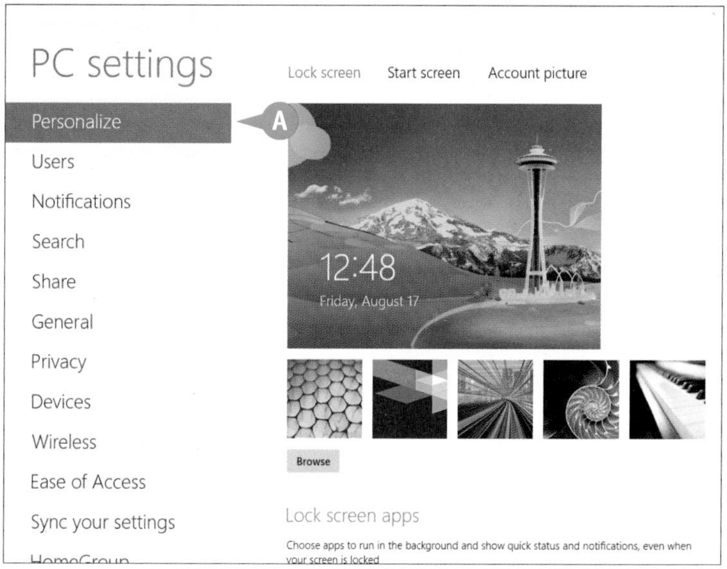

TIPS

Is there a faster way to open the PC Settings app?

Probably the fastest way to open the PC Settings app is to press ⊞+I and then press Enter. If you are using a tablet, swipe in from the right edge of the screen to display the Charms menu, tap **Settings**, and then tap **Change PC Settings**.

If I know which tab of the PC Settings app I want to use, is there a quick way to display it?

Press ⊞+W to open the Settings search pane, and then begin typing the name of the tab or setting you want. For example, if you want to go directly to the Users tab, type **users** and then click **Users** in the search results.

Change the Start Screen Background

To give Windows 8 a different look, you can change the default Start screen background.

The Start screen background is the area that appears "behind" the tiles. It consists of an abstract pattern formatted with a green color scheme. If you find yourself using the Start screen frequently, the default background might become tiresome. If so, you can liven things up a bit by changing both the background pattern and the background color.

Change the Start Screen Background

1. Open the PC Settings app.

Note: See the previous section, "Open the PC Settings App."

2. Click **Personalize**.

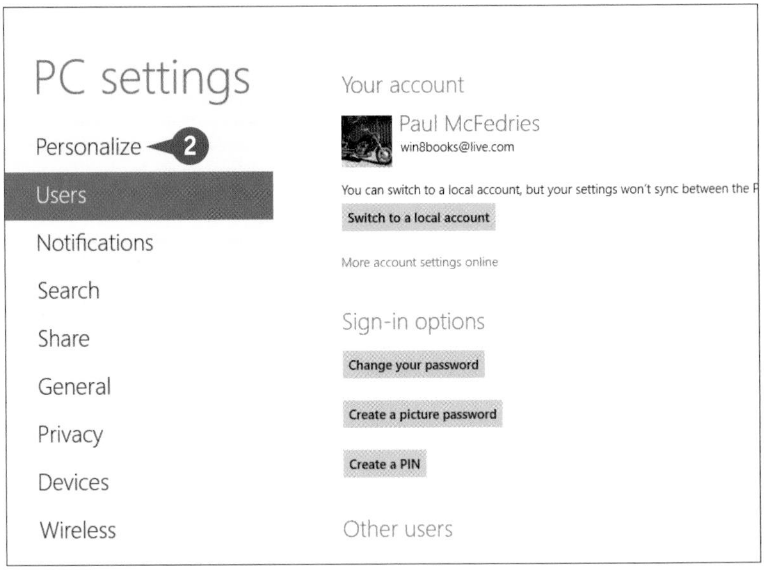

3. Click **Start screen**.

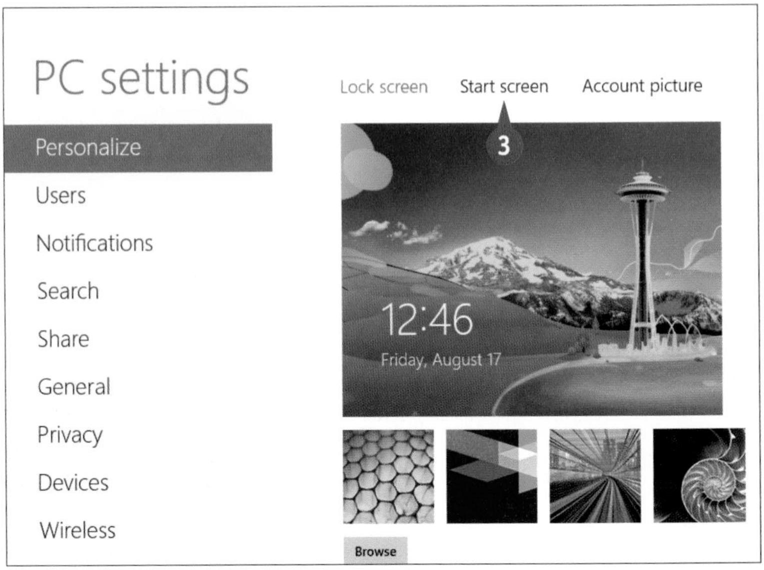

4 Click the background image you want to use.

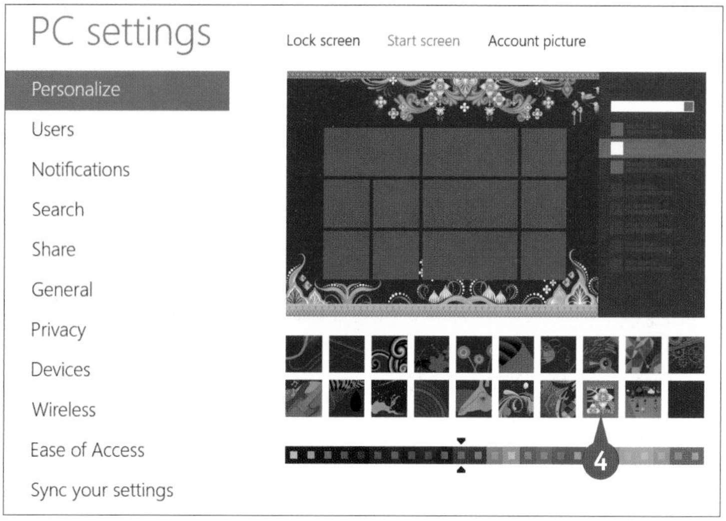

5 Click the background color you want to use.

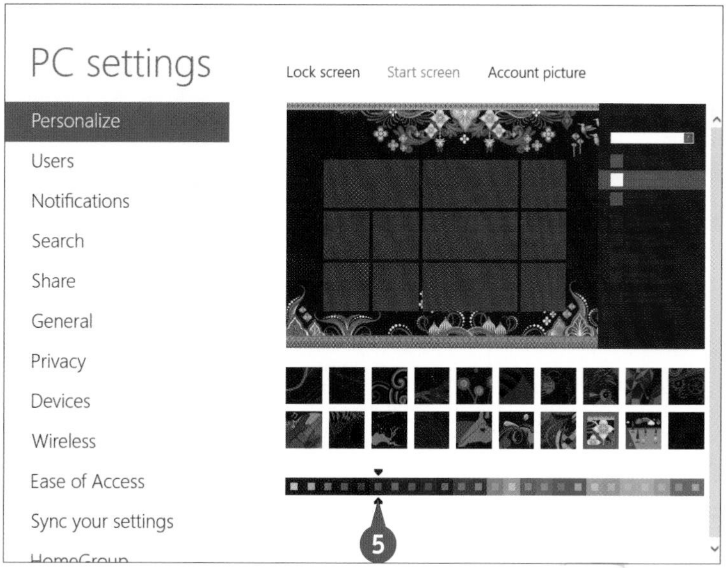

TIP

My eyesight is not what it used to be. Is there a way to make the Start screen more readable?
Windows tends to use fairly subtle colors and fairly small text, so the screen can be hard to read if your eyesight is poor. The solution is to switch to High Contrast mode, which uses white text on a black background. You can also increase the size of the screen elements.

To set this up, open the PC Settings app, click the **Ease of Access** tab, click the **High contrast** switch to **On**, and click the **Make everything on your screen bigger** switch to **On**. Note, too, that you can also switch between the regular screen mode and High Contrast mode by pressing Shift+Alt+Print Screen. (Make sure you use the left Shift and left Alt keys for this.) When Windows asks you to confirm, click **Yes**.

Change the Lock Screen Background

If you frequently lock your computer, you can change the Lock screen background to something more interesting.

As discussed in Chapter 12, locking your computer is a useful safety feature because it prevents unauthorized users from accessing your files and your network. If you find yourself looking at the Lock screen frequently, you might prefer to see something other than the default image. Windows 8 comes with several system pictures that you can use, or you can use one of your own pictures.

Change the Lock Screen Background

1. Open the PC Settings app.

Note: See "Open the PC Settings App," earlier in this chapter.

2. Click **Personalize**.
3. Click **Lock screen**.

(A) You can choose a system picture.

4. To use one of your own pictures, click **Browse**.

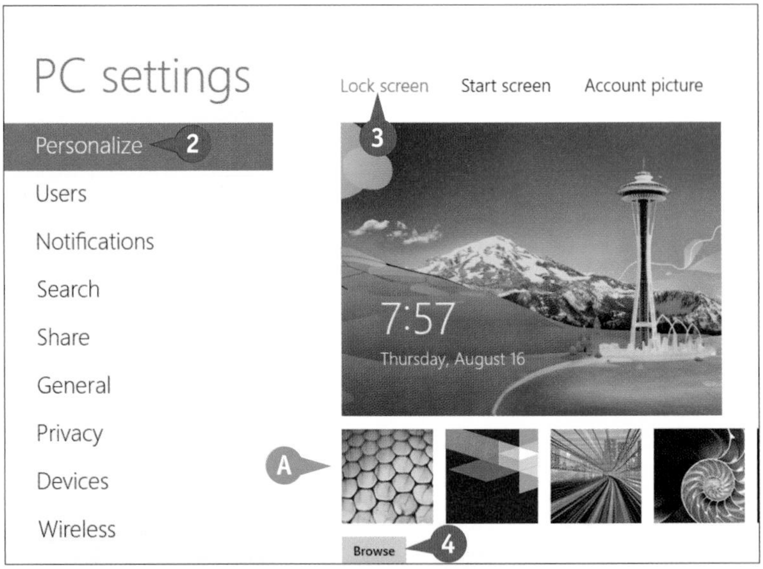

5. Click **Files**.
6. Click the folder that contains the picture you want to use.
7. If the picture resides in a subfolder, click that subfolder to open it.

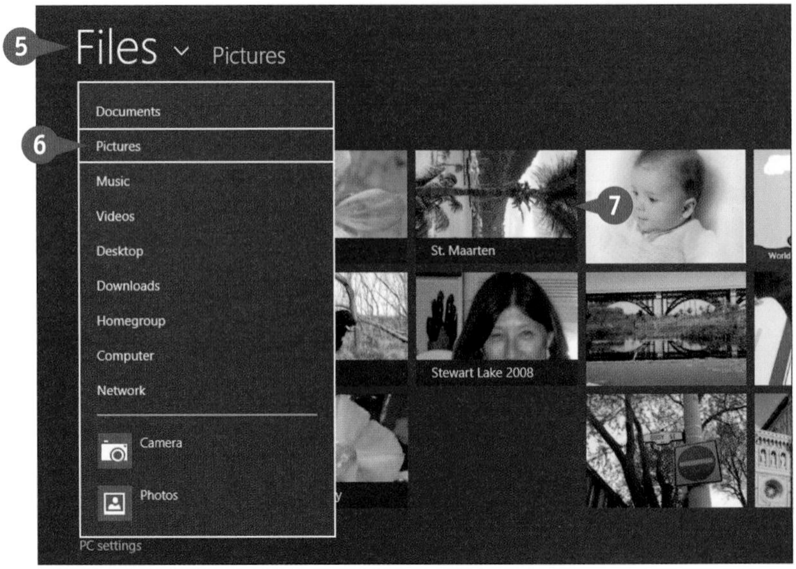

8 Click the picture you want to use.

9 Click **Choose picture**.

The image appears the next time you lock your computer.

TIP

Can I change the desktop background?

Yes, by following these steps:

1 Press ⊞+W, type **desktop**, and then click **Change desktop background**.

The Desktop Background window appears.

2 Click the **Picture location** ▾ and then click the background gallery you want to use.

3 Click the image or color you want to use.

The picture or color you selected appears on the desktop.

4 Click **Save changes**.

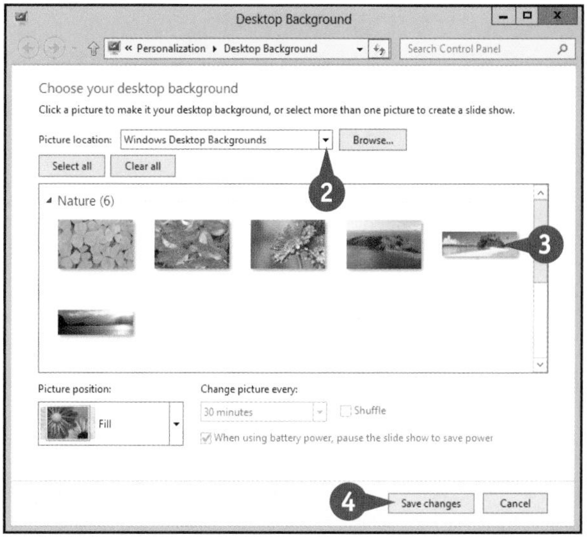

Add an App to the Lock Screen

If you frequently lock your PC, you can make the resulting Lock screen more useful by adding one or more apps.

When you lock your PC, Windows 8 displays icons for apps that have had recent notifications. For example, the Mail app shows the number of unread messages, and the Messages app shows the number of new text messages. The Lock screen also shows any new notifications that appear for these apps.

If you lock your computer frequently, you can make the Lock screen even more useful by adding icons for other apps that support notifications.

Add an App to the Lock Screen

1. Open the PC Settings app.

Note: See "Open the PC Settings App," earlier in this chapter.

2. Click **Personalize**.

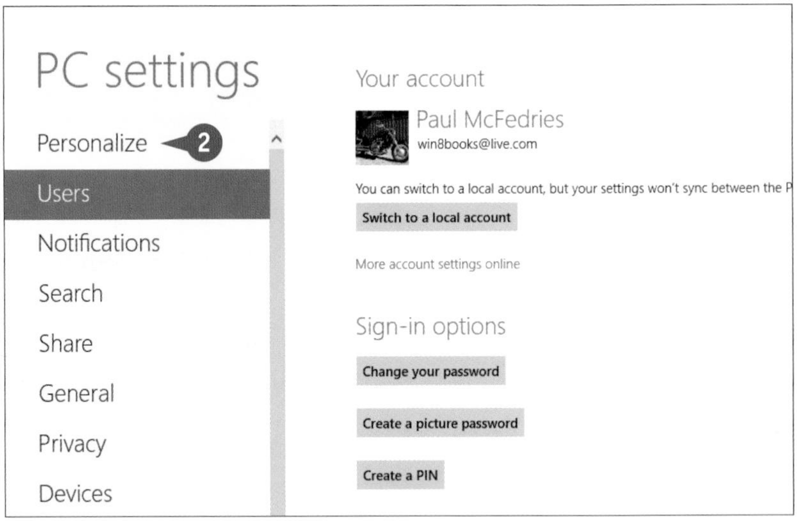

3. Click **Lock screen**.

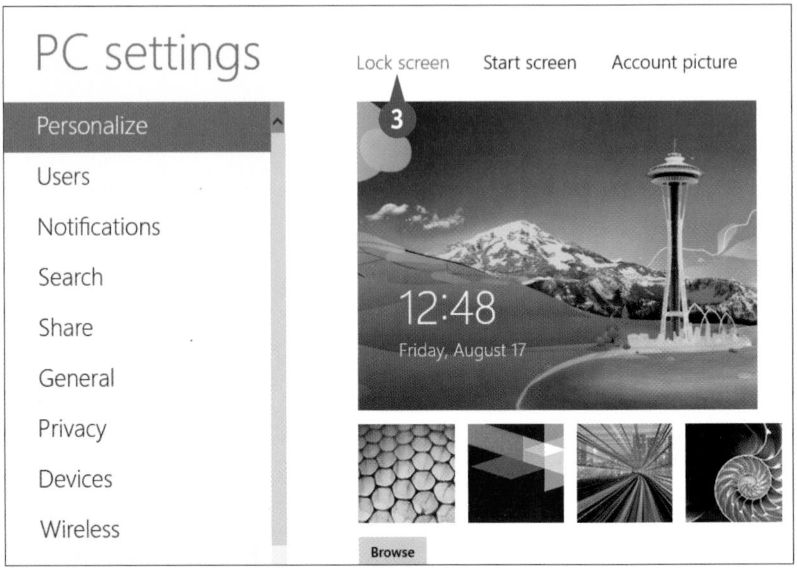

4 Click **Add** (+).

Windows 8 opens the Choose an App window.

5 Click the app you want to add to the Lock screen.

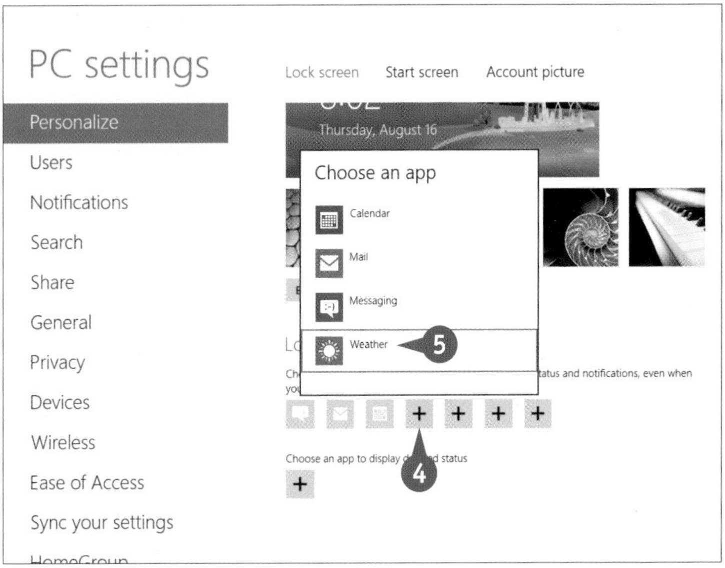

6 To add an app to display detailed status, click **Add** (+).

7 Click the app.

Windows 8 puts the new settings into effect and the apps appear on the Lock screen the next time you use it.

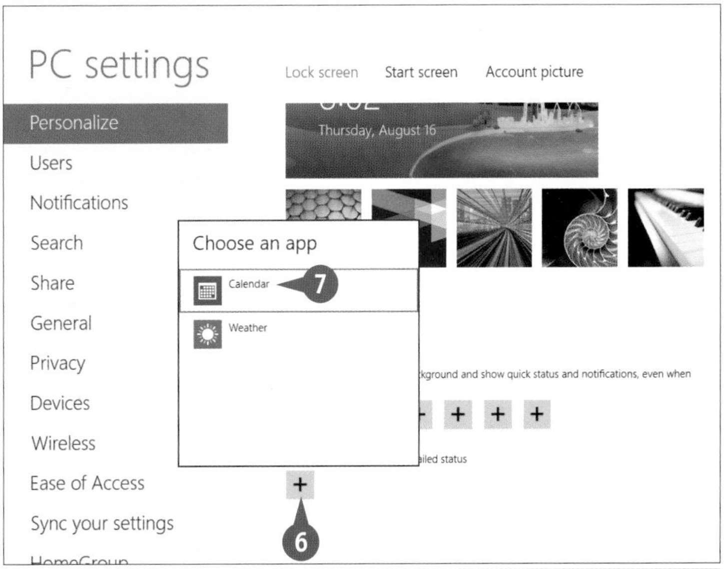

TIP

What is the difference between quick status and detailed status?

Quick status means that the Lock screen shows only a small icon for an app, and that icon displays the number of recent or unread items, such as the number of unread e-mail messages in the Mail app (A). Detailed status means that the Lock screen shows more information from the app. For example, if you have an upcoming event in the Calendar app, the Lock screen shows the details of that event, including the event title, location, and time (B).

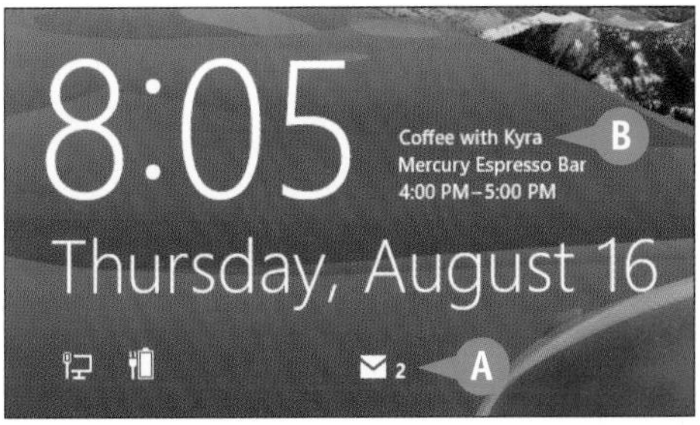

Synchronize Settings between PCs

You can make Windows 8 easier to use, more consistent, and more efficient by synchronizing your settings, customizations, and data between multiple devices.

If besides your Windows 8 desktop computer you also have a Windows 8 notebook, a Windows 8 tablet, and a Windows 8 phone, using the same Microsoft account on each means you can synchronize data between them. You can sync customizations (such as backgrounds and themes), system settings (such as languages and regional settings), Internet Explorer data (such as favorites and history), app settings, and more. This gives you a consistent interface across your devices, and consistent data so you can be more productive.

Synchronize Settings between PCs

1. Open the PC Settings app.

Note: See "Open the PC Settings App," earlier in this chapter.

2. Click **Sync your settings**.

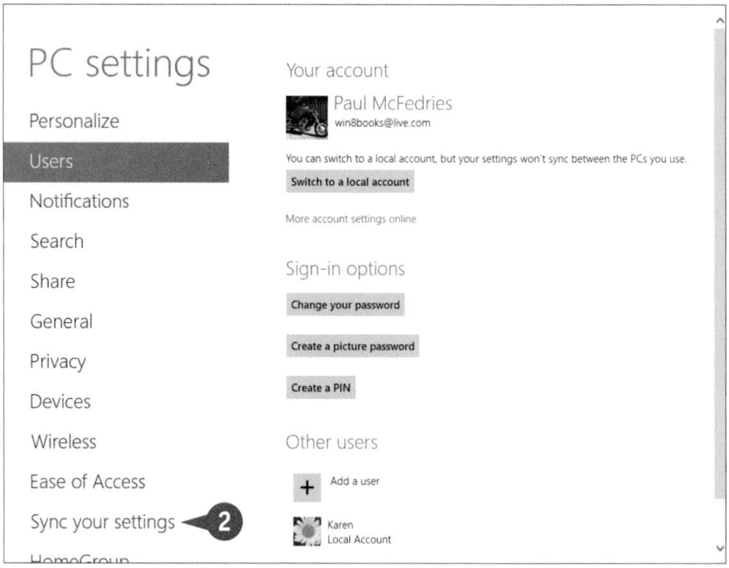

Windows 8 displays the Sync Your Settings screen.

3. Click **Sync settings on this PC** to **On**.

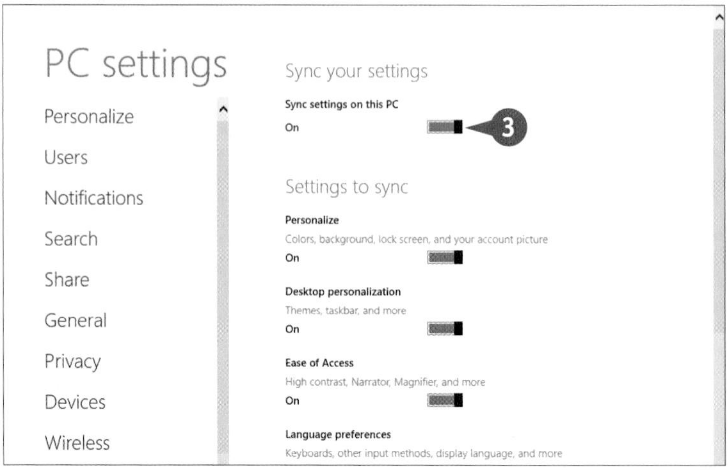

4 Under Settings to Sync, click the switch to **Off** beside each type of setting that you do not want to include in the sync.

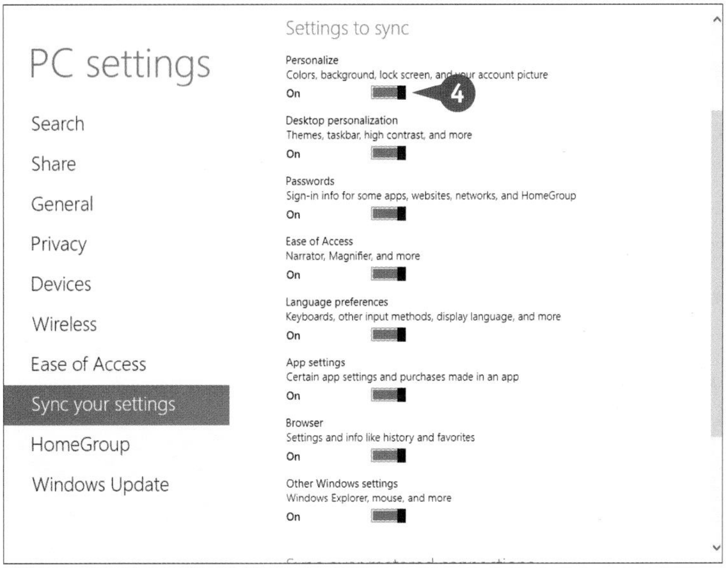

TIPS

Can I prevent syncing during those times when I am using a metered Internet connection that allows me only so much data?

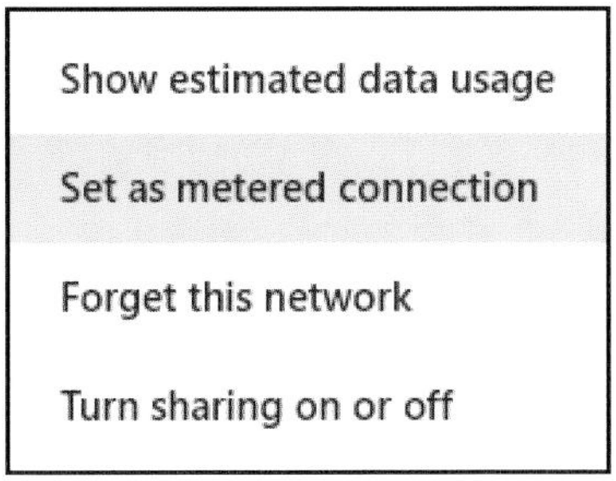

By default, Windows 8 does not sync with other PCs when you are using a metered Internet connection. However, you have to tell Windows 8 when you are using a metered connection. Press + , click the **Network** icon (), right-click your Internet connection, and then click **Set as metered connection**.

If I am using a metered Internet connection, is there a way to sync between PCs anyway?

Yes, you can configure Windows 8 to sync over a metered Internet connection. Follow steps **1** and **2** to display the Sync Your Settings screen, scroll to the bottom of the screen, and then click the **Sync settings on metered connections** switch to **On**.

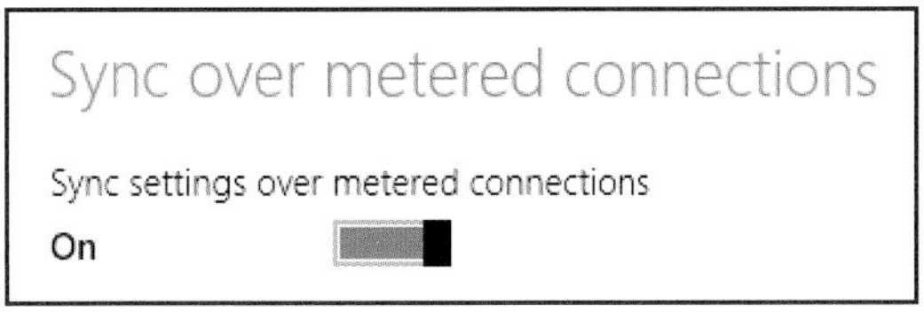

Access an App's Features

You can gain access to all of a Windows 8 app's commands and settings by displaying its application bar.

By design, Windows 8 apps appear simple and uncomplicated. They take up the entire screen, and when you first launch them you usually only see a fairly basic interface. However, almost all Windows 8 apps include a number of features — commands, settings, views, and so on — that you cannot see at first. To access these features, you must display the application bar (sometimes called the app bar), a strip that appears along the bottom (or sometimes the top) of the screen. You can then click the feature you want to use.

Access an App's Features

Display the Application Bar

1. Open the Windows 8 app you want to work with.
2. Right-click the screen.

A The application bar appears.

B The icons inside the application bar represent the app's features.

Note: In some apps, the application bar appears at the top of the screen, whereas in other apps you see two application bars, one on the bottom and one on the top of the screen.

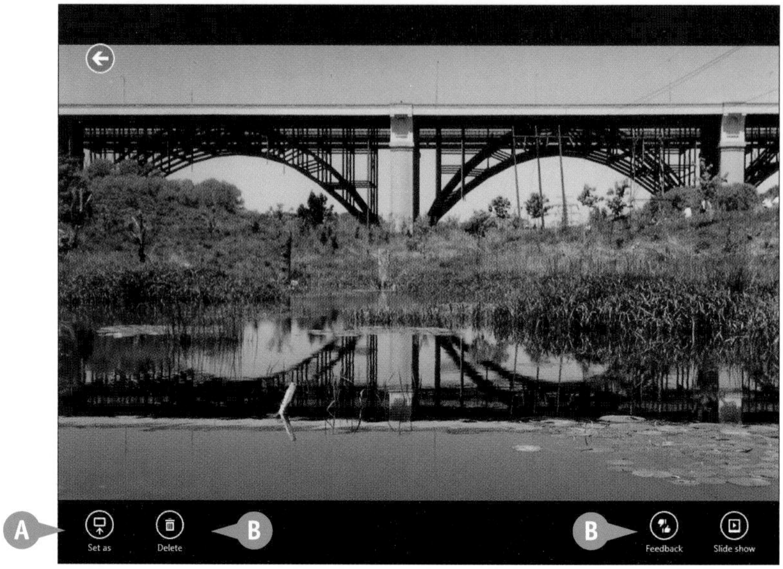

Hide the Application Bar

Note: If you click an application bar feature, the app automatically hides the application bar. You only need to hide the application bar by hand if you decide not to select a feature.

1 Click an empty section of the app screen outside the application bar.

C The app hides the application bar.

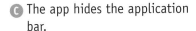

TIPS

Is there a faster way to display and hide the application bar?

If your hands are already on the keyboard, then probably the fastest way to access the application bar is to press ⊞+Z. To hide the application, press ⊞+Z again.

How do I display and hide the application bar on my Windows 8 tablet?

To access the application bar on a tablet, either swipe up from the bottom edge of the screen, or swipe down from the top edge of the screen. To hide the application bar on a tablet, tap an empty section of the screen outside the application bar.

Pin an App to the Taskbar

If you spend more time using the desktop than the Start screen, you can place your favorite apps a mouse click away by pinning them to the taskbar.

Pinning an app to the Start screen was covered earlier in this chapter, but that is helpful only if you use the Start screen regularly. If you use the desktop more often and you have an app that you use frequently, you might prefer to have that app just a single click away. You can achieve this by pinning that app to the taskbar.

You can pin an app to the taskbar either from the Start screen or from the desktop.

Pin an App to the Taskbar

Pin an App Using the Start Screen

1. On the Start screen, type the name of the app you want to pin.
2. In the Apps screen search results, right-click the app you want to pin.
3. Click **Pin to taskbar**.

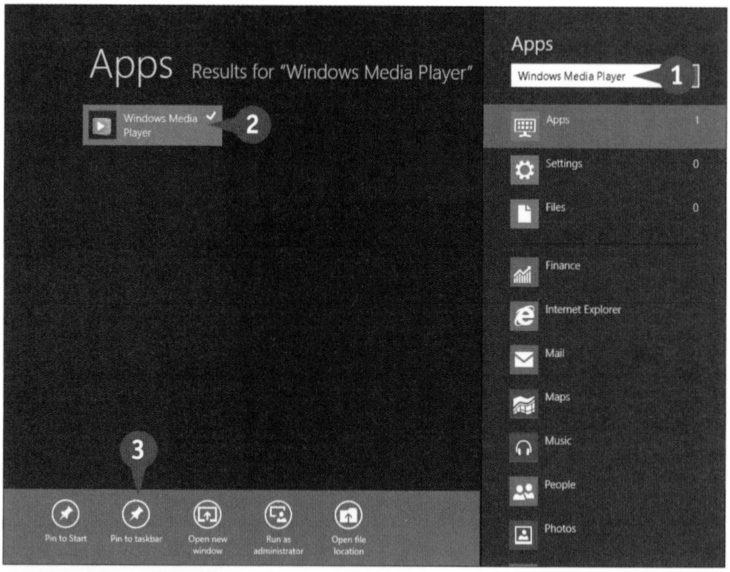

4. Press [Windows]+[D].

   The desktop appears.

A. An icon for the app now appears in the taskbar.

Pin a Running App

1. Launch the app you want to pin.
2. Right-click the running app's taskbar icon.
3. Click **Pin this program to taskbar.**
4. Click the **Close** button (×).

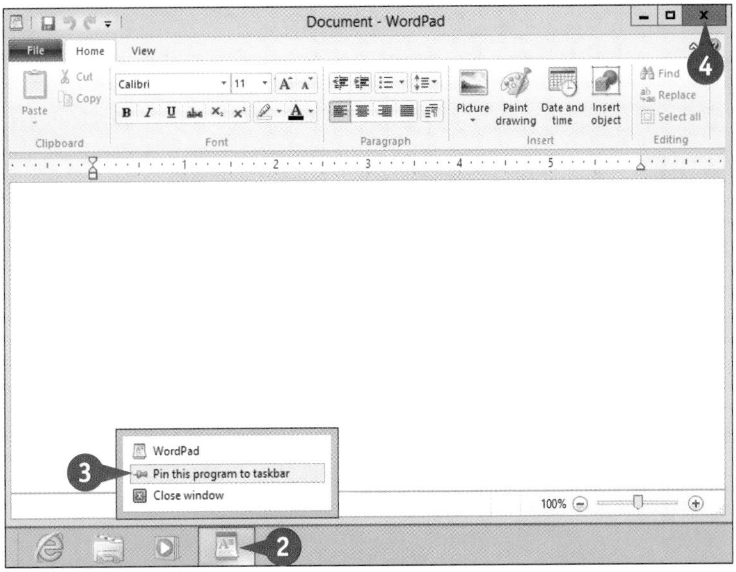

Ⓑ An icon for the app remains on the taskbar.

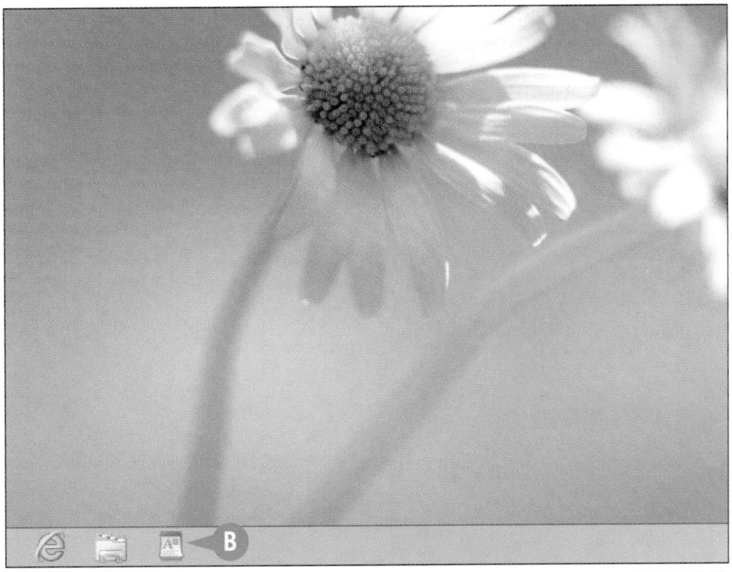

TIPS

Can I change the order of the taskbar icons?
Yes. As you drop app icons onto the taskbar, Windows 8 displays the icons left to right in the order you added them. If you prefer a different order, click and drag a taskbar icon to the left or right and then drop it in the new position. Note that this technique applies not only to the icons pinned to the taskbar, but also to the icons for any running programs.

How do I remove an app icon from the taskbar?
If you decide you no longer require an app pinned to the taskbar, you should remove it to reduce taskbar clutter and provide more room for other taskbar icons. To remove a pinned app icon, right-click the icon and then click **Unpin this program from taskbar**.

CHAPTER 14

Maintaining Windows 8

To keep your system running smoothly, maintain top performance, and reduce the risk of computer problems, you need to perform some routine maintenance chores. This chapter shows you how to delete unnecessary files, check for hard drive and other device errors, back up your files, and more.

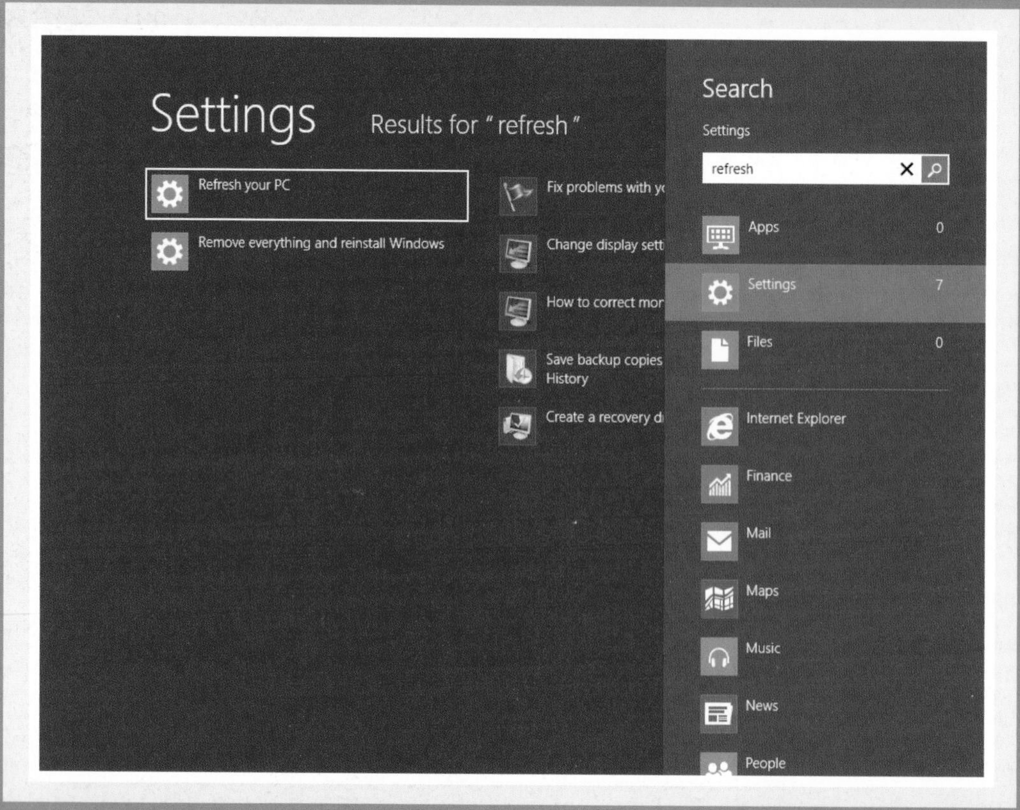

Check Hard Drive Free Space

To ensure that your PC's hard drive does not become full, you should periodically check how much free space it has left.

This is important because if you run out of room on your hard drive, you cannot install more programs or create more documents, and your PC's performance will suffer.

Of particular concern is the hard drive on which Windows 8 is installed, usually drive C. If this hard drive's free space gets low — say, less than about 20 or 25GB — Windows 8 runs slowly.

Check Hard Drive Free Space

Note: You can also check the free space on a CD, DVD, memory card, or flash drive. Before you continue, insert the disc, card, or drive.

1. On the Start screen, type **computer**.
2. Click **Computer**.

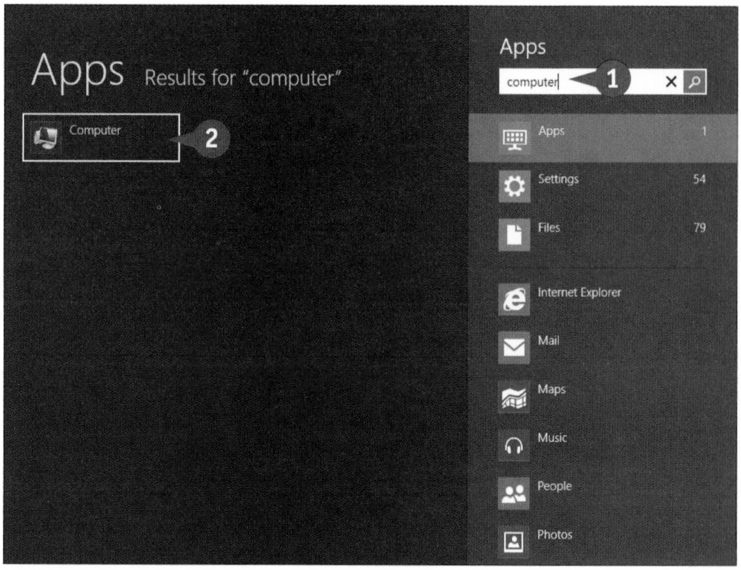

The Computer window appears.

3. Click the **View** tab.
4. Click **Tiles**.

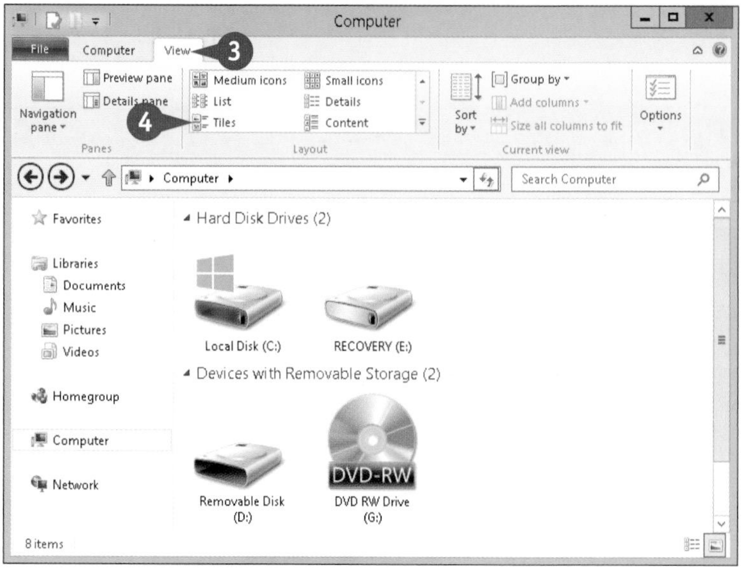

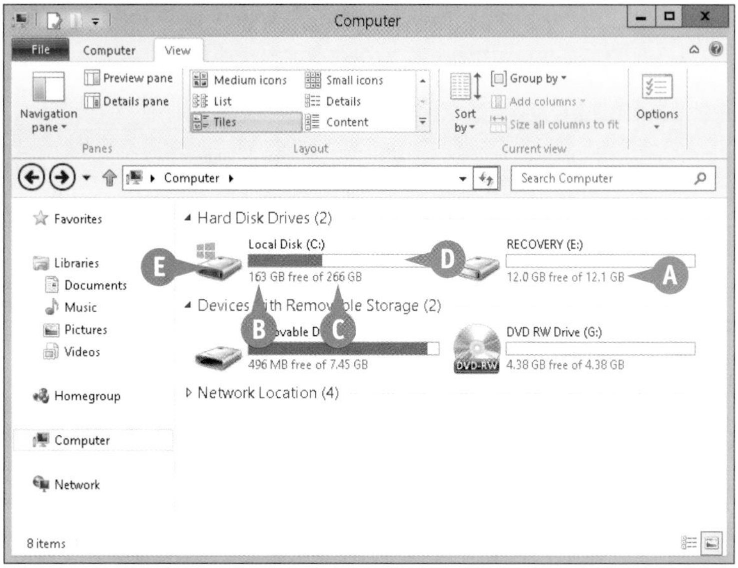

Ⓐ Information about each drive appears along with the drive icon.

Ⓑ This value tells you the amount of free space on the drive.

Ⓒ This value tells you the total amount of space on the drive.

Ⓓ This bar gives you a visual indication of how much disk space the drive is using.

Ⓔ Windows is installed on the drive with the Windows logo (▦).

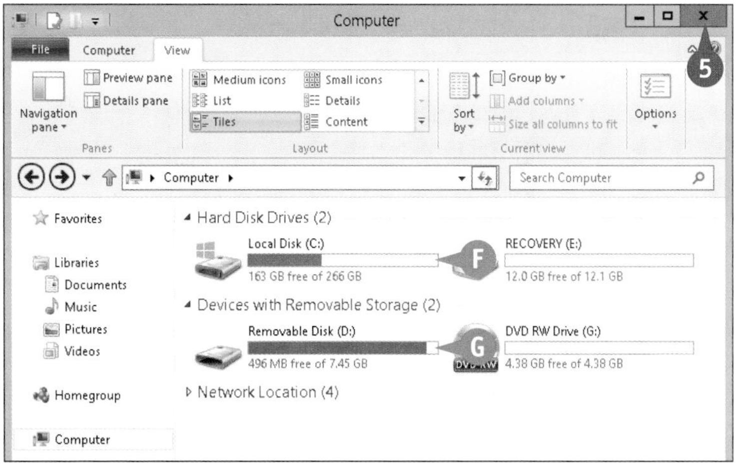

Ⓕ The used portion of the bar appears blue when a drive still has sufficient disk space.

Ⓖ The used portion of the bar turns red when a drive's disk space becomes low.

❺ Click the **Close** button (✕) to close the Computer window.

TIPS

How often should I check my hard drive free space?
With normal computer use, you should check your hard drive free space about once a month. If you install programs, create large files, or download media frequently, you should probably check your free space every couple of weeks.

What can I do if my hard drive space is getting low?
You can do three things:

- **Delete Documents**. If you have documents — particularly media files such as images, music, and videos — that you no longer need, delete them.
- **Remove Programs**. If you have programs that you no longer use, uninstall them (see "Uninstall an App" in Chapter 2).
- **Run Disk Cleanup**. Use the Disk Cleanup program to delete files that Windows 8 no longer uses. See the next section, "Delete Unnecessary Files."

Delete Unnecessary Files

To free up hard drive space on your computer and keep Windows 8 running efficiently, you can use the Disk Cleanup program to delete files that your system no longer needs.

Although today's hard drives are quite large, it is still possible to run low on disk space, particularly because today's applications and media files are larger than ever. Run Disk Cleanup any time that your hard drive free space gets too low. If hard drive space is not a problem, run Disk Cleanup every two or three months.

Delete Unnecessary Files

1. Press ⊞+W.

   The Settings search pane appears.

2. Type **disk cleanup**.
3. Click **Free up disk space by deleting unnecessary files**.

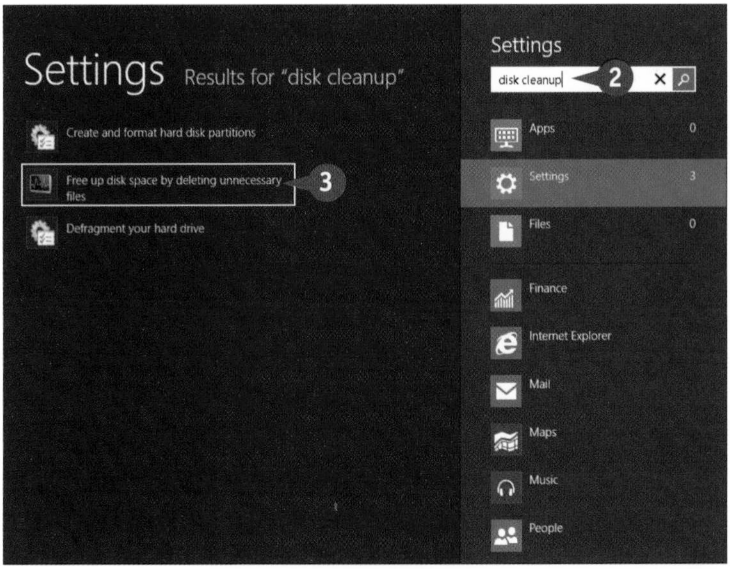

   If your computer has more than one drive, the Drive Selection dialog box appears.

4. Click the **Drives** ▾ and then click the hard drive you want to clean up.
5. Click **OK**.

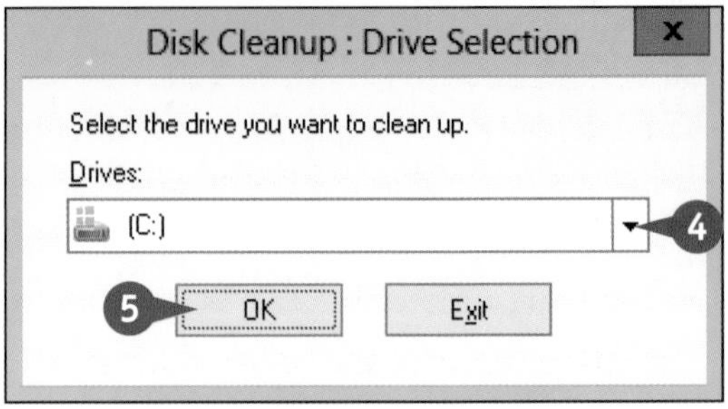

After a few moments, the Disk Cleanup dialog box appears.

A This area displays the total amount of drive space you can free up.

B This area displays the amount of drive space the activated options will free up.

6 Click the check box (☐ changes to ☑) for each file type that you want to delete.

C This area displays a description of the highlighted file type.

7 Click **OK**.

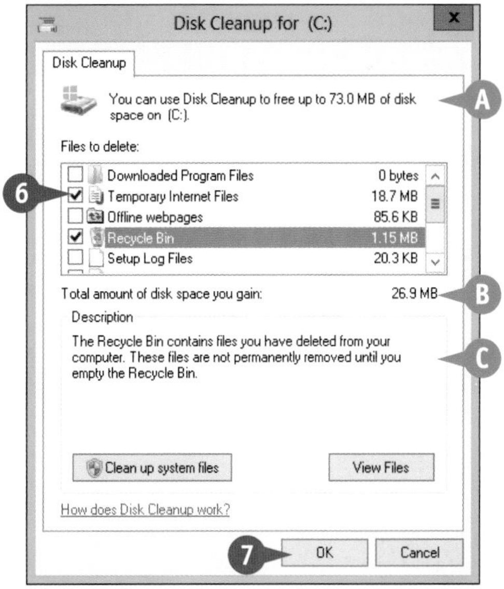

Disk Cleanup asks you to confirm that you want to delete the file types.

8 Click **Delete Files**.

TIP

What types of files does Disk Cleanup delete?

It deletes the following file types:

- **Downloaded Program Files**: Small web page programs downloaded onto your hard drive.
- **Temporary Internet Files**: Web page copies stored on your hard drive for faster viewing.
- **Offline Webpages**: Web page copies stored on your hard drive for offline viewing.
- **Recycle Bin**: Files that you have deleted since you last emptied your Recycle Bin.
- **Temporary Files**: Files used by programs to store temporary data.
- **Thumbnails**: Miniature versions of images and other content used in folder windows.

Refresh Your Computer

If you find that your computer is running slowly or that frequent program glitches are hurting your productivity, you can often solve these problems by resetting your PC's system files.

The Refresh Your PC feature reinstalls a fresh copy of Windows 8. It also saves the documents, images, and other files in your user account, some of your settings, and any Windows 8 apps that you have installed. However, Refresh Your PC does *not* save any other PC settings (which are reverted to their defaults) or any desktop programs that you installed.

Refresh Your Computer

1. Press ⊞+I.

   The Settings pane appears.

2. Click **Change PC settings**.

The PC Settings app runs and selects the General tab.

3. Click **Get started**.

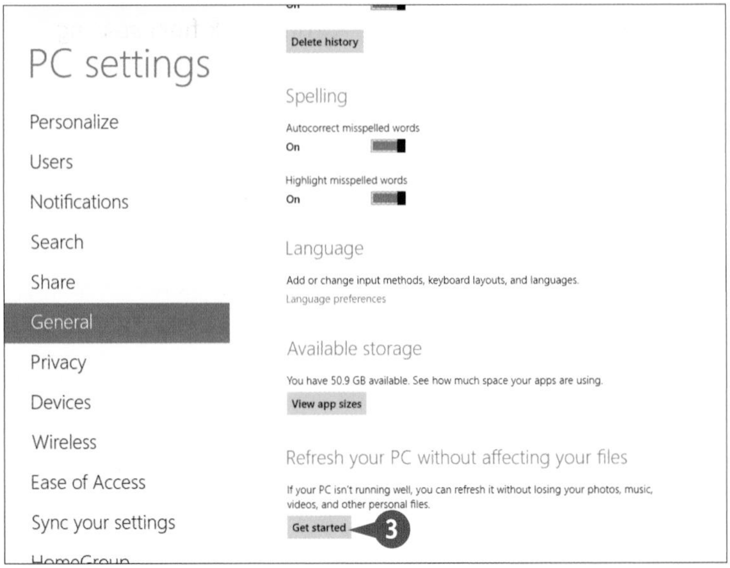

Refresh Your PC explains the process.

4. Insert your Windows 8 installation disc or a Windows 8 recovery drive.

Note: See "Create a Recovery Drive" to learn how to create a USB recovery drive.

5. Click **Next**.
6. Click **Refresh**.

Refresh Your PC reboots the computer and refreshes the system files.

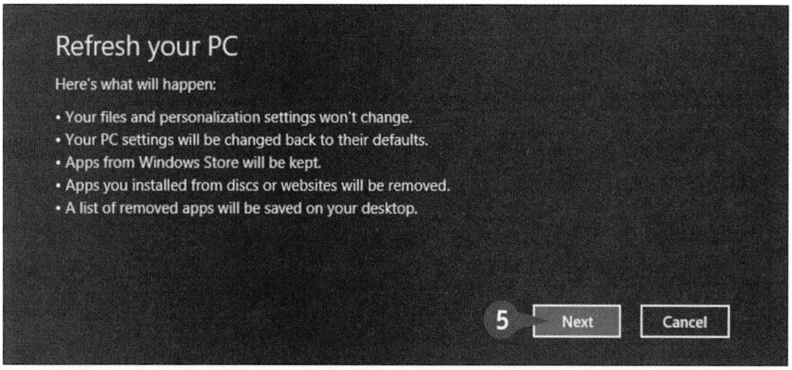
Refresh your PC
Here's what will happen:
• Your files and personalization settings won't change.
• Your PC settings will be changed back to their defaults.
• Apps from Windows Store will be kept.
• Apps you installed from discs or websites will be removed.
• A list of removed apps will be saved on your desktop.
5
Next
Cancel

Ready to refresh your PC
This will take a few minutes, and your PC will restart.
6
Refresh
Cancel

TIP

How do I refresh my computer if I cannot start Windows?

If system problems are preventing Windows 8 from starting, you can also run Refresh Your PC from your Windows installation media:

1. Insert the media and then restart your computer.
2. Boot to the media.

Note: How you boot to the media depends on your system. In some cases, you see a message telling you to press a key; in other cases you select the media from a menu.

The Windows Setup dialog box appears.

3. Click **Next**.
4. Click **Repair your computer**.
5. Click **Troubleshoot**.
6. Click **Refresh Your PC**.
7. Click **Next**.
8. Click **Windows 8**.
9. Click **Refresh**.

Create a Recovery Drive

You can make it easier to troubleshoot and recover from computer problems by creating a USB recovery drive.

If a problem prevents you from booting your computer, then you must boot using some other drive. If you have your Windows 8 installation media, you can boot using that drive. If you do not have the installation media, you can still recover if you have created a recovery drive. This is a USB flash drive that contains the Windows 8 recovery environment, which enables you to refresh or reset your PC, recover a system image, and more.

Create a Recovery Drive

1. Insert the USB flash drive you want to use.
2. Press ⊞+W.

   The Settings search pane appears.
3. Type **recovery drive**.
4. Click **Create a recovery drive**.

   The User Account Control dialog box appears.
5. Click **Yes**.

Note: If you are using a standard account, enter your PC's administrator credentials to continue.

The Recovery Drive Wizard appears.

6. Click **Next**.

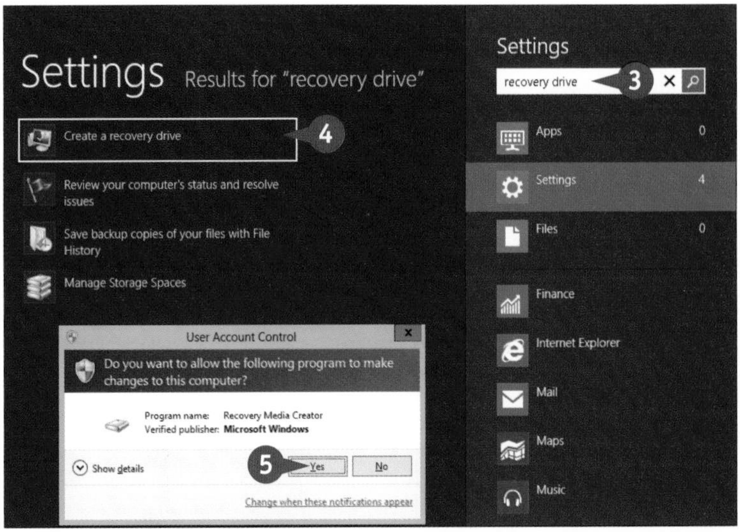

Settings Results for "recovery drive"
Create a recovery drive
Review your computer's status and resolve issues
Save backup copies of your files with File History
Manage Storage Spaces
Settings
recovery drive
Apps 0
Settings 4
Files 0
Finance
Internet Explorer
Mail
Maps
Music
User Account Control
Do you want to allow the following program to make changes to this computer?
Program name: Recovery Media Creator
Verified publisher: Microsoft Windows
Show details
Yes
No
Change when these notifications appear

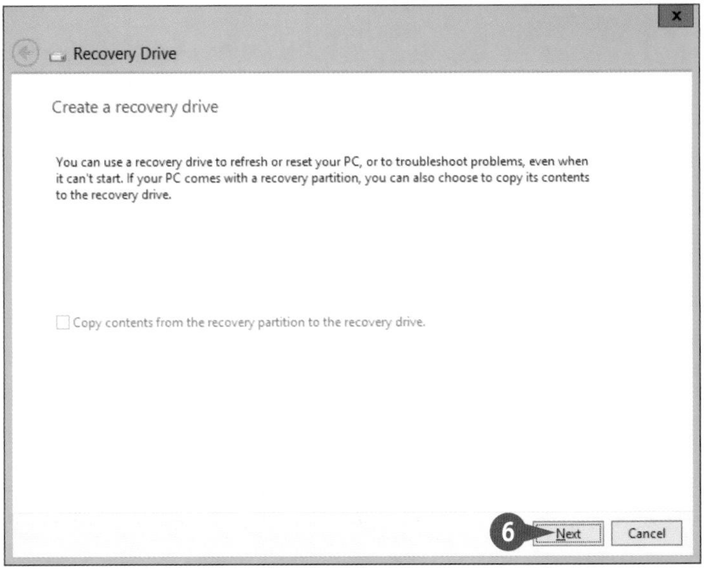

Recovery Drive
Create a recovery drive
You can use a recovery drive to refresh or reset your PC, or to troubleshoot problems, even when it can't start. If your PC comes with a recovery partition, you can also choose to copy its contents to the recovery drive.
Copy contents from the recovery partition to the recovery drive.
Next
Cancel

The Recovery Drive Wizard prompts you to choose the USB flash drive.

7. Click the drive, if it is not selected already.
8. Click **Next**.

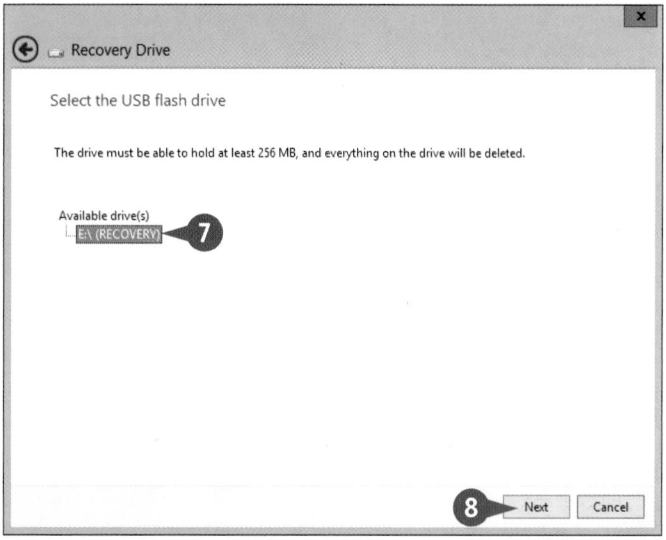
Recovery Drive
Select the USB flash drive
The drive must be able to hold at least 256 MB, and everything on the drive will be deleted.
Available drive(s)
E:\ (RECOVERY)
Next
Cancel

The Recovery Drive Wizard warns you that all the data on the drive will be deleted.

9. Click **Create**.

The wizard formats the drive and copies the recovery tools and data.

10. Click **Finish** (not shown).

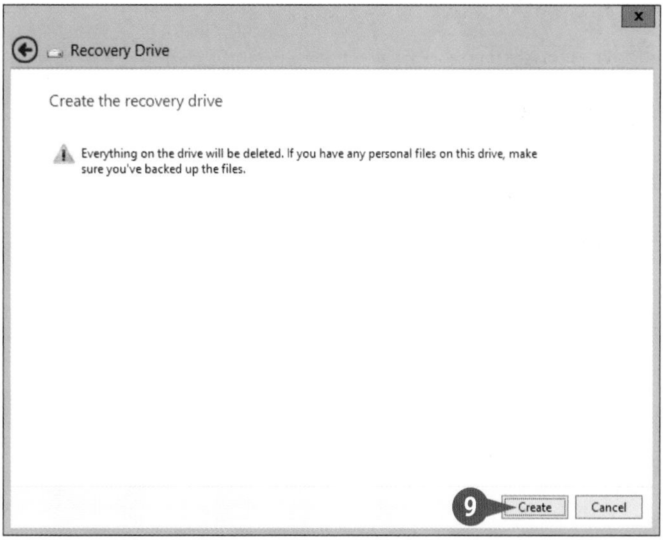
Recovery Drive
Create the recovery drive
Everything on the drive will be deleted. If you have any personal files on this drive, make sure you've backed up the files.
Create
Cancel

TIPS

Can I use any USB flash drive as a recovery drive?

No. To use a USB flash drive as a recovery drive, the drive must have a capacity of at least 256MB. Also, Windows 8 erases all data on the drive, so make sure the flash drive does not contain any files you want to keep. If it does, be sure to move those files to a different drive before you begin this procedure.

How can I make sure the recovery drive works properly?

To make sure your recovery drive works properly, you should test it by booting your PC to the drive. Insert the recovery drive and then restart your PC. How you boot to the drive depends on your system. Some PCs display a menu of boot devices, and you select the USB drive from that menu. In other cases, you see a message telling you to press a key.

Safeguard Your Computer with a System Image Backup

To protect against your system hard drive failing or otherwise becoming unusable, you can create a system image backup.

The worst-case scenario for PC problems is a system crash that renders your hard drive or system files unusable. Your only recourse in such a case is to start from scratch with either a reformatted hard drive or a new hard drive. This usually means that you have to reinstall Windows 8 and then reinstall and reconfigure all your applications. However, if you create a system image backup, you can restore your system quickly and easily.

Safeguard Your Computer with a System Image Backup

1 Press ⊞+W.

The Settings search pane appears.

2 Type **file recovery**.

3 Click **Windows 7 File Recovery**.

The Windows 7 File Recovery window appears.

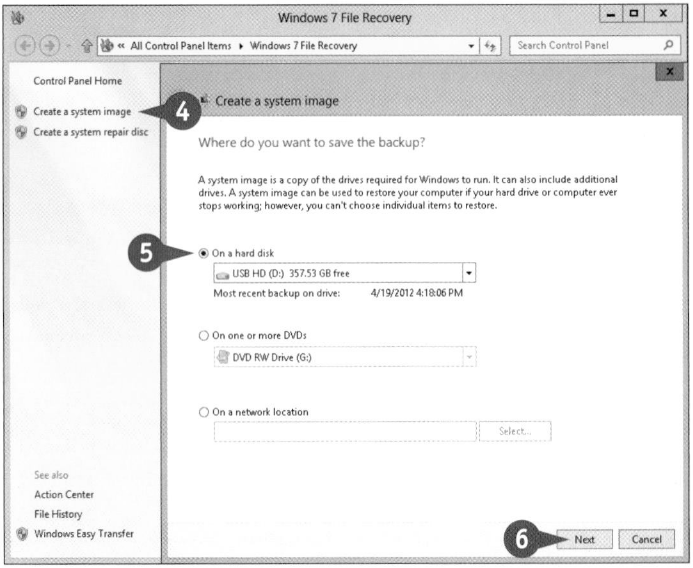

4 Click **Create a system image**.

The Create a System Image Wizard appears.

5 Select a backup destination (○ changes to ◉):

On a hard disk: Select this option to use a disk drive on your computer.

On one or more DVDs: Select this option if you want to use DVDs to hold the backup.

On a network location: Select this option if you want to use a shared network folder.

6 Click **Next**.

The Which Drives Do You Want to Include in the Backup? dialog box appears.

7. Select the check box beside each extra drive you want to add to the backup (☐ changes to ☑).
8. Click **Next**.

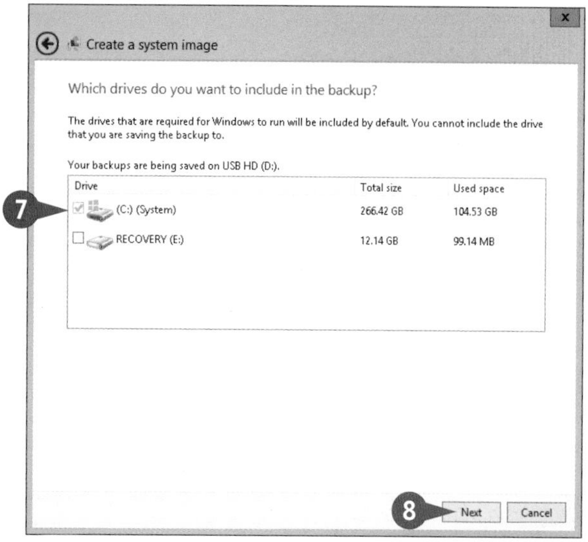
Create a system image
Which drives do you want to include in the backup?
The drives that are required for Windows to run will be included by default. You cannot include the drive that you are saving the backup to.
Your backups are being saved on USB HD (D:).
Drive
Total size
Used space
(C:) (System)
266.42 GB
104.53 GB
RECOVERY (E:)
12.14 GB
99.14 MB
7
8
Next
Cancel

Windows 8 asks you to confirm your backup settings.

9. Click **Start backup**.

Windows 8 creates the system image.

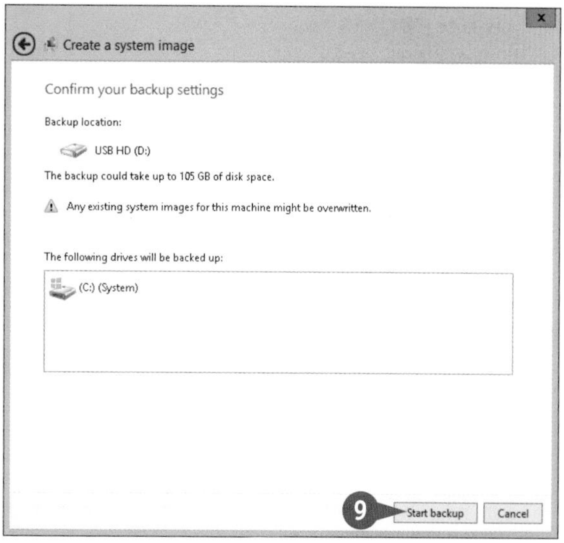
Create a system image
Confirm your backup settings
Backup location:
USB HD (D:)
The backup could take up to 105 GB of disk space.
Any existing system images for this machine might be overwritten.
The following drives will be backed up:
(C:) (System)
9
Start backup
Cancel

TIPS

Windows 8 asks me if I want to create a "system repair disc" when the backup is done. Do I need this?

You do not need a system repair disc if you already created a USB recovery drive, as described in the previous section, so click **No**. If you do not have a USB recovery drive and you do not have a USB flash drive to create one, click **Yes**, instead.

How do I restore my system using a system image?

If worst comes to worst and you are forced to start over with a formatted or new hard drive, you need to restore the system image. If you have a USB recovery drive, boot to it and then click a keyboard layout; if you have the Windows 8 install media, boot to it, click **Next**, and then click **Repair your computer**. Click **Troubleshoot**, click **Advanced Options**, and then click **System Image Recovery**.

Keep a History of Your Files

You can make it easier to recover earlier versions of your files by saving copies of your files to an external drive.

There may be times when backing up a file just by making a copy is not good enough. For example, if you make frequent changes to a file, you might want to copy not only the current version, but also the versions from an hour ago, a day ago, a week ago, and so on. In Windows 8, these previous versions of a file are called its *file history*, and you can save this data for all your documents by activating a feature called File History.

Keep a History of Your Files

Set the File History Drive

1. Connect an external drive to your PC.

Note: The drive should have enough capacity to hold your files, so an external hard drive is probably best.

2. On the Start screen, press ⊞+W.

   The Settings search pane appears.

3. Type **history**.
4. Click **File History**.

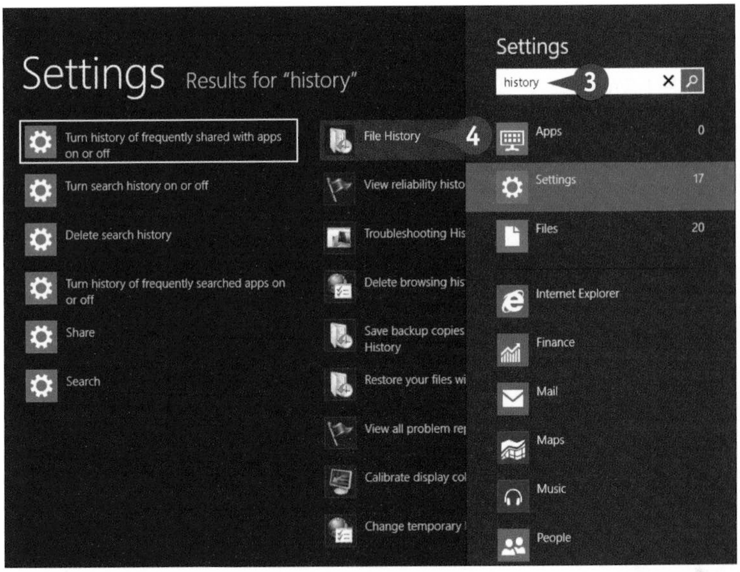

The File History window appears.

A. If Windows 8 detects an external hard drive, it displays the drive here.

If this is the correct drive, you can skip steps **5** to **7**.

5. Click **Select drive**.

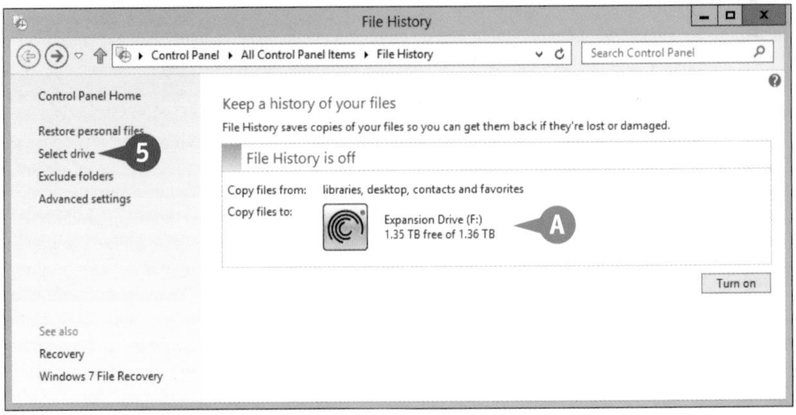

The Select Drive window appears.

6 Click the drive you want to use.

7 Click **OK**.

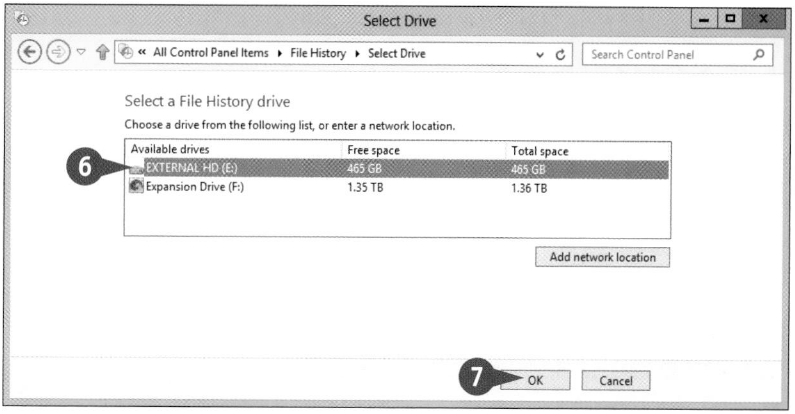

Activate File History

1 Click **Turn on**.

Windows 8 activates File History and begins saving copies of your files to the external drive.

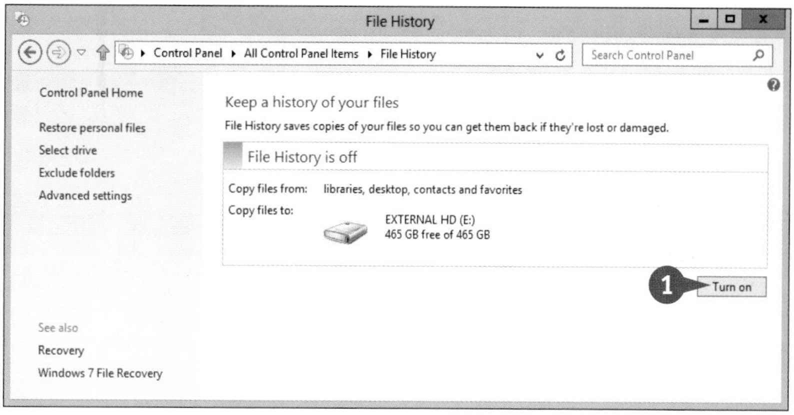

TIPS

What can I do if I do not have an external hard drive?
If you do not have an external drive, or if your drives do not have enough capacity, you can use a network folder to store your file history. In the File History window, click **Change drive** and then click **Add network location**. In the Select Folder dialog box, open a computer on your network, select a shared folder to which you have permission to add files, and then click **Select Folder**.

Is it okay to disconnect the external hard drive temporarily?
If you need to remove the external drive temporarily (for example, if you need to use the port for another device), you should turn off File History before disconnecting the external drive. Follow steps **1** to **4** to open the File History window and then click **Turn off**.

Restore a File from Your History

If you improperly edit, accidentally delete, or corrupt a file through a system crash, in many cases you can restore a previous version of the file.

Why would you want to revert to a previous version of a file? One reason is that you might improperly edit the file by deleting or changing important data. In some cases you may be able to restore that data by going back to a previous version of the file. Another reason is that the file might become corrupted if the program or Windows 8 crashes. You can get a working version of the file back by restoring to a previous version.

Restore a File from Your History

1. On the Start screen, press Windows + W.

   The Settings search pane appears.

2. Type **history**.
3. Click **File History**.

   The File History window appears.

4. Click **Restore personal files**.

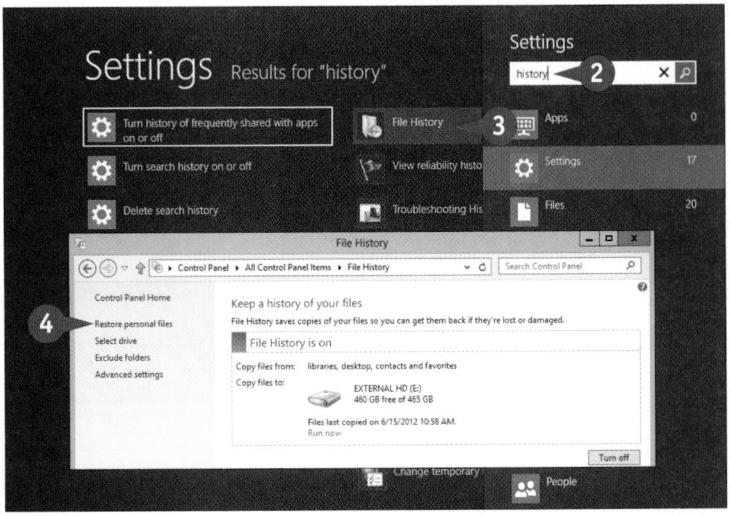

The Home - File History window appears.

5. Double-click the library that contains the file you want to restore.

6 Open the folder that contains the file.

7 Click **Previous Version** (⏮) until you open the version of the folder you want to use.

8 Click the file you want to restore.

9 Click **Restore to Original Location** (↺).

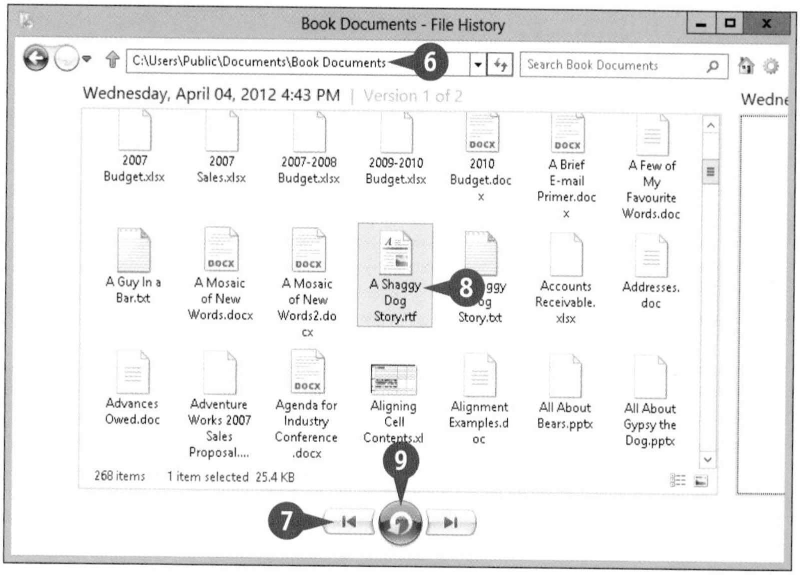

If the original folder has a file with the same name, File History asks what you want to do.

10 Select an option:

Click **Replace the file in the destination folder** to overwrite the existing file with the previous version.

Click **Skip this file** to do nothing.

Click **Choose the file to keep in the destination folder** to decide which file you prefer to keep.

Windows 8 restores the previous version.

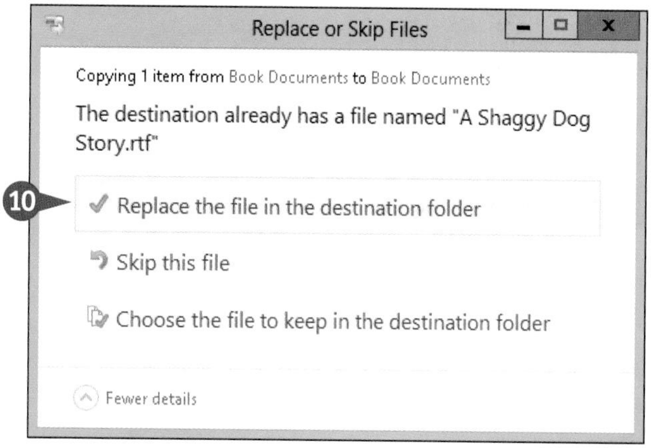

TIPS

Is it possible to restore an entire folder?
Yes, because Windows 8 also keeps track of previous versions of folders, which is useful if an entire folder becomes corrupted because of a system crash. Follow steps **1** to **7**, click the folder you want to restore, and then click **Restore to original location** (↺).

What should I do if I am not sure about replacing an existing file with a previous version of the file?
If you are not sure whether to replace an existing file with a previous version, click **Choose the file to keep in the destination folder** in the Replace or Skip Files dialog box. In the File Conflict dialog box, activate the check box beside both versions (☐ changes to ☑), and then click **Continue**. This leaves the existing file as is and restores the previous version with (2) appended to the name.

Check Your Hard Drive for Errors

To keep your system running smoothly, you should periodically check your hard drive for errors and fix any errors that come up.

Because hard drive errors can cause files to become corrupted, which may prevent you from running a program or opening a document, you can use the Check Disk program to look for and fix hard drive errors.

Check Your Hard Drive for Errors

1. Press ⊞+E.

   File Explorer appears.

2. Click **Computer**.
3. Click the hard drive that you want to check.
4. Click the **Computer** tab.
5. Click **Properties**.

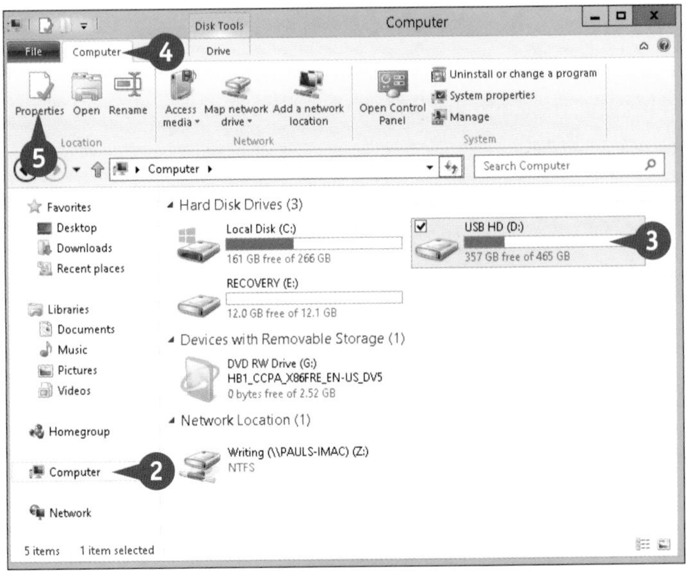

The hard drive's Properties dialog box appears.

6. Click the **Tools** tab.
7. Click **Check**.

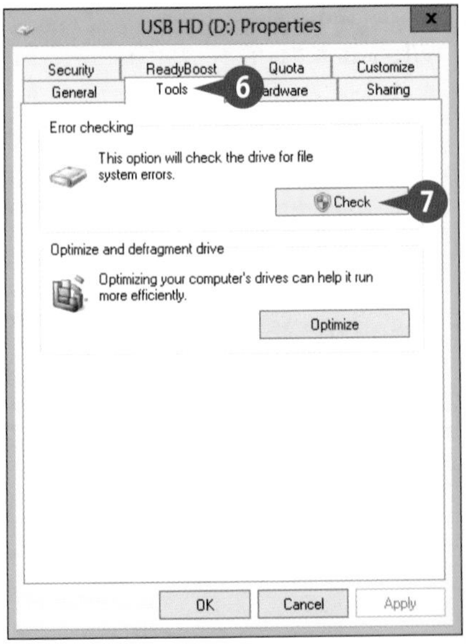

Ⓐ If Windows 8 tells you that the drive has no errors, you can click **Cancel** and skip the rest of these steps.

8 Otherwise, click **Scan drive**.

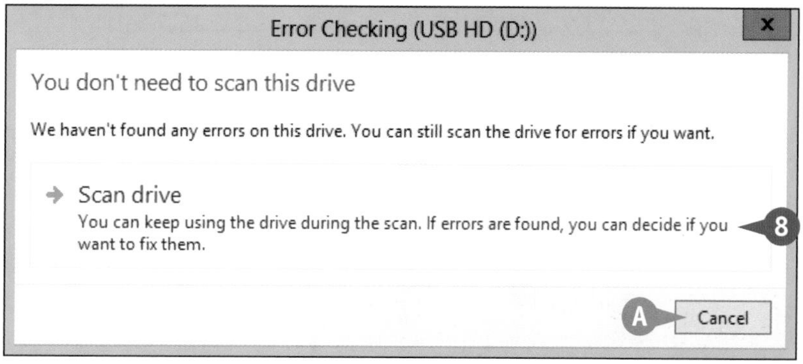
Error Checking (USB HD (D:))
You don't need to scan this drive
We haven't found any errors on this drive. You can still scan the drive for errors if you want.
Scan drive
You can keep using the drive during the scan. If errors are found, you can decide if you want to fix them.
8
A
Cancel

Windows 8 checks the hard drive.

9 When the check is complete, click **Close**.

Note: If Check Disk finds any errors, follow the instructions the program provides.

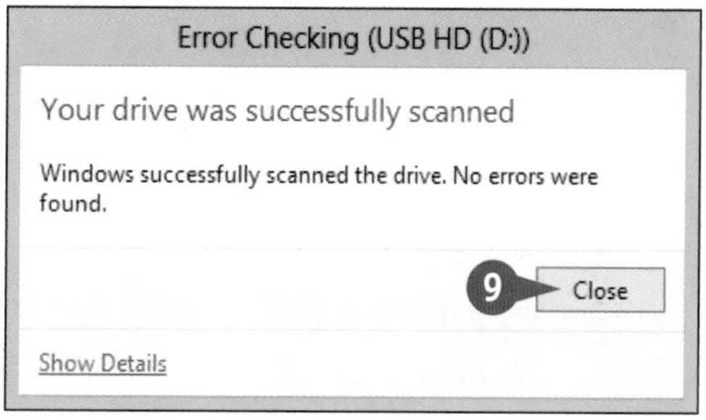
Error Checking (USB HD (D:))
Your drive was successfully scanned
Windows successfully scanned the drive. No errors were found.
9
Close
Show Details

TIPS

What is a "bad sector"?

A *sector* is a small storage location on your hard drive. When Windows 8 saves a file on the drive, it divides the file into pieces and stores each piece in a separate sector. A bad sector is one that, through physical damage or some other cause, can no longer be used to reliably store data.

How often should I check for hard drive errors?

You should perform the basic hard drive check about once a week. Perform the more thorough bad sector check once a month. Note that the bad sector check can take several hours, depending on the size of the drive, so perform this check only when you will not need your computer for a while.

Check Your Devices for Errors

To help ensure that your system is operating smoothly and efficiently, you should periodically check for errors associated with the devices attached to your computer.

Device errors usually mean either that you cannot work with a device entirely, or that the device behaves erratically or unexpectedly. You can use Windows 8's Devices and Printers feature to check your installed devices for errors. You can also use Devices and Printers to troubleshoot your problem devices, and in most cases Windows 8 will be able to fix the problem automatically.

Check Your Devices for Errors

Check for Devices with Errors

1. Press ⊞+W.

   The Settings search pane appears.

2. Type **view devices**.
3. Click **View devices and printers**.

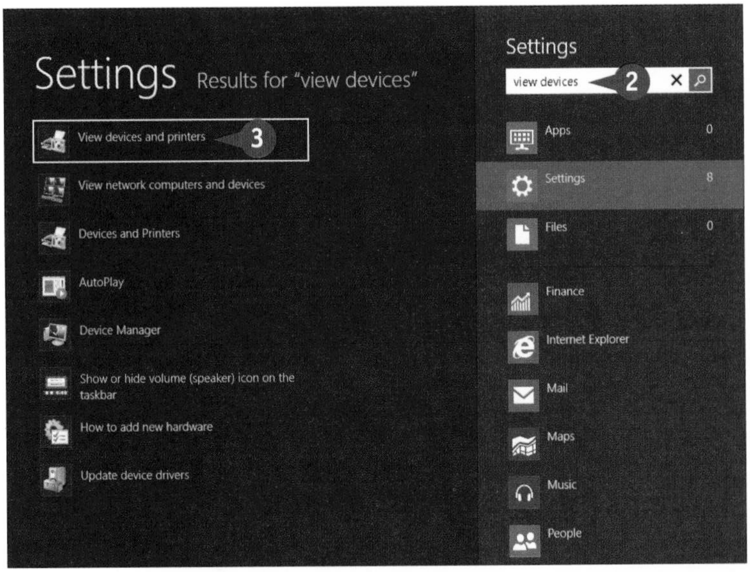

The Devices and Printers window appears.

4. Examine the device icons for errors.

A. Windows 8 indicates devices with errors using this icon (⚠).

Begin Device Troubleshooting

1. Click a device that has an error.
2. Click **Troubleshoot**.

The Devices and Printers troubleshooting wizard appears and displays the first fix.

3. Click **Apply this fix**.

   Devices and Printers 7 applies the fix. If this did not solve the problem, Devices and Printers displays the next fix.

B. If you are certain this fix is not the solution, click **Skip this fix**, instead.

4. Repeat step **3** until the problem is resolved.

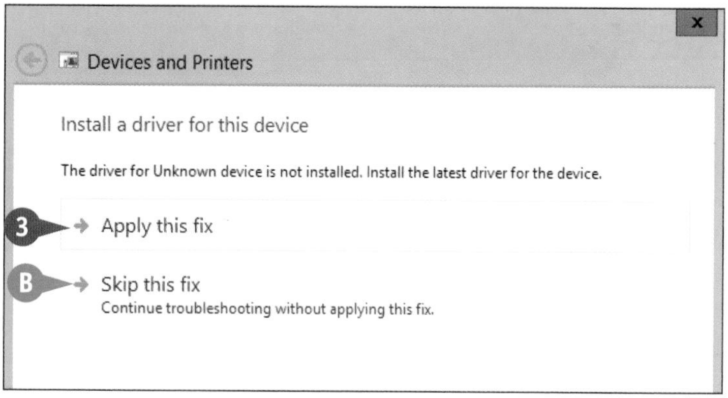

TIPS

What is a device driver?

A *device driver* is a small program that Windows 8 uses to communicate with a particular device. Many hardware problems are the result of either not having a device driver installed, or having an incorrect driver installed. Most devices come with discs that have the correct device driver, so you should insert that disc when troubleshooting. You can also obtain the latest device driver from the manufacturer's website.

What do I do if Devices and Printers cannot solve the problem?

Devices and Printers can solve many types of device problems, but not all of them. For example, if your device is broken or defective, Devices and Printers can do nothing to fix it. In that case, you need to either return the device to the manufacturer for repair or replacement, or take it to a local computer shop for fixing.

Defragment Your Hard Drive on a Schedule

You can make Windows 8, and your programs, run faster, and your documents open more quickly, by defragmenting your hard drive on a regular schedule.

File fragmentation means that a file is stored on your hard drive in multiple pieces instead of as single piece. This is a performance drag because it means that when Windows 8 tries to open such a file, it must make several stops to collect the various pieces. A lot of fragmented files can slow down even the fastest hard drive. Defragmenting improves performance by bringing all those pieces together, making finding and opening each file faster.

Defragment Your Hard Drive on a Schedule

1. Press ⊞+W.

   The Settings search pane appears.

2. Type **defrag**.
3. Click **Defragment and optimize your drives**.

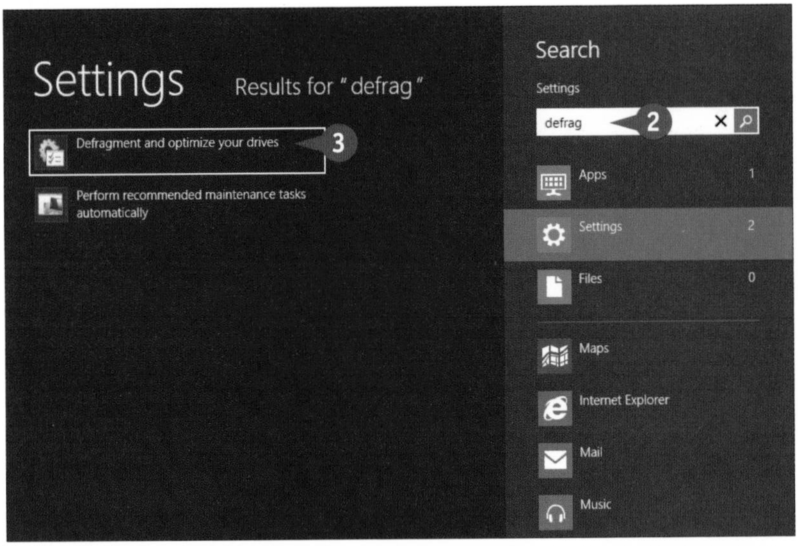

The Optimize Drives window appears.

4. Click **Change settings**.

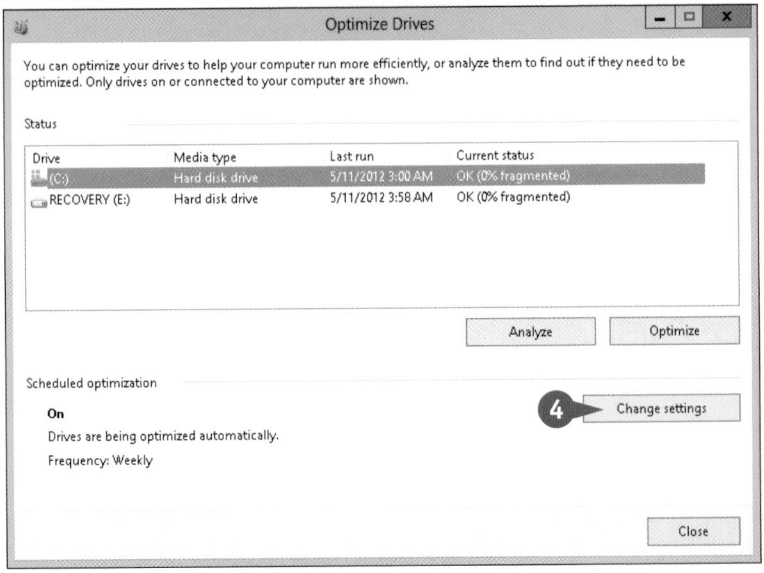

The Optimization Schedule dialog box appears.

5 Click **Run on a schedule (recommended)** (☐ changes to ☑).

6 Click the **Frequency** ▾ and then click the frequency with which you want to defragment (Daily, Weekly, or Monthly).

7 Click **OK**.

A The new schedule appears here.

B If you want to defragment your drives now, click **Optimize**.

8 Click **Close**.

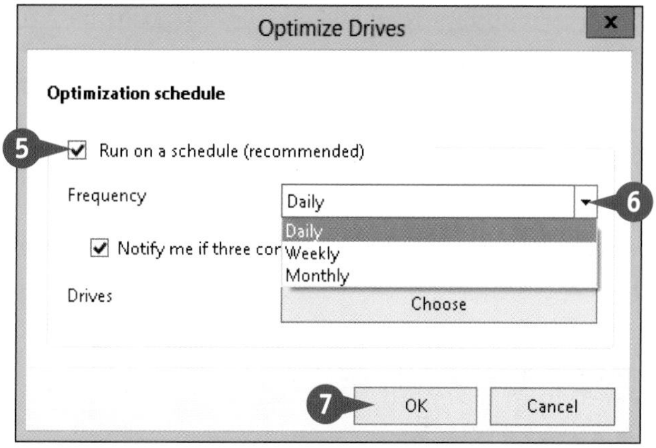

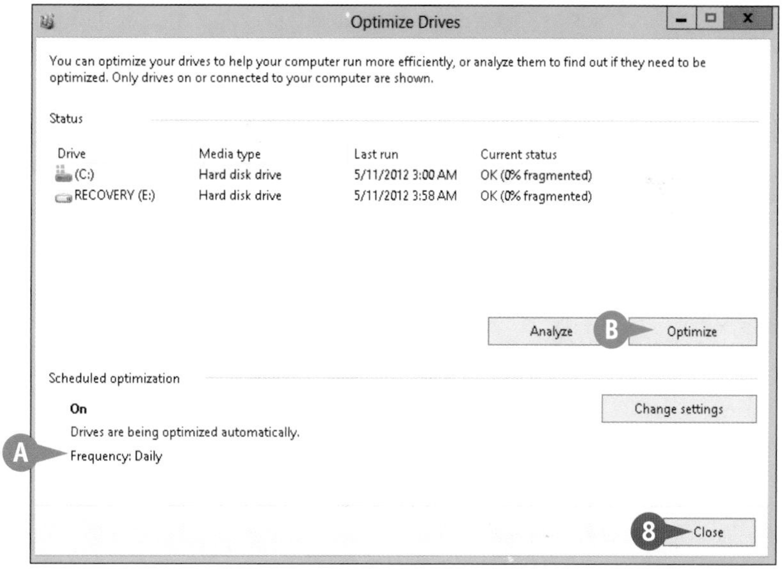

TIPS

How often should I defragment my hard drive?
This depends on how often you use your computer. If you use your computer every day, you should defragment your hard drive weekly. If you use your computer only occasionally, you should defragment your hard drive monthly.

How long does defragmenting my hard drive take?
It depends on the size of the hard drive, the amount of data on it, and the extent of the defragmentation. Budget at least 15 minutes for the defragment, and know that it could take more than an hour.

Create a System Restore Point

If your computer crashes or becomes unstable after you install a program or a new device, Windows 8's System Restore feature can fix things by restoring the system to its previous state. To ensure this works, you need to set restore points before you install programs and devices on your computer.

Windows 8 automatically creates system restore points as follows: every week (called a *system checkpoint*); before installing an update; and before installing certain programs (such as Microsoft Office) and devices. These are useful, but it pays to err on the side of caution and create your own restore points more often.

Create a System Restore Point

1. Press ⊞+W.

   The Settings search pane appears.

2. Type **protection.**
3. Click **Create a restore point.**

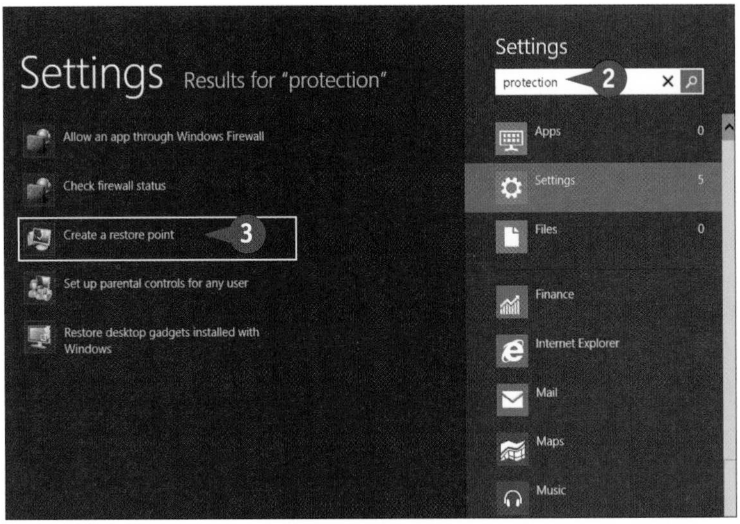

The System Properties dialog box appears.

A The System Protection tab is already displayed.

4. Click **Create.**

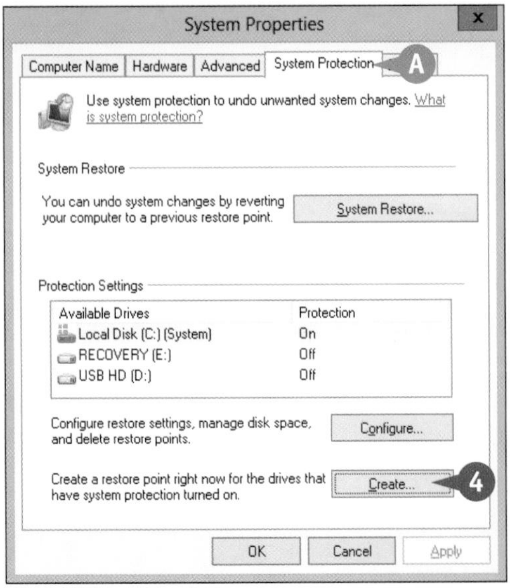

The Create a Restore Point dialog box appears.

5 Type a description for your restore point.

6 Click **Create**.

System Restore creates the restore point.

Windows 8 tells you the restore point was created successfully.

7 Click **Close**.

8 Click **OK** to close the System Properties dialog box.

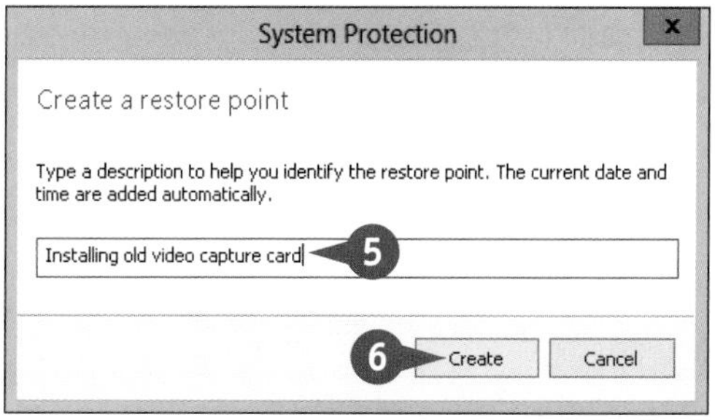

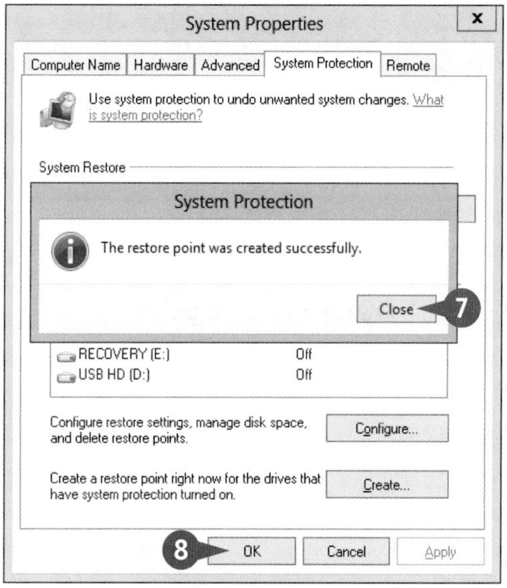

TIP

When should I create a restore point?

To be safe, you should create a restore point before you install any software, whether you purchased the program at a store or downloaded it from the Internet. You should also create a restore point before you add any new hardware devices to your system.

Apply a System Restore Point

If your computer becomes unstable or behaves erratically after you install a program or device, you can often fix the problem by applying the restore point you created before making the change.

If after you install a program or device you notice problems with your system, the easiest solution is to uninstall the item. If that does not work, then your next step is to revert to an earlier restore point. Windows 8 reverts your computer to the configuration it had when you created the restore point, which should solve the problem.

Apply a System Restore Point

1. Press ⊞+W.

   The Settings search pane appears.

2. Type **protection**.
3. Click **Create a restore point**.

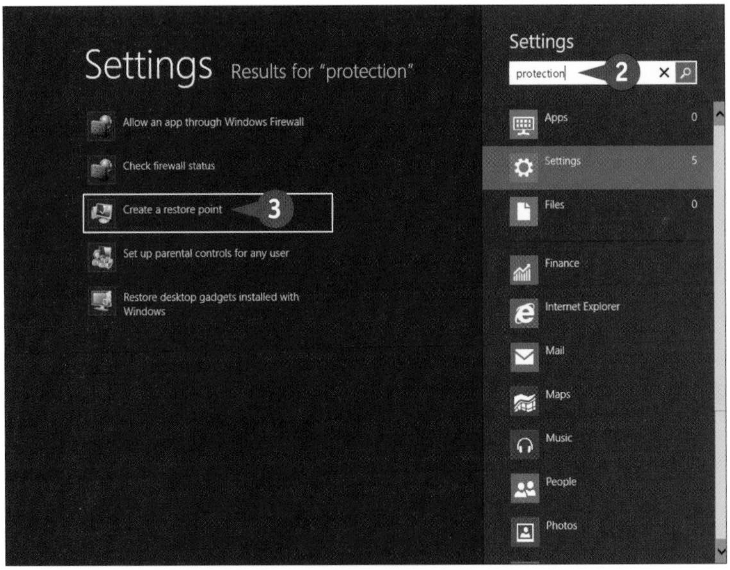

4. Click **System Restore**.

   The System Restore window appears.

   Ⓐ System Restore might show the most likely restore point here. If this is the restore point you want, or if you do not see a restore point, skip to step **8**.

5. Click **Choose a different restore point** (○ changes to ◉).
6. Click **Next**.

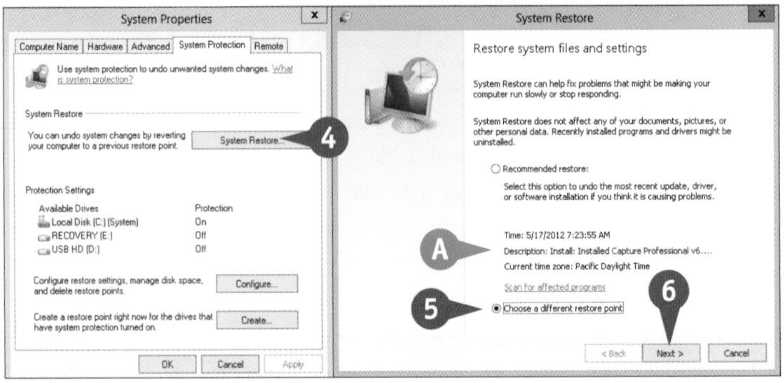

The Choose a Restore Point window appears.

7 Click the restore point you want to apply.

B If you do not see the restore point you want, click **Show more restore points** (☐ changes to ☑).

8 Click **Next**.

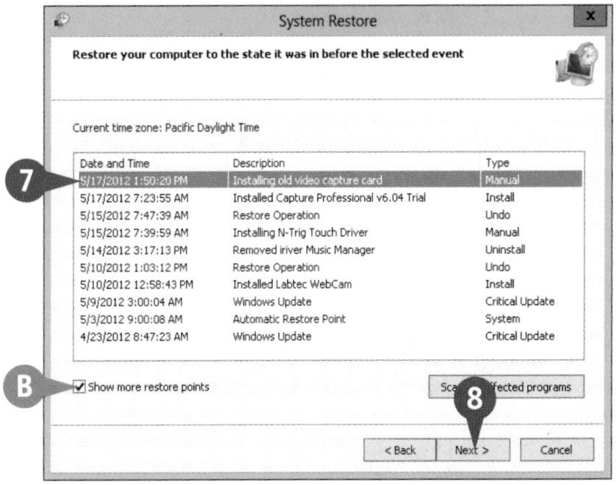

The Confirm Your Restore Point window appears.

9 Click **Finish**.

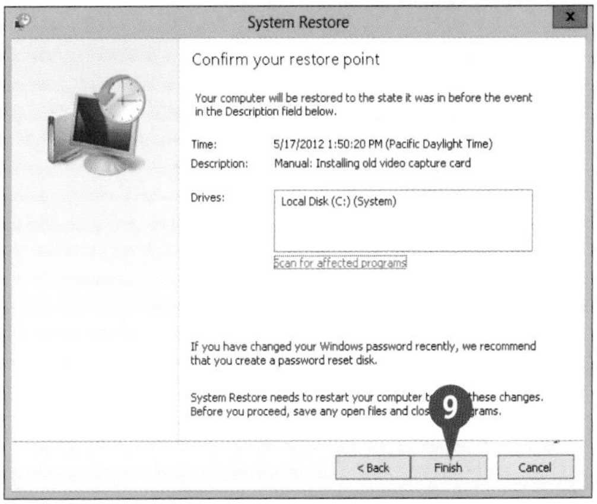

System Restore asks you to confirm that you want to restore your system.

10 Click **Yes**.

System Restore applies the restore point and then restarts Windows 8.

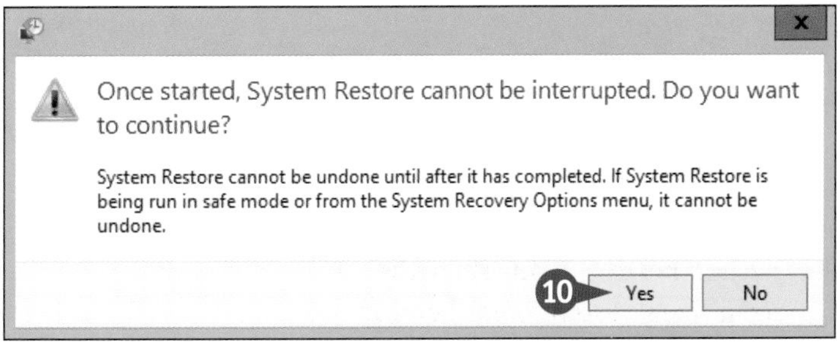

TIPS

Will I lose any of my recent work when I apply a restore point?

No, the restore point reverts only your computer's configuration back to the earlier time. Any work you performed in the interim — documents you created, e-mails you received, web page favorites you saved, and so on — is not affected when you apply the restore point. However, if you installed any programs after the restore point, you must reinstall those programs.

If applying the restore point makes things worse, can I reverse it?

Yes. Follow steps **1** to **6** to display the list of available restore points on your computer. Click the **Restore Operation** restore point, and then follow steps **8** to **10**.

Index

D

E

F

G

H

I

J

K

L

M

Q

R

S

Y

Z

ml 1-13